SHAKESPEARE, THE MOVIE, II

Following on from the phenomenally successful *Shakespeare, The Movie*, this volume brings together an invaluable new collection of essays on cinematic Shakespeares in the 1990s and beyond. *Shakespeare, The Movie, II*:

- focuses for the first time on the impact of postcolonialism, globalization, and digital film on recent adaptations of Shakespeare;
- takes in not only American and British films but also adaptations of Shakespeare in Europe and in the Asian diaspora;
- explores a wide range of film, television, video, and DVD adaptations from Almereyda's *Hamlet* to animated tales, via Baz Luhrmann, Kenneth Branagh, and 1990s' *Macbeths*, to name but a few;
- offers fresh insight into the issues surrounding Shakespeare in film, such as the interplay between originals and adaptations, the appropriations of popular culture, the question of spectatorship, and the impact of popularization on the canonical status of "the Bard."

Combining three key essays from the earlier collection with exciting new work from leading contributors, *Shakespeare, The Movie, II* offers sixteen fascinating essays. It is quite simply a must-read for any student of Shakespeare, film, media, or cultural studies.

Contributors: Michael Anderegg, Lynda E. Boose, Richard Burt, Thomas Cartelli, Peter S. Donaldson, Katherine Eggert, Donald K. Hedrick, Diana E. Henderson, Barbara Hodgdon, Douglas Lanier, Courtney Lehmann, James N. Loehlin, Laurie Osborne, Katherine Rowe, Amy Scott-Douglass, and Susan Wiseman.

Richard Burt is Professor of English at the University of Florida, Gainesville. His most recent books are *Unspeakable ShaXXXspeares: Queer Theory and American Kiddie Culture* (1998) and *Shakespeare After Mass Media* (2002). **Lynda E. Boose** is Professor of English and Women's Studies at Dartmouth College. Her most recent book is *Shakespeare, The Movie* (1997).

SHAKESPEARE, THE MOVIE, II

Popularizing the plays on film, TV, video, and DVD

Edited by
Richard Burt and Lynda E. Boose

LONDON AND NEW YORK

First published 2003

Simultaneously published in the UK, USA and Canada
by Routledge
29 West 35th Street, New York, NY 10001
and Routledge
11 New Fetter Lane, London EC4P 4EE

Routledge is an imprint of the Taylor & Francis Group

Typeset in Baskerville by
Florence Production Ltd, Stoodleigh, Devon
Printed and bound in Great Britain by
MPG Books Ltd, Bodmin

Library of Congress Cataloging in Publication Data
Shakespeare, the movie II: popularizing the plays on film, tv, video, and
DVD/Richard Burt, Lynda E. Boose, editors.
p.cm.
Includes bibliographical references and index.
1. Shakespeare, William, 1564–1616 – Film and video adaptations.
2. English drama – Film and video adaptations. 3. Film adaptations.
4. Popular culture. I. Burt, Richard, 1954–
II. Boose, Lynda E., 1943–
PR3093.S543 2003
791.43′6–dc21 2002155445

British Library Cataloguing in Publication Data
A catalogue record for this book is available from the British Library

ISBN 0–415–28298–5 (hbk)
ISBN 0–415–28299–3 (pbk)

CONTENTS

List of illustrations vii
Notes on contributors ix

Introduction: Editors' cut 1
RICHARD BURT AND LYNDA E. BOOSE

1 **Shakespeare, "Glo-cali-zation," race, and the small screens of post-popular culture** 14
RICHARD BURT

2 **"Remember me": technologies of memory in Michael Almereyda's *Hamlet*** 37
KATHERINE ROWE

3 **James Dean meets the pirate's daughter: passion and parody in *William Shakespeare's Romeo + Juliet* and *Shakespeare in Love*** 56
MICHAEL ANDEREGG

4 **Sure can sing and dance: minstrelsy, the star system, and the post-postcoloniality of Kenneth Branagh's *Love's Labour's Lost* and Trevor Nunn's *Twelfth Night*** 72
KATHERINE EGGERT

5 **Race-ing *Othello*, re-engendering white-out, II** 89
BARBARA HODGDON

6 **Shakespeare in the age of post-mechanical reproduction: sexual and electronic magic in *Prospero's Books*** 105
PETER S. DONALDSON

7 **A *Shrew* for the times, revisited** 120
DIANA E. HENDERSON

8 Mixing media and animating Shakespeare tales 140
LAURIE OSBORNE

9 Nostalgia and theatricality: the fate of the Shakespearean stage in the *Midsummer Night's Dreams* of Hoffman, Noble, and Edzard 154
DOUGLAS LANIER

10 "Top of the world, ma": *Richard III* and cinematic convention 173
JAMES N. LOEHLIN

11 Shakespeare and the street: Pacino's *Looking for Richard*, Bedford's *Street King*, and the common understanding 186
THOMAS CARTELLI

12 The family tree motel: subliming Shakespeare in *My Own Private Idaho* 200
SUSAN WISEMAN

13 War is mud: Branagh's *Dirty Harry V* and the types of political ambiguity 213
DONALD K. HEDRICK

14 Out damned Scot: dislocating *Macbeth* in transnational film and media culture 231
COURTNEY LEHMANN

15 Dogme Shakespeare 95: European cinema, anti-Hollywood sentiment, and the Bard 252
AMY SCOTT-DOUGLASS

16 Shakespeare and Asia in postdiasporic cinemas: spin-offs and citations of the plays from Bollywood to Hollywood 265
RICHARD BURT

References 304
Filmography 323
Index 329

ILLUSTRATIONS

I.1 Animated menu trailer for *Moulin Rouge DVD* 2
I.2 Curtains open on animated menu trailer for special edition DVD of *William Shakespeare's Romeo + Juliet* 3
I.3 Lovers kiss in animated menu trailer film clip from *William Shakespeare's Romeo + Juliet* 4
I.4 Off the wall digital Shakespeare 5
I.5 Shakespeare, thou art translated 6
1.1 Shakespeare, homeboy 16
2.1 Design for a mental memory theater, John Willis, 1621 40
2.2 Luhrmann's "wooden O" 45
2.3 Video soliloquy 47
2.4 Video memoir 48
2.5 Editing video memories: Hamlet's inner life on screen 48
2.6 Shot/response shot: crossing the screen barrier 50
2.7 Old Hamlet dissolves through the Pepsi machine 51
16.1 Shakespeare goes Bollywood 273
16.2 Bollywood goes Shakespeare 274
16.3 Computing *Hamlet* 289
16.4 Filling in the blanks with *Hamlet* 290
16.5 Buddhist Hamlet 293
16.6 Hamlet's polaroid photo of defaced Buddha 294
16.7 Tea or Hamlet? 295
16.8 To interbe or not to interbe? 296

CONTRIBUTORS

Editor

Richard Burt is Professor of English at the University of Florida, Gainesville, and the author of *Unspeakable ShaXXXspeares: Queer Theory and American Kiddie Culture* (1998) and *Licensed by Authority: Ben Jonson and the Discourses of Censorship* (1993). He is the editor of *Shakespeare after Mass Media* (2002) and the *Administration of Aesthetics: Censorship, Political Criticism, and the Public Sphere*, and co-editor of *Shakespeare, The Movie: Popularizing the Plays on Film, TV, and Video* (1997) and *Enclosure Acts: Sexuality, Property, and Culture in Early Modern England*. Burt is currently writing two books: *Ever Afterlives: Renaissance Remakes on Film and Video* and *Rechanneling Shakespeare across Media: Post-diasporic Citations and Spin-offs from Bollywood to Hollywood*. E-mail: burt@english.ufl.edu

Co-editor

Lynda E. Boose is Professor of English and Women's Studies at Dartmouth College. She has published numerous articles on Shakespeare and Renaissance culture. She co-edited *Shakespeare, The Movie: Popularizing the Plays on Film, TV, and Video* (1997), and an article on rape in Bosnia appeared in *Signs*. E-mail: lynda.boose@dartmouth.edu

Contributors

Michael Anderegg is Professor of English at the University of North Dakota. He is the author of *Orson Welles, Shakespeare, and Popular Culture* (1999), *David Lean* (1984), *William Wyler* (1979), and the editor of *Inventing Vietnam: The War in Film and Television* (1991). E-mail: michael_anderegg@und.nodak.edu

Thomas Cartelli is Professor of English and Chair of the English Department at Muhlenberg College. He is the author of *Repositioning Shakespeare: National Formations, Postcolonial Appropriations* (1999) and *Marlowe, Shakespeare, and the Economy of Theatrical Experience* (1991). Cartelli is at work on two additional books: *Producing Disorder*, a study of the construction of misrule in early modern England and New England, and *New Wave Shakespeares*, a study of modernist and postmodern encounters with the Bard, from which the present essay is drawn. E-mail: cartelli@muhlenberg.edu

Peter S. Donaldson is Professor of Literature at M.I.T. and Director of the Shakespeare Electronic Archive. He is author of *Machiavelli and Mystery of State*,

Shakespearean Films/Shakespearean Directors and of a series of multimedia essays on Shakespeare on film including "Digital Archives and Sibylline Sentences: *The Tempest* and the 'End of Books.'" E-mail: psdlit@mit.edu

Katherine Eggert is Associate Professor of English at the University of Colorado, Boulder. Her publications include *Showing Like a Queen: Female Authority and Literary Experiment in Spenser, Shakespeare, and Milton* (2000), as well as essays on Spenser, Shakespeare, and new historicism. Her essay "Age Cannot Wither Him: Warren Beatty's Bugsy as Hollywood Cleopatra" appeared in *Shakespeare, The Movie*. She is currently working on a study of alchemy in early modern English literature. E-mail: katherine.eggert@colorado.edu

Donald K. Hedrick is Professor of English at Kansas State University, where he was founding Director of the program in Cultural Studies. He has published in film, architectural history, Shakespeare, language and cultural theory, and has been a Visiting Professor at Cornell, Colgate, Amherst College, Charles University in Prague, and the University of California, Irvine. He co-edited with Bryan Reynolds *Shakespeare Without Class: Misappropriations of Cultural Capital* (2000), and his most recent essay is "Advantage, Affect, History, *Henry V*" in *PMLA*. Hedrick's current projects are on early modern entertainment value and movie trailers. E-mail: hedrick@ksu.edu

Diana E. Henderson, Associate Professor of Literature at M.I.T., is the author of *Passion Made Public: Elizabethan Lyric, Gender, and Performance* and numerous articles, including essays on early modern drama, poetry, and domestic culture, Shakespeare on film, James Joyce, and Virginia Woolf. Her current book manuscript is entitled *Uneasy Collaborations: Shakespeare across Time and Media*. E-mail: dianah@mit.edu

Barbara Hodgdon, Adjunct Professor of English at the University of Michigan, is the author of *The End Crowns All: Closure and Contradiction in Shakespeare's History*, *The First Part of King Henry the Fourth: Texts and Contexts*, and *The Shakespeare Trade: Performances and Appropriations*; she is currently editing *The Taming of the Shrew* for the Arden Shakespeare and co-editing, with William B. Worthen, the *Blackwell Companion to Shakespeare and Performance*. E-mail: hodgdonb@umich.edu

Douglas Lanier is Associate Professor of English at the University of New Hampshire. He has published articles on Shakespeare, Marston, Jonson, Milton, the Jacobean masque, and literature pedagogy in a number of journals and collections. His most recent publication is *Shakespeare and Modern Popular Culture* (2002) in the Shakespeare Topics series for Oxford University Press. He is currently working on a project concerning literary representations of disaffected intellectuals in early modern England. E-mail: doug.lanier@unh.edu

Courtney Lehmann is Assistant Professor of English and Film Studies at the University of the Pacific, and Director of the Pacific Humanities Center. She is an award-winning teacher, and author of *Shakespeare Remains: Theater to Film, Early Modern to Postmodern* (2002), as well as co-editor (with Lisa S. Starks) of two collections of Shakespeare and screen criticism: *Spectacular Shakespeare: Critical Theory and Popular Cinema* (2002) and *The Reel Shakespeare: Alternative Cinema and Theory* (2003). E-mail: clehmann@uop.edu

James N. Loehlin is Associate Professor of English and Director of the Shakespeare at Winedale program, where he directs three or four Shakespeare plays every year. He is the author of *Henry V* in the Manchester University Press Shakespeare in Performance series and editor of *Romeo and Juliet* in the Cambridge Shakespeare in Production series. He is currently preparing a stage history of Chekhov's *The Cherry Orchard* for Cambridge University Press. E-mail: jnloehlin@mail.utexas.edu

Laurie Osborne is Associate Professor of English at Colby College. She has published *The Trick of Singularity: Twelfth Night and the Performance Editions*, as well as several essays on Renaissance audiences and Shakespeare in film and popular culture. Her recent work includes "Harlequin Presents: That 70's Shakespeare and Beyond" in *Shakespeare after Mass Media*, "Shakespeare and the Construction of Character" in *Shakespeare Yearbook*, and "Clip Art: Theorizing the Shakespearean Film Clip" in *Shakespeare Quarterly*. E-mail: leosborn@colby.edu

Katherine Rowe is Associate Professor of English at Bryn Mawr College and the author of *Dead Hands: Fictions of Agency, Renaissance to Modern* (1999), as well as articles on Shakespeare, Renaissance drama, and early modern psychology. Her current projects include a co-edited anthology, *Reading the Early Modern Passions: Essays in the Cultural History of Emotion* (2003), and a study of contractual relations in Stuart drama. E-mail: krowe@brynmawr.edu

Amy Scott-Douglass is an Assistant Professor of English and Comparative Literature at California State University, Fullerton. She has published on Margaret Cavendish, and is currently completing a monograph on paratextual materials to books by seventeenth-century Englishwomen entitled *The Female Preface*. E-mail: ascott-douglass@fullerton.edu

Susan Wiseman teaches English at Birkbeck College. She is the author of *Drama and Politics in the English Civil War* (1998) and co-editor of *Refashioning Ben Jonson: Gender, Politics* (1998) and *The Jonsonian Canon and Women, Writing, History, 1640–1740* (1992). E-mail: s.wiseman@bbk.ac.uk

INTRODUCTION

Editors' cut

Richard Burt and Lynda E. Boose

I

Richard Burt

Since *Shakespeare, The Movie* went to press in 1997, Shakespeare adaptations, spin-offs, and citations on film and television have continued to gallop apace, and Shakespeare has continued to race at the forefront of new cinematic technologies. The German modern adaptation *Rave MacBeth* (dir. Klaus Knoesel, 2001), for example, was the first film to be shot on Sony's new generation of 24-p (progressive scanning) 1080 cameras.[1] Similarly, Kristian Levring's Dogme95 film *The King is Alive* (2000) was among the first to be shot entirely on digital film, and Michael Almereyda's *Hamlet* (2001) includes extensive footage shot on a digital camcorder. Our new subtitle acknowledges a related development: Shakespeare on film is now seen in post-theatrical release not only on video but on DVD as well, and DVDs are seen both on television screens as well as computer screens.[2]

The essays in *Shakespeare, The Movie, II*, mostly new, a few reprinted as they were in the previous volume, and a few others updated, focus on the 1990s and the millennial resurgence of Shakespeare on film and television that began with Branagh's *Henry V*. The sheer volume of Shakespeare films and television productions has made total coverage of them impossible, and the aim is less to provide an update than it is to consider how film itself and television have changed in the 1990s in the wake of globalization and digitalization. Whereas *Shakespeare, The Movie* aimed to go beyond a dialogic model of text and film, in which a Shakespeare film is evaluated in terms of how faithful it is to the original, and arrive at a more cinematic model in which a Shakespeare film is examined as an object worthy of critical attention in its own right, *Shakespeare, The Movie, II* acknowledges how Shakespeare's popularization on DVD has involved the transformation of film itself. If the "original" text had been displaced by the secondary film, viewed prior to reading, the DVD edition has now effectively displaced the film viewing. We are now invited to attend not only to a given Shakespeare film as shown in theatrical release and on the DVD but to a series of DVD extras such as menu trailers, deleted scenes, audio commentaries, interviews, "making of" documentaries, music videos, video games, and so on. Taking Shakespeare on DVD into account also involves taking into consideration the circulation of film and television adaptations not only in cinematographic and televisual contexts but, more broadly, in other mass media such as comics, novelizations, advertising, video games, and live performances in theaters of various kinds.[3] In transforming film, the digitalization of film on DVDs has also transformed both the way in which films are produced and viewed. Indeed, DVDs are so often released in multiple editions, each with more added features, that the president of a DVD distribution company commented in 2002 that "the initial release of the motion picture in movie theaters is becoming, to a large extent, little more than a preview trailer for the subsequent purchase of the DVD" (Lyman 2002).[4]

In this introduction, I would like to consider two ways in which Shakespeare's popularization has been altered and expanded by digitalization and globalization, the first being film's circulation and alteration in other media and the other being a shift from national to transnational cinemas. I want to focus first on a small feature of many DVDs, the animated menu trailer, as seen on two DVDs, Baz Luhrmann's *Moulin Rouge* (where a character in the film calls the poet (Ewan McGregor) Shakespeare) and the "Special Edition" DVD of *William Shakespeare's Romeo + Juliet*, released about six months after the release of the *Moulin Rouge* DVD had appeared. Historicist Shakespeare film and television criticism typically focuses on the moment when a film or program was first released, asking why a particular play was filmed at a particular time, often locating it in relation to some widely known extra-cinematic event that occurred around the same time. The animated menu trailers on the Luhrmann DVDs challenge this kind

Figure I.1 Animated menu trailer for *Moulin Rouge DVD.*

of historicism, however, by alerting us to the way a film's multiple release in different media allows the film to be seen in multiple versions on multiple screens. This multiplicity complicates any attempt to historicize film by linking its meaning to a single historical moment.[5] The two Luhrmann DVD animated menu trailers acknowledge a much more complex temporality of reception by functioning not only as double previews (reframing the film itself as a trailer for the DVD edition and framing the menu trailer as a trailer for the DVD edition) but as retrospective "postviews" as well.

The *Moulin Rouge* animated menu trailer recapitulates a narrative of media transformations in the history of film already present in the film titles. The trailer recapitulates the opening of the film itself, which begins in a movie theater with the curtains closed, and then a conductor appears as if the viewer were actually in a live theater. The soundtrack then begins. After the film credits roll, the first sequence of *Moulin Rouge* is presented as if from a silent film.[6] On the DVD animated menu, the theater appears with curtains closed, and then the menu options appear on the screen as a Tinkerbell-like fairy holding up a bottle of absinthe appears in the upper right of the screen. Whereas the film *Moulin Rouge* charts a move forward from theater to silent film to celluloid film with digital special effects to suggest a postmodern updating of 1900 Parisian Bohemia, the DVD reframes those transitions according to a different temporality, as the gains of extra features on the DVD but also as the loss of the movie-theater viewing experience.

The animated menu trailer of the second DVD "special" edition of *William Shakespeare's Romeo + Juliet* is a mini-allegory of the double temporality of the menu trailer as preview and postview. We first see the theater of the Sycamore Grove (from the film) digitally altered as a classical-looking proscenium stage, with palm trees behind, icons from the film across the bottom of the stage, and the menu options where the seats would ordinarily be.

Figure I.2 Curtains open on animated menu trailer for special edition DVD *of William Shakespeare's Romeo + Juliet.*

As the theater curtains open and the camera pulls back from the stage, we see a trailer within this animated menu trailer composed of film credits and then clips taken from the film, including Romeo's and Juliet's first kiss, digitally altered to appear as if they were taken from a silent film, with a sunset seen more fully in the background.[7]

The animated menu trailer(s) recall the experience of film itself in a movie theater as something in the past, nearly unavailable as an alternative to the DVD, at best capable of being reanimated by this supplementary edition. Indeed, from one point of view, the DVD's extra features and multiple editions are less a struggle to provide the definitive version of the film than they are attempts to compensate for the loss of the now largely unattainable experience of watching the film in a movie theater.[8]

Film on video and DVD involves a shift in reception from historical to posthistorical time. "Media cross one another in time," Friedrich Kittler writes, "which is no longer history" (1986/1999: 115). The horizon of reception is hence far from limited to the moment of release, then. The horizon is composed of multiple viewing possibilities that reframe the initial theatrical viewing, if it occurred at all, in media that are often old and new (DVDs textualize film, for example by dividing scenes up into chapters) and that are both increasingly integrated – such as the computer as home theater – and dispersed – such as cell phones and portable DVD players.

The consequence is that film reception has become posthistorical. Prior to video and DVD, that is, the experience of viewing film might be considered historical. As Stanley Cavell notes, "movies . . . at least some movies, maybe most, used to exist in something that resembles [a] condition of evanescence, viewable only in certain places at certain times, discussible solely as occasions for sociable exchange, and never seen more than once, and then more or less forgotten" (1982: 78). Moreover, the horizon of reception is multiplied by the coexistence of DVDs and VCRs. Although the adoption of DVD in the US has occurred more quickly than it has with any other technology, even television, DVDs will likely not replace video cassettes the way CDs almost totally replaced

Figure I.3 Lovers kiss in animated menu trailer film clip from *William Shakespeare's Romeo + Juliet.*

records and audio cassettes both because the release of DVD versions of earlier films on video has occurred at a very slow rate and because a large volume of (increasingly inexpensive) VCRs continue to be sold (Pike-Johnson 2002). This is not to say that historicist film criticism has no value; it is, rather, to acknowledge the challenge to historicist criticism, the need to what Žižek calls "over-rapid historicization" (1989: 50). In *The Fright of Real Tears*, Žižek advises:

> One should avoid . . . the historicist trap: . . . unique circumstance does not account for the "truth" and universal scope of the analysed phenomenon. It is precisely against . . . hasty historicizers that one should refer to Marx's famous observation apropos of Homer: it is easy to explain how Homer's poetry emerged from early Greek society; what is much more difficult to explain is its universal appeal, i.e. why it continues to exert its charm even today.
>
> (2001, 8).[9]

The second significant way in which Shakespeare's popularization has been transformed since the first edition is by globalization and the emergence of transnational cinema. Transnationalism marks cinematic production from the start. As Ella Shohat and Robert Stam point out in their essay on media spectatorship in the age of globalization, "the dispersed nature of the globalizing process, and the global reach of mass media, virtually oblige the critic to move beyond the restrictive framework of the nation state" (1996: 145).[10] Along similar lines Mitsuhiro Yoshimoto writes:

> Production, distribution, and consumption of films is no longer possible outside of influences of global capital which transgress national boundaries. In other words, the idea of nationality does not seem to provide the most useful way of thinking about the junction of cinema and global capitalism.
>
> (1996: 108–9)

Figure I.4 Off the wall digital Shakespeare.

We can appreciate the inter-connection between cinema's digitalization and globalization by considering an extraordinarily self-reflexive moment in the documentary *Kurosawa* (dir. Adam Low, 2001) in which we see, from the street, a screening of *Throne of Blood* (*Kumonosu jo*, dir. Akira Kurosawa, 1957), the celebrated adaptation of *Macbeth* set in feudal Japan, in a strikingly multimedia and multilingual setting in downtown Tokyo. The final minutes of *Throne of Blood* are being broadcast on a huge television screen on the side of a building in a Tokyo shopping area. As the camera zooms in closer, we see a sign in English saying "Ships United Arrows" and two Gap clothing company logos to the left of the "Flags Vision" screen, with a small USA on the lower right of the video frame. And on the screen, Lord Taketori Washizu (Mifune Toshiro), the samurai equivalent of Macbeth, is being pierced by a multitude of arrows. As Washizu gets the *coup de grâce* with an arrow in his neck, the word "arrows" (as well as "gap" and "ships") on the left comes into clearer focus. After Washizu falls down dead, we see the audience leaving the cineplex art-movie theater, with a name foreign to Japan, "Lumine 2", where they have just seen the film inside.[11]

The screening of *Throne of Blood* both outside and inside a cineplex transforms our sense of what is foreign Shakespeare, what is native, and hence poses a challenge to postcolonial Shakespeare criticism. Kurosawa's film, itself an adaptation of a text foreign to Japan, is positioned next to identifying US- and Japanese-owned corporations with English logos (Flags Vision is a Japanese company) which are of course foreign in Tokyo. To be sure, the foreign status of *Throne of Blood* has always been contested: it is a Japanese film according to Kurosawa and nearly all Western film critics, but an international, highly Westernized film according to many Japanese.[12] The fact that the documentary, funded by the BBC and in English, is addressed to a Western audience estranges the already strange Japanese Westernization of Kurosawa's "Japanified" Shakespeare. The screening of *Throne of Blood* in an art-house cinema named "Lumine" positions Kurosawa's film as foreign for its Japanese audience (the

Figure I.5 Shakespeare, thou art translated.

film is foreign, that is to say, as much because it is directed by Kurosawa as because it is an adaptation of Shakespeare) but "foreignizes" it for the Western audience as well; that is, the name "Lumine" is foreign to native Japanese speakers and to contemporary native English (and French) speakers as well.[13] "Lumine" is an obsolete English word derived from an Old French word meaning to illuminate, initially in manuscripts. "Lumine" also implicitly signals Kurosawa's international reception, particularly in the US (George Lucas and Steven Spielberg, being notable supporters), and in France (Chris Marker did a documentary on the making of *Ran* entitled *AK*, in 1985), where the Japanese that replaces Shakespeare's language is in turn translated accurately into French as *Le Château de l'araignée* [*The Castle of the Spider's Web*].[14]

Along the lines of the menu trailers in the Luhrmann DVDs, the multimedia (re)screening of *Throne of Blood* in Tokyo multiplies the screens (on the wall, in the theater, on the television showing the documentary) such that an opposition between the foreign Shakespeare play and the indigenous Kurosawa film seems impossible to maintain; everything is "foreignized." The screens on which the film is shown differ, to be sure: one external, seen without sound, for free, and in passing so that a given film clip acts like a movie trailer; the other internal, seen with sound, paid for, and in its entirety. Yet even this distinction between internal and external breaks down. The external film image, the surface, is not really a ghostly double or simulacrum of the original (which is not seen by us in the theater); rather, the number of the theater – 2 – echoes the two Gap clothing logos, reminding us that the film print shown inside is not original but itself already a copy, a double, a specter.

How we are to make sense of this multimedia screening of *Throne of Blood* is far from clear. Though the word "arrows" in the partially seen corporate logo to the left of the screen image tantalizingly and somewhat comically suggests a parallel between the word "arrows" and the arrows piercing Lord Washizu in the film, there is not a hermeneutic relation between them but a gap, or gaps, as it were, separating the commercial word and the screen image next to it. Indeed, the conjunction of film clip and logo is purely coincidental, an accident. (Kurosawa's) Shakespeare is being shipped like an arrow, so to speak, but the film does not follow a trajectory by which it arrives at a final destination, like the arrows that kill Washizu at the end of *Throne of Blood*. Hence, there is no point or moment, either, at which we cross a border clearly marking (Western) Shakespeare in Asian films from Asia in (Western) Shakespeare films, the indigenous Shakespeare from the foreign.[15]

Just as the Luhrmann animated menu trailers challenge existing historicist film strategies, so too the rescreening of Kurosawa challenges many of the dominant strategies of relocating resistance for subversion in anti-institutional and popular uses of Shakespeare. These new venues for screenings of film and the new features often found on DVD editions of film are supplementary to the film as seen in theatrical release, but whether they are in any way subversive or subaltern is open to debate.[16]

II

Lynda E. Boose

The essays in *Shakespeare, The Movie, II* engage new developments in Shakespeare, cinema, television, DVD, and other technologies and mass media in a variety of ways.

The problem with trying to be *au courant* is not simply that new Shakespeare films and television programs will have been released and broadcast by the time a given collection or monograph is in print but that the very media by which Shakespeare is produced and reproduced date one's work.[17] Popular culture has arguably been displaced by digital culture and, like film, academic criticism is being transformed by digital culture. As editors, we want to acknowledge, then, that the variety of essays in *Shakespeare, The Movie, II* reflects this transitional moment in academia: as we move from print to online books and make use of websites, older modes of criticism and, more crucially, of publication seem less and less adequate both to the object of criticism and to the criticism itself.

In "Shakespeare, 'Glo-cali-zation,' Race, and the Small Screens of Post-popular Culture" Richard Burt argues the heterogeneity of popular culture and its mass mediatization call into question assumptions about Shakespeare, popular, and elite culture shared by the Left and the Right. Focusing on Shakespeare's relation to popular culture as it relates to pedagogy, race, and nationalism in the US and the UK, Burt traces the impact of what he calls "glo-cali-zation," the collapse of the local and the global into the "glocal" and the retention of "Cali" (or Hollywood) as the discursive center of the film industry, on Shakespeare on film and television from the late 1990s into the millennium. Burt also notes that television and film now often overlap, as many of the contributors to this volume make clear (see also Willems 2000). The reproduction of Shakespeare film on DVD has occurred at the same time Shakespeare has moved from the big screen to the small screen (and television programs, once relatively evanescent, appear on DVDs and video cassettes as entire seasons).

In " 'Remember me': Technologies of Memory in Michael Almeryeda's *Hamlet*," Katherine Rowe observes that recent work on Shakespeare and film has tended to leave the text behind in order to move beyond questions of cinematic faithfulness. Yet this reasonable impulse effectively obscures the ways cultural practices based on older technologies – such as playtexts and writing – persist in and shape our uses of the newer forms, such as film and video. Almereyda's film *Hamlet* offers an opportunity for comparatist analysis of what Michel Serres would call the "polychronic" nature of these technologies: the early memory technologies allegorized in Shakespeare's play; the multimedia practices illustrated in John Willis's 1621 manual, *The Art of Memory*; the mnemonic grammar of television and video editing; and even the forms of quotation we use in scholarly discussions of printed and audio/visual texts.

The next three essays concern shifts in UK and US national cinemas and Shakespeare as well as race. In "James Dean meets the Pirate's Daughter: Passion and Parody in *William Shakespeare's Romeo + Juliet* and *Shakespeare in Love*," Michael Anderegg argues that Baz Luhrmann's *William Shakespeare's Romeo + Juliet* and John Madden's *Shakespeare in Love* reconstitute Shakespeare's popular romantic tragedy for a turn-of-the-millennium audience. Both films are homages to Shakespeare and to his play and at the same time popularizations that sacrifice Shakespeare's otherness in order to appeal to a contemporary audience. And both films testify to the continuing fascination of *Romeo and Juliet* as an iconic text in popular culture. Katherine Eggert, in "Sure Can Sing and Dance: Minstrelsy, the Star System, and the Post-postcoloniality of Kenneth Branagh's *Love's Labour's Lost* and Trevor Nunn's *Twelfth Night*," explores this changing relation between Shakespeare's position in British and US film, television, and other mass media. It is not surprising that the films and television programs

Hodgdon examines in her essay on 1990s *Othellos*, "Race-ing *Othello*, Re-engendering White-out, II," do not easily contrast in terms of how Shakespearean and how English they are. Both the US-produced film *O* and the ITV version of *Othello* modernize the language.[18] Hodgdon examines three recent films – Oliver Parker's *Othello* (1995), Andrew Davies's ITV *Othello* (dir. Geoffrey Sax, 2001) and Tim Blake Nelson's *O* (2001) – each an example of a different genre – the "Shakespeare remake," the television docudrama, and the Shakespeare high-school film. Reading how each version of the play aligns with and (re)mediates contemporary events – the aftermath of the O.J. Simpson trial, Britain's Stephen Lawrence case, and America's recent wave of high-school violence – she explores how these re-performances circulate metanarratives of race and engage with cultural tropes of white paranoia.

Peter S. Donaldson's "Shakespeare in the Age of Post-mechanical Reproduction: Sexual and Electronic Magic in *Prospero's Books*" registers in part how what used to be the province of the art film, digital media, have now already become commonplace in the mall film. Donaldson maintains that *Prospero's Books* gives recent and psychoanalytic readings as a story about Prospero's attempts to control female sexuality and appropriate the birth-giving powers of the maternal a technological inflection, associating Prospero's (Sir John Gielgud) magic with the power of digital media to create enhanced illusions of life. Because the film relies so heavily on digital-image technologies and foregrounds their workings, *Prospero's Books* is not only a reading of *The Tempest*, but also a metadigital or metacomputational allegory: it links new media to the wonder-working technologies of the Renaissance. Greenaway's avant-garde film strategies have since been played out in new cinematic territory as the art film has hybridized with the popular film, as in Julie Taymor's *Titus* and Almereyda's *Hamlet*, in which Sir John Gielgud is literally decentered by Ethan Hawke.

Diana E. Henderson and Laurie Osborne both engage Shakespeare and youth culture. Henderson explores the teen film in her updated version of her essay, "A *Shrew* for the Times," considering both the possibilities and ghosts lurking in spin-offs such as *10 Things I Hate About You*. Henderson maintains that *The Taming of the Shrew*'s frequent representation on film and video during periods of antifeminist backlash is more than coincidental. Although adapters have long striven to make the story more palatable by creating extratextual moments of subjectivity for Katherine and emphasizing an erotic bond between the principals, the problematic nature of the changes themselves suggests the need for an esthetic that will offer an alternative to textual fidelity in filming Shakespeare.

In "Mixing Media and Animating Shakespeare Tales," Laurie Osborne argues that the second series of *Shakespeare: The Animated Tales* builds on the first series because of the provocative ways that these *Tales* self-consciously meditate on the mixture of media at work in animation. The cel animation of *Julius Caesar* and *Othello* pushes the boundaries of animated representation of character whereas the puppetry of *The Winter's Tale* and *The Taming of the Shrew* self-consciously foregrounds the blends of artistic forms in the plays through distinctive uses of sculpture and movement, folk tales, and conventional puppet shows. *Richard III* and *As You Like It* play out still more vividly the interaction of different modes of artistic production represented within the plays as well as with the animations. As a consequence, the artistic productions of *Shakespeare: The Animated Tales* serve as a useful gateway into a consideration of our current multimedia Shakespeare.[19]

The relation between live Shakespeare theater production and film adaptation is addressed by Douglas Lanier in his essay "Nostalgia and Theatricality: The Fate of the Shakespearean Stage in the *Midsummer Night's Dreams* of Hoffman, Noble, and Edzard," which deals with the representation of live theater in three *Midsummer Night's Dreams*, and by James N. Loehlin in his updated essay " 'Top of the World, Ma': *Richard III* and cinematic convention." In the film adaptations of *A Midsummer Night's Dream* by Michael Hoffman, Adrian Noble, and Christine Edzard, the insistent theatricality of Shakespeare's play, according to Lanier, becomes bound up with nostalgia for some utopian – or at least preferable – cultural past with which Shakespeare is metonymically linked. Hoffman links *Midsummer* with heritage film and its preoccupation with the last hurrah of European aristocratic culture before the advent of modernity, while Noble and Edzard re-imagine *Midsummer* through the rosy perspective of childhood and children's culture, that moment putatively before the fall into adulthood and the demands of the symbolic. Loehlin examines the way Richard Loncraine's *Richard III* (1995) modernizes the history it tells by appropriating the cinematic codes of genres like the British heritage film and the American gangster movie. For this updated version, Loehlin has added a discussion of the recently rediscovered 1912 *Richard III* starring Frederick Warde, a film that anticipates Loncraine's in placing a flamboyantly theatrical performance in a distinctly cinematic setting. The differing concerns with theatricality and nostalgia in these works illuminate cinema's ambivalent relationship to Shakespeare's persistent association with the stage.

Urban locations figure prominently in 1990s and millennial Shakespeare-related films, with the road and the road movie as possible alternatives to the urban film noir. Consider the romantic comedy *Head Over Heels* (dir. Mark S. Waters, 2001): set in New York City, the main character, Jim Winston (Freddy Prinz), an undercover FBI agent, walks his dog, a great dane named Hamlet, and runs into his love interest.[20] The lead woman character, Amanda Pierce (Monica Potter), tells him she gets the joke. She is herself a kind of Hamlet figure, unable to decide, on the basis of *Rear Window*-like spying from her apartment with her roommates on him in his apartment, if he is suitable romantic material or a deadly stalker. Thomas Cartelli in "Shakespeare and the Street: Pacino's *Looking for Richard*, Bedford's *Street King* and the Common Understanding" and Sue Wiseman in "The Family Tree Motel: Subliming Shakespeare in *My Own Private Idaho*" explore the ambiguities of a romance with Shakespeare, the urban street, and rural road.[21] Cartelli focuses mainly on Al Pacino's efforts to assimilate Shakespeare to the rhythms and emotions of the American street in his docu-dramatic film *Looking for Richard*. Pacino does not so much seek to "stage" Shakespeare as he does to restructure our experience of the play by maximizing the dramatic potential of individual moments of the playtext in a manner that resists the American theater's slavishly colonial devotion to the full Shakespearean script. In a sustained coda to his essay, Cartelli extends his discussion to a more recent filmic exploration of *Richard III*, James Gavin Bedford's *The Street King* (aka *King Rikki* or *Rikki the Pig*), in which irony, more than the earnest quest for emotional truth, characterizes the effort to translate Shakespeare's tragedy into the idioms of the street. Wiseman acknowledges that, in Van Sant's film *My Own Private Idaho*, Shakespeare may not save a critique of American masculinity, but he does authenticate the decidedly different cultural narrative of the paternal and filial street bonds of gay hustlers versus those of inhabited privilege and social legitimacy, a narrative that self-consciously invokes within scenes it self-consciously quotes – via Orson Welles's *Chimes at Midnight* – from the *Henry IV* and *Henry V* plays.

Donald K. Hedrick's essay "War is Mud: Branagh's *Dirty Harry V* and the Types of Political Ambiguity" throws into relief a significant trend away from the national Shakespeare cinema that preceded the wave of Shakespeare films that followed Branagh's *Henry V* (1989). Characterized by its visual representation under the sign of dirt, Branagh's film adds to the historically changing charisma of Henry in ways that draw not only from American film but from American military ideology. Branagh accordingly creates the political complexity cultural critics usually unpack, but a conservative ambiguity rather than, as in Shakespeare, a critical one: Branagh's is neither pro-war nor anti-war since he excuses the King because of the muddy nature of war, excuses war because of the dark side of the King. Directing, playwriting, ruling, and military action are conjoined politically as the organization of movement. In "Out Damned Scot: Dislocating *Macbeth* in Transnational Film and Media Culture," Courtney Lehmann takes up the emergence of post-national cinemas and Shakespeare in relation to a surge of *Macbeth* adaptations in the 1990s, including Michael Bogdanov's television adaptation (1998), spin-offs such as *Macbeth: The Comedy* (dir. Lisa LiCalsi, 2001), and the porn adaptation, *In the Flesh* (dir. Stuart Canterbury, 1999). Lehmann demonstrates how the Scottish play has become a post-Scottish film and television phenomenon, arguing that *Macbeth* has emerged not only as a symptom of global capitalism's relentless reterritorialization of the very idea of the nation state, but also as an affirmation of the perverse states of mind that perpetuate it.

The final two essays address much neglected areas of Shakespeare in film studies: European and Asian cinemas. In "Dogme Shakespeare 95: European Cinema, Anti-Hollywood Sentiment, and the Bard," Amy Scott-Douglass looks at Thomas Vinterberg's *The Celebration* [*Festen*] (1998) and Kristian Levring's *The King is Alive* (2000), two films out of the Danish minimalist cinema movement, Dogme95. This essay considers the films' borrowings from and uses of *Hamlet* and *King Lear*, and places the films and the Dogme95 movement in the context of European/American debates about cinema at the turn of the millennium. In his essay "Shakespeare and Asia in Postdiasporic Cinemas: Spin-offs and Citations of the Plays from Bollywood to Hollywood," Burt looks at a number of Shakespeare-related films that involve the Asian diaspora, including that of Australia, in the Bollywood film *Dil Chahta Hai*, Bollywood in Luhrmann's *Moulin Rouge*, England and New York in Merchant Ivory's *The Golden Bowl*, the New York streets in *China Girl* and Almereyda's *Hamlet*, and the Malibu of the *Hamlet*-citing teen "chiller" *The Glass House*. Burt argues that present models of postcolonialism and the diasporic imaginary do not adequately address the complexity either of transnational cinemas or of Shakespeare's global migrations.

Notes

1 See *Rare Macbeth* webpage: <http://www.german-cinema.de/archive/film_view.php?film_id=580>.
2 DVD manufacturers and retailers are quoted by Lyman 2002.
3 See Burt 2002a.
4 "Directors have embraced the format so enthusiastically, much more than they ever did with VHS," Mr. Feingold said. "As a result, they're getting involved right from the beginning in the making of the extra DVD material and taking a much more hands-on approach to the

DVD release. It can't help but have an impact" (Lyman 2002). See also Geuens 2002. On the use of film clips as trailers in Shakespeare classes, see Osborne 2002.

5 To be sure, film itself resists this kind of historicist criticism.

6 The theatrical frame in film is nothing new, of course. Marcel Carne uses it at the opening of his film, *Les Enfants du paradis* (1945), which also makes frequent Shakespeare allusions.

7 Compare the Luhrmann menu trailer to the use of clips from silent Shakespeare films at the beginning of *Theatre of Blood* (dir. Douglas Hickox, 1973). These clips set up Edward Lionheart (Vincent Price) as a has-been and inadequate Shakespearean. The opening credits of *Scotland, Pa* (dir. Billy Morrissette, 2001) also roll over a full-screen clip from the end of a *McCloud* television series (aired 1970–7), effectively silenced by the soundtrack music and made archaic by being shown in black and white (the show was broadcast in color). Trevor Nunn's *Merchant of Venice* (2001) also begins with what is made to look like silent film footage of Venice as the credits roll, and then the performance of the play starts as the camera cuts to a television stage set.

8 On the film, see Donaldson (2002).

9 Žižek makes a similar point in 1989: 49–50.

10 Shohat and Stam point out that the theoretical challenge in addressing global media is to avoid either euphoria or melancholy:

> The globalization thesis . . . often descends into teleological assumptions of global integration and uniformity or into unidirectional accounts of cultural imperialism and obliteration. There is a corresponding tendency among those who assert the primacy of the local to mythologize independence from international power structures and to romanticize indigenous cultural forms.
>
> (1996: 146)

11 There is a similar estrangement in reading the letters at the right-hand bottom of the Flags Vision screen. They are apparently "USA" but because of their altered shape look like "Lisa." The Flags Vision website has headings in English, but the text is in Japanese. See <http://www.flags-vision.co.jp>.

12 On the way Western critics of the film have tried to identify *Throne of Blood* as a Japanese film, see Yoshimoto 2000: 253–8.

13 The final shot of the BBC documentary returns to the wall screening of *Throne of Blood* and pulls back and upwards to reveal the Lumine cinema nearby, as if looking down from the perspective of Kurosawa's ghost.

14 See the French DVD, part of a six-film DVD Kurosawa collection available in France only. Chris Marker's documentary is on the French DVD, *Le Château de l'araignée* [*The Castle of the Spider's Web*]. Kurosawa's film was itself indebted to French cinema. For its particular debt to Melies, see Forsyth 2000: 284.

15 On the post-hermeneutic, see Burt 1999 and Burt 2001.

16 See, for example, Dipesh Chakrabarty's critique of Western historicism in *Provincializing Europe* (2000). Chakrabarty argues that we must go "beyond historicism" to account for marginal groups, and he opposes the Bengali *addas*, a discussion without a specific point or duration and Heidegger's notion of ontic-belonging to Marxist notions of history, which bring with them a notion of linear progression that efface what Chakrabarty calls "heterotemporalities," other possible futures already present in the past. Though Chakrabarty directs his critique at a European philosophy of history, it applies equally well to postcolonial critiques of Eurocentrism. Current versions of postcolonial Shakespeare criticism, especially in invoking the precolonial and thereby implying a teleology toward the colonial, reinscribe precisely the kind of linear history and its attendant exclusions that Chakrabarty rightly criticizes. This kind of historicism has produced contorted attempts to read *Othello* as a play about colonialism. (To be sure, Othello was once enslaved, he tells us, but by other Africans, not by Europeans.)

17 See Willems (2000), for example, which focuses only on video, not on DVD.

18 A film Hodgdon does not take up in her essay in this volume, the adult spin-off *Hotel O* (dir. Roy Karch, 2002), also mentions Shakespeare (and O.J. Simpson).

19 Charles Lamb was foundational for the *Shakespeare: The Animated Tales* series, as Osborne notes in her essay. But in Louisa May Alcott's *Little Women*, Shakespeare comes to the US via the German Professor Bhaer. In the 1990s in the US, Shakespeare has also massively appeared in children's books, including a pop-up Shakespeare, Shakespeare with CD-ROM. Linda Johns (a pen name?) wrote a toilet-training book called *To Pee or Not to Pee* (1998), illustrated by Dana Regan, and published by All by Myself Books. *Kids Discover* did a special issue on Shakespeare.

20 See <http://us.imdb.com/Title?0192111>.

21 Queer sexuality has also made its appearance in a number of films since *Shakespeare, The Movie* appeared, including a gay teen in *Scotland, Pa*; the lesbian adaptation *Macbeth: The Comedy* (dir. Lisa LiCalsi, 2001); a lesbian scene in *Orange County* (dir. Jake Kasdan, 2002); and a lesbian character who cites Shakespeare in *Lost and Delirious* (dir. Lea Pool, 2001).

1

SHAKESPEARE, "GLO-CALI-ZATION," RACE, AND THE SMALL SCREENS OF POST-POPULAR CULTURE

Richard Burt

"I don't like Shakespeare. I'd rather be in Malibu."

Anthony Hopkins[1]

Dislocation, dislocation, dislocation

In *Orange County* (dir. Jake Kasdan 2002), Mr. Burke (Mike White), a high-school English teacher, asks his students who comes to mind when they hear the names "Romeo" and "Juliet." One student responds, "Claire Danes," and another adds "Leonardo DiCaprio." Overlooking the constantly raised hand of the film's protagonist, Shaun Brumder (Colin Hanks), Mr. Burke says that another person was involved in "that movie" (Baz Luhrmann's 1996 *William Shakespeare's Romeo + Juliet*) who "in some ways is as famous as Leonardo DiCaprio," and then holds up a Folger edition of *Romeo and Juliet*, and names "William Shakespeare." The scene hardly ends up confirming Shakespeare's status as a literary writer, however.[2] Mr. Burke proceeds not to value literature and print over film but the opposite, as the film's satire of literature's low value among adult as well youth culture is driven home. "And some great movies were based on [Shakespeare's] plays," Mr. Burke comments, and then ticks off the titles as Shaun looks increasingly puzzled: "*Hamlet, West Side Story, The Talented Mr. Ripley, Waterworld, Gladiator, Chocolat.*"[3]

Yet the film undercuts its satire of a present indifference to esthetic distinctions between literature and film as well as among films (which *Hamlet* is being referred to?) by consistently devaluing literature in the serious and non-serious moments of the film. Shaun wants to become a writer and go to Stanford University, and his story, first seen in the beginning, shares the same title as the film, "Orange County." Shaun's girlfriend, Ashley (Schuyler Fisk), ends her praise for his short story by saying "it could be a movie," and when Shaun suggests that Toni Morrison be invited as the graduation speaker, the school Principal (Chevy Chase) opts instead for pop star Britney Spears. Similarly, a Stanford student who wants to become a writer lists novels, short stories, and screenplays as his interests, and says he has a television project going on vampires which, he explains, is really about "the reunification of Germany – but still funny."

By the end of the film, Shaun decides that it is best both for him and for his writing to remain "on location" in *Orange County*. It turns out that the collapse of elite and pop culture evident in Shaun's high-school English class also obtains at Stanford. Shaun meets a female student who is reading Faulkner and who invites him to a party. He takes her up on the invitation, but when Shaun asks her at the party if she likes Faulkner, she shrugs and says "it's pretty boring" and that maybe she'll "get the CliffsNotes." When her friends walk up to them, Red Hot Chili Peppers' "Butterfly" plays and the women excitedly move to the dance floor and do the very same dance routine the cheerleaders did earlier to the same song at Shaun's high school. Moreover, the Stanford English professor Marcus Skinner, played by Kevin Kline, with whom Shaun wants to study, is equally disappointing. Unlike the serious teachers Kline played in *In and Out* (dir. Frank Oz, 1998), where he cited Shakespeare, and *The Emperor's Club* (dir. Michael Hoffman, 2002) or Robin Williams played in *Dead Poets Society* (dir. Peter Weir, 1986), this English professor offers Shaun only empty praise ("it's very good") and empty criticism ("you need an ending"). Given the universal triumph of popular culture even in elite higher education, it makes no difference if Shaun goes to Stanford, the Harvard of the West Coast, or the fictional Orange County University, where Shaun's girlfriend Ashley has been accepted.

Yet the very universality of popular culture also undercuts Shaun's rationale for staying in Orange County so he can be a writer. By the end, when Shaun cites the examples of James Joyce and William Faulkner as writers who did not leave their regions or cities of origin, the idea that writing is tied to the writer's location has become meaningless. Shaun immediately corrects himself in the case of Joyce, and he is simply wrong about Faulkner, who did leave the South and go to Hollywood to write screenplays. There is no *locus classicus* for writing in the film, then.

Orange County's satire of the low value accorded literature in contemporary high-school pedagogy and in our culture moves beyond the earlier comic reversals of literature and film in *Clueless* (dir. Amy Heckerling, 1995), which actually did involve knowledge of a recognizable and canonical Shakespeare film, Franco Zeffirelli's *Hamlet* (1992), and *Last Action Hero* (dir. John McTiernan 1992), which did show a clip from Olivier's *Hamlet*. In *Clueless*, Mel Gibson was a mnemonic device for Cher (Alicia Silverstone) that allowed her to identify the character in *Hamlet* who delivers a cited line correctly and impress the guy she likes; and in *Last Action Hero*, Danny Madigan's (Austin O'Brien) memory of the Jack Slater (Arnold Schwarzenegger) action film he has seen before class allows him to leave Olivier's version behind as he fantasizes his own trailer-length *Hamlet* as action film. Yet in *Orange County*, nothing other than the lead movie stars is considered memorable about "that film," *William Shakespeare's Romeo + Juliet*, not even its name. Shakespeare's foundational status as printed text and even as canonical film is emptied out, and star fan trivia games such as "six degrees of separation" count as knowledge.

In a failed and rather futile attempt to tie writing to location, *Orange County* shows how difficult it is to place and locate Shakespeare in the wake of the digitalization and multimediatization of film and what I call, if I may be permitted a neologism that also contains a pun, "glo-cali-zation." By "glo-cali-zation," I mean both the collapse of the local and the global into the "glocal" and the retention of "Cali" (or Hollywood) as the center of the film industry. Shakespeare film adaptations significantly blur if not fully deconstruct distinctions between local and global, original and copy, pure and hybrid, indigenous and foreign, high and low, authentic and inauthentic, hermeneutic and post-hermeneutic, English and other languages. Consider Figure 1.1, taken from the opening of *The Street King*, a modernized adaptation of *Richard III* (dir. James Gavin Bedford, 2002), set in contemporary Los Angeles. What begins as a spray painting of Shakespeare very similar to the Droeshout portrait ends up a modernized, bandannaed, beauty marked, and much hairier Shakespeare, wearing dark glasses and an earring as a cross, with two spray-painted Spanish words, "plata" (silver) and "plomo" (lead), gang slang for a strategy called "bullets or bribes."[4] The graffiti artist has signed off as well as "LCN."

The global city Los Angeles, the site of *King of the Streets*, is not exclusively American or Western. It has been called the Third World capital of the world (Rieff 1991) and the site of "forces that marginalize ever-shifting populations into internal third worlds" (Sawhney 2002). Moreover, Los Angeles is part of what Pico Iyer (2000) calls a post-imperial, post-global order, a world of jetlagged speed, flux, mediatized-interconnection, and rhizomatic newness, and of what Marc Auge (1995), along similar lines, calls the "supermodern non-places" of the airport transit lounge, supermarket, and highway, that have outstripped our earlier notions of "place." As glo-cali-zation collapses the local into the global, cultural centers and margins are no longer opposed as high to low culture, authentic to inauthentic, serious to parody, sacred to profane, and so Shakespeare cannot rightly be placed squarely on the side of hegemonic, dominant culture or counter-hegemonic, resistant subculture. Nevertheless, when it comes to cinema, glo-cali-zation keeps "Cali" (as in California) or, more specifically, Hollywood, as the central point of discursive reference, through a center hybridized by the white suburbs of Orange County and the gang warfare of south central Los

Figure 1.1 Shakespeare, homeboy.

Angeles.[5] Shakespeare is still going Hollywood, even if Hollywood is only a discursive point of reference rather than the center of actual film and television production.

In the remainder of the present essay, I examine how Shakespeare's glo-cali-zation has accompanied both his decanonization and decolonization via film, television, advertising, and other media, in the US and the UK. While adaptations of Shakespeare, as *The Street King* testifies, have become more multiracial and multicultural, the heterogeneity and multiplicity of Shakespeare's decanonization and decolonization does not amount to a liberated "popularization" that one could oppose to institutional, elite Shakespeare, however. The present era of mass media is effectively one of post-popular culture, if indeed popular culture as such ever existed (see Burt 2002a). Liberals who want to redeem the popular as political (or protopolitical) and elitist neoconservatives and reactionaries who want to trash it cannot convincingly account for the ways mass media have transformed Shakespeare's status and reproduction.[6] In this essay, I want to focus on several related aspects of that transformation: Shakespeare's televisualization and post-popular culture; a new phase in the postcolonial relation between the US and the UK; and race in relation to US and UK film and television advertising. Shakespeare on film is not only seen more frequently on the small screens of television sets and computer monitors than on the big screens of movie theaters, but has also more frequently been produced for television in the late 1990s than for film, and most Shakespeare films went straight to video and DVD. Shakespeare (or "Shakespeare") is less a foundational origin that might authorize either a progressive or conservative agenda than he is a nodal point whose position and presence, when recognized, are relative to the media in which he appears.

Post-popular Shakespeare

At an earlier historical moment when Shakespeare and high culture were regarded as sacred in the West, when Shakespeare was a token of Englishness used to legitimate Britain's imperial power (Viswanathan 1989; Loomba 1997) or to legitimate a division between high and low cultures in the United Sates (Levine 1988), there was an investment among colonizers and the (post)colonized in distinguishing between the authentic and the inauthentic Shakespeare. Any critical potential of a parody was gutted by virtue of its not being "really Shakespeare." Now the distinction between authentic and inauthentic Shakespeares is not even made consistently, much less policed. Few academic critics want to ask anymore how Shakespearean a given adaptation of a given play is because we all know there is no authentic Shakespeare, no "masterpiece" against which the adaptation might be evaluated and interpreted. To be sure, one can easily tell the difference between the Quarto or Folio *King Lear* and the made-for-television, Shakespeare-language free, US Western adaptation, *King of Texas* (dir. Uli Edel, 2002), directed by a German filmmaker and starring Patrick Stewart as John Lear, set in 1842 in the newly created Republic of Texas just after the Mexican–American wars and the Alamo. My point is that virtually no one cares to make it.

Even in contemporary Britain, productions of Shakespeare such as the made-for-television *Othello* (dir. Geoffrey Sax, 2001) drop the language of the play and modernize it, then, without explanation or apology, put it on PBS "Masterpiece Theater" in the US. Trevor Nunn's PBS *The Merchant of Venice* (2001) was broadcast in the US a few months earlier in the same PBS "Masterpiece Theater" series, using the language of the play. Yet the "Masterpiece Theater" introducers and the educational material for the two productions did not in any way differentiate them by their distance from the original play they were adapting.

A consequence of the present lack of interest in differentiating modern-language film and television Shakespeare adaptations from Shakespeare adaptations retaining the language is that earlier ideas about popularization no longer hold. Conservatives might think of popularization as equivalent to simplification, secondary to a more expensive and supposedly better, more authentic version. A liberal like Orson Welles might, by contrast, think of popularization through film and radio (or even comic books) as introductions to the real thing. In either case, the popular is seen as secondary to the original. Insofar as there's a Shakespeare in many present adaptations at all, he seems to inhere in the plot. The implicit claim is that the Shakespearean language is not universal but the plots, narrative conflicts, and/or character issues are. Yet plot and character are what traditionally was taught as inessential, borrowed, not-Shakespeare. Popularization does not return us, then, to the fuller, original and essential Shakespeare; it *is* the essence of Shakespeare.

The present indifference to how Shakespearean a given film or television adaptation may be poses problems both for neoconservative and reactionary commentators such as Lynn Cheney and George Will, as well as for self-identified liberal academics. The problem for liberals is that there is no longer a Shakespeare icon, a token of Western imperial power, out there to subvert from the margins; the center is already decentered, the original is already hybrid, the authentic is already a simulacrum. The problem for the conservatives is that there is no Shakespeare at the center for them to uphold. To be sure, one can still find stereotypical right- and left-wing uses of Shakespeare. And on the Far Right, the Alamogordo Christ Community Church of New Mexico held a "holy book burning" of Shakespeare along with Harry Potter books (because they promote witchcraft) on December 30, 2001.[7] On the hawkish Right, commentator Ken Adelman argued on National Public Radio's "All Things Considered" (August 26, 2002) that the US should go to war with Iraq, based on an analogy he drew between the then-current circumstances and the situation Othello faced in Shakespeare's play of the same name. Adelman argued that in the play *Othello*, as the Venetians face the Turkish fleet, they have no clear idea whether that fleet consists of 107 ships, 140, or considerably fewer. Yet they have the "big picture," and based on that picture they decide to go to war. Adelman urged that the US do the same against Saddam Hussein, because the US also has the big picture.[8] And just before the US-led invasion of Iraq in 2003, the US Defense Department distributed copies of *Henry V* to US soldiers (Shulevitz 2003). Liberal uses of Shakespeare are just as common. During an April 3, 2002 episode of the liberal *The West Wing*, for example, Donnatella Moss (Janel Moloney), a member of President Bartlett's (Martin Sheen) staff, recommends that her old high-school English teacher, Mrs. Molly Morello (who is retiring), should get a Presidential Proclamation for, among other things, teaching *Twelfth Night* to students at her house on the weekends after it was banned by the Madison school district in the 1960s.[9]

Yet educational testing as well as new media complicate these easy oppositions. Indeed, the very educational reforms promoted by George W. Bush threaten to take Shakespeare out of the middle-school curriculum. In a *New York Times Sunday Magazine* essay by James Traub about George W. Bush's educational reform bill passed in 2001, Shakespeare's *Romeo and Juliet* figures prominently.[10] Traub compares two New York middle schools both in terms of the economic class of the students and how much the schools resist testing:

> Scarsdale could afford to [ignore testing] because the culture of the school is the exact opposite of the culture that has brought standards-based reform into being: the internal pressure to succeed according to the highest standards is so intense that external motivations are superfluous. And so in the eighth-grade English class I sat in on at the Scarsdale Middle School in the weeks leading up to the E.L.A. test [the New York State English language arts exam], the kids were wearing masks and cloaks and performing a scene from *Romeo and Juliet*, which they planned on studying for a good eight weeks. . . . In Mamaroneck, *Romeo and Juliet* turned out to be a luxury that simply couldn't be afforded. Dee O'Brien, the eighth-grade English teacher, was also an actress and theater producer; she had planned a comprehensive unit on the play until she suddenly realized, in December, that the E.L.A. test had been moved up from June to March. As she said to the class the day I was there, "That whole project got knocked to smithereens because we couldn't juggle the time between finishing the project and doing the practice for this exam." And so O'Brien handed out sample tests and had her students give them to one another to evaluate. . . . The kids seemed genuinely upset about missing out on Shakespeare.[11]

A related irony for conservatives who embrace Shakespeare and the classics is that Bush's national reform became law by using a single state, Texas, as a model. According to Traub, "there is in any case a fierce debate over the data, especially in Texas, which President Bush has pointed to as proof that standards-based reform works. But one reason that the standards-and-testing element of the new education law found such broad support is that many independent scholars and experts have been persuaded that the system does work in Texas." Though the law allows the states to make up their own tests, critics see the law as a new kind of federalism, hardly what one would expect from a conservative President: "In places like Scarsdale, school is communal identity. Those hurricane units and Colonial fairs are what Scarsdale is about, as those performances of 'Romeo and Juliet' are what Mamaroneck is about. These schools are extensions of the community – not of the state. And to one degree or another, the communities see the new doctrine of one-standard-for-all as an assault on their cherished particularity." Like globalization, then, the federalization of education through national "standards" assaults the local and the particular.

In addition to educational reforms, the other complicating factors for both conservatives and liberals are mass media and new electronic communications technologies. Shakespeare is invoked in recent accounts of the decline of English and higher education such as Patrick Bratlinger's *Who Killed Shakespeare?* (2001) and Bill Readings's *The University in Ruins* (1996). Except for parts of the first chapter, Bratlinger's book is not about Shakespeare at all. Bratlinger begins each chapter with an epigraph from Shakespeare (identified only by "Shakespeare" and the title of the work) or one that comments on Shakespeare. Readings points out that Shakespeare was central to an Arnoldian antitechnological esthetic that was crucial to the university of ideas and the nation state. "The importance of the technological specter," Readings writes, "can be realized when one realizes that for Arnold, as for Eliot and Leavis after him, Shakespeare occupies the position that the German Idealists ascribed to the Greeks: that of immediately representing an organic community to itself in a living language" (1996: 78).

For liberals who support the popularization of Shakespeare as an educational process, mass media has made the popular impossible. In his fine book, *Orson Welles, Shakespeare, and Popular Culture*, Michael Anderegg writes, for example:

> What made the culture of nineteenth-century America – including the plays of Shakespeare – at all "popular" was the interaction between production and reception, actor and audience, speaker and listener. By definition, of course, radio, recordings, television, the movies, and all other forms of mass communication are antithetical to such a relationship. Not only is there no genuine interaction between sender and receiver, but there is precious little interaction among the various receivers themselves. The whole notion of popular culture, when the term is used in a positive sense, nearly ceases to have meaning in the twentieth century. For most people most of the time, the consumption of culture is an individual, private experience. Without attempting to make too absolute a distinction, it might be suggested that . . . a production of Shakespeare in front of an audience of two hundred is (or can be) popular culture; a television transmission of a Time-Life BBC Shakespeare play viewed by five million people . . . can in no way be thought of as popular in this sense. (1999: 165–7)

In Anderegg's idealizing, nostalgic narrative of Welles's career, mass culture has effectively made popular culture impossible. On the other side, the private reading experience has also been compromised. Reactionary elitist Harold Bloom, who claims in *Shakespeare and the Invention of the Human* that he only reads Shakespeare and never goes to theatrical performances, admitted in an interview that he went to see *Shakespeare in Love*.[12]

This fall back into a myth of the popular by the liberal critic and this catching up to present-day film by the reactionary critic are, in my view, inadequate responses to the end of literary culture and the displacement of esthetic taste by the laws of cool. Alan Liu comments bluntly that "Literature as traditionally understood no longer survives as an autonomous force. . . . Since the eighteenth through the nineteenth centuries, literature has merged with mass-market, media, educational, political, and other institutions that reallocate, repackage, and otherwise 'repurpose' its assets" (2002: 62). He adds that literature has "lost its distinction on the gradient that blurs together textuality and information, imagination and entertainment, authors and celebrities, and publishers and conglomerates" (2002: 61–2).

New pedagogical developments in relation to Shakespeare draw increasingly both on film and digital media, and while they register the decline of literary culture, they do not show that Shakespeare is simply being dropped or dumbed down. To be sure, Al Pacino held up the CliffsNotes edition to mock his own inability to understand the play during *Looking for Richard* (1996). And there are similarly parodic uses of Cliffs Notes-style graphics ("Clitt Notes") on the covers for two porn compilations, one called *Much Ado About Nuttin'* (dir. Anon., 2001) and the other *Julius Eats'er* (dir. Anon., 2001).[13] But the line between serious and parodic is not so clear when it comes to educational materials for some adaptations. The website for *Scotland, PA* (dir. Billy Morrissette, 2001), a spin-off of *Macbeth* set in 1970s McDonald's fast-food culture that retains virtually none of the language of the play, includes a study guide for the film, written by an academic, also called CliffsNotes.[14] The guide for this rather parodic film is not a subversive parody but quite serious, however, and includes a table of contents with sections on the characters, the actors, the purpose of the film, and so on. Similarly, websites for an "ad-rap-tation" of *The Comedy of Errors* called *The Bomb-itty of Errors* in 1999 and a 2001 Broadway revival of *Kiss Me Kate* included extensive study guides.[15] And, in a further twist, the screenwriter for a *Sopranos*-like, gritty TV series called *Kingpin*, reputedly *Macbeth* set in a Mexican drug cartel, said in an interview that, after getting a green light, "he hired a largely Latino writing staff and boned up on his Shakespeare: 'I literally bought the CliffsNotes to *Macbeth*'" (Hart 2003; see also Hinson 2003).

Yet these examples do not show a cultural decline into either post-Shakespeare or ex-Shakespeare. Consider a website advertisement for Apple computers that makes use of Richard III, with "A horse, a horse, my kingdom for a horse!" at the top in large letters, and then text accompanying two photos about Glenwood Public School's digital video film, using iMac and iMovie2 of their traditional, period-dress production of the play, performed by elementary school students. The teacher is quoted as saying "I wanted to do my pupils' acting talent justice with the *Richard III* production, while giving the children a multimedia project to challenge their skills, to crown their achievement, and as a record of their abilities."[16] More ambitiously, a Glenridge high-school class in Arizona did a film called *Star Wars Macbeth* (2000) in which parts of the play are recast using *Star Wars* costumes and characters (Han Siward, Admiral Seyton, and Malcolm Calrissian).[17]

There was a plan in the UK in 2001 to drop Shakespeare and all other English literature from secondary-school exams. As John Clare writes: "The plan recommends that Shakespeare and the entire English literary canon be abandoned in favor of media studies, the 'moving image' and 'information reading,' which includes the study of web pages and e-mail" (2001). Yet clearly, media studies and Shakespeare do not necessarily conflict. The point is rather that present pedagogical uses of digital film, streaming video, and Shakespeare have no longer defined politics in the way Welles's productions were aligned with the New Deal, nor are new media being harnessed to the kinds of populist critiques leftist Shakespeare critics have produced over the past two decades.[18] Shakespeare's "popularization" often involves stupidity (Burt 1999). In an episode of the late-night cartoon *South Park* (dir. Trey Parker, July 8, 2001), for example, Terrance and Phillip part ways, and Phillip ends up playing Hamlet. The kids find Phillip and convince him to perform at an Earth Day festival with Terrance, where they show at the last minute a highly abbreviated version of *Hamlet*.[19] Even those Shakespeareans who might attempt to redeem Terrance and Phillip's farting as some kind of proto-political resistance to adult authority, will be hard pressed to include it in the limits of the resistant popular conspiracy theories about Shakespeare's authorship. The 1990s has seen the expansion of challenges to Shakespeare's authorship through the Internet and journalistic coverage and documentaries such as *The Shakespeare Conspiracy* (dir. Michael Peer, 2001) and *Much Ado About Something* (dir. Mike Rubbo, 2002), the former about the Earl of Oxford and the latter about Christopher Marlowe being the true author of Shakespeare's works.[20]

Kings of Texas, or Shakespeare in the bush revisited

As the difference between hermeneutic and post-hermeneutic Shakespeares has become less pressing, the small screens of the television and computer have become the dominant places for viewing, and televised Shakespeare has overtaken filmed Shakespeare. Shakespeare has, of course, also shown up frequently on television, in the UK as early as The Beatles doing a scene from *A Midsummer Night's Dream*, episodes of comedy series such as *Monty Python* and *Blackadder*, thrillers like *A Midsummer Nightmare* (dir. Don Leaver, 1996), and soap operas like *EastEnders*. He similarly shows up in US television in situation comedies such as *Frasier*, *The Simpsons*, *Bette*, and *South Park*, melodramas like *The West Wing*, *Felicity*, *Dawson's Creek*, *Boston Public*, *The Gilmore Girls*, and "tween" shows like *Lizzie McGuire*, *Malcolm in the Middle*, *The Proud Family*, *Degrassi*, *Hey Arnold!*, and teen fare such as *Buffy the Vampire Slayer*, among others.[21] Yet television directors of Shakespeare films no longer think of television as a diminishment, as Laurence Olivier did when he objected to his *Richard III* (1955) being shown on black and white television sets in the US (Manvell 1979: 131–2). To be sure, Shakespeare on film is by no means coming to an end because of television, as Roger Manvell, writing in 1987 (p. 258), thought it might.[22] Yet the dominance of television is registered if not allegorized in films such as Baz Luhrmann's *William Shakespeare's Romeo + Juliet* (1996), which closes and ends with a television turning on and turning off and a television newscaster giving the prologue and epilogue; Michael Almereyda's *Hamlet* (2000), which closes with a television broadcast of the epilogue; and made-for-television adaptations such as Michael Bogdanov's *Macbeth* (1998), which shows the title on a television set.

We can grasp more concretely how Shakespeare's glo-cali-zation and the big screen to the small screen challenge both Left and Right accounts of popularization by turning to Patrick Stewart's acting career as a subShakespearean and his made-for-television adaptation of *King Lear*, *King of Texas*. Co-produced by TNT (Turner Network Television) and Hallmark Entertainment and starring Patrick Stewart, *King of Texas* straddles the divide between high Shakespeare (art cinema) culture and low (television) culture. As producer and actor in *King of Texas*, Stewart invites comparisons less to Shakespeareans such as Laurence Olivier, who did do a UK television *King Lear* with an all-English cast, including Diana Rigg and John Hurt (dir. Michael Elliott, 1984), in the course of making increasingly trashy American films, than to Branagh, whose *Love's Labour's Lost* (2000) was the last in a series of increasingly Americanized film Shakespeare adaptations, this one cutting two-thirds of the play.[23] And even more than Branagh, Stewart has been a hybrid figure who has straddled popular culture and Shakespeare. Stewart has played Lear and other Shakespeare roles on stage and television, but he is not now known as a Shakespearean actor, as are Olivier and Branagh.[24] Stewart is best known for his role as Starship Captain Jean-Luc Picard in *Star Trek: The Next Generation* and several *Star Trek* film off-shoots. As Picard, Stewart carried a copy of Shakespeare's works with him and often cited from it. Whereas Olivier performed Lear on television, Stewart has never done a movie Shakespeare role. Even the *Star Trek* films Stewart has starred in do not cite Shakespeare (others do).[25] Stewart used an international cast and production team, much along the lines of Kenneth Branagh's Shakespeare films made after *Henry V* (1989).[26] (By contrast, an all US production of a *Richard III* western comedy entitled *Texas Dick: Shakespeare in the Pecos* never got funding to produce more than a promotional trailer in 1996.)[27] When asked why he was so drawn to directing westerns, German director Uli Edel responded: "I think it has to do with my origin as a German. In Germany, we grew up with Westerns. For some reason, the Germans have a very strong affinity for Westerns. To dream about this endless sky and endless horizon, that's something I saw in a lot of Westerns and that's what drew me to them."[28] Unlike Branagh, who tried to do Shakespeare as an American musical in *Love's Labour's Lost*, Stewart has no investment in doing an authentic western. *King of Texas* was actually shot in Mexico, not Texas. Irish actor Colm Meaney (Mr. Tumlinson, based on Albany), also from *Star Trek: The Next Generation* (and *Star Trek: Deep Space Nine*) where he played Chief Miles O'Brien, can't manage the Texas accent. The actor who plays a Mexican character named Menchaca (Steven Bauer, born Rocky Echaveria), the equivalent of *Lear*'s France, was actually born in Cuba.

To be sure, the idea of *Lear* as a western is not new. As Edel said in an interview posted on the TNT webpages (no longer fully in existence) for the film: "When Patrick Stewart approached me to do *King Lear* with him, I started to think about Anthony Mann, the old western director. He planned his whole life to do a *King Lear* version and never could get the money from the studios. Even Howard Hawks said that Shakespeare's *King Lear* could become a wonderful Western." (Edel is apparently unaware of *Broken Lance* (dir. Edward Dmytryk, 1954), a remake of *House of Strangers* (dir. Joseph L. Mankiewicz, 1949), that made the original's connection to *King Lear* more apparent.) What differentiates *King of Texas* from past Shakespeare adaptations as westerns is not only that it mentions Shakespeare's *King Lear* as the source in the opening credits but that it is a made-for-television western.[29] *King of Texas* attempts to rise above television by belatedly citing scenes from western films, including the desert of the *The Good, the Bad, and the Ugly* (dir. Sergio Leone, 1966), the cattle drive in *Red River* (dir. Howard Hawks, 1948), Mercedes McCambridge as the jealous, vindictive, and murderous Emma Small in *Johnny Guitar* (dir. Nicholas Ray, 1954), and the final, nihilistic machine-gun battle in *The Wild Bunch* (dir. Sam Peckinpah, 1969). The effect is occasionally comic, particularly when Patrick Stewart often sounds like Jeb (Buddy Epsen) in the *Beverly Hillbillies* television series, and Rip, the only black character, suggests the sheriff in *Blazing Saddles* (dir. Mel Brooks, 1974).[30] Stewart's *Lear* as western television adaptation fails, in any case, to use Shakespeare either to reassert Britain's cultural dominance or to generate a critique of the post-imperial US in Shakespeare's name; the exchange of Shakespeare's language for Shakespeare's plot and character in *King of Texas* and Stewart's non-Shakespearean status mark the extent to which a neocolonial UK Shakespeare or postcolonial US Shakespeare have been bypassed by a televisual, hybridized Shakespearean as television series actor, American and international mode of reproduction.

Breedin' Shakespeare

Shakespeare's decanonization and colonization has similarly transformed British adaptations both on film and on television.[31] The relation between British and US Shakespeare has taken a different turn in terms of mass media, approaching what Katherine Eggert calls in her contribution to this volume, "post-postcolonialism." One index of this shift is Judi Dench's 1998 Oscar for Best Supporting Actress as Queen Elizabeth in *Shakespeare in Love* (dir. John Madden, 1998). This award might appear to confirm the Anglophilia of Hollywood and Britain's neocolonial status in relation to the US. After all, Dench won for her role as arguably England's foremost imperial Queen, even if her appearance on film was limited to eight minutes. Yet the award also followed a shift in Dench's career away from her roles in Shakespeare films such as Branagh's *Henry V* (Mistress Quickly) and television adaptations such as Trevor

Nunn's 1979 *Macbeth* and Peter Hall's *A Midsummer Night's Dream* (1968), and toward roles such as "M" in the James Bond film *Golden Eye* (1995).[32] Moreover, *Shakespeare in Love* was co-written by an American, Marc Norman, with an American actress, Gwyneth Paltrow, and ends up on the shores of Virginia.[33] Queen Elizabeth, yes; Shakespeare, no (unless Hollywoodized as a romantic comedy). Along similar lines, consider the difference between Johnny Rotten drawing on Richard III via Olivier's *Richard III* (1955) film and soccer star David Beckham and his wife naming their son Romeo. Whereas Rotten drew on English cinematic and theatrical Shakespeare traditions for his punk-rock persona, at least one journalist acknowledged that the Beckhams may not have used Shakespeare as their source for Romeo:

> Our scene may not be laid in fair Verona, but the Beckhams may have looked to the tragic love story of *Romeo and Juliet* for inspiration when naming their second son. . . . Of course, if music be the food of love, Posh and Becks didn't need to look far for ideas. Dire Straits' "Romeo and Juliet" could have been playing on that special night nine months ago, or perhaps the proud parents are fans of Showaddywaddy member Romeo Challenger, mini-rapper Lil' Romeo or So Solid Crew's Romeo.[34]

Shakespeare's mass mediatization has succeeded so well that Shakespeare no longer has foundational and hence even neocolonial status. And it is notable that most of the UK television programs and adaptations are available on DVD and video only in the UK or not at all. Even Branagh's more Americanized *Love's Labour's Lost* flopped at the box office.

That Shakespeare came to occupy a post-postcolonial status in the later 1990s and into the millennium may be seen in British television and film as well. The perceived failure of British television in comparison with US television was made quite clear by the head of BBC Four in August 2002. As Matt Wells writes, "BBC Four's chief executive last night attacked British television as 'dull, mechanical and samey,' saying that most innovative programming now comes out of the United States" (2002). When it comes to films and television, even when using Shakespeare, the US has apparently become the neocolonial power. Consider Colin Firth, Lord Wessex in *Shakespeare in Love*, as Shakespeare in an episode of *Blackadder* (1999).[35] Though Firth might seem to be cast as the romantic winner this time around, he again turns out to be a loser, this time as a writer. When Blackadder meets Shakespeare, after having traveled back to early 1600s London in a time machine gone out of control, he asks Shakespeare to autograph the frontispiece of a script of *Macbeth*, and Shakespeare graciously obliges. As he leaves, Blackadder pauses, however, adding "just one more thing" and he then floors Shakespeare with a punch, explaining "this is for every schoolboy and schoolgirl for the next four hundred years. Have you any idea how much suffering you are going to cause? Hours spent at school desks trying to find one joke in *A Midsummer Night's Dream*? Years wearing stupid tights in school plays and saying things like 'What ho, my lord' and 'Oh, look, here comes Othello, talking total crap as usual'." Blackadder goes on to fault Shakespeare on film as well, but a UK rather than US adaptation: "Oh, and [he kicks Shakespeare, who's still on the ground] that is for Ken Branagh's endless uncut four-hour version of *Hamlet*." Shakespeare is of course in the dark and asks "Who's Ken Branagh?"[36]

A BBC film comedy, *Maybe Baby* (dir. Ben Elton, 2000), anticipates the head of BBC Four's critique of British television by two years, and defends rather weakly against it.[37] Elton – who was also the co-screenwriter of the *Blackadder* "Back and Forth" episode – based the film on his own novel *Inconceivable*, about an infertile white English couple, Lucy Bell (Joely Richardson) and Sam Bell (Hugh Laurie). Sam works for the BBC and Lucy works as an advertising agency publicist. Initially, Sam is opposed as unromantic to a handsome and famous actor named Carl Phipps (James Purefoy) to whom Lucy is attracted, and the contrast is based on their knowledge of Shakespeare. Like Shakespeare in *Shakespeare in Love*, Sam's impotence is tied to his writer's block, but, unlike Shakespeare, Sam has little interest in poetry and sex. Lucy, however, is interested in Shakespeare and in sex, so she can have a baby. Though she did not complete her degree, she says at a dinner party that she is just about to take it up again and that she is doing a Shakespeare module for a distant-learning project. On their way home afterwards, Lucy and Sam have sex in a park, and when they finish, Lucy says that she is "reminded of a scene [she's] been doing in [her] course on *A Midsummer Night's Dream*." Sam doesn't take her seriously, but she adds that she "meant the magic where Hermione [*sic*] and Lysander lie down to sleep in the enchanted wood." (Apparently she forgot about Hermia's lines, "lie further off yet, do not lie so near . . ./Lie further off; in human modesty"). Lucy asks Sam if he remembers the scene, and he answers "sort of." She presses on, adding that she remembers Sam "used to read [her] sonnets when [they] were first together." But again he puts her off like a wet blanket. After he gets up and walks off, we see her looking rather forlorn on what has turned out to be some disenchanted evening.

Lucy first meets Sam's apparent opposite, Carl, in a scene following the sex-in-the-park scene, and when Carl says that he really wants "work that stretches [him], challenges [him]," the first of a series of anal references is made as Lucy responds that the North Welsh Language Shakespeare Company is looking for "a friendly and enthusiastic Bottom. That would be quite challenging." Carl quickly turns Shakespeare into a quite heterosexual account, however. In a later scene, Lucy is asked as "our resident Shakespeare scholar" for a Shakespeare text Carl can use at a benefit. She suggests "Sonnet 18" and asks him if he knows it. Carl says "No," and so she recites from memory the first quatrain, and then he finishes the sonnet, as lute music kicks in. The agency head, Sheila (Joanna Lumley), quips that Carl "is in perilous danger of turning me back into a heterosexual."

This contrast between the romantic and productive Shakespeare lover and the unromantic, blocked unShakespeare would-be breeder breaks down as Cole plays the part of Sam in an autobiographical script he has written, and even more decisively when, near the end of the film in a *Romeo and Juliet*-like balcony scene, Sam recites from memory sonnet 116 to Lucy. The parallel between the two men is noticeable at an even earlier moment when Sam appears to take a sperm sample out of his ass (where he's kept it warm) when he drops it off at the gynecologist's office. The similarity between Carl and Sam is reinforced by the fact that neither man is fertile, in contrast to a black co-worker and friend of Sam's, played by Adrian Lester, seen with his wife and baby. And *Maybe Baby*'s pro-BBC and English-film stance is constantly undermined, despite the use of special appearances by English movie and television stars Emma Thompson as a gynocentric, hippie feminist, Joanna Lumley of *Absolutely Fabulous*, and comic Rowan Atkinson as a gynecologist, in a number of ways, including the opening soundtrack, a cover of Buddy Holly's "Maybe Baby" by Paul McCartney; the use of

American slang (a particular way of saying "Hello," with the emphasis on the second syllable, as popularized in *Clueless*); and by the representation of the BBC management, headed by a young Turk who wants to produce more films like the "three released last year" that "the Americans quite liked."[38] Moreover, Sam is demoted to daytime television, and his film script, supposedly a success when the film is released, is made by a Scottish film writer and director, a character who is a parody of Ewan McGregor named Ewan Proclaimer (Tom Hollander, who is actually English). Proclaimer initially pitches a script to Sam for a "comedy" called *Sick Junkies*, a belabored to the point of being obvious satiric reference to *Trainspotting* (dir. Danny Boyle, 1996). Sam rejects the script partly on the grounds that the person making it just wants to go to the States the first chance he gets. Yet Ewan does not in fact go to the States, and he makes explicit the anal view of male creation associated with Sam and Carl, telling Sam at one point "My shite [writing] shits on your shite [writing]."

The relation of the film's stars to Shakespeare indicates a wide range of engagements from the high theatrical to the popular (on film and television), from Emma Thompson's roles in then husband Branagh's *Henry V* (1989) and *Much Ado About Nothing* (1993), and as Shakespeare-citing heroines in the British comedy *The Tall Guy* (dir. Mel Smith, 1989) and British/American adaptation *Sense and Sensibility* (dir. Ang Lee, 1995), to Adrian Lester in Branagh's *Love's Labour's Lost*, to Joely Richardson's more remote connection via her father, Tony Richardson, who filmed *Hamlet* (1969) with Nicol Williamson, to James Purefoy who has performed various Shakespeare roles with the RSC, to Rowan Atkinson in *Blackadder* episodes, some of which in addition to "Back and Forth" cite Shakespeare, to Hugh Laurie's engagement as Shakespeare in a *Blackadder* sketch with Atkinson for an AIDS benefit in 1989.[39] Despite these different attempts to use stars and Shakespeare in popular English contexts, it is telling that *Maybe Baby* was a total flop, distributed in the US by USA Films. The lead actor, Hugh Laurie, has made it in the US starring as the father, Mr. Little, in *Stuart Little* (dir. Rob Minkoff, 1999) and *Stuart Little 2* (dir. Rob Minkoff, 2002).[40]

Black stars and authenticity in Shakespeare advertising

We can further understand how Shakespeare's glo-cali-zation relates to television and the US as postcolonial subject of the UK by turning to two television advertisements in the US and the UK involving African-American actors and Shakespeare.[41] Racial difference is mediated by the actors' stardom, achieved often less through Shakespearean roles than by non-Shakespearean roles. Consider two television advertisements using Shakespeare with James Earl Jones and Samuel L. Jackson, both of whom are famous in relation to *Star Wars*: Jones as the voice of Darth Vader in the first three films and Samuel L. Jackson for his role as Jedi Master Mace Windu in *Star Wars, Episode One: The Phantom Menace* (dir. George Lucas, 2000), *Star Wars, Episode Two: Attack of the Clones* (dir. George Lucas, 2002), and the forthcoming *Star Wars: Episode III* (dir. George Lucas). A commercial for Bell Atlantic that ran in 2000 using Jones as Othello may be read as Jones's reply to the way he played himself in the romantic comedy *True Identity* (dir. Charles Lane, Jr., 1991). In that film, British comic Lenny Henry's character, Miles Pope, replaces Jones as Othello in a New York stage production after Jones is struck by the villain's car and hospitalized with a broken leg.[42] The Bell commercial begins as theatergoers are going to see James Earl Jones as Othello, identified in the theater marquee and then in New York style playbills. Jones was the spokesman for Bell Atlantic at the time. As the audience sits down, we see Othello on stage wearing, Darth Vader-like, a big cloak with his back turned to us. Othello, we see, is being played this night by a stand-in, J.J. Walker, best known for the 1970s television situation comedy *Good Times*, who turns and smiles mischievously at the camera. The commercial then cuts to Jones holding a Bell telephone book, saying "Don't settle for stand-ins," and then makes the pitch for Bell. The commercial ends back in the theater as the audience gasp at Walker crying over a Desdemona (played by a blonde actress) he has apparently actually murdered, but Walker then smiles and winks at the camera to show that he really can act.[43]

Whereas Jones wants to be identified as the real Othello and a serious Shakespearean (he is interviewed briefly in Pacino's *Looking for Richard*), Samuel L. Jackson, who has not performed in Shakespeare productions, was nevertheless hired by Barclays Bank to do a series of television advertisements that ran in 2002, using lines from *The Comedy of Errors*. An article in the London *Times* noted "Barclays has stuck with Hollywood stars for its *Fluent in Finance* campaign, dropping Sir Anthony Hopkins in favor of Samuel L. Jackson . . . to appeal to younger consumers" (Nugent 2002).[44] In the last ad of the campaign, Jackson recites the following speech:

> Upon my life, by some device or other
> The villain is o'er-raught of all my money.
> They say this town is full of cozenage,
> As, nimble jugglers that deceive the eye,
> Dark-working sorcerers that change the mind,
> Soul-killing witches that deform the body,
> Disguised cheaters, prating mountebanks,
> And many such-like liberties of sin:
> If it prove so, I will be gone the sooner.
> I'll to the Centaur, to go seek this slave:
> I greatly fear my money is not safe.

Helen Nugent comments, "Hiring a Jedi master to encourage us to bank with Barclays may have seemed like a masterstroke, but even Mr. Jackson can't make sense of the scripts. Apart from the advert based on an extract from Shakespeare's *Comedy of Errors*, the scenes are incomprehensible. . . . It's all very uncool, isn't it Mr. Jackson?" Though the last line "I greatly fear my money is not safe" seems to be the point of the speech, the effect is comically undercut for anyone who knows the play by the appearance of a real centaur, rather than an inn named the Centaur. Whereas Shakespeare earlier legitimated the African-American actors such as Ira Aldridge and Paul Robeson, who went on to perform Shakespeare, (an incomprehensible) Shakespeare is now legitimated by a cool African-American movie star.

Shakespeare without Shakespeare? The canonization of post-popular culture

Whether Shakespeare can be performed well without using the language of his plays is usually a question critics ask in relation to foreign theatrical performances (Dennis Kennedy 1993). The usual defense of what Kennedy calls "foreign Shakespeare" is that there is something essentially Shakespearean about the foreign production even if Shakespeare's language has been lost in translation. In the case of Shakespeare on film in English, we have seen that Shakespeare's language often drops out. The distinction between Anglophone and foreign Shakespeares is eroding as native films modernize the language and as foreign films such as *The King is Alive* and *Rave MacBeth* are made in English with American actors, some of them movie and television stars. As Shakespeare has been dispersed globally and "Englished" and "Americanized," Hollywood remains central as a measure of the highest value for any non-US national cinema. Even films that define themselves as part of a national cinema against Hollywood are nevertheless marketed in terms of their value in the US. Across the bottom of the British video-box cover for Jeremy Freeston's *Macbeth* (1997), for example, is written "Winner 30th US International Film and Video Festival", and the back of the Michael Bogdanov *Macbeth* (1998) video-box cover compares the film to Baz Luhrmann's *William Shakespeare's Romeo + Juliet.*

The glo-cali-zation of cinema marks the end of cultural imperialism rather than the ascendancy of a monocultural US cinema. Curtis Breight comments, for example:

> As film becomes increasingly international on the cusp of vast changes in whatever we call the new information industries *in toto* (including but not limited to satellites, telecommunications, film, music, computers, CD ROMS, books, animation, etc.), Shakespeare is being used both as a means of global communication and a touchstone for struggle within tumultuous societies such as the USA. . . . Shakespeare is not just some ideological tool by which a single dominant group reproduces it own cultural and economic hegemony.
>
> (1997: 297)[45]

Yet the infinite variety of Shakespeare's glo-cali-zations do not, in my view, amount to some liberatory decanonization and decolonization of Shakespeare through film and so-called popular culture.[46] For popular culture itself has a history and has begun to be canonized (see Nelson 2002). The beginning of the millennium has seen the critical devotion to older films, albums, and so on, that are unknown to a younger generation of viewers and listeners for whom popular culture begins with Madonna and Prince. What has become "post-popular culture" now has its own educational apparatus.

To some critics, the canonization of post-popular culture might seem to mark a new and advanced stage in the instrumentalization of culture, another form of capitalist containment along the lines Theodor Adorno and Max Horkheimer articulated in *The Dialectic of Enlightenment.* The collapse of high-culture Shakespeare and popular Shakespeare, the present indifference to the distinction between hermeneutic and post-hermeneutic Shakespeares, might be grasped as the end of any authentic resistance from "the people." Commenting on Heiner Müller's *Hamletmachine*, Richard Halpern says the play "welds the numbing, repetitive succession of tyrants to the numbing, receptive enactment of *Hamlet.* Not only does Shakespeare's play empty its own meaning through constant performance, but in doing so it symbolizes the performance of history, which has become unendurably routinized, and thus caught in the tolls of the *Hamletmachine*" (1997: 273). Halpern's analysis of Müller in relation to the Arnold Schwarzenegger Hamlet of *Last Action Hero* confirms that the same kind of entanglement holds equally true for the mall film.

Yet the unendurable repetition and routinization Halpern notes in the production of theatrical and cinematic Shakespeare seems increasingly to hold for the critical reception of Shakespeare itself, particularly of the avowedly historicist and political variety, which seems content to play over and over again the greatest hits of the 1980s Shakespeare criticism parade. I concede I have no more "genuinely" historical or radical or authentic mode of criticism to advance as an alternative to what I find to be the largely stultifyingly predictable work that advertises itself as politically progressive. I do think that the present moment, a moment that most Shakespeare critics would, I think, acknowledge is far from exciting, does offer us the opportunity for critical self-examination, if only through a corrosive and possibly self-defeating dialectical negativity.

Rather than view Shakespeare's (dis)location in global cinemas in terms of liberatory popular culture or a repressive simulacrum thereof, I would like to consider Shakespeare's status in post-popular culture by engaging Fredric Jameson's work on what he calls the "geopolitical esthetic" (1995) and an "esthetic of cognitive mapping" (1991: 51), which he defines as "a pedagogical political culture which seeks to endow the individual subject with some new heightened sense of its place in the global system" (1991: 54). The metaphor of mapping itself is inadequate and, Jameson rightly says, has to be immediately junked the moment it is introduced: "In our time the referent – the world system – is a being of such enormous complexity that it [can] only be mapped and modeled indirectly, by way of a simpler object that stands as an allegorical interpretant, that object being most often in postmodernism itself a media phenomenon" (1995: 169).[47] According to Jameson, "all allegories . . . are necessarily allegories of representational failure" (1992b: 177). Allegory meets the sublime, in other words.

What I find particularly interesting about Jameson's attempt to map the esthetic allegorically is his concession that allegorization is always interpretive simplification, dependent for an "allegorical interpretant" on an "*analogon*" or "simpler object." For Jameson, political, utopian criticism therefore takes on a restorative function: "In the absence of Utopia, things, remaining as they do, contingent and 'unequal' to their own concepts, have to be pumped back up and patched together" (1995: 45). For Jameson, the aims of Marxist criticism are the dialectical reconciliation of all antagonisms and "the Utopian escape from commercial reification" (1995: 204). Social relations stand outside of allegory and media technologies. According to Jameson

> a lot of histories of ideas have often taken technology or science as a kind of ultimately determining instance. I think that's a mistake in the sense that we always secretly, maybe without knowing it, think of technology as an allegory of social relations. And these allegories can be of various kinds, especially in the modern period the airplane, the steamship, the automobile were figures of enormous energy. Today the technology of the computer is rather this figure of networks. But I think it always also means a new model of human relationships. One must always look at technological descriptions in order to detect that layer of allegory of social relations that they accordingly to me always contain.[48]

It is perhaps no accident that Jameson focuses on film so often to allegorize social relations or that Slavoj Žižek uses film and popular culture to illustrate Lacanian theory

(1991, 1992), and it is worth noting that one of Jameson's books, *The Seeds of Time*, cites a line fom *Macbeth.*

I would agree with Jameson that what Žižek might call a sublime failure is the condition of any allegorization of Shakespeare's cinematic glo-cali-zations. Yet, in my view, the failure is so radical that it necessarily hobbles any restorative attempt to patch things together; in other words, if allegory always fails, then things cannot be adequately pumped up so as to be patched together. Instead of lamenting the end of iconoclastic, popular Shakespeare that one could argue subverts institutional Shakespeare (but what is left of institutional Shakespeare?), we might consider the status "allegorical interpretant," as simplified *analogon* puts into question the status of political criticism itself. Can such criticism produce much more than an always already dumbed-down "mapping" of digital culture, already obsolete by the time it is readable? If not, it follows that utopian critique in Shakespeare studies, at least, has to face up to the ways in which academic allegories of social relations ventriloquize the popular, speak for the people, fantasize that the academic and the popular are at least congruent, if not identical. Shakespeare's glo-cali-zations suggest the reverse: we may not learn everything we want to know about academia even if we are not afraid to ask post-popular culture, and vice versa.

Notes

1 See Grobel 1994.

2 The DVD edition of *Orange County* excerpts the classroom scene with *Romeo and Juliet*, which the screenwriter calls the best scene in the film on the DVD audio commentary, as well as a similar scene (not in the film) involving *Macbeth* and the television sitcom *Friends*, as "intersticials" (promo spots) that originally aired on MTV just before the film was released on January 11, 2002.

3 A very similar joke occurs at the end of the episode "Teen Angels" (dir. James Quinn, #56, third season, original air date, December 19, 1998) of the CBS television sci-fi melodrama, *Early Edition*, about a divorced man, Gary Hobson (Kyle Chandler), who gets the *Chicago Sun-Times* a day early and so can intervene to prevent future disasters. In this episode Hobson and his friend, Chuck Fishman (Fischer Stevens), pretend to be a substitute and a student-teacher, respectively. The student-teacher has to lead a class on *Hamlet*, which he has never read. (He has a copy of the Arden version and flips through it, concluding "no pictures!") He gets a brief plot summary from a student and then compares the play to a film he has seen, *Anaconda* (dir. Luis Llosa, 1997). The students initially resist, but then get drawn into a discussion of the film. A brighter student asks "But what does all this have to do with *Hamlet*?" "Facing your fears," he says. This moral drawn from *Hamlet* as *Anaconda* is carried through the episode. A young woman breaks up with her overly possessive and rather violent boyfriend, who then tries unsuccessfully to shoot the student-teacher. Hobson and Fishman are found out at the end and dismissed by the school principal. The student-teacher says he would like to continue teaching anyway, and he enthuses:

> Shakespeare's covered. The plays are just like films. *Macbeth*? It's just like *I Know What You Did Last Summer*. Driving along and killing a guy, and then they're haunted by his ghost. Exactly the same thing. Exactly the same thing. And *The Tempest*? *Ernest Goes to Camp*. The same thing! And then there's *Zorro*. That play about the girl and boy? *Romeo and Juliet*.

The hero does not accept his friend's Fluellenesque analogies, of course. Episode 84 of the fourth season of *Early Edition* was called "The Play's the Thing" (dir. Deborah Reinisch, original air date August 4, 2000) and Episode 18 of the second season was called "The Quality Of Mercy" (dir. Fisher Stevens, original air date April 25, 1998). The animated cartoon *The Simpsons' Hamlet* segment (March 17, 2002) of season thirteen, episode 283, "Tales from the Public Domain" (dir. Michael B. Anderson), ends on a similar note. After Homer reads his version, Lisa comments, "And that's the greatest play ever written." When Bart demurs, Homer says "It's not only the world's greatest play, but it was made into a great movie – *Ghostbusters*!" In the HBO movie *Cheaters*, there is a brief mention of Shakespeare's sonnets. The teacher (Jeff Daniels) asks his students what kind of verse the sonnets are in. The central literary reference in the film is *Paradise Lost*.

4 The Arellano Felix cartel has officially adopted this slogan as a strategy. See <http://www.sandiegomag.com/issues/june99/blood.shtml>.

5 To be sure, Hollywood is far from the only game these days. And even so-called Hollywood films are dislocated from that site. (Vancouver and Toronto both have become favorite filming sites.)

6 See Burt 2001 for a fuller critique of dominant accounts of popular culture in Shakespeare studies. See John Collick, *Shakespeare and Cinema* (1989) and Anderegg (1999). Even the Luhrmann *Romeo + Juliet* was heavily integrated on its theatrical release in the US with television. The week before its cinematic premiere saw numerous advertisements and a half-hour long special on the making of the film. And the 1990s also saw the release on video and DVD of earlier television adaptations of Shakespeare.

7 March 2002, "Burning Sensations," "How Would-be Censors Promote Free speech," by Jeremy Lott: <http://reason.com/0203/cr.jl.burning.shtml>.

8 I thank my former colleague Stephen Clingman for alerting me to this interview.

9 Third season, Episode seventeen, "Stirred." Original air date April 3, 2002. Story by Dee Dee Myers, directed by Jeremy Kagan. My thanks to Billy Houck for drawing my attention to this episode. For more details on it, see <http://bartlet4america.org/char/others.html>. On *Twelfth Night* actually being banned by a US school: "In 1995, a teacher in New Hampshire was fired for refusing to remove pro-gay books from her classroom. A statewide policy barring instruction that has 'the effect of encouraging or supporting homosexuality as a positive lifestyle alternative' also led . . . to the banning of Shakespeare's *Twelfth Night*." (http://www.libr.org/Juice/issues/vol3/LJ_3.36.html). The year after, "a group of parents and educators filed a lawsuit February 15, 1996, in the United States District Court in Concord, N.H., challenging a homophobic censorship policy passed by the Merrimack, N.H. school board August, 1995. The policy had led to removal of several books, including Shakespeare's *Twelfth Night* from a high school English class." (http://www.youth.org/loco/PERSONProject/Handbook/States/newhampshire2.html). Shakespeare also shows up in the third season finale of *The West Wing*, episode 322, "Posse Comitatus" (May 22, 2002; writer Aaron Sorkin, director Alex Graves). President Bartlet attends an RSC-style *Wars of the Roses* (1963) and *This England – The Histories* (2001) adaptation of the three *Henry VI* plays. The funeral of Henry V and the death of York were featured and the play seemed to comment – like the end of *The Godfather* (dir. Francis Ford Coppola, 1972) – on the story of the finale. Alison Janney's boyfriend (Mark Harmon) was killed while retrieving a bunch of red and white roses for her, which lay next to his body. As York is killed, the President has ordered an assassination of the Qumari defense minister. The President's interest in Shakespeare stands out as somewhat eccentric by virtue of comments on how unusual reading and theatre-going are in the US and about baseball being the American national pastime. This Anglophilic performance is not authentically Shakespeare. As a *The West Wing* website notes:

> The song sung by the Shakespeare Company at the end of the segment of the *Wars of the Roses* . . . is called "Patriotic Chorus" by Stephen Oliver. It was originally composed as the Finale of the mock-Victorian revisionist *Romeo and Juliet* which closes Part One of the 9 hour-long, 1983 Royal Shakespeare Company production of Dickens' *The Life and Adventures of Nicholas Nickleby* which was an

actual hit in London's West End and on Broadway in the early 80's. One would assume that the RSC and the "endlessly long", high-brow nature of both plays would have created the intellectual resonance for Sorkin. And the originally tongue-in-cheek words and tune, a send-up of typical Victorian xenophobia, have a certain irony as played over the assassination of the Qumari defense minister. The music at the end contained the following lyrics, among others:

> England arise! Join in the chorus!
> It is a new made song you should be singing.
> See in the skies, flutt'ring before us
> what the bright bird of peace is bringing!
>
> http://westwing.bewarne.com/third/3–23posse.html.

10 James Traub, "The Test Mess," April 7, 2002: <http://www.nytimes.com/2002/04/07/magazine/07TESTING.html?ex=1019212849&ei=1&en=9dc90a92c9ca1012>.

11 Traub continues: "After class, I asked O'Brien . . .: Why not just teach Shakespeare? She said she could not afford to assume that her charges would do just fine on their own. What if other teachers got better results than she did? And so she, too, was teaching to the test, but . . . she kept coming back to how much she missed Shakespeare."

12 See also the Cornell President Hunter Rawling's allusion to *Shakespeare in Love* and mention of Shakespeare in his introduction to Bloom as Cornell commencement speaker in 1999: <http://www.news.cornell.edu/Chronicle/99/6.10.99/Bloom.html>. A review of *Shakespeare in Love* says the film endorses Bloom's book: <http://www.metroactive.com/papers/metro/12.24.98/shaksprelove-9851.html>.

13 For similarly parodic porn adaptations, see *Naughty College Student Girls #19* (dir. S. Taylor and Andree Madness, 2001). The last episode (#19) begins with a woman named Krystal quizzing her boyfriend about *Romeo and Juliet*. She strips off an item of clothing each time he gets the answer right. The questions are nearly impossible to get wrong: "Who are the main characters? What are the names of the feuding families?" He answers correctly, then they have sex. See also *Sexspeare: The Uncensored Lusty Works of William Sexspeare* (dir. Shawn Ricks, 2003).

14 <http://www.lot47.com/scotlandpa/press.html>. Professor David Linton of Marymount College in Manhattan wrote the study guide.

15 <http://www.kissmekateontour.com/html/study_guidecon.htm>.

16 <http://www.apple.com.au/edu/k12/products/imovie/glenwoodshakes.html>.

17 For *Star Wars Macbeth* (2000), available only on the Internet, go to <http://www.glenridge.org/macbeth/>.

18 The 1990s saw the emergence of several youth-related film and television genres that have continued into the millennium. Perhaps most visible is the Shakespeare-citing teen film, including *O* (dir. Tim Blake Nelson, 2001), *Not Another Teen Movie* (dir. Joel Gallen, 2001), *American Pie* (dir. Paul Weitz, 1999), *Get Over It* (dir. Tommy O'Haver, 2001), *Lost and Delirious* (dir. Léa Pool, 2001), and *Soul Survivors: Final Cut* (dir. Stephen Carpenter, 2001). On this genre, see Burt 2001. Referencing also proliferated in children's television programs such as Disney's *The Book of Pooh* (original air date September 1, 2001), *Between the Lions* (original air date February 6, 2002), and the video *Baby Shakespeare* (dir. Julie Aigner-Clark, 2000). The most interesting innovations are in the new market known as "tween" programming, composed of ten–fourteen year olds. Like most television programming, "tween" shows are heavily multicultural and multiracial, and Shakespeare comes up in a pedagogical context that often links him to theatrical performance and to film or television. "Romeo Must Wed," for example, an episode of the Disney-animated television series *The Proud Family* (as in "We're Black and Proud Family"), is about a romance between the heroine, fourteen-year-old Penny Proud, and a Chinese boy from Hong Kong named Kwok, whose parents arranged his marriage before he was born. The episode's title derives from the interracial action and hip-hop film *Romeo Must Die* (dir. Andrzej Bartkowiak, 2000), which is also mentioned by

Penny's friend Dijonay in the episode, but quotes liberally from Shakespeare's *Romeo and Juliet* as it is being rehearsed and then performed by Kwok and Penny as Romeo and Juliet, and again when Penny/Juliet raps her final lines in the Capulet tomb set to rap music (using the original text). For details, go to <http://www.tvtome.com/ProudFamily/season1.html#ep21>. (Original air date on the Disney channel, Friday May 24, 2002.) Similarly, when assigning students Acts of *Romeo and Juliet* and asking them to stage them in a period of their choice, a teacher in an episode of *The Gilmore Girls* says that her favorite student production was one that put it in a *Jerry Springer Show* setting. For more details, go to <http://www.tvtome.com/GilmoreGirls/season2.html>. See also *The Gilmore Girls* episode "The Deer Hunters" (original air date October 26, 2000) and the animated cartoon *Hey Arnold!*, episode 318, "School Play" (original air date March 10, 1999), about a school production of *Romeo and Juliet*. See <http://www.netvista.net/~del_grande/arn_318.html>.

To my mind, by far the most canny and most cynical tween program is Disney's *Lizzie McGuire*, which makes use of animation and first-person narrative from Lizzie and frequently breaks out at random into clips from videos by the star Hilary Duff, identified as the "*Lizzie McGuire* soundtrack" on Radio Disney, and there are book spin-offs, a movie spin-off, and a Lizzie clothing line. An episode entitled "Lizzie in the Middle" involving *Romeo and Juliet* is an allegory of the downside of tween stardom. The references to *Romeo and Juliet* become increasingly mediatized and infrequent, the last being a pop song about Romeo and Juliet. "Romeo Must Wed" aired again on Friday, August 23, 2002 (7.00 P.M.), immediately preceding the *Lizzie McGuire* episode involving *Romeo and Juliet*. (My thanks to my daughter Nora for alerting me to the *Lizzie McGuire* episode.) See <http://www.tvtome.com/LizzieMcGuire/season2.html#ep46>. The word "tween" comes up in a scrabble game in the *Lizzie McGuire* episode, August 23, 2002, 7.30–8.00 P.M. See also a *Malcolm in the Middle* episode called "High School Play," original air date December 10, 2001, in which Malcolm plays the changeling boy in a production of *A Midsummer Night's Dream* (written by Maggie Bandur and Pang-Ni Landrum, directed by Jeff Melman). On the website, *Malcolm's Journal*, there is an entry describing the episode. See <http://www.fox.com/malcolm/journal/211.htm>.

19 Episode #70, "Terrance and Phillip: Behind the Blow," season 5 (July 8, 2001). My thanks to Marcia Eppich-Harris for alerting me to this episode. For more details, go to http://www.tvtome.com/tvtome/servlet/GuidePageServlet/showid-344/epid-59095>.

20 John Maybury's *Marlowe* (2003), starring Johnny Depp as a heterosexual Christopher Marlowe and Jude Law as Shakespeare, was still in production at the time this book went to press.

21 For earlier US television shows, see Burt, 1999. *Monty Python's Flying Circus*, "Hamlet," series 4, episode #43: <http://www.mwscomp.com/mpfc/mpfc.html#series4>. *Monty Python's Flying Circus*, series 2, "The First Underwater Production of Measure for Measure"; *Monty Python's Flying Circus*, "The Hospital for Overactors," episode 25 (*Richard III*); *Bette*, season one, episode 9, "Or Not to Be" (dir. Andrew D. Weyman), original air date, December 13, 2000. See <http://www.tvtome.com/tvtome/servlet/EpisodeGuideSummary/showid-16>. An episode of *Boston Public* with Shakespeare involved the student-teacher Lisa Greer teaching the Shakespeare class. After the administration stops her, vice-principal Guber attempts to lead the class in a discussion of *Macbeth*. The students preferred Lisa's comments about a sexual subtext of Lady Macbeth's speech to the vice-principal's more sanitized interpretation. A later episode (November 19, 2001) opened with a diatribe by a young black male student about a Shakespeare conspiracy. Summaries of other *Boston Public* episodes using Shakespeare – Chapter 10 (January 15, 2001), Chapter 17 (April 16, 2001), and Chapter 26 (November 19, 2001) – may be found at <http://tvcentral.thewebsitez.com/boston_public.htm>. A *Felicity* episode ("Finally," December 15, 1998) about plagiarism had a reference to Shakespeare and a later one to *Hamlet*. An ad for *Shakespeare in Love* aired during the episode. The final episode of the fifth season of *Buffy, the Vampire Slayer* cites a line from *Henry V* (#100, "The Gift," May 22, 2001, dir. Joss Whedon). There was a Shakespearean reference in an episode of the UK's most popular soap, *EastEnders*, original

air date, July 29, 2002: <http://www.guardian.co.uk/Archive/Article/0,4273,4472043,00.html>. My thanks to Takashi Kozuka for this reference and link. For details on episodes of the other shows mentioned, see notes 32, 38, 39, and 40 below.

22

> It would seem now that the grand period of Shakespearean adaptation for the cinema (from Olivier's *Henry V* to Kurosawa's *Ran* – a forty year span) may well be over, with ever-increasing costs balking potential producers. But this is not true of television, a good medium for the intimate, less spectacular aspects of the plays. (Manvell 1987: 258).

My thanks to Kenneth Rothwell for this reference.

23 Since *Dead Again* (dir. Kenneth Branagh, 1991), Branagh has tended to move between Shakespeare adaptations and 'lower' film genres.

24 On Branagh's career, see Burnett 2002. It is also worth comparing Stewart and Branagh to Sir Ian McKellen. When Branagh plays a non-Shakespeare role such as Gilderoy Lockhart in *Harry Potter and the Chamber of Secrets* (dir. Chris Columbus, 2002), he is typically referred to in the press as a Shakespearean or in connection to his Shakespeare films. See "Shakespearean Actor Kenneth Branagh will Play the Flamboyant Professor Gilderoy Lockhart in *Harry Potter and the Chamber of Secrets*" (http://filmforce.ign.com/harrypotter/articles/315478p1.html); "Shakespearean Actor Kenneth Branagh will Play the Flamboyant Professor Gilderoy Lockhart in *Harry Potter and the Chamber of Secrets*." (http://www.branaghcompendium.com/gilderoy_ken_cast.html); "Thespian Kenneth Branagh, Best Known for his Film Versions of such Shakespeare Works as *Henry V* and *Much Ado About Nothing*" (http://www.hollywood.com/sites/harrypotter/feature/channel/movie/id/1097020). McKellen's Shakespeare work on stage, television, and in film (*Richard III* 1995, Shakespeare references as English director James Whale in Hollywood in *Gods and Monsters*, dir. Bill Condon, 1998) is not similarly referred to in publicity for his more famous roles as Magneto – opposite Patrick Stewart as Professor Xavier – in *X-Men* (dir. Bryan Singer, 1999) and Gandalf in *Lord of the Rings* (dir. Peter Jackson, 2001). See <http://www.lordoftherings.net/film/cast/ca_imcke.html> and <http://news.bbc.co.uk/1/hi/entertainment/film/1361833.stm>.

25 On *Star Trek* and Shakespeare, see Burt 1999 and Dionne 2002. In addition to Olivier, many other Shakespeareans have also done television adaptations, including Derek Jacobi and Maurice Evans. It is worth noting that Branagh has never done television Shakespeare. (To be sure, his Renaissance Theatre company's stage version of *Twelfth Night*, directed by Branagh, was adapted for TV in 1988. Interestingly, IMDb says Branagh is co-director, but the video cover says "Directed for television by Paul Kafno." My thanks to Neil Dowden for this information.) Stewart's American analogue might be Kevin Kline, who has played roles in mall movies such as *In and Out* and *Soap Dish*, recording his aspiration to be a Shakespearean.

26 *King of Texas* was not the first international western to cite Shakespeare. The 1976 spaghetti western *Get Mean* (dir. Ferdinando Baldi, 1976) ends with an imitation of Shakespeare's *Richard III*: <http://us.imdb.com/Title?0074570>. Also, part of the St. Crispian's Day speech from *Henry* V was recited by actor Billy Zane playing an English traveling actor in *Tombstone* (dir. George P. Cosmatos, 1993).

27 International casting in film became increasingly common in the late 1990s. See Annette Insdorf, "Like the World, Casting Is Going Multinational," *New York Times*, November 8, 1998: 13, 31.

28 The website remains in smaller form at <http://www.tnt.tv/Title/Display/0,5918,341986,00.html>.

29 Michael Anderegg refers to Orson Welles's *Macbeth* as a "Shakespearean Western" (1999: 97), and *Scotland, PA* references the televised western through its latter-day, urban, back East incarnation in *McCloud*.

30 Whatever its faults, *King of Texas* is light years beyond the hopelessly incompetent and self-congratulatory liberal-minded NBC television adaptation *Tempest* (dir. Jack Bender, 1998),

starring Peter Fonda as Gideon Prosper and set in the Deep South during the American Civil War.

31 See Burt 1999 and also Cartelli 1999.

32 Dench's role as Hecuba in Branagh's *Hamlet* shows her increasing marginality with respect to Shakespeare, as does her role in *Tea with Mussolini* (dir. Franco Zeffirelli, 1999), where Joan Plowright's character is the one associated with Shakespeare.

33 Czech-born co-writer Tom Stoppard, who engaged, of course, in his own popularization of Shakespeare – *Rosencrantz and Guildenstern Are Dead* and *Dogg's Hamlet, Cahoot's Macbeth* – came on board late in production of *Shakespeare in Love*. See Burt 1999 and Burt 2000.

34 "Romeo Beckham. No one quite knows why the Beckhams have called their second son Romeo. We present a web guide to the name that's taken centre stage." Bobby Stansfield, *Guardian*, September 2, 2002, <http://www.guardian.co.uk/netnotes/article/0,6729, 784945,00.html>.

35 The screenwriters are Richard Curtis and Ben Elton.

36 For more UK films involving British abjection and Shakespeare, see *Withnail and I* (dir. Bruce Robinson, 1987), *Shiner* (dir. John Irvin, 2000) and *My Kingdom* (dir. Don Boyd, 2001) – the last two gangster films that draw on *King Lear* – and *Beginner's Luck* (dir. James Callis and Nick Cohen 2001), about a theater troupe of teenagers who travel from London to Paris performing *The Tempest*. A British reviewer of *My Kingdom* writes:

> *My Kingdom* is likely to make a modest splash, although critical support could give it a boost and it represents a very honourable achievement for all concerned. Lack of major names, outside [Richard] Harris, nominated for a British Independent Film award, and Lynn Redgrave in a small but significant role, will not help internationally.
>
> (Johnston 2002)

37 *Maybe Baby* follows in the wake of Trevor Nunn's all-UK *Twelfth Night* and *Merchant of Venice*, which also opens with use of black and white silent film footage before going to video. On Nunn's *Twelfth Night*, see Boose and Burt, 1997: 176–80.

38 For an interesting contrast in the way Shakespeare is used to differentiate English and American theater, see Emma Thompson as Kate Lemmon (she drops some Shakespeare references here and there) in the British romantic comedy *The Tall Guy*, in which an American named Dexter King (Jeff Goldblum) is doing a musical of *The Elephant Man* with Rowan Atkinson as Ron Anderson.

39 *Blackadder: The Shakespeare Sketch* was directed by Stephen Fry and performed on September 18, 1989. Rowan Atkinson's character was unnamed, but he was apparently a member of the Blackadder family. See <http://www.lackadderhall.com/specials/shakespeare_sketch.htm>. An episode called *Blackadder* "Back and Forth" that included Shakespeare also aired March 6, 2001 on PBS. For the text and some photos, go to <http://www.firth.com/BA.html>. It is also available on DVD.

40 Perhaps another index of Shakespeare's changing status as token of English colonialism is the film adaptation *Mansfield Park* (dir. Patricia Rozema, 1999). While the film gives full attention to the issue of slavery and Antigua in the novel, Shakespeare's frequent presence in the novel is reduced to the name of Fanny's horse ("Shakespeare") – Fanny's "refuge" – in the film. See Henry Crawford's comment in Chapter 13 that he "could be fool enough at this moment to take on any character that ever was written, from Shylock or Richard III to the singing hero of a farce in his scarlet coat and cocked hat" and Tom's, in the same chapter: "How many a time have we mourned over the dead body of Julius Caesar and to be'd and not to be'd in this very room for his amusement?" In Chapter 14, the young characters reject *Hamlet*, *Othello*, and *Macbeth* as possible plays to perform, and in Chapter 34, Henry Crawford mentions Shakespeare and sees that Fanny has been reading *Henry VIII*. See <http://www.planet.eon.net/~bplaroch/litJA.html>.

41 For further discussions of Shakespeare and African-American popular culture, see Burt 2002a, pp. 17–25, p. 26, n. 17, and Burt 2002b and 2002c. An exchange about Shakespeare

in the African-American romantic comedy, *Class Act* (dir. Randall Miller 1992), heightens a contrast between two black students, Duncan (Christopher Reid), upper middle class and brilliant but ineffectual, and Blade (Christopher Martin), lower class and street smart but crass. The two have exchanged identities. Ellen (Karyn Parsons), a young woman interested in Duncan, whom she mistakenly takes Blade to be, brings up Shakespeare in a bawdy context. "In *Much Ado About Nothing*, Shakespeare says, 'I will live in thy ear, die in thy lap, and be buried in thy eyes'" [5.2.102–3]. Blade responds with an indifferent "So?" and she explains, "Well, in Shakespeare's day 'to die' meant to have a sexual orgasm." At this point Blade lights up: "Yo! You mean my man Shakespeare wrote about a guy poppin' some coochie?! I mean 'making love?'" Ellen says "Well, I guess you could say that." The comedy of the scene turns, predictably enough, on the way Shakespeare's citation serves a desublimated, bawdy turn. The comedy *Deliver Us from Eva* (dir. Gary Hardwick, 2003) is an African-American spin-off of *The Taming of the Shrew* (see Holden 2003); Gabrielle Union, who plays Eva, also played Bianca's best friend, Chastity, in the *Shrew* spin-off *10 Things I Hate About You*. Though *Deliver* does not mention or allude directly to Shakespeare or the *Shrew*, it does play with the frame of the play by adding a brief clip after all of the credits have played in which a gay hairdresser turns out to be straight: he has only pretended to be gay so he won't be fired. This tailpiece offers a tacked-on supplement to assuage or possibly increase any residual anxieties or discomfort (black) male viewers may feel at the end of the film, which reverses the *Shrew*. Eva, Kate's analogue, is fully in charge as we see, from behind, her and Ray (L.L. Cool J.), Petruchio's analogue, ride off on a white horse, which has just thrown Ray, with Ray sitting behind Eva, who holds the reins. In *Bringing Down the House* (dir. Adam Shankman, 2003), a racist, spinster heiress played by Joan Plowright owns an all-white bull dog named William Shakespeare. There is a later slang reference by Peter Sanderson (Steve Martin) to African-Americans as "dogs" that gets him thrown into his pool. The dog Shakespeare is also mentioned at the end of the film outside a black club. And in *Hollywood Shuffle* (Robert Townsend 1987), aspiring African-American actor Bobby Taylor (Robert Townsend) meets a barber who tells him he can do anything, including Shakespeare. At the end of the film, we see Taylor onstage as King Lear.

42 See Burt 2002a for a discussion of the film.

43 The commercial aired April 10, 2000. Interestingly enough, James also made a guest appearance as Norman in episode 4. 15 of Frasier (1993) entitled "Roz's Krantz & Gouldenstein Are Dead" (original air date March 11, 1997).

44 My thanks to John Briggs for this reference.

45 See also Lucy Mazdon (2000) on the American remaking of French films.

46 For a critique of the concept of popular culture, see Burt 2002a.

47 In an interview, Jameson responds to a question about cognitive mapping by saying:

> My point was that it was cognitively unmappable, because the map itself is not a genuine representation. It is a substitute for representation. All of these models you're speaking about are attempts to overcome the problems of linguistic representation with something visible. What I meant originally by global mapping was to sense, how this new system holds together that somehow economically and even politically and socially it seems to be too vast.
>
> (http://www.heise.de/tp/english/inhalt/co/7127/1.html)

48 See <http://www.heise.de/tp/english/inhalt/co/7127/1.html>.

2

"REMEMBER ME":

Technologies of memory in Michael Almereyda's *Hamlet*

Katherine Rowe

> We are always simultaneously making gestures that are archaic, modern, and futuristic. Earlier I took the example of a car, which can be dated from several eras; every historical era is likewise multitemporal, simultaneously drawing from the obsolete, the contemporary, and the futuristic. An object, a circumstance, is thus polychronic, multitemporal, and reveals a time that is gathered together, with multiple pleats.
>
> Michel Serres, *Conversations on Science, Culture, and Time*

In his influential, late twentieth-century account of modernity, Pierre Nora attributes the impoverished condition of modern memory to the proliferation of new technologies. As Nora tells it, our modern condition of memory is technological dependency as well as loss. The communications and storage media we depend on to shore up the past also ruin it. They offer only "sifted and sorted" fragments of its actual plenitude (Nora 1989: 8). That plenitude consisted in a time of unmediated "true memory" and in "skills passed down by unspoken traditions, in the body's inherent self-knowledge, in unstudied reflexes . . . social, collective [and] all-encompassing" (Nora 1989: 13). What remains to us now is "a mode of historical perception which, with the help of the media, has substituted for a memory entwined in the intimacy of a collective heritage the ephemeral film of current events" (Nora 1989: 7). In a trenchant critique of Nora's theory, John Frow outlines its underlying nostalgia. Nora's model depends on a set of structuring contradictions "between a realm of authenticity and fullness of being, and the actually existing 'forms of human association.'" It displays a "spirituality independent of the materiality of the sign; it is unstructured by social technologies of learning or recall; it is incapable of reflexivity (it cannot take itself as an object), and its mode of apprehension is thus rooted in the 'inherent self-knowledge' and 'unstudied reflexes' of the body; it is organically related to its community and partakes of the continuity of tradition."[1] Periodizing in a way that abjects modernity, Nora projects the split between these different forms of mnemonic experience onto the advent of a modern representational technology, film. As Frow observes, this pattern repeats itself with successive modern representational forms: against an idealized vision of the forms that precede it, each new technology appears impoverished.[2]

Recent apologies for new media – particularly electronic media – contest their social and phenomenological impoverishment. Yet these apologies betray a similar desire for immediate experience projected into an idealized past. Recent examples are Allucquère Roseanne Stone's vision of electronic community and Malcolm McCullough's idea of virtual "handicraft." The former argues for the social and collective nature of electronic communication, the latter for a skill-based understanding of electronic design. In making these arguments, both critics project their media back, across the void of modernity, into the idealized plenitude of traditional, artisan community. Virtual handicraft has the Benjaminian quality of being "thrown," McCullough tells us, retaining the maker's unique and direct impressions as clay does a potter's hand. Little if anything of earlier modes of making is lost in this progressive vision, while much is gained that serves human memory and desire. What's missing from such progressive, technophilic models is real cost–benefit analysis: a fuller account of the needs we bring to any given technology, an exploration of the different losses and gains intrinsic to the varied media that serve those needs. Our current and past memory technologies are both mediated and phenomenally rich in ways that serve some interests but not others. Instead of a richer account of these qualities, nostalgic arguments like Nora's offer invidious contrasts, while apologic ones offer celebratory analogies.

In what follows, I emphasize the limitations of both these stances: limitations in the ways they periodize technology and idealize its relations to individual and cultural memory. My text is the Western locus of memory to which we regularly return to play out the conflict between a desire for presence and the technologies that mediate and shore up our losses – *Hamlet*. Michael Almereyda's 2000 adaptation of the play foregrounds this conflict, in an extended meditation on the resources film and digital video bring to the problem. In exploring the different technologies dramatized in the film, I am responding in part to Frow's call for a fuller account of the specific representational forms which structure Western invocations to memory (Frow 1997: 223–4). As an alternative to Nora, Frow suggests we should conceive of memory as always already technological: a function of the cognitive and social practices of representation that mediate past experience (indeed all experience) and selectively describe it for the present. "Technology," in this root sense of art or craft (*tekhne*), denotes a range of devices and practices:

> . . . on the one hand storage-and-retrieval devices and sites such as books, calendars, computers, shrines, or museums; and on the other hand particular practices of recall – techniques of learning acquired in school, structured confession or reminiscence, the writing of autobiography or history, the giving of evidence in court, the telling of stories related to an artifact or a photograph, and even such apparently immediate forms of recollection as the epiphanic flash of involuntary memory or the obsessive insistence of the symptom.
>
> (Frow 1997: 230)

Frow draws this integrated model of cognitive and social praxis, liberally quoted below, from early modern theories of memory – particularly the art of mental "writing." Writing serves him as the trans-historical type of all the forms and practices named above, which select, sort, and reproduce the matter of the past as a text. This technophilic alternative to Nora is enormously appealing, in part because its embrace of mediated, textualized experience seems to free us from the unproductive desire for presence, and with that desire, from the perception of loss. Yet a progressive account of memory-as-technology does not get rid of the problems Nora raises – specifically the problem of loss – any more than Hamlet's "tables" allow him, in his most famous moment of remembrance, to "wipe away" the memory of his mother (1.5.99). By reducing loss to nostalgia, Frow stops short of a richly comparatist exploration of the different ways various representational forms constrain and serve human memory. Oddly, what is missing most urgently from Frow's analysis is a broader recognition of the historically composite nature of the specific technologies through which individuals and cultures remember. Michel Serres reminds us that any technology develops polychronically, a "disparate aggregate" of technical solutions, practices and uses arising from multiple historical contexts.[3] Over time, any given technology may turn out to be neutral to the desire for immediacy, the embrace of mediation, or perceptions of belatedness and loss. The same technical solution may serve some of these impulses at different moments, or even serve conflicting impulses at the same time. Finally the meaning of immediacy itself and its relation to memory technologies may change significantly in different periods. This is true for the figure of "writing on tables" that dominates early modern memory arts. It is equally true for the modern memory arts of the moving image.

The first observation a Serresian critic might make about Almereyda's *Hamlet* is that the viewing experience most of us have of the film is not, in fact, cinematic. Most readers of this essay will have watched the film – if they have at all – on VHS or DVD, forms that begin to simulate something like a print-based experience that allows for non-linear reading, replay, and even (in the case of DVD) delivers the text in chapters. This point may seem a quibble. In fact, it is an important instance of the polychronic needs we bring to any representational form (and not incidentally, an important element of Almereyda's *mise-en-scène*). As a medium, film exists largely as an experience in memory. For all the phenomenological richness and collective social experience of the cinema, we tend to view films only once in this way, only to return to this experience in memory: in later conversation, commentary (as in this essay), or classroom analysis. Unredacted, uncited, unrehearsed films do not have a robust existence. For those with access to video and DVD, the loss of the social and esthetic impact associated with cinema may balanced by the more quotable, rehearsable and transmissable experience supported by video replay.

To pursue the polychrony of film and video further, however, we need a fuller account of the earlier memory arts that these media inherit and renovate. For a film like *Hamlet*, this means looking back not only to some of its film predecessors (for a sketch of the form and uses of film in Shakespearean adaptation), but also to Shakespeare's text and the memory arts it invokes. Recent work on Shakespeare and film has tended to leave the text behind in order to move beyond the limitations of the fidelity model of adaptation (how faithful is the film to the play being the only question the text seems to answer). This reasonable impulse effectively obscures the ways older practices of memory persist in and shape our uses of the newer forms. The same impulse makes it harder for us to see how Shakespeare's own plays allegorize their relation to media that were both new and old at the time of their earliest performance and publication. Almereyda adapts an allegory of earlier memory technologies worked out in Shakespeare's *Hamlet*. As an experiment in polychronic reading, then, this essay begins with those early technologies, sketching the multimedia practices of early modern memory as illustrated in John Willis's 1621 manual, *The Art of Memory*, and as evoked (much more anxiously) in Shakespeare's play.

Memory was understood in early modern Europe as a cognitive and social discipline that marshals past knowledge and experience for present uses.[4] In this model, recollection satisfies present needs by means of – rather than in spite of – technologies of representation that "sift," "sort," and otherwise manipulate the matter of the past. This view, essentially technophilic, emphasizes the different kinds of cognitive leverage different forms of representation and remembering environments provide. Early modern memory arts draw on theatrical environments and practices, writing and printing, painting and emblem books, religious observance, and so on. John Willis relies on all of these media when he sets out to popularize the classical memory arts. Willis translates his own earlier treatise in Latin to English, so as to expand its potential audience: anyone aspiring to the status of civil gentleman but lacking, perhaps, the classical education that might sustain civil subjectivity. The arts Willis describes are accessible in part because they depend on familiar technologies of representation and storage. These include an anachronistic mix of classical and early modern technologies: the tablets (Hamlet's "tables") in which ideas may be cognitively inscribed; pamphlets; books ("tables" again, but also books for collective reading like missals); emblems; the mental house or theater in which ideas can be placed until future need, often as moving and audible scenes (Willis 1621: 13). "Idea" is Willis's technical term for the visual metaphors in which we commit matter (events, information) to memory. Willis describes several orders of memory ideas, including scenes of human figures in motion – a smith working, a "duell fought between two combatants" – and important sayings inscribed on "tables" and hung on the wall (Willis 1621: 12–15).[5]

For Willis, writing and *mise-en-scène* are not just metaphors for cognitive activities but practical constraints on such activity. The mental memory theater Willis describes has precise dimensions and optical limits. For example, how we store ideas depends on where our mind's eye is positioned as we face our mental theater. Imagine your mental house or theater "wide open to our view," he advises, with a stage "one yard high

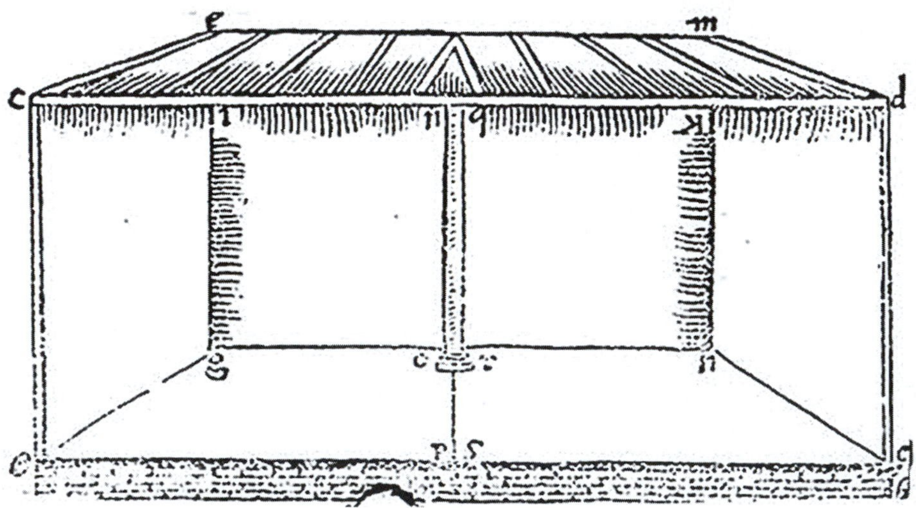

Figure 2.1 Design for a mental memory theater, John Willis, 1621.

above the level of the ground whereon we stand" (Willis 1621: 3). "Such a fashioned Repositorie are we to prefix before the eyes of our mind, as often as we intend to commit things to memory, supposing ourselves to be right against the midst thereof, and in the distance of two yards there from" (Willis 1621: 8).

Willis's memory arts depend on modes of visual perception that combine theatrical spectation with reading. He is specific about the material conditions of *mise-en-page*, or layout, as well as architecture, in ways that may seem extraordinary to modern readers. For example, he takes pains to explain the proper shape of letters, line spacing, marginal citation conventions, and capitalization involved in mental writing – as well as the materials involved. Your table should be plain, sturdily framed (of broad oak), and the right size for what you write on it. Most importantly, your letters should "be all of such bignesse as that they may plainly be read by him that standeth on this side of the Repositorie; like unto the writings which we see in Churches." Thus, when remembering important sayings – sententiae – it is best to inscribe them on the tables of your brain using large initials, that can be clearly seen by your mind's eye as they hang on the wall:

> A single word and quotation, must be written in a tablet one foote and an halfe broad, and a foote high; and their first letter must be a great Romane capitall letter of extraordinary bignesse above the rest, and the transcendencies of the small letters also, if there be any must be drawne much higher or lower than is usuall in common writing. For by this meanes they are the more easily attracted by the visuall facultie, and transferred to the memory.
> (Willis 1621: 33–5)

The imperative to keep ideas at the right size positions the memorial subject simultaneously as a reader and a spectator, as the allusion to Church writings suggests. Here the differences between Willis's plain-style memory theater and the more elaborate, multi-roomed memory houses of his classical sources show clearly. Willis's remembering subject takes the position of a fixed spectator: never turning to view his other rooms (coded by color) but apparently substituting each one into the same spatial configuration in front of him, as needed. The optical constraints of this fixed spectatorial position are particularly evident in the case of remembered objects (in general, Willis emphasizes memory for idea/things – *res* – over memory for text – *verba*). Objects that are too big to fit on the mental stage or too little to be seen need to be metaphorically reduced or enhanced. To remember a pearl, for example, you'd have to mentally pile a bushel of pearls on your stage (Willis 1621: 16). To remember something enormous or sublime, like a city or mountain – "whose Idea in the full bigness, cannot be contained in a place of the Repositorie" – you'd have to paint it in small on the wall in your theater (Willis 1621: 17–18). Such formal techniques for manipulating remembered things help to optimize their retrieval. Retrieval typically means, for Willis, recombining the matter in memory to suit the needs of a given occasion, not playing it back sequentially. Prodigious artificial memories were distinguished by the degree to which they could recombine and reverse the matter in memory. Familiar examples include the monks who could recite any Psalm backwards, or run through the sequence starting anywhere, or redact random verses as you call out their numbers (Carruthers 1990: 82).

The point to be taken here is the profound shaping force that early modern technologies of representation – architecture, theatrical performance, written texts – were understood to have on cognitive processes. Like other Renaissance arts, memory arts were distinguished from the "natural" memory of an embodied mind shaped by outside forces, both physical and social. With practice, a civil gentleman might use such arts to discipline and improve his natural faculties (Willis 1621: A4). These arts protected against both inordinate environmental pressures and the organic failures of memory intrinsic to humoral cognition – vulnerable to environmental impressions from the outside and unruly humors within.[6] The immediacy and force of humoral affections were understood to be such that forgetting past impressions might be as difficult as remembering them. The ability to filter and forget impressions – as well as to train the memory to sort more significant matter – was a requirement for successful remembering as critical as retention (Sullivan 1999).

The interplay of impressions in this material psychology seems especially fraught in Shakespeare's *Hamlet*. The question of whether internal disciplines actually work – and the ways in which technical supplements support or fail them – turns out to be a critical problem in the play.[7] The problem is most acute, I would suggest, precisely at a moment in which the polychronic nature of one dominant technology – writing on tables – shows most clearly. That is, when Hamlet formally accepts the Ghost's charge, "remember me:"

> . . . Remember thee?
> Yea, from the table of my memory
> I'll wipe away all trivial fond records,
> All saws of books, all forms, all pressures past
> That youth and observation copied there,
> And thy commandment all alone shall live
> Within the book and volume of my brain,
> Unmix'd with baser matter. Yes, by heaven!
> O most pernicious woman.
> (1.5.97–105)

Much critical attention has been paid to these lines. They serve here briefly to emphasize three points. First, the "pressures past" recorded in Hamlet's memory are simultaneously bodily and immediate (fond, youth) and deliberate (observation). Second, immediacy is here an obstacle to true memory rather than – as for Nora – its privilege. Hamlet needs to forget the combined impressions of his natural and artificial memory – which he cannot quite succeed in doing, as the pun on "baser matter" makes clear. Matter implies, of course, both the rhetorical matter – "trivial fond records" – of early modern education, and the physical matter of the affections and humors, their frailties conflated with *mater*. The spontaneous break of memory in line 1.5.104 which recalls Hamlet to his mother suggests it may be as difficult to wipe away artful impressions (the Latin of a classical education or of Roman Catholic observance) as natural ones. Indeed, the pun suggests it is impossible to distinguish the two.

The third point to be taken here returns us to the question of the historicity of memory technologies like writing on tables. Scholars have tended to gloss the figure as either a reference to the ancient technology (and memory metaphor) of tablets or a concrete object (like ivory writing tablets) that Hamlet carries. Significantly, as Peter Stallybrass and Roger Chartier remind us, the word "table" in the early modern period denotes a range of book technologies, from archaic to cutting edge. Recent discoveries by Stallybrass, Chartier and several collaborators suggest a third referent, a new form of portable notebook with treated, eraseable leaves.[8] They invite us, accordingly, to read this passage as an exploration of the strengths and limitations of different kinds of writing-on-tables in the period. Ancient wax tablets were reuseable but somewhat challenging to erase, and they never entirely lost impressions – a fact that Shane Butler reminds us made them a formidable source of forensic evidence for scholars like Cicero (Butler 2002: 66–7). In the context of Hamlet's pun on matter, it is tempting to associate this form of storage with the weaknesses of a humoral memory: not easily wiped of impressions in a way that permits reordered priorities of recall. In response, Hamlet reaches for the latest technology to redress the failures of an earlier one. He looks to a portable repository, invitingly separable from the matter of an embodied mind, and more easily wiped. If, as Stallybrass and his coauthors urge, we resist the temptation to collapse "table," "book," "volume," and writing into a single kind of technology, Hamlet seems to be groping through a variety of storage forms here, seeking the one that best serves the functions of sorting and reordering the matter of the past. Judging by the force of spontaneous recollections that follow – his mother's affections, sententiae about smiling villains – the attempt is at best a partial success.

The transitional, polychronic nature of early modern technologies such as Hamlet's tables provides some insight into the stances towards memory in recent film adaptations of Shakespeare. In particular, the early examples help explain their preoccupation with anachronism, their sense that the matter of the past is reversible and manipulable, and their notion that Shakespeare's plays are particularly congenial to such manipulation. These preoccupations slant what Peter Donaldson has called the "media allegory" in Baz Luhrmann's *Shakespeare's Romeo + Juliet* (1997), with its out-of-control culture of mass media and advertising (Donaldson 1999: 62). Film and video technologies become the focus of a similar allegory of recording media in Almereyda's *Hamlet.* Both filmmakers subscribe to the non-nostalgic notion of memory as a cognitive and social techné. Acts of memory, for them, serve as opportunities to assess the adequacy of different technologies in relation to present needs, not to past actualities. Almereyda's Hamlet seems at first to personify the psychological costs and mnemonic impoverishment Nora attributes to modern media, when we encounter him absorbed in a melancholy session of video replay. In fact, Almereyda's film probes both the strengths and limitations of different memory technologies, including photography, film, video, and digital video. The film also serves to remind us that these media, like earlier forms of artificial memory, are historically composite technologies that incorporate multiple stances towards remembering – technophilic, nostalgic, skeptical – often at the same time.

This approach is different enough from other film adaptations that it is worth marshalling a few examples for comparison. For adapters like Kenneth Branagh, for instance, the Shakespearean text functions as the material trace of lost experiences to be reconstructed as fully as possible, against the relentless rush forward of history. Barbara Hodgdon describes Branagh's *mise-en-scène* as a continual negotiation between the demands of audience accessibility and authenticity (Hodgdon 2003). His choice of source text for debated line readings in *Hamlet* (1996) – Harold Jenkins's magisterial Arden edition – suggests Branagh's affiliation to the project of reconstruction.[9] As several scholars have observed, this project is actually a double one: to reconstruct both a lost theatrical and a lost cinematic experience. His films explore the increasing difficulty of achieving the experience of immersion established so powerfully in

Olivier's classic Shakespearean oeuvre (Donaldson 1999; Hodgdon 2003). Olivier's adaptations seemed to answer the problems of editorial reconstruction with the seamlessness of cinematic suture, restoring us to a fullness of experience not present in the partial text. At the same time, Olivier reveled in the technical mediation that made this renovation possible, to the point almost of exposing his technical resources. His glee is particularly clear in *Hamlet* (1948). In a famous moment in Gertrude's closet, for example, the vertiginous sweep of Olivier's camera gradually reveals the mnemonic force of cinema, commanding its audience to an audition that returns the past to the present. By contrast to the early modern technologies the playtext evokes, this moment of audition emphasizes a supremely successful technical management of memory and emotion. Addressing the Ghost, Hamlet indicates the camera in a way that explicitly calls attention to the cinematic moment. First, he seems to assert the camera's ghostly oversight and prowess: ". . . Look you how pale he glares./His form and cause conjoin'd, preaching to stones,/Would make them capable" (3.4.25–7). Then he wards off that force, still in the meta-cinematic mode, addressing the camera in the second person, "Do not look on me." For Branagh, by contrast, the authority of this second-person address comes hard, if at all. Olivier's camera-work and the Shakespearean text together serve as the origins whose authenticity is affirmed by proclaiming their loss.[10] Accordingly, his revivals frame the past nostalgically: its beauty and power are most visible and authentic at the moment that we recognize it as no longer ours.

For Luhrmann, Almereyda and Julie Taymor, by contrast, Shakespeare's plays serve as robust compendia of traces of the past, to be recycled according to specific investments. Taymor describes *Titus Andronicus* as a "complete . . . dissertation on violence" (Schechner 1999: 46). The play offers a systematic survey of knowledge about violence that anyone thinking about the topic right now will benefit from. Luhrmann and Almereyda come to their plays for similar reasons: seeking commonplace knowledge on specific topics, many times renovated and circulated. Neither authenticity nor accessibility are the main concerns of these directors, as their embrace of anachronism and play with cinematic distance makes clear. In this context, the practice of "sifting and sorting" this knowledge – far from reductive, as Nora imagines it – turns out to be fundamental to its cognitive and emotional utility for those who remember. Memory, understood as both a cognitive and social phenomenon, reworks traces of the past according to present interests, anxieties, and desires; as Frow observes: "rather than being the repetition of the physical traces of the past, [memory] is a construction of it under conditions and constraints determined by the present" (1997: 228). Like the temporality of a text, the temporality of memory is

> not the linear, before-and-after, cause-and-effect time embedded in the logic of the archive but the time of a continuous analeptic and proleptic shaping . . . In such a model the past is a function of the system: rather than having a meaning and a truth determined once and for all by its status as event, it's meaning and its truth are constituted retroactively and repeatedly.
>
> (Frow 1997: 229)

For these filmmakers, as for Willis, accurate retrieval of the matter of the past is less important than its effective use. Thus, technologies of recording and retrieval in their films are marked by their belatedness in regards to present needs: both the older technologies of book and theater, and apparently cutting-edge technologies of modern communications and transport, that proliferate in their hypermodern, urban settings. Luhrmann and Almereyda layer technologies in a way that regularly feels anachronistic, altering the viewer's sense of distance from the modern *mise-en-scène* and from the Shakespearean text. It can be hard to tell which feels the most stylized and belated. The clash between the archaic language (delivered flatly) and the modern settings (delivered with visual energy) might suggest an esthetic progressivism. But Luhrmann's use of a high-speed delivery service ("Post Haste") that arrives too late to give Romeo news of the Friar's ruse reverses the relation, framing modern technology in decidedly belated terms. Less obvious anachronisms can be just as telling. Absurdly, in a story that supposedly takes place in AD 2000, Almereyda's Hamlet transmits Claudius's message to England via floppy disk rather than e-mail. The choice is dramatically necessary, of course. Yet the just-in-time-delivery economy of the web is wholly absent from the film.

All technologies in these Shakespearean worlds tend to lag behind our needs of them. But nostalgia is not the only register in which the films address this problem. A brief example from Luhrmann's *Romeo + Juliet* reminds us that such lags are features to be reckoned with in most representational forms and practices, and always have been. Like Taymor, Luhrmann finds Shakespearean language and dramatic conventions readily available to his present interests. Indeed, they seem as available and current as the conventions of Australian Mardi Gras or the earlier film *Priscilla Queen of the Desert* (Donaldson 2002: 72). When Luhrmann's director of photography, Donald McAlpine, calls Shakespeare a great "Australian," he speaks only partly tongue in cheek (Luhrmann 2000: laserdisc commentary track). The matter of *Romeo and Juliet* communicates no more or less legibly in a global context than local Australian matter. Luhrmann adapts Shakespeare in part because he's interested in the global transport of performance forms. He is surprisingly confident about the degree to which performance conventions remain legible across time and geopolitical boundaries. If the past is a foreign country, it's simply subject to the same challenges and opportunities of translation that apply to all cultural exchanges under globalism. Luhrmann's figure for such global translations is Shakespeare's "wooden O," stood up vertically, on end. The setting, a blasted-out cinema palace, introduces us to Romeo in the middle of a solitary experiment in love-melancholy:

Figure 2.2 Luhrmann's "wooden O."

This blasted theater is a global conduit through which we receive conventional matter from far-away places. Romeo's stale Petrarchisms travel West as we look East through the center of a proscenium arch, into the rising sun. They hark forward in time as we listen back to their archaic patterns: "Why then, O brawling love, O loving hate!/O any thing, of nothing first create!" (1.1.176–7). Romeo's oxymorons exemplify the conventional matter that will pass through this setting later in the film: Mercutio's drag performance, the Western shootout in which he dies. The Petrarchan conventions are thin and outdated, but their belatedness makes them recyclable for Luhrmann as for Shakespeare. Romeo's musings are conveyed by multiple vehicles here: the modern soundtrack, his handwriting, his note book (a commonplace book?), the limousine, the theatrical setting. A longer clip would show us other modes of transport: TV screens, radio, more cars. To the extent that we recognize this setting as a vertical "wooden O," we're being asked to see these diverse vehicles not as anachronisms but as historically composite technologies, like the composite car described by Michel Serres: a combination of ancient technologies (the wheel), modern ones (internal combustion engine), and the latest composite plastics (Serres 1995: 45). As Ovid is to Petrarch and Petrarch to Shakespeare, so Shakespeare is to Luhrmann: a source of commonplace conventions for interiority to be reworked and reapplied in surprising ways. However, where the composite technologies of a car present themselves as seamlessly integrated – so well, indeed, that it can be hard to recognize their historical heterogeneity – Romeo's Petrarchan toolkit for conjuring subjectivity emphasizes the very fact of borrowing. Its appeal is the belatedness of its own devices and the engaging dissonance such belatedness can generate.[11]

The media allegory in Almereyda's *Hamlet* focuses more narrowly on technologies of memory. His preoccupation is the way film and video mediate past experience, both for the individual and the community. Yet Almereyda is more concerned than Luhrmann with the trade-offs these different technologies entail. For Almereyda's Hamlet, the personal video is *the* technology of interiority among a variety of modern media, including telephones, television, photography, film, and so on. All but one of Hamlet's soliloquies are framed as video sequences that he has composed. As he dies, we see his life flash back in the same grainy black-and-white collage. Like Willis's visual topoi, Hamlet's videos create narratives of the past not for the purpose of accurate retrieval but in response to present interests and desires. The formal features of film and video supply a cognitive grammar for the mind as it stores and recombines the traces of the past. Whereas for John Willis, as I noted, the constraints of *mise-en-page* and *mise-en-scène* governed the way in which ideas are stored and retrieved, Almereyda's key constraints are the framed screen (film or video) and the conventions of editing that create a continuous experience out of fragmented images. We see this in Hamlet's first soliloquy, which unfolds characteristically, in a home video. Before the opening credits, we enter the film through a video collage that turns out to be what Hamlet watches as he works at his desk. While the audio track voices over his melancholy thoughts – "I have of late . . . lost all my mirth . . ." – Hamlet's gestures link the work of his editing hands, moving on the track pad, with his mental experience.

The clips Hamlet has spliced into this video look at first like what Pierre Nora would call the "sifted and sorted historical traces" of a lost past: Renaissance painting, military footage, cartoon monster (Fig. 2.3). They seem like fragments of collective memory, a loose collection of "pop images and simulacra" through which, as Frederic Jameson warns, we may be "condemned to seek History . . ." in the nostalgic mode (Jameson

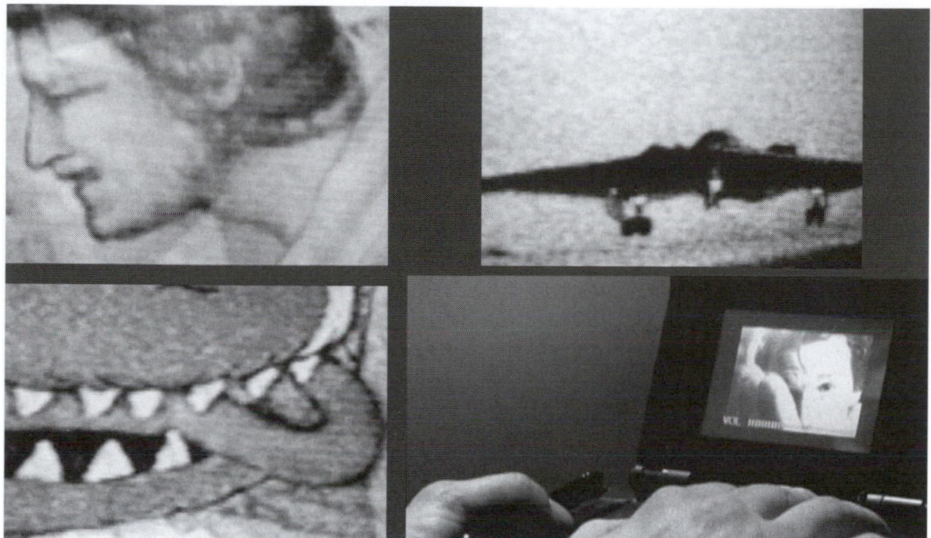

Figure 2.3 Video soliloquy.

25; cited in Frow 1997: 218). But what Almereyda sees in these screens is a composite vehicle like Luhrmann's Globe. What Hamlet seeks in his videos is not history but a connection between collective experience and his own loss. We are asked here to understand his interiority in terms of the video record he manipulates.

The grainy, shimmery quality of the video image, and the way Hamlet addresses the camera in this video-within-the film, recall early video memoires by Sadie Benning and others in the 1980s (Fig. 2.4). These are already belated conventions for video soliloquy that use a dated technology of their own. The camera we see in Hamlet's hands early in the film is a Pixelvision camera rigged to a digital recorder. The watery, shifting signature of Pixelvision images echoes other imagined breaks through clear surfaces in the film, into private and protected space. When Ophelia later imagines herself diving into the pool to escape Polonius's relentless toadying and exposure, the surface breaks into a similar screening, protective pattern of bubbles.

At a different level, however, we're asked to recognize that our *perception* of interiority depends on much older technologies of self. The next time Almereyda offers us a video soliloquy, he emphasizes the composite technologies that transmit a shared past. Once again, we watch Hamlet replay a home video of his parents in a second soliloquy, on the "weary, stale, flat and unprofitable" uses of this world. A medium shot establishes Hamlet (from behind) seated at his desk. Then the camera reverses to a medium shot from the other side of the desk. A stack of books at the bottom of the screen complete a frame with the two monitors on either side (it is hard to see in this shot, but we see later that there is a photograph lying on top of the books).

The books and monitors work together to put Hamlet's inner life on screen for us. Indeed, this window into his thoughts will expand in a zoom to include the whole screen. The zoom reorients our attention to a different set of frames as well. From foreground to background, our field of view is defined by the two screens Hamlet sits between: the

Figure 2.4 Video memoir.

monitors between the camera and his body, and the window behind him, with its striped reflections, that serves as backdrop. As the clip continues and the camera zooms in, Hamlet plays and replays his father's image, offering us what will become a signature action for Old Hamlet, as he brushes his hand across his temple and ear (Fig. 2.5).

The emphasis of all these video soliloquies is Hamlet's editorial process. There is no possibility of knowing the past in this film except through captured images processed by the self. The opportunity to process in this intimate way makes these traces more than simulacra. Hamlet forges an authentic connection to the past, if not a perfect one. We know this, I hazard, because of the conventions of cinematic reversal on which this

Figure 2.5 Editing video memories: Hamlet's inner life on screen.

connection depends. Two kinds of reversal are in play here. The first is the reversibility of video traces of the past: rewound, edited, played back again by hand. These videos explore the notion, critical to recent art-house filmmaking, of digital media as so-called "haptic" technologies, serving a sense of touch as well as sight. Almereyda offers the protected, psychic experience afforded by Hamlet's camera-holding and by his editing as an analogy and extension to earlier modes of representation and storage. Shakespeare's Hamlet, like Willis's memorial subject, remembers according to the cognitive structures of "book and volume" and the theater; we know the ins and outs of his experience by watching him manipulate conventional matter – "trivial, fond saws" or a player's speech – in strategic and occasional ways. Similarly, Almereyda's memory arts depend on the representational constraints of film and video.

Our sense that Hamlet has an authentic memorial experience with his videos depends, accordingly, on a second kind of reversal: the way the scene itself is edited: in a series of eye-line cuts that come very close to the standard convention of shot/response shot. The scene stages Hamlet's meditation in alternating shots of Hamlet's face and the video he plays with. Tellingly, as he replays and stops the images he internalizes his father's gesture, hand to the temple. Shot/response shot cuts are a staple of continuity editing, often used to establish the fiction of intimate exchange. In classic cinema, the technique involves cuts that switch point of view back and forth between two characters in dialogue. The camera stays on the same side of the two characters, but reverses its angle across an imaginary line that runs 180 degrees between them. We sit at person A's shoulder, watching person B react as A talks (as if we're seeing what A sees). Then we sit at person B's shoulder and watch A react as B responds. Shot/response shot is a cinematic trope that makes us feel party to an intimate exchange, creating the fiction that we can know both points of view simultaneously. Using this convention for example, Olivier lets us know that Claudius suspects and hates Hamlet and that Hamlet requites the feelings. In sequences like this, alternating shots are sutured together so as to "seem to constitute a perfect whole," assuring the viewer that "his or her gaze suffers under no constraints" (Silverman 1988: 12).

Turning back to the editing sequence from Almereyda's film, we can see Almereyda adapting this device and referencing its classic effects. The camera cuts from our view of Hamlet through the monitors, to the video he watches. Then it reverses to a close shot of his eyes, then reverses again to the wider shot of his hand editing the video. In these tight, alternating shots we watch Hamlet react to the video, then see the video player respond to Hamlet's manipulation. As in classic shot/response shot the camera stays on the same side of both figures. What would be the 180-degree line falls about at the plane of the monitor screen. There is a kind of naturalized emotional transmission that happens in these reversals, intimate enough that Hamlet internalizes his father's gesture from shot to response shot. At this moment, digital video editing looks intensely kin to a handicraft, a medium of trained as well as spontaneous gesture passed on as organic experience.[12]

Whereas the spectator in Willis's memory theater remains in a fixed optical relation to the matter stored in memory, the camera work in classical shot/response shot moves us along a defined axis within the field of dramatic action. The conventions of cinema sustain this diffused, mobile spectating position for the remembering subject in Almereyda's film. As the story unfolds, Almereyda's editing affords even greater play across the barrier of the screen past. Indeed, in Hamlet's first encounter with the ghost,

Figure 2.6 Shot/response shot: crossing the screen barrier.

Old Hamlet appears easily out of the screen past. The camera itself crosses the screen barrier, taking the spectators over and returning, bringing the ghost back through its plane with us (Fig. 2.6). The sequence is gradual, and it is important to notice some of the differences between this shot arrangement and classical shot/response shot. As the actors cross, the camera switches not only point of view but also moves from one side to the other, eventually tracking around to reverse position with the spectators. As the scene begins, Hamlet wakes up to a phone ringing. Then the Ghost appears on the balcony. After a series of medium shots establish emotional connection between the dead and the living, the Ghost easily crosses the screen barrier, the glass wall of the 180-degree line that had been a backdrop for the video soliloquy. The dialogue that marks this crossing is the Ghost's command – "mark me" – and Hamlet's acquiescence – "I will." There is no apparent emotional barrier between father and son here, a fact that's emphasized by the Ghost's behavior as he tells of his death. The Ghost repeats his gesture (this time handkerchief to poisoned ear), then reaches to touch Hamlet in the same place, holding his head close. As the scene unfolds, the actors and camera circle until they have reversed positions from their opening arrangement. Hamlet and the Ghost stand roughly where the camera had positioned the spectator as the scene opened. At the same time, the editing resolves into more classic arrangements of shot and response shot, with a less mobile camera. With the wall of memory technologies as backdrop – photographs, monitors, digital editor, even a film reel on the desk – the sequence hits its climax and they embrace. This Ghost is tangible and emotionally available (despite casting of Sam Shepard).

The shot/response shot structure repeats throughout the film, most often in the flexible mode of the first soliloquy than in the classical mode, moving both actors and spectators across the screen/surface boundary as we see here. Almereyda's conceit is that this crossing is the condition of intimacy between the self and others. Intimacy results from the projection of self simultaneously behind and in front of a screen, a projection that makes the self accessible because it provides a cognitive grammar for transmitting and internalizing multiple points of view. Yet for Almereyda's Hamlet, as for Shakespeare's, this is a purely private experience, apparently untransmittable to others. The real conflict in the film and the source of Hamlet's melancholy is not the technical mediation of experience, but its social circulation. At first the easy circulation of public images seems to be precisely the problem. The private and autonomous record digital video makes possible appears as a necessary protection against the appropriation of memory technologies by large corporate systems. (A shot of a huge Panasonic screen launches the first video soliloquy.) The struggle over who controls the technologies of memory emerges as the opening credits roll, in the scene of a press conference where Claudius presides as the new CEO of Denmark Corporation. As it films the paparazzi filming Claudius's speech, Hamlet's camera serves as a "particular" rather than a "common" lens – picking up on the oppositional stance Gertrude describes in 1.2.75:

QUEEN: . . . Thou know'st 'tis common, all that lives must die,
Passing through nature to eternity.
HAMLET: Ay, madam, it is common.
QUEEN: If it be,
Why seems it so particular with thee?

(1.2.72–5)

In this public scene we are invited to see Hamlet's manipulations of his own video record as oppositional: a resistance to the official counter-memories of the corporate-media-advertising-complex that swallowed his father. The Ghost's dissolve through the Pepsi machine, gateway to the underworld, captures the nature of this threat.

In this context, Hamlet's obsessive replays serve not to slow the rush of present into the past but to privatize memory records for meditation and self-reflection. He gets the matter and inspiration for the "to be" speech from found footage taped from the TV; the soliloquy emerges in fragments (as if in a play on the different Folio and Quarto versions), to emerge in its most familiar Folio form only through editing and playback.

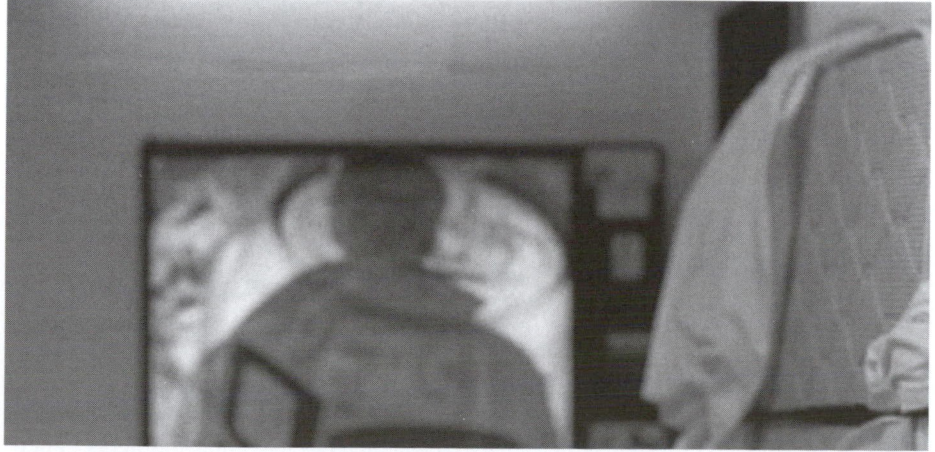

Figure 2.7 Old Hamlet dissolves through the Pepsi machine.

Replay and collage here serve to appropriate found footage from the media environment and recycle it for private purposes. With *The Mousetrap* video, Hamlet seeks to do more than trap Claudius. He edits his found footage in this video-within-the-film so as to expose the "real" interests behind Claudius's media show. In the process, he attempts to retrieve the memory of his mother's affection for his father from behind the counter-memory of her lust for his uncle.

When Hamlet turns to the conventions of cinema in this way, Almereyda introduces a different set of concerns than the problem of who controls modern mnemotechnologies. Indeed, that concern turns out by the end of the film to be secondary to the problem of how well modern media technologies extend the social self: providing for intimacy with others as well as self-reflection, meeting the demands of occasion, as Willis understands memory to do. In order to trap his uncle, Hamlet needs a medium that serves collective experience: the arena of the screening room where he premiers *The Mousetrap* as a "film/video." The found footage in *The Mousetrap* works differently from Hamlet's home videos, stitching together fragments of familiar images in a way that evokes a variety of earlier forms associated with the cinematic experiences of visual presence. These include sequences from silent films, stop-motion footage, advertising footage, and film pornography.[13] In stitching these sequences together, the film/video vividly evokes Bruce Conner's cinematic formalism, addressing the viewer aggressively in Conner's "second-person" mode, "reworking the already coded and manipulated cultural material of the movies" and peripheral media like advertising (Jenkins 1999: 187).[14]

The Mousetrap generates strong individual and collective responses in Hamlet's on-screen, theater audience, as some of the other imaging technologies in the film do (Ophelia's photographs for example). Home video technologies, by contrast, are now so individuated that we really have no idea if we can go around handing our version of the past to someone else – as Ophelia does her photographs – and expect it to be legible. It is worth remembering back even a short time to the period in which Almereyda's film premiered, at the turn of the century: a period in which such technologies seemed permanently untouched by the common standards that ensure what the industry calls "interoperability." As many as eight different formats competed on the market at the time, as a contemporary article in the *New York Times* "Circuits" section lamented. At the time of writing, no industry standard ensures that this medium may be exchanged between different users or support a shared experience of different pasts.[15] From Almereyda's point of view this is a contemporary challenge as pressing as the threat of corporate control. The apotheosis of technically extended experience, in his film, is not for Hamlet to transcend mediating technologies but to inhabit them in a way that is fully portable and transmissible to others. Our solution to the social and cognitive demands of memory technologies, Almereyda argues, is a necessarily composite work-around. Once the memory of Old Hamlet's death cycles through the shared venue of cinema audition, its powerful affects may extend in turn to private modes of audition: the scene of Claudius, in his limo, repenting his rank offense in front of a small TV screen. For such purposes, Almereyda suggests, video allows us to receive and process content in intimate ways. Yet cinema provides the cognitive grammar that organizes that content in socially legible terms and produces it as shared knowledge. The claim is particularly clear in Hamlet's final moments. There video supplies the grainy, black-and-white final memories of Hamlet dying, products of intimate collection, sorting, and recollection. But those memories are also shots from the film: meaningful because conflated with and recycled through our cinematic audition.[16]

> "The text of a film is unattainable because it is an unquotable text."
> Raymond Bellour, *The Analysis of Film*

In its print form, this essay is caught between polychronic interests and desires of its own – interests that derive from the modern technologies of film and video and the older craft of the scholarly essay. Ideally, you would be reading this essay in a web-based version of the kind AHR pioneered in 2000. In such a format, readers might read, hear, and view audio-visual quotations, in the form of playable clips embedded in the text.[17] The few stills offered here capture the esthetic dimensions of film – a patterned sequence of moving images and sounds – as poorly as a print quotation of a poem would if it reproduced only the outline of the poem on the page. Without a medium that quotes the work in its own material dimensions, this essay has no cinematic text to close-read. Raymond Bellour explained the problem eloquently in 1975. Print quotations reproduce print "by a reduplication whose fascination has been fully felt by modern thought. . . . This effect . . . lies in the undivided conformity of the object of study and the means of study, in the absolute material coincidence between language and language" (2000: 22). By selecting and sorting the matter of a work (so as to illustrate, exemplify, and jog the reader's memory) print quotation produces a print work as a text. To the extent that the textuality of any work becomes visible only in this possibility of quotation, Bellour reminds us that stills paradoxically open up the textuality of the film just at the moment they interrupt its unfolding:

> In a sense [this] is really what is done when a reader stops at a sentence in a book to re-read it and reflect on it. But it is not the same movement that is frozen. Continuity is suspended, meaning fragmented; but the material specificity of a means of expression is not interfered with in the same way. The cinema, through the moving image, is the only art of time which, when we go against the principle on which it is based, still turns out to give us something to see, and moreover something alone that allows us to feel its textuality fully.
>
> (2000: 26)

For as long as it remains feasible to host, readers may explore alternative modes of quotation by reading an online version of this essay with playable clips, at <http://www.brynmawr_edu/filmstudies/writing/index.html>. Yet in the larger analysis, double publication of this kind represents the duct-tape solution to a system of scholarly communication that lags behind our current needs.[18] For reasons that are largely economic, legal, and social – not technical – academics in the languages and literatures have, as a group, been slower than other fields to explore the resources of online publication beyond electronic delivery and the electronic archive.[19] The currently murky state of fair-use law for cinematic texts has kept film studies to the limited mode of quotation that Bellour described more than twenty-five years ago. Like theorists of the novel – who work with a form also defined by its esthetic copia and extensiveness

– we reproduce film texts by condensing, summarizing, and naming generic moves and tropes. But we do so in a medium that radically obscures the material specificity and internal dimensions of that text.

If online publication offers a viable alternative mode of quotation, what it adds is phenomenological complexity.[20] But what is at stake in that addition is discursive complexity. In any print quotation of a print original, the selective process of quotation will be relatively more visible to a reader than it is in a still of a moving image. Scholarly quotations serve academic discourse in a variety of ways, to be sure. Yet to my mind the most urgent of these is the way in which quotation inevitably exceeds the writer's account of a work. That excess sustains a critical dialogue between writer and reader in which a reader tests, compares, and evaluates the writer's selective assertions on the basis of her or his own experience of the text in play. Sparking disagreement as well as assent, print quotation sets an intellectual standard for scholarly discourse that our current conventions for writing on film do not meet. When the institutional conditions for scholarly discourse do not sustain our key intellectual values, scholars have an obligation to articulate those values and experiment with the technologies that will support them. Quotation is not, of course, our only interest when we choose venues and media of publication. Still it makes a good case for attending more carefully to the polychronic nature of our scholarly protocols. Reading the web-based version of the essay you may more easily disagree or elaborate on my reading of Almereyda's film; but how easily can you scribble your thoughts in the margins? And will it still be there should you wish to read it? We too readily lament the costs or celebrate the benefits of different technical solutions before we explore the actual trade-offs they entail in a searching way.

Acknowledgments

For their generous technical and scholarly insights, which now go way back, I owe thanks to Kim Benston, Scott Black, Richard Burt, Tom Cartelli, Ralph Del Giudice, Peter Donaldson, Nora Gully, Gretchen Hitt, Jenny Horne, Nora Johnson, Jonathan Kahana, John Norman, Lauren Shohet, Rod Matthews, Kristin Poole, Richard Rowe, Lyn Tribble, Julian Yates; also Lyn Tribble's graduate seminar on Shakespearean Optics, Temple University, and the undergraduates in English 250 at Bryn Mawr.

For Warren Jacobson, *in memoriam*.

Notes

1 Frow is quoting from Bryan Turner 1987: 151, 222.

2 Frow reminds us of the persistence of this pattern. For Walter Benjamin, the newspaper and novel destroy the "chasteness" and embedded life of storytelling. For Fredric Jameson, photography offers the same challenge to the fullness of the novel. For recent critics of electronic media, like Margaret Morse, television is the impoverished newcomer.

3

> In order to say "contemporary," one must already be thinking of a certain time and thinking of it in a certain way . . . what things are contemporary? Consider a late-model car. It is a disparate aggregate of scientific and technical solutions dating from different periods. One can date it component by component: this part was invented at the turn of the century, another, ten years ago, and Carno's cycle

is almost two hundred years old. Not to mention that the wheel dates back to neolithic times. The ensemble is only contemporary by assemblage, by its design, its finish, sometimes only by the slickness of the advertising surrounding it.

(Serres and Latour 1995: 45)

4 See the work of Frances Yates, Mary Carruthers, Laurie Maguire, and more recently, Garrett Sullivan.

5 On the uses of imagined scenes and persons (from personal acquaintance or from classical texts), see, for example, the *ars memoriaie* of Jacobus Publicius, in his *Artes orandi, epistolandi, memorandi* (Venice: Erhard Ratdolt, 1485) and of Peter of Ravenna (Petrus Ravennus, *Phoenix sev Artificiosa Memoria*, Vicentiae: 1600, discussed in Carruthers 1990: 109).

6 See John Sutton (1998) on Galenic theories of mind, unruly humors, and memory. Both Jacobus Publicius and Peter of Ravenna testify to importance of humoral crasis – balance – to a functioning memory, and to the force of the affections in laying down impressions.

7 Techniques of internal discipline were part of what scholars have described as a national project of self-fashioning, the object of increasingly anxious self-reflection in early seventeenth century England. Mary Floyd-Wilson (2003) makes a powerful case that Shakespeare's plays, *Hamlet* included, systematically and anxiously explore this project. See also Michael C. Schoenfeldt (1999), Reid Barbour (1998), and Gail Kern Paster (1993).

8 Chartier *et al.* (2002).

9 Jenkins repaid the favor, testifying in an interview to the synaesthetic force of Branagh's film, as he waited in suspense to see if Branagh accepted his emendation of "diest" for "diddst" in Laertes's late speech (Rosenbaum 2002: 68).

10 "Nostalgic essentialism . . . affirms the reality of an origin by proclaiming its loss" (Frow 1992: 225).

11 Petrarchan self-reflexiveness of this kind has both its anxious and triumphal modes. On Petrarchism and early global encounters, see Greene (1999). On the anxiety of market influence and recent film Shakespeares, see Lanier (2002). For influential critical accounts of Luhrmann and electronic media, see Donaldson (2002) and Barbara Hodgdon (1999).

12 We see Hamlet's hand on the video machine twice here; by contrast, we do not see the hand clicking the remote in similar scenes of viewing in Luhrmann's *Romeo + Juliet.*

13 See Richard Burt's discussion of Almereyda's *The Mousetrap* in this volume, Chapter 16. On film pornography and fictions of presence, see Williams (1989: 295–6).

14 The "snow" screens that punctuate Hamlet's video collages recall the skittering strips of blank film leaders that punctuate Connor's shorts. Video "snow" serves as the textual record of a video recorder turned off – no longer recording – reminding us that what we are looking at is a material record of something no longer recording (Connor's signature gesture).

15 The latest models seek to address this problem by providing digital data storage in a mode that allows easy uploads to the internet for e-mailing and display. See Taub (2002).

16 Thanks to Richard Burt for calling this to my attention.

17 See AHR's inaugural online issue at <http://www.historycooperative.org/journals/ahr/105.1/index.html>.

18 See Richard Lanham (1993) for the notion that technology always lags behind our needs of it.

19 There are important exceptions to this, such as the *Rosetti Archive* at UVA, Alan Liu's The Voice of the Shuttle, the Perseus Project, the Shakespeare archives at MIT and UPenn, pioneered by Peter Donaldson and Rebecca Bushnell, as well as a few peer-reviewed journals such as *Postmodern Culture.*

20 See Jerome McGann (2001) on the rich interpretive environment digital media offer to those interested in a scholarly discourse about texts that combine word, sound, and image.

3

JAMES DEAN MEETS THE PIRATE'S DAUGHTER

Passion and parody in *William Shakespeare's Romeo + Juliet* and *Shakespeare in Love*

Michael Anderegg

> "Believe you me, we're not the first butchers of the Bard"
>
> Baz Luhrmann, *Romeo + Juliet* Special Edition DVD (2002)

> "The Elizabethan theatre was a similar set-up to Hollywood in many respects. Collective writing, rapid writing on commission, repeated re-use of the same subjects, no control for writers over their own products, fame only among other writers, . . . even Shakespeare's curious retirement to run a public house [!] resembles the escape to the ranch that everybody here is planning."
>
> Bertolt Brecht, *Journals 1934–1955* (Santa Monica, July 7, 1943)

Baz Luhrmann's *William Shakespeare's Romeo + Juliet* (1996) and John Madden's *Shakespeare in Love* (1998) can both be described as postmodern retellings of the best-known romantic tragedy in Western literature. Both films find ways to stand in awe of *Romeo and Juliet* even as they undermine its highbrow credentials. Luhrmann essentially puts the play in quotation marks, almost as if his gun-wielding teens had been dragooned into a high school production and had then found themselves swept away by the force of its romantic vision. *Shakespeare in Love* pretends that the play originates in the hackwork of a thieving playwright in search of a saleable commodity which then becomes magically transformed by the promptings of desire into a transcendent expression of love's truth. Each film is a testimony to the malleability of *Romeo and Juliet* as a cultural object in the modern and postmodern moment. Before looking at both films in some detail, a brief excursus into earlier mass media appropriations of Shakespeare's play will help to reveal some of the sources of its continuing fascination as an iconic text in popular culture.

I

On February 21, 1954, CBS Television's *You Are There* took its viewers back to "December 26, 1594: The First Command Performance of *Romeo and Juliet*." This evening's episode, like all of the others in this popular middlebrow series, was structured to resemble a news special, complete with reporters and on-the-scene interviews, and, like the series as a whole, it lay claim to be founded solidly on the historical record. It would not have taken very long, however, for an informed viewer to discover that, series anchor Walter Cronkite to the contrary, "all things" on this particular evening were not quite "as they were then." The theater historians who might have tuned in would have been intrigued to discover that, among other interesting details, a Globe-like thrust stage had been constructed at Court for the players; presumably, someone involved with the production wanted television viewers to experience an "authentic" open-air Elizabethan theatrical performance even if, in this instance, it was taking place indoors. William Shakespeare, furthermore, very likely did not, as he does here, play Mercutio in *Romeo and Juliet*. And, although scholars differ on this point, it seems likely that Richard Burbage, if he had the actor's instinct and the actor's ego we can be reasonably certain he had, would (given the choice) have opted to play Mercutio, not, as he does on this occasion, the less colorful and less flamboyant Romeo. Although the work of the various *You Are There* writers continues to be praised for its "accurate portrayals of historical events" (Horowitz 1983: 93), history, in this particular episode, has been replaced almost entirely by speculation. At least we don't have Queen Elizabeth coming to the playhouse, as she will in *Shakespeare in Love*: Shakespeare, quite properly, goes to her. She does, however, appear to find in Shakespeare's romantic tragedy analogies to her own emotional life, much as Judi Dench's Elizabeth discovers, in the later film, that love can indeed be spoken of truly in a play.

This *You Are There* episode usefully serves to introduce my several concerns for the remainder of this discussion: the centrality of *Romeo and Juliet* in Shakespeare offshoots and the way Shakespeare becomes positioned in contemporary popular film as at once highbrow and lowbrow, a sign of culture and a vehicle for puncturing cultural pretension. Among the more peculiar aspects of "the first command performance of *Romeo and Juliet*" is that, as far as history is concerned, the dramatized incident never happened. It is, of course, possible that *Romeo and Juliet* was presented at Court for Elizabeth, but no trace of any such performance exists. The teleplay writer (McCarthyism victim Abraham Polonsky, writing under an assumed name) here went out of his way to dramatize a non-event even though history could have provided him with specific dates on which one or another Shakespeare play was presented at Court. *Shakespeare in Love* engages in the analogous fiction of reconstructing the very first performance of *Romeo and Juliet* at the Rose Theatre in 1593, an event for which there is an equal absence of evidence; we have, in fact, no record of any performance of the play before 1598. In both instances, the writers simply wanted to construct their narratives around *Romeo and Juliet*, no matter how inconvenient in terms of history or even legend such a choice might be.

This fascination with *Romeo and Juliet* is not surprising: of all of Shakespeare's plays, it is probably the most frequently performed, most often filmed, and most likely to be re-written, transformed, parodied, bowdlerized, or burlesqued. It may be the play that, perhaps only after *Hamlet*, means "Shakespeare" to most people. In popular culture in particular, *Romeo and Juliet* becomes a kind of shorthand for Shakespeare and, for that matter, for love tragedy in general.[1] When *I Love Lucy* had Orson Welles as guest star, Lucy wanted to be Juliet to his Romeo. When Andy Griffith, who made a series of comic 45 rpm recordings in the late 1950s, sends his country bumpkin persona to the theater for the first time, we hear the latter's reaction in "What it was was *Romeo and*

Juliet." *West Side Story*, musical play and film, with great success retold the travails of Shakespeare's young lovers in the context of racially divided gang wars in 1950s Manhattan. Franco Zeffirelli's 1968 adaptation is among the most popular of Shakespeare films. And then there are the jokes: "O Romeo, Romeo, wherefore art thou, Romeo?" – "Down in the bushes, the damn ladder broke." Among the twenty-plus *Romeo and Juliet* films from the silent era noted by Robert Hamilton Ball (1968: 217), we have such parodies and imitations as *Juliet and Her Romeo*, *Doubling for Romeo* (with satirist Will Rogers), *Romeo and Juliet* (a Mack Sennett version, with cross-eyed comedian Ben Turpin), *Romeo Turns Bandit*, etc. In some of these early films, as in later ones, *Romeo and Juliet* is the play within the film, as in Edison's *Bumptious as Romeo*: "The climax," according to Ball's source (the film is lost), "comes in a balcony scene where the entire palazzo collapses on the unfortunate actor" (Ball 1968: 67).

What is it about *Romeo and Juliet* that lays it open to such treatment? One answer might be that the story as Shakespeare tells it is already a comedy, upon which a tragic denouement has been more or less arbitrarily imposed; at some point, we are supposed to stop laughing and start crying. But where, exactly, is that point? There is, undeniably, something inherently funny about adolescent passion, even to the young. Shakespeare was quite aware of this, which is why he created Mercutio, the cynic within the play who channels off our impulse to laugh at the lovers. The play's tragic ending, especially, is, at one level, ridiculously avoidable. However much *Romeo and Juliet* may be seen as a highly valued cultural object, the fact remains that it has, in the words of Stanley Wells, "undergone adaptation, sometimes slight, sometimes substantial, in ways that are implicitly critical of the original" (1996: 49). The impulse to burlesque *Romeo and Juliet*, moreover, may also stem from male anxiety about something so un-masculine as romantic love, especially when carried to a tragic conclusion. Parody and burlesque, in this light, serve as defense mechanisms against a powerful, poetic evocation of love and death that at once makes the play a popular favorite and something of an embarrassment. *William Shakespeare's Romeo + Juliet* and *Shakespeare in Love* are among the latest incarnations of Shakespeare's love story, and both exhibit, albeit in very different ways, the tension between satiric playfulness on the one hand and high seriousness on the other that the play has always inspired.

II

At first glance, Baz Luhrmann's *William Shakespeare's Romeo + Juliet* could be mistaken for yet another (mis)appropriation of Shakespeare's play for purposes of parody or even burlesque, a hip (hop?) retelling aimed at an irredeemably low-brow audience of clueless teenagers inhabiting an intellectually bankrupt culture. *Romeo + Juliet* (a less cumbersome title I will generally use from now on) simultaneously encourages and undermines such a reading.[2] Throughout the film, Luhrmann sets up expectations and then subverts them, freely manipulating past, present, and future time, wedding richly poetic language to pop-culture imagery, theater to film, employing cinematographic and editing styles that evoke both MTV and the "historical" avant-garde. He simultaneously flatters and critiques the teen culture from which his film appears to draw its inspiration and primary *raison d'être*. As the film begins, a television set occupies the screen – a retro 1970s/1980s model. We are at once in the present-day world of mass communication ("a world," as Peter Donaldson [2002: 62] observes, "saturated by image, where mass media and corporate power have triumphed even more decisively . . . than in real life"), and yet the first object we see is already archaic. We are, vaguely, in the past, a feeling reinforced by the montage of images drawn from later points in the film, as well as, vaguely, in the future. As the Chorus makes clear, this is a story already told, already done; its end is in its beginning. The opening sequence fragments into a cacophony of sound and image, even as the words of Shakespeare's Prologue are given a solidity and, by repetition (twice spoken, but also repeated as both verbal and visual language), redundancy. Barbara Hodgdon identifies a tone that "ricochets between Wall-and-Moonshine tongue-in-cheekiness and playing it straight, between selling Shakespeare as one-off visual in-jokes and tying its scenography, almost over-explicitly, to the word" (1999: 89). We will be given Shakespeare's words, this initial sequence tells us, but the seeming promise turns out to be something of a deception, as words will not play so central a role as we are led to suppose.

The following sequence, of the first "brawl," stylistically continues the melding of the modern and the archaic. This bravura sequence – and something similar could be said of Shakespeare's opening scene – acts as a "grabber," a powerful, dramatic, somewhat deceptive means of gaining the attention of an audience. Deceptive because, in Luhrmann's case, the stylistic flamboyance that characterizes this opening does not accurately represent the tonal ground of the film; what it succeeds in doing, most of all, is providing a "cover" for what follows. For all of its cinematic verve, Luhrmann's *Romeo + Juliet* is a highly theatrical film (as the director readily acknowledges), its style clearly drawn from Luhrmann's work in opera as much as from his forays into advertising and rock videos. As James Loehlin observes, "*William Shakespeare's Romeo + Juliet* continually and playfully juxtaposes contemporary kitsch with the high-culture world of Shakespeare, classical music and Renaissance art and architecture" (2000: 124).

Indeed, what many critics have identified as Luhrmann's "MTV style" can be more accurately described as a mix of early experimental cinema and modernist video art. Music videos themselves are, with some exceptions, stylistically archaic and unadventurous (Dali and Buñuel set many of the parameters in *Un chien andalou* [1929]): irrational editing patterns, impressionistic imagery, expressionist decor, surreal juxtapositions, all presented with a strong dose of "*épater les bourgeois*" (which might be translated, in the present instance, as "screw the parents"). Rock video, developed in the early 1980s, was already cliché-ridden and ossified by the early 1990s, having settled into a very few, rigid moves, most of them founded on already shopworn cinematic clichés. Luhrmann draws on a far richer range of allusions and on a wider variety of stylistic choices than can be encapsulated by the reference to MTV. In this sense, the photographic qualities of Luhrmann's film coordinates with his *mise-en-scène*; a future that is really a past; a "there" that is really "here;" a story that is freshly being told yet again – the effect intensified by the way Luhrmann ratchets up the sense of fate and foreknowledge already present in the play: this is a story already over before it begins. What is most "postmodern" about the film is its ransacking of the past both for its subject matter and for its style.

If the opening sequences – the Prologue and the fight – serve to establish the film-maker's bona fides as cinema, the sequence that follows very much introduces us to the world of theater. We find Romeo sitting on the stage of a ruined movie house, his image constructed in a theatrical, self-conscious fashion, cigarette in hand, hair tousled, sports coat over his open-necked shirt, jotting down his presumably Petrarchan conceits into a small notebook. Later, Mercutio, too, makes a flamboyantly "theatrical" entrance. Not only is he in drag, but he almost immediately appears on the same stage earlier associated with Romeo. Although this stage set is infrequently seen, it features in some of the most important moments in the film: Romeo's entrance, Mercutio's entrance, and Mercutio's death. At the end of the last-mentioned sequence, a lap dissolve associates the stage as well with Juliet's bed and thus by extension with the "bed"/bier on which Romeo and Juliet die. The final setting in the film, the Capulet tomb, may be the most theatrical of all: a set illuminated by hundreds of candles and dozens of neon crosses, a neo-baroque wedding of sixteenth- and twentieth-century light sources, self-consciously decorated as no church or tomb has ever been, and seemingly prepared in advance for the lovers' final meeting.

Even in the act of bringing Shakespeare's play up to date, Luhrmann does little more than, say, David Garrick did in the eighteenth century: he makes it into a recognizable contemporary cultural object, and shows himself alert to the sensibilities of an audience whose tastes and feelings are conditioned by the culture in which they are immersed. This can, of course, be accomplished in a variety of ways, of which bringing the film "up to date" in terms of its *mise-en-scène* is only one. The pastiche element of the film is not, as in so much "vulgar" postmodernism, an end in itself, however. Luhrmann's strategy is to deprive the viewer of specific markers for pinning down time and place too precisely. This need not be interpreted as "dumbing down" – Zeffirelli, for his 1968 film, though he re-creates a Renaissance world in the *mise-en-scène*, does something quite similar for a late 1960s audience, stripping from Shakespeare's play much of what did not conveniently fit into the cultural moment and the cultural attitudes he wanted to highlight, something obvious enough at the time and even clearer in retrospect.

Luhrmann has claimed, with a seeming absence of irony, that his goal was "to do a sort of Elizabethan interpretation of Shakespeare" (2001: DVD Special Edition), which would in part explain his insistence on retaining Shakespeare's language – or, at least, a reasonable percentage of it – rather than creating a verbal language of his own: the sixteenth-century syntax and vocabulary serve as necessary links between the pastness of the tale and the presentness of the *mise-en-scène*; or, as Elsie Walker puts it, "The obvious disjunction between the verse and the setting in Luhrmann's film throws the verse *and* its filmic context into a kind of defamiliarizing relief" (2000: 138). *Romeo + Juliet*, in fact, employs Shakespeare's dialogue in a variety of ways, depending on the occasion. At times, the film can simply pretend that the language and "poetic" diction are not alien to contemporary sensibilities. A line like "thy drugs are quick" fits easily into the drug culture of the Capulet ball sequence (even though, in this particular instance, the words have been transplanted from one point in the play to another). At other times, the language is allowed to remain "Shakespeare"[3] – so, for a critical example, the sonnet lines Romeo and Juliet recite at first meeting are spoken in their entirety in spite of the fact that the meaning of the imagery is not self-evident. Luhrmann, presumably, would not have wanted to cut one of the most famous passages in Shakespeare; but, beyond that, Shakespeare's sonnet transports us momentarily back to the sixteenth century and in so doing collapses the worlds of Verona and Verona Beach. For further insurance that this scene will "work," Luhrmann – again with the precedence of Zeffirelli – gives us the meeting of Romeo and Juliet in effect several times over through time expansion and repetitive editing patterns, and he precedes the sonnet meeting with the fish-tank meeting where the exchange of glances and the matching of identities have already been made.

But if Luhrmann's young lovers speak the language of Shakespeare, they project images drawn from popular culture. Leonardo DiCaprio's Romeo, a more complexly drawn character than Claire Danes's Juliet,[4] combines a number of cultural signifiers: first of all, inevitably, we have DiCaprio's own image as a kind of asexual love object for adolescents; then the sensitive, essentially white-bread teen, roughly equivalent to Richard Beymer's Tony in *West Side Story*; and, very consciously, the James Dean allusions, especially the latter's incarnation of Jim Stark in *Rebel Without a Cause* (which could itself be seen as a loose *Romeo and Juliet* adaptation). These reference points, needless to add, are not all necessarily aimed at the 1990s teen audience that would constitute the obvious target of the film's production and marketing strategies, an audience for whom James Dean might be only slightly more (or slightly less) familiar than Shakespeare. Luhrmann's film is cunningly designed to appeal to the parents and even the grandparents of that "natural" audience. Nonetheless, the various elements that go to make up the image of Romeo in the film are available to any savvy youth who has absorbed, whether at first, second, or third hand, those cultural markers. The image of Juliet, on the other hand, though less allusively defined than Romeo's, appeals to a special kind of nostalgia for girlhood innocence, not so much lost as never available in the first place. Even a jaded sixteen-year-old can be imagined yearning for the kind of protected, cocoon existence Claire Danes, costumed as she is like an American Girl doll, lives out in Luhrmann's film, a world of parental protection and direction (as well as, it must be noted, of parental control and physical violence).

In a piece for *Variety* ("Fox doth use its wiles to sell Shakespeare"), John Brodie claims that "[m]uch credit for the pic's surprising success was the studio's understanding from the outset that this was a teen picture, not a movie for eggheads" (1996). Apart from the somewhat quaint use of the word "eggheads," Brodie expresses here what many reviewers identified as Luhrmann's condescending to his audience. But this view is itself simplistic and unsophisticated. In making Shakespeare's play "acceptable" to a contemporary audience, a filmmaker will find it necessary to disguise, gloss over, or entirely repress much in the play that might be off-putting or incomprehensible. If the question that a Shakespeare film needs to ask of its audience is "Do you accept the revelation of the human condition that Shakespeare achieved 400 years ago can be relevant and be freed again today," as Luhrmann himself states it (Fox Video Laser: 1997), then the answer is probably "no." There are many ways Shakespeare is not one of us: many ways, indeed, in which he was already not "one of us" by, say, 1750. In his aptly titled essay "The Challenges of *Romeo and Juliet*," Stanley Wells addresses the perceived problematic of Shakespeare's play: "The history of critical and theatrical reactions to the play demonstrates the fact that Shakespeare worked in a far more literary mode than has been fashionable in the theater of later ages, and that its literariness has often been regarded as a theatrical handicap" (1996: 4). Wells identifies the type of material often cut – long speeches that recapitulate what the audience has already seen, "self-conscious and even ostentatious intellectualism" as expressed in complex wordplay, and passages of "false emotion."

Among Luhrmann's many alterations and omissions, the following are especially in line with Wells's observations: the virtual elimination of the scene where the Nurse reports Tybalt's death to Juliet; the discovery of Juliet's supposed death by the Capulet household; the killing of Paris at the tomb; the comic musicians; Friar Lawrence's appearance at the Capulet tomb and his subsequent desertion of Juliet. Other scenes are severely reduced: Juliet's 45-line "potion" soliloquy is pared down to two lines; the ball scene lacks most of Capulet's exchanges with Old Capulet and other characters; and the Nurse's interchanges with her servant, Peter, are gone. What a number of these cuts have in common is that they can be thought of as eliminating either rhetorical excess or violations of decorum – or both at once. These are pressure points in Shakespeare's play, places where his failure to adhere to classical principles and, by anticipation, neoclassical rules have in the past been regarded as close to scandalous. These are the elements of Shakespearean drama presumed to be indigestible for a contemporary audience: both *Shakespeare in Love*, which pretends to take us back to the origins of *Romeo and Juliet*, and Luhrmann's film, which projects Shakespeare's play into the twenty-first century, elide or gloss over the very same elements, the elements that run counter to the idea of Shakespeare as a screenwriter, an entertainer, "one of us."

One strategy for translating the highly rhetorical essence of *Romeo and Juliet* into acceptable modern terms is to make what is public in the play private on the screen. Juliet's reception of the news of Tybalt's death and Romeo's banishment, a serio-comic scene of misunderstanding – the Nurse, as usual, cannot seem to get to the point – is almost entirely eliminated, and what remains of it is transformed into an internal meditation by Juliet alone in her bedroom. What is passionate intensity in Shakespeare's play is a passive, puzzling reflection in the film. Juliet, in fact, suffers most from this avoidance of rhetoric and of the tragi-comic. Shakespeare created a Juliet quite capable of dissimulation and irony as well as anger and fierce determination. Her love for Romeo quickly, if temporarily, turns to hatred when she hears the news of Tybalt's death; she engages in elaborate and deceitful wordplay, allowing her mother to think that she is mourning for Tybalt when, in fact, she is yearning for Romeo; she dismisses her nurse with angry finality ("ancient damnation") when the latter encourages her to marry Paris; she fools her father with a hypocritical pretense of submission even as she plots her rebellion against him; she doubts the motives of the Friar, temporarily seeing him, with mature insight, in a Machiavellian light, as she prepares to swallow the potion (and her potion soliloquy as a whole reveals her to be a young woman of vivid, if morbid, imagination). Claire Danes's Juliet, robbed of these enriching traits, emotions, motives, and inconsistencies of character, is an ideal Victorian Juliet, perhaps, but she is far from the Juliet Shakespeare created. Neither a contemporary teenager nor a Shakespearean heroine, the Luhrmann Juliet has little social or cultural grounding apart from the baroque Catholicism that decorates her immediate environment.[5]

More significant than the cuts and transpositions, however, is the way Luhrmann interprets Shakespeare's text, and in particular, his focus on the doomed nature of Romeo and Juliet's love. By placing his emphasis on fate, Luhrmann robs the lovers of agency, of responsibility for their own actions and choices. Fate, of course, plays a crucial role in Shakespeare's play, which is one reason why some critics deny it tragic stature. *Romeo and Juliet* is a tragi-comedy not merely because it mixes tragic and comic elements but because its tragic elements are also comic: much of the misfortune in the play has a comic dimension, and what is the denouement but a comedy of errors? Any production of the play has to come to terms with preventing the image of Romeo and

Juliet dead in the tomb from seeming preposterous. In one way, Luhrmann adds to the sense of sheer bad luck by having Juliet wake up before Romeo dies – all Romeo had to do is glance over at Juliet before he drinks the poison, and the story would have a happy ending. Shakespeare continually modulates between the apprehension of inexorable fatality and a recognition that humans can choose to act in some other way. The coda, almost entirely cut (though not for the first time – if *Shakespeare in Love* is to be believed, even Shakespeare failed to include it), exists in part to allow the surviving characters, as well as the audience, to contemplate the complex intertwining of human error and sheer bad luck. Shakespeare's ending also emphasizes the larger dimensions of the tragedy. As G. Blakemore Evans has emphasized, "To bring the curtain down on Juliet's death, an ending dear to the Victorians, borders on the melodramatic and sacrifices Shakespeare's finely held balance between the personal tragedy of the lovers and the larger social implications of the feud" (1984: 44–5). Luhrmann includes a coda, but it is highly abbreviated and fails, deliberately, to achieve any sense of social integration. The young lovers "become merely another lurid image for a media-besotted culture, body-bagged victims in a grainy news video" (Loehlin 2000: 130). The twice-repeated "all are punished," spoken by "Captain" Prince, words that simply recognize a tragic fact in the context Shakespeare provides, sound more like a threat of retribution in the film.

Among the last words we hear at the end of *Romeo + Juliet*, "we hope your rules and wisdom choke you" come not from Shakespeare but from Radiohead, and they affirm a generational conflict that, in truth, we have not actually experienced, except intermittently, in the course of the film itself. "The moral of the story," one of the film's producers asserts, "is that if you teach hatred to your children, you lose them" (Laserdisc commentary track). This is, no doubt, what countless viewers and audiences have wanted *Romeo and Juliet* to be about. But it is not, except very superficially, what Shakespeare seems most concerned with. To understand the play as primarily centering on the "generation gap" (or, alternately, with the dangers of teen suicide) is to misrepresent its essence.[6] Shakespeare, I would argue, goes out of his way to suggest that the Montague and Capulet parents may be, in today's parlance, "over-protective," almost too concerned to keep their children away from the harsh world they must ultimately inhabit. "Oh where is Romeo – saw you him today?", Lady Montague inquires (in both play and film), "Right glad I am he was not at this fray" (1.1.107–9). At the same time, the older generation seems eager to keep the peace: Capulet, notably, though he discovers a Montague at his family celebration, refuses to countenance any disturbance that might spoil his daughter's coming-out festivities, and even acknowledges of Romeo that "Verona brags of him/To be a virtuous and well-governed youth" (1.5.66–7). The impulse for Romeo and Juliet to create and inhabit a world of their own is not necessarily a response to the failures of the parents.

Shakespeare's *Romeo and Juliet* is in fact a double-edged sword when employed as a glorification or even validation of the young and a concomitant condemnation of grown-up values. In the social world of Shakespeare's play, it is the young – masters and servants – who maintain the deadly feud, a feud that has been inherited, it is true, from generations of parental figures, but also a feud of which the adults have become weary, as Capulet's attitude towards Romeo indicates. The irrelevance of parents is made especially clear in *West Side Story* where they essentially disappear. And, although *Romeo and Juliet* is inevitably remembered as a tale of young lovers whose love is forbidden by parental interdict, nothing of the kind actually takes place in Shakespeare's play. The fact is that Romeo and Juliet make no effort to discover whether or not they could marry: Juliet's eagerness to become Romeo's wife, almost as if the very act of falling in love had been a kind of self-deflowering, precludes all other avenues. Friar Lawrence's assumption that by marrying Juliet to Romeo he can effect an end to the feud actually makes a good deal of sense: unfortunately, he does not have the opportunity to find out. The deadly impetuosity of the young make such an outcome impossible.

At least as far back as Franco Zeffirelli's Old Vic production of *Romeo and Juliet* in 1960, directors have tended to treat the feud as, to a greater or lesser extent, adolescent hi-jinx, a kind of masculine showing off, not to be taken too seriously. Zeffirelli's 1968 film became the best-known version of this approach, and a similar impulse can be detected in Luhrmann's film as well. The advantage is that one can maintain a comic tone – and this is part of Shakespeare's strategy as well – almost uninterruptedly until the death of Mercutio; the disadvantage is that it tends to undermine the *gravitas* of the words spoken by the Prince, whose language ("purple fountains issuing blood," etc.) make it quite clear that the feud has been and continues to be a matter of deadly force. Luhrmann has an added problem Zeffirelli did not have to worry about, in that the presence of guns makes it even more difficult to treat the opening segment as light-hearted good fun. In the end, Luhrmann has it both ways. With all of the exchange of gunfire, it is unclear who, if anyone, is actually killed (the one character who appears to have been shot – and in the head at that – pops up a few scenes later with a bandage on his arm). Consequently, when matters turn deadly, it seems almost accidental, and the responsibility for the tragic turn of events does not so much lie in the feud as in the actions of Romeo, Tybalt, and Mercutio. On this point, at least, Luhrmann cannot be faulted for flattering his teenaged audience: the blame the parents game is ultimately no more convincing in *Romeo + Juliet* than it was in *Rebel Without a Cause*. In the end, it is the children who must either grow up (as Jim Stark does in *Rebel*) or be destroyed; society is almost irrelevant.

III

Shakespeare films, much like contemporary Shakespeare projects of various kinds – the restored Globe, the Stratford, UK, and the Stratford, Canada, festivals – can be seen as, in the words of Dennis Kennedy, instances of "cultural tourism" and "edutainment" (Kennedy 1998), except that instead of traveling in space, the cinema cultural tourist travels in time. *Shakespeare in Love*, a film about Shakespeare as well as a Shakespeare film, notably partakes of the tourist experience, serving as a good advertisement for the newly "restored" Globe Theatre which opened for business on Bankside not long before the film went into production. Both the film and the theater engage in an archeological approach to Shakespeare and to the Elizabethan theatrical world that simultaneously functions as a highly commercial crowd pleaser (the Globe was voted the top tourist attraction in Europe by an organization of travel journalists [Kennedy 1998: 182]); *Shakespeare in Love*, as of 2001, had grossed $250 million worldwide "and still counting" (Miramax DVD 1998). In both venues, the turn of the millennium audience is taken back 500 years to the beginning of the modern era, a moment when art, entertainment, and commerce became inextricably intertwined into a purely secular mix. *Shakespeare in Love*, of course, does not require its audience to sit on hard benches or, even more of a challenge, to stand in the pit for three-plus hours, as modern-day tourists can and do at the Globe. In editing together moments from rehearsals and a performance of *Romeo and Juliet* with the amorous and entrepreneurial adventures of the film's own characters, the space of first the Rose and then the Curtain Theatres is energized and cut up into acceptable temporal and physical chunks: "Shakespeare," once again, becomes a series of purple passages and action sequences, as he had been in nineteenth-century American culture (Levine 1988; Uricchio and Pearson 1993). And what we do see of Shakespeare on the Tudor stage is further dynamized through editing and camera movement into the more familiar cinematic space to which the spectators are accustomed. Just as the film's Shakespeare does not have to work too hard to compose *Romeo and Juliet*, so the audience does not have to work too hard to absorb it. As Courtney Lehmann remarks, "What gets truly mystified in this film . . . is not love, but labor" (2002: 134).

Indeed, another name for the film could be *Shakespeare Without Tears*. We may note, for example, that whereas Shakespeare's *Romeo and Juliet* ends tragically, *Shakespeare in Love* ends sentimentally. There can hardly ever have been any question of a conventionally "happy ending" for the film, and not only because the writers did not want to alter history. The "happiest" – or, at least, the most emotionally satisfying – ending for a love story, as writers, including Shakespeare, have known from time immemorial, is one where the love is brought to an end even as it reaches its highest pitch: young lovers should never become old lovers; what we want is a love that cannot die. Will is explicit about this: "You will never age for me, nor fade, nor die." Love, too, should not require too much work. Particularly popular among male authors is the version where the woman dies and the man lives on to keep his memories of her in amber – think *A Farewell to Arms* or *Love Story*. (Less often, the man dies or disappears and the woman lives on – see *West Side Story*, a *Romeo and Juliet* adaptation, and, of course, *Titanic*, starring Leonardo DiCaprio; the formula works almost as well either way.) *Shakespeare in Love* is very much in this tradition, but with a twist: Shakespeare lives on to write his plays and to be re-united, presumably, with his faithful wife, Anne; his true love, Viola de Lesseps, is transformed into "Viola," a fictional character in one of Will's plays.

The creative process, too, is at once painful and painless as *Shakespeare in Love* imagines it, and the way creativity as theme is played with functions both as a source of much of the film's humor and as a means of at once honoring Shakespeare and cutting him down to size. Indeed, the film is in general ingeniously designed to appeal to a variety of audiences, to both flatter the susceptibilities of those for whom "art" is pretty much a bore as well as the more or less "academic" or "educated" audience, the teachers and students who can recognize the allusions to Elizabethan theater and sixteenth-century culture. Every high-school graduate, for that matter, will have read, or at the least been to some degree exposed to, *Romeo and Juliet*, and the film can expect to be seen, both in its original theatrical release and in its subsidiary form on video, by ninth graders everywhere. But even viewers unfamiliar with Shakespeare will appreciate the manner in which the transformation of "Romeo and Ethel the Pirate's Daughter" ("good title," the banker, Fennyman, remarks) into *Romeo and Juliet* serves to define the nature of artistic "inspiration." A play like *Romeo and Juliet* evolves through stages in the poet's mind as the original "pitch" idea ("there's this pirate") magically ("it's a mystery") turns into art which is also profitable entertainment. The joke, of course, is that *Romeo and Juliet* could never have been named anything very different from what it is, since Shakespeare borrowed his plot and characters from a poem, *The Tragical Historye of Romeus and Juliet* (1562), that was itself based on earlier versions of the same well-known and popular story. Like many a joke in the film, this one serves both to assert and to occlude the communal nature of early modern writing practices. It may also serve to occlude the extent to which *Shakespeare in Love* itself "borrows" significantly from other treatments of the subject, including the novel *No Bed for Bacon*, the play *William Shakespeare* by Clemence Dane, and even, perhaps, the episode of *You Are There* with which I began this discussion.

Writing itself, in this film, is an uneasy mixture of superstition, inspiration, "living life," and simple mechanical labor. The familiar writer-at-work montage sequence for once works convincingly since for an Elizabethan writer, writing is, at a minimum, a visible, mechanical process involving much sharpening of pens, dipping quills into ink, and salting paper. For the most part, however, this William Shakespeare lives out the Romantic image of the writer who seeks and sometimes is given inspiration from a variety of sources. We see and hear him pick up some of his best lines from the sights and sounds of London life, a populist base for his flights of fancy. One activity Shakespeare does not appear to indulge in, oddly enough, is reading. Clearly, at the same time that we are told that Shakespeare is just another cog in the "business of show," the film does not want him to be as hard-headed as the historical Shakespeare must have been. Writer's block? The playwright had only to turn to Plutarch or Holinshed or Giraldo Cinthio. That we never see the film's Shakespeare resort to books is certainly curious, since he is perfectly happy to ransack other people's spoken words and verbally expressed ideas. Without involving ourselves too far in a Derridean maze, it seems worth noting the extent to which the film privileges speech over writing – indeed, so much so that Shakespeare seems incapable of writing anything that he has not first either heard or spoken himself. Again, the filmmakers want it both ways. On the one hand, Shakespeare is a hack, stealing ideas right and left, but on the other hand he is a genius who turns the dross of everyday life into immortal poetry.

Furthermore, while the "real" Shakespeare was influenced and inspired by reading other writers, our Will gets his inspiration for the plot and characters of a heterosexual romance directly from his friend, the homosexual poet-playwright Christopher ("Kit") Marlowe, a crucial if vaguely defined presence in the film. Neither the name of Marlowe nor the name of the avowed homosexual actor who plays him, Rupert Everett, appears in the credits for the film and no reference is made to Marlowe's sexual preference. Interestingly, it is almost immediately after his conversation with Marlowe that Will is captivated by a "boy," Tom of Kent. That this boy is in fact a girl, Viola de Lesseps, allows for a variety of comic moments and, perhaps, some coded messages. For those in the know (the *Sonnets* and all that), Shakespeare is allowed a *soupçon* of same-sex desire; for everyone else, a bit of cross-dressing confusion and farce. Shakespeare, presumably, is drawn to a lovely boy because that lovely boy is really a lovely girl – or is the lovely girl attractive to him because she looks like a lovely boy? In any case, it is in the act of chasing a boy ("Romeo") that he finds his Juliet. In the *As You Like It*-style love scenes between Will and "Tom" one may agree, with Richard Burt, that "It is never in doubt that Shakespeare is attracted to the woman underneath the boy . . . when kissed by her/him, he does not realize her/his dual identity, and responds with shock and astonishment" (2000: 214). True enough, though I would substitute "slightly taken aback" for "shock and astonishment." But what does it mean to be attracted to the woman underneath the boy? That Shakespeare cannot see through Viola's deception is, of course, perfectly in accord with the "impenetrable disguise" convention of his own plays – he is, amusingly enough, fooled by the very theatrical practice he regularly employs. The subtext, however, suggests something else: it is a boy that Shakespeare lusts after, and it is more or less incidental that "he" should turn out to be a "she." Or, perhaps, Will simply cannot tell the difference. Even the water-taxi driver comments that Viola's disguise "wouldn't fool a child." Most viewers would no doubt agree with Sujata Iyengar that "Biological sex becomes manifest in this film to assert that true love is always heterosexual" (2001: 123), but it is equally manifest that we can find traces of another reading on the margins of the text. On the DVD commentary track, John Madden claims that he would have liked Viola to perform her love scenes with her masculine wig and mustache but had to drop the idea because of "scheduling" problems. One cannot help but wonder, however, if the decision did not have more to do with a fear that a queer reading was becoming too naturalized for all concerned.

What the film does do, with great skill and panache, is substitute cross-dressing for cross-gender sexual desire. For a modern audience, it is particularly striking and even "educational" to see Juliet played by a boy and Romeo played by a girl. In the *Romeo and Juliet* rehearsal scenes, the film audience is allowed to experience what, in spite of Viola's earlier comment about "pip-squeak boys in petticoats," was an undoubted truth, which is that if the play-acting was sufficiently sincere, the gender of the actor did not really matter. And the cross-dressing – or, better, "cross-speaking" – continues in the bedroom as Will and Viola act out the roles, respectively, of Juliet and Romeo, which allows for the inter-cutting of these scenes with the rehearsal of the balcony scene from Shakespeare's play at the Rose Theatre. At the same time, of course, the gender confusion adds a certain frisson to the sexual play of the lovers. And Will himself literally cross-dresses when he disguises himself as Viola's chaperone. Here, however, the disguise is unconvincing; together with the comically droll performance of Jim Carter/Ralph Bashford as Juliet's Nurse, this may be the film's way of suggesting as well the limits of Elizabethan stage conventions.

The discourse surrounding the film, especially the documentary and the various commentary tracks packaged with the DVD, reveals much about the contradictory (or, perhaps, only paradoxical?) way "Shakespeare" has been constructed. Of particular interest are the comments by the screenwriters, Marc Norman and Tom Stoppard. *Shakespeare in Love* is the product of serial collaboration, the Brit Stoppard revising the script written by the American Norman. Amusingly enough, Norman and Stoppard, separately interviewed, speak, most of the time, as if the other did not exist (though Norman does, at one point, tell us that adding Ned Allyn as a character was Stoppard's idea). One would not know, from listening to them, that Stoppard was, at least ostensibly, a glorified script doctor for Norman. Students of the theater have had little difficulty in finding "obvious signs of Stoppard's hand: eclecticism; conflating a previous era with a modern one; cultural observations about both; verbal wit" (Levinson 2001: 168). It is tempting, though perhaps unfair, to assign all that is best in the script to Stoppard, and the rest to Norman (the popular press, much to Norman's irritation, often made that very assumption).[7] Ironically, collaboration – the simultaneous and/or successive work by two or more individuals on a play – is one aspect of Elizabethan writing practice that is most like Hollywood.

Although *Shakespeare in Love* flirts with the idea of collaboration, the screenwriters never quite let go of the "Shakespeare as lone genius" image. In the DVD commentaries, Norman is the "low brow" who brings everything down to his level. He makes some of the most obvious and pat or most egregiously fatuous comments, indulging enthusiastically in the stale "if Shakespeare were alive today . . ." game. "If Shakespeare were alive today," Norman claims, "he'd have a three-picture deal at Warner Brothers, he'd be driving a Porsche, and he'd be living in Bel Air." Just as nineteenth-century schoolmasters thought that Shakespeare must have taught school in his youth, so the screenwriter wants to claim Shakespeare for one of his own. In 1593 (when the film is set), Shakespeare, Norman assures us, was "not a magical, mysterious, genius playwright." Rather, "he was broke, he was horny, and he was starved for an idea." On the other hand, Stoppard, commenting on the casting of Joseph Fiennes, says: "His [Fiennes'] face suggests that he wrote the plays – you feel, yes, this man could be a genius." Relishing the film's central paradox, Stoppard comments that "while demystifying Shakespeare, [the script] also revealed the opposite, the deep mystery of Shakespeare." Tom Stoppard, in any case, is not afraid of the "g" word: he has been called a genius himself; Norman, on the other hand, *auteur* of, among other films, *Zandy's Bride* and *Cutthroat Island*, is in little danger of being tagged with that particular label.

Fiennes, in fact, plays Shakespeare in a manner sufficiently complex to encompass both readings. He gives an intelligent, witty, and spirited performance, but it is also an oddly guarded one. John Madden remarks at one point that Fiennes "has a kind of privateness about him, a slightly hidden quality" (Miramax DVD). Another way of looking at this would be to say that there is a strong element of narcissism to his performance: we never quite believe that this Shakespeare loves anyone more than he loves himself – even writing is a form of auto-eroticism. Fiennes to some extent works against the grain of the script and refuses any play for the audience's sympathy (though both Gwyneth Paltrow and Judi Dench won Oscars for their performance, Fiennes was not even nominated). This is a Shakespeare with a mission, and that mission is to be Shakespeare. He has his eye fixed throughout on the main chance. He remains unknowable not because he is acting out some proto-Romantic notion of what genius might be, but because at heart he does not want to be known.

The manner in which the screenplay to *Shakespeare in Love* was developed plays itself out in the language of the film. Words spoken "spontaneously" by the characters are eventually transformed, as if by alchemy, into the language of *Romeo and Juliet*. In "real life" Will and Viola speak of the owl and the rooster; in the play, this becomes the nightingale and the lark. Frequently, the Norman/Stoppard script provides pseudo-Elizabethan dialogue of astonishing flatness, something of which the writers are presumably aware, although one cannot be certain. At times, the dialogue verges on the nonsensical, syntactic confusion merging with sheer banality: "If I could write the beauty of her eyes," Will says to "Thomas," "I was born to look in them and know myself" (the first phrase is from Sonnet 17, the second a *non sequitur*); or, "love denied blights the soul we owe to God." What is the point of this, if not to flatter the audience's suspicion that Shakespeare's language is, at some level, itself nonsense, fancy words that do not really mean very much? At other moments, the writing is just silly.

"For sixpence a line," Will tells his "shrink," "I could cause a riot in a nunnery;" "pay attention," Ned Allyn (Ben Affleck) tells Fennyman, "and you will see how genius creates a legend." Even for pastiche, this is all pretty bad. Assuming the badness is deliberate, the point may be to suggest how difficult it is to write like Shakespeare. Which points to another, different joke: writing (and talking) like Shakespeare is something Shakespeare himself has a hard time with. In the end, the film wants both to value poetry and to devalue it. Even the jokes, like Henslowe's injunction, "Speak prose," marries the philistinism of the man of business with the audience's own presumed impatience with fancy words. When push comes to shove, Viola is moved to say, "I love you, Will, beyond poetry." Sex, as Viola also reveals, is better than plays, as love is truer than poetry. At the same time, the film's emotional high point is the performance of *Romeo and Juliet*, an unambiguous celebration of art over mere life.

IV

Both *Romeo + Juliet* and *Shakespeare in Love* can be (and have been) devalued for their "low-brow" treatment of Shakespeare and the Shakespearean text. Both films, however, attempt, each in its own way, to answer the hard question any film dealing with Shakespeare's life and work must confront: how do you make the work of a writer dead for 400 years seem relevant to present-day audiences? One answer, of course, is that you do not need to: Shakespeare remains relevant to us today; indeed, that is precisely what makes Shakespeare Shakespeare. The circular argument, needless to say, begs a lot of questions. The strategy, in any case, is always to bring Shakespeare to us, not to take us back to Shakespeare. Or, rather, as *Shakespeare in Love* demonstrates, to take us back to Shakespeare by bringing Shakespeare to us, to collapse past and present, to deny that there is such a thing as "pastness" altogether. "History," from this point of view, is always "now." The publicists knew precisely what the film was up to: "Refreshingly contemporary, *Shakespeare in Love* is ultimately the tale of a man and woman trying to make love work in the 90s – the 1590s" (*Pressbook*). In discussing the characters and situations they have constructed, the participants in *Shakespeare in Love* continuously look for analogies: Ned Allyn is the Tom Cruise of his day (Madden, Ben Affleck); "It's Dallas, it's J.R. with different props" (Colin Firth). Baz Luhrmann, too, finds equivalents: "If Shakespeare was writing a screenplay, it would be . . . *Something About Mary* set on the *Titanic*" (Special Edition DVD).

Shakespeare in Love, like *Romeo + Juliet*, continually negotiates this balance between past and present, between then and now. The film's opening nicely encapsulates the effect: we move smoothly from the Miramax logo (a stylized view of the Manhattan skyline) to the Universal logo to the initial scene which, though set in 1593, is introduced to us via a rapid steadicam camera movement, and reflects back on those two initial corporate logos: Fennyman the money-lender is torturing Henslowe the producer. When, after some discussion, Henslowe promises Fennyman a new work by Shakespeare, Fennyman balances the costs and gains of putting on a play. "The writer and the actors," he concludes, "can be paid out of the profits." "But," Henslowe responds, "there are no profits." "Exactly," Fennyman answers with obvious satisfaction. To which Henslowe, with unconcealed admiration, can only reply: "I think you have hit on something, Mr. Fennyman." As often in the entertainment culture of advanced capitalism – which, *Shakespeare in Love* wants us to believe, is not so different from the entertainment culture of Elizabethan England – the hand that feeds is not only bitten but relishes the pain. This is, in one sense, as much a movie about money as it is about Shakespeare.

Shakespeare in Love and *Romeo + Juliet* want to make Shakespeare "relevant" to a turn of the millennium audience and at the same time to make something "new," something that is at once sincere and playful, at once homage and pastiche, at once a meditation on Shakespeare's characters and themes and a multiplex hit. And both films succeed in part because, while taking Shakespeare (more or less) seriously, they also rely on generic codes and conventions that are at the heart of the movies. These are films highly aware of themselves as participating in movie culture, institutionally and generically. With *Shakespeare in Love*, that awareness is expressed through a self-reflexive commentary on the vicissitudes of filmmaking itself. *Romeo + Juliet*, on the other hand, draws on narrative and stylistic conventions of international cinema: critics, as well as ordinary viewers, have identified allusions to Sergio Leone westerns, to John Woo, to Busby Berkeley musicals and *Paris is Burning*, to *Priscilla, Queen of the Desert* and *Rebel Without a Cause*. All of this is so self-conscious that there hardly needs a critic come from a screening to tell us this; Luhrmann and company are perfectly happy to make the connections for us. And both films reflect, and take advantage of, the peculiar hybridity of contemporary filmmaking practices. *Romeo + Juliet* has American stars, an Australian director, and a largely Australian and Mexican crew; financed by an American major, it was filmed mainly in Mexico. *Shakespeare in Love*, an "independent" film, is nevertheless financed in part and released by Universal, a major studio; it features an Anglo-American cast, and one American and one British screenwriter.

In presenting their versions of romantic tragedy, the creators of *William Shakespeare's Romeo + Juliet* and of *Shakespeare in Love*, in spite of comments they may sometimes make to the contrary, saw themselves, unsurprisingly, not as iconoclasts or vulgarians, but as conservers or restorers intent on breaking down the cultural encrustations that have made Shakespeare "highbrow," rarefied, effeminate, and boring. Luhrmann, as much as John Madden and company, claims to be taking us back to the "real" Shakespeare, to the "original" *Romeo and Juliet*; his aim was to free Shakespeare from "the accumulation of . . . 'club' Shakespeare, which kind of dates to, really, the Victorian period" (Special Edition DVD; Luhrmann never mentions Zeffirelli). Far from desecration, these filmmakers are involved in a salvage operation. Jonathan Bate, King Alfred Professor of Literature at the University of Liverpool, happily endorses Luhrmann's achievement: "The best Shakespeare is always Shakespeare made contemporary," which is why "one of the great achievements of our time is Baz Luhrmann's *Romeo and Juliet* film" (Special Edition DVD). To please Jonathan Bate and Stephen Greenblatt, on the one hand, and Miramax's Harvey Weinstein, on the other, may seem a large ambition, but it is one to which the creators of both films, directly and indirectly, aspire, and if the circa $200 million each film has brought into the box office is juxtaposed to the generally enthusiastic critical reception each has enjoyed from academics and non-academics alike, they appear to have succeeded.

Notes

1 Stephen Buhler (2002) shows how "Romeo and Juliet have been depicted and transformed in mass-marketed pop music directed primarily at young audiences" since the 1950s.

2 While some have seen Luhrmann's film as fluctuating "between splendid thrusts of disruption of received authority and an ultimately time-pleasing reiteration" of Shakespeare's text "as it has been historically and ideologically fixed" (Modenessi 2002: 65), others have argued that *Romeo + Juliet* "is not simply an 'easy,' 'mindless' modernization but a re-contextualisation of the play which merits close analysis" (Walker 2000: 125).

3 Courtney Lehmann notes that, with the exception of Claire Danes, Lurhmann's cast members "articulate the couplets in a way that draws attention to their forced, artificial, and constraining nature" (2001: 208)

4 As José Arroyo (1997: 9) remarks, "[Romeo] is the one who bears the brunt of feeling: it's his face in close-up most of the time indicating how he wants, longs, feels and sometimes, eyes hidden by tears, suffers." This is, in a sense, a reversal of the dynamics of Shakespeare's play, where Juliet is clearly the one who articulates much of the play's emotional texture.

5 On the other hand, Crystal Downing (2000: 127) argues that "the film's self-conscious postmodern idiom intensifies Juliet's ironizing gestures, thus drawing our attention to the artificial construction of Romeo's identity".

6 Jonathan Goldberg (1994: 220) finds that "rather than breaking the filial bond, Romeo and Juliet reinsure it; it is the brotherhood of Romeo and Juliet that they secure."

7 Writing in *Variety*, for example, Adam Dawtrey and Monica Roman (1998) reported that Stoppard "substantially overhauled" Norman's script; such comments led Norman to respond in *Hollywood Reporter* (Harris 1999) that "Stoppard did what we call a dialogue polish," though he aknowledges that "he added some important ideas."

4

SURE CAN SING AND DANCE

Minstrelsy, the star system, and the post-postcoloniality of Kenneth Branagh's *Love's Labour's Lost* and Trevor Nunn's *Twelfth Night*

Katherine Eggert

Writing in 1850 in the Boston-based *Literary World*, an anonymous reviewer of Thomas De Quincey's *Biographical Essays* expresses the fear that, however much Shakespeare has triumphed upon the mid-nineteenth-century American stage, Americans cannot truly comprehend the language of the Bard (Anon. 1999: 159).[1] An American audience, still in its cultural infancy, requires both literalism and spectacle: "the story must be told as to children; every circumstance made out and presented with a literal fidelity; instead of having it suggested that 'the flask is red with wine,' we must be informed that there is 'just one pint and a half in that bottle there upon that table, which you see standing in the middle of the stage'" (160). However many productions of Shakespeare they attend, Americans thus prefer theatrical entertainments of a much baser sort: "We want to see and hear everything. Our amusements must be served up to us in solid 'chunks'. . . . Of this we have a capital and favorable illustration – in the unvarying patronage of the Ravels, in pantomime, and the black-featured minstrelsy of Christy" (160). Unconscious of the finer points of Shakespearean verse, "of a difference between Shakespeare and Bulwer," Americans turn to preliterate entertainment: minstrelsy and pantomime, song and dance (160).

But the spectacles discussed by this reviewer are more than just preliterate: they are nationalized and racialized, and their audience appeal only demonstrates that "American" theatrical culture is a no man's land, poised as it is between the equally foreign influences of both "low" African-American and "high" European culture. Although the two companies mentioned by the reviewer, Christy's and Ravel's, seem on the face of it to present quite starkly the contrast between these two competing spheres of cultural influence, African-American and European, each company freely mixed these two "un-American" modes of entertainment. Christy's Minstrels, the company in permanent residence at New York's Mechanics' Hall beginning in 1847, performed blackface shows that included not only standard "plantation" and "free black" minstrel numbers, but also parodies of such high-culture imports as Italian and English opera (Mahar 1999: 23–6). The Ravel company, a French troupe of acrobats, ballet dancers, and pantomime artists who appeared regularly in New York theaters and on national American tours between 1832 and 1848, did present a more obviously European brand of entertainment than did the Christy Minstrels, specializing in "romantic ballet, new wonders of physical virtuosity, and scenarios which united these elements (ballet and physical feats) plausibly and with continuity of dramatic action in the pantomime" (Schneider 1979: 242). Nevertheless, among the Ravels' most enduringly successful acts were several versions of a play about Jocko, "the noble ape who meets a tragic end" that had been popularly portrayed by the early nineteenth-century French pantomimist Mazurier (Towsen 1976: 147; Senelick 1979). These Jocko pantomimes implied to their audience that the Ravels, too, trafficked in African-derived entertainment. Even at the time, the tragic story of Jocko the ape was viewed as a thinly veiled allegory of an African man; Prussian naturalist Adelbert von Chamisso, whose account of his sea voyage to Alaska in 1815–18 was published in 1836, remarked of the antics of an ape brought on board ship that he found "encounters with apes instructive. . . . They are the truly genuine animal, the one on which mankind is based. Mazurier knew it well; he played Jocko as [Edmund] Kean did Othello."[2]

The way that the terms of Chamisso's analogy bleed into each other – Mazurier the pantomime is to Kean the Shakespearean actor as Jocko the ape is to Othello – has not only the racist effect of bestializing the African, but also the anti-literary and anti-esthetic effects of robbing the Shakespearean character of language, and robbing British high culture of the poetry that many see as its best achievement. Arguably, the reception of Shakespeare in America combines all these effects – racial themes, and non-literary, spectacular theatrical presentation – into one, in a fashion that will prove to be the enduring legacy of mid-nineteenth-century American theater for contemporary productions of Shakespeare. The unsophisticated American not only prefers minstrelsy or pantomime to Shakespeare, but also experiences Shakespeare as if the plays similarly were composed only of music and movement: currently, says our 1850 reviewer, "Shakespeare, without the accessories of scenery, costume, and the tumult of merely stage-scenes and passages, if he presented himself, simply in his character of a poet, would be scarcely more than Milton" (Anon. 1999: 160). To an American weaned on low-culture theatrical spectacle, Shakespeare's plays are all the better if they are staged as the equivalent of minstrel presentations bastardizing African-derived songs in blackface, or of European pantomimes taking their American audience's measure in showy acrobatics and dance.[3] Thus our reviewer glumly abandons American theatergoers to the minstrel show and the Ravel revue, consigning them to a life of inferior servitude to a true, British literary language. Americans labor in the rearguard of their British cultural superiors, speaking not their masters' language, but the blackface version of African-American dialect: "We cannot as yet quite digest Shakespeare – he is rather too much for us: so we must needs disport for awhile on 'Mose;' while other nations run before, and command the ropes, we must be content to take 'de but of the machine'" (162).

The real danger is that Americans might never learn better, and the lower-class version of Shakespeare – lively spectacle, rather than decorous poetry – might permanently dominate the American stage. The reviewer's reference to "Mose" is telling here. Not a blackface character but rather a "Bowery b'hoy" whose "rubric invoked Irishness [although] no single ethnic profile defined him" (Lott 1993: 81), the minstrel-show figure of "Mose" personified the rowdiness that, one year prior to the writing of this review, had erupted in the Astor Place riot, a demonstration of New York working-class resentment that coalesced around partisanship of the American actor Edwin Forrest against his rival, the genteel English Shakespearean actor William Charles Macready (Lott 1993: 66). Known for his commanding physique and arresting gestures in "democratic" roles such as Jack Cade and Spartacus, the American Forrest presented a truly physical theatrical spectacle, a "muscular and exuberant style" to counter the classically trained Macready's mellifluous elocution of Shakespearean verse (Moody 1958: 32). In May 1849, when the two actors were staging dueling Macbeths at two New York theaters, Macready's English Macbeth at the Astor Place Opera House sparked a confrontation outside the theater between some 10–15,000 working-class New Yorkers and the Seventh Regiment of the US Army. Forrest's supporters did not, by any means, win the battle: twenty-three of them were killed. However, they may have helped win the theatrical war, allowing an American Shakespeare to take precedence over a British one. Macready beat a hasty retreat to Boston and then to England, entering an embittered retirement a mere two years later, whereas Forrest enjoyed a soaring reputation and more than twenty more years of phenomenal theatrical success in his homeland (Moody 1958: 233–6) – this, for an untutored actor who was judged to have "no intellectual comprehension of what he was about" (Moody 1958: 38). The ultimate victor in the Astor Place riot is American Shakespeare, which substitutes style for substance, emotion for language, and bodies for text.

Kenneth Branagh's *Love's Labour's Lost* (2000) and Trevor Nunn's *Twelfth Night* (1996), the London-based film productions that are the topic of this essay, are quite a distance, both temporally and geographically, from the New York Shakespeare rivalries of the 1840s. Yet I wish to suggest that the narrative I have set out here – in which America, initially the subaltern obliged by its inferior cultural status to attend to a Shakespearean language it does not understand, ultimately revises high culture by translating Shakespeare either into a nonlinguistic spectacle, or into a racialized, colonial, and distinctly non-British language, or into some combination of both – can still govern the presentation of Shakespeare in contemporary film. This point may be obvious: whether they applaud or decry the democratization of Shakespeare in contemporary popular culture, critics generally agree that Shakespeare without Shakespeare, stripped as much as possible of Shakespearean language and translated into American popular idiom, has triumphed. Michael Bristol, for example, asserts that while the canonical Shakespeare whose "value is said to be embodied in concrete textual material" underwrites the Shakespeare of popular allusion in cartoons or musical comedies or television situation-comedies, the latter, far more successful Shakespeare may be accessed purely on the basis of a vague familiarity with his works, not by means of any real acquaintance with the text (1996: 90). And Richard Burt argues that dumbed-down or "loser" Shakespeare, Shakespeare *sans la lettre*, has even become the new and paradoxically "cool" gold standard of American Shakespearean presentation (1999: 1–12).

Less discussed, however, is the response of the British Shakespeare industry to the triumph of this American Shakespeare. While the British seem to have maintained the upper hand in prestigious stage productions of Shakespeare, dominance on film has been quite another matter. With the notable exceptions of films by Laurence Olivier and Kenneth Branagh, American film productions of Shakespeare, though not always the critics' or scholars' favorites, have enjoyed the cultural popularity and ubiquity that appertain worldwide to the Hollywood film industry of the twentieth and twenty-first centuries. (Continental European or European-American productions, especially those directed by Franco Zeffirelli, have perhaps held second place.) As a result, I would argue, the geographical vectors of cultural imperialism have reversed themselves from those delineated by the 1850 reviewer who despaired of Americans' appreciating Shakespeare. While Shakespearean language is still devalued by both American producers and audiences, Shakespeare productions that cater to an American taste for spectacle and distaste for dialogue are now considered to be the superior ones. One might well expect, then, that British Shakespeare films would be the last bastion of script-based Shakespeare, holding the fort against anti-high-culture, dumbed-down spectacles. But in what we might term the post-postcolonial relation in which America and Britain now find themselves – one in which, culturally and economically speaking, the colonizer is now the colonized – British producers of Shakespeare films are to be found not fending off the barbarians at the gates, but rather absorbing and repeating the customs of the new overlords.

The result of this inversion is a curious discursive stance that comprises a range of somewhat contradictory British Shakespearean responses to the American Shakespeare-on-film hegemony. First, nostalgia: the wish to re-invert cultural influence so that Shakespeare is England's own again – a wish that, like all nostalgic wishes, recognizes its own futility. Second, mockery: the parodic imitation of Hollywood, which in the light of the post-postcolonialism I have proposed might be seen as a bizarrely postmodern, white-on-white version of the colonial mimicry identified by Homi Bhabha, where the colonial power fashions an "almost the same but not quite" version of itself that in turn "mimes the forms of authority at the point at which it deauthorizes them" (Bhabha 1994: 91). And third, affection and desire: a genuine love for Hollywood and for what it represents, namely, the charismatic ability (and the financial backing) to compel the attention of an adoring audience. The sum effect is a new twist on what Renato Rosaldo has called "imperialist nostalgia," in which the colonial agent longs for, and reproduces as tribute or museum display, the very culture it has destroyed (1993: 69–74). As the former colonizer for which Shakespeare was part of the arsenal of cultural imperialism, England now is in the position of mining itself nostalgically for cultural artifacts, the chief of which is Shakespeare himself. British productions, and especially film productions, of Shakespeare thus bear the traces both of a nostalgia for England's ascendant past, and of a recognition of its current subordinate status.

This recognition is particularly acute in Branagh's *Love's Labour's Lost* and Nunn's *Twelfth Night*. Certainly, these two productions are very different, both in their treatment of Shakespeare and in their film-industry affiliations. Branagh's film is the more Americanized, Hollywood-centered production, the more "mainstream" both in its eagerness to attract an American and youthful audience, and in its having garnered prestigious Hollywood backing. Its credits declare that it is "presented" by no less than Martin Scorsese, the epitome of Hollywood director-*auteurs*, and Stanley Donen, director of many of the most prestigious Hollywood musicals of the post-World War II decades, including *On the Town* (1949), *Seven Brides for Seven Brothers* (1954), and, most monumentally, *Singin' in the Rain* (1952), the film typically cited as the best-ever Hollywood musical. As the Donen lineage would suggest, *Love's Labour's Lost* is also notably spectacular rather than text-centered. Branagh lops the Shakespearean script by about half, bringing in the film at an astonishingly short 93 minutes, and substitutes song-and-dance numbers intended to evoke the mood of the omitted dialogue and scenes. *Twelfth Night*, in contrast, is the more stage-centered and seemingly authentically "English," as

Nicholas R. Jones has described it: "Nunn's film, on the face of it, steers clear of the 'cutting-edge': its style is verbal, meditative and restrained – in short, 'British.' 'The performances are muted, the text relatively undisturbed, the poetry well spoken and expressive, the cinematography unobtrusive" (2002: par. 2). *Love's Labour's Lost* was financially backed by Miramax, widely credited with bringing the art-house sensibility into mainstream films of the 1990s and early 2000s – as evidenced by such commercial successes as *Pulp Fiction* (1994), *The English Patient* (1996), *Shakespeare in Love* (1998), and *Chocolat* (2000). *Twelfth Night*, in contrast, was backed by Fine Line Features, which generally produces films that, though often critically successful, do not jump the line from art house to mainstream – e.g., David Cronenberg's *Crash* (1996) and Lars von Trier's *Dancer in the Dark* (2000). The two films' casting also seems to reflect their American-versus-British, big-budget-versus-small sensibilities. Branagh's increasing turn toward American film stars for his Shakespeare films (Denzel Washington, Michael Keaton, and Keanu Reeves in *Much Ado about Nothing* (1993); Billy Crystal, Charlton Heston, Robin Williams, and Jack Lemmon in *Hamlet* (1996); and Alicia Silverstone and Nathan Lane in *Love's Labour's Lost*) initially appears to be the obverse of Nunn's use of heavy-hitting British stars like Ben Kingsley, Helena Bonham Carter, and Nigel Hawthorne in central roles. And yet, despite their differences, both films in fact allegorize an anxiety about the relation between the British and American film industries, an anxiety that consists of the blend of attitudes toward Hollywood I mentioned above – nostalgia, mockery, and affection. This blend is accomplished through the several kinds of filmmaking technique I examine in this essay, including homages to Hollywood; references to the careers of previous Shakespeare-film directors; racial- and ethnic-minority casting; and the use of music and dance. Together, these techniques model the relation between British and American Shakespeare as a postcolonialist relation – just as it was in 1850, except that now the British Shakespearean actor risks occupying the position of the minstrel.

Love's Labour's Lost wears most of its Hollywood homages on its sleeve, most obviously its debts to Hollywood (primarily RKO and MGM) musicals of the 1930s, 1940s, and 1950s. The opening title of the film, cursive script superimposed on draped red satin, imitates the Technicolor titles in which MGM specialized, whereas the musical numbers trace a history of, in particular, Fred Astaire's and Ethel Merman's stage and film musical careers from the late 1920s to the mid-1940s.[4] Costume functions as another cue. In an early scene set in a library, the gentlemen's open-front academic gowns disclose the fact that their basic costume – lightweight flannel pants, open-collared white shirts, and neckties jauntily worn in the place of belts – duplicates, as Charles Taylor (2000) notes in his review of the film, the frequent film attire of Astaire. Similarly, the lovers' color-coded attire, which identifies which woman will pair with which man (or mis-pair with which man, in the musical number that replaces the Masque of the Muscovites), derives from the color-coding of (particularly female) costume to clarify romantic assignations in Technicolor musicals like *On the Town*. *Love's Labour's Lost* also revives the "feature number" tradition of the classical Hollywood musical with the appearance of its one genuine Broadway-musical star, Nathan Lane in the role of Costard, in a knowingly kitschy, pull-out-all-the-stops ballad-tempo version of "There's No Business Like Show Business." We are perhaps reminded that Astaire himself, who when he came to Hollywood was judged physically uncongenial to leading-man roles, was initially slotted into feature numbers that would showcase his phenomenal dancing talents.[5]

But to notice Branagh's homage to the classic Hollywood musical style is not to explain either its motives or its effects. Why should Branagh make *Love's Labour's Lost* in 1999–2000? A different analysis of this topic might consider Branagh's effort, unpopular at the box office though it was, as contributing to what might be a turn-of-the-century revival of the film musical as a popular and critically successful genre.[6] My concern here, however, is the place of *Love's Labour's Lost* in Branagh's own career, which itself is indebted, as has often been noted, to that of his predecessor British Shakespearean actor-director-producer, Laurence Olivier. Arguably, *Love's Labour's Lost* is yet another in a series of Branaghian attempts to outdo Olivier, this time not by remaking one of Olivier's great Shakespeare films, but by temporally relocating Branagh's own Shakespearean-filmmaking career to a time before Olivier's began. After all, *Love's Labour's Lost* is insistently set in 1939. The film is punctuated by "Cinetone News" segments, narrated by Branagh himself, that suggest the gentlemen's retreat takes place during the "Sitzkrieg" that preceded open hostilities between Germany and Britain in World War II; and it closes with a coda that first sends the gentlemen off to war and then sees them safe at home, reunited with their lady-loves, in front of Buckingham Palace on VE Day. With his customary audaciousness in relation to Olivier, Branagh concludes most of the action of his film before Olivier had even thought of directing *Henry V* on film, retroactively establishing Branagh's own movie as launching the sound era's greatest wave of filmic Shakespeare. Further, in this light *Love's Labour's Lost*'s nostalgic moment is also a device that returns filmic Shakespeare to its rightful British origins. The glory days of British film Shakespeare are just ahead; the Shakespeare film heyday of the 1970s and beyond, where Shakespeare becomes the property of Italians, Americans, and (perhaps worst of all) Australians, is displaced into the distant future. And Branagh himself, who has already exceeded Olivier's count of major Shakespeare films directed and who has declared his intent to direct more – Olivier made three; Branagh has made four and counting – proleptically corrects Olivier's abdication of the Shakespeare-on-film throne to other, non-British directors.[7]

We may read the corrective nostalgia of this move as having personal as well as nationalistic motives. For Branagh is charting a retrospective course *vis-à-vis* not only the history of film, but also the careers of Shakespeare, of Shakespeare's heroes, and of other, non-British directors of Shakespeare on film.[8] Having progressed forward in the Shakespearean canon from *Henry V* (1599) to *Much Ado about Nothing* (*c.* 1600) to *Hamlet* (1600–1), Branagh retreats to *Love's Labour's Lost*, whose date is uncertain but cannot be later than 1598. (Most scholars who have worked on the issue date the play at 1594–5.) And his shift toward the less mature end of the Shakespearean oeuvre is matched by his playing a role whose age does not suit his own. Forty years old when *Love's Labour's Lost* was released, Branagh seems to have rejected the age-appropriate progression of his previous Shakespearean film roles, from the young King Henry when Branagh was thirty, to the slightly jaded Benedick when he was thirty-three, to the truly jaded Iago when he was thirty-five, to the world-weary Hamlet when he was thirty-six. Branagh's retreat to the Hollywood golden age of *Love's Labour's Lost*, then, may be seen somewhat cynically as a middle-aged man's attempt to regain his own golden age, to become younger than Hamlet – or younger even than Benedick or Henry V, since Berowne (in a Branaghian invention) acquires the adult-soldier status of Henry and Benedick only in the closing minutes of *Love's Labour's Lost*. In this regard Branagh may be contrasted to his predecessors in the actor-director Shakespeare-film *auteur* tradition: Olivier (b. 1907), who after making *Henry V* (1944) and *Hamlet* (1948) at ages 37 and 41, respectively, went on to the more mature roles of Richard III (1955) and Othello (1965); and Orson Welles (b. 1915), who after debuting in his age-traversing masterpiece *Citizen Kane* (1941) at 25, moved in his 30s and 40s to mature Shakespearean film roles in *Macbeth* (1948), *The Tragedy of Othello* (1952), and *Chimes at Midnight* (1965).

Of course, by his turn to filmed Shakespeare in the late 1940s Welles was already Hollywood poison, and his Shakespeare films, though brilliant, are marred by low production values. Similarly, and as I have noted, Olivier's career as a ground-breaking film director of Shakespeare was more or less over after *Hamlet*. We must consider, then, whether Branagh's mid-life retreat to comic-lover youth is a defense not only against his own middle age, but also against directorial has-been status (Burt 2002b: 15). And yet to acknowledge predecessor has-beens is also to acknowledge the fear that one has already slipped into that role – a fear that surely must haunt the maker of such commercial flops as *Peter's Friends* (1992), *Mary Shelley's Frankenstein* (1994), and *A Midwinter's Tale/In the Bleak Midwinter* (1995/1996). *Love's Labour's Lost*'s gestures of homage to Woody Allen bear this mark, the mark of the once-great toast of Hollywood whose installations of himself in nostalgia-film leading-man roles (such as in *The Curse of the Jade Scorpion* (2001)) look increasingly hubristic, if not simply pathetic. Having played the sexually hapless lead character, Allen's customary screen persona, in Allen's *Celebrity* (1998), Branagh has taken an even closer look at the Woody Allen career trajectory than most directors have. All of these associations may encourage us to take a closer look at the time frame of *Love's Labour's Lost*: while the glory days of British Shakespeare-on-film lay ahead in 1939, the glory days of early British cinema lay behind, as an ill-advised "quota system" installed in 1927 to protect the British film industry had the unintended effect in the 1930s of encouraging the production of badly made British films (Low 1985: 33–53).

I wish to propose that the bad British production is precisely Branagh's reference point in *Love's Labour's Lost*. Branagh's failure to achieve a nostalgic reincarnation either of the heyday of British film or of his own youth is not, in my view, merely a directorial slip-up, but rather part and parcel of the overdetermined amateurism of the film – amateurism that cheerfully devalues the past by offering an obviously inauthentic simulacrum of it. At first, the film's deployment of the simulacrum seems to function in only one transatlantic direction: American fakery duplicates English authenticity. In a BBC interview on the set of the film, Branagh takes pleasure in the filmic art of explicitly inaccurate re-creation, defined as the replacement of English originals by American replicas:

> BBC: This is a fantastic set – what is it meant to be?
>
> BRANAGH: Well, it's a kind of fantasy Oxbridge. It's actually inspired by some colleges at Yale University, where in fact, having built their college several hundred years after most of the Oxbridge colleges, they then distressed them. They actually poured acid down the walls and made them all much older looking, so there's a certain ye olde thing which is also redolent of some kind of movie college sets that we wanted to evoke for this musical.
>
> (Anon. n.d.a)

The joke is that eventually even American kitsch becomes "classic." Whether Yale colleges designed to resemble Oxbridge, or 1930s college-film sets designed to resemble Yale, the American replicas have finally acquired enough age to amass nostalgia value. A similar dynamic is at work in Branagh's use of American song "classics," used in the film not to enhance Shakespeare but to supersede Shakespeare, so that, for example, "Let's Face the Music and Dance" replaces the Masque of the Muscovites and "There's No Business Like Show Business" replaces the Pageant of the Nine Worthies. The supplanting of Shakespeare by American popular culture is perhaps most pointedly staged just before the gentlemen's declarations of love in the "Cheek to Cheek" number. Branagh, playing Berowne, begins to tap-dance on a library table in percussion to his speech, in essence embodying Shakespearean metrics as he audibly explicates the rhythms of iambic pentameter. This marriage of poetics to spectacle is extremely short-lived, however; soon the dance overtakes the verse, the song dominates the dance, and eventually the four gentlemen float up to the dome of the library in an absurd homage to both the "I Love to Laugh" number from *Mary Poppins* (1964) and the Fizzy Lifting Drink scene from *Willy Wonka and the Chocolate Factory* (1971) – two more American film adaptations whose popularity has entirely surpassed that of their British literary sources.

Here, however, is where *Love's Labour's Lost* begins to complicate the submission of British Shakespeare-on-film to the hegemony of Hollywood. Silly as it is, the turn at the end of the "Cheek to Cheek" number from classic 1930s American musical film to kitschy 1960s and 1970s American musical film, from Irving Berlin to *Willy Wonka*, also serves a less comedic purpose: it illustrates how Branagh's film determinedly assumes the "almost but not quite" status that, Bhabha argues, is foisted upon the colonial mimic and that in turn functions to deauthorize the colonial authority. Once the song and dance of Fred Astaire metamorphose into the song and dance of Dick Van Dyke – whose *Mary Poppins* Cockney chimney sweep is both improbably lovable and abysmally accented – we can easily see that *Love's Labour's Lost* never truly proposes to pull off the hat trick of surpassing the antique with its reproduction. This devotion to the bad imitation is evident even when we consider the basic structure of dual replication in the film. Reviving not only Shakespeare but also the classic Hollywood musical, Branagh forces on his viewers the recognition that although he and most of the remainder of his cast may be virtuosos in the first kind of performance, they are mere hacks at the second. (Or, in the case of Silverstone, bad at both.) Nodding to Astaire, the transcendent genius of dance in American film, is like nodding to *Singin' in the Rain*: a gesture that will always demonstrate the tribute's secondary status. Thus Branagh's and the rest of his cast's poor imitations of Astaire have the effect not only of *revealing* this production as in some way second-rate, but of *designating* this production with that status.

At the same time, however, *Love's Labour's Lost* tars American popular culture with something of the same brush, exposing it as derivative even in its ascendancy. The signal moment in this regard is the dance number "I've Got a Crush on You," which stands in for the gentlemen's sonnet-reading in Act 4, Scene 3. Adrian Lester as Dumaine – the sole black male actor in the cast, and an award-winning performer in several major stage musicals[9] – performs the one star dance turn of the production: not exactly Astaire, but closer than the rest. That the black dancer is the best performer reminds us that Astaire is *not* on the scene, and that the kinds of cultural triumphalism that Astaire enacted are not a possibility here. Astaire, we must remember, embodied

American cultural imperialism at its appropriative pinnacle: modeling his work after that of brilliant African-American dancers like Harold and Fayard Nicholas, Astaire ultimately also trumped the European classical tradition, so that European ballet artists like Nureyev and Baryshnikov came to describe Astaire (and not, say, the Nicholas brothers or Bill "Bojangles" Robinson) as the American dancer to whom they were most indebted (Kroll 1987). In *Love's Labour's Lost*, in contrast, the British actor of African ancestry easily outdoes the American and the other British players alike by being the best dancer on the set. While British musical performance does not ultimately trump American – Lester is largely hobbled in the rest of the film, forced to perform at the level of the other, less accomplished singers and dancers – the result is that Astaire, one of the finest artists of American film, is designated simultaneously as an object of envy, and as a cultural parasite; as secondary, if not second-rate.

Branagh, in contrast, inhabits a world in which, whenever British actors go to Hollywood, the first-rate are condemned to be secondary. Branagh's poor dancing and merely competent singing in *Love's Labour's Lost* distance him not only from Astaire the musical performer, but also from the star persona that Hollywood actors like Astaire embody. Despite being the star of the film, despite being perhaps the most celebrated Shakespearean actor of the 1990s and early 2000s, and despite his efforts to acquire the blend of personal and professional life on which the movie-star reputation has historically depended,[10] Branagh is *not* a star in the Hollywood sense: not the actor whose recognizable and likeable personality remains essentially the same from film to film, no matter what role the actor takes (Dyer 1979). It is a dilemma dramatized in Branagh's *A Midwinter's Tale*, where an English actor-director must choose between British Shakespearean penury and a well-paid existence as a Hollywood B-movie side-kick: the British actor in Hollywood is generally relegated to character roles. The male British actor, in particular, tends to play the villain. (Think, for example, of Laurence Olivier in *Marathon Man* (1976); Alan Rickman in *Die Hard* (1988) and *Robin Hood, Prince of Thieves* (1991); and Anthony Hopkins in *The Silence of the Lambs* (1991).) Branagh has even used this phenomenon to his self-conscious directorial advantage, casting the great British Shakespearean actor Derek Jacobi as the villain in both his Hitchcock homage *Dead Again* (1991) and *Hamlet*. Of course, all aging Hamlets play Claudius somewhere down the road, but the villain's role seems the inexorable endpoint of the British male actor's career. Branagh himself has found his widest audience in such roles of late; not only did he play a formidable Iago to American star Laurence Fishburne's Othello in Oliver Parker's 1995 film production, but his turn as the impotent, paraplegic, and allegorically named gadgetician-villain Dr. Loveless in *Wild Wild West* (1999) no doubt brought him more viewers than all his Shakespeare films combined.

As the role of Dr. Loveless demonstrates, British actors in American films often end up playing a caricature of Britishness: for British men in villain roles, this means portraying characters who are usually megalomaniacal, often sexually compromised, and always too clever by half – qualities that never stand up to the American hero's virility, sense of fair play, and dogged competence. Thus the British actor in Hollywood takes a role reminiscent of that occupied in Hollywood for so many years (and arguably, even today) by the African-American actor: the role of the minstrel, who must play unpleasant caricatures of his or her racial or national origin in order to make a decent living. Just as postbellum African-American entertainers had to don blackface in order to play before white and African-American audiences alike (Rogin 1996: 43) and then had to carry on in humiliating Mammy and Uncle Tom roles in Hollywood film, so too does the British actor earn his or her keep not by playing Shakespeare, but by parroting back to Hollywood its own ignorant, xenophobic view of an "exotic" culture.

I do not wish to press this analogy very far. Obviously, the British actor is not the victim of racism, and has never suffered the injustices perpetrated from the antebellum era to the present upon African-American entertainers. In fact, quite the reverse: British actors, who often have developed their art in a national, publicly funded filmmaking and theater industry that is theoretically independent of Hollywood concerns, tend to enjoy considerable cultural authority in the United States and command true respect in Hollywood for their dramatic training. As well, and as I discuss further below, for a British actor knowingly to adopt the minstrel's part is to raise the specter of the British Empire's own colonialist enterprises, and its own appropriations of subjected cultures for the purposes of theatrical amusement. Nevertheless, *Love's Labour's Lost* and *Twelfth Night* both circle around the topic of minstrelsy – to some extent claiming the minstrel's position as the British Shakespearean actor's own, but to some extent attempting to displace minstrelsy onto representatives of the American star system.

One response to occupying the minstrel's role, as Tommy L. Lott has pointed out, is to parody the hegemonic culture of the audience that is entertained by such simplistic representations (1999: 94–9). And certainly parody, and the parodic undermining of Hollywood's dominance, is a strategy adopted by many British actors and filmmakers. Yet *Love's Labour's Lost*, in my view, does not undertake a full-fledged parody of American popular culture, perhaps because parody, while it does not quite release the parodist from an obligation of debt to the object that is mocked, at least endeavors to place the parodist somewhat outside that object's sphere of influence. Branagh, Hollywood-lover that he is, clearly does not wish to live beyond that pale (Crowl 2000, 2002). After all, *Love's Labour's Lost* is a film that views even Britain's finest hour, its entry into war against the Nazis, through the lens of the American film *Casablanca* (1942), to which the scene of the lovers' final parting when the war begins (men in fedoras bidding goodbye to their tearful beloveds as a propeller plane awaits) is a blatant homage. Instead, Branagh tends to engage in complicity with notions of race that comport with a stereotypical white sensibility. Take, for example, his casting of non-white Hollywood stars Denzel Washington (who is African-American) and Keanu Reeves (whose father is of Hawaiian/Chinese descent) as the fraternal outsiders – Don Pedro and Don John, respectively – in *Much Ado about Nothing*.[11] Non-whiteness thus seems to explain why, despite their disparate personalities, Don Pedro and Don John are both excluded from the marriage bonds at the end of the film. *Love's Labour's Lost* is even more egregious in this respect: the film skates rather too closely to offensive stereotypes when it insinuates that white people can't dance, and black people can. (Although it mitigates such a suggestion somewhat by the casting of Carmen Ejogo as Maria, Ejogo, of Nigerian and white descent, displays no real talent as a dancer.) If the British Shakespearean takes part in something resembling minstrelsy, then for Branagh this minstrelsy is something that must be not celebrated for its satirical potential, but rather displaced as quickly as possible, in hot-potato fashion, onto actors whose race or ethnicity makes them "eligible" for such a position.

Any performance of *Love's Labour's Lost* requires ethnic jokes, of course; and Timothy Spall fulfills our expectations by playing Don Armado, the braggart Spaniard, with the exact accent and many of the mannerisms of Manuel, *Fawlty Towers*' hapless Spanish waiter (played by German-born and British-raised actor Andrew Sachs). In other ways, though, Branagh seems to solve the play's racial-insult problem by silently erasing ethnic presences. Rosaline, the dark mistress who, Kim Hall argues, is "whitened" by Berowne's rhetoric (Hall 1995: 90–1), is played by the fair-skinned Natascha McElhone; and not only the Muscovites but also the mute "Blackamoors" who accompany them are excised from the shooting script.[12] But in having Nathan Lane play Costard, Branagh introduces a new ethnic presence, one whose participation in the American minstrelsy tradition is clearly, if briefly, evoked: the American Jewish entertainer. Lane to some extent simply embodies all (non-black) ethnicities: a Jewish performer himself, he plays Costard as borrowing various shticks from such great ethnic vaudevillians as Groucho Marx (the voice), Milton Berle (the plaid sport coat and the unabashed randiness), and Señor Wences (the Spanish-accented hand puppet). For one moment, however, Lane impersonates a specific Jewish star of vaudeville, Broadway, and Hollywood, one whose fame and fortune relied heavily upon blackface minstrelsy: Al Jolson. In the "There's No Business Like Show Business" number, Lane shifts into a Jolson impression during the verse that goes, "Top of that, your pa and ma have parted,/You're broken-hearted, but you go on." Lane's Jolsonesque exclamation after these lines, "No, Mama, Papa!," turns the song, ever so briefly, into the "My Mammy" number that was Jolson's signature piece in his most famous film, *The Jazz Singer* (1927). As Mark Winokur (1996) and Michael Rogin (1996) have both argued, the Jewish star in 1920s and 1930s Hollywood enacted on film the struggle to invent him/herself as genteel and "white," unlike the immigrant or blackface characters he or she played. Branagh's film returns the Jewish actor to that moment, both historically and thematically, and thus reinscribes the assimilation of race and ethnicity into dramatic, musical, and dance entertainment as a purely American problem. But in that case, a talent for singing and dancing must also be an American purview. When the King urges Branagh/Berowne not to let the "There's No Business Like Show Business" pageant proceed ("Berowne, they will shame us. Let them not approach" (Shakespeare 1998: 5.2.509)), we understand that, unlike in the play – where the king fears being embarrassed by the bad acting of the lower classes – here the shame accrues to the British actors, about to be shown up by the vastly superior American performer Lane. The price of second-rate performance that Branagh pays is evidently justified by its goal: a whitened, Anglicized presence for Branagh, and, by extension, for British Shakespearean film.

An alternate, and more radical, approach is one that Branagh does not seem to consider in *Love's Labour's Lost*: he might have fully embraced the minstrel's position, developing a new kind of stardom for the British Shakespearean actor. This post-postcolonial British-Shakespearean minstrelsy might reference the history of race and colonialism in the British Empire as a means of exploring the Bard's current peculiar place at both the center and the margins of popular culture. Such a strategy might not be too far-fetched for an actor brought up as a Protestant in Northern Ireland, who might well understand what it means to be simultaneously a representative of the cultural elite, and a member of an embattled and territorially marginalized minority. Branagh, however, has publicly deployed his Irish origins not to explore this paradox, but rather to disclaim the "cultural elite" label and to associate "Irishness" with verbal facility rather than with a history of colonialist conflict: "I feel more Irish than English. . . . I feel freer than British, more visceral, with a love of language. Shot through with fire in some way. That's why I resist being appropriated as the current repository of Shakespeare on the planet. That would mean I'm part of the English cultural elite, and I am utterly ill-fitted to be" (Witchel 1999: C7). And if Branagh does not exploit these associations in his film of *Henry V*, with its explicit themes of British conquest and of the splintered internal colonialism of British national identity, it should not be surprising that he fails to do so in a lightweight comedy. A film that undertook such a project, however, would force us to reconsider the post-postcolonial relation of Britain to the United States, to shift our sense of Shakespeare as being simply the refined tool, or perhaps even the producer, of colonial hegemony. Perhaps such a film would demonstrate that Shakespeare, in the context of the Anglo-American exchanges I have been considering here, has become his own subaltern. I do not mean that Shakespeare is in the position of the voiceless and history-less subaltern as Gayatri Spivak (1988) describes him/her – the subaltern, that is, of always unrepresented indigenous populations – but, rather, that Shakespeare is in the position of the "indigenous elite" that Spivak posits as the third term between the colonizer and the repressed peonage: the subaltern who does speak, but speaks in order that his language may please and ultimately conform to the colonizing interests.

For an idea of what, exactly, this kind of Shakespeare sounds like when he speaks, we may turn to Ben Kingsley's Feste. While Nunn's *Twelfth Night* presents itself as an ensemble production (specifically, a Royal Shakespeare Company/National Theatre ensemble production, with a dash of the West End thrown in; see Jones 2002: para. 6), the film features stars recognizable to an American filmgoing audience, Kingsley and Helena Bonham Carter. Moreover, Bonham Carter's American breakthrough role in a non-art-house film, *Fight Club* (1999), was still ahead of her at the time of *Twelfth Night*'s release. Thus, for the American audience in 1996, or at least the few who saw the film, Kingsley was the true star of *Twelfth Night*. Kingsley's mass-audience film fame at that point relied on a single role, his 1982 Best Actor Oscar-winning performance as Mahatma Gandhi. It is a role we are meant to recollect, with something of a shock, when Kingsley's Feste breaks at two moments into mimicry of a colonial-Indian native soldier. The first such mimicry accompanies nonsensical lines that vaguely suggest an exotic people ("Malvolio's nose is no whipstock, my lady has a white hand, and the Myrmidons are no bottle-ale houses" (Nunn 1996: 42)). The second follows Sir Toby's "Dost thou think, because thou art virtuous, there shall be no more cakes and ale?" and accompanies Feste's line, "Yes, by Saint Anne, and ginger shall be hot i'the mouth, too" (Nunn 1996: 49). The association is obvious: spicy, gingery food is Indian. And so, too, is Ben Kingsley, in a roundabout way: he was born Krishna Bhanji, in Yorkshire, England, to a half-Jewish English mother and an Indian-descended father who immigrated from Kenya. Just as Branagh has cast non-white actors for the unassimilable roles in *Much Ado About Nothing*, so too does Nunn cast the non-WASP Kingsley in the prototypical outsider's role of the Shakespearean fool.

What is remarkable about Kingsley's Feste, then, is that although he retains the role's trappings of vagrancy and poverty, he is hardly the utterly subordinate subaltern that his brief moments of Indian playacting might indicate. Feste wears the shapeless and worn clothes of a tramp, but his accent is as upper class as the aristocratic characters', his bearing indistinguishable from theirs. He is, most of all, a serious clown, one whose reaction shots often silently register the knowing point of view that contrasts with the confusion of the other characters, and that makes him, in filmic terms, the stand-in for the director/author/*auteur*. The film even insinuates that Feste has engineered or at least foreseen the main plot, Viola's masquerade and revelation of identity: at the end of the film, Feste returns to Viola a necklace she discarded during the events that led up to her crossdressing as Cesario. Let me stretch the point: if there is a Shakespeare figure in this film, Feste is it. But Kingsley as Feste/Shakespeare also bears the mantle of his previous role as Gandhi, author of modern India and, improbably, all-American hero, canonized in a big-budget film produced by "Indo-British Film Productions" but bankrolled by Hollywood's Columbia Pictures. Kingsley carries his multiple colonial identities, American and Indian, into *Twelfth Night*. As a result, even in a film that hypostasizes a limitless British Empire (so that when one travels to Illyria, one still ends up in Victorian England), the *auteur* of *Twelfth Night* is, remarkably, the least British of all.

These connotations of racial and national origin redefine Feste's skills as Shakespearean fool: just as with Adrian Lester in *Love's Labour's Lost*, we notice that it is the non-white entertainer who really *can* sing and dance. This is the case even though Kingsley's musical performances in the film are marked as "English"; Kingsley plays the traditional folk instruments of concertina and guitar, and he sings "O Mistress Mine" and "Come Away, Death" to traditional tunes. However, his best song, "O Mistress Mine," is bracketed by the two instances cited above in which he imitates an Indian colonial soldier. Given Kingsley's own multivalent ethnic identity, it becomes difficult to discern which is his real mode of mimicry, whether he is an Indian mimicking British aristocrats to the point of passing for one, or whether he is a Briton mimicking an Indian to the point of momentarily going native. In either case, however, Feste's multiple personae are defined by an immigrant/colonial axis of exchange, as opposed to, say, by the British regionalism that often is used to mark lower social caste in British Shakespearean performance. (Unlike his Indian accent, Feste's rural English accent as Master Topas is manifestly fake, and we later discern that he has simply imitated the garb and accent of the priest who marries Olivia and Sebastian.) We even hear a hint of Kingsley's "other" immigrant ethnicity when he briefly slips into a stereotypically comic Jewish accent – as if he were pronouncing "went" as "vent" – in the lines, "Vent my folly! Tell me what I shall vent to my lady? Shall I vent to her that thou art coming?" (Nunn 1996: 102). More subtle than his Indianness but just as startling, his Jewish-vaudevillian moment marks Feste's character as culturally fluid and culturally fluent in a way that Branagh is generally unwilling to let his British actors be.

In short, Kingsley's Feste redefines Shakespeare as the author who spans the former British Empire – although not in the way imagined by the Boston *Literary World* reviewer who in 1850 hoped that, one day, American audiences would be able to digest Shakespeare in his pure form; or by Maurice Morgann, who in 1777 envisioned an America that, even though newly freed from British rule, would speak Shakespeare as a native language: "the *Apalachian* mountains, the banks of the *Ohio*, and the plains of *Sciota* shall resound with [Shakespeare's] accents" (1963: 233). Shakespeare, as it turned out, did not conquer the empire. But neither would it be correct to say that the empire has conquered Shakespeare. The kinds of post-postcolonial exchange I describe are similar to those discussed by Richard Burt in his new study of Shakespeare citation in black popular culture, where "Shakespeare cannot be placed exclusively on the side of dominant culture or on the side of counterhegemonic resistance" (Burt 2002c: 202). While making *Twelfth Night*, Nunn chafed against having to mold Shakespeare to American expectations, protesting that "Hollywood executives and southern California audiences . . . conspired to force him to provide explanatory introductory materials establishing not only the story line but also Feste's role as narrator, observer, and (it is suggested) orchestrator of all that follows" (Buhler 2002b: 152; see Nunn 1996: introduction). Yet this is a somewhat disingenuous complaint from the fantastically successful director of musicals such as *Cats*, *Sunset Boulevard*, and *Les Misérables* – stage shows designed to transfer seamlessly, in all their long-running and profitable glory, between the West End and Broadway. Moreover, Nunn's musicals demonstrate the adaptability of literary properties from one culture to another, as long as they are adapted into a primarily spectacular production: in the case of *Cats* and *Sunset Boulevard*, for example, literary or filmic properties, once turned into spectacular musicals, may be translated from their American origins into British adaptations that enjoy phenomenal American success.[13] Viewed in the context of Nunn's directorial career, Kingsley's Feste, with his multiple racial and cultural affiliations and with his songster expertise, seems to mark the irruption into *Twelfth Night* of the truly culturally transferable art form, exemplified by Shakespeare as musical theater.

British Shakespeare film as a post-postcolonial minstrel form accommodates all these elements: the song, the dance, the spectacle; the simultaneously celebratory and cynical, exuberant and weary attitude toward the formerly colonial audience and its dumbed-down entertainment demands. For Nunn's *Twelfth Night* hardly takes unadulterated pleasure in the former colonial's occupancy of the Shakespeare *auteur* role. Indeed, one sign of the mixed feelings provoked by that occupancy might be the melancholy air connoted, in part, by the film's temporal confusion. While most of *Twelfth Night*'s costumes – especially those of Malvolio, Sir Toby, Andrew Aguecheek, and Olivia's servants – set the piece in an *Upstairs, Downstairs*-like 1890s, Olivia's Pre-Raphaelite gowns and the gentlemen's uniforms derive from somewhere around the 1840s, well before the apex of the British Empire. This admixture of time frames leaves us unsure about the future of British colonial ascendancy: is the Empire waxing yet, or is it about to see its decline? Similarly, the film's celebration of youthful love is balanced by its being an autumnal piece, shot through with the mourning shared by Viola and Olivia in the opening scenes. The knowingness of *Twelfth Night*'s nostalgia for youth and for rising empire betrays the inevitable failure attending upon Branagh's attempts in *Love's Labour's Lost* to recapture British dominance in the Shakespeare-on-film industry. *Twelfth Night* displays a realization that a temporal reversion does not really forestall the long, slow slide into being second rate.

I think it is not accidental that the new British Shakespeare minstrelsy is best demonstrated in the genre of film comedy. Not only are minstrelsy and comedy historically connected, but for the last several hundred years Shakespearean comedy has shared the status ascribed to the races represented in minstrel practice: secondary, lesser. This secondary status has extended to Shakespeare on film, where the most acclaimed productions have been either tragedies, or the anomalous *Henry V*. To film a Shakespearean comedy is to know that one's production, despite its high-culture imprimatur, will never be designated "great," that it will never be taken seriously (Jackson 1994: 99). The last pre-credit moments of *Twelfth Night* – where Feste, alone on the headlands overlooking the sea, sings, cavorts, and repeats that "we'll strive to please you every day" – act out the recognition that to please is to serve, and to serve the Shakespeare mass market is to speak in a language that non-Britons can understand, even if it is a debased language or non-language of comedy and pantomime.

Hence the weird desperation of this scene, as Kingsley, so very focused, thoughtful, and serious in most of his performance in this film, laughs in an unmotivated and even slightly psychotic fashion. An actor whose stage and film roles have looked like a picture gallery of villainy, ethnicity, and sometimes ethnic villainy – from Othello (Royal Shakespeare Company, 1985) to Gandhi; from the saintly Jewish accountant Itzhak Stern in *Schindler's List* (1993) to the icy Jewish gangster Meyer Lansky in *Bugsy* (1991); from the sadistic South American Dr. Miranda in *Death and the Maiden* (1994) to Satan in *Tuck Everlasting* (2002) – Kingsley, the best speaker of Shakespearean verse in the illustrious cast of *Twelfth Night*, swears repeatedly in this scene to please us every day, as if he knows his next Oscar nomination will be for another stereotypical British villain's part. In his role as the absurdly pumped-up, crazily enraged criminal Don Logan in *Sexy Beast* (2001), Kingsley takes part in another permutation of British minstrelsy: the nouveau British gangster film. This genre begins to answer, in a way that may be horrifying to Shakespeareans, this question: if even British cinema has given up on Shakespearean dialogue, what kind of script does it substitute instead? The answer has to do with a post-postcolonial interdependency of filmic influence. New British gangster films like *Lock, Stock and Two Smoking Barrels* (1998), *Love, Honour and Obey* (2000), *Snatch* (2000), *Sexy Beast*, and *Gangster No. 1* (2002) translate Quentin Tarantino's hip, rap-influenced dialogue in *Reservoir Dogs* (1992) and *Pulp Fiction* into British regional accents, usually Cockney ones like Don Logan's. This language, as Kingsley delivers it in *Sexy Beast*, takes on an extraordinary nonsensical lyricism that, in the context of the film's generic derivativeness, ultimately connects it to the rat-a-tat-tat ethnic-character dialogue of 1930s gangster films (Winokur 1996: 139) – the very films that, in the same era in which *Love's Labour's Lost* is set, were blamed for undermining traditional English values (Taylor 2000: 164–5). Despite the character's "Englishness," Kingsley's Don Logan speaks a language that voices the history of an ethnically accented American popular entertainment. In the process Kingsley both perfects the "muscular and exuberant" style that launched American Edwin Forrest upon his Shakespearean triumphs, and joins in the remaking of British film as a new kind of minstrel show, one that, for better or worse, is far more likely than Shakespeare to please us every day.

Notes

This essay is indebted to the scholarship and comments of Mark Winokur, as well as to the timely suggestions of Adélékè Adéèkó, Richard Burt, Tom Riis, John-Michael Rivera, Charlotte Sussman, and the members of Samuel Crowl's 2002 Shakespeare Association of America seminar on Shakespearean comedy on film, particularly John Ford.

1 See Lawrence W. Levine, who argues that the nineteenth century saw the gradual conversion of Shakespeare "from a popular playwright whose dramas were the property of those who flocked to see them, into a sacred author who had to be protected from ignorant audiences and overbearing actors threatening the integrity of his creations" (1988: 72).

2 "Ich finde den Umgang mit Affen behlehrend. . . . Sie sind das ganz natürliche Tier, das dem Menschen zum Grunde liegt. Mazurier wußte es wohl; er spielte den Jocko wie Kean den Othello" (Chamisso 1964: 565; my translation).

3 While blackface minstrel shows rarely presented anything resembling "authentic" African-American music or dance, most white American audience members believed they did. Eric Lott (1993) notes a number of prominent nineteenth-century white American writers –

including Margaret Fuller, Mark Twain, and Walt Whitman – who regarded the minstrel depictions of African-American entertainment culture as accurate (15–20). A twist on my point that American audiences viewed Shakespeare performances through eyes trained by minstrelsy is the fact that minstrel shows often adapted or cited Shakespeare; see Browne (1960), Collins (1996), and MacDonald (1994).

4 In a forthcoming essay, Peter Christensen notes that *Love's Labour's Lost*'s score "is dominated by six songs written for five of the ten (nine at RKO) Astaire–Rogers musicals: 'No Strings,' 'Cheek to Cheek,' and 'Let's Face the Music and Dance' by Irving Berlin; 'I Won't Dance' and 'The Way You Look Tonight' by Jerome Kern; and 'They Can't Take That Away from Me' by the Gershwins." The remaining four songs in the film are "I'd Rather Charleston," from the 1926 version of the Gershwin stage musical "Lady, Be Good!" starring Fred and Adele Astaire; "I Get a Kick out of You," an Ethel Merman number in the Cole Porter stage and film musical *Anything Goes*; "I've Got a Crush on You," originally written by the Gershwins for Gertrude Lawrence in the stage musical *Treasure Girl* and used in many different stage and film musicals thereafter; and "There's No Business Like Show Business," the Ethel Merman signature number from Berlin's *Annie Get Your Gun*. (Peter Christensen, "*Love's Labour's Lost*: Branagh's Revitalization of the Fairy Tale Musical," forthcoming in *Shakespeare and Renaissance Association of West Virginia Selected Papers*. I am grateful to Professor Christensen for permitting me to cite his essay before publication.)

5 Astaire's first film appearance was in *Flying Down to Rio* (1933), in which he and Ginger Rogers partnered in the feature dance number "The Carioca," which became an enormous hit and propelled them toward their starring roles in later films. Astaire also dances a "wild man" solo tap number that is indebted to African-American dance in ways I discuss later in this essay.

6 See, for example, *Moulin Rouge* (2001) and *Hedwig and the Angry Inch* (2001), films that became darlings of, respectively, mainstream and independent-film awards nominations in 2002. Woody Allen's *Everyone Says I Love You* (1996), which Branagh mentions as an inspiration for his work, is a similarly under-remarked precursor in this revival; see Anon. n.d.b.

7 Deborah Cartmell argues that Branagh's *Henry V* performs exactly this same kind of nationalistic revivification through militaristic nostalgia: "the fighting spirit of the British combined with the immortal lines of Shakespeare provide an ideal British export, a force to be reckoned with abroad" (2000: 107). Mark Thornton Burnett similarly sees *Love's Labour's Lost* as successfully forging a new future for Shakespeare on film, despite (and partly because of) its plethora of Hollywood homage (2002: 100–1).

8 To this list we might add that Branagh is retracing his own history of filming Shakespeare to rethink how far a filmmaker must go to make Shakespeare popular; see Douglas Lanier (2002a), who argues that *Love's Labour's Lost* reverts to the optimism for a truly populist Shakespeare that Branagh expressed in *Henry V*.

9 Lester was nominated for Britain's Olivier award for his 1993 performance as Anthony in Stephen Sondheim's *Sweeney Todd*, and won the Olivier for his 1996 performance as Bobby in Sondheim's *Company*.

10 Branagh has been romantically and/or maritally linked to his female co-stars in most of the pictures he has directed. He dated and then married Emma Thompson (with whom he co-starred in *Henry V*, *Dead Again*, *Peter's Friends*, and *Much Ado about Nothing*), dated Helena Bonham Carter (*Mary Shelley's Frankenstein*), and has been rumored to have dated Alicia Silverstone (*Love's Labour's Lost*). For the blending of the actor's personal and professional lives in the emerging Hollywood star system of the 1920s, see DeCordova 1990: 98–151.

11 While Washington's casting as *Much Ado*'s Don Pedro drew praise for being "color-blind," no one seems to have noticed that the villain is played by a man who is of one-quarter Asian and one-quarter Pacific Island descent. Thus Neil Taylor argues, for example, that the casting of Washington is "an attempt to move into a world where, if there are stereotypes, they are neither national nor racial" (2000: 271).

12 Branagh did initially film some of the dialogue from the Masque of the Muscovites; the deleted scene is included in the DVD version of the film. One hopes that he deleted it partly

because Adrian Lester in his dark, wooly "Muscovite" wig and beard looks like a racist caricature of a black man, a virtual stand-in for the Blackamoors that Branagh excises from Shakespeare's play.

13 *Cats* and *Sunset Boulevard* may be especially apt properties for transcultural adaptation; T.S. Eliot, author of *Old Possum's Book of Practical Cats*, is perhaps the most Anglophile of American writers, whereas the film *Sunset Blvd.* (1950), which traces the history of American film from the silent era through the 1950s, was directed by the Austrian-born Jewish Billy Wilder, and stars German-born Erich von Stroheim, along with American-born Gloria Swanson (née Svennson) and William Holden.

5

RACE-ING *OTHELLO*, RE-ENGENDERING WHITE-OUT, II

Barbara Hodgdon

For *Time*'s Lance Morrow, writing just the day before the O.J. Simpson verdict, "The easiest meaning of the trial is that we live in a golden age of high trash, an Elizabethan epoch of lowest-common-denominator, everything-is-entertainment daytime drama that in Judge Ito's courtroom composes, day by day, its masterpiece – its soap, Santa Monica Othello" (1995: 28). In the aftermath of its last episode, as that drama moved to other time slots and the talking cures began, one emerging cultural scenario began to resemble Maurice Dowling's 1834 *Othello Travestie, An Operatic Burlesque Burletta*, where, at the close, Desdemona rises from the murder bed to accuse Iago, who deters Othello from cutting his throat, and all heartily agree with Roderigo's "Let the past be all forgot" (Dowling 1834: 36). But, once tragedy had given way to a pulp-fiction horoscope of race, sex, celebrity, justice and injustice, there was no catharsis. Nor, in a nation demonstrating its deep divisions by symbolic action and by calls for equal treatment by law, for citizen oversight of the police, and for protection against domestic abuse, did communal forgetting seem possible. Over a year later, as the outcome of the Browns' and Goldmans' wrongful death civil suit brought a multi-million-dollar judgment against Simpson, the genre shifted once more. By taking the "uppity negro" down from the top, white America had composed another ending, exacting the perfect capitalist revenge.

What love had to do with it

Long before that judgment, however, Shakespeare's *Othello* had moved from high trash back to high culture and been reclaimed from its temporary sojourn as a media bite for Nicole's and O.J. 's story. Two months after Simpson's acquittal, Oliver Parker's film of *Othello*, starring Laurence Fishburne, Irène Jacob and Kenneth Branagh, opened in New York just in time for the 1995 Christmas season. Although Amy Taubin, whose review appeared (most aptly) next to that of *Father of the Bride, Part II*, found it "so incoherently directed . . . that it wasn't until hours after I left the theater that I thought of OJ" (Taubin 1995; see also Maslin 1995), in many respects Parker's film represents an ideal post-O.J. *Othello* which functions as a performative instrument of culture somewhat analogous to Simpson's civil trial. If the story of Nicole and O.J. was about what passes for love in the culture these days, the story of Desdemona and Othello, according to Parker, was about their "all-consuming love . . . which flies in the face of conventions of the time. I wanted," he remarked, "to reinvest the tragedy with passion and romance, because without romance there is no real tragedy" (Jones 1995; Parker quoted in Rafferty 1995: 127).

Anchored by Laurence Fishburne's Othello and Kenneth Branagh's Iago, Parker's film represents the first mainstream *Othello* to cast a black actor in the title role. Although Fishburne's Oscar-nominated performance as the abusive Ike Turner in *What's Love Got to Do With It*, Brian Gibson's 1993 film of Tina Turner's autobiography, *I, Tina*, makes an uncanny fit with O.J.'s history, he plays Othello precisely against such stereotypes of black masculinity and on his own terms – what he calls, in words reminiscent of those of O.J.'s defense lawyer Johnnie Cochran, "not playing it according to the white man" (Fishburne quoted in *USA Weekend*, January 5–7, 1996: 1). As Othello, Fishburne is a powerfully controlled, self-possessed figure, radiating a quiet, reserved dignity from a magnificent physical presence: his ownership of the role differs markedly from that of Olivier and distinguishes him from Branagh's reptilian Iago, whose leather outfit hints at a Theweleitian brown-shirt identity that the review discourse, which consistently coupled the film with Richard Loncraine's *Richard III* (1995) and compared Branagh's performance to that of Ian McKellen's neo-fascist Richard, confirmed (see, for instance, Bowman 1996; Corliss 1996). Most reviewers labeled Fishburne as a Shakespearean outsider, also faulting Desdemona, the French-speaking Swiss actor Irène Jacob, and the Venetian Doge (Gabrielle Ferzetti) for mangling verse rhythms. Fishburne's voice, which couples a soft African-American sound to vaguely exotic or "foreign" intonation patterns, not only disappointed critics' desire for the explosive raw blackness assumed by a racialized unconscious but also evoked national linguistic prejudices favoring Branagh's "native" British facility with Shakespeare, both of which furthered Iago's performative power (see, for example, Alleva 1996; Kauffman 1996).[1]

What race has to do with it is certainly up there on the screen in the film's opening shots, where a gondola containing a black man and a white woman plies a Venetian canal. Briefly, the man covers his face with a white mask, a gesture which not only glances at spectators' surveillance but also reads as an in-joke for an *Othello* in which a black star plays a "white" man. But looking, in this film as in any *Othello*, is more than Euro-sightseeing. Immediately, scenes shift rapidly through Desdemona's clandestine marriage; her furtive return to her father's house; the Duke's response to the Turks' invasion; Roderigo and Iago calling up Brabantio; and Othello and Desdemona before the Senate, including an illustrative flashback of Desdemona's fascination with Othello's travel tales. Of these, the marriage, shot in close-ups of faces and joined hands, seen through bars by Roderigo and glossed by Iago's words, connects race and sex through looking relations, signaling the film's strategy for asserting Iago's control over narrative and gaze that will eventually entrap Othello. Exactly what love (and sexual attraction) has to do with it, however, comes fully into view when, at a sumptuously Zeffirelli-esque banquet, Irène Jacob's Desdemona performs a graceful "Moorish" dance for Othello which concludes as she blows him a kiss – a discreet though definite invitation that yields to mid-shots of her dancing with Othello and then with Cassio, smiling up at each. As banquet gives way to bedchamber, Desdemona, fully dressed, poses before a white-curtained bed while, in calculated close-ups and mid-shots, Othello removes his boots and belt. Partly as a result of their shared dance, the two appear equally eager to consummate their marriage; backing away from Othello's steady advance, Desdemona teases him to come to her. But as the traveling camera cuts to a long shot over Othello's shoulder and then to a closer shot of Desdemona, she looks momentarily startled, even fearful, and because the camera never shows Othello's face, he remains unreadable. That interruptive cut not only opens up the space between them, turning their encounter into an attack, but, because the camera that follows Othello is not subjective but outside his experience, the sequence works to confirm a voyeuristic surveillance that also aligns with the spectator's gaze, already maligned by Roderigo and Iago.[2] Consequently, the ensuing mid-shots of Othello and Desdemona in the bed, showing her white breast and his black body, and a climactic emblematic shot of their two hands joined in close-up against white bed linens strewn with rose petals, feed a white male viewer's potentially racist, miscegenistic specular economy.

Whether perceived as a romantic-erotic love scene or, in one critic's view, as a "bed scene" backed by a "lyrical shlock-rock" soundtrack reminiscent of Zeffirelli's 1968 *Romeo and Juliet* (see Brantley 1996; Denby 1996), the film redirects both readings by intercutting Desdemona's and Othello's love-making with shots of a country couple making "the beast with two backs" in a rude wagon, under which Iago slithers to the despondent Roderigo; as he whispers that Desdemona loves Cassio, the film intercuts the previous image of Desdemona laughing up at Cassio as the pair dance. Juxtaposing the two spaces permits the one to bleed over into the other, serving, finally, less to mark the difference between "romance" and "sex" or between what occurs in each than to put fantasy, driven largely by Iago's language, to work. And because it also seems as though Iago may be putting a clandestine make on Roderigo, the overall impression of what Parker called "passion and romance" is overtly, repellently sexualized. On the basis of this sequence alone, the film earns its R-rating: "includes violence, partial nudity and sexual situations (under 17 requires accompanying parent or guardian)." Moreover, its racialized point of view appears to be licensed by Shakespeare's authority or, perhaps more appropriately, by Branagh's talent for turning Shakespeare's language into contemporary colloquial idiom.

If the film foregrounds exotic eroticism as the key to Desdemona's and Othello's relationship, that is hardly a neutral term, for its representation of erotic (or romantic) sexuality is consistently encompassed within "dirtied" looking relations, a strategy the later temptation sequence enhances, rewriting the pleasures and dangers of such looking and replacing one passionate couple with another. Iago's questioning takes place in conventionally masculine spaces, as he and Othello practice with long staves on the castle green and, later, in the armory, where Othello, loading a pistol, responds to Iago's seemingly off-handed remarks. As with the love scene, the sequence positions them apart and brings them together; this time, however, the voyeuristic viewing position is inside rather than outside the frame, occupied first by Iago and eventually by Othello himself. Initially, Othello controls Iago's moves, even to pointing his now-loaded gun at him ("By heaven, I'll know thy thought"), but as Iago's insinuations take hold, a series of conventional shot/reverse shot set-ups shifts that dynamic to turn Othello in on himself while simultaneously fracturing his subjectivity. That crisis becomes transparently obvious as voice plays with and against image in one particular series of shots. As Othello muses, "Yet how nature, erring from herself . . ." and Iago concurs with "Ay, there's the point," an extreme close-up of Iago's profile is matched by one of Othello's eyes, which keys a flashback cut-in of Desdemona laughing up at Cassio as they dance, Iago's words glossing both images. Then the shot widens slightly, bringing Iago's nose and lips in profile into the frame: although his lips move, there is no sound, as though the image Othello conjures up not only has replaced but exceeded language.

However transparently (and conventionally) this flashback technique registers the covert and overt control of one subjectivity through another, and however much they are marked as Iago's projections, the line between the projected and the real is consciously and consistently blurred. Not only does Fishburne slip between an Othello-self and one whose imaginary takes on Iago-like contours, but Parker himself seems to be listening to an inner Iago, for his repeated cut-ins of remembered scenes resemble Branagh's *Henry V* (1989), which resorts to sentimental flashbacks of Falstaff in order to flesh out Hal's youthful tavern past. And however clearly marked as generated by Othello, because they are also what viewers see, they edge toward ocular proof, disabling the trope of "men should be what they seem." Following this sequence, which positions Othello and Iago as bound subjects, Othello fabricates his own visual evidence. Nude to the waist, he approaches the white-curtained bed and parts its curtains with a knife to see Desdemona and Cassio naked in the bed. He closes his eyes against the sight ("My life upon her faith"), and the next shot repeats the image of his and Desdemona's clasped hands on the sheet ("if she be false, then heaven mocks itself, I'll not believe it"), which yields to an inset flashback of Brabantio ("Look to her, Moor, if thou hast eyes to see. She has deceived her father and may thee."). As though deliberately sending up the perennial time problem of *Othello*'s narrative, at this point the film shifts into "real" time to reveal that Othello has generated this scenario while in bed beside Desdemona. Rising, he wraps himself in a white sheet and leaves the castle, observed through a doorway by Iago. A later fantasy, which brings on his epileptic fit and is cued by Iago's "lie with her, on her . . .," unfolds as a montage of soft-porn images of Desdemona and Cassio, their tongues and limbs intertwined, their hands caressing each other's thighs and legs. And this time, signaling that Iago's "ocular proofs" have become rooted in Othello's psyche, Othello and Iago cut their palms with a dagger, sealing their vow in a bloody handclasp that replaces the previously repeated close-up of Desdemona's and Othello's hands against the flower-strewn wedding sheets. Avoiding any suggestion of a homosexual coupling in favor of stressing the military code of honor that demands the deaths of Cassio and Desdemona, Parker's *Othello* (like the Simpson trial) is one in which justice becomes the provenance of men.

This repetitive imaging of Desdemona's body or, more precisely, her body parts, makes her an especially contradictory ground for engendering fantasy. Throughout, she is doubly represented, doubly seen: one face is that of the forthrightly confident woman who speaks before the senators, tries to soothe her angry father and pleads Cassio's case to Othello; the other shows her open smile transformed by Othello's licentious imaginings, scripted by Iago. The film uses (and uses up) her body to feed those fantasies, forcing her into the place assigned her by male desire and especially suited to *Othello*'s scopic economy (see Hodgdon 1990). Just as the tabloid press put Nicole's body on show in verbal and pictorial images stressing her sexual agency and attempting to implicate her in her own death, a similar figuration of Desdemona's sexual agency is keyed by the film's poster image, a close-up of Desdemona and Othello which shows her nuzzling Othello's ear. Fascinatingly contradictory, it not only appears to be colorblind (the warm skin tones of both faces erase color distinctions) but also, by making Desdemona active and Othello passive, creates a disturbing dissonance between the two.

Even more significant, however, is the displacement at work here, for showing Desdemona whispering into Othello's ear (his eyes are half open, hers are shut) aligns her perversely with Iago. As a teaser for Parker's R-rated trope of "all-consuming love," it is of a piece with his penchant for reducing *Othello* to a series of emblematic illustrations, which underline familiar snippets of text. Because many of these are associated with Iago ("green-eyed monster," "beware, my lord, of jealousy"), the strategy enhances his control of the cinematic apparatus and its ability to objectify and blame women – even, as the poster image of "Adam and Evil" suggests, to re-mark them with his own actions and desires, turning them into substitutes of himself. Or, as when Iago finally arrives at the ideal means of exploiting Desdemona and "turn[ing] her virtue into pitch," he grabs a smoldering log from the fire and rubs soot over his hands, deliberately injuring himself before putting his hand over the camera to block out the lens. Less a means of keeping viewers from looking at him than a way of controlling what they see, his gesture knowingly marks him as the film's "true" author, in control of both Shakespeare's text and the camera, capable of making his own cinematic transitions, of fading out of and into the frame, even popping up (as he does in the ensuing conversation with Roderigo) like a jack-in-the-box. Later, in his own "bed scene," when Emilia brings him the handkerchief, he rolls on top of her, brutally and quickly invades her body, retrieves the handkerchief, inhales its scent and throws it up in the air, where, against a black background, it falls slowly down, a "trifle lighter than air" – this *Othello*'s analogue for the Simpson trial's infamous "planted" glove.

Such fugitive, phantom connections between O.J.'s and Othello's history, of course, fade away in the film's final narrative moves. After all, one consequence of the shift from high trash to high tragedy is that, whereas the close of Simpson's trial canonized him in the court of public opinion, canonical Shakespeare decrees that the ideal black male figure Fishburne has created – the one that "plays against the white man's rules" for the role – must murder and then kill himself. For Fishburne's Othello, Desdemona's murder is an intensely private ritual. Dressed all in black, he blows out the lamps lining the corridor to her bedchamber and, exhorting her to pray, pours water into a golden basin held between his knees, dipping his hands in it and moving them over his tattooed scalp, his eyebrows and face, as though purifying his body for the deed. Although Desdemona struggles and resists her assailant, her "Nobody, I myself" is not spoken: when Emilia discovers her death and closes her eyes, Othello immediately confesses, depriving her of the agency which, elsewhere, the film's representational strategies had implied. About to be arrested, Othello shrugs free of the officers' grasp and, encircling his neck with a cord, stabs himself in the gut, crawls to the bed to kiss Desdemona and fall beside her, his body and Emilia's framing hers to provide an overt illustration of Iago's own primal scene.

Although this is not the film's final image,[3] it is the one that reroutes the experience of the play to align Parker's *Othello* with the theatricalization marking the Simpson trial and its fabulation in the press, implicating it in the politics of cultural signification (see Blau 1992: 68). Much as the Holocaust has altered the meanings of Shakespeare's *The Merchant of Venice*, the Simpson trial, at least for a while, has made *Othello* perhaps the timeliest of Shakespeare's plays for late twentieth-century America. Moreover, Parker's film is the perfect post-O.J. *Othello*, at least for a white America, precisely because, in Terrence Rafferty's phrase, it is "hopelessly Iago-centric" (1995: 127). For in spite of Parker's desire to reroute the experience of the play away from the constructed paths of the racial unconscious and toward "all-consuming love . . . passion and romance," what emerges offers evidence of the persistent tensions between race and sex uppermost in American culture that led, in John Taylor's words, to the "triumph of murder as an American performance art" (1994: 82). If the image of the "loaded bed" is what marks the limits of *Othello*-as-entertainment, the point at which spectators chastise themselves for sharing Iago's voyeuristic pleasure, Parker's film represents that bed, to which Iago crawls, curling his body into the tableau as its "director," if not its author, as his ultimate artistic creation, the conclusive "ocular proof" of the perversely racialized, misogynistic imaginary that split a nation that thought itself united into two. During the early days of Simpson's trial, Johnnie Cochran was quoted as saying, "Give me one black man on that jury"; tracing the shifting boundaries between filmed Shakespeare and other performative instruments of culture, however, gives him the lie. All that was necessary, in order to reinscribe the white (re)production of black men back onto America's troubled national imaginary, was one white man – uncannily enough, an English Iago capable of reasserting the terms by which whiteness can triumph over blackness, even in the crucible of a public discourse over a racially mixed bed that desires it otherwise.

Making it real: white backlash

Much like the topical connections surrounding original Shakespearean performances, the links between *Othello* and the O.J. narrative have faded (though not entirely disappeared): old news, after all, ceases to command attention in a Warhol world of fifteen-minute fame. But the questions those connections raised concerning the ideological and symbolic intertwining of race and power as well as a growing white paranoia continue to energize public debates. Nearly a decade later, two *Othello*-dramas – one British, one American; each belonging to very different genres – serve not only as litmus tests of the width and depth of the racial divide in each society but also suggest the highly visible as well as phantasmic forms that race-consciousness assumes in different cultural landscapes. Taking *Othello* into a territory where high tragedy travels towards realistic drama, each reshapes the narrative through a particularized cultural context, re-invents characters' motivations, conveys Shakespeare's language in contemporary idiom, and attempts to iron out flaws in believability that, since the days of Thomas Rhymer, have troubled spectators and critics alike. Perhaps most significantly, each creates a space for a counter-narrative that offers to contest, though not erase, the racist conventions of performance that haunt most *Othello*s (see Gates 1995: 57).

Of the two, *Othello*, a 2001 ITV production, uses Shakespeare's plot to interrogate the explosively racialized politics surrounding the history of Stephen Lawrence, a black teenager brutally beaten and murdered by racist thugs at a bus stop in Eltham, southeast London, in 1993. The original investigation was bungled, and none of the five white men widely suspected (and publicly accused) were convicted; an official inquiry (prompting resignations high up within the Metropolitan Police) accused the police of institutionalized racism and violence in what became an ongoing national scandal reminiscent of that following America's equally infamous Rodney King case in 1992 (see Gooding-Williams 1993). Despite immense efforts by the police to clean up their image, it was seven years before the Lawrence family was able to present a civil case against those suspected of murdering their son, but this collapsed and no one has been convicted. In 1999, ITV aired *The Murder of Stephen Lawrence*, an award-winning docu-drama starring, among others, Hugh Quarshie, an actor who has spoken publicly about colorblind casting as well as the role of Othello, as Neville Lawrence, Stephen's father (Quarshie 1999). In an interview, Andrew Davies, *Othello*'s scriptwriter, speaks of how the Lawrence case gave him the idea of making his John Othello the first black commissioner of the London Metropolitan Police, thereby also mounting a tangential critique of Tony Blair's (or any government's) cynical administrative strategies, especially in making bold political gestures that will play well in the media.[4] As with Shakespeare's Venetian Doges, who need Othello to protect their property and reputation, Davies's Othello is a token designed to enhance government's image – a black man put in the right place at the right time to do the state some service. And if British viewers hardly needed reminding of connections between the Lawrence case and Davies's *Othello* – a memorial at the Eltham bus stop had been vandalized in 1998 – that intersection was driven home for American viewers by PBS's decision to air *The Murder of Stephen Lawrence* just the week before *Othello*, both on Masterpiece Theater, January 21 and January 28, 2002, respectively.

Interweaving features of Shakespeare's plot with a parallel story of an incident in which police officers beat and kill Billy Coates, a black man, Davies fashions a double narrative – half Shakespeare, half police procedural – that resituates Othello's story within a racially saturated field of visibility. Seen in a brief sequence filmed with a hand-held camera to mimic "on the scene" footage, Coates's beating at first seems designed simply to draw John Othello (Eamonn Walker) away from an officers' banquet, but by the time he arrives at the scene, Coates has died in hospital and TV crews are filming a full-scale riot in the black community. Striding through smoke from an explosion to stand on the raised steps, he confronts and quiets the outraged crowd (an uncanny echo of Henry Fonda's Lincoln in John Ford's *Young Mister Lincoln* [1939], who gradually calms an angry lynch mob about to storm a county courthouse), promising them that if Coates was unlawfully killed he will find the killers and give his brothers and sisters "justice under the law." After the forced resignation of the former (white) commissioner (exposed in the tabloids for making a racial slur), Othello, appointed in his place over his mentor, Ben Jago (Iago, Christopher Eccleston), announces his policy ("zero tolerance for racism, zero tolerance for misconduct") to senior officers and, privately, to Jago: "If they think it's all right to beat a man to death they don't belong in the Met: they belong in prison because they're violent animals."

Initially, then, the film represents Othello, not as a black man who offers a pretext for racism but as one responding to racism within his own professional institution. Yet once the trial of the police officers for Coates's murder is dismissed and Othello fails to get justice, the film fails to articulate why he isn't immediately dismissed or doesn't offer to resign (instead, it's Jago who makes that offer): like the issue of whether or not he loses credibility within the black community, that question gets erased, subsumed into Shakespeare's final narrative moves. Indeed, even as the investigation into Coates's killing begins, Othello becomes a shadowed presence, seen behind a one-way window while Jago interrogates the officers (as he puts it, "You play with your wife's tits while I do your work for you"), all of whom parrot the same phrases, claiming that Coates went for his knife ("he went mad, sir – ape shit"; "I was in genuine fear for my life") and that they used only approved methods of restraint. Finally, the youngest, Roderick (Roderigo, Del Synott), tearfully admits that what set off the beating was Coates waving his penis and asking the officers, "Hey bitches, you come to get some?" Recalling the repeated references to Rodney King's "ass" in the LA policemen's testimony, Judith Butler writes: "There is within the white male's racist fear of the black male body a clear anxiety over the possibility of sexual exchange"; doubly dangerous, the black body presents not just the threat of sodomy but the fear that in crossing a physical distance, whiteness will be endangered, sullied, by that proximity (1993: 18). Perhaps most disturbingly, Othello himself will become like the officers who beat Coates when, attacking Michael Cass (Cassio, Richard Coyle) in a parking garage, he not only does precisely what the police did but turns himself into the familiar cliché figure of the violent black man assaulting, first, a white man and then, as Shakespeare's plot demands, a white woman.

But this *Othello* does not begin as a police procedural or an indictment of racial discrimination. Rather, it opens on an extreme close-up of a closed eye, its lids flickering; cutting to another extreme close-up of lips moving, though with no discernible sound, the film establishes sight and sound as grounded in Desdemona's/Dessie's (Keeley Hawes) body and as rhetorical tropes that drive a narrative in which both are called into question. For a viewer who knows *Othello*, it might seem that the film begins with its ending, especially as the next shot is an extreme close-up of Othello's eyes, followed by a close-up of his hand covering Dessie's, black on white. But then, as though coming to life, she opens her eyes to see Othello smiling down at her and, as the camera pulls back, she rises into his arms. A scene of double watching that connects Othello's look with that of viewers, it is then interpreted through voice-over (later revealed as Jago): "It was about love – not race, not politics, but love: as simple as that. She loved him as well as she knew how; he loved her more than a man should love a woman. Tragedy, right? No other word for it." Now seen in a limousine, Jago speaks directly to the camera, "I loved him, too, you know." With extreme economy, the film sets up the question of negotiating between what is seen – and heard – and a reading imposed on that visual evidence.

Voice-over, of course, constitutes cinema's most authoritative speaking position, but the sneering, slightly nasty tone of this narration turns its speaker into a caricature of credibility. Unlike the attractively manipulative Iagos of Branagh or Ian McKellen, Jago's solicitations of viewers are consistently over the top, his tabloid-reporter consciousness cheapens everything; like ex-Commissioner Sinclair Carver (Bill Paterson), who remarks that black officers lack "brains as big as their pricks," he is – if only to the viewer – overtly racist. A fiercely envious (as well as jealous) loner, he's a control freak, especially in his dealings with women: his relationship with Lulu (Rachael Stirling) appears driven by attempting to emulate Othello (as she says, "Your mate got himself a posh girl, so you thought you'd get one too") and by a misogynous imagination that covers contradictory homoerotic desire. And because the film is composed of short, often jagged sequences (thus pushing theatrical conventions towards TV drama), Jago's voice-overs occur frequently enough to bridge between segments detailing two investigative procedures – the one aimed at discovering the "truth" about Coates's killing, the other constructing a tissue of lies – to suggest, somewhat disturbingly, that the film, by privileging his in-your-face address, conspires with Jago. Throughout, Jago undercuts both Dessie and Othello. He mocks, in a close-up of his mouth, Dessie's voice ("I feel so safe with him"); watching the pair at the Prime Minister's reception, he sneers, "How easily he slides into the way of it." After Othello appoints him second in command, a series of frantic, hand-held shots shows Jago addressing the camera ("stupid patronizing ape, token nigger") and then breaking off ("Well, well, what a passionate performance"), acutely marking his hysterical response to a perceived lack of identity, to being passed over, displaced. Much later, in shots intercut with Dessie and Othello making love, he accesses a White Bunker chat room, sending off a message (imaged in fragments – "jungle bunny . . . commissioner . . . white tart . . . wife") that leads to neo-Nazi thugs threatening Dessie, prompting Othello to insist that she have police protection and so bringing Cass into Jago's scenario.

When with Othello, Dessie repeatedly is seen – and voiced – as a sex object; early on, she appears dressed in a white satin nightgown, an indolent, body-obsessed houri who rises to embrace Othello ("I think about you all the time; I don't know what to do with myself when you're not here"). When with Cass, however, Dessie not only is marked as active (she jogs competitively) but as a professional interviewer and writer about the arts, an interest Cass shares. And since the pair play – and talk – well together, it is even possible to imagine a relationship between them. Dessie's words to Othello – "I was like a blank sheet waiting for you to write your name on me" – aptly describe her shadow function in a narrative where, consistently, it is men who shape her identity and articulate her past – her father, Othello, and Jago, who falsely constructs her "wild" sexuality and projects it into the present. Reduced to a cipher, a sign of "woman," she herself is framed as a fetish, much like the golden silk dressing gown, her gift to Othello and the film's substitute for the handkerchief, which figures in their love-making, so when Othello finds Cass wearing it, his immediate, hysterical conclusion is that Cass also has replaced him in bed.

"I loved him too, you know": Jago's opening words well might be spoken by any number of Shakespearean characters who move from adolescent male bonds to bonding with women. Whereas that move is not at issue in Shakespeare's *Othello*, it is in this remake, for neither Othello nor Jago are shown as capable of negotiating the liminal territories between homosocial, homoerotic, and heterosexual bonds. Jago plays with women, using Lulu and Dessie to his advantage: ultimately, manipulating both serves to advance his own career path; Othello, on the other hand, seems sexually obsessed as well as sexually naïve, his fragile masculinity haunted – even in possession. Confessing his fear of losing Dessie ("I wake so I can watch her . . . dream – am I in them? I watch her eyelids tremble, her mouth whisper, feeling that I'm at her mercy"), Othello puts himself at the mercy of Jago's intimations ("Who knows what's going on in their heads – they like it more than we think they do") and machinations; and as the camera pushes in to capture Othello and Jago in close-up, Othello vows that if he thought Dessie and Cass were lovers, he'd kill them both. Indeed, the two men arguably turn into hysterics, much like the heroes of Vincente Minelli's *The Cobweb* (1955), Elia Kazan's *East of Eden* (1955) and Douglas Sirk's *Written on the Wind* (1956) – domestic melodramas in which oedipal themes predominate and where plot patterning makes the heroes consistently look inwards, at each other or at themselves, often resulting in outbursts of inner violence, which the characters turn against themselves. In that they reproduce cultural patterns of domination and exploitation, such narratives are vehicles for diagnosing characters in ideological terms by presenting them as victims of external forces, thus placing questions of "evil" or/and responsibility on a social and existential level (see Elsaesser 1987: 55–6, 64; Rodowick: 1987, 276–7). A genre that arose in response to and aligned with post-war threats to political and ideological stability, the so-called male weepie is ideally suited to interrogate this *Othello*, shot through with the phenomena of white paranoia and social betrayal – the fear that white men are losing their places because black men are "taking over," usurping what rightfully belongs to whites. And although *Othello* tries to maintain a plausible, believable "reality TV effect," the two characters' hysterical excess overwhelms and stands in jarring contrast, producing a somewhat schizoid film.

It is, of course, Othello's own excess which fuels the narrative's final moves. At dinner with Dessie, Jago and Lulu, Othello recounts his history – a slavery narrative of his grandmother and old Joshua, who (like Caliban) "could show you every inch of the isle where my family worked and died"; speaking of how, after coming to England, his people got "leftovers, other men's leavings," he confesses, to his shame, that he wanted to be white. When Cass interrupts ("Someone's been telling lies, sir"), an outraged Othello attacks him verbally but lunges at Dessie; pulled off by Jago, the two men embrace. Later, alone with Dessie, Othello not only turns her into a slave ("Who else had you?") but also, by accusing her of being damaged goods, into just another "leftover" ("Let's palm her off on the black man; nobody else will have her"). After a frightened Dessie leaves, he throws himself on their bed, crawling across it like an animal, smelling the sheets, his excess capped by a fantasy sequence where a superimposed image of Cass reaches out towards him from Dessie's computer screen, a double displacement in which Othello himself is both replaced and feminized. Even Dessie's murder – in Othello's mind, revenge for feminine betrayal ("You were never mine – always with someone else in your dreams"; "Look at her, she's asleep – no one would guess what a whore she was") – yields, after Jago's revelation of her innocence, to an exchange of close-ups – and declarations of love – between the two men, marking the conclusion of their love story. As though suddenly remembering Dessie (or Shakespeare), the film then repeats its opening shots – extreme close-ups of Dessie's and Othello's clasped hands, Othello's eyes, Dessie's mouth – before shots of Othello holding a gun, the "loaded bed," and a close-up kiss yield, at an off-screen gunshot, to Jago's face.

Cued by the Prime Minister's responses ("Too soon . . . woman trouble . . . bloody shame . . . great experiment, best to turn it over to a safe pair of hands"), the finale shows what "safe" means, exposes restoring order as putting (another) white racist in charge of the Met. Taking his rightful place after the "big black bastard" has been erased from the picture seen earlier of Othello posing for an official photograph as commissioner, Jago walks into the final shot to adopt a similar pose, wearing the same dress uniform, holding the same white-plumed hat, his voice-over repeating his opening words ("It was love – simple as that. Don't talk to me about race, don't talk to me about politics"). Then, as the camera pushes in to a close-up on "It was love," yet another "truth" comes (literally) to light – in this as in all *Othello*s, a loaded term. Disappearing in a blur of white-out, Jago's fading image foregrounds whiteness as the invisible dynamic of cultural production and interrelation, the normalized center – the "everything," the connection to masculinity as well as to power – against which its others are delineated. Simultaneously, of course, whiteness, as Richard Dyer writes, is nothing, for "its power lies, in part, in its ability not to name or admit its particularity, and thus its limits" (1992: 142).

According to the film's website plot synopsis, "Shakespeare's classic tale of jealousy, love and obsession enters the millennium." Yet the "millennium" it addresses seems much more like a repetition compulsion or memory of the past than a symptom of present-day hopes, shared by British and American culture alike, for an equitable future of race (and gender) relations – or for their representation in the media. Yet if this *Othello* takes an ambiguous, conflicted, and contradictory attitude towards both race and gender, perhaps, given Jago's denial that love has anything to do with either race or politics, that's all it can do. Certainly deflecting the question has been a perennially successful debating strategy even (or especially) when, as here, it results in white blindness – call it cultural protectionism.

Hoop dreaming

"Trust. Seduction. Betrayal." The tag lines for Tim Blake Nelson's *O* (2001) might as easily describe Parker's or Davies's *Othellos* or, for that matter, any subsequent performance of the play. But this is not your father's – or mother's – *Othello* for, although *O* remains almost slavishly close to Shakespeare's narrative, Brad Kaaya's script, which draws on his own experience of being black in an almost all-white private school and his memories of being allowed into a world from which others like him were excluded (Anon. 2001: 22), substitutes a verbal register that produces a highly intelligent "tradaptation" (Garneau 1989: 7–8), an upscale *Classic Comics Othello* that pulls in three popular niche markets: teen films, sports, and Shakespeare.[5] And, as with any Shakespearean update – for instance, Baz Luhrmann's *William Shakespeare's Romeo + Juliet* (1996) – much depends on location, location, location: in this case, the highly charged ante-bellum setting of Palmetto Grove Academy, a South Carolina prep school where the Othello figure is a star ringer imported to give the school's basketball team a championship season. Like Luhrmann's *Romeo + Juliet*, *O* addresses a number of hot issues: teenage sex, interracial relationships, parents' limited control, and boys with guns; but despite its similar reliance on equally hot teenage stars (Julia Stiles as Desi Brable/Desdemona, Josh Hartnett as Hugo/Iago, Mekhi Pfifer as Odin/Othello), Nelson's film reinvents a genre that came to prominence with *Clueless* (dir. Amy Heckerling, 1995), and, throughout the 1990s, spawned releases ranging from *Romeo + Juliet*'s flash and flamboyance to Gil Junger's *10 Things I Hate About You* (1999), and Michael Almereyda's *Hamlet* (2000).

Anxious to avoid yet another "teening down" of the classics, Nelson was determined not to pander to the usual clichés circulating in such films – that all young adults care about are dating, proms, and who's wearing what. One measure of his success comes from Amy Taubin, who, in not only faulting *O*'s actors for exhibiting "a composure and attention span out of keeping with teenage behavior" but by accusing the film of "so badly blurring the distinction between adolescents and grown-ups that it could be used to make the case for treating minors as adults within the criminal justice system" (2001: 80), marks (however negatively) its sophisticated attitude towards young adults, its refusal to condescend. To its credit, *O* represents the secondary-school milieu as a crisis culture where adolescents define their relation to the world through performances of maturity, a microcosm of a larger culture that idolizes sports heroes and is shot through with violence. As Nelson writes, "What makes *O* credible in executing the considerable leap from war and statecraft to basketball and high school is the reality that this specifically adolescent combination has lately resulted in the American phenomenon of teenagers killing teenagers." Moreover, he notes that although commentators attribute teenage violence to national pathologies such as alienation or anomie, "the classmates of the killers in these incidents have mentioned ostracism, a love triangle, friction at home: each time, the impulse to kill was personal" (2002: 8, 15). Indeed, an epidemic of shootings in Jonesboro, Pearl, Eugene, Springfield, and Edinboro during the year or so leading up to photography made an uncanny match with the film's represented events (*O* Press Kit 2001: 7). Almost too uncanny: notoriously, *O* was held from distribution by Miramax in the wake of the Columbine shootings (April 20, 1999, less than two weeks into the final edit), which provoked Washington legislators to call on Hollywood to police itself. Though films with similar target audiences contained far more violence, one difference, writes Nelson, was that *O* was *real* (Nelson 2001: 15) – and, I might add, quintessentially *American*.[6]

O's poster isolates Pfifer's O, wearing a jersey which stresses his physique and holding a basketball hoop, his signature and trophy, high above his head; posing him at bottom center against an inner-city landscape, the image fixes him as a black athlete rising above his origins. Flanking him, above, the faces of Julia Stiles and Josh Hartnett, teen poster-stars, market the film's generational appeal to white spectators. Although they do not exchange gazes, their placement not only suggests a potential relationship between them but also hints that the film may tell a story other than that of *Othello*. Although that is not the case, both *O* and its poster-image do circulate traces of O.J. Simpson's story, signs of the space it continues to occupy in the American cultural imaginary. Even if one reads Odin James's name and his sports-star status simply as one-off in-jokes, the poster has another tangential connection to his history, recalling the doctored *Time* magazine cover (June 27, 1994) featuring a blacked-up mug shot of Simpson with the headline banner "An American Tragedy" that appeared as the story broke. Here, however, it is Stiles's image that is altered: giving her fuller lips, changing the set of her eyes, and darkening her complexion turns her into a mulatto-like figure – a re-marking that, as it turns out, does echo in the film. Yet, although the poster seems poised to address black and white spectators alike, it also reads as a near-blatant sign of how *O* loads the representational deck, relying on strategies that approach, even as they also work to overturn, familiar stereotypes.

However inaccurate, stereotypes serve, bell hooks argues, as substitutions, stand-ins for what is real; rather than "tell[ing] it like it is . . . they are a fantasy, a projection on the Other that makes them less threatening . . . a pretense that one knows when the steps that would make real knowing possible cannot be taken – are not allowed" (1997: 170). As it happens, *O* walks a wobbly line through this territory. Although it is minimally believable that Odin James might be the *only* black student in a present-day prep school (even one in the deep South), certainly the sense of him as an "extravagant and wheeling stranger" is made more radical by situating him among "similarly dressed scions of former slave-owning families" (*O* Press Kit 2001: 6). And despite the students' worship of O (he makes them look good by winning games), portraying him within such an ideological cinema-scape points to a somewhat unchallenged transmission of racial hierarchies that not only weakens resistance to their falsity but also strengthens their racialized legitimacy. Inevitably, too, other black bodies are cast as members of the opposing basketball team in the climactic playoff game, as cheerleaders for that team, as a drug dealer (to Hugo and O), and as a ball boy at the slam-dunk contest where, high on drugs himself, O loses his cool. Yet O also is hot-wired to other, arguably more positive stereotypes. He's a cocky, street-smart black bomber, a superstar Michael

Jordan or Magic Johnson clone warring on a prep-school court: at the center of the film's sports spectacles, watched by all eyes, he's the Most Valuable Player with special prowess, flash and style, able to fly like a dark hawk – the team mascot associated with him and also with Hugo.

Here, too, race is sound, which operates in several ways, juxtaposing high to mass culture entertainment and white noise to black – even conflating the two. At the level of spoken language, Kaaya's script naturalizes "blackspeak" – 'hood idioms such as "homey" and "Yo" – to the white students, but this is less obvious in the finished film; indeed, when O says Desi can't call him "nigger" (despite her claim that her people coined the word), the film offers a mini-lesson on identity politics, on who can say what to whom. But it is in its soundtrack where *O*'s aural play becomes most complex. Combining modern orchestration for strings with Elizabethan instruments, Jeff Danna's score deliberately refers to the story's antecedents, signaled first by *O*'s stunning opening, where the "Ave Maria" from Verdi's *Otello*, sung by the boys choir from the Paris Opera, plays softly behind an image of white shapes surrounding an oriel window that resolve into doves, grounding the visual both in the hero's name and in a somewhat clichéd emblem of purity and sanctity. Led by Hugo's voice-over ("All my life I always wanted to fly like a hawk"), the camera pans a hawk's soaring flight (are the doves its prey?) across a basketball court; then, as O's face appears in close-up, Roscoe's "Ridddaz" cuts in, establishing rap – raced black, aggressively subversive of white culture – as *O*'s dominant sound.[7] Arguably, its dialogic, rhythmic linguistic structure functions as a verbal substitute for Shakespeare, but it also works to displace the questions of power, racism, and class it verbalizes away from "character" and into sound (see Rose 1989: 37–8). And since rap also is popular with white adolescents – part of a wider trend of experimenting with performing other (potentially transgressive) identities – it is perfectly at home in the genre and in this particular film, for by making a noise that isn't "white," it adds an aurally racialized layer to issues that *O* plays out, whether by commenting on the image or leading the action by interpreting images. If at times, as when it backs the basketball games or scenes between O and Desi, the black beat signifies black heat, it also plays behind Mike Casio's (Cassio, Andrew Keegan) attack on Roger (Roderigo, Elden Henson), the first sign of an escalating violence, and, later, introduces Hugo's and O's conversation in the workout-room temptation sequence.

In its representation of basketball culture, *O* is all about the construction of manhood through socialization in sports, and that context intensifies the homosocial and homoerotic bonds locking O, Hugo, and Mike together as teammates – "boys," writes Nelson, "with the drive, stamina, and competitiveness of men" (*O* Press Kit 2001: 7). As in *Hoop Dreams* (dir. Steve James, 1994) and *White Men Can't Jump* (dir. Ron Shelton, 1992), films with which *O* shares topics and tropes, on the court – where Hugo's and Mike's ball-handling takes second place to O, the star player and slam-dunk genius who's got game – blackness rules. That also is the case off-court, for after O has made the winning play in the game with which the film opens, Coach Duke Goulding (Martin Sheen), Hugo's father, not only gives O the MVP award but, in a formal presentation before the entire student body, embraces him, announcing, "I love him like my own son." Just as Davies's *Othello* fleshes out Iago's notorious "motiveless malignity" by making professional displacement motivate Jago's plotting, *O*'s narrative is driven by the envy of a white boy who loses his place to a black man. Here, situating displacement in terms of a family dynamic that forces Hugo to rival O for his father's attention and admiration shifts not just its affective power but also, more significantly, its ideological charge. For one thing, because this scenario is about letting someone "other" into a family history, it touches on miscegenation, though less through the romantic narrative, where that issue becomes contradictory, than through the father–son story. For another, whereas in Davies's *Othello*, Jago's displacement works to critique racist behaviors, *O* attempts to separate race from envy or, perhaps more appropriately, to collapse one history into another – a move that (whether consciously or unconsciously) pretends to avoid such critique altogether.

Unlike Davies's Jago, Hugo's response to being overlooked and sidelined does not take on hysterical contours; rather, and especially in contrast to Branagh's and Eccleston's omniscient, over-the-top performances, Hartnett's is highly controlled – intelligent, cool, consistently compelling. Following all cinematic (and theatrical) Iagos, his is the dominant consciousness and the dominant desire: a dissembling hustler, he balances intense poise and stilled panic that the camera records, at several points, in extremely formal shots, pulling away to show him abandoned by his father or pushing in as, covering his face, he recognizes that his plot has gone too far. Rather than turning Hugo into a device for deluding spectators, *O* is as interested in his history as in his control over O;[8] indeed, the film does not manipulate his gaze repeatedly in order to subordinate O or turn him into an object. When that does happen, as in the hospital where O is taken after a fall knocks him out, Emily (Rain Phoenix) shares Hugo's envy, a slow pull-back capturing them watching Desi and O embrace from a distance. Earlier, too, when O and Desi lie together in the dorm room that Emily and Desi share, repeated cut-aways to Emily mark her desire to be like them.

Far from attempting to co-opt or Hollywood-ize ostensibly racial themes to capitalize on their perceived trendiness, *O* – or at least its characters – seem to desire to "be" black. Just as Hugo's initial voice-over reveals his obsession with wanting to fly like a hawk – that is, to be like O – blackness is something that Desi (her name a shorthand for desiring subject – or object) shares Hugo's wish for blackness or, perhaps more simply, she does not want to be O's "other." That desire first surfaces in her dorm room, with Black Star's lyrics – "Black people unite and let's all get down/We got to have what? We got to have that love" – underscoring their caresses and their conversation. But it becomes even more pointed in their tryst at The Willows motel (one of *O*'s few Shakespearean in-jokes[9]), where Desi's "I want you to have me however you want" not only suggests that sexuality – and its transgressive potential – are wedded to blackness but figures her desire to be "made black" by consuming O's body language. Arguably, *O* can be read as a (tragic) counter-clone of *Bye, Bye Birdie* (dir. George Sidney, 1963) in which O's ability to talk the talk and walk the (sexy) walk function as the equivalent of Conrad Birdie's pelvic grind (borrowed from Elvis who, in turn, borrowed it from black culture): singing "You've gotta be sincere – you've gotta feel it here", he not only wipes out an entire Ohio town but transforms the heroine's sense of herself, giving her access to sexual privilege that (in the 1960s) previously accrued only to males (see MacPherson 1997: 290–2).

More significantly, however, the motel sequence offers a staging of racial memory that re-performs the past in the present tense, for, in the white imaginary, the idea that black men rape white women constitutes and sustains the illusory basis for lynching. Playing into that fantasy, the scene becomes even more risky than, say, Othello's and

Desdemona's sexual encounter in Parker's film, in part because what I will call the "high tragedy barrier" has broken down or been erased by a situation that replicates " the real." Moreover, not only is the controlling point of view associated with O rather than with Desi but the sequence, articulated solely in terms of image and soundtrack, juxtaposes his seeing to her sound – precisely what she will lose when, later, his kiss turns into murder.[10] Following a highly erotic sequence of near-abstract extreme close-ups of body parts, her white skin against his blackness,[11] what began as consensual sex turns to date-rape or, in Taubin's apt term, to a "hate-fuck" (2001: 80), when, looking into the mirror, O sees, not himself, but Mike. Not only does the mirror shot image a fantasized homoerotic relation that suggests a floating sexuality, it also momentarily turns O into a white boy, a threat to his identity that he plays out in anger, despite her telling him to stop, on Desi's body. Matched to O's rhythmic thrusts, the pace of the music – Outkast's "Even the sun goes down . . . heroes eventually die . . . nothin' is for sure, nothin' is for certain, nothin' lasts forever" – intensifies towards his climax. As the scene concludes with close-ups of both, Desi's hand touching O's neck, the film cuts to the preening doves (her emblem as well as O's); ambiguous and troubling, the shot hints that she really liked it. Yet as the pair leave the motel the next morning and get into the car without speaking, a long shot clearly figures the distance that has opened between them. It is the last time they are seen together until, much later, O turns Desi's desire to have it his way back on her, accusing her of not being a virgin because she knew what she wanted. But the motel scene also echoes in another way when, at the slam-dunk contest, O "rapes" the backboard, shattering its glass backing before holding the hoop high over his head and, in a near-symbolic gesture that insists on his prowess and his identity, refuses to give up the ball to the (black) ball boy.

Here, and from this point forward, O becomes less and less articulate, his verbal language given over to body language as his character's primary signifier – at least until, after Desi's murder, he evokes the cliché of violent black masculinity only to overturn it in the film's substitute for Othello's Aleppo speech: "I ain't no different than y'all. My mother wasn't no crack head; I wasn't no gangbanger . . . it wasn't a hoodrat, drug dealer that tripped me up. It was this white, prep school mothafucka right here." Then, turning to Hugo, O looks dead into his eyes: "You tell 'em, where I came from didn't make me do this." More Hamlet than Othello, O turns his story over to an even more imperfect teller than Horatio or Lodovico just before shooting himself; freeze-framing the shot, the film sets his suicide apart from the other deaths, and a last glimpse of him shows his body spread out "like a bird fallen to the ground." As Verdi's "Ave Maria" keys in over a slow-motion sequence evoking familiar news footage – shots of the bodies, eye-witness reports, the suspect being put into the police car with TV cameramen running after – the film, obeying O's charge, gives Hugo its last words: "I always wanted to fly like a hawk . . . take flight . . . soar above everyone and everything . . . O was a hawk . . . he soared above us . . . now everyone's gonna pay attention to me, because I'm going to fly, too." Since he has been arrested for Emily's murder, it is difficult to imagine how Hugo will fulfill his desire. But the character's self-delusion is not the point here. What matters is that having the last word is white masculinity's privilege, its ideological strength and weakness, granting its others the power to define what it is (see DiPiero 1992: 133).

O offers no final answers, no deft conclusion – except, perhaps, for its prophetic tag line, "Everything Comes Full Circle." The most that can be said is that Nelson's film represents an intervention that moves, against its origins, towards a counter-hegemonic retelling of Shakespeare's *Othello*. O's own last words, indicting racism's root cause, may not be enough, but at least *O* dreams itself as a critical film that frankly addresses the contradictions encoded in its contemporary re-location. How to negotiate those issues further – both within the culture and in film, its dominant mode of visual representation – is anybody's guess. Catching occasional flickers of *Do the Right Thing* (1989), *Summer of Sam* (1999), and *Eve's Bayou* (1997), I'm left wondering how a Spike Lee or a Kasi Lemmons might tackle Shakespeare's *Othello*. Might they, one wonders, frame up a visual – and aural – field that would enable seeing its racial ethics and textual erotics with a difference?

Notes

1 Notably, the black press praised Fishburne's performance: see Anon. 1996.

2 Although the film does not quote it precisely, these moments recall ones from Orson Welles's *Othello* (1952), where a high-angle shot from the point of view of a windowed eye/I observes Othello and Desdemona on the murder bed at the close. See Hodgdon 1990.

3 Following this tableau, the film fades into a sunset at sea, where Cassio, standing in a longboat, presides over Desdemona's and Othello's watery funeral rites, an image that also quotes Welles's *Othello*.

4 On Davies's *Othello*, see <http://www.pbs.org/wgbh/masterpiece/othello/html>, which also links to the site for the Stephen Lawrence case.

5 The DVD version of *O* includes, on a second disk, Dmitri Bukhovetsky's 1923 silent *Othello*, starring Emil Jannings, a somewhat curious choice but probably an accident of copyright availability.

6 In his DVD commentary, Nelson points out features of *mise-en-scène* – the Hawks' team uniforms, banners, streamers, the repeated use of the American flag – deliberately chosen to drive home the point that *O* is an American story; Nelson's commentary also is extremely sensitive to the relation between actors' work and camera set-ups.

7 Like most recent films targeted at young adult audiences, *O* is a high-concept film, marketing features (such as CDs) that can be accentuated and extended within its social appropriation (Wyatt 1994: 39–44). My thanks to Elizabeth A. Deitchman for conversations about the score, especially its use of rap.

8 *O*'s website focuses at least as much if not more on Hugo than on O or Desi, suggesting Hartnett's popularity among viewers. A majority of the user comments come (apparently, though it is always difficult to mark internet genders precisely) from young women, who speak of their attraction to Hartnett and their surprise at a role that violates their expectations of his star persona. Confessing that she cried at the end, Natalie (July 25, 2002) attributes that to "Josh's character [being] so evil . . . but also because this kind of thing happens in real life, and in fact could happen in my school . . . high school is a violent place . . . full of jealousy and betrayal." See <http://www.othemovie.com>.

9 Did *Shakespeare in Love* (dir. John Madden, 1996) kill the early modern in-joke?

10 The sequence preceding this one, where Emily brings Hugo the scarf that O has given to Desi (the film's analogue to the handkerchief), also anticipates his silencing of Emily (not incidentally quoting Desdemona's murder in Orson Welles's *Othello* (1952), where Othello draws the wedding sheet over her face). Pushing Emily down on his bed, Hugo caresses her face with the scarf before stuffing it in her mouth; juxtaposed to the motel sequence and linked to it with a musical bridge, the film joins two potentially troubling sexual scenarios.

11 On the web, one user (Sabienna, March 12, 2002) comments: "Don't watch this with your parents." Kaaya's script goes beyond the film's representation, blatantly evoking stereotypes of black male sexuality and verging towards soft porn. See also the modernized adult film adapation of *Othello, Hotel O* (dir. Roy Karch, 2002).

6

SHAKESPEARE IN THE AGE OF POST-MECHANICAL REPRODUCTION

Sexual and electronic magic in *Prospero's Books*

Peter S. Donaldson

Prospero's Books offers a striking interpretation of *The Tempest*, similar to recent feminist and psychoanalytic accounts, in which Prospero attempts to control female sexuality and "appropriate" the birth-giving powers of the maternal body. Greenaway gives such a reading of *The Tempest* a technological inflection. By associating Prospero's "magic" with the ability of the new medium of digital cinema to create enhanced illusions of life, Greenaway recasts central questions of the play in contemporary terms. And by associating his own electronic medium with earlier wonder-working technologies – the voice of the magus, the printed pages of the Renaissance book – the film suggests that we are still living in the era of Renaissance magic, perhaps at a time toward the end of that era when, to quote Donna Haraway, "our machines are disturbingly lively, and we ourselves frighteningly inert" (1985: 68).

Artificial life and digital cinema

In Peter Greenaway's version of *The Tempest*, Prospero is not just the "master manipulator of people and events, but their prime originator" (Greenaway 1991: 9). With the possible exception of Miranda, Caliban, and Ariel, Prospero actually creates the world of the island, including its plants and animals, its buildings, the spirits who inhabit it, and the shipwrecked characters from the mainland who are cast up by the tempest. This creation takes place in two ways, both involving books. The first combines the roles of dramatist and magus. Prospero conjures with words he himself has written, the words of *The Tempest*:

> On his island of exile, Prospero plans a drama to right the wrongs done to him. He invents characters to flesh out his imaginary fantasy to steer his enemies into his power, writes their dialogue and having written it, he speaks the lines aloud, shaping the characters so powerfully through the words that they are conjured before us.
>
> (Ibid.)

The working of Prospero's magic is presented in the film in several ways: spirits hold up a mirror in which Prospero beholds the scenes his pen evokes or screen overlays show Prospero's cell and his writing utensils as well as the world he is calling into being. At times, when the levels of illusion and reality, or present narration and memory, proliferate, there are three and four images on the screen at once, one nested in another, each permitting a partial view of the screen beneath. Often the foreground screen shows, in huge close-up, Prospero's hand and quill inscribing parchment in a beautiful italic hand. Lest we think that the temporal primacy of writing makes this a programmatically deconstructive Tempest, it may be useful to note that the text that Prospero is writing remains authorized not only by its Shakespearean origin but by the continued presence of its fictional author as well. The handwritten words we see on the screen are, essentially, transcriptions of an authorial intention and serve to reactivate that intention as oral discourse.[1] That is not to say that the "book" Prospero is writing is not important. The material inscription of Prospero's verbum mirificum is central to the design of the film, for the reinscription of *The Tempest* by its main character makes Shakespeare's play one of twenty-four wonder-working books – "Prospero's books" – which are the technical glory of the film.

These books, like the text Prospero is writing, are used by Prospero to create the world we see in the film. But Prospero hasn't written them. In the fiction of the film, they are the books, the "volumes that I priz'd above my dukedom," which Gonzalo gave to Prospero to take into exile. As described in the script, they provide an epitome of Old World knowledge and technique, with a cabalistic or hermetic flavor. There are books on navigation, education, farming, colonial administration, herbals, bestiaries, mythologies, and so on (ibid.: 11–12). These are not ordinary books, not even ordinary books of Renaissance magic like the Athanasius Kircher texts from which Greenaway drew his inspiration, for when opened, the books come alive with movement and animation. In the Book of Water there are "rippling waves and slanting storms. Rivers and cataracts flow and bubble" (ibid.: 17); the Book of Mirrors has pages that are "covered in a film of mercury that will roll off the page unless treated cautiously"; the Primer of Small Stars' pages "twinkle with travelling planets"; the pages of the Anatomy of Birth "move and throb and bleed" (ibid.: 20). Many of the special effects described in the filmscript are realized in the film, some even more impressively than in the script, as when small live animals – salamanders, toads and insects – come to life and walk off the pages of the Bestiary. The script describes Prospero as using these books to create the physical and human environment of the island:

> Prospero walks among books that blow and rustle in the contrary winds. There are a great many of them . . . for Prospero's initial twenty four books have begotten thousands more . . . Covering the whole screen at one point is one very large book – maybe four metres by seven . . . – The Book of Mythologies. This is the "example book," the template for Prospero's imaginings to people the island. With this book – a primer and textbook of his humanist education – Prospero populates the island.
>
> (Ibid.: 57)

For Greenaway, the technologies used to create this book on screen are analogs of Prospero's generative magic. The magic voice, the manuscript text of *The Tempest*, the printed books of Renaissance hermetism and technique, and the wonderworking "arts" of late twentieth-century digital cinema form a continuum that links our age to Shakespeare's.

Greenaway describes his own image-processing system in loving detail (ibid.: 28–33), and speculates that Prospero himself would have approved of its use in the "manufacture of magical volumes" because he

> would no doubt call upon the most contemporary state-of-the-art techniques that the legacy of the Gutenberg revolution could offer. The newest Gutenberg technology – and to talk of a comparable revolution may not be to exaggerate – is the digital, electronic Graphic Paintbox.
>
> (Ibid.: 28)

Digital image technology is present in the film by analogy: the multiple "windows" summoned and dismissed by Prospero's "art" evoke the scene of digital composition; the quill pen with which Prospero writes has acquired the functionalities of the electronic stylus; the repeated shots of Gielgud's writing fingers may allude to the medium of composition through the ambiguity of the word "digital," which can refer to works of the hand or the effects of computation.[2] Subtler references – should we call them metacomputational or metadigital? – help to explain the extraordinarily restrictive, stilted blocking and dancing style of *Prospero's Books*. It is an attempt to make live performers on film look as much like computer animations as possible. Prospero is a double for Greenaway, the digital cinema artist, as much as for Shakespeare the playwright.

Like the Elizabethan stage, the contemporary arts of digital image-making and computer-enhanced animation trouble the margin between representation and originary creation, between licit and illicit forms of artistic endeavor, between "white" or natural magic (which is only technology, however marvelous its successes) and something beyond ordinary technique, no longer called necromancy, which, like forbidden or questionable forms of Renaissance magic, aims at rivalling or supplanting the natural world and its modes of reproducing itself.

The discourse in which the new medium of digital cinema is described by its practitioners speaks of artificial worlds, and, at its most explicit, of artificial life. In a sense, these writers are extending claims for artistic creation that derive, ultimately, from Renaissance artistic and poetic theory. Sidney can say, for example, that the poet, disdaining the limits of the laws of nature "doth grow, in effect into another nature, in making things either better than Nature bringeth forth, or, quite anew, forms such as never were in Nature" (1965: 100). In the *Apology for Poetry* it is not in mirroring Nature but in rivalling and surpassing Nature's power to "bring forth" forms that highest claims of art consist. The inventors of photography were to make analogous claims: "The Daguerrotype is not merely an instrument which serves to draw nature; on the contrary, it is a chemical and physical process which gives her the power to reproduce herself" (Daguerre, as cited in Gernsheim and Gernsheim 1968: 81). Greenaway's claims for digital creation echo claims to a creativity that replaces or betters natural creation which have been revived at the advent of every substantial advance in representational technology since the Renaissance. Giving nature the power to reproduce "herself," Daguerre's potent metaphor for photochemistry, is a

Greenaway motif in *Prospero's Books*. The next section of this essay deals at length with the film's images of birth and reproduction, but there is one passage in the film-script that is particularly resonant in relation to Daguerre – it is the moment when Prospero's hand reaches into the frame in which the Anatomy of Birth is displayed to caress the animated engraving of the body of his wife at the moment of giving birth (Greenaway 1991: 70);[3] later, Prospero will act literally as a midwife at the birth of Caliban (ibid.: 88).

It is surprising how closely theorists of the new media used to create the bestiaries of *Prospero's Books*, from which "live" toads and other small creatures arise, follow the pattern of Prospero's creations as Greenaway imagines them. Roger Malina, for example, places digital image-making in the context of other computer-based efforts to create artificial life. Some of these "life forms" are no more than robots or enhanced animated images:

> Workers in artificial life such as Randall Beer have been developing artificial insects, such as miniature robots capable of maneuvering around computer circuit boards to carry out circuit repairs. Artist Vernon Reed has been for some years creating cybernetic jewelry that can be viewed as a precursor to cybernetic art insects.
>
> (Malina 1990: 36)

But, as Malina recognizes, the cybernetic art insect – a phrase that neatly describes a number of the creatures that Prospero's books produce[4] – may not represent the closest approach to artificial life that the computer can claim. Microrobots are impressive, but digital art can claim to be like life in more profound ways. One of these ways is its simulation of personhood. Because computer software can be designed to be responsive, adjustive to the user, it is less a passive tool like a paintbrush, however sensitive, and more like a collaborator, whose suggestions, redrafts and sketches introduce a second consciousness into the artistic process. A further claim (which merits equal scepticism) is that computer art is generative in ways that rival human reproduction.

A different kind of reproduction is made possible by software – this is what I will call post-mechanical reproduction (although a more descriptive term such as "generative reproduction" is needed). The goal of post-mechanical reproduction is to make copies that are as different as possible from each other, but constrained by a set of initial rules. The prototypical type of post-mechanical reproduction is of course sexual and biological reproduction (Malina 1990: 37; see also Verostko 1987). Most interestingly in regard to Greenaway's reworking of *The Tempest*, Malina regards "compassion" as both the limit and the challenge of digital generativity. Acknowledging that male dominance has affected the development of the computer, pushing development toward war games and toward mind–body dualism, Malina ends his paper by calling for a redirection of computer art toward "a technology of compassion."[5] "A technology of compassion" is an ambiguous phrase in contemporary discourse. It might once have meant only that technology would be directed by compassion, or used for ends determined by compassion. As used by proponents of artificial intelligence and others, it can mean that the technology itself might be compassionate, that computer programs might be written that would emulate human compassion. To quote Donna Haraway again, more fully:

> Late twentieth-century machines have made thoroughly ambiguous the difference between natural and artificial, mind and body, self-developing and externally designed, and many other distinctions that would apply to organisms and machines. Our machines are disturbingly lively, and we ourselves frighteningly inert.
>
> (Haraway 1989: 68)

Such a statement differs from older humanist protests against mechanization (for example F.R. Leavis's objections to C.P. Snow, or Joseph Weizenbaum's (1976) critique of artificial intelligence). Haraway, like Greenaway, finds the margin between the human and the machine troubling, but also glamorous and exciting, even liberating, as her title implies.

The idea that "compassion" marks a limit or a challenge to attempts at creating simulations of life is a crucial one in Greenaway's reading of *The Tempest*.[6] The structure of *Prospero's Books* depends upon this idea. Prospero can conjure people into existence, but his magical creation is incomplete:

> the characters walk and gesture, act and react, but still they do not speak. Their life-giving words are not their own, they continue to be the mouthpiece of Prospero, the master dramatist. . . . Then there is a twist, a rearrangement of events, a reversal. When his enemies are totally in his power, Prospero is admonished by Ariel for the ferocity of the revengeful humiliation he forces on them, and he repudiates his plans and turns again to forgiveness. The characters that his passion for revenge had created now speak for the first time with their own voices, brought to a full life by his act of compassion.
>
> (Greenaway 1991: 9)

The concluding sequences of *Prospero's Books* hover, as this passage does, and as the theorists of digital art and artificial intelligence do, between regarding "compassion" as a human quality that cannot be artificially produced, and regarding it as the final achievement or necessary condition in the creation of artificial life.

Greenaway stages the end of *The Tempest* as a renunciation of the magician's tools of trade, including, in this version, the quill pen and the magic animated volumes. The pen is broken, all the volumes are snapped shut with dust flying and cast into the waters of Prospero's immense Roman bath. The tools of cinematic illusion, too, are renounced, for, according to Greenaway, at the end

> Prospero/Shakespeare breaks the theatrical filmic illusion by appealing directly to his audience . . . and all his audiences . . . and his last audience in his last play . . . as he takes leave of the island, the theatre and possibly his life.
>
> (Ibid.: 164)

Much of this section of the film is impressive, even moving in its multi-layered attempt to "humanize" both Prospero and the other characters, who now speak for the first time. But the film's pace (always almost slow motion), its rigid blocking, oppressively rectilinear composition, bizarrely heavy costumes, and extremely low-key style of dialogue even in the scenes in which the other characters do speak undermine the turn toward acknowledging the autonomy and independent life of others. This effect is so pronounced as to suggest that Greenaway intends (as in all his films) to undercut whatever Romantic or humanist impulses he sets in motion.

Ariel, Miranda, and Caliban are not wholly engendered by magic as are the tiny creatures that hop from the pages of the magic books, but they are creatures "new created" by Prospero's potent art, and in accordance with the film's central premise do not fully exist until they speak in their own voices. Yet, despite the script's apparent commitment to bringing them to a "full life," the film itself does not or cannot present their voicing as a convincing mark of independence and autonomy. The sequence in which Ariel first speaks is compelling. With the conspirators under Prospero's power, the youngest of the Ariels,[7] a golden-haired cherub, looks over Prospero's shoulder to read what he is writing, and reads aloud the end of the passage in which Prospero exults over his enemies, now "all confin'd together." At this point, Ariel takes the quill from Prospero and writes, followed in turn by each of his elder siblings or clones. It is they who write the script for Prospero's conversion to mercy. When they have finished writing, Prospero takes the book back, we see a halting, childish hand instead of Prospero's confident italic, and he reads the lines in which Ariel admonishes him to allow his "affections" to "become tender." At the end of the passage ("the rarer action is/In virtue than in vengeance; they being penitent,/The sole drift of my purpose doth extend/Not a frown further"), Prospero breaks his quill in two, Ariel's hands are seen to snap the book shut, and then follows a series of shots in which all of the twenty-four books are snapped shut in a definitive turn away, it would seem, from the scripted toward the interactive, driven by this powerful moment of recognition of self and other. But what follows does not allow the other characters more than the perfunctory autonomy conferred by the fact that they speak.

The conspirators are confined by a bright blue charmed circle; their movements are restrained and even puppet-like; Miranda and Ferdinand are no exceptions. In the final moments of the film, Prospero's face is presented in freeze-frame, and the camera tracks back from it, while Ariel runs toward the retreating camera and then leaps, in slow motion, toward us and over it, in what Greenaway, on the evidence of the filmscript, intended as a moment of final liberation in which the image of Prospero would be reduced, as it were, to the manufactured, filmed image it really is, allowing space for others. However, it is possible to read this moment very differently, as Prospero's continuing direction of the action, even in the absence of his moving form and voice; as the authorial sponsorship of a licensed enfranchisement over which Prospero and the canonical text of *The Tempest* retain authority. Instead of seeing Prospero as very small and immobile, we can see him as the originator of the film in an enhanced, permanent way. As the voice-over, which is the most dominant and dominating of all vocal positionings in cinema (Silverman 1988), Prospero has been the central cinematic figure until this point, and has been used exclusively by Gielgud and by the narrator who describes the books, so now the image of Prospero remains fixed at the vanishing point, the implied origin of all that we see on the screen. Because this is so, Ariel's slow-motion run toward the retreating camera, and his leap up and apparently over it out of the image and into audience space does not convey the feeling of independence from Prospero that the script implies for this moment. Rather, Prospero seems to suffuse the space; he has become one with the point of origin of the image, the point of convergence of a perspectival space that emanates from his unchanging simulacrum.

This effect whereby Prospero, far from renouncing his powers, is installed as a permanent, authorizing presence, is reinforced by the conclusion Greenaway gives to the tropes that center on textuality and its relation to authorial intention. All of the wonder-working books are closed and thrown, one by one, into the water, to the accompaniment of fireworks, explosions, burning acid, and other displays of destruction and dispersal. But Caliban saves two of them – the plays of Shakespeare and a slim volume – the book Prospero has been writing – which will be bound into it as its first section. As Ferdinand and Miranda are joined together just before the final shots of the film, the text of the First Folio *Tempest* (not the manuscript Prospero has been writing) unscrolls as an overlay on the screen, in large gilt letters. The manuscript that is no longer seen, like Prospero's still image, mystifies origins, makes them inaccessible even as they continue to influence the future. Though this is a work in which books come apart, are dispersed, are seen to be written, *Prospero's Books* ends in a series of powerful images that remystify the book as the inscription of an originating discourse that is both artistic and magical.

"An undergoing stomach": male birth and midwivery in *Prospero's Books*

Several recent critics have argued that Prospero's magic in *The Tempest* may be understood as an attempt to control a dangerous and threatening female sexuality, and to replace it with a kind of sanitized, non-physical generativity that is gendered male. I place *Prospero's Books* in the context of such interpretations, and suggest that Greenaway's technological version of Prospero's "life-giving" magic can illuminate some aspects of the current discourse relating the human world to the new electronic technologies. *Prospero's Books* is part of an extensive discursive shift that includes aspects of cyberpunk, "technoporn," extreme versions of artificial intelligence and virtual reality theory, and other attempts to reconfigure desire and sexuality in terms of human/machine interaction. Greenaway's work – *Prospero's Books* as well as his other films – may be regarded as a soft-core, high-culture manifestation of what Constance Penley and Andrew Ross call "technoculture" (1991). *Prospero's Books* portrays Prospero's magic powers as an "appropriation" of maternal power, and in doing so may suggest a psychoanalytic framework for understanding the "technophilia" of the present cultural moment, and its preoccupation with "disturbingly lively" machines.

Kay Stockholder, in a brilliant paper entitled "Sexual Magic and Magical Sex" (1989), has argued that the magic in *The Tempest* is "both generated by and based on revulsion from and fear of women's sexuality." The strict sexual morality Prospero enforces, the demonization of sexuality in his accounts of Sycorax and Caliban, and much else in the play suggest that magical control is necessary to protect his hopes for a generative, spiritual, and redemptive love relationship for Miranda from his own fear that sexuality is inherently cruel and corrupt. But in Stockholder's reading, Prospero's magic does not merely control, but derives from and usurps female potencies – the "bad" magic of Sycorax as well as the nurturant and compassionate aspects of Shakespeare's "good" female characters. Power thus "passes from female to male figures"; Prospero appropriates female qualities "while keeping female figures subject to male authority by defining compassion as an aspect of his magic." His magic, then, both controls female sexuality and competes with it, replacing "feminine" nurture and care-giving with modes of concern, compassion and forgiveness that are fused with his willful and magical (I would add, "technical") control.

Janet Adelman is even more direct in claiming that *The Tempest* enacts a usurpation of specifically maternal powers:

> Prospero's reappropriation of control at the beginning of *The Tempest* is nearly diagrammatic: even before the play has begun the maternal body has been defined as dangerous and banished in the form of Sycorax . . . Prospero's use of Medea's words to describe his own magic suggests the extent to which his reappropriated control is based firmly on her banishment.
>
> (1992: 237)

Adelman is most persuasive, here and throughout her book, in discovering submerged metaphors of birth, and in analyzing the strategies by which fears associated with birth from the mother are defused and redirected. For her, Ariel's release from the "cloven pine" is a kind of birth, as is the voyage from Milan:

> Miranda's passage to the island is similarly mediated by a birth-act, the fantasized pregnancy – he "groan'd" under his "burthen"; her smiles "raised in [him]/An undergoing stomach to bear up/Against what should ensue" (1.2.156–8) – that imagistically remakes her wholly her father's daughter.
>
> (1992: 237)

"Thus able to control the maternal body," Adelman continues, "Prospero seems able to reshape the world in the image of his own mind." Adelman, however, places somewhat greater credence than Stockholder in Prospero's turn toward compassion and self-recognition at the end. For her, the cost of Prospero's magical control is isolation from others which he begins to overcome when Ariel prompts him to the recognition that it is "less than human to refuse the vulnerabilities of human feeling" (*ibid.*).

Such an account of *The Tempest* would, if technologically inflected, be close to the reading proposed by *Prospero's Books*, implicitly in the film itself and explicitly in the filmscript. For Greenaway, Prospero's magic is associated with sexuality – with a kind of regressive yet efficacious autoeroticism that creates, indeed, gives birth to things and to people. Like the Prosperos of Adelman and Stockholder, Greenaway's protagonist is self-enclosed despite his attempts at magical generativity, is beset by images of bloody, violent, and excremental birth, and, toward the conclusion attempts – but only attempts – to break out of the solipsism his magical control imposes by recognizing others and allowing them voice, and through "compassion," which here, as in Stockholder and in the discourses on computer-created life,[8] may be read as yet one more appropriation, or reappropriation, of the feminine.

The film begins with what Greenaway likes to call a "bravura, virtuoso" sequence that links writing and magic as works of the hand. Perhaps the most exciting part of Gielgud's performance in *Prospero's Books* comes here, at the start, when he responds to his own writing as a cue for his speech. Having imagined, and thought the word "Boatswain!" as a line for a character in the play he is writing about his imagined revenge and restoration, Prospero sees his own written mark as if for the first time and recites it with surprise, in a kind of auditory mirroring, the freshly inscribed page serving as script. Though he has just written it himself, Gielgud responds to the word (which we also see written on an immense image, overlaid upon the scene of its writing) as if responding to the writing of another, with approval and delight. That there is an element of regression in such delight is conveyed in many ways – Prospero speaks the line in a Roman bath, waist-deep in water; the storm he is imagining begins as a single drop of water, seen in immense close-up splashing into his own outstretched palm. The image suggests a connection between writing and masturbation in a paradigmatic way, recalling Derrida's playful critique of Rousseau's fear of the dangerous "supplementarity" of writing and of autoeroticism. A connection between magic and psychological regression is also suggested: Ariel's supernatural, seemingly inexhaustible urine stream, splashing into the bath as he swings on a trapeze above the surface of the water, is overlayed upon a scene of storm upon the high seas – and when a toy boat Prospero sets to drift in the bath is drenched by the stream, the ship carrying Prospero's enemies founders. Later, in a flashback to Prospero's life as Duke of Milan, we discover that the toy ship is one of Miranda's childhood toys. As the storm scene develops, spirits hold up an immense ornate mirror before Prospero, and he watches the scene he has conjured as if in a mirror. Prospero's pen, his voice, the toy boat, and the preternatural waterings of Ariel all seem necessary to create the magic storm – Greenaway wants us to see it as the product of an erotically tinged infantile fantasy.

But the project – Prospero's project – of making his imaginary dramatic creation "real" entails breaking free of the constraints of infantile wish fulfillments, both erotic and agressive, with which the "magic" begins. The moment at which the characters become real, and "speak in their own voices" is the point at which Prospero accepts rebuke and shows compassion. Yet it is possible to understand compassion not as a rejection of magical thinking, but, as Stockholder suggests, as a magical appropriation of the "feminine".

If we follow the logic of the filmscript, nearly all of the many inhabitants of the island are literally Prospero's creations, conjured into being with the help of his magic. Even the shipwrecked Italians are, in Greenaway's account, "creatures that his passion for revenge has created."[9] Miranda is born from her mother, who appears in the film, and is named, like Shakespeare's daughter, Susannah. Yet her appearance does not wholly answer contemporary questions, such as those of Stephen Orgel (1986), about her absence, for she never speaks, even through Prospero, and her childbirth scene is made to seem, in a remarkable sequence, to proceed from the pages of a book, Vesalius's "lost Anatomy of Birth." As this book is first described, we see Miranda's birth-scene, intercut with the pages of the wonder-working anatomy, in which animated dissections are presented, as well as a childbirth scene that may be an alternate presentation of Miranda's birth itself. As Prospero recounts this scene to the sleeping Miranda on the island, Susannah, naked to the waist, appears at the side of Miranda's bed while she is sleeping, and silently pulls down the skin of her abdomen as if she were a living anatomy lesson, revealing a blood-saturated mass of internal organs, including a uterus swollen with her pregnancy. The absent mother – actually the dead mother, for she appears not only in the Anatomy of Birth, but also in the Book of the Dead, as the last entry in a register of deaths that extends from Adam to Susannah, "Prospero's wife" – returns when summoned by Prospero's thoughts. This apparition at the bedside not only makes birth terrifying, but also links the image of the unconscious Miranda to other scenes of blood just shown: the story of Miranda's birth is intercut with the massacre in which Prospero lost his political power, a scene of twitching bodies, pikes penetrating every bodily opening, and a blood-and-corpse-filled bathtub. The shots of the Vesalius Anatomy alternate with these shots, and connect the blood of birth to that of massacre and dissection.

The illustration of the Anatomy of Birth which is presented at greatest length shows a large operating theater, on which a woman in childbirth is placed at right angles to the screen, her head to the rear of the image, a cloth draped between her legs. The shot, both in its careful perspectival arrangement and in its blocking of what, in the logic of the composition should be the si(gh)te of greatest interest, recalls Dürer's famous engraving of the perpective artist at work, with the body of his female model aligned along the axis of his sight line, a cloth between her legs.[10] Other Greenaway films are similarly preoccupied with connections between linear perspective and female sexuality. In *A Zed and Two Noughts*, the obsessive object of attention is the "foreshortened" body of Mrs. Bewick, the legless, pregnant lover of the twin zoologists who are the film's protagonists. Often seen through the round circle of the iron bed rail, at the center of the image along the axis of sight, the bedclothes that cover Mrs. Bewick's reproductive organs indicate the film's thematic center. The perspectival vanishing point and the point of origin of human life coincide. In *Prospero's Books*, the horrors of childbirth seem to procede from the biological facts of birth, and from a terror that inheres in female anatomy. Yet, if one attends to the deployment and the blocking off of the gaze of the spectator, as well as to the fact that the blood we actually see is a product of either political fratricide or anatomical dissection, a scientific analog of the inquiring, objectifying aspects of the male gaze, it is possible to understand the horror that attends these scenes as a projection of Prospero's violent fantasies.

As in many other parts of the film, the script is not only more explicit (more "graphic" as the slang expression has it), but also more interactive. The loss of the texture of interaction between the twenty-four wonder-books and the rest of the world of the film constitutes the most significant difference between script and book. Technical limitations may have determined this shift – but it may also represent a pulling back from the script's bolder approach to the themes of *The Tempest*. So, for example, the magic books do come alive in the film, but the living creatures that emerge from their pages do not, as the script leads us to expect, leave the frame but remain confined to the tight close-ups in which the books are presented. We do not see Prospero using the books to fill his world with artificial life. In the birth scenes, too, the Anatomy of Birth is more sequestered in the film, intercut with, but not sharing a continuous space with the narrative of the massacre or the narrative of Miranda's early life. In the script, Prospero opens the Anatomy as he recites the history of Antonio's rebellion to the sleeping Miranda. The open pages of the book enact the story of Miranda's birth and then, as the book is replaced by a mirror brought into the room, the story of Susannah's death:

> As he turns the pages . . . Prospero's fingers appear to become covered in blood . . . the organs of the body become three dimensional – small reproductions of the liver, the spleen, the heart, the intestine . . . then red ink floods the page . . . then black ink. There is the sound of babies crying . . . and then exultant singing . . . as Prospero and we contemplate a handsome and awesome drawing of a woman giving birth . . . we surmise that the woman

> is – was – Prospero's wife. The diagram's discrete figures and dotted lines are animated. Prospero's fingers enter the frame and caress his wife's body. A woman materialises behind Prospero – leaning lightly on the back of his chair – she is alternately a Titianesque nude and then the Vesalius figure – flayed – her blood vessels and nerve endings and internal organs displayed and marked with black figures and numbers as in the book . . . she leans lightly over and kisses Prospero on the cheek. The kiss leaves a blood-red mark on his withered cheek.
>
> (Greenaway 1991: 70)

A mirror is then brought into the room by Prospero's spirits, and he sees Susannah's corpse laid out for her funeral. In the film, as noted previously, Susannah does appear in Miranda's room and silently opens her abdomen as if she were a living anatomical picture. But the interactive elements of the script – the hand reaching into the book and the bloodstaining kiss – are absent from the film. Again, the world of the "books" remains separate from the rest of the setting, and, in this case, that separation intimates a psychic defense against the disturbing associations connected with the birth of Miranda and the body of her mother.

Prospero's Books embodies the general reading prosposed by Stockholder and Adelman. Birth is presented as so disturbing that Prospero's efforts to recast the facts of birth in masculine, magical terms seem a relief. Insistent patterns of birth imagery also move both Caliban and Ariel into the sphere of Prospero's quasi-maternal ambitions. Caliban's actual birth from the body of an immensely swollen, lewdly hairless Sycorax is closely juxtaposed to two symbolic "births." Ariel's release from the cloven pine is presented in a way that recalls Stockholder's reading of the passage as a fantasy of retentive birth, and Caliban descends, at Prospero's command "Come forth!" from a foul sewer-pipe or cloaca into a pit of filth.[11] In each case, Prospero's magic is presented as giving the characters a second, or supplementary, birth by male command.[12] There is a sense that Prospero is compelled, perhaps by his hatred for the natural course of birth *inter faeces et urinam*, to engineer magical, highly controlled, morally "purified" substitutions for motherhood. If Prospero attempts to replace maternal birth, both by literally creating many of the characters through his magic and by reinscribing others as his "creatures," he also attempts, in both the play and the film, to control Miranda's sexuality, in an effort, as Stockholder suggests (1989: 11–12), to control his own. In *Prospero's Books*, the rigorous control over the relationship between Ferdinand and Miranda is intensified and extreme, and underscored by Prospero's ventriloquial control over their words. The film's pervasive and idiosyncratic recourse to nudity is also, paradoxically, a defense against sex. The troops of naked dancers and extras function as a kind of *a fortiori* argument against the possibility of incestuous feelings. For example, when Prospero first approaches Miranda's bed, he is accompanied by an attractive naked female "spirit." Prospero ignores her, and in fact never is seen to glance at any of the naked denizens of his island, male or female, even for an instant. That does not imply that he is without sexuality, but that he controls it. Indeed, by creating hordes of naked attendants, he multiplies occasions to manifest his control. If the autonomy of the other characters was to have been one mark of the success of Prospero's project of creation and reformation of self and other, the spontaneous sexual relationship between Ferdinand and Miranda was to have been another. The filmscript's treatment of the erotic union of the couple, would, if it had been realized in the film, have made an impressive central scene. Recognizing both the scripted and the spontaneous character of "love at first sight" Greenaway had the Ariels, like Raphaelesque putti, mediate the scene through texts, checking at each moment of the infatuation to see what was written in the *Book of Love*, before whispering the appropriate lines to Ferdinand and Miranda (lines spoken of course by Prospero). At one point Ariel even acts as couturier, gathering Miranda's diaphanous gown behind her to display her body more clearly, as if fitting Botticelli's Aphrodite for a wedding dress (103–6; see also 123). None of this appears in the far less witty and more stilted "love scene" in the film, and, unbalanced by such major recourse to an eroticism that was to have been both mythic and literally "textual," the supposed attraction between the couple seems merely formal, rote, and overcontrolled.[13]

The betrothal masque is likewise overcontrolled. The movements of the dancers – male and female, nude and semi-nude – parody sexual passion. At times the dancers mechanically jerk their long hair, pulling it out to the side in a burlesque of hair-flying or windswept ardor; at other times they mime the gestures of piercing their breasts with arrows, clockwork victims of Cupid, cloned postmodern descendants of Bernini's St. Theresa. They are "real" performers, but in the fiction of the film, they have been literally created by Prospero, and do his bidding, reacting with somewhat abrupt and robotic obedience to his will. Like Prospero's ventriloquism, the jerky and unconvincing eroticism of the film is partly diagnostic, meant, perhaps, as a criticism of a self-loving, overcontrolling, unself-knowing character whom Greenaway understands to be a "moralising scold and a petty revenger, a benevolent despot, a jealous father" (1991: 12) as well as a master magician and dramatist. They instance his control over sexuality, a control that empties it of spontaneity and renders it machine-like.[14]

If Eros is rendered mechanical in several senses in the film, it is also true that, in the making of the film, Greenaway thought of his relation to machines (especially computers running image processing programs) in erotic terms. The filmscript describes these programs as ushering in a new "Gutenberg revolution," and, to exemplify the "paintbox images" that play so large a role in *Prospero's Books*, Greenaway provides a double-page reproduction of two states – a daytime and a night-time version – of one of the animated characters originally planned for the film. Though, in fact, she never appears in the finished film, this figure of "the juggler" is worth discussing precisely because, in her melding of the erotic and the creative, she is so unlike the almost endless succession of naked figures, with their bobbing breasts, "wagging dicks" (as the *Village Voice* reviewer called them), and mechanical toylike movements in the film. She represents a spontaneous and unruly sexuality that is absent from the film:

> Prospero looked for jugglers. He looked for twinkling eyes and the smell of sweat and pepper. . . . After a quick appraisal, for Prospero could not be seen to spend too long on such a humble appointment, the most likely candidate proved to be a naked, bright orange bacchante with wide hips who juggled balls and fruit, scientific instruments, and defenceless small animals. . . . For Prospero this little laughing, orange, juggling creature played the juggling part during the day, but was a professional fornicator at night. Maybe the roles were interchangeable. She dyed her body orange by laying in a wet iron-pit and her partners soon knew each other. Every marked fornicator could see so

> many others on the beach the next each morning. The juggler's eagerness to please Prospero in her diurnal role eventually affected her nocturnal fee. For she asked her satyrical clients for objects to juggle with, preferably brightly colored, for she had a notion that Prospero had been colour-blinded by reading too many black-and-white books. She savoured the eccentric object: a potato shaped like a dwarf'd foot, a pebble with holes like eyes, a Venus fruit-nut scarred to suggest rape, a petrified apple bitten by Eve.
>
> And then a reversal occurred. She began to exchange her roles. Trying to annex quality in her nocturnal clientele by exhibitions of her skill, she juggled with mathematical solids, splashing herself with her own stale milk, fearful that her orange body could not be seen among the dark columned corridors. The clients grew bored and moved to other pastures to browse their sensual taste. . . . Continuing to confuse her responsibilities, she began to accept professional advances by day, especially from the lazy imitation scholars who ought to have been pretending to read the books in Prospero's library. Finally she perfected juggling and fornicating by day and by night as simultaneous activities. In disappointed exasperation, Prospero turned his head the other way and sought his fool elsewhere.
>
> (Greenaway 1991: 28–9)

"The juggler" was invented to display and allegorize computer "paint" software, showing how discrete forms can be altered in shape and color with a stylus used in conjunction with a tablet or "palette" of colors. At a touch, colors – the orange body of the juggler, the dark blue of the night in which she works – can taint or bleed into one another, can be made to stain, as, in the story, her milk and her iron-oxide pigment stain adjacent figures. In Greenaway's description, the paintbox is a medium that defies conventional categories, blurs boundaries, partakes of a freedom that is erotic yet "professional." The paintbox leads one away from the library and toward the iron-pit, a locus of creativity gendered female not only by its association with the independent and enterprising activity of the juggler/fornicator, but also the hint of uterine blood conveyed by its color and its iron-rich chemical composition. Yet – though the juggler allegorizes the very medium in which Greenaway has produced Prospero's marvels, and especially the computer-animated books that are the film's technical glory – Prospero disdains her, and does so at the precise moment at which she has achieved a complete inter-penetration of day- and night-time activities and realms. And Greenaway, as director, rejects this character, too, for she never appears in the film, and the meaning she carries, of the fusion, beyond conventional limits, of eros, creativity, and skill, is rejected as well. Sex, in *Prospero's Books*, is either rigidly controlled or excremental. Women are either pure beings, like Miranda, foul witches, like Sycorax, or robotic naked dancers, whose movements follow the rhythms of Prospero's clock-work paradise like the animated dolls in Coppelia. The juggler, though no less literally an artifact of male imagination than Shakespeare's women or Greenaway's, is more lively invention than the female representations in the film. Like other contemporary *Tempests*, Greenaway's includes a Sycorax and, in addition, a wife for Prospero (named Susannah), and the many female dancers, spirits who serve Prospero's will. But Greenaway's most interesting attempt to come to terms with female sexuality, that is, with the body of the mother, was invented to help explain the workings of his own electronic equipment. She exists under a kind of suppression, only in the (published) script. Greenaway's fertile vision of a world populated by books; his vision of Prospero's hand stroking the body of his wife, dying in childbirth in the pages of a lost work by Vesalius; the "textual" Cupids who prompt Miranda and Ferdinand in their love-making – all these are consigned to the medium of print, either by self-censorship or by the limits of a medium that seemed, in the planning stages, to have no limits.

It is easy to agree with Greenaway that we are in the midst of a new "Gutenberg revolution" in communication technologies. But we are in the early phases of that revolution, when it is also easy to overestimate the potential of new tools and to misjudge their power to liberate or to enhance creativity. Perhaps this is the reason that, despite the technological virtuosity of *Prospero's Books*, many of the boldest features of Greenaway's interesting and contemporary interpretation of *The Tempest* appear, it sounds strange to say, "only in the book."

Notes

1 See Rodolphe Gasché's distinctions between deconstructive and non-deconstructive conceptions of "text" (Gasché 1986: 279–83).
2 See p. 108, and n. 3 below.
3 The hand that reaches into the artificial world and interacts with the representations of people and objects in it also evokes the "data glove" of virtual reality experiments:

> What gives virtual reality its realism is, in part, the expansiveness of its scope, which is related to the universality of mathematics. But an even more important factor is our immersion in it, our ability to interact with an alter ego. Interfaces form bridges between the real and the virtual and back again. We cross them to inhabit a strange place that is both concrete and abstract. A human hand grasping a real sensor holds, at the same time, a virtual paintbrush or the controls of a virtual space vehicle. Since a hand can be described with numbers as readily as any denizen of virtual reality, we too can "live" in these synthetic universes. We visit a territory we can probe, inquiring about and interacting with its residents to bring to life with equal ease bizarre fantasies as well as sedate realities.
>
> (Binckley 1990: 18)

Like *Prospero's Books* the digital cinema literature is replete with puns that confound the digits of the hand and those of mathematics. When Binckley met the digital artist David Em at an exhibition and asked him what he had been working on lately, Em, who had returned to sculpture, held up his hands and said "digital art!" (ibid.: 13).
4 Prospero's insects and toads may remind us, in turn, of John Dee's "flying crab" and other instances of artificial life in the world of the Renaissance magus. See Yates 1964: 147–8.
5 Malina's remarks on compassion were made in response to a paper by Sally Prior not printed in *SIGGRAPH 1990*.
6 It is also what distinguishes humans from replicants in *Blade Runner* and other works of science fiction that deal with the cyborg–human boundary.
7 There are three Ariels in the film, of similar appearance but different ages.
8 See above, pp. 108–9. "Compassion" was the issue raised by Sally Prior in regard to artificial life at the Adelaide Conference. In this, as in other ways, Shakespeare's play prefigures the terms of the continuing debate about the fate of "the human" in a technological age.
9 See Orgel 1986: 64.
10 See Freedman 1991. Greenaway makes many explicit references to perspective in the script of *Prospero's Books*; see, for example, Greenaway 1991: 42, 121.

11 The pipe through which Caliban descends to the pit is described as "like a tunnel to a distant privy used by incontinent giants" (Greenaway 1991: 92). The Book of the Earth is Caliban's "signature" text. When opened during the visit to Caliban's pit in the film, it is spattered with raw eggs, urine, and excrement.

12 The birth imagery in the script is again more detailed, and there is even a strong suggstion, as in Stockholder's psychological scenario, that Ariel is Sycorax's child. In addition, Prospero himself attempts to act as midwife at Caliban's birth (Greenaway 1991: 87–92).

13 It would be interesting to know why so much of this scene was altered in a film that displays so much nudity. It may be that the very centrality of Miranda's body to the design of the film, its blatant and underscored to-be-looked-at-ness could not be filmed for a high-culture audience now at least partly aware of the feminist critique of such cinematic displays. Yet, without this scene, the film seems not to make one of its major interpretive points.

14 Some reviewers suggest a relationship between *Prospero's Books* and pornography which may be worth developing. The group nude scenes may allude to group sex scenes in one subgenre of contemporary film pornography, and perhaps ultimately to Sade. At several points, Greenaway creates a unisex version of Felicien Rops's "Pornocrates," with male as well as female figures naked except for garters, scarves, gloves, and hat. But Greenaway's is an orgy that never happens, and was never meant to happen, an orgy by allusion. In its mechanical approach to sexuality, *Prospero's Books* may be seen in the context of the recent history of "technoporn." Recent essays that provide a useful introduction to the discourses that connect computers and sexuality in the 1980s and 1990s include Buckley 1991, D'Alessandro 1988, and Springer 1991.

7

A *SHREW* FOR THE TIMES, REVISITED

Diana E. Henderson

Of all Shakespeare's comedies, *The Taming of the Shrew* most overtly reinforces the social hierarchies of its day. Lacking the gendered inversion of power and the poetic complexity of Shakespeare's romantic comedies, this early play might seem less likely to capture the imagination of modern audiences and producers; we might expect it, like its farcical companion *The Comedy of Errors*, to be filmed infrequently and almost obligatorily as part of canonical projects such as the BBC TV Shakespeare series. Quite the converse is true. More than eighteen screen versions of the play have been produced in Europe and North America, putting Shrew in a select league with the "big four" tragedies, and outpacing those comedies scholars usually dub more "mature."[1] What accounts for this frequent reproduction of an anachronistic plot premised on the sale of women?[2]

Part of the answer lies in a venerable tradition of adaptation. Discussing David Garrick's Catharine and Petruchio, Michael Dobson points out that seemingly minor changes in the text "mute . . . the outright feudal masculinism of *The Taming of the Shrew* in favour of guardedly egalitarian, and specifically private, contemporary versions of sympathy and domestic virtue" (1992: 190). Garrick's version provides the source for a performance tradition that tames not only the "shrew" but also the text. Here "Dr. Petruchio" consciously assumes his boorishness as part of a therapy program for a disturbed Katherina. This Petruchio is a far cry from Shakespeare's blusterer, knocking his servant Grumio soundly as he comes to wive it wealthily ("if wealthily then happily") in Padua. Such attempts to obliterate gender struggle ultimately collapse the leading couple into a single entity, "Kate-and-Petruchio," replicating the play's narrative movement and its ideology. Viewing the story in a euphemized and relatively untroubled way from Petruchio's perspective remains the norm in almost all modern video versions – though not, intriguingly, in the two feature films starring Hollywood's most famous couples of their respective generations, Mary Pickford and Douglas Fairbanks Sr., and Elizabeth Taylor and Richard Burton. The films' differences derive both from the unusual box-office power of their leading ladies and also from their directors' cinematic choices.

These choices strive to create a female subject position for Katherine, adding gestures, glances, and private speech to the script's most notorious silences. The erasure of the Christopher Sly induction from filmed versions of *Shrew* removes the play's most common theatrical "excuse" for its gender politics (i.e., it's all a prank, or a drunkard's wish fulfillment). In the very necessity of using the camera's eye to produce a second perspective on the story, modern filmmakers both reveal the potential of their medium to provide an alternative "frame" to the script's use of Sly and call attention to the text's troubled relationship to Katherina as shrew-heroine. Their choices also highlight the continuing difficulties involved in imagining a woman as the dramatic subject as well as object of narrative desire, and especially the interrelated muteness and mystery associated with woman-as-knower. Yet while the use of the camera to gesture at female subjectivity deserves special attention, ultimately each foray is displaced by a more conventional "solution" in representing femininity.

Both modern theater and film have removed the ironic potential of a cross-dressed boy playing Katherine. Thus they make all the more central their basic reliance on modern culture's enshrining of the heterosexual love plot and the presumed link between love and marriage. The familiarity and tug of this domestic fantasy helps explain *Shrew*'s obsessive return to the screen – particularly during the decades of "backlash" when advances in women's political participation outside the home have prompted a response from those who perceive a threat. The timing of the *Shrew*s reinforces this cultural connection. In addition to five silent shorts between 1908 and 1913, "spin-offs" such as *Taming Mrs. Shrew* attest to the popularity of the story during the heyday of suffragism.[3] Soon after suffrage came another silent (1923), and finally United Artists' *The Taming of the Shrew* of 1929, the only movie in which Pickford and Fairbanks co-starred. It claims pride of place as the very first of all Shakespeare "talkies."

Having been supplanted by more sophisticated remarriage narratives and screwball comedies during the Depression Era, *Shrew* returned as an ur-text for two musicals in the 1940s.[4] Soon after, the next set of "faithful" *Shrew*s (as well as the filmed version of *Kiss Me, Kate*) coincided with the enforced return to domesticity of the women who had provided World War II's "swing shift"; Rosie the Riveter was supplanted by Kate the Happy Housewife, as sponsored on television by Westinghouse and Hallmark. All these 1950s productions adopt Petruchio's perspective; on television he is a "frame speaker" who gets the first or last word, while in *Kiss Me, Kate* his character doubles as the narrator for the titular musical-within-a musical. The new homeviewing technology gave *Shrew* new resonance, as it not only promoted female consumerism but quite literally kept women in their homes. And despite its stylistic innovations and dazzling tempo, Zeffirelli's feature film for the swinging sixties retained this emphasis on domesticity – though the motivation and effect of its domestic desires may be interpreted in a radically different way. Indeed, because of an unusual alliance between the director's and Katherina's perspective vis-à-vis the narrative, the unexpected subtext of this farcical film reveals female silencing and isolation, the issues that *Shrew* ballads of Shakespeare's day were quite blatant in promoting but which stage and film versions of the modern era have anxiously tried to suppress.

The third wave of *Shrew*s appeared not in the cinema but back on the TV screen, during the decade following the emergence of "women's liberation." Between 1976 and 1986, five *Shrew*s (including one parodic rewriting) appeared on North American television – setting a frequency record for productions during the era of sound recording. The most telling cinematic innovation in several of these is a post-"sexual revolution" directness in emphasizing the erotic appeal of Petruchio's body as a motivation for Kate's conversion. The centrality of sex appeal is particularly powerful in two versions based on theatrical performances, both broadcast on PBS: the 1976 video of the American Conservatory Theater (ACT) production (dir. William Ball), and Joseph Papp's 1981 video repackaging of scenes from the New York Shakespeare Festival's Central Park production. By contrast, Jonathan Miller's putatively historicist and undeniably sober *Shrew*, made for the BBC Time-Life series, was the perfect production to usher in the neo-conservative 1980s.[5] Miller set his production in opposition to what he perceived as "American" "feminist" versions less true to Shakespeare's text; he identified this foreign enemy with Papp (Miller 1986). Ironically, the stars of Papp's own video, *Kiss Me, Petruchio*, appear to share Miller's sexual politics: in interspersed backstage moments creating another version of a "frame" story, Meryl Streep and Raul Julia deny that the play's gender representation constitutes a problem.[6] Indeed, by replicating Julia's stage energy and sexual appeal through its angled close-ups and fast-paced intercuts, *Kiss Me, Petruchio* seduces. For very different reasons, so does the send-up of *Shrew* on the US network television series *Moonlighting* (1986), which seems wildly progressive in simply advocating marriage as a "fifty–fifty" agreement. A sign of the times, indeed.

The clustering of filmed *Shrew*s correlates with those decades when feminism has induced conservative responses and when the media are actively encouraging women to find their pleasures in the home; moreover, *Shrew* occurs at moments of new viewing technologies and is promptly reproduced in the new media before most if not all other Shakespeare plays. The agents of culture seem anxious to make sure *The Taming of the Shrew* is preserved, even as our science progresses: from moving pictures, to the first Shakespeare talkie, to early television drama, to Zeffirelli's first popularized "younger generation" Shakespeare film, to the world of network TV spoofs and home videos – and now beyond, to one of the first Shakespeare spin-off "teenflicks," *10 Things I Hate About You* (dir. Gil Junger, 1999).[7]

In choosing to erase the Sly frame and use actresses for the female roles, *Shrew*'s filmmakers increase the inset story's claims to social reality, already abetted by the transfer to a normatively realist medium. As Barbara Hodgdon has effectively argued, film's tendency to reify the voyeuristic and consumerist logic of the play's presentation of sexuality also reinforces the tendency to view Kate as a spectacle, bound by an economy in which her pleasure derives from placating "her" man; the female spectator who identifies with Kate, not wishing to deprive herself of what is represented as the means to heterosexual pleasure, thus participates in her double-bind. Patriarchal inscription becomes inevitable and self-consuming for woman, with intended subversion revealed as always already inscribed as a sub-version in the dominant discourse.

While finding this analysis compelling and descriptive of the narrative logic of most filmed *Shrew*s, I resist regarding patriarchal reinscription as a formal necessity, as this discounts some striking film moments as well as the agency (and responsibility) of the filmmakers. My aim is not to deny that all the *Shrew*s we currently have are works of ideological containment, but rather to suggest that despite their ultimate closing down of possibilities, their use of the camera and voice do temporarily work otherwise, and could be employed and extended in ways that might lead away from a co-opted and conservative gender politics. By looking closely at such moments of filmic adaptation and perspective play, my aim is not to argue about the prior existence of female subjectivity in Shakespeare's text nor to ignore the relative meagreness of those moments that catch my eye as causes for celebration within a bleak cultural canvas; rather, it is to affirm the significance and resonance of local artistic choices within our ideological frame, and hence the need to acknowledge their particular cultural agency and consequences. This is true whether the version announces its "fidelity" to Shakespeare or not, and whether it sticks to Shakespeare's playtext (itself an unstable "object") or "spins off" in new directions.

To this end, I focus briefly on five films and four television shows that epitomize their generations' dominant patterns in representing *Shrew*; all are works that were constructed for screen viewing through editing and/or scripting, rather than being video recordings of theatrical performances. In *Kiss Me, Petruchio*, the actual scenes from *Shrew* are filmed theater, but the intercutting of backstage interviews and commentary by audience members constructs a new narrative logic specifically for the camera. Finally, in this edition I turn to the most recent film *Shrew*, *10 Things . . .*, as indicative of new trajectories and styles in "popularizing" Shakespeare – but not in any fundamental way changing the overarching thesis of my argument. By combining a chronological discussion with emphasis on the use of the camera to create a second "authorial" perspective, I hope to illuminate both the attempts to expand the representation of Kate as subject, and the particular cultural "solutions" and frustrations tied to the eras of their production. Viewing these *Shrews* historically, we can better understand their duplicitous, shrewd cultural work.

Early *Shrews*

The silent short films and early talkies establish the basic filmic patterns and modifications to *Shrew* that have been reproduced throughout the twentieth century. D.W. Griffith's direction of Biograph's brief 1908 *Shrew*, the first extant moving picture version, gains it a place in film history; Robert Ball regards it as one of Griffith's "fumbling experiments to express himself artistically in a new form" (Ball 1968: 62). Paving the way for several patterns in *Shrew* representation, Griffith's Petruchio laughs at Katherine's physical assaults and brings his whip to the wedding; in keeping with the "improvement" of Petruchio on film, there is no final wager on Kate's behavior but rather an offering of flowers. As interesting as the film is Biograph's promotional material, which begins with a moralizing message clearly applied only to Katherine: "If we could see ourselves as others see us what models we would become" (cited in Ball 1968: 63). This language foreshadows Jonathan Miller's 1980s statement that Petruchio gives Kate "an image of herself" (1986: 122) and Meryl Streep's matching explanation of Kate's visual education. In each case (as in so many traditional narratives, including those of Golden Age Hollywood cinema), a woman uses her eyes not to view (and hence potentially criticize and judge) others, but rather to see an objectification of her inadequate self. Through this "proper" viewing of herself through the culture's eyes, Katherina is indeed transformed into a model of femininity.

The first *Shrew* produced in the era of women's suffrage, Edwin J. Collins's twenty-minute British & Colonial production of 1923, accounts for Katherine's transformation in terms superficially more amenable to independently minded women. One of the many narrative title cards explains: "By noon the next day, though famished and weary for want of food and rest, the Shrew deep in her heart admired the man whose temper is stronger than her own."[8] Here is the "two of a kind" logic that fits *Shrew*'s pop spin-offs and that some critics apply to Zeffirelli's film as well, arguing that this wild couple stands in opposition to the tame, mercantile society of Padua; here too begins the representation of Katherine as the desiring subject erotically drawn to an alpha male, a pattern dominating the late twentieth-century *Shrews*. In the 1923 silent film, Petruchio's strength is signified by the invulnerability of his body to her fists and fury, gendering the female as the one who is subject to physical suffering. When she hits him to punctuate her warning to "beware my [wasp] sting," she hurts only herself: enacting a classic comic trope, he laughs while she nurses her own hand. Again deleting the final wager, the film ends with Kate firmly transplanted to her new home and cured of her "vile" temper, laughing and kissing Petruchio as she sits in his lap.[9]

United Artists' feature film of 1929 shares this final image of the happy couple, but the backstage context informing Sam Taylor's movie is more complicated. Whereas the other silent *Shrews* prefigure the norms that predominate in the sound era, this version reveals the struggles and momentary counterimages that encourage us to look closely. Made at the moment of transition from silents to talkies when many theaters were not yet equipped for sound, the movie was released in both formats; this knowledge helps explain the extreme gesturing and slow pace of the early scenes, and adds to one's appreciation of Douglas Fairbanks Sr.'s spirited entry and almost throwaway delivery. It does not, however, explain his bungling of famous lines ("I come to wive in Padua – wealthily"). For that, we must turn to Mary Pickford's autobiography:

> the strange new Douglas acting opposite me was being another Petruchio in real life . . . I would be waiting on the set for him till nearly noon. . . . When Douglas finally showed up, he wouldn't know his lines. They had to be chalked on enormous blackboards, and I had to move my head so he could read them. . . . With dozens of eyes focused on us every minute of the day I couldn't afford to let my real feelings be seen.
>
> (1955: 311–12)

Pickford was hardly an impartial observer: during *Shrew* her marriage to Fairbanks was disintegrating. But even if read skeptically, her tale of the traumas of playing Kate (and play[Kat]ing Fairbanks, to invoke Hodgdon's pun) resonates in later actresses' accounts, most notably those of Fiona Shaw.[10]

While director Sam Taylor's writing credit for the film created an uproar at the time, more enduringly troublesome is the acting advice he had relayed to Pickford, against her own better judgment: "We don't want any of this heavy stage drama; we want the old Pickford tricks." The result, Pickford notes, was that "Instead of being a forceful tiger-cat, I was a spitting little kitten."[11] The "set was tense with unspoken thoughts" as her suggestions were overriden: "The making of that film was my finish. My confidence was completely shattered, and I was never again at ease before the camera or microphone." Internalizing *Shrew*'s dynamics, Pickford gave up her unpopular attempts to become something other than America's Sweetheart, soon abandoning her career as an actress for behind-the-scenes employment.

Despite her Shirley Temple timbre and pout, Pickford nevertheless was given equal time on screen, with added speeches and close-ups creating a sense of her ongoing agency, albeit in solitude or silence. The film's more equivalent representation of Kate and Petruchio includes giving them duelling whips, duelling soliloquies, and duelling eavesdropping scenes. Echoing Garrick's script, Katherine gets the last lines of the "wooing scene" as a soliloquy (a form she lacks in Shakespeare), using Petruchio's animal-taming metaphors to refer equally to herself and her rider/falcon:

> Look to your seat, Petruchio, or I'll throw you.
> Katherine shall tame this haggard or if she fails,
> I'll tie up her tongue and pare down her nails.

Though the scene begins with a phallic parody in which Katherine visually assesses their respective whip-length and retreats upon discovering that Petruchio's is longer, both this and the previous scene broadcast an ironic send-up of the usual Fairbanks hero. Gremio and Hortensio exchange sidelong winks and glances behind Petruchio's back when he delivers his braggadochio catalogue of experience ("Have I not heard lions roar?"), and he breaks down in near-hysteria at the prospect of a "woman's tongue." In a remarkable dissolve, we continue to hear Fairbanks's laughing reiteration of "a woman's tongue" as the scene shifts to the unhappy face of Baptista, being chastised by Katherina in her first speech of the film (earlier, we only saw her, and briefly). Thus the director's edit serves to mock Petruchio even as it confirms the narrative's logic that he plays a necessary role in taming Katherina's dangerous tongue.

Both through this visual choice and textual modifications, the following scene accentuates the fear of uncontrolled female speech, whose power is in some part confirmed as Katherina exits with a curse (borrowed from Gremio's part) which silences her father: "you may go to the devil's dam." She later uses her tongue as well as body parodically when waiting before the wedding, imitating Petruchio/Fairbanks's sweeping arm gestures, swagger, and incessant "ha ha" as she describes his behavior. Both speech and visuals collude in deconstructing Petruchio's dominance, reaching a climax when the man who began by leaping over walls ends up reeling in pain from her blow to his head (with a jointstool), murmuring "Have I not heard lions roar?" in woozy bafflement. While the film alters the story to undo Petruchio's harsh agency in effecting a change, Katherina's speech must nevertheless be tamed, a sign of her tender feminine heart when she discovers her husband's vulnerability. Uniquely among "straight" screen *Shrews*, Katherine's final assertion of voice does not require the disappearance or rejection of Bianca: Pickford's famous final wink after her abbreviated last speech, the film model for later winks at the audience, is here clearly aimed at her sister, and is acknowledged as such: behind the patriarchal ventriloquizing remains a conspiracy of "unspoken thoughts," a female subculture whose bond is unbroken. Though her words have become tame, Katherine remains the one who sees more than her husband, creating a silent connection between her perspective and the filmmaker's own. In concert with the shift from an invulnerable to a wounded Petruchio, these adaptations – while hardly presenting a challenge to the social world of Padua – preserve a "separate sphere" for woman as agent. Kate thus sustains her own gaze and the illusion of self-creation from a subaltern position, becoming the sneaky servant rather than the Stepford wife of patriarchy. And in what seems on screen to be their "merry war," Pickford and Fairbanks together provide a prototype for the great Hollywood comedies to come, in which equally important co-stars mix screwball antics with subtler repartée than this transitional film affords.

A *Shrew* in the home

The camera's eye works quite differently in US television's first *Shrew*, the Westinghouse Studio One production broadcast June 5, 1950 (dir. Paul Nickell). Whereas the Pickfair film represents an ironic visual contest between the sexes, this *Shrew* suggests a gap between the viewer's expectations about a "classic" and what the new technology will reveal. The hour-long video begins with a visual joke premised on our sense of historical distance from the past, a distance the immediacy of live, modern-dress performance will then work to deny. Beyond a stone arch labelled "Padua," we survey a painted backdrop with a monumental column dominating an ancient townscape; then the camera tracks back to reveal the modern world of sidewalk cafés as Petruchio (Charlton Heston dressed in trenchcoat, hat, and sunglasses) enters on a bicycle and reiterates "Padua." Shorn of all that might distance this story from an American viewer (including the master/servant relations and class stratification that complicate the text's power relations), this version relentlessly reiterates conventional post-war ideas of gender difference. Even the radios Betty Furness hawks during a commercial break are gendered.[12] Having downed a beer in one gulp, pleased-with-himself Petruchio laughingly pronounces his modernized version of Grumio's couplet: "Katharine the curst!/Of all titles for a woman, this one's the worst"; slapping her ass and chuckling to himself throughout the play, he appears entirely satisfied to embody those attitudes that two decades later would be called male chauvinism. The transformation of Lisa Kirk's Katherine, meanwhile, is played out through frequent costume changes. As if to replicate the recent displacement of the silver screen's strong women by "softer" sweethearts, Kirk begins in a riding outfit clearly evocative of Katherine Hepburn's trousered look (she beats blonde Bianca, who wears an off-the-shoulder dress, with the riding crop), but with her courtship and marriage this Kate changes to the "proper" dresses that accentuate her hourglass figure. The new medium of television also accentuates a cartoonish vision of Katherine; Kirk's Broadway background ill prepared her to convey gesture subtly on screen, and she mugs in silent close-up while Petruchio talks in the middle distance. She is done a further disservice by director Paul Nickell's decision to give her a voice-over "soliloquy" of lamentation in Act 4 (the speech usually addressed to Grumio) while she silently gestures her hunger straight at the camera: in both cases, she appears less angry than mad. Nickell's treatment of Kirk could not be more remote from the use of voice-over for soliloquies in Olivier's films of himself as Henry V and Hamlet, in which the actor's pensive face becomes an occasion for esthetic adulation. By contrast, this vocal/visual experiment in the new technology serves, like the production as a whole, to legitimate the domestication of women. Unlike Petruchio, who gets to speak directly to the camera in his soliloquies outlining his plan, Katherine is shown silently mouthing comments at the end of the "wooing scene" and then closemouthed at this moment of putative self-expression; but she does get to speak directly to the camera in the final speech, as she reminds all those happy homemakers about their duties to their husbands. Meanwhile, a grinning Petruchio casually eats grapes. The hour concludes with Kate's sustained wink to the camera while engaged in her third stolid kiss with Petruchio. She is thus allowed to address the TV audience as a unified speaking subject only when she has learned to manipulate the system and stand by her man.

Stylistically at the opposite end of the spectrum, the other US television *Shrew* of the 1950s nevertheless shares with the Westinghouse version an air of confidence and nonchalance in regard to its subject matter. Moreover, for all its visual wit and parody, the 1956 Hallmark Hall of Fame production (dir. George Schaefer) starring Lilli Palmer and Maurice Evans concludes similarly to the 1950 "realistic" version.[13] The divide-and-conquer logic implicit in most productions, wherein Bianca must be revealed as the "real" shrew when Katherine is tamed, is accentuated by transferring the widow's lines to the younger sister (see Miller 1986: 122). In this regard, both the 1950s television *Shrews* seem to have taken a step backward in time from Pickford's finale. And as in the 1950 production, Palmer's Katherine shifts her gaze from Bianca to the camera during her final speech when pronouncing that "women are so simple"; deploying the new intimacy of the television screen to make herself a guest in our home, she smiles as she calls us "unable worms." The play had opened with an oblique use of lines from the Sly Induction, when Grumio invited the audience to watch these "antic players," addressing the TV camera as he said "Come, madam wife." Now all the madam wives of middle America discover the purpose of their spectatorship as Katherine goes down on her knees, earning a final kiss from her husband and lord. Despite Maurice Evans's friendly reappearance after the curtain calls (in order to advertise subsequent programs), the feminine mystique of the play's conclusion has not been ironized by this "romp."

A *Shrew* alone

Ten years later, Elizabeth Taylor similarly performed Shrew's final speech without irony – and indeed without any lead-in request from her Petruchio, for she launches into her chastisement immediately upon re-entering the banquet hall (having dragged along the other women on her own initiative as well). The result was to naturalize Katherine's assertions as her own spontaneous feelings, flamed by her indignation at unruly wives and empathy for her husband's unexpressed desires. In this, art imitated life. For Taylor herself chose to perform the scene "straight" to the surprise of both director Franco Zeffirelli and co-star Richard Burton, and her husband was touched:

> The usual trick is for the actress to wink at the audience . . . Amazingly, Liz did nothing of the kind; she played it straight . . . and she meant it.
>
> Full of that Welsh passion, Richard was deeply moved. I saw him wipe away a tear. "All right, my girl, I wish you'd put that into practice."
>
> She looked him straight in the eye. "Of course, I can't say it in words like that, but my heart is there."
>
> (Zeffirelli 1986: 216)

Complete with Taylor's stated inability to own the powers of language, this incident epitomizes the paradoxical nature of Zeffirelli's 1967 film, in which Katherina is presented far more empathetically and with greater agency than in most video versions, yet employs that agency to naturalize a traditional sex-gender system all the more doggedly.

With similar irony, there is a surprising undercurrent of melancholy and nostalgia for home within this fast-paced lark of a film designed to appeal to the 1960s younger generation. Those raised on MTV may find the contemporary reviews of this *Shrew* bemusing, for their worries about the disorientation caused by busy sets and camerawork seem almost quaint given the subsequent speed-up of our visual culture.

Moreover, this concern with pace tends to displace detailed analysis of why the film makes unusual choices, such as presenting a predominantly boorish Petruchio and an often tearful Katherina, whose isolation is accentuated by sentimental music and lingering close-up shots. Some have regarded the movie solely as a vehicle for the co-producing star couple, but in this paradoxical tempo one finds marks of the director's own sensibility, representing through the images of *Shrew* the same emotions that his autobiography articulates regarding his fractured and romanticized childhood. His tendency to empathize with the social outcast becomes the occasion for cross-gender identification with Kate, as the camera repeatedly adopts her perspective and adds private moments in which we see her thinking.

An illegitimate child, Zeffirelli felt both beloved and abandoned. He was raised sequentially by a peasant wetnurse, his professional but socially ostracized mother (who died when he was six), and his unmarried aunt. His father, who occasionally visited his mother, at which time the "family" all shared a bed, remained in other ways distant from the little boy; his father's wife memorably hounded the child as a "*bastardino*" and haunted his dreams (her harassment becomes his autobiography's framestory). What Peter Donaldson notes in regard to Zeffirelli's other films also applies to his *Shrew*, providing a subtext for his empathetic representation of Katherina's perspective: "Mourning for his mother's death and absence, grief for his own exclusion from the parental relationship . . . and the effort to find a place in a fragmented family leave their mark on Zeffirelli's work in film" (1990: 147).

Zeffirelli's sensibilities are split and seemingly contradictory, befitting the topsy-turvyness of life in the 1960s. His favorite movie of the year was the Beatles' *Help!* and he got its buffoon-villain Victor Spinetti to play Hortensio, as well as hiring disaffected Roman *capelloni* ("long-haired ones") for the university scenes. At the same time, Zeffirelli insisted that the Italian premiere of his film be the English-language version, to please any of the old English ladies still surviving in Florence who had shared in his own youthful discovery of filmed Shakespeare through Olivier's *Henry V* – a film he credits with having liberated him from paternal authority by giving him the confidence to choose an artistic career.[14] In a version of subjectivity akin to that which the film grants Katherine, he became free to follow the master(s) of his own choosing. As director of *Shrew*, he creates a fantastic version of "home" as screen image, displacing his own illegitimacy, his absent/present father, and the Florentine scandal that precipitated his mother's death, and replacing them with a cultural inheritance from the Bard, Italian *cinéma-verité*, and the visual splendors of the Italian Renaissance (a pattern later extended in his autobiographical film *Tea with Mussolini*). Zeffirelli concludes the account of his childhood by remarking "I still have difficulty in trusting love when it is offered. This is something that has marked my entire life" (1986: 9). Within his representation, the farcical frenzy slows only when his camera lingers on those who are emotionally isolated, unsure, or far from home. The movie embodies the appeal of "traditional values" for those self-creators who were only partially transformed by the sixties sexual "revolution."

The plaintiveness of the moments when one sees Katherine's isolation and sense of betrayal and the balancing tenderness of attention to gestures of gentleness provide an unexpected counterpoint to this *Shrew*'s energetic opening. Such moments also sentimentalize the story more thoroughly than does Taylor's particular (though consistent) choice in the banquet scene. Throughout the film, the pauses are pregnant, and sympathy goes to the outcast: Katherina hurt and crying in defeat after the protracted wooing chase, as she realizes she has been betrothed against her will; locked in a darkened room while the men chortle in the public hall; looking anxiously to her father for support as she faces unfamiliar applause before her wedding; unintentionally witnessing the backroom transaction selling her (the transfer of the massive dowry her father has paid Petruchio); Katherine and Petruchio awkwardly preparing for bed; Katherina alone again, sobbing in the unfamiliar, wrecked bed in Petruchio's home; and then, in a key shift as she takes control of domestic space, a newly sympathetic Petruchio looking at his wife's working alliances with his re-clothed servants; melancholy Katherina sitting amidst the wreckage of her promised clothes; Petruchio uncomfortably focusing on his drink at the banquet and waiting to see if Katherina will come at his bidding; and Petruchio surprised to find her gone after he finally achieves his long-desired kiss. All these extratextual moments create another layer of storytelling, allowing Katherina as much subjective presence as Petruchio.

The dynamics of power change radically at the moment when Katherina discovers her means to control: housekeeping. While it is easy enough for the critic to point out the patronizing gender assumptions informing this means of attaining "power" (and Zeffirelli's political pronouncements affirm his conservatism on some gender issues), it is also important to recognize the seductiveness of his representation, rooted in another aspect of Zeffirelli's social vision: his sense of allegiance to and nostalgia for peasant life. Not only does Katherina remake herself as the force of culture and domestic beauty in opposition to Petruchio's ruffian masculinity, but she does so through an alliance with servants. She transforms the dusty barrenness of Petruchio's bachelor home into a lively arcadian villa, in which lady and grooms share featherdusters and wear similar homemade clothes. (Tellingly, the scene of Grumio's tormenting Kate with the prospect of beef and/or mustard is omitted.) Here too Katherine's newly chosen way of life – not exactly "slumming" but finding solace in a working vacation from her privileged social position – matches a powerful memory from Zeffirelli's youth. He had spent summers in Borselli with his wetnurse's family, in a world later lost through the parallel changes of his growing up (and the death of his individual caretaker) and the culture's development (the displacement of the age-old peasant economy). Ironically, it was only in that "simple peasant town" that Zeffirelli "had a sense of permanence" (1986: 10–11). The director's affection for this world in which the children picked out dead ticks from the wool and all the clothes were homemade overdetermines the more obvious messages produced by similar actions on film (Petruchio's boorishness in proudly displaying his dog's ticks at Hortensio's table; Katherina's "capture" in the woolbin; her rustic home decorating); it also deepens the film's nostalgic desire to embrace a past in which class as well as gender are mystified. After comically recording the skepticism of laborers who hear Lucentio's outburst of academic desire upon entering Padua, the rest of the movie presents the people as a jolly chorus to the public scenes – an energetic film correlate to a theater audience's response, but also one that re-creates feudalism as the good old days. It counters critical attempts to read Kate and Petruchio as carnivalesque opponents to a rigidly monolithic society: this jolly, frolicking Padua is not represented in a way so amenable to Bakhtinian schematization.

Conversely, the ironies and wit of Zeffirelli's *Shrew* defy over-simple interpretation of this as a conservative film. In addition to its unusual crediting of Katherina with interiority akin to the director's own, it is also a work of pop art in postmodern style. For the film, as Holderness observes, is a minefield of parody. The fact that it is the giant prostitute who breaks into tears at the domestic fervor of Katherine's grand finale makes her action equally available for sentimental or ironic interpretation.[15] Moreover, the stress on Baptista's "selling" of his daughters provides a counter-theme to the romanticized home. This is especially true in the film's mid-section, where Zeffirelli delivers a 1–2–3 punch showing Katherine isolated and silenced at her own wedding festivities. First Katherine, humiliated by Petruchio's loud, late arrival, tries to yell "I will not" at the altar in response to her wedding vows – but Petruchio literally stops her mouth in an unerotized kiss before the last word, at which point the entire congregation loudly celebrates. Next Katherine is shown half-buried by the congratulatory crowd, desperately yelling "no" and "father" despite the crowd's indifference to her will. We then appear to shift mood with Katherine as she graciously thanks guests at the reception while a musical consort plays; this, however, is merely the prelude to her witnessing, beyond a doorframe, the handshake and transfer of dowry funds from her father to her husband, an action confirming her isolation. She stands silently gazing from outside the space of a more orderly transaction than took place at church. This sequence of isolating moments, which highlights the culture's traffic in women, works in concert with an undercurrent of violence and the shifting use of the camera's perspective to create a more complicated film than has been fully credited.[16]

Who's zoomin' who?

Zeffirelli's perspective play, in and out of Kate's vantage point, makes obvious the shaping potential – and ironic open-endedness – allowed by artful use of that other movie "subject," the camera. Such play is especially appropriate for representing the subjectivity of a character who, though called a shrew, seldom gets a word in edgewise. Fiona Shaw observes, "Along comes a man to tame the noisy one. And for almost five acts we never hear her speak"; but Paola Dionosetti rightly adds that although Petruchio gets the lines, "Kate has eyes everywhere" (Rutter 1989: 1). The more socially progressive versions work to equalize the battle of wills by showing Katherine in thought, or by constructing visual matches. In Zeffirelli's film, the balance shifts in keeping with his visual priorities as well as emotional sympathies.

While critics swoon over her eyes and bustline, the camerawork not only accentuates Taylor's feminine beauty but mimics her positionality: showing her first as a single watchful eye above the street action; viewing her viewing; pausing to watch her pausing to think; concluding scenes when she concludes her sequence of emotions and decision-making. Indeed, it is Bianca's usurpation of Katherine's viewing position at the window that initiates Kate's attack on her sister, prompting the mock-horror sequence that actually unites the camera's perspective with Kate's own gaze. This affinity between the camera and Kate holds true after the wooing sequence, when the camera returns to join Katherina in her darkened room looking out rather than moving on with the men in the hall; gone is the scene of bartering over Bianca, leaving Katherine's solitary smile to close the narrative's first section. Similarly, in the wedding scenes her looks counterbalance Petruchio's blustering comedy and she again has a solo moment to end the sequence, when she pauses on donkeyback at Padua's gate recognizing that neither direction holds much promise. She is seen last in the travel scene (in which Kate actively schemes to intercept the other riders, rather than merely suffering as in Grumio's textual account), and she gets both the nuptial bed and the last image on her wedding night – all the more remarkable since Petruchio's soliloquy is virtually cut.

By presenting Petruchio as a material creature at the start (a choice often criticized despite its textual defensibility and cinematic usefulness), Zeffirelli allows these camera shots to establish Kate as the movie's silent thinker. This subjectivity remains even after her gain in power causes a shift of empathy embracing Petruchio (now quieter, smarter, and sadder than before she started cleaning house). Because we have already seen Katherina plotting, acting unexpectedly, and only afterwards understood her motives, her final "straight" delivery of her major speech benefits from that sense of anticipation: when Petruchio turns to find her gone, he experiences the surprise that we, filmically, have been trained to expect. Yet we do end up looking at the world from Petruchio's rather than Katherine's vantage. The ironies in this conclusion are legion: the actress's unexpected choice of sincerity is overriden by the director who thereby sustains his own vision by crediting the character with more artfulness than the actress professes. As such, this version shares with so many other productions a power struggle not only between the protagonists but also between director and actress. What remains indisputable is the complexity of cameraplay in the Zeffirelli film, and its crucial effect upon the representation of Katherine.

Back to the future

The five television variations on the theme of *Shrew* appearing in North America between 1976 and 1986 demonstrate the range of stylistic interpretation the play continues to afford; they also reveal how meagerly the previous decade's political upheavals informed those productions deemed worthy to broadcast. Despite radical theatrical reinterpretations such as those of Charles Marowitz and Di Trevis, the hallmark of these TV productions (with the obvious exception of the last, a network spoof) is textual fidelity. The most notable shift has been an explicitly sexual one. In trying to make a recalcitrant text appeal to both sexes, the productions and camerawork for both the ACT and Papp videos celebrate the male body as erotic object; that body is well represented by the charismatic, slyly self-parodic figures of Marc Singer and Raul Julia. For the "me generation," sexual passion (leading automatically to true love) provides the quick-fix to explain away the societal dynamics of power in Katherine's "taming" – or so Meryl Streep's backstage commentary seems to imply in the video aptly entitled *Kiss Me, Petruchio.*[17] Raul Julia's Petruchio plays the sexual Svengali, his perspective credited as fully reasonable and his body the prize worth any price; as Julia himself asserts (in comments that shift between the third and first person), Petruchio "is very self-confident . . . [and] feels he can make the best husband in the world, and he can, too . . . I'm here to make money . . . and any father [with the money for a dowry], he's getting a good bargain." The video seems to confront the potentially offensive aspects of the play right away, with Petruchio performing his post-wedding assertion of ownership ("she is my goods, my chattel . . .") – the only speech recorded twice, in and out of context. What we are soon told, however, is that we should not have been identifying with the audience members who boo – or if we do, our protest has already been as domesticated as Katherine herself (Streep: "They boo because they don't see it"; Julia: "I love it when they boo and hiss Petruchio, because that means Petruchio is making them feel something."). Throughout, offstage cuts deflect potential criticisms of the production, as do camera pans of the audience (we are shown women laughing at the end of the "wooing" scene as Petruchio sits on Katherine announcing she will become as "conformable as other household Kates"). Because the actors are commenting during a performance, they understandably adopt the perspective they have created for their characters. In Julia's case this adds an unintended layer of comedy; however, Streep's replication of Katherine's "conversion" – seeing the world through the eyes of patriarchy – is more disturbing, particularly because she does not show comparable imagination in understanding Katherine's former "shrewish" identity. Onstage, she performs a cartoon catalog of "masculine," anti-social behavior (stomping on flowers, "pumping up" for a fight); although she always appears smart and funny, none of these actions is presented with the nuanced psychological realism she accords to the reformed Katherine. The video accentuates this by allowing her voice-overs to explain the latter part of the play, whereas Julia's comments dominate during the first half. In a voice-over during the tailor scene, as Kate sits with the torn gown in hand, Streep asserts "Really what matters is that they have an incredible passion and love; it's not something that Katherine admits to right away but it does provide the source of her change." Then, as Katherine silently gives the dress to Petruchio, Streep makes the leap to his perspective (thereby legitimating what she never directly confronts, the inequity of behavioral reformation and her infantilization in this putatively mutual scene of passion and love): "What Petruchio does is say I'm going to take responsibility for you, and I'm going to try to change you for your better, make you as great as you can be." Both actors presume throughout that Petruchio does not need to be (could not be?) improved.

The focus solely on the leads and the constant need for the actors to justify the narrative testify to the play's intractability; Streep's exasperated attempts ultimately underscore the interpretive work necessary to make sense of Kate's fate, and leave one agreeing instead with Ann Thompson's sense that "we can no longer treat *The Shrew* as a straightforward comedy but must redefine it as a problem play in Ernest Schanzer's sense: . . . 'so that uncertain and divided responses to it in the minds of the audience are possible or even probable'" (1979: 41). Perhaps the video's most appealing choice is to allow audience members to voice the tensions that the actors try so hard to erase. In the viewers' responses a gender gap appears. None of the men interviewed expresses discomfort, whereas the women divide: most express reservations, though one (speaking in concert with her male partner) fully enjoys this "fabulous love story."

A jolly conclusion recapitulates the performance's emphasis on Petruchio as sexual prize, as if to defuse the social hierarchy: Kate begins to drag him off to bed during the final lines, and then he concedes to exit in her direction during curtain call. While a woman in the audience gets the last word (noting that "It's a fantasy that is dangerous for men" and that she feels "very ambiguous"), the last image is Streep patting Julia's ass as they exit – as if this role-reversal of Heston's fifties' slaps constituted a restoration of equality.

When a wooer goes a wooing . . .

Comparison between this production's and Zeffirelli's rendering of the climactic scene of *Shrew*'s first two acts, the initial encounter between Katherine and Petruchio (2.1.178–269), reinforces the crucial role of the camera in establishing empathy and shaping the script's significance.[18] To achieve the dowry that has motivated his suit, Petruchio must obtain "the special thing . . . That is, her love" which her father regards as "all in all" (2.1.124–5). Nevertheless, as in the parallel "wooing scene" in *Henry V*, it is not clear that Katherine's consent is actually required: Petruchio's reply "Why, that is nothing" (2.1.126) not only indicates his confidence that he will make her yield but also how little evidence it takes for the men of Padua to decide she has been won. Both in the play and in criticism, Katherine's own last words of the act, her refusal to marry ("I'll see thee hanged on Sunday first!"; 2.1.288), are overriden and supplanted by Petruchio's brazen assertion – directly contrary to what he knows of her "private" behavior, and consistent with his decision to invert the truth verbally to get his way – that "'tis incredible to believe/How much she loves me" (2.1.295–6). Indeed, to make *Shrew* into a romantic comedy, one needs to make Petruchio a truth-teller in spite of himself or else motivate an even more "incredible" reversal later (having Katherine fall for him when he deprives her of all forms of ownership). Neither subtext is psychologically implausible in a world of contorted desires and socially endorsed abjection, but to say so removes the lightheartedness associated with farce and may make a viewer uneasy. Once the complexity of real-life psyches intrudes, slapstick can look distressingly like domestic violence, and the problem of Kate's consent is not evaded but compounded.

In the Papp production, the eroticized male body which provides an explanation for Kate's desire is thus invoked most insistently in the initial encounter. The scene allows Julia to dominate playfully and seductively without seeming overtly violent. Thus Petruchio tickles, carries, and encloses Katherine, but only she actually slaps, hits, and spits; nevertheless, she is the one who is left breathless and lying on the floor, while he retains his poise and humor. When Kate strikes Petruchio to "try" whether he is a gentleman (the scene's only scripted violence), he does not flinch. When she spits in his face in response to his request to "kiss me, Kate," he pauses and then delightedly licks his lips to ingest her spittle. Although Streep makes the most of her wittier lines, she is clearly confronted with a superior force here, whose apparent invulnerability to abuse or opposition is only a step less absolute than Fairbanks's laughter as he is whipped. The tide of inevitability that Petruchio had predicted is thus for the most part fulfilled in these performances through the men's delighted embodiment, and Kate's resistance seems both doomed and counterintuitive. These are the sexual dynamics captured by the camera most frequently in twentieth-century *Shrews*.

By contrast, the extended farcical chase in Zeffirelli's movie defuses the scene's focus, transforming Petruchio's relentless verbal enclosure of Katherine into an unpredictable game in which neither words nor rooms can effectively enclose energy: both their bodies hurtle precariously through space, walls, and ceilings. Petruchio does show his persistence, using his head to raise the trap door upon which Kate heavily sits (thus giving a visual punch to the bawdry of his "tongue in [her] tail" retort). But the camera's giddy tracking from room to courtyard to barn to roof and back down through roof to woolbin conveys the film's ongoing message that Kate may eventually be trapped but not easily tamed. The end of the scene brings a shadow of violence, but in doing so acknowledges a change of mood as well: when Petruchio pins down Katherine in the woolbin, the stick in her hand (with which she has been pounding his head) is forced across her throat, while the camera angling down upon her head and heaving breast comes close to Petruchio's perspective of dominance. This eroticized shot puts Katherine in the position of countless female victims in movie thrillers, cowering with a knife at the throat. Zeffirelli earlier used a conventional horror movie sequence in open parody, with Kate in the unseen killer/monster position of the camera closing in upon Bianca as the screaming victim. Thus the shift in Katherine's placement underscores her succumbing to the superior force of Petruchio and the coincidence of that position with eroticized femininity. She will later reclaim equanimity through her greater intelligence and her adoption of a matron's role, but here – and in her subsequent collapse on the floor in tears – she is first revealed as vulnerable in body and spirit. Even as Petruchio looks on tenderly and helps her to her feet, this "wooing" concludes by uneasily signalling his power and her abjection, not her consent. Here again Zeffirelli's practice implies the possibility of a more extensive use of the camera to suggest another perspective on Shakespeare's story.

Coda: all's well . . .?

The silliest of the 1980s *Shrews* constantly parodies Zeffirelli's film, and goes further in modifying Shakespeare's text to create a space for modern love. Replacing the Sly frame with a homework-resisting schoolboy who wants to watch television, the *Moonlighting Shrew* (dir. Will McKenzie, 1986) begins with some self-reflexive comedy about the most widespread modern addiction and its target audience. And by placing the series' stars in Shakespeare's plot (sort of), we get a market-pleasing three-for-the-price-of-one dose of character deconstruction: when Cybill Shepherd plays Maddie Hayes plays Kate, and Bruce Willis plays David Addison plays Petruchio, who can say what's "really" going on? One joke involves Willis/Addison/Petruchio presenting his parchment list of dowry demands, which includes a winnebago, rights to direct, and other TV contract items; having earlier quoted other Shakespeare lines ("wrong play"), he now realizes "wrong scroll." As much a send-up of contemporary media as of Shakespeare, the show nevertheless displays a commonsense consciousness of the textual tensions scholars spend so much energy explaining away, and uses its overdetermined characters to comment on how times do change (as in Willis's comic aside after his pre-wooing soliloquy, which devolves into the Steinian mantra "the man is the man is the man . . .": "if you're a man, you gotta love the sixteenth century"). Willis's rock-'n'-roll wedding number, "Good Lovin'," invokes the familiar medical trope but converts Dr. Petruchio into the patient ("I said doctor, Mr. M.D.,/can you tell me what's ailin' me? . . . he said all I really need is good lovin'"). Of course, singing "I got the fever, you got the cure" to a Katherina bound and gagged at the altar takes "commentary" over the top. The looney-tunery of his post-wedding courtship (at which point Shakespeare's plot is entirely rewritten to replace coercion with mutual respect) reanimates a classic cartoon sequence: upon Petruchio's third gift offering at a hostile Katherine's door, her hand shoves a stick of dynamite into his suit-of-armor's visor; he "looks" at us, walks off camera, and then the picture jiggles with the unseen explosion. Inverting the sun and moon speech to allow Katherine her own eyesight, the show carries further Shakespeare's comic logic, allowing hierarchies (artistic as well as gendered) to evaporate without pain. Unlike the Papp video so titled, when Kate here says "Kiss me, Petruchio" and sweeps him into her arms, role reversal gives the story a new lease on life, without victims. And for those who wish to find a Petruchio motivated by true love rather than money, this version makes his culminating gesture the renunciation of the dowry (which here is involved with the wager). An unabashed

American wish-fulfillment of painless change resulting in equality for all, this sunny moonlit *Shrew* announces it is now the best of times, when the messages a schoolboy learns from his "Atomic Shakespeare" resemble those in "Free to Be . . . You and Me."

Postscript: the beat goes on

The last *Shrew* film of the twentieth century signals the new energies and box-office priorities of its times: *10 Things* is among the first loose "spin-offs" using Shakespeare's stories and specific references, though almost none of the text, in order to make a movie popular with (even as it mocks) the high school crowd. Nevertheless, like its predecessors, this jaunty little film still grapples with the contrary impulses of reproducing Shakespeare (his story, his "spirit") and crafting a narrative amenable to its putatively enlightened post-feminist viewers. On the one hand, Shakespeare has become a flexible enough figure to appeal to the rapping black English teacher and his feminist student nemesis as well as be identified with the nerdy smart boy. Where the source story cannot be reformed adequately to fit this world, the film follows in the footsteps of *Moonlighting* and simply changes the story. Yet the female tongue of *Shrew* persists as a "terrorizing" threat even now, transforming the otherwise attractive, once-popular Kat Stratford (Julia Stiles) into a "heinous bitch." Her insults and references to feminist literature are enough – along with reports of the occasional well-placed knee-kick – to make the thought of a date with Kat a horror, inducing even the neediest misfits to scream, laugh, and flee. Like Petruchio, Patrick Verona is lured to court Kat by the offer of money, but the times require his reluctance in accepting the bribe, his ongoing discomfort, and finally his transformation of bribe into gift; thus he provides Kat with the guitar that can help her sustain her rebellious self-image even as she accepts interpellation into the traditional romance plot. In one sense, Patrick's evolution from (seeming) bad boy to sensitive stud corresponds with the movement of the film as a whole, which gradually shifts perspective from mocking its cartoonish caricatures (the a-v geek, the white Rastas, the Prada-loving Bianca) to humanizing them: Patrick, Bianca, Kat, and even the girls' father "grow up" as the story progresses, as they learn to see (and reveal themselves) beyond farcical surfaces. The Gremio/Hortensio surrogate Joey – the male narcissist who works as a model, and hence is rich enough to bribe Patrick – is the only major character left out of this re-viewing process,

The famous film *Shrew* "wink" returns in *10 Things*, but with gender-inverted hipness. Now it signals misguided sexual arrogance on the part of males: first Patrick tries winking at Kat (prior to his sentimental education), and Joey reiterates the gesture after inviting Bianca to a party – but at himself, in a hallway mirror. Joey's self-involved wink epitomizes his complacent delusion throughout the story, as he has just unwittingly revealed his limited vocabulary to Bianca. However, the shift in "who's winking who" also reveals how thoroughly the causes for female subaltern behavior have been erased in this film, to the extent that Kat's anger at patriarchy can become a running joke. There are no white males in authority positions at the high school, and at home Mr. Stratford is a beleaguered overprotective dad whose wife left him three years prior. Indeed, along with Joey, the only potential "bad guys" of this film are the absent mother and Bianca's backstabbing black girlfriend Chastity. Joey becomes the scapegoat replacement for an erased social order, and thus is gradually revealed to be the cause for almost all the anti-social and conflicted behavior – even that between females. In the most ironic of these cases, Kat's feminism turns out to be a reaction to Joey's having rejected her because she would not continue their sexual relationship (itself a one-night stand occasioned by the combination of Kat's mother's desertion and peer pressure). Like her "statement" of ripping down prom posters and lecturing Bianca about doing things for her own reasons, Kat's politics are reduced to predictable personal responses to her own emotional vulnerability. Whether an internally driven critique of high school values would be possible, given the consumerist MTV world parodied here, remains a moot point; even Kat's supposedly radical stance of questioning what is "popular" has been incorporated into the English classroom as a banner slogan. *10 Things* certainly does not require its audience to pursue such thinking, instead substituting yet another gorgeous hunk as the reward for female acceptance of normative romance. As embodied by Heath Ledger, this Petruchio is both physically invulnerable and gentle, asking a drunken Kat to "open your eyes" and see the green in his as her reward. He may sing "Can't take my eyes off of you" to Kat, but as he does so he makes himself the real (and disarmingly sweet as well as comic) spectacle. The camera endorses his increasing allure, even as it reveals his anxiousness and bad judgment in hiding his original mercenary motive. When the Zeffirelli wooing scene is finally quoted here by having Kat and Patrick play paintball among haystacks, all we get is a lingering kiss in the hay and acceptable romping, not a hint of the earlier film's physical violence in "subduing" the shrew.

But ultimately, the shrew must have her taming speech, and in this, *10 Things* remains true to the dynamics – that is, the jarring disjunction – of Shakespeare's final scene. Signaling its affiliation to Shakespeare as text, Kat's climactic public oration takes place in English class, a response to the assignment to write "your own version of" Shakespeare's sonnet 141, "In faith I do not love thee with mine eyes." An ironic choice, given film's reliance on the eye to reveal, rather than contest, the heart's judgment – but this central conceit of the sonnet will have no bearing on Kat's "poem." Nor will poetic craft. Kat does query whether she should write in iambic pentameter (which results, absurdly, in her again being kicked out of class – as befits a teen film, in which all adult actions should appear ludicrous). Yet nothing could prepare one for the dreadful "poem" she voluntarily performs. While the film has earlier "detached" from Kat's perspective on occasion (when she is doctrinaire in her anti-prom stance, for example), here the incongruity truly baffles. How could a reader of *The Bell Jar* who is bright enough to gain admission to Sarah Lawrence (despite spending much class time in the guidance counselor's office) come up with the nursery doggerel that begins:

> I hate the way you talk to me
> And the way you cut your hair.
> I hate the way you drive my car.
> I hate it when you stare.

and concludes:

> But mostly I hate the way I don't hate you,
> Not even close,
> Not even a little bit,
> Not even at all.

Dr. Seuss would be abashed. Not even rhyme, not even rhythm, not even verse at all. Moreover, this act of "poetic" self-confession drives Kat to tears and yet another hasty exit from the classroom – and not for the obvious reasons accountable were she an English teacher. Rather, we are directed to see this performance, addressed to Patrick, as a sign of "love," emotionally embarrassing but ultimately "worthwhile" since the next sequence shows her approaching her car at day's end to discover the guitar gift and Patrick, in that order. Taming this shrew means temporarily erasing her intelligence and sarcasm, and replacing them with emotional submission: we have been here before. While the final exchange – without peers listening – confirms the value of the newly educated Patrick and allows Kat her chosen future, the oddity of her "sonnet" performance resembles the voluntary strangeness of Liz Taylor's and many an earlier Shrew's final speech. Quickly moving out to "frame" the ending with Kat's favorite band improbably performing on the school roof, the filmmakers of *10 Things* are arguably as tongue-in-cheek about this sentimental interpellation as anybody – or one might say, as Richard Burt does in the service of a quite different reading, that the music tracks "cover" not only earlier bands but also the film's own "cheap trick" in popularizing Shakespeare. Certainly Kat became more attractive to Patrick in the traditional Hollywood manner as the object of his gaze, when she was dancing at the club and then when vulnerably drunk. Sisterhood may be more powerful these days, with Bianca learning to stand up for her boyfriend and her sister by punching Joey twice in the nose and then kneeing him in the groin for herself – but beyond the slapstick reversals, girls talking political rather than heterosexual remain uncool.

10 Things presents a shrew who is overprotective rather than jealous of her sister; from her window, Kat watches Bianca with melancholy sympathy rather than Liz Taylor's fury. And Patrick's ultimate acknowledgement that he "screwed up" is, given both the text and film traditions of *Shrew*, a refreshing addition – prior to his more conventional move to "stop her mouth" (as in *Much Ado*) by kissing. Of course, it is easier to play with *Shrew* in spinoff form, without the textual specifics, and the cleverness of *10 Things* (like *Clueless*) resides primarily in enmeshing the generic conventions of a teen movie with a "literary" classic. But in its attempts at allusion and in its free departures, *10 Things* (like the *Moonlighting* spoof) continues to remind one of the recalcitrance of Shakespeare's story, once the plot progresses from farce to marriage.

As Graham Holderness concludes, if historical analysis "fails to engage with contemporary sexual politics, then the play will continue to speak . . . for the same repressive and authoritarian ideology" (1989: 117). In Zeffirelli's emphasis on the visual, he suggests that artful camerawork and conceptual adaptation could yet produce a textually grounded but truly modern *Shrew*: a fully filmic version that would address rather than replicate the gender hierarchy that continues to haunt most screen versions. Until that time, viewers may take solace in freely adapted spin-offs and the farcical throwaways of the *Moonlighting* grapple:

PETRUCHIO: Where there's a will –
KATHERINA: There's a won't.

Perhaps this new millennium will produce a more experimental filmic rendering of Shakespeare's resistant tale. For the present, by studying the subtler differences and historical reflections of the many twentieth-century *The Taming of the Shrews*, we may learn more – if not about a golden world, at least about this brazen one.

Notes

1 This number excludes spin-offs. Since the publication of the first version of this essay, much work has been done on film Shakespeare, including Rutter's broader survey of femininity and the gaze in Jackson (2000), and Richard Burt's essay (2001) on *10 Things* (to name only two of the most directly relevant essays), as well as Hodgdon's expansion of her crucial *PMLA* essay in *The Shakespeare Trade* (1998).

2 While aware of the shiftiness of meaning in comedy and of the ways people ironize or evade some of the text's less pleasant implications, the work of Boose, Newman, and Marcus has demonstrated, and companion plays such as Fletcher's *The Woman's Prize* confirm, that the text responds to the particular gender issues of its time.

3 A link with contemporary gender issues occurs in the spin-off *The Taming of the Shrewd* (Knickerbocker, 1912), in which a suffragist who has neglected her housework is "tamed" by her husband's arousal of jealousy when he escorts another woman to one of her political meetings (Ball 1968: 149).

4 See Hirschhorn (1981: 236) on *Casanova in Burlesque* (1944). The famous musical was *Kiss Me, Kate*, debuting on Broadway in 1948 and made into a film by George Sidney in 1953.

5 Radical only in its departures from theatrical tradition, this BBC TV museum piece unabashedly celebrates the order achieved through female submission – and makes John Cleese seem not very funny as part of that project. The show was broadcast on the BBC in June 1980, soon after Thatcher's election; in the US on January 26, 1981, at the beginning of Reagan's presidency.

6 Although the stage director was Wilford Leech and the video director was Christopher Dixon, I refer to this as the Papp *Shrew* because the video foregrounds Papp's proprietary control.

7 In a related "first," in 1964 *Kiss Me, Kate* was the first US musical to be adapted for British television (Rothwell and Melzer 1990: 275).

8 Cited from the Folger Shakespeare Library Archive's 35mm print. Another title card tells us that this Petruchio follows in the tradition of Garrick's "masked" educator: "In order to tame the Shrew, Petruchio determines to be more unreasonable than her in all things."

9 Visually, this Shrew epitomizes the style Collick characterizes as quintessentially and conservatively British, replicating the Victorian stage spectacle in its elaborate costumes, proscenium-like sets, and statically full-front camera work. Collick (1989: 33–57) interprets it as symptomatic of a desire to define an English, as distinct from a US, style and tradition; see also Rothwell and Melzer 1990: 270–1.

10 Shaw remarks upon her parallelism with Kate as an actress alone among men in rehearsal, a gendered isolation which men don't [often] experience: "the sense of the terribly clouded confusion that overwhelms you when you are the only woman around. That was Kate's position, and it was mine: she in that mad marriage, me in rehearsal. Men, together, sometimes speak a funny language" (Rutter 1989: xvii).

11 Pickford 1955: 311. The 1966 version removes "with additional dialogue by Sam Taylor," replacing it with "Adaptation and Direction by Sam Taylor." Although the cutting of lines and variation from "pure" Shakespeare aroused criticism in 1929, the development of film theory and practice would confirm the necessity of true screen adaptation – including line cuts as well as the discovery of visual equivalencies and distinctively filmic motifs.

12 These radios are rhetorically and physically differentiated: the young man wants the "swell-looking job in the dark green cabinet" with the "powerful" reach; whereas the ivory compact is a "big favorite with the girls because it's light as a feather." Having been given the properly sexed radio, the couple dances away together.

13 Extending a pattern introduced by the 1929 film's opening with a Punch and Judy puppet show, this production uses *commedia dell'arte* techniques; the constant movement of acrobats,

dancers, and clown-nosed servants combines with active camerawork to create an energetically three-dimensional look within the bare studio "setting."

14 See Zeffirelli 1986: 224 and Holderness 1989: 55–6 on *Help!,* and Donaldson 1990: 148–9 on the role of Olivier's film.

15 On the use of metafilmic parodies, see Holderness 1989: 64–7.

16 None of this undermines the farce or enjoyment that the film affords.

17 The stage directors' motivations for emphasizing the male body lie outside the scope of this essay. My aim is to outline the filmic effects of such choices, and how (even if informed by alternative sexualities and unconventional desires) when combined with a traditional narrative they reflect the dominant ideology of their times – in this case, making a patriarchal text more palatable to a predominantly heterosexual public affected by the "sexual revolution."

18 Line citations for *The Taming of the Shrew* refer to the Cambridge edition edited by Thompson in 1979.

8

MIXING MEDIA AND ANIMATING SHAKESPEARE TALES[1]

Laurie Osborne

When the Folio of Shakespeare's plays was first published in 1623, that text presented both the collected and the divided works of the playwright. The divisions along the lines of dramatic genre in that collection are typographically marked both by subtitle and by renewed pagination; the comedies, histories and tragedies create alliances between plays which we now sometimes separate – romances, problem plays, tetralogies. The shift from one mode of production to another, from performance to print, served both to ally Shakespeare's plays and to distinguish between them. The apparent unity of the Folio thus both reveals and disguises the very different materials drawn together in these plays, most noticeably the chronicle histories which Shakespeare has transmuted into dramatic properties.

Similarly, other reproductions of Shakespeare in alternative forms reveal the impulse both to collect Shakespeare's plays and to divide them. In the engravings of Boydell's Shakespeare, in the performance texts of nineteenth-century directors ranging from John Philip Kemble to Henry Irving, and in the silent films of the late nineteenth century and early twentieth century, reproductions of Shakespeare unite groups of "major texts" while at the same time often dividing them along the lines of genre, significant characters or scenes, or even abridgeable texts. Such "union in partition" definitely continues in film in the twentieth century.[2] Beyond the group of plays first presented in silent pictures, individual *auteurs* as diverse as Laurence Olivier, Orson Welles, Akira Kurosawa, Grigori Kozintsev, and Franco Zeffirelli have produced their own "canons" of Shakespeare, often taken up by later filmmakers like Kenneth Branagh. We have accepted, or at least tolerated, each new mode of production re-creating Shakespeare's plays using its own media and addressed most closely the relationship between film and stage performance. It has seemed clear that film is film and stage is stage, separated as surely by modes of production as the genres in the Folio are separated typographically.

However, as a number of critics have pointed out, each new mode of production depends on a mixture of media. In *Shakespeare, Cinema, and Society*, John Collick carefully delineates a wide range of sometimes conflicting features from Victorian stage craft to political cartooning which helped give silent film its means of communication (1989: 12–32). Although moving from such icons as the silent films to *Shakespeare: The Animated Tales* may seem a serious step down on the cultural ladder, the similarities in necessary abbreviation, the dominance of visual images, and a radically new representation of Shakespeare's plays ally the two forms. Moreover, animation offers its own radical innovation by mixing the still image with frame-by-frame motion in ways which can preserve both media in tension – painting and film. The new film conventions in the *Tales* produce self-conscious revelations of conflicting modes of production, raising the issue of mixed media in Shakespearean productions as we enter an era of multimedia Shakespeare.

The mixed modes of production, which characterize the series taken as a whole and the productions of the second series taken individually, demonstrate that the multiple media that are beginning to converge in reproductions of Shakespeare relate directly to colliding materials within the plays. Shakespeare's mixing of language and genres becomes the model for the mixed media that might seem to fragment or diminish the plays. In turn, the mixture of materials in these animations provide an interpretive model, especially evident in the second series of *Animated Tales* which builds on the first six tales.

In the first series, *Shakespeare: The Animated Tales* offered an instant diversity of animation styles by producing thirty-minute versions of six plays using three distinct techniques. Three of these, *Macbeth* (dir. Nikolai Serebirakov, 1992), *Romeo and Juliet* (dir. Efim Gambourg, 1992), and *A Midsummer Night's Dream* (Robert Saakianz, 1992), took the very recognizable form of cel animation. Although the visual style differed markedly from the darkly shadowed *Macbeth* to the lushly rounded and colorful *A Midsummer Night's Dream*, the movements, visual transformations, and limited perspectives of cel animation linked these cartoons. This mode of production also distinguished them both from the potentially similar oil-painting animation of *Hamlet* and from the stop-action animation of puppets in *Twelfth Night* (dir. Marcia Muat, 1992) and *The Tempest* (dir. Stanislav Sokolov, 1992). Immediately the first series both joined a group of plays and unexpectedly divided them by varying animation techniques, in the process provoking the interest of film reviewers and garnering an Emmy for the animated *Hamlet* (dir. Natalia Orlova, 1992).

The second series of *Animated Shakespeare Tales* has drawn markedly less attention because it lacks the novelty of the first series; the initial project's ambitious animation and its multinational combination of Welsh producers, English actors, and Russian animators were now familiar.[3] But neither series has occasioned much critical analysis from Shakespeareans – even from those concerned with film.[4] These animations deserve such analysis because *Shakespeare: The Animated Tales*, especially in the second series, has developed dynamic relationships between Shakespeare's texts and the specific features of the several distinctive styles of animation. The interaction between the highly valued but traditionally laborious artistry of Russian animation and Western technology, like line test equipment brought in by Welsh and English producers during the first series, led to a heightened self-awareness in the second. Moreover, lacking the abundance of research and Western film materials provided for the first series, the directors more fully explore the effects of mingling modes of production. As a result, these animations self-consciously foreground animation techniques and record provocative collisions of differing modes of production.[5] They employ imagery that grows from the plays' text while also exploiting the unusual features of animation which emphasize how new modes of production refashion and reinstate mixed media in the Shakespearean canon.[6]

Animating Shakespeare's plays goes beyond bridging the now familiar gap between filmed and staged performances or even the more tenuous boundary between film and video; these tales link the extremes of Shakespeare and cartoon; high culture and low culture; art and (to some eyes) reductive kitsch. Within the tales more familiarly constructed in cel animations, the animators challenge assumptions about animation that Russian film theorist Sergei Eisenstein first expressed in his analyses of Disney. Ironically, Eisenstein invokes Shakespearean genres to argue that animation is inherently comic: "In Shakespeare's tragedies, people change. In Shakespeare's comedies, the characters are transformed constantly . . . by disguising themselves, or undergoing physical transformations through magical means. In Disney – they turn into each other" (1988: 39). Thus Eisenstein draws attention to "the literalization of metaphor" (39) which animation shares with comedy and argues that "poetry's principle of transformation works comically . . . given as literal metamorphosis" (40). The animators of the second series strikingly revise this premise when they turn the literalization of metaphor which Eisenstein locates only in comedy into a principle for tragedy as well.

In a noteworthy sequence in the animated *Julius Caesar* (dir. Yuri Yulakov, 1996) where Brutus fully embraces the conspiracy, the animators use both exterior film movements and the flexibility of image transformation to portray Brutus's choice to join the conspiracy. Despite the often-held view that "the animated film . . . employs metamorphosis (and stroboscopic motion) in lieu of conventional cuts and thereby erases the remnants of its frame-by-frame construction" (Small and Levinson 1989: 70), the tale offers an animated series of jump-cuts: [long shot of Brutus reading] "Speak [cut to medium shot], strike [cut to close-up], redress" (*JC*: 2.1.47). This common film cut thus draws attention to the frame-by-frame construction of the piece even while other elements of the sequence register the metamorphoses noted by Eisenstein. For example, Brutus is reading Cassius's message from a scroll which itself took the form of a snake in Cassius's hands. As Brutus reads from the letter, the film-like jump-cuts draw attention to the nearing decision. But then the close-up of Brutus undergoes its own transformation as he dissolves in flames which in turn become Cassius. The presented camera action of the feigned jump-cut meshes with Brutus's internal convictions; then the very outlines of the character prove unstable as he turns into Cassius. The effect, however, is hardly comic, although it does represent a provocative literalization of the metaphor.

The imagery incorporated in the scroll of conspiracy and the shifting boundaries of the characters animate the language of the play. As the scroll/serpent is brought to him, Brutus's own language locates the serpent as a potent image in the context of worrying about how the crown might change Caesar's nature (square brackets within quotations throughout this essay indicate lines that do not appear in the *Animated Tales*): "[It is the bright day that brings forth the adder/And that craves wary walking]. Crown him that,/And then I grant we put a sting in him" (*JC*: 2.1.14–16). This animation plants the image of the serpent in the scroll well before Brutus decides to think of Caesar "as a serpent's egg,/[Which hatch'd, would, as his kind, grow mischievous/]And kill him in the shell" (*JC*: 2.1.32–4). Although the script severely curtails the textual elaborations of this metaphor, the animators emphasize it even before Brutus's speech and identify the serpent not as Caesar but as Cassius's tempting of Brutus.

If the snake metaphor is literalized before it actually appears in the text, the enflaming of Brutus is literalized well after Cassius comments in Act 1 that "[I am glad/ That my weak words have struck thus much show/ Of fire from Brutus]" (*JC*: 1.2.176–7). Although he has not yet managed to convince Brutus of the necessity of killing Caesar and, in fact, these lines do not appear at all in the *Animated Tale*, his speech provides the metaphor which the animators make literal to demonstrate that Brutus has embraced Cassius's cause. The displaced animations of these metaphors interpret the play and demonstrate Cassius's influence on Brutus's noble personality: they underscore a central mode of Shakespeare's character development in this play by literally showing one character turn into another but with serious rather than comic effect.

Thus the animators also test Eisenstein's vivid contrasting of "the self-contained independence of the outlined character and an independence of his actions" in animation with Shakespearean unity which Eisenstein defines as combining action and character such "that a trait of personality determines the course of action and then an action, in turn, molds the personality of the character" (1988: 61). Eisenstein's distinction between animated and Shakespearean characters grows from his perception that, in Disney's productions, actions and emotions are registered outside of characters with trembling lines of shock, for example, which separate the outlined character from what he says or does rather than creating the organic unity assumed to be part of Shakespearean characters. The *Animated Tales* scriptwriter frames a similar proposition: "Animation, Leon Garfield thinks, gives you the opposite of theatre. 'In the theatre it'w [sic] the actor who creates the part; in animation, it's the animator'" (quoted in Buss 1992: 28). By singling out the animator, Garfield identifies the *image*, rather than the actor, with the creation of character. Both current views of character in Shakespeare and the representations of animated interiority have changed so that the cel animations of recent series create what Alan Sinfield might call "character effects" (Sinfield 1992: 52–79). Their images subtly underscore how Shakespeare presented character development and motivation from outside the outlines of his supposedly organic characters.

For example, as in *Julius Caesar*, the cel animation in *Othello* (dir. Nickolai Serebirakov, 1996) also draws directly on speeches of the characters, but the animation extends well beyond literalizing metaphor. Desdemona's evocative description of the maid of Barbary and her willow song – both verbal expressions rather than actions advancing the plot of Shakespeare's play – become a series of images in the tale. Even though the Barbary maid and her lover obviously appear outside of the animated Desdemona, subject to her voice-over description, the sequence registers Desdemona's experiences and the imagery from speeches cut in the production. At the turning point in the couple's devotion, as the maid reclines in his lap, a white, fluttering moth arrives. The death's head of its body (shown in close-up) foreshadows her death later in the sequence. More curiously, the moth, which drifts between the couple, appears reflected (or perhaps imbedded) in the eye of the maid's lover just before he vanishes.

This image enacts Desdemona's perception that Othello grows neglectful because of the handkerchief; in the playtext, he has threatened that "[if she lost it,/Or made a gift of it, my . . . eye/Should hold her loathed]" (*Oth.*: 3.4.60–2) and urged her to "[make it a darling like your precious eye]" (*Oth.*: 3.4.66). He claims that there is "magic in the web of it/ . . . [/The worms were hallowed that did breed the silk]" (*Oth.*: 3.4.69, 73). During Othello's radically curtailed speech, the tale shows the Egyptian woman holding a handkerchief which turns into the same kind of moth that reappears in the scene of the Barbary maid. The whiteness of the moth, the death's head, the mummy-shape of its body, and its apparent penetration of the lover's eye all associate it with Desdemona's handkerchief, even though the *Animated Othello* cuts the description of the handkerchief's origins.

The animation of the Barbary maid's death, drowned Ophelia-like amid the hanging willow leaves that were at first Desdemona's hair, thus represents Desdemona's experiences while foreshadowing and explaining her passivity on her deathbed. Taken from Shakespeare's set piece of the tale and set against the willow song, this animated cutaway integrates the maid's tale and Desdemona's personality even though the two are physically separate in the animated scene. Moreover, this sequence also shows that Shakespeare's text itself includes such externalizations despite claims about the organic unity of Shakespeare's characters. These external events – the lover's departure and maid's death – develop Desdemona's character.

As interesting as these cel animations are in representing conflicting modes of characterization in Shakespearean drama, the more immediate and compelling collisions of artistic modes occur within the other four *Tales*. *The Winter's Tale* (dir. Stanislav Sokolov, 1992), *The Taming of the Shrew* (dir. Aida Ziablikova, 1996), *Richard III* (dir. Natalia Orlova, 1996), and *As You Like It* (dir. Alexei Karakov, 1996) take the opportunity of their innovative modes of production to test the interdisciplinary artistry in their own work as well as mixed media in Shakespeare's plays. Although Terence Hawkes suggests that the animated tales will "be of no use. They are packages of stories based on the Shakespearean plots, which themselves were not original. So they aren't going to provide much insight into Shakespeare" (quoted in Lewis 1992: 12), the very repackaging underscores Shakespeare's own strategies for reworking his sources. As a result, these four *Animated Tales* not only create compelling visual tensions between sculpture, painting, engraving, film, and puppetry, but also invoke the ways such tensions between different art forms (including those of performance) traverse the plays.

The stop-motion photography of the puppet animation captures the tiny changes the animators must make to produce the kind of realistic movement which earned *The Winter's Tale* the 1996 Emmy for Best Animated Feature: "Each puppet is constructed around a metal jointed skeleton (or "armature") which holds the limbs in exactly the position desired by the animators. Heads can be changed to display different expressions and even eyeballs can be moved with a pin" (*Guardian* 1992: E14). When the first series used this technique, the puppets and their carefully manipulated movements enabled an exploration of Prospero's magical abilities to control stillness and motion and the fantastic twinning of *Twelfth Night*. The second series builds on these explorations by incorporating still more explicit invocations of the underlying artistry of puppetry.

Like *The Tempest*, *The Winter's Tale* explores the magical boundary between stillness and movement in the context of puppets. This *Tale* initially concentrates the viewers' attention on the destruction of mobility. Since the animated *Winter's Tale* cuts all of Hermione's verbal interactions with both Polixenes and Leontes in the second scene, the latter's aroused jealousy takes root from seeing his wife and his friend across the courtyard, sheltered amid columns. Neither the supposed lovers nor the husband actually moves that much, an immobility which is more than made up for by Mamilius who plays, dances across the courtyard, hides from his nurses, and cheerfully jumps onto and off of his toys. In fact, the child puppet noticeably enacts even references to movement. When Leontes announces, "I have tremor cordis on me; my heart dances,/but not for joy; not joy" (*WT*: 1.2.110–11), Mamilius comes dancing into a fire-lit room where his father broods. All this realistic, childlike movement on the part of the Mamilius puppet paves the way for the blow of his death. The loss of Mamillius is all the more touching because he has been such an engaging and active small figure. The announcement of the permanent removal of the most mobile figure apparently leads also to his mother's immobility in death. The stillness of Sicilia's wintry landscape is now complete.

At the same time, the animation of *The Winter's Tale* explores the magical dimensions of the play in ways which foreground the movement of puppetry. Stanislav Sokolov, who animated both this tale and *The Tempest*, suggested during an interview that "animated film has more concentrated powers of expression, as well as a capacity for giving concrete form to fantasy that is impossible in any other medium" (Buss 1992: 28). Certainly Sokolov's animated *Winter's Tale* underscores (and in some cases invents) the fantastic in the play. The bear and the incursion of Time are unusual, even supernatural elements within the playtext, but Sokolov brings in sprites which dance around Leontes's head like flames as he condemns his daughter first to be burnt and then to be abandoned. Moreover, the ghost of Hermione literally appears in an interpolated scene on the boat with Antigonus. Both these concrete fantasies spring from some textual cues, but they visually exceed what Shakespeare offers and enforce particular readings of events. For example, the floating spirits which surround Leontes may be the evil counterparts of the spirits which Antigonus asks to protect the child: "Come on, poor babe./Some powerful spirit instruct the kites and ravens/To be thy nurses" (*WT*: 2.3.185–7). Even so, the effect of these near transparent and flame-like creatures is to mitigate Leontes's jealousy and his wanton destructiveness of an innocent child. Yes, the devils made him do it – complete with horns and near transparent figures.

Even more obviously, the appearance of Hermione's ghost while Antigonus bears the child away on a boat seems merely a literal rendering of the account Antigonus gives of his dream about Hermione when he lands in Bohemia – with a few important omissions:

> [I have heard (but not believ'd) the spirits o' th' dead
> May walk again. If such thing be, thy mother
> Appear'd to me last night; for ne'er was dream
> So like a waking. To me comes a creature,
> Sometimes her head on one side, some another –
> I never saw a vessel of like sorrow,
> So fill'd, and so becoming; in pure white robes,
> Like very sanctity, she did approach
> My cabin where I lay; thrice bow'd before me,
> And (gasping to begin some speech) her eyes
> Became two spouts; the fury spent, anon
> This did break from her:] "Good Antigonus,
> Since fate, [(against thy better disposition)],
> Hath made thy person for the thrower out
> Of my poor babe, [according to thine oath,]
> Places remote enough are in Bohemia,

> There weep and leave it crying; and for the babe
> Is counted lost forever, Perdita
> I prithee call't. [For this ungentle business,
> Put on thee by my lord, thou ne'er shalt see
> Thy wife Paulina more." And so with shrieks,
> She melted into air.] . . .
>
> (*WT*: 3.3.15–37)

The speech becomes Hermione's rather than Antigonus's, with most of *her* language intact. However, the description of her appearance and behavior in the text does not match the ghostly Hermione who speaks in the *Animated Tale*; that figure, though clothed in white as during the trial scene, spouts neither tears nor fury. The words are much the same, but the tone is gentler – no shrieks or extended weeping bracket this speech in Sokolov's *The Winter's Tale*. Without Antigonus's commentary, the audience is left to assume that this is Hermione's ghost indeed. If Leontes's crime is softened by the apparent supernatural intervention, Hermione's death is made all the more certain with her lifeless body and her apparently real ghost.

At the same time, the "ghost" reactivates Hermione, this time drifting puppet-like above Antigonus as the evil spirits were suspended around Leontes's head. An overlay effect allows these floating figures to invoke puppetry while distancing them in contrast to the fully present puppets in the scene. The figure of Time emphasizes puppetry more concretely. Echoing vividly Ariel's floating appearance as the Harpy in *The Tempest*, Time also combines the winged image of Leontes's evil spirits and the hovering whiteness of Hermione's ghost. These interjections of fantasy in the form of translucent puppet-figures, floating on wires in the frame, functions as prelude to the culmination of the dynamic between stillness and motion which occurs, naturally enough, during the unveiling of the statue.

Hermione's stillness, like that of the sleeping Miranda in *The Tempest*, is that of a puppet not moving. In *The Winter's Tale* we do not have the advantage of watching Hermione "fall asleep," so we lack assurance of her ability to move at all. By seeing and hearing her "ghost" rather than hearing Antigonus's dream, we are led to accept her death in the *Animated Tale*. The omission of comments that she might move only draws even more attention to the fact that she is, as a statue, an immobilized puppet. In fact, when Paulina animates her, she must do so by invoking Hermione's former movement, that is, her collapse during the trial scene. The bright light which whitens still more the veil around the statue echoes the all-white vision of Hermione during her trial, both dressed in white and illuminated by light from a window in an otherwise darkened room. Her immobility as accused and as corpse in that scene has already been revised by the movement of her whitened ghost on the boat. During the recognition scene, the dynamic between the stasis of the statue with fresh paint on her cheek and her movement within the drama of the reunited family underscores Shakespeare's invocation of the plastic arts; in the *Animated Tale*, the "concentrated expression of fantasy" forges the connection between the still image/puppet brought to motion and the statue brought to life, markedly without either Paulina's or Leontes's comments that she seems to breathe or move. By explicitly invoking the magic of puppetry where still sculpted figures come to life and move, the animators thus create the fantastic within an interplay between filmed movement and sculpture.

As *Twelfth Night* did, the *Animated Taming of the Shrew* seems to call for bodies, even wooden ones, in the parts being played and exploits the depth of field which the puppets allow more readily than other animated forms. However, the animators have chosen to use the available perspectives in order to emphasize the self-conscious puppet performance of Kate's *Taming*. As a result, this animation in particular draws attention to its formal use of puppets in ways which draw traditional puppet theater together provocatively with Shakespeare's shrew taming.

The puppetry of the *Animated Taming* is reworked through the context of the frame tale of Christopher Sly. Even though a half-hour production calls for all the cuts possible, the producers make the deliberate choice to set up the internal show, entitled on the curtain before it "The Taming of the Shrew," as a puppet show. In so doing they create a conflict between the conventions of puppet shows – where Yu M. Lotman argues that the puppet players are a given and therefore invisible – and the filmed puppeteering where clearly inanimate figures are moved little by little to convey the sense of motion (Lotman 1981: 39). Although the animators did not adopt the suggestion of scriptwriter Leon Garfield and academic coordinator Roy Kendall that they produce the frame story in cel animation and the taming of Kate in puppetry (and thus introduce mixed animation in one production), they do vividly emphasize the puppetry at the core of the tale (Kendall 1996: 29). In fact, at several points where the production *could* allow Kate's story to emerge from the metatheatrical context, the tale sets up self-conscious devices like the near-spherical narrator who handles the curtain or the use of that same curtain as the backdrop for Petruchio's horseback ride to Verona which recall the frame and set limits of the puppet show. These features help to reproduce the remarkably unironic version of Kate's taming which the Lord offers to Sly.

This version cuts most of Petruchio's soliloquies revealing his proposed shrew-taming strategies. Without his suggestion that he will woo her in her own humor, his cheerful brutality seems motiveless even though the physical violence of his treatment of Kate is not emphasized. For example, he does not smack her "tail" during their courtship as do other filmed Petruchios; instead the animated production punctuates their first scene together with tap-dance foot movements and sounds rather than any fist fights. The result is an oddly understated *Shrew* where everything is played "straight" including Kate's speech of submission which seems to carry no tinge of the irony we have come to expect from contemporary productions. Possibly, the relative absence in the puppets of subtle changes in facial expression – so crucial to other tamed *Shrews* in showing Kate's responses – flattens the effect of a comedy whose very physicality has produced notable exuberance on film. However, I think an even more subtle set of generic considerations influence the puppet *Shrew* – this play, with its farcical violence between the male and female leads, runs all too close to Punch and Judy, that classic of puppet theater. The production's palpable efforts not to victimize Kate physically do not eliminate the resonance of the punched Judy version of marriage.

Because the frame of the tale is crucial, this version of *Taming*, though radically abbreviated in other ways, invents the closure of the Sly plot, not even using the text of *The Taming of the Shrew* as some productions do (1992: 88–9). This version proves that the lesson Sly thinks he has learned about dealing with shrews is completely inadequate, as the Innkeeper forestalls his use of Petruchio's shrew-taming tactics by hurling Sly once again out of the tavern to fall into a slovenly, huge-bellied position comparable to his first appearance. The added ending reverses the violence of the generic puppet confrontation since Punch gets punched.

In their use of puppetry, *The Winter's Tale* and *The Taming of the Shrew* tend in opposite directions: *Winter's Tale* equates puppet stillness with the art of sculpture which Shakespeare has drawn into his dynamic of time and seasonal revival, whereas *Taming* invokes traditional puppet theater as the backdrop for Shakespeare's staging of narrative Shrew tales. Both tales exploit their modes of production to display while interpreting Shakespeare's mixed media, the blending of plastic and dramatic arts on the one hand and the combination of folk-tales and theatre on the other.

In the cases of *Richard III* and *As You Like It*, the blend of media in the animation techniques themselves becomes an interpretive model. These *Tales* use comparable animation techniques drawn from painting. When the *Animated Hamlet* came out, this technique drew considerable attention:

> The production of *Hamlet* was a remarkable achievement as it uses one of the most difficult animation techniques of all – painting on glass. This creates a final result with all the attractive textures of a moving oil painting . . . the animators paint directly on to sheets of glass which are suspended beneath the camera. They use a thick ink which dries slowly. After a frame is exposed to the film, tiny changes are made to the painting by scraping away some ink and adding a little more as necessary. It is a painstaking process . . . with painting on glass, all of the work takes place under the camera with the surface of the same sheet of glass gradually transformed from the first frame of a scene to the last.
>
> The difficulty of this technique means that it would be completely impractical to produce 24 paintings for every second of *Hamlet*. Instead several frames at a time are shot of each painting, dissolving into several frames of the next. This approach also helps to give a more fluid look to the movements.
>
> (*Guardian* 1992: E14)

Hamlet's success and distinctiveness led the second series directors to adopt that method to explore self-consciously an animation technique which has been so vividly and consistently likened to oil painting. As one journalist described the *Hamlet* of the first series, "at times you almost believe that you're watching a kinetic unfolding of the *Hamlet* story etched by Rembrandt" (Andreae 1993: 14). *Richard III* strongly echoes the earlier oil painting animation, exploiting the ghosts and darkness of that play, whereas *As You Like It* uses watercolors (Kendall 1996: 33). As a consequence, the comedy offers both more color and more extreme variations in visual style. Both tales, however, incorporate a striking degree of self-consciousness about the dependence of their animation upon stained glass, painting, and etching.

Designed by Natasha Orlova, who also directed *Hamlet*, *Richard III* possesses the same density and darkened richness of the earlier production. Orlova's Richard is a creature haunted by his own grotesque shadow as well as by ghosts. Also like *Hamlet*, in *Richard III* "the insanely laborious method of painting each image on glass" has resulted in cuts which focus the tale around the title character to the exclusion of those who react to him and set his actions in vivid familial and political contexts within Shakespeare's plays. Perhaps inspired by the local space of the single plane of glass, covered "with black etching ink mixed with Vaseline, the base . . . pulled off with fingertips, refined with brushes, then underlit" (*Radio Times* 1992: 30), noticeable rearrangements end up interleaving and reversing aspects of the text, revising Richard while emphasizing him.

At first glance, *Richard III* seems derivative of both the earlier *Hamlet* and of *Macbeth.* As in the cel animation of the Scottish play, *Richard III* also produces insistent images of shadows and stained glass. In the context of this form of animation, however, both the shadows which come to represent Richard's murderous nature and especially the "stained glass window" images emphasize the under-lit images on glass which form the basis for this kind of animation.

The shadows that Richard casts throughout the first half of the play, most noticeably over Anne in the wooing scene, are more than just signals of depth and perspective. Shadows appear to swallow the young princes when they enter the tower. They recur when Tyrrell visits the princes to kill them – shadows from either side of the frame reach in, collide and snuff out the lighted boys as they sleep. The resulting darkness then shatters into crows in flight. Already associated with Richard because one has emerged from his eyes in the transition from Clarence's imprisonment to Anne's wooing, the crows form a flock until one swoops down to land and literally becomes Richard, shaking loose a dark cape which surrounds him as if he himself were a shadow.

Closely interconnected with these shadows, the persistent images of stained glass both open Richard's villainy and symbolically shut it down. As Richard of York admits his nature – "Since I cannot prove a lover (To entertain these fair spoken days) I am determined to prove a villain" (*RIII*: 1.1.28–30) – his disclaimer of lover-status is set against an image of golden back-lit lovers, the shadow of an embrace projected on an ornately framed window. In fact, the camera "pans" past a series of elaborately framed windows all back-lit so that the figures within seem projected upon their glass, neatly combining the light, shadow, and painted glass which produce the animation.

The most dramatic of several such "window" images is also marked subtly by shadows, the faint traces of Richard and Buckingham as they leave "Towards Ludlow then" (*RIII*: 2.3.154) to greet the princes. Their faint shadows appear to move behind the large stained-glass scene which comes to occupy the whole frame. The camera cuts to a still closer view of window representation of two warriors being slain as the narrator recounts how the Queen's two brothers are put to death. A static scene marked out on glass explicitly replaces the mobile scenes on glass that we have been watching.

However, shadows and stain do not remain separate once Richard is declared king. As Buckingham toasts his ascension to the throne, the wine spills, flooding the screen with red that subsequently, as the camera pulls back, turns out to be the red of Richard's enormously long coronation cloak. The spilt wine, like the overflowing and murderous shadows which engulf the princes soon after, is so forcefully associated with Richard's villainy that Buckingham's slight resistance to killing the heirs apparent is accompanied by an image of his swirling his wine, but *not* spilling it. And after Richard's final disturbed night's sleep before the battle that claims his life, he spills his own wine as he starts away from his shadow which looms, apparently, on every side. The blood-red wine has fully superceded the golden yellow of the "glorious summer of this sun of York" (*RIII*: 1.1.2) which opened the *Tale.*

Throughout this *Animated Tale,* floods of shadow or color oppose the crisp outlines of the stained-glass image. From Richard's first rejection of the embracing figures crisply outlined within the window frame, he has moved from shadows overtaking the screen to the bloodbath of red to the whitely shadowed figures of the ghosts which lighten the shadows of his tent and urge him repeatedly to "despair and die" (*RIII*: 5.3.126). His death then gives way to an image that echoes and improves upon the initial lovers in the window. As the voice-over narrates the resolution of the War of the Roses, Richmond and Elizabeth appear in a fully detailed embrace in just such a window frame. The "living couple" in the window replaces both stained-glass containment and engulfing shadows as the *Animated Tale* resolves England's civil war. However, Richmond's speeches in the play are entirely absent before this scene, and Elizabeth – as well as the other women, including Anne – appear in the *Tale* only on parapets and beyond the castle walls, barely visible or only at the margins of the painted images of Richard. Thus, the restoration of the royal couple within the frame which initiated Richard's jealousy does not quite restore the forces who oppose Richard throughout the play's text and who are so often cut in the *Animated Tale*. Richard has become so closely allied with the very method of animation that apparently he cannot be fully banished.

In contrast, *As You Like It* plays with the ideas of surface, the limitations of the still, flat image brought to motion. While one reviewer complains that "the oil and pastel painted compositions of *As You Like It* are . . . more like illustrations than full bodied animations" (Gilson 1996: 2F), in fact the illustrated quality of this *Tale* seems quite deliberate. From its very opening, *As You Like It* insists on both its origins in the alterations of surfaces (whether the surface of glass or cel) and its dependence on earlier types of images. The film opens with a shot of the play's title, panning down past a windmill to a town at the corner of two rivers, all in black-and-white line drawings. However, those images – evocative of Renaissance woodcuts – turn out to be inscribed on the back of Charles the wrestler. The transformation of a series of pseudo-Elizabethan still images into the mobile, powerful, yet ultimately defeated body of Charles foregrounds both the power of the surfaces in this animation technique and their vulnerability in the creation of genuinely mobile and successful animation.

That image style – the black-and-white Elizabethan woodcut – henceforth becomes a notable motif in a production whose other images are blurred and colorful. These designs appear at significant places in the production – notably those moments when the play itself seems to draw in other genres – and gradually change in representation to become both more active and more colorful. Although the narrative from Lodge of the lion's assault on Oliver appears in the blurred colors of the major narrative (implying that event is comparable to the fantasies of the forest), Jaques's Seven Ages of Man speech, the most famous set piece in the play, and the few aphorisms about women which Rosalind retains in this production both appear as woodcuts which recall the surfaces and contrasts in the opening.

The Seven Ages speech is framed as a combination of theatrical production and Elizabethan comic strip – the Duke and Jaques toast each other before the banquet's tablecloth which then parts as if it were a curtain to reveal an interplay of several woodcut images. The opening image, like that on Charles's back, reveals an extensive scene. It displays the surroundings of the theater, this time populated by figures that disappear one by one as the voice reveals that "all the men and women [are] merely players" (*AYL*: 2.7.140). "Their exits" (*AYL*: 2.7.142) is the cue for a skeleton to rise from a coffin pictured at the front and go into the theater. There the only hint of color is the dark red curtain at the back of the stage from which Jaques briefly emerges. The curtain and the appearance of Jaques within the woodcut mark the beginning of a revision of the static Elizabethan woodcut into mobile narrative.

As Jaques declaims, "his acts being seven ages" (*AYL*: 2.7.143), those ages appear as seven separate frames of a comic strip sliding by, with the the curtain still visible in the upper corners of the frame. The sole animation in this sequence is the single figure, first flung as the babe from left to right into the next frame of "mewling schoolboy" but after, moving on his own, in stick-figure jerkiness, from one stage to the next, until in the sixth age, a skeleton enters the frame from the right and sits across from the sickly figure on the bed. The last stage – "sans teeth, sans eyes, sans taste, sans every thing" (*AYL*: 2.7.166) – interestingly enough returns our view to the table in the forest and to the contrasting animation of the rest of the *Tale*. The shift in visual style in the Seven Ages speech underscores the shift in verbal style and the intrusion of a set piece into the ongoing action of the playtext while the opulence of the colorful feast undercuts its gloomy conclusion. Jaques's all-encompassing speech reducing a man's life to a series of scenes becomes the occasion for activating the woodcuts. This animation includes mobile figures within the woodcut as opposed to the still woodcuts which were wholly immobile on Charles's back until he moved. Here the still image becomes both internalized and metatheatrical, not the limit set on this form of animation, but its prerequisite.

Although the *Animated Tale* noticeably leaves out the more negative stereotyping of women's behavior from Rosalind's "love-prate," her characterizations of women ultimately lead to the final, most active woodcut scene. Her initial invocations of the various postures she will adopt when curing Orlando, with a few noteworthy omissions (in brackets), appear as a series of simultaneous images of her, "At which time would I [being but a moonish youth,] grieve, [be effeminate, changeable, longing and liking,] proud, fantastical, apish, [shallow], inconstant, full of tears, full of smiles" (*AYL*: 3.2.400–4). This sequence portraying the seven stages of women's love ends with the figures becoming masks which drift like leaves amongst Orlando's sonnets scattered in the water, matching perhaps the variability of his invocations of Rosalind. The resolution of this dispersal of Rosalind's character occurs after masks and poems alike pour off the waterfall and a single mask dominates the screen, saying, "And thus I cured him" (*AYL*: 3.2.411–12).

This markedly externalized representation of Rosalind's words contrasts the rest of the representation of Rosalind's love-prate. In the next scene between Orlando and Ganymede, Rosalind makes one of the few cynical statements about courtship and marriage that she is allowed to keep in this production, "Say 'a day,' with the 'ever.' No, no. Orlando. Men are April when they woo, December when they wed. Maids are May when they are maids, but the sky changes when they are wives" (*AYL*: 4.1.139–42). In the playtext, what follows is a misogynist litany of "feminine" behaviors: "[I will be more jealous of thee than a Barbary cock-pigeon over his hen, more clamorous than a parrot against the rain, more newfangled than an ape, more giddy in my desires than a monkey. I will weep for nothing, like Diana in the fountain, and I will do that when you are disposed to be merry; I will laugh like a hyen and that when you are inclined to sleep]" (*AYL*: 4.1.142–9). In other words, in the play's text, Rosalind follows the comments about husbands and wives with an account of the weather that changes in wives.

However, without even being spoken, the speech is both represented and undone by the woodcut images that appear within the animated scene. These final woodcuts are projected into the space beside Rosalind's head as the animated equivalent of the comic-book "thought bubble." They offer visual enactments of the metaphoric identification of men and women with the seasons in a woodcut-image style that explicitly links Rosalind's aphoristic comments given above to the Seven Ages speech. Even more important, this woodcut cartoon represents the pleading of the suitor followed by his neglect and pursuit of another woman once he has wed. The sky changes when the scornful, angry wife pursues her husband as he visits his lover and then chases him back to his own house has a strong narrative motive within the animated scene for her "shrewish" behavior. Thus, as the woodcuts become more animated, they display the revisionary potential of the animated image. This sequence effectively reinterprets the taint of overt misogyny so noticeable in Rosalind's assertions about women within Shakespeare's playtext. More important, the animation takes Rosalind's claim that Orlando will meet "*your wife's wit going to your neighbor's bed . . . And she will say she came to seek you there*" (4.1.168–9, 171) and transforms the wife's witty excuse for adultery into her justifiable anger at her husband's in the animated imagery. Unlike Jaques's speech which generalizes and even flattens the cycle of human experience until the return to the alternate animation style opposes that reductive narrative, here the woodcut images explain and even contradict the aphorisms spoken adjacent to them.

Through embedding these woodcut images in the more fluid, but still noticeably static, images of this mode of animation, the animators create a contrast which enlivens the movement of the principal story while emphasizing the blurring of genres and materials within *As You Like It*. Drawn from a pastoral romance by Thomas Lodge and liberally including misogynist texts and aphorisms, *As You Like It* demonstrates that Shakespeare combined stasis with motion, the set piece or narrative moment with headlong action. The animation of this tale plays the static image against the animated movement in ways comparable to Shakespeare's willingness to play written narratives from Thomas Lodge as theatrical action, to enliven set speeches in the context of staged dinner conversations or courtships.

As these analyses demonstrate, the modes of production in *Shakespeare: The Animated Tales* illuminate as much as they might collide with the Shakespearean text. In the tragedies of *Julius Caesar* and *Othello*, the extension from literalized metaphor into externalized characters within their cel animation demonstrates how profoundly metaphor and narrative can work to create the effects critics once took as unity in character. The stasis of *The Winter's Tale*, culminating with the animating of Hermione's statue, contrasts with *Taming*, which deliberately exploits puppet theater itself. These *Animated Tales* bring the artifice of Shakespeare's use of artistic forms outside drama to the foreground by examining their own artistic materials. In *Richard III* and *As You Like It*, the self-consciousness about artistic borrowing becomes the mode of interpretation in an animation form which has itself been categorized more as painting than animation. These productions go beyond drawing upon the verbal imagery or other art forms when they use their production techniques, staining glass, and inscribing surfaces, as their means of interpreting both history and comedy.

Examining productions like the *Animated Tales* is crucial at a time when we face Shakespearean productions which overtly combine multiple forms of these plays at the same time. In 1996, Sony released the CD-ROM *Othello: The Interactive Guide*,[7] providing maps, film clips, study guides, screenplay texts; the next year, they released *Hamlet: A Murder Mystery*,[8] a CD-ROM game based on and excerpting from Kenneth Branagh's

1996 film of *Hamlet*. The former blends text, an Elizabethan guide, a "theater district," and assorted commentary, whereas the latter is in essence an adventure game, offering two choices: "To be" where players will collect their ten wits to save Denmark, and a guide to studying the play entitled "Not to be."[9] Even the more scholarly Voyager *Macbeth* (1994), edited by A.R. Braunmuller, combines an audio performance of the text, video clips from several film *Macbeths*, hundreds of images from paintings and etchings, as well as an extensively annotated text. By the early twenty-first century, the many media in which Shakespeare can be produced are being drawn together to entertain and to teach; the flourishing CD-ROMs, websites, and DVDs raise the pressing question of how we should approach new productions of Shakespeare, where mixed media become multimedia. *Shakespeare: The Animated Tales* provides an excellent starting place, as they test their own multiple, converging modes of production and meditate on Shakespeare's own mixture of creative forms.

Notes

1 This essay is a revised and updated version of my 1998 essay, "Mixing Media in Shakespeare: Animating Tales and Colliding Modes of Production," *PostScript: Essays in Film and the Humanities* 17(2): 73–89, reprinted here with the permission of the journal.

2 William Shakespeare, *A Midsummer Night's Dream* (3.2.210), in *The Riverside Shakespeare*, ed. G. Blakemore Evans (Boston: Houghton Mifflin, 1974). All further references to Shakespeare's plays come from this edition.

3 In addition, Roy Kendall, academic co-ordinator for the series, was involved in other projects and therefore did not have the time to publicize the second series as extensively (Kendall, telephone interview, November 12, 1996).

4 Two exceptions are Osborne 1997 and Coursen 2002.

5 The line test camera allows animators to project how a panned sequence will look in line drawings rather than having to produce the sequence and then discard it if the animation idea does not pan out (Kendall, telephone interview, November 12, 1996). The equipment brought in during the first series is being used in the second where the line test camera operator is acknowledged in the credits.

6 Roy Kendall 1996: 9–10 notes that these strategies originate in the first series and are perhaps inspired by Leon Garfield's scripts.

7 *Othello: The Interactive Guide* (1996) Academic Advisor Arlene Steibel. Castle Rock Entertainment/EEME Interactive. Educational CD-ROM.

8 *Hamlet: A Murder Mystery* (1997) Academic Advisor Arlene Steibel. Castle Rock Entertainment/EEME Interactive. CD-ROM game.

9 Thanks to Tammy Glover for this information.

9

NOSTALGIA AND THEATRICALITY

The fate of the Shakespearean stage in the *Midsummer Night's Dreams* of Hoffman, Noble, and Edzard

Douglas Lanier

For all their varied approaches to adaptation and their equally varied performances at the box office, the Shakespeare films of the 1990s might be understood in retrospect as participating in a much larger *fin de siècle* project, the recuperation of traditional literary culture for an age of mass media. At the heart of the recent Shakespeare film boom has been a desire definitively to disengage Shakespeare from the theater, to refute the proposition that the special nature and power of Shakespearean drama is rooted in the specific medium for which he wrote, live stage performance. That proposition has become increasingly problematic throughout the twentieth century as the professional theater has moved decisively to the margins of cultural production, displaced by the newer, putatively more democratic dominants of film and video. Were Shakespeare's works to be regarded as indelibly theatrical, they – and, more importantly, the cultural capital they represent – would risk being mired in an outmoded, coterie format, the cultural equivalent of Betamax. What film adaptations of the 1990s share is an assertion of the radical *mobility* of Shakespearean content, the capacity of Shakespeare's writing to transcend the particularities of his chosen medium and its unproblematic affinity with more contemporary media, particularly film and TV. Nowhere is this assertion more explicit than in the final moments of *Shakespeare in Love* (dir. John Madden, 1998), when Shakespeare, in the wake of the triumphal stage performance of his *Romeo and Juliet*, begins writing *Twelfth Night*, his valentine to Viola de Lesseps, his newfound secret muse. As Shakespeare puts his pen to page and outlines the opening scene in voice-over, we see no playhouse enactment of his script-in-progress but rather Shakespeare's "unmediated" imagination, one that, judging from the slo-mo of the watery shipwreck and Viola's stride across an emphatically widescreen beach, operates cinematically. That is, if this scene gives Viola a means for transcending the marriage market that binds her throughout the film, it also provides Shakespeare a means for transcending the stultifying artificiality and conventionality of the Elizabethan theater that heretofore has rendered him artistically impotent. To stress the extent to which Shakespeare's writing relies upon live stage performance for its full meaning and power, then, would entail swimming against the tide of recent screen Shakespeares and insisting upon an antiquarian authenticity that risks relegating Shakespeare to the dustbin of history.

It is noteworthy, then, that questions about Shakespeare's association with the stage remain stubbornly in play in recent film adaptations, suggesting perhaps that there may remain something fundamentally theatrical about Shakespeare that resists full appropriation by the cinema. *A Midsummer Night's Dream* provides a useful test case, for on several levels the play insistently thematizes the particular species of imaginative (mis)perception upon which live stage performance depends. The play's exploration of how the lovers' romantic perceptions of each other are shaped (and misshaped) by fantasies both willed and imposed is elaborated in the concluding play-within-the-play, where we are made aware of how fully stage performance relies upon its audience's willingness to deny the objective evidence of their eyes and imaginatively to collaborate in the actors' creation of a fictional world.[1] Three recent films of *A Midsummer Night's Dream*, directed by Michael Hoffman (1999), Adrian Noble (1996), and Christine Edzard (2001), take up and extend the play's insistent theatricality in very different ways and from distinct national and institutional perspectives. Despite their differences, it is striking how in all three films the concern with theatricality becomes bound up with various forms of nostalgia, recourse to some body of allusions that evokes some utopian – or at least preferable – cultural past with which Shakespeare is then loosely, metonymically linked. As these works explore different conceptions of Shakespeare's relationship to modernity's signature medium, film, they model different ways of recuperating Shakespeare as a signifier of traditional culture in ways that illuminate the associations and anxieties that persistently attend upon Shakespeare's theatricality.

As several reviewers noted, the initial establishing shot of Michael Hoffman's *William Shakespeare's A Midsummer Night's Dream* unmistakably evokes Branagh's *Much Ado About Nothing* (1993). Both open with postcard-perfect vistas of a mythic rural Tuscany unsullied by modernity, so sensual and fertile that the patriarchal impulse to control women's sexuality – Egeus's exercise of authority over Hermia, Claudio's public humiliation of Hero – comes off as an especially perverse violation of the natural milieu. Yet the resemblance is only superficial. Branagh imagines Messina as an extended family in which differences of class and rank are muted (with the exception of Dogberry and his men), its joyous "natural" communalism epitomized by the opening picnic and group-bathing sequence and the film's closing dance. By contrast, Hoffman's opening sequence emphasizes the aristocratic pleasures of country-house living, the over-abundant foods, fabrics, china, crystal, and silver being laid out for the royal wedding. The camera encourages the viewer to take surreptitious delight from the antique finery laid out before us, placing us almost in the position of the dwarves who pilfer luxury items as cooks scurry about the kitchen. This display of opulence is carefully cordoned off from any hint of class-based exploitation: the army of smartly dressed servants are all anonymous, silent, and dutifully in the service of privilege, under the eye of Theseus, lord of the manor, who looks down from above with satisfaction upon their preparations. That we are to link this spectacle of wealth with cultural heritage is made clear by the mythological statues and paintings scattered throughout Theseus's house and grounds and, later, by the operatic arias on the soundtrack. In short, from the start Hoffman's *Dream* situates itself firmly within the conventions of heritage cinema, in which nostalgia for an upper-class lifestyle and its material accoutrements is wedded to the high-cultural cachet of literary "classics" adapted for film. The characters of heritage cinema are often concerned with holding on to their elite class status in the face of its slow loss to modernization, and the viewers of these films are invited to indulge vicariously in the sensual delights of aristocratic finery.[2] The unstable relationship between class status, systems of property, and romantic passion, a hallmark of heritage films and a place where they register a certain ambivalence about elitism and materialism, also dominates Hoffman's opening scenes. Theseus's power over his estate is immediately qualified by Hippolyta's resistance to her husband-to-be's erotic overtures, she preferring the Mendelssohn overture she hears on the Victrola to his blandishments. Egeus's insistence that Hermia marry Lysander becomes the signal example of the tension between patrician heritage (codified, significantly enough, in books), and the vagaries of (primarily women's) independent passions, a harbinger – so the opening title cards hint – of feminism and with it modernity.

The film's nostalgic strain also dominates the Italian town of Monte Athena with which Theseus's country house is incongruously paired. The shots of the piazza offer romanticized glimpses of long-lived rhythms of village labor and leisure, all as Verdi's "Brindisi" from *La Traviata* extols the joys of wine and love. As in the visual tour of Theseus's palace, the emphasis falls on authenticity of place and period (underlined by location shooting), and the sensual delights of the Tuscan café and marketplace. At its center is Bottom, presented here as an aristocratic wannabe who enjoys his own dapper image in the glass and fancies himself a man of means and a ladykiller. Like Theseus, Bottom is the seeming master of all he surveys, despite the donkey that trots by as he comes into frame, but that vision is quickly destroyed by the arrival of his shrewish wife who complains that he is a "worthless dreamer" and later by the boys who cruelly pour wine on his head as he commands the crowd with his impromptu acting in the marketplace.[3] The subplots of the lovers and of the mechanicals are recast in terms of fantasies of (male) aristocratic privilege, in both cases blocked in different ways by the wills of independent women. If Theseus presents the governing fantasy of the film, Bottom presents the recognition that it is merely a fantasy, Bottom's dream. What gives Bottom's characterization added resonance – beyond Kevin Kline's affecting performance – is that it poignantly engages the very desires heritage film is calculated to prompt: the middle-class baby-boomer's dream of an aristocratic life of leisure and high culture, here presented as a compensatory fantasy for the inevitable accommodation to the realities of family responsibility and middle-age.

Hoffman's fairy realm, by contrast, seems to push against many of the heritage elements that so characterize the village of Monte Athena. For one thing, the forest is filmed on what is patently a sound stage, its stagey artificiality emphasized, for example, by the low-tech special effects and creaky, hand-cranked mechanics of Titania's elevated bower. For another, the iconography of the fairy world is a mélange of various, predominantly Mediterranean sources – Etruscan, Greco-Roman, Indian – all filtered through Renaissance painting and Pre-Raphaelite fairy lore. Indeed, Hoffman foregrounds the very process of postmodern pastiche as we watch the fairies appropriating various luxury items pilfered from Theseus's palace, divorcing them from their original uses and turning them into "pure" esthetic objects. Whereas Hoffman's handling of the Athenian frametale stresses lavish cinematic verisimilitude and historical fidelity, his approach to the fairies and forest is far more self-consciously theatrical and postmodern in its look and tone. The fairies also express what remains unsaid in Monte

Athena: weariness about service to aristocrats, voiced as early as Puck's first encounter with one of Titania's attendants in a forest singles bar and referenced again with the looks the fairies exchange as Titania and Bottom prolong their tryst; and acknowledgment of women's desires and desire for erotic power, played out in Titania's advances upon the clueless but grateful and ever-tumescent Bottom.[4] Titania becomes the vehicle for Bottom to live out the dream of upper-class privilege – in a short interpolated sequence he is crowned as Titania's consort – and male potency he can only play at in Monte Athena. Though that lived fantasy is qualified for the viewer throughout by the clear cinematic unreality of the fairy realm, the fairies nevertheless represent a contemporary outlook – paradoxically presented as ancient and pan-cultural – that the film seeks to integrate with the heritage world of Monte Athena. In Theseus's palace, images of the fairies have become mere decorative ornaments of the elite, unremarked by anyone but Bottom, symbols of a culture of petrified privilege that cannot acknowledge the passions and independence for which these images stand. Through the intervention of the fairies in the forest, we are meant to think, the lovers encounter a mythologized principle of erotic vitality both contemporary and putatively timeless. By heeding Hippolyta's urging and aligning himself with the lovers, Theseus rejects the deadened patriarchal privilege represented by Egeus and reconciles heritage culture with the demands of modernity (in a way that rewrites the often tragic turn of most heritage films). Bottom's brief encounter is no less transforming, though his brush with royal status and erotic vitality remains a matter of dreamy nostalgia, not a real change in station, a point underlined when he watches with bittersweet wistfulness as the fluttering fairies pause before the window of his tiny flat and then leave him behind.

So understood, the film would seem to align the play with a rather conventional Leavisite opposition of conventionality and vitality were it not for elements that complicate such a reading. First, as Courtney Lehmann (2002) has argued, for all the film's focus on independent women as harbingers of modernity, it also points to their potential for shrewishness. In this Bottom's wife is not so much the exception as the rule. Hippolyta rejects Theseus when he somewhat reluctantly enforces Athenian law and later even rides off in mid-speech as he boasts about his hounds; after crowning Bottom as her consort, Titania instructs one fairy in a pointed aside "Tie up my love's tongue, bring him silently," and by the time Bottom complains of his hairiness she is hardly listening to him at all; once rejected by Lysander, Hermia turns almost instantly from sweet lover to vengeful bitch, though she directs her ire at Helena. As if to give this potential a mythological foundation, Hoffman includes among the idyllic images in Titania's bower two Janus-faced female figures who worship a fearsome Medusa. For Lehmann this potential articulates one of the film's key sites of anxiety, the loss of power of the turn-of-the-century male in the face of the women's movement:

> . . . it is the sacred donkey that leads us to empathize with Bottom as the hopeful romantic in us all and, therefore, to see his disillusionment as the site of the film's real violence. But at the bottom of this sacralizing epistemology of transcendent love with little women is an ass-backward approach to gender relations that rewrites the romance topos as a form of cinematherapy for men, brilliantly positioning them as the real victims of a genre – and a gender – that has suffered historic abuses in the name of love.
>
> (Lehmann 2002b: 269)

Read in this manner, the film offers two different forms of masculinist nostalgia: the first in the person of Theseus, who harkens back to a moment and social system before the advent of modern feminism and who points the way to accommodating patriarchal power with the demands of feminine passion; and second in the person of Bottom, for whom status and potency are always no more than a compensatory, temporary illusion, either an act he plays out on the piazza or stage or a past glory that at the movie's end he recalls and recognizes as lost. The address of recent heritage films, most commentators agree, have been "widely understood as feminine, if not female" (Vincendeau 2001: xx); it has also been amenable, Richard Dyer points out (2001: 43–8), to the concerns and tastes of a homosexual male audience. One aim of Hoffman's *Dream*, then, is to recalibrate heritage film – and heritage culture generally, of which Shakespeare is a part – to a more heteromasculine orientation.

Equally interesting is the film's concern with the technology of modernity, the principal examples of which are the bicycle and the phonograph, each of which anticipates key emblems of modernity, the automobile and the cinema. The bicycle is explicitly identified in the opening sequence as a sign of the coming age: "The good news: The bustle is on the decline, allowing for the meteoric rise of that newfangled creation, the bicycle." Appropriately enough, it is identified with Helena, the woman who takes the active role in romantic pursuit, and it becomes the means by which Hermia and Lysander escape the Athenian edict into the wood. What's more, it quickly becomes assimilated into the ancient/contemporary fairy world: Puck at first travels on the back of a giant tortoise (an allusion to Valerio Cioli's statue of Bacchus in Florence's Boboli Gardens), but he quickly embraces the more modern mode of transport when he comes across Lysander's bicycle. Though the phonograph is less ubiquitous in the film, it is symbolically the more resonant. At first the fairies treat the records and phonograph components naively, as yet more bright objects for their amusement. Yet when in Titania's bower Bottom is served sweetmeats on a record, he takes and plays it (the selection is "Casta Diva") to the amazement of his lover and her entourage; their admiration for his feat of technological magic leads them to declare "Hail, mortal," the crucial prelude to Bottom's becoming Titania's consort. Just as in the case of Hippolyta in her opening appearance, the phonograph exerts a romantic power capable of enthralling women, a power that within the film is not securely in the control of men. It is significant that the recording erases the theatrical component of opera, transforming it into "pure" disembodied music. Released from the artificiality of dramatic performance, so the implication goes, its ability to seduce the listener is magnified. What the phonograph exemplifies, in short, is a reconciliation between heritage culture and modern technology. Bottom's one moment of power over Titania springs from the power of modern technology wedded with "classical" romantic content, in a way that divorces opera from the taint of the theatrical. And all with an object that evokes at once the advent of mass media and the quaint charm of an antique.

The phonograph bears metathematically upon Shakespeare, film and theater, for like the phonograph, film has become the preferred contemporary means to extend the cultural life of a "classical" commodity while stripping it of the theatricality so inimical to the dominant naturalistic esthetic of mainstream media. On the early modern stage that theatricality was a resource, nowhere more so than in *A Midsummer Night's Dream*, where the suspension of disbelief – the capacity imaginatively to transform the evidence of the eye – emerges as one of the play's central concerns, a source of anxiety and critique as the male suitors and Titania easily change lovers, but also of utopian transformation and fulfillment of desire. The play's final act makes precisely this connection. Theseus stresses the ways in which imaginative re-perception allows the wedding party to perceive both the botched reality of the mechanicals' performance and the fiction they seek to portray, all of which he identifies as a mark of *noblesse oblige*:

> Our sport shall be to take what they mistake,
> And what poor duty cannot do,
> Noble respect takes it in might, not merit.
>
> (5.1.90–2)[5]

By contrast, Hoffman tends to blunt Shakespeare's foregrounding of theatricality. Symptomatically, Theseus's "lunatic, lover, and poet" soliloquy is truncated – there is no mention of the poet at all – and thereby becomes not a commentary on the nature of fiction or volatility of the imagination but rather an expression of skepticism about the ancient gods. So too is underplayed the link between the audience's imaginative experience of dramatic performance and Hippolyta's quizzical observation about "all their minds transfigured so together" (5.1.24). Instead, the final scene is pressed into the service of the high versus popular cultural divide, re-focused on the competition between well-meaning amateurs and cultural professionals, Bottom, Quince, and company pitted against a panoply of practiced acrobats, dancers, choristers, and actors offering classical entertainments, including an Othello in the midst of strangling Desdemona. The last of these, a moment of over-the-top action and rhetorical flight, an emblem of Shakespeare at his most theatrical, points to the kind of high-flown, stagey Shakespeare Hoffman is determined to reject.

The film is most remarkable for its treatment of Francis Flute's portrayal of Thisbe, particularly his/her death which concludes the mechanicals' play-within-the-play. Up to that moment, the film offers a relatively conventional theatrical lampoon (with the exception of Starveling's improvised Moon), a catalogue of performative misfires – even a botched "bit with a dog" *à la Shakespeare in Love* – that amuses the aristocrats and offends the stuffy Philostrate. Quince, the play's author, is anguished as he watches his script being butchered by its translation into stage performance. The play of Pyramus and Thisbe demonstrates the failings of theater as a medium: absurdly grandiose and old-fashioned, prone to errors and accidents, patently unbelievable. And Flute's Thisbe epitomizes those failings: from the moment he is cast, his cross-dressing elicits snickers from his fellow mechanicals, as does the preposterous falsetto, "proper" for the part, into which Quince coaxes him. Flute's early appearances in the play-within-the-play prompt a similarly bemused reaction from the male lovers (the women are far more sympathetic), so much so that he finds it difficult to get through the performance, despite backstage coaching from Quince. As in *Shakespeare in Love*, the cross-dressing of early modern theater exemplifies how fundamentally the medium violates the canons of photographic verisimilitude – canons crucial to the "authenticity" of heritage cinema – and presents romance, in the words of Viola DeLessups, as "the artful postures of love." In this case, cross-dressing also exemplifies the medium's potential to emasculate its male practitioners, a point which extends to Bottom's compulsive and finally self-humiliating penchant for grandiloquent performing.

When Flute takes the stage to give his final speech, he begins in falsetto, but met by laughter, he quickly drops the drag act, doffs his wig, and offers a deeply felt, *in propria voce* rendition of Thisbe's death soliloquy. The startling shift in style is underlined by the cinematography. Whereas much of the play-within-the-play is photographed so as to emphasize the proscenium frame and thus the theatrical audience's perspective, Flute's performance is captured in medium close-up, an intimate point-of-view appropriate for his deliberately understated manner. It is Flute's heartfelt naturalistic performance of Thisbe's grief, certainly not the absurd poetry of the speech, that dominates the sequence and ends up winning the day. Instead of reacting with laughter and condescension, the wedding party is deeply touched, and on behalf of Theseus Philostrate awards the actors a pension with the equally understated compliment, "very notably discharged." What Flute's Thisbe accomplishes, in short, is a purge of the taint of the outmoded stage – in particular a rejection of theatrical cross-dressing – and a legitimation of cinematic naturalism. Flute demonstrates, if only momentarily, how Shakespeare's poetic language, the very stuff of cultural heritage, might be made compatible with the conventions of American mainstream film acting. Given the film's concern with the ways in which the coming of (feminist) modernity imperils traditional male status, it is certainly significant that Hoffman's validation of modern acting (and the medium with which it is associated, film) takes the form of a purgation of male effeminacy. If the film offers only nostalgic dreams of male aristocratic status, all situated in the past, what it also offers is the possibility that cultural heritage, with a crucial shuffling of medium, can become a source of masculine legitimation. Just as Bottom is given a compensatory fantasy of class mobility and sexual potency, so the play-within-the-play becomes a compensatory fantasy for Shakespearean theater, made powerful and popular insofar as it demonstrates its capacity to deny its own theatricality.

The vexed status of Shakespearean theater is central in a very different way to the concerns of two recent British film adaptations of *A Midsummer Night's Dream*, Adrian Noble's from 1996 and Christine Edzard's from 2001. Though the two adopt different strategies of adaptation, they share an active embrace, rather than a rejection, of Shakespearean theatricality. Noble's film springs directly from his visually dazzling, highly praised 1994 Royal Shakespeare Company (RSC) stage production, filmed with minimal accommodation to cinematic convention, so much so that, in a judgment echoed by several reviewers, "the production always looks like a play which has been videoed rather than a film in its own right."[6] The Athenian forest, for example, is imaged as a vast stage dominated by a handful of symbols meant to evoke the surreal dreamscapes of Magritte.[7] Such virtuosic effects as doors rising magically from the floor, Puck descending through a sky filled with hanging light bulbs, or the lovers wrapped in chrysalis-like sheets simply reproduce Noble's inventive staging on screen. With perhaps the exception of the opening bedroom sequence, the film's *mise-en-scène* actively flaunts its artificiality: lighting favors primary colors and is concerned with illuminating mood more than features, and sets typically have the look of sets rather than actual locales. Even the actors' performances seem calibrated more to stage than screen, one indication of which is their penchant for engaging the audience by looking directly at the camera. Though Noble shows a preference for close-ups throughout much of the film, a choice that may explain why the production has the feel of a film made for television (it was co-produced by Channel 4), the actors' delivery – particularly that of Alex Jennings, who plays Theseus and Oberon – tends toward the declamatory rather than the conversational, and longer speeches trimmed in Hoffman's adaptation are here included in their entirety. Theatrical performance is even more insistently in the foreground of Edzard's film. Perhaps taking her cue from Olivier's *Henry V*, she structures her adaptation like a Chinese box. The film opens with a staging of *A Midsummer Night's Dream* for schoolchildren. Soon students from the audience take up the parts, with the scene shifting to contemporary London; and with the forest scenes the production becomes a period-dress performance in high Victorian pictorialist style. Late in the film Edzard works backward through these stylistic frames until for the mechanicals' play we return to the schoolhouse theater and student audience with which the film began. Unlike Olivier's film, however, Edzard's production does not arrive in its center at conventional cinematic realism. Even in the lushly staged nature scenes Edzard includes reminders of stage artifice: the theater is slowly transformed into the forest by festooning it with greenery, and storm effects are created by flashes of light on stage flats we can clearly see in the background. The fact that children play the parts also heightens our awareness of the performance as a performance. Despite the production's considerable charm, we are never fully allowed to suspend disbelief.

This embrace of theatricality has a specific cultural horizon – the still robust tradition of live Shakespearean performance in British culture. More specifically, both films engage what has become the dominant institutional form of that tradition – the kind of subsidized directors' theater produced by the RSC and the Royal National Theatre, high concept productions that aim to realize interpretations of professional directors and designers.[8] Without doubt this form of production has reinvigorated the performance of Shakespeare's work and drawn new audiences to live theater, but it has not been without negative effects. First, it has tended to focus audience attention on production design rather than on Shakespearean language. Second, because directors' Shakespeare is concerned with creating productions that function as "interpretive essays" (Smallwood 1996: 117), it has tended to address itself to audiences already familiar with the plays from other performances, that is, to that informed subset of spectators capable of appreciating the director's particular concept and its place in intellectual, critical, and stage traditions (see also Sinfield 1985: 164–72). Third, this mode of production also has tended to undermine the collaborative contributions of actors, since as a matter of practicality they are expected to serve a production design established well before rehearsals begin. The cultural prestige accorded to major directors and their productions has also pushed regional and community Shakespearean production to the margins and thereby contributed to their diminished vitality and influence. Lastly, even the Arts Council subsidies that have underwritten the rise of directors' Shakespeare has also shielded it from pressures of the popular marketplace and allowed it to present itself as a "quality" alternative – one implicitly class-coded – to the vulgar or vapid productions of mass culture. In short, the result has been that directors' Shakespeare has tended to widen the gap between Shakespeare and popular audiences, to contribute to the elitist and intellectual reputation of contemporary Shakespearean theater, this irrespective of the political orientations of particular productions or the ambitions of companies like the RSC to bring live Shakespearean performance to the masses.

Both Noble and Edzard address the problem of directors' Shakespeare by evoking nostalgia for an earlier moment in the history of the Shakespearean stage, the late Victorian period in which Shakespearean theater was still a genuinely popular art, the moment before British culture's "fall" into modernity, mass media, and the highbrow/lowbrow divide. The crucial symbolic vehicle for this nostalgia is the figure of the child. Noble and Edzard offer quite different types of children's Shakespeare: Noble presents his film as if it were the dreamwork of a boy who has fallen asleep reading Arthur Rackham's illustrated edition of *A Midsummer Night's Dream*; in an even more thoroughgoing move, Edzard puts the play's performance almost entirely in the hands of child actors (and in the opening and closing scenes features child audiences). In both cases, children become the means for returning Shakespeare and Shakespearean performance to an earlier golden age of cultural "innocence," a time before Shakespeare became invested with directorial preoccupations and prejudices and highbrow standards of "proper" performance. Children, the reigning conceit of these films suggests, provide the pre-socialized, innocent eye that allows us to appreciate *Dream* anew and as it really is, without the intervening distortion of directorial preconceptions and unencumbered by modern notions of "quality." In both films this childlike perspective also functions, I will be arguing, as the foundation for imagining a (re)popularized form of Shakespearean performance. In the case of Noble, the Boy serves as a surrogate director and audience for the play whose vision of the script renders it congruent with late Victorian children's literature, a set of works that has the status of popular classics. The forest sequence in Edzard's film also references Victorian iconography – that of Victorian fairy lore, pictorialist productions of *Dream*, and such books as E. Nesbit's illustrated *Children's Shakespeare* (1900) – as a way of connecting its amateur children's production with various popular forms of Shakespeare from the past. In both films but in quite different ways, the figure of the child brings together several interlocking associations: nostalgia for the interpretive innocence of childhood; nostalgia for the cultural moment in which Shakespearean theater qualified as popular culture; nostalgia for a response to the play and its performance that emphasizes childlike wonder, popular sentiment, and charm rather than critical attention to darker questions of adult sexuality and power.

The most striking change in Adrian Noble's production of *A Midsummer Night's Dream* as it passed from stage to screen was his addition of the Boy through whose imaginative eye we see the production. In an oblique reference to *Peter Pan*, the film's opening sequence gives us a portrait of the sources of the Boy's imagination. The camera travels down through a moonlit sky into an open window and surveys the Boy's bedroom as he sleeps, revealing all manner of vintage toys and books, with heavy emphasis on those from the turn of the century – puppets, teddy bears, a harlequin, a rocking horse, a toy theater[9] – the shot culminating in a close-up of Rackham's illustrated edition of *Dream* which the Boy holds in his arms. Clearly Noble intends to link a nostalgic sensibility – and Victorian Shakespeare – with childhood innocence, a theme he has pursued in several of his theatrical productions.[10] Yet in the context of film Shakespeare, we might note that this sequence also prompts nostalgia for the children's culture that predated the advent of modern media and mass reproduction, a world before comic books, television, CDs, and video games in which childplay involved greater degrees of active performance and imagination. The literary end of that culture is epitomized by "classic" children's books from or evoking the period – Lewis Carroll's *Alice in Wonderland* (1865), Edward Lear's *The Owl and the Pussycat* (1871), L. Frank Baum's *The Wonderful Wizard of Oz* (1900), J.M. Barrie's *Peter Pan* (1904), and P.L. Travers's *Mary Poppins* (1934). As many commentators have documented, Noble's *Dream* is filled with sly allusions to these works: the Boy's fall down a stovepipe into the mechanicals' rehearsal shed resembles Alice's fall into the rabbit hole and Dorothy's fall into Oz; the fairies travel via floating umbrellas like Mary Poppins; Bottom and Titania's moonlit voyage in a red umbrella is meant to recall the Owl and the Pussycat.[11] Among the many effects of this opening sequence and body of allusion is to recuperate Shakespeare's "classical" status but without the baggage of high culture. Demonstrating *Dream*'s deep affinity with perennial children's favorites allows Noble to make the case for Shakespeare's play as a kind of popular classic and to ally his self-conscious theatricality with the primal processes of children's play. Situated in the company of children's classics, Noble's *Dream* emphasizes the difference between his film Shakespeare and contemporary media-saturated mass culture, but in a way that dodges the charge of elitism or intellectualism.

The opening sequence of the film and the continued presence of the Boy also recodes the often ostentatiously symbolic imagery of the production. In the stage production that imagery and the fantasies it brilliantly expressed had their origin in Noble's reading of the play as an erotic dream, akin to Peter Brook's famous white-box production of 1970. Recasting *A Midsummer Night's Dream* as the Boy's dream allows Noble to take his production design out of the domain of high-cultural allusion and upmarket eroticism and set it instead in the company of children's literature, where psychoanalytic symbolism is in the service of a far more "democratic" realm of experience, the child's passage to adulthood. As Gary Jay Williams observes of the stage version, "the production missed – or avoided – many opportunities for engaging issues of contemporary interest" (1997: 256), particularly those of sexual politics. The film version redoubles that avoidance. In it, the dream vision springs from the Boy who through a process of associative elaboration invests mundane objects – light bulbs, umbrellas, doors – with significance and melds them with the Shakespearean narrative. This process is set in motion by the Boy's fascination with and incomprehension of the dynamics of adult sexuality, particularly those of his parents, for whom Theseus/Oberon and Hippolyta/Titania are clearly fictional stand-ins. We first glimpse Theseus and Hippolyta through the Boy's eyes as he peers at their erotically charged opening exchange through the keyhole of their chamber door (appropriately painted red). The Fairy King and Queen seem to magnify qualities of their Athenian counterparts, Oberon a volatile, sometimes wry father capable of evoking fear with his roars, Titania an eroticized mother both enticing and potentially engulfing. The psychoanalytic subtext Noble establishes through the Boy does not follow a conventional Oedipal trajectory, for Shakespeare, not Sophocles, becomes the principal means for him to navigate his developmental crisis. *A Midsummer Night's Dream* allows him to engage anxieties and forbidden pleasures associated with adult sexuality without rivalry with the father. It also allows him to express his deep longing for a family, a desire that moves from Theseus and Hippolyta, to the mechanicals, to Bottom and Titania, and finally in the concluding tableau to the entire theatrical cast.

Most important, the Boy functions as an embedded surrogate for Noble himself, a means, I want to argue, for him to recast the image of the high-concept director and his relationship to the play, its players, and the public. Certainly the Boy allies Noble's directorial vision of the play with childlike innocence and popular sentimentality, but he also allows Noble to occlude the position of intellectual and institutional mastery that he as director might otherwise be thought to occupy. Though the Boy is presented as the source for this *Midsummer Night's Dream*, typically undercut are those moments where he seems actively to intervene in or impose his desires upon the play's action. He creates the bubbles that enable the entrance of the fairies only after he watches Puck create the bubble that bears the image of the Indian boy (a version of the Boy himself). When Oberon reveals his plan to induce love in Titania and Demetrius, he and Puck watch each other at opposite ends of the Boy's toy theater, the Boy supplying a figurine of Helena, Oberon and Puck the love-in-idleness flower. At the end of this same scene, shots of the Boy handling puppet strings above his toy theater are intercut with shots of Puck and Oberon rising on umbrellas and Titania's fairies dancing. Whether or not we are to think the Boy is actually manipulating the characters is deliberately left unclear, as if Noble were purposely avoiding any hint of directorial control. The same ambiguity hovers over the relationship between shots of the lovers embracing after their relationships have been mended and shots of the Boy gleefully spinning: is he conjuring these unions or merely celebrating them? Indeed, throughout much of the film the Boy takes the role not of active participant but of passive observer, highly empathetic with the characters if not always understanding their motives or actions. Modeling responses to characters and events – he is touched by Helena's plight, delighted by the fairies, intimidated by Theseus and Oberon, amused by the mechanicals – the Boy tends to assimilate the position of the director with that of the audience, watching and reacting to an autonomous dream world rather than actively creating or imposing a high concept on the play. The play and its characters are presented as a fantasy space within which the Boy's inchoate, primal anxieties, and desires can be given imaginative shape and played through, a co-operative therapeutic enterprise rather than an interpretive essay. To put the matter bluntly, the Boy's centrality to the film encourages us to misrecognize the cultural politics that underlie the high-concept director's Shakespeare that has become the forte of the RSC. Through him, the nostalgia with which the film opens – for childhood, for pre-war Britain, for performative play, for an innocent eye – can be reconciled with those modes of modern theatrical production that now dominate professional Shakespearean theater.

The final scenes of the film ostentatiously celebrate the power of theater, focusing especially on the relationship between director and company. That celebration takes two forms. Noble's staging of the mechanicals' play follows the same general contours as Hoffman's: both are performed on small proscenium stages without Quince's first prologue, and they share a certain good-hearted earnestness and many of the same comic touches (Bottom's manhandling of Wall and Quince's concern about getting "Ninus' tomb" right, for example). Tellingly, the attitude of the newly-weds toward the players is far less condescending than in Hoffman's version, and their responses are not as clearly divided along gender lines. Most of their sharper barbs are simply excised, and it is Theseus who dominates the commentary that remains, alternating between gentle bemusement and deep sentiment. The play's key performance belongs not to Thisbe but to Bottom, whose rendition of Pyramus's grief over his dead beloved momentarily pulls at the heartstrings of the wedding party, particularly those of Hippolyta and the Boy. Bottom's text concerns remembrance for the woman he has lost – "O wherefore, Nature, didst thou lions frame?/Since lion vile hath here deflower'd my dear:/Which is – no, no – which was the fairest dame/That lived, that loved, that liked, that look'd with cheer" (5.1.286–9) – and its bitter-sweet quality is emphasized by a yearning violin motif that swells underneath. The nostalgic mood is compounded by the fact that Bottom appears to deliver these lines to Hippolyta, the woman who in her incarnation as Titania he seems dimly to recall at play's end. Given Hippolyta/Titania's role as the Boy's surrogate mother figure, Bottom's heartfelt delivery also puts into play an intimation of the Boy's impending loss of maternal protection as he enters maturity, a resonance that may explain why he is so deeply moved by Bottom's speech. The performance is of course a star turn for Bottom and the actor who plays him, Desmond Barritt, a demonstration of the power of unsophisticated conviction in live performance, a quality also found in the gleeful delight with which Bottom and Flute dance their childlike Bergomask.

Once again, throughout this final scene the Boy occupies two positions at once, as a kind of director – he pulls the curtain for the mechanicals' play, and their performance takes place in a life-size version of his toy theater – and as spectator – we see him watching the play both from backstage and from a privileged seat alone in the dress circle. And after the mechanicals' play ends and the bell of midnight tolls, attention turns more fully to the Boy's relationship to the company. Puck escorts him through the theater's backdoor where are revealed the fairies, floating magically toward the two on the shimmering moonlit sea, a return to the dreamlike night-time world of the bare-stage forest which now takes on a quasi-religious quality. The fairies are accompanied by solemn choir music, and Oberon's blessing resembles a form of baptism, far more a talisman against the encroaching concerns of adulthood than a blessing upon the newly-weds (the couples are by this point entirely forgotten). That is, the ritual the fairies perform is directed toward theater; their reappearance assures that though the play is over, the stage will remain a "sacred" space, free of any return to adult reality. Noble concludes with a striking image: after the cast rush back onto the stage, they lift the Boy aloft, passing him from one to another as the Boy pretends to fly and then is gently brought to earth, a return to the nostalgic *Peter Pan* motif with which the film began. The theater company now serves as the Boy's substitute family (unfortunately the image also resembles a therapy-group exercise), the means by which he can retain his innocence into adulthood. This moment evokes a familial conception of the theatrical company supposedly at the heart of the repertory system, an ideal very much in evidence in Branagh's Shakespearean films.[12] Yet in its final moments the film reveals, perhaps despite itself, the contradictory agenda it wants to pursue. The image of the Boy integrated into what has become his extended family is calculated to obliterate any distinction between director and company and to remind us of the anti-elitist nature of the production. Yet in the final tableau it is the silent (omni)present Boy who occupies center-stage, the one whose fantasies conjure the action and whose desire for imaginative "flight" the company serves. What's more, as a form of curtain call, the actors look up in the final shot to directly engage the viewer's eye, an act that unwittingly underlines the differences between theater and film. Onstage, such a gesture breaks the barrier between the audience and the fictional space of the performer. On film, however, the tableau tends only to reveal how fully the performers do not and cannot share the reality of the spectator, how the cast and the dream world they portray remain trapped within the confines of the screen.

In *A Children's Midsummer Night's Dream*, Christine Edzard engages the reigning institutional form of Shakespearean theater even more directly, with an approach more radical and paradoxically even more backward-looking than that of Noble. Her experiment in staging extends her interest in the intersection between Shakespeare and contemporary urban culture begun with her film *As You Like It* (1992), which resituated the Forest of Arden in London's run-down Docklands. For her *Midsummer* Edzard assembled a cast of eight- to twelve-year-old schoolchildren from eight underprivileged inner-city schools in Southwark, children from all manner of ethnic and class backgrounds with no acting training and very little experience with Shakespeare. The range of accents and abilities is precisely the point. Edzard's production makes the case that Shakespeare and the cultural capital he represents can become the common property of the emergent New Britain, not merely the province of the largely college-educated, bourgeois audiences of the "proper" theater. Even fluffed lines (many not edited out) and the occasional lack of polish contest the sense of monumentality typical of directorial Shakespeare, "highlight[ing] qualities of provisionality and spontaneity"[13] and recapturing a sense of performance as play. The inevitable resonance between the multicultural child cast and Shakespeare's mechanicals only underlines the populist orientation of the production. Edzard's film rejects the often unarticulated canons of performance and interpretation – matters of accent, class, and cultural background, expectations of sophistication, the imperative of interpretive innovation – that govern "proper" performance of Shakespeare in contemporary theater. It is a telling sign that despite her considerable track record as a filmmaker (her screen adaptation of Dickens's *Little Dorrit* (1987) was critically acclaimed and her controversial version of *As You Like It* (1992) was admired by some), *A Children's Midsummer Night's Dream* was rejected for financing by "official" funding sources like the British Arts Council, a fact Edzard proudly trumpets in the credits.

Lest the oppositional nature of her approach be missed, Edzard creates a frame for the film that sets up a stark opposition between her children's production and "proper" Shakespeare. The film opens in an Elizabethan-style theater in which schoolchildren have gathered to see a performance of *A Midsummer Night's Dream.* Several moments into the performance when the camera moves from long to medium shot, we are startled to learn that the performers are life-size puppets voiced by such RADA-trained stars of the British stage as Derek Jacobi and Samantha Bond. Though the puppets are skillfully manipulated, they make abundantly clear how wooden Shakespeare performance in its professional form has become. The sense of a false authenticity is bolstered by the period costumes that the puppets wear, a contrast to the school blazers and sweaters of the schoolchildren. The voice-work too magnifies this impression. The performers run their lines with precise, clipped articulation characteristic of professional Shakespearean theater, and speak with Received Pronunciation, reinforcing the association between "proper" Shakespeare and Oxbridge elitism, particularly when measured against the varied accents of the children. Throughout these puppet performances, a tinny sound quality mocks the full-bodied vocal tone these professional actors are capable of, and it reminds us that these ventriloquized vocal performances issue from elsewhere, clearly mediated through otherwise unseen systems of technology and training, like the visible strings that control the puppets' movements. Perhaps more subtle is the association of the sound tone with the mass media: it is as if we are hearing a BBC radio broadcast of the scene rather than a genuinely live performance, the flawlessly spoken text rendered utterly disjunct from the actors' bodies. At every turn the puppets' presentation undercuts the distinctive elements of theatrical performance: presence and spontaneity.

From the start, the cultural authority of the professional theater is allied with the opening scene's exercise of parental tyranny, a link reinforced by the jaunty superciliousness with which Derek Jacobi delivers Theseus's lines. The puppet Theseus takes Egeus's side against his daughter without the slightest hesitation or regret and adopts a condescending tone as he chides Hermia. (The fact that Hippolyta is represented by an African puppet – the only non-white in the initial group of characters – adds hints of racism and imperialism to the portrait of Theseus and stands in marked contrast to the multiracial cast of children. As if to underline the difference, Oberon, so often doubled with Theseus, is played by Jamaican-English Dominic Haywood-Benge.) As Theseus lectures the puppet Hermia, a girl in the audience (Jamie Peachey) leaps to her feet and takes up Hermia's part with the resonant line, "I would my father look'd but with my eyes" (1.1.56). It is a startling moment of double resistance, of Hermia against adult patriarchalism and of the student audience against respectful obeisance before a "proper" display of high culture. As the scene progresses, the emphasis falls more squarely on the latter, for Hermia's outburst prompts other students to take up the parts of Demetrius and Lysander and the children to move from restlessness to outright rebellion as they cheer Hermia and boo Theseus. During Theseus's longer speeches the camera becomes less interested in the performance onstage than in the increasingly active, independent response of the youthful audience. Once Theseus and company exit, the child actors take over performance of the play, and the production becomes a modern-dress adaptation staged in modern London locales – the school theater, the children's bedrooms, a city park – until the entrance of the fairies. This opening sequence suggests the need to move Shakespeare from heritage culture mired in staid decorum and reverence for the past to an active engagement with the multicultural, urban British present and the new generation that occupies it. With the takeover of the students Edzard demonstrates that "the new ownership of Shakespeare permits a thrilling geographical and discursive mobility" (Burnett 2002b: 4). One might add that the children's rejection of "proper" performance, their movement out of the schoolhouse theater into contemporary reality, is also a rejection of the apparatus of academic Shakespeare in which they as students are enmeshed.

With the arrival of the fairies the production style shifts yet again. Their presence, punctuated by childish dancing and songs, transforms the school theater by degrees into a lush, realistic forest, complete with a moonlit pond, and when the lovers reappear they – as all the cast members – are now dressed in period costume similar to that which originally adorned the puppets. This approach to the forest scenes strikes a compromise between cinematic verisimilitude and theatrical artificiality. For Mark Thornton Burnett, the shift in style suggests "that the puppets have been subsumed by, and reincarnated in, the players" (2002: 5); the children have taken up the mantle of authenticity once reserved for "proper" Shakespearean performers. Even so, the tone is never allowed to lapse into adult solemnity, for as the lovers and Titania undergo their romantic exchanges, various fairies mock their travails with by giggling and repeating their lines and cutaway shots picture fairies offering comically sententious commentary on the action. *A la* Brecht, the naturalistic scene is disrupted by our constant awareness of the gap between the child actors and the adult roles they play, one effect of which is to draw our attention to details of Shakespeare's language. This awareness also serves thematic ends: the imperfect performances dovetail with *Midsummer*'s concern with errors and mistaking, and we are encouraged to read the lovers' couplings and uncouplings in terms of the fraught dynamics of teen romance. The relative immaturity of pre-teen boys in relation to pre-teen girls, very much apparent in the actors' performances, amplifies the impression of callowness from Demetrius and Lysander and lends a subtle girl-power edge to Hermia's and Helena's assertiveness. Though one might see resonances between the child actors in the film and the child actors of the early modern British stage, the lush forest scenes evoke more strongly the precious pictorialism that so dominated Victorian productions of *A Midsummer Night's Dream* and, with it, nostalgia for the heyday of popular Shakespearean theater in the last century. Edzard's production design, with its emphasis on charming fairies in naturalistic gardens, is a daring rejection of modernist and postmodernist theatrical styles and the institutional apparatus they serve, an attempt to recover a now antiquated style of stage production but without the repressive imperial and gender ideologies that were its handmaidens. The style of the central section, that is, is calculated to make Edzard's children's production heir to a lost golden age of popular Shakespearean performance.

At the end of the forest sequence, Edzard rather quickly backs through the stylistic frames she has established to arrive once more at a school performance of Shakespeare, now of the play's final scene. The awakening of Bottom and the lovers becomes the occasion for returning us to the present day and to a contemporary cinematic style filled with intercut narratives and voice-overs. Though we hear Theseus and Egeus briefly in voice-over, the visual emphasis is on the four lovers and Bottom making sense of their dream experiences and, in the case of the lovers, adopting a more mature perspective on their romances. Appropriately enough, Edzard cuts the moment in which Theseus overrules Egeus in favor of Hermia, so that the stress falls on the agency of the young lovers rather than on the intervention of one parent figure over another. This cut also leaves in place for the final scene Theseus's overbearing authority, a foil against which the children continue to rebel. In fact, the final scene returns with even greater force to the cultural politics of "proper" Shakespearean theater. For the performance of the mechanicals' play, Edzard sets up two rival audiences, first, the wedding party played by puppets and segregated on a proscenium stage at the back of the theater, and second, contemporary schoolchildren who are seated above and around the playing area, in modified theater-in-the-round style. Throughout the performance of "Pyramus and Thisbe" the puppet adults make snide commentary on the action, even stepping on the actors' lines. The response of the schoolchildren is key, and again the girls tend to take the lead. We watch them listen intently and empathetically, reacting spontaneously to the performances, laughing at Bottom's Pyramus peering through the chink, screaming with fear at the Lion, lamenting the deaths of the lovers, and applauding the players enthusiastically at the end of each segment. At the same time, the children express mounting disgust at the rude behavior of the puppet newlyweds, shaking their heads and repeatedly turning to shush them as they disrupt the performance. In effect, this reverses the roles of parent and child: the puppet adults act like unruly kids as they try to project over the mechanicals' play their own canons of good taste and proper performance, and the students are forced to discipline their ill manners. In the course of the film, the puppets and the entrenched canons of performance they represent have been shunted off to the margins, and they are replaced by a more communal and participatory, less elitist and intellectual style of production, one in which the children share the acting space with the players and are in the best position spatially and culturally to appreciate their earnest efforts. The final shots reinforce this ideal, for Oberon's final blessing is directed at the theater itself and it is handled as a group song as the credits roll; after Puck delivers his epilogue and the credits continue, the music begins again, this time with the sounds of the audience joining in. Edzard concludes, that is, with endorsement of an egalitarian "poor theater" for the masses that stands in contrast to the dominant high-concept, high-cultural production style of director's Shakespeare. It is significant that the mechanicals' performance takes place in a wooden Elizabethan-style theater, for the play's production style seems intended to evoke what I have called "the Globe myth" (Lanier 2002b: 144–5), the notion that the communal atmosphere often imagined for performances at the original Globe Theater is inherently democratic and authentically Shakespearean.

Laudable as Edzard's ideals may be, the film raises a number of questions about how achievable they are in this medium and style of staging. One is the production's difficulty with accommodating irony. The segregation of responses to the final scene into two distinct modes of perception, for example, arguably blunts the scene's point, placing emphasis on the charms of the children's acting (the players' errors become endearing) rather than on the complexity of imaginative perception demanded by this performance and, indeed, by theatrical performance in general. Indeed, Puck is the only character capable of appreciating the ironies of the narrative, a quality nicely expressed by Leane Lyson's deadpan performance. What is more, in her effort to recover a sense of post-cynical innocence and wonder, Edzard, like Noble, rejects any direct intrusion of "hard" politics – questions of class, empire, gender, race, sexuality – into the thematics of the play. Though the movement from modern dress to Victorian pictorialism underscores the production's theatricality, it also prevents many contemporary issues and analogues from being engaged in any more than a cursory way. The emphasis on charm means that the more nightmarish elements of the play are left unaddressed – neither the lovers nor Bottom and Titania suffer any real danger or pain in this Edenic fairy wood. Most important is the controversial premise upon which this children's performance is founded, the notion that untrained, unspoiled children can give us access to a Shakespeare free of the interpretive baggage and glossy technique that so concern professional directors and actors. In his comments on the play (Stockman 2001), Oliver Stockman, producer of Edzard's film, unpacks this set of essentially romantic oppositions: where theater professionals "embellish," children "speak plain" and allow Shakespeare's play to come to the fore unadorned; the actor must use "tricks" and "skills" to perform a role, but the child simply "sees, hears and feels the character and the action"; while actors (and directors) are concerned with polish and virtuosity, the child, absorbed in an imaginative act of "intense faith," produces a performance that may be "rough and clumsy" but which also exudes "honesty"; acting professionals are overly preoccupied with their own status, but children "take the play seriously." It remains debatable whether or not the production in fact bears out these assumptions. As many reviewers noticed, at times the children's line readings betray their lack of understanding of the text (though, countered others, the same might be said for professional actors). More to the point, the film never bares its own directorial and institutional apparatus. After all, the notion that this is genuinely a children's production of *A Midsummer Night's Dream* is something of an illusion. As the credits reveal, theater and film professionals were involved throughout its creation – in its design, in coaching the actors and musicians, behind the camera, in post-production.

The film depended for its success upon its close association with local schools, and the indisputable educational value of the enterprise dominated the press coverage at its release.[14] That this production offers us access to a children's vision of the play unmediated by academic or cultural professionals seems dubious. Indeed, the charge might be raised that Edzard's children's production is yet another manifestation of directors' Shakespeare, one that obscures its own high-concept design behind the faces of adorable children. The question might be posed bluntly: is the film's interest genuinely in children's understandings of Shakespeare, or are children simply being used to stage an oppositional production design, to signify as neo-romantic symbols of innocence?

Lastly, and perhaps most important, absent is any consideration of the relationship of the film medium to the kind of communal "poor" Shakespearean theater Edzard advocates. Edzard's camera allows for special effects and use of locations otherwise impossible for a school theater production, but arguably it also undermines the very participatory amateur production style it advocates. As spectators of the film we experience a pre-recorded performance with which we cannot interact; the impression of spontaneity and communalism is conveyed by the fact that we watch the recorded responses of a child audience of which we are not – and cannot be – a part. My experience of *A Children's Midsummer Night's Dream* has been shaped by the fact that I watched the video of the production in my American home, far from the specific sociocultural context that gave these performances their primary meaning and power. The film medium allows the production to be preserved and experienced in a wide variety of cultural milieux, but that permanence and mobility – and my ability to read the film closely – comes at the price of theatrical performance's distinctive liveness,[15] the frisson of actors and audience present to each other, the local particularity of each performance context, the communal imaginative act that stage performance necessarily requires, the potential to alter the performance in light of changing audience responses, the sheer danger and exhilaration of performing live. As an interpretive essay on the virtues of children's production of Shakespeare, Edzard's film has enormous value and cumulative power. As an attempt to practice the very theatrical communalism it praises, however, it shares with Noble's film and, indeed, other British films of Shakespearean theater – among them Kenneth Branagh's *In the Bleak Midwinter* (1995) – a certain blindness about the nature of media. One is tempted to call it a childlike innocence about film and its relationship to the embattled Shakespearean stage.

In a provocative recent study, Michael Gilmore (1998) has argued that the British affinity for theater and the American affinity for film reveals a deep structural opposition that underlies an extraordinary array of differences between British and American culture. As Gilmore himself acknowledges, that cultural opposition may be becoming irrelevant to the contemporary scene as cultural products become increasingly mediatized and travel with ease across national borders. Even so, the three films of *A Midsummer Night's Dream* under discussion suggest that in the case of Shakespeare this opposition remains very much in play, though with a degree of paradox. All three films are self-consciously concerned with the institutional conditions that govern the cultural survival of Shakespeare in performance, and all three reach back to earlier moments in theatrical or cultural history, particularly those at the turn of the nineteenth century, to legitimate their own practice and prompt nostalgia for a popular Shakespearean theater. Hoffman's American production considers the consequences of modern mediatization for the theater (and for gender relations) with some ambivalence, but his *coup de théâtre* in the mechanicals' play aims at purging theatricality in order to make the playing of Shakespeare fit (for) the American multiplex. Noble and Edzard, on the other hand, are far more engaged with the distinctively British question of how to produce Shakespeare for the stage in a form as popular as the cinema. Indeed, the desire to recover a popular orientation and appeal Shakespearean theater is imagined once to have had, a popularity now enjoyed by film, may go along way toward explaining why these productions take the form of movies. More generally all three films reveal Shakespeare's persistent association with the stage and with theatricality, despite the concerted mediatization of his canon in the last decade. That association may suggest a finally incommensurable incompatibility between Shakespearean stage plays and the nature of contemporary mass media commodities, or it may suggest that for all its liabilities, Shakespearean theatricality is still a potentially valuable cultural resource, one bound up with notions of cultural heritage and one to which filmmakers are eager to lay qualified claim. But whatever its reason for persisting, that association affirms that the cinema has not yet found a form of production that fully accommodates one of Shakespeare's most distinctive qualities.

Notes

1 This is, of course, a staple of criticism about *A Midsummer Night's Dream*. For a classic discussion of the play's metatheatrical dimensions, see Calderwood 1971: 120–48.

2 For the debate over recent heritage cinema, see Higson 1993, Hill 1999, Sargeant 2000, Vincendeau 2001.

3 The boys' cruel prank is a vestigial limb of an earlier script (Hoffman 1997) in which Bottom's amateur company is plagued by competition with a professional company of boys led by the schoolmaster Antonio (a passing shot of Antonio in the square remains in the film's final cut). In that earlier incarnation, the boys humiliate Bottom by showering him with donkey dung and braying, a perhaps too heavy-handed foreshadowing of his transformation. This original subplot thematizes the film's alliance with populist Shakespeare over academically "proper," stilted Shakespeare; it ends with Antonio's troupe, dressed in Roman togas and reciting their lines in singsong rhythms, being rejected in favor of the mechanicals. Indeed, the earlier script generally has a decidedly more populist orientation. Another motif concerned a cruel foreman who, for beating an underling and calling him a pig, was turned into a wild boar by Puck. Throughout the film the boar-man is harassed and chased, in effect given a taste of his own cruelty, until as Puck speaks his epilogue the foreman awakens from what he thinks is a dream.

4 The operatic theme consistently associated with Titania, "Casta Diva" ("chaste goddess") from Bellini's *Norma*, hardly squares with her frank, woman-on-top enthusiasm for sex, though it is likely that Hoffman is conceiving of the aria as an indication of Bottom's romantic idealization of Titania.

5 All quotations from *A Midsummer Night's Dream* in this chapter are taken from *The Norton Shakespeare*, edited by Stephen Greenblatt *et al.* (1997).

6 Dickson 1997. For a fuller discussion of the relationship between the stage and film productions, see Jensen.

7 The production's connections to the surrealism of Magritte are easily overstated, since the image of the light bulb and the use of moonlit water may have its origins in Robert Lepage's 1992 production for the Olivier Theater in London, and doors, Gary Jay Williams notes, "have become almost international theatrical analogues of the poststructural idea of subjectivity" (1997: 256).

8 For discussions of "directors' Shakespeare," see Wells 1976 and Smallwood 1996.

9 To be sure, there are a few twentieth-century examples in their midst: an antique radio, metal toy cars, an electric lamp with a cartoon donkey motif. Nevertheless, even these few anachronisms are treated as if they were of a piece with the otherwise consistently late nineteenth-century decor. This kind of anachronism also surfaces in Noble's visual references to children's literature throughout the film. Though most are to turn-of-the-century examples, Noble also includes an ostentatious reference to the film *E.T. the Extra-Terrestrial* (dir. Steven Spielberg, 1982) when Bottom, Titania, and the boy ride a motorcycle through the night sky in front of a silhouette of the moon. Once again, Noble hardly acknowledges the anachronistic quality of the reference, preferring instead to weave it into what Burnett has called the "collective children's memory" that pervades the film and to treat it as yet another example of "classic" children's literature (see Burnett 2000: 92).

10 Note, for example, the links with *Peter Pan* and *Alice in Wonderland* in Noble's production of *As You Like It*, noted by Samuel Crowl (1992: 68 and 134), or Noble's 2002 staging of a musical version of *Chitty Chitty Bang Bang* at the London Palladium.

11 See Burnett 2000: 92. He emphasizes the link to Victorian *fin de siècle* anxieties on 97–8.

12 For further discussion of the company ideal in Branagh's films, see Lanier 2002a, esp. 151–3.

13 Burnett 2002b: 169. My reading of the film is indebted to Burnett's superb discussion.

14 For examples, see Brooks 2000, Allen 2001, Johnston 2001, and Kinnes 2001.

15 For an illuminating discussion of "liveness," see Auslander 1999.

10

"TOP OF THE WORLD, MA"

Richard III and cinematic convention

James N. Loehlin

In the mid-1990s, within a few months of each other, three film adaptations of *Richard III* reached the screen. Al Pacino's *Looking for Richard* (1996) followed an actor known primarily for film work as he explored Shakespeare's play, largely within the conventions of the stage. The other two films featured stage actors, who had successfully played Richard III in the theatre, adapting their performances to the medium of cinema. In Richard Loncraine's 1995 *Richard III*, Ian McKellen played Richard as a fascist dictator against a backdrop of 1930s Britain. In *The Life and Death of Richard III* (dir. James Keane), made in 1912 but rediscovered in 1996, Frederick Warde's histrionic stage performance was captured in a large-scale and confident film that is the first surviving American feature. All of these films raise important questions about Shakespeare, theatre, and cinema. How does visual imagery supplement, undermine or replace Shakespearean text? What is the relation between the conventions of theatrical acting and the technical possibilities of cinema? How do Shakespeare films function in the arenas of high and popular culture? This essay concentrates on the McKellen/Loncraine film, and its successful exploitation of the conventions of popular cinema. I conclude with a brief afterword about the Warde film, which provides a telling early instance of the way cinema forces a redefinition of Shakespearean performance.

The Shakespeare movies of the new wave that followed Kenneth Branagh's *Henry V* (1989) – Franco Zeffirelli's *Hamlet* (1990), Branagh's *Much Ado About Nothing* (1993), Oliver Parker's *Othello* (1995), Trevor Nunn's *Twelfth Night* (1996), and Richard Loncraine's *Richard III* – are mostly made in what Jack Jorgens has termed the "realist" mode (1977: 7).[1] "Realist" films, in Jorgens's typology, lie between "theatrical" films that simply transfer stage performances to the screen and "filmic" versions that substantially reimagine the play in terms of the esthetics and resources of the new medium. The Burge/Olivier (1965) and Orson Welles (1952) versions of *Othello* are representative of these two poles; Oliver Parker's version is a typical "realist" film. Baz Luhrmann's *William Shakespeare's Romeo + Juliet* (1996), with its kinetic visuals and awkwardly naturalistic acting, falls somewhere between the filmic and realist modes.

The realist Shakespeare film is characterized by the sort of mid-range naturalistic acting, cinematography, and editing that is used in most Hollywood films. The characters are represented as "real people," in plausible make-up and costumes, and the film relates the narrative straightforwardly without calling attention to the medium. Such films are not, of course, realistic in the sense of imitating anyone's actual experience of the world; but such cinematic conventions as continuity editing and soundtrack music are so universal that they are no longer even perceived by most viewers. The new wave of Shakespeare films, aiming for a share of the mainstream Hollywood audience, buys into Hollywood conventions, to the extent that Parker's *Othello* was marketed in Columbia Pictures print ads as an "erotic thriller" that was "as accessible as *Fatal Attraction*." Yet while the other new Shakespeare films employ mainstream conventions in a straightforward, unselfconscious way, the Richard Loncraine *Richard III* embraces and exploits those conventions to make a striking and imaginative Shakespeare film that remains every inch a movie.

Ironically, Loncraine's *Richard III*, like the Stuart Burge/Laurence Olivier *Othello*, originated as a stage production. Richard Eyre directed Ian McKellen as *Richard III* at the Royal National Theatre in 1990, and McKellen's desire for a filmed version of the performance led to the collaboration with Loncraine, a director of television advertisements and commercial films with no background in the theatre or Shakespeare (McKellen 1996: 26–7). It is from Richard Eyre's production that the film takes its single most important interpretive choice: resetting the action to 1930s Britain and presenting Richard as a fascist dictator. Yet the film exploits the historical parallel more pointedly than the stage production did, and McKellen's performance, which was stiff and mannered on stage, is subtler and more effective on screen. In the theatre Eyre's production was a grim, humorless history lesson, which drew theatrical excitement chiefly from McKellen's ability to perform complicated tasks with his one good hand while rattling off long verse speeches in a clipped parade-ground accent. Loncraine's film, by contrast, is a witty and incisive retelling of the story that capitalizes on cinema's power as popular narrative entertainment.

Loncraine exploits to the full the narrative drive of modern mass-market movies, creating an energetic, primarily visual method of storytelling. Scenes and even speeches are broken down and intercut into short, clear sequences whose impact is supported by establishing shots, music, and visual paraphrases; the words serve to reinforce or complicate a visual meaning that precedes them. Barbara Freedman notes that Loncraine is adapting a method developed in the early talkies: "a separation of action from speech" (2000: 65). Loncraine's method allows him some of the interpretive flexibility that Dennis Kennedy ascribes to foreign directors working on Shakespeare in translation; the text loses pre-eminence through its reproduction in a new medium (Kennedy 1993: 5). In the end, Loncraine's film doesn't advance a particularly sophisticated or original reading of *Richard III*; but the sum of its parts is in this case greater than the whole. The inventive insouciance with which the film treats individual characters, scenes, and images makes it a consistently engaging riff on Shakespeare's text, which it plays off against a number of other signifying systems.

The text itself is severely cut; the film makes little reference to the events of the *Henry VI* plays, beyond establishing the fact of a civil war in which the York family has triumphed. Queen Margaret, the vengeful spirit of the house of Lancaster, is gone entirely, as are many of the supporting characters. Those that remain, however, are often expanded and developed through non-Shakespearean appearances. Queen Elizabeth (Annette Bening), Lady Anne (Kristin Scott Thomas), and the young Princess Elizabeth (Kate Steavenson-Payne) – who doesn't even appear in the text – are all given added prominence and in some cases additional lines. The film's emphasis on visuals over text, together with its 1930s setting, actually allows a greater degree of characterization to various minor figures. Richard's henchmen, for instance, are carefully differentiated within the hierarchies of rank and class. Tim McInnerny's Catesby is a cold-blooded, opportunistic civil servant; Adrian Dunbar's Tyrell is a sadistic young non-commissioned officer; Bill Paterson's Ratcliffe is Richard's doggedly loyal batman, who never realizes the full extent of his superior officer's villainy. In spite of the fact that most of their lines are cut, these three characters are more memorably depicted than in most stage productions.

Loncraine's method of witty visual storytelling is especially evident in the three linked sequences that begin the film. Loncraine gets nearly ten minutes into the film before using a single word of Shakespeare; by the time Richard begins his opening speech, the film has introduced not only the setting and background of the story but all the principal characters and their relationships. Kenneth Branagh attempted much the same thing in *Much Ado About Nothing*, but his overblown pre-credits sequence of galloping horses and heaving bosoms served mainly to convey a general (and somewhat deceptive) sense of the lusty, busty romp he was presenting the film to be. Loncraine's opening, by contrast, is dense, economical, and multi-layered.

The first sequence, before the credits, shows the headquarters of Henry VI and Prince Edward during the civil war. Henry is merely shown as old, pious, and weary, but Edward is given a succinct modern characterization as one of the young Eton-bred officers who perished at the Somme. He is almost a caricature of naive Edwardian Englishness: clean-cut and open-faced, his uniform neatly pressed, he eats his dinner with a photograph of his wife on the table and a loyal dog at his feet. Suddenly a tank crashes through the wall, and the Prince is gunned down by a man in a gas mask: in a moment the world has changed. A monster out of the wartime drawings of Otto Dix, McKellen's Richard Gloucester executes the old King, then pulls off the mask as the title appears, each glowing red letter accompanied by a gunshot.

The credits sequence that follows shifts to a world of post-war elation. A limousine glides over sunny Westminster Bridge; a shrieking blond princeling scampers away from his indulgent governess; the royal family poses for a formal photograph. The scene then moves to a palace ballroom, where a stylish chanteuse croons a jazz version of Marlowe's "Come Live With Me and Be My Love." The ballroom sequence subtly introduces virtually every character and relationship in the film. The aging, doting King Edward IV dances with his young wife; the audience learns both that he is ill, and that members of the court don't approve of her. A series of brief, across-the-room takes reveals Richard's social and physical unease, his collusion with Buckingham, and his strained, oppressive relationship with his mother, the Duchess of York, played imperiously by Maggie Smith. Richard's plotting takes effect as Clarence is quietly led away by Brakenbury and his guards; meanwhile Richmond dances with Princess Elizabeth, who will eventually secure his claim to the throne. The Queen's brother Rivers makes a brash entrance to embrace his sister; the prominence given this moment suggests both the Woodvilles' unpopularity at court and the highly significant roles they will have in the film. Above all, the sequence reveals that the film will operate not so much as a series of textual exchanges, but through a pattern of interwoven and overlapping visual codes derived from historical and film iconography.

The film's primary level of meaning comes from its setting in twentieth-century Britain. The story of Richard's rise and fall provides a critical perspective on the current crisis in the monarchy and on the spectre of fascism that haunted British politics from the blackshirts of the 1930s to the National Front of the 1970s. Richard is iconically linked to Hitler by his haircut and moustache, but his uniform and accent identify him as an upper-class British officer like Sir Oswald Mosley, the charismatic leader of the British Union of Fascists. The film's link between fascism and the ruling class also builds on the figure of King Edward VIII, whose pro-German sympathies might have led to a political crisis had he not abdicated the throne in 1936 in order to marry the American divorcée Wallis Simpson. These historical resonances give some political impact to the film's central story of a modern England ruled by an aristocratic dictator.

Loncraine exploits those resonances through a series of powerful visuals, the most obvious being the scene wherein Richard, through Buckingham's stage-management, is hailed as king by the citizenry. Richard and his henchmen, wearing black uniforms, converse with the Lord Mayor and his retinue in a lobby festooned with red-and-black posters bearing nationalistic slogans from the play: "this noble isle," "glorious summer," "the time to come." Then Richard enters the auditorium and mounts a platform decked with red banners and microphones; the camera backs away at a low angle as Richard raises his right arm to the chanting crowd. This scene essentially duplicates one in Richard Eyre's stage production, but on film it gains an added power from its similarity to Leni Riefenstahl's depiction of the Nuremberg rallies in *Triumph of the Will*.

Throughout *Richard III*, the film medium allows Loncraine to create a convincing alternative reality. In the theatre, the 1930s milieu seemed arbitrarily tacked on, presented mainly through costuming; on film, Loncraine establishes an uncanny historicity through a superabundance of visual detail – Bentley limousines, Abdulla cigarettes, Sten guns, newspapers, railroad cars, and recognizable English locations, including several examples of the quasi-fascist architecture of 1930s London. Mid-way through the film Loncraine succinctly defines his milieu, and wittily acknowledges his medium, when he shows Richard watching black-and-white newsreels of his own coronation in the royal screening room.

The film complicates and deepens its historical parallel by casting American actors in the roles of Queen Elizabeth and her brother Lord Rivers. No doubt the decision was partly economic: Annette Bening and Robert Downey, Jr. are well known and bankable actors, and they figure disproportionately in all the film's publicity. But they also figure prominently in the story Loncraine's film, as opposed to Shakespeare's text, is telling. Queen Elizabeth, the low-born, social-climbing wife of the dying Edward IV, is played by Bening as a Shakespearean Wallis Simpson, gate-crashing the Royal Family with her playboy brother in tow.

The presentation of the Woodvilles as American *arrivistes* is an effective interpretive choice, despite some clumsy line readings. Bening's Elizabeth develops in complex and interesting directions; in the end, she becomes one of the most important characters in the film, making several non-Shakespearean appearances and taking some lines from the excised Queen Margaret. Evidently Loncraine felt the need for a pole of positive identification to counterbalance Richard, since Richmond only appears late in the play and is scarcely developed. Bening's Elizabeth grows in moral stature through the film, is never seriously tempted by Richard's attempt to woo her daughter, and presides in person over the daughter's marriage to Richmond. Within the film's historical framework, Bening could be read as America growing from an indifference to fascism to come to Britain's rescue in World War II.

The film's primary level of meaning, then, is a retelling of the *Richard III* story in the context of modern British fascism, against the background of the 1930s and World War II. However, the film operates at several other levels based on the kinds of cinematic codes it employs. Kathy Howlett points out that even the film's quotations of fascism, reproducing the clichés of Hollywood spectacle, are "less historical than cinematic" (2000: 128). The iconography of Nazism is only part of a whole range of movie imagery on which the film draws. Loncraine exuberantly quotes various popular genres, from science fiction (Richard's audible breathing in a gas mask suggests Darth Vader from *Star Wars*) to the slasher film (Lord Rivers is stabbed from under the bed while having sex with an airline hostess) to the western (Richard's use of a truck-mounted machine gun in the final battle replicates William Holden's last stand in *The Wild Bunch*).[2] *Richard III* can also be read as an inspired conflation of two principal cinematic genres: the British "heritage film" and the American gangster movie.

The first of these is a staple of the modern British film industry, somewhat derided in Britain but extremely popular in the United States. A wide-screen variation on the success of *Masterpiece Theatre*, the modern heritage film probably began with *Chariots of Fire* but really hit its stride with the tremendous success of *A Room with a View*, the first of Merchant and Ivory's popular anglophilic adaptations of anglophobic Forster novels. The recent film versions of Jane Austen, Henry James, and Virginia Woolf are examples of the ongoing heritage phenomenon. Heritage films are costume dramas of a particularly English sort, wherein the conflicts and sufferings of the beautiful, articulate characters are always mitigated by the reassuring presence of white linen and sunny meadows, leather armchairs and bone china. Most of these films are exquisitely made and acted, and their romantic nostalgia is difficult to resist.[3]

Richard III seems at times to be a parody of a heritage costume drama: the idea of "Englishness" is often held up as ironic. In the opening scene with Prince Edward, the loyal dog is shown chewing an ugly piece of raw meat while the Prince tidily cuts up his roast beef. The juxtaposition is suggestive, and the camera lingers on the slavering dog longer than his plot function – sensing the approaching tank – seems to warrant. The glamour of the early scenes of the "glorious summer" of the Yorks is similarly qualified. Interiors are a little too crowded with period detail, so the effect becomes showy and gaudy; the York ladies dine alfresco in their mourning frocks, on a carpet laid out rather absurdly in the middle of a field; the elegantly dressed Royal Family looks enervated and cadaverous in the bleak seaside sunshine. The parodic effect becomes overt when the heritage treatment is accorded to some of the ugliest buildings in Britain, from the Brighton Pavilion to St Pancras railway station – which stands in for a royal palace – to the Speeresque Shell-Mex Building, where Richard makes his headquarters. Costumes and locations change constantly and surprisingly, to the accompaniment of Trevor Jones's jazzy score, so that the film provides the visual pleasure of heritage film while making cynical fun of it and the wholesome, hierarchical "English" values it represents.

Richard III also co-opts the heritage tradition by using a number of actors in roles similar to those for which they are well known to international audiences. Nigel Hawthorne exploits the sympathy accorded to his King George III as a sweet-natured, trusting Clarence, while Jim Carter, Charles James Fox in *The Madness of King George*, plays another dissolute politician as Hastings. Edward Hardwicke reprises his bluff, honorable Dr Watson as Lord Stanley, played as a sturdy RAF officer, always set off from Richard's black-clad henchmen by his blue aviator's uniform. Kristin Scott Thomas, as a drug-addicted, love-starved Lady Anne, adds to the series of unhappy neglected women she has played in costume dramas ranging from *A Handful of Dust* to *Angels and Insects* to the modern heritage film *Four Weddings and a Funeral* (*The English Patient*, released just after *Richard III* in 1996, gave her another in this line of roles). With the exception of Thomas as Anne, none of these actors has much time to develop a characterization; the film relies on the associations they already carry with them as a kind of cinematic shorthand.

The other set of codes the film uses belongs to a very different genre, the American gangster film. Here, the connection is more complicated, since the gangster genre itself is related to the rise-and-fall archetype partly defined by Shakespeare's *Richard III*. The uncanny similarities between them have been noticed before, most notably by Bertolt Brecht, who anticipated Loncraine by fifty years in linking gangsters, Richard III and Hitler, in *The Resistible Rise of Arturo Ui*. Brecht intended his play, which charted the rise of a clownish Hitler figure to the head of Chicago's greengrocery trade, to undermine Hitler's self-mythologizing. In Brecht's words, "Ui is a parable play, written with the aim of destroying the dangerous respect commonly felt for great killers" (cited in Manheim and Willett 1977: 458). The Shakespearean allusions in Brecht's play are cuttingly ironic – the clownish Ui is shown studying Shakespearean declamation with a ham actor – and the gangster parallels serve to reduce Hitler to a petty crook. Loncraine's *Richard III* likewise resonates with the gangster genre, but not in a way that reduces Richard's stature. The gangster element of *Richard III* capitalizes on the crude-but-effective psychology of the archetype and the energy of its pop-culture manifestations.

The gangster underworld, with its violence, passion, and feudal conflicts of loyalty, has served several Shakespeare film adaptations, including *The Bad Sleep Well* (Kurosawa's version of *Hamlet*, 1960), the *Macbeth* adaptations *Joe MacBeth* (dir. Ken Hughes, 1955) and *Men of Respect* (dir. William Reilly, 1991), and several Romeo and Juliet spin-offs. Yet Loncraine's *Richard III*, while not given an explicit underworld setting, in many ways follows the classic gangster film even more closely. The American gangster film was defined by a trio of movies from the early thirties. *Little Caesar*, *The Public Enemy*, and *Scarface: The Shame of a Nation* established the guidelines for hundreds of films in a genre that continues into the present day. Like the Elizabethan tragedies, *Richard III* among them, that focus on an overreaching Machiavellian anti-hero, the gangster film is built on a structure of identification and alienation. In violating the moral and political laws that constrain the viewer, the gangster, like Tamburlaine, the Jew of Malta or Richard III, provides a focus for audience identification and wish-fulfillment. Once the viewer's trangressive desire is vicariously satisfied – when the gangster reaches the "top of the world" – he may be safely rejected, and his fall and destruction assuage the viewer's guilty conscience.

In the classic gangster movie, which Loncraine's film parallels, deliberately or not, with uncanny precision, the anti-hero is an ambitious man who feels unfairly excluded from society (Shadoian 1977: 2–11; Rostow 1978: 27–30). He may be set apart by low or shameful birth, but his marginality often has a physical manifestation as well, such as Paul Muni's disfiguration in *Scarface* or James Cagney's mental illness in *White Heat*. The hero is often haunted by bitterness, shame or some unfulfilled psychological need, usually related to his family. His father is almost always dead, though he may remain a stern presence in the background, but the hero's most important personal relationship is generally with his mother. His rise to power is often motivated by a need to impress her and win her love, yet it invariably somehow alienates her or causes their separation (cf. *Scarface*, *The Public Enemy*, and especially *White Heat*). The hero has difficulties with other women; he often wins, and then neglects, a beautiful wife, who may become his enemy and/or victim (cf. *Scarface* and *White Heat*). The hero's daring and ruthlessness earn him the admiration of the audience and of a small group of followers. In the early part of the story he may work tirelessly to help his family or organization gain dominance over others; he then moves up within the organization through guile and assassination. Certain scenes and sequences are common to virtually all gangster films: a montage of crimes by which the hero rises; a conference at which the hero reveals his new power to his former colleagues, often making an example of one who challenges him; a scene in which the hero adopts new clothes or mannerisms to go with his new position. The hero is almost always helped in his rise by a close associate or pal, whom he later rubs out for a perceived or actual betrayal. When the hero reaches the top he begins to forfeit audience sympathy; he becomes paranoid, violent, and increasingly isolated as outside forces rise against him. He may be haunted by his past deeds; he begins to reveal his weakness. Cornered, he rises to a final heroic moment of defiance before being destroyed.

Shakespeare's play bears some correspondances to this pattern, but Loncraine's film follows it almost exactly. All the elements are there: the troubled relationships with the mother and wife; the bloody elimination of rivals (Clarence, Rivers, and the princes); the meeting where the hero reveals himself (making an example of Hastings); the physical transformation as he reaches the top (adopting a black dress uniform and having his portrait made); the betrayal by, and elimination of, the right-hand man (Buckingham); the fear and isolation; the final moment of defiance. The film's 1930s setting lends it many of the trappings of gangsterism – black limousines, jazz, swanky clothes, machine guns – but more importantly Loncraine follows the rhythms of a Hollywood movie rather than an Elizabethan history play. In the stage production the 1930s setting seemed artificial, at odds with the dramatic structures of the play. The text of *Richard III* is one of Shakespeare's longest, and it is characterized by large, formally structured scenes and heightened, balanced rhetoric. Loncraine's fast editing, jaunty music, and deep textual cuts shape it to the swift rise and fall of the gangster film template, so that the narrative and design seem all of a piece.

McKellen's Richard is invested with many of the psychological qualities of the gangster archetype. In spite of its fascist parallel, Loncraine's film doesn't read Richard's rise in primarily political terms. McKellen's Richard isn't motivated by nationalism, racial ideology or a military-industrial complex, but by a lack of maternal affection. Like Cagney's Cody Jarrett in *White Heat*, McKellen's Richard is obsessed with his mother, and his criminal career is linked to a childhood rejection. Maggie Smith's Duchess of York hasn't come around to doting on her son in the way Ma Jarrett does – her attitude is closer to that of the rejecting mother in *Scarface* – but she exercises a comparable psychological influence. She is given a disproportionate number of lines in the screen adaptation; indeed she takes over some of the lines, and some of the qualities, of the vengeful old Queen Margaret. In the opening ballroom scene, she applauds Richard only grudgingly, and he notes her disapproval. After the deaths of Clarence and Edward, Richard is present for, and visibly wounded by, his mother's remark that "I for comfort, have but one false glass/That grieves me when I see my shame in him" (2.2.53–4). Her final, departing curse is made a pivotal scene in the film, and Smith delivers it with ferocity. It gives McKellen his only moment of real vulnerability: as the Duchess departs, Richard stands, frozen with fear and anguish, while his aides watch him uncertainly, his power undermined for the first time. Her words return in Richard's nightmare, in place of the textual curses of his victims. Throughout the film, whenever his mother mentions his deformities of body or character, Richard shows pain and panic. The implication is clear: she has rejected him for his crooked body, and that rejection has warped his soul. McKellen's notes in the screenplay refer to "the emotional barrenness of Richard's childhood," and his mother's "disappointment and disgust with his physique"; McKellen observes that "perhaps it was from his mother that Richard learned to hate so deeply" (1996: 144, 236). This psychological reading of the character is a little simplistic, and perhaps politically naive, but it reinforces the film's connections to the gangster genre and makes the bitter anguish of McKellen's Richard vivid and intelligible.

McKellen's performance is far more successful on film than it was on stage, in my view, partly because the proximity of the camera breaks through the surface armor of his icy characterization. As in the stage production, McKellen eschews the traditional majesty and charisma associated with Olivier, who flaunted sexual magnetism and athletic vigor in spite of his limp and hump. Though McKellen gives asides and soliloquies directly to the camera, as Olivier did, he rarely ingratiates himself; he is no charming Vice-figure but a haggard, sleepless killer.[4] Yet while McKellen's stage performance was rigid, unvaried, and not integrated with the rest of the production, in the film his work comes across as more nuanced and complex. The camera catches his relationships to the other characters in subtle details: the amused affection with which he offers chocolates to Tyrell, the glinting malice with which he flatters Hastings just before condemning him; the mute contempt with which he rejects the sexual offers of the miserable Lady Anne. McKellen's performance remains highly self-contained, but it resonates with other elements of the film's production style in tantalizing, sometimes enigmatic ways, and it remains continually involving.

The final moments of the film provide a good instance of its complex allusiveness and effective use of the medium. The Battle of Bosworth takes place in the environs of the Battersea Power Station, an abandoned industrial monstrosity on the south bank of the Thames. Pursued by Richmond, Richard climbs to the top of a giant structure of metal girders, from which he falls into the flames below. The sequence makes literal Richard's rise and fall, like any number of film climaxes where the anti-hero climbs upward in a last desperate attempt, only to fall back defeated. Yet this ending also specifically recalls the "top of the world" finale of one of the classic gangster pictures, *White Heat.* In that film James Cagney, pursued by the police to the top of a gasworks, shoots into the tanks and destroys himself in a fiery explosion after proclaiming, "Made it, Ma, top of the world!" In *Richard III*, McKellen, atop the Battersea Power Station, holds out his hand to Richmond and the audience and invites us to accompany him, "If not to heaven, then hand in hand to hell." As he topples grinning into the flames, the soundtrack plays Al Jolson singing "I'm sitting on top of the world."

This ending works on a number of levels, suggesting with equal pertinence the heroic, self-defining suicide of the greatest of movie gangsters and the fall into the hell-mouth of the medieval devils who are Richard's theatrical ancestors. Further, Richmond's final smirk to the camera calls into question the apparently simple relation of good and evil in the film's fascist parable: will the cycle of tyranny merely begin again, according to Jan Kott's cynical reading of Shakespearean history? The jaunty music on the soundtrack adds to the irony of the ending, as well as cementing the link to the gangster genre. The specific use of Jolson alludes to a defining moment in film history, the introduction of sound in *The Jazz Singer*: the first time words and images were used together to create the layered texture of modern film that *Richard III* exploits so effectively.

The above observations unpack some of the moment's range of meanings, but they by no means exhaust it.[5] Roland Barthes, in an essay in *Image/Music/Text*, locates three levels of meaning in a moment from Eisenstein's *Ivan the Terrible*: a narrative level, the message; a symbolic level, what Barthes calls the "obvious" meaning; and a third level, what he calls the "obtuse" meaning. The obvious meaning uses familiar, established codes, while the obtuse meaning is "a signifier without a signified" that exists outside the level of articulated language and rational analysis; it can be apprehended but not described (1977: 54). As Barthes puts it, "the obtuse meaning appears to extend outside culture, knowledge, information . . . it belongs to the family of pun, buffoonery, useless expenditure." Barthes associates this meaning specifically with films and their plenitude of signification: "It is at the level of the third meaning, and at that level alone, that the 'filmic' finally emerges. The filmic is that in the film which cannot be described, the representation which cannot be represented" (64). The ending of Loncraine's film seems to me to go beyond its "realist" mode into this realm of layered and elusive meanings. It is readable both in terms of the surface narrative of a Shakespearean dictator's rise and fall, and in terms of the signifying network of cinematic codes and conventions to which the film repeatedly alludes. Yet the image of McKellen's laughing face receding into the flames has a disturbing comic strangeness that can't be fully accounted for at either level. He seems to be mockingly aware of meanings just beyond the viewer's grasp, just "over the shoulder" of the obvious meaning, in Barthes's phrase (1977: 61). The multivalent power of signification evident in such moments gives film its potential as a medium for myriad-minded Shakespeare, a potential that Loncraine's *Richard III* effectively realizes.

Postscript: Frederick Warde's *The Life and Death of Richard III* (1912)

In 1996, while the Loncraine/McKellen *Richard III* was playing in American movie theaters, another *Richard III* film came to the attention of cinema scholars. William Buffen, a retired projectionist from Portland, Oregon, donated *The Life and Death of Richard III* to the American Film Institute, having carefully preserved the fragile nitrate print for over thirty years without realizing its significance. Made in 1912, it is the earliest surviving American feature film, running nearly an hour on five reels. Produced by M.B. Dudley, directed by James Keane and starring stage veteran Frederick B. Warde in the title role, it is a remarkable document that is now central to the study of early cinema and Shakespearean filmmaking.[6] In particular, *The Life and Death of Richard III* makes clear what a devastating challenge the cinema presented to theatre as a vehicle for Shakespeare. In this milestone from the very beginnings of cinema, the narrative power of the screen comes across powerfully, while the Victorian histrionics at the center of the film look flatly ridiculous.

Frederick Warde was at a severe disadvantage in the title role, having to mime Shakespeare without the use of language. Indeed, Warde toured with the film on its initial release, providing some of the text that was necessarily absent from a silent picture. Barbara Freedman argues that by performing alongside the film, Warde found "a unique means of countering what the silent film had truncated, distorted, and silenced" (2000: 48). This form of multimedia performance may have been part of the film's design; it opens and closes with a shot of Warde, without make-up and in a modern suit, bowing and nodding as if to an audience. According to the *Charleston News and Courier* of January 12, 1913,

> While the eyes rest in the intermissions between the five reels, Mr. Warde entertains the audience with dramatic recitals of famous passages in the play, elucidating them at the same time. During the showing of the pictures he explains the situations. The result is amazingly good. In educational value, from the historical viewpoint, it is better than the presentation of the play itself.
>
> (Ball 1968: 159)

Robert Hamilton Ball, writing before the film's rediscovery, suspected that the film depended heavily on Warde's live accompaniment: "Whether it could have stood on its own feet without Frederick Warde's explanatory intercessions is highly questionable" (1968: 162). Viewing the film now, it is clear that it does. The adaptation is cogent and streamlined; the silent images tell the story with clarity and dramatic effect. Viewed nearly a century after it was made, the film seems to me an ambitious, well-crafted, and confident piece of filmmaking, with one glaring shortcoming. The problem with *The Life and Death of Richard III* is Warde's own performance. The cinema, with its new language of movement and image, proved merciless to the traditions of nineteenth-century theatrical acting.

Frederick Warde was by no means a bad actor; he had had a long and distinguished stage career when he first went in front of the cameras, at age 61, to film *Richard III.* He had toured with Irving in England, played Romeo opposite Adelaide Neilsen, and alternated the roles of Iago and Othello with Edwin Booth. Yet in film acting Warde felt himself out of his element. In an interview given at the time of filming, Warde complained of the pragmatic approach of director James Keane:

> The director of the company simply told the other actors what to do, telling them when to look glad or sorry, when to shout and when to fight, without telling them why they did any of these things. It was another matter for me. I simply couldn't act without saying my lines, and I had to suppress all sense of the ridiculous to go through with the thing in such surroundings.
>
> (*Brooklyn Eagle* interview, 1912, *Richard III* DVD)

Warde's reservations about Keane's methods are understandable, but in practice the other actors, even the extras, look much more natural and convincing than Warde does. In Warde's autobiography some years later, after he had made a few more films and his own son had become a film director, he softened his tone toward the cinema: "I had much to learn and considerable to unlearn but the director and photographer were very considerate, although my ignorance of the necessities of the camera must have tried their patience almost to the limit" (1920: 306). Clearly Warde had come to recognize the limitations of his own approach and the possibilities of the new medium of the twentieth century.[7]

The problems with Warde's performance have largely to do with scale. Warde is acting for a theatre audience, while Keane is making a movie. A comparison with a 1911 British film of *Richard III* shows the technical and creative advance made by Keane, and the degree to which it forced a re-evaluation of Shakespearean acting. The 1911 film simply uses a fixed camera to record a performance by Frank Benson in the Shakespeare Memorial Theatre. The fact that the camera is kept at a distance, that what the viewer sees is visibly constrained by the limits of the stage, actually allows Benson's performance some of the ferocity and vigor it evidently had for theatre audiences. In the Keane/Warde film, by contrast, it is precisely the skills of the filmmakers that place Warde's hamminess in such pitiless relief. Every stagy flourish of gesture or expression is seen too close, so that Warde seems to be playing to the galleries far behind the viewer.

Keane's camera details every slight miscue in Warde's performance. At one point he has to make two attempts to draw his sword; he later has some difficulty picking up his gloves. His black page-boy wig looks absurdly youthful, as the camera catches every line on his craggy face. His forward lean and stamping, arm-swinging walk often make him look too big for the frame. His gestures are grotesquely exaggerated; he wipes blood from his sword with extravagant relish, and celebrates his successful wooing of Anne with a hearty slap of the thigh. These moments, which might have played well enough on the nineteenth-century stage, can't survive under the unblinking stare of the camera.

Despite the shortcomings of Warde's performance, the film is clearly a major achievement. There is nothing sophisticated in its interpretation of the play; Richard's villainy is gleeful and unmotivated, his fall swift and well deserved. But the story Keane tells is compelling in its simplicity, and provides ample material for visual excitement. Compositions are bold and dynamic, especially in crowd scenes; soldiers and processions sweep in serpentine and diagonal patterns toward the camera. The production design is sumptuous and impressive, with fine period costumes borrowed from the New York stage. The interior castle settings are rather crude, with obviously fake stone walls, but the outdoor locations are effective. Many shots are memorable: a duel between two mounted knights in an open field, an ambush over a stone wall that runs perpendicular to the camera, a troop of soldiers galloping directly at the screen. Most vivid of all is Richmond's approach to England in a fully rigged medieval ship.

In terms of cinematic technique, the film is conservative; it makes little use of the cross-cutting and camera movement that were being pioneered by D.W. Griffith in the early 1910s. Most of *Richard III*'s seventy-odd shots are taken with a stationary camera from middle distance, and often a single length of film is used to record an entire scene. Yet Keane puts the evolving language of film to judicious use. In the scene in which Buckingham and the citizens plead with Richard to take the throne, Keane cuts between a room in the palace and an exterior balcony as Richard moves in and out to respond to the crowd. The scene's parallel editing establishes the contrast between the public face of politics and the behind-the-scenes workings of power. In the scene of Richard's coronation, the camera pans with Richard as he ascends the throne.

The combination of crowd and camera movement gives an impressive sense of grandeur, and the depth of field and stately ceremony make Warde's gestures for once seem appropriate.

Though Keane uses editing and camera movement only occasionally, he proves adept at what André Bazin was to define as *mise-en-scène* cinematography, changing the relationship of elements within the frame so as to convey visual meaning.[8] The death of Lady Anne, a scene invented by Keane, is particularly effective in this regard. The action occurs in three distinct planes, all held simultaneously in focus. Anne lies in the foreground, well illuminated. Behind her, in darkness, stands an attending physician visible only in silhouette. In the third plane, an illuminated passageway, Richard appears, back-lit and with his face mostly shadowed. He draws the physician from Anne's side, giving him a poison to place in the drink. Richard hovers in the background while Anne drinks and dies, with all three planes of action remaining in focus, but contrasted by lighting and relative size. The scene anticipates the frightening effects of F.W. Murnau's *Nosferatu* as well as the deep-focus camera-work of Gregg Toland in the films of Orson Welles.

Throughout, the film gives the sense of a new medium just being discovered, one for which the ground rules are not yet fully established, but which offers nearly limitless possibilities for visual storytelling. Keane was no Griffith or Murnau; his narrative style is pragmatic rather than innovative, but it is clear, forceful and well suited to his material. *The Life and Death of Richard III*, the very first feature-length Shakespeare film, throws down a gauntlet against the theatre as the primary medium for Shakespeare. By showing that a play can be communicated intelligibly without the language, and that the histrionic traditions of the stage may sometimes be less effective than cinema's manipulation of images, it forces a redefinition of Shakespearean performance. At the beginning of the twentieth century, the cinema made existing theatrical conventions obsolete; the theatre had to reinvent itself in order to compete. *The Life and Death of Richard III* shows the first stage of that process, one that has been going on now for a century, and shows no signs of abating.

Notes

1 The recent proliferation of Shakespeare on film and video has provided examples of all three of Jorgens's modes. The Trevor Nunn and Janet Suzman versions of *Othello*, both based on stage performances adapted for television, remain in the theatrical mode, whereas both Derek Jarman's *The Tempest* and Peter Greenaway's *Prospero's Books* can be described as filmic. But the majority of the commercial Shakespeare films released since *Henry V* remain realist productions grounded squarely in the conventions of naturalistic cinema.

2 Barbara Freedman notes a number of other possible quotations, as well as the film's allusions to non-cinematic media genres such as television commercials and rock videos (2000: 66).

3 In an illuminating essay in *Sight and Sound* magazine, Claire Monk discusses the ambivalent relationship to the heritage genre of another recent British film, Christopher Hampton's *Carrington*:

> *Carrington* treats its audience to the visual, literary and performative period pleasures associated with that critically despised but highly exportable British product, the heritage film, while pointedly seeking to distance itself, through various strategies, from the supposed conservatism these films were so often

> condemned for in the 80s and early 90s, particularly their innate escapism, and their promotion of a conservative, bourgeois, pastoral, "English" national identity. (1995: 33)

In my view *Carrington* mostly fails in this endeavor, at times revealing a self-righteous hypocrisy equivalent to that of many of its Bloomsbury subjects, while *Richard III* is more successful.

4 For a dissenting view see Christopher Andrews's article on three screen Richards; he sees McKellen's performance as deliberately seducing the viewer (2000: 90–1). Barbara Freedman notes that McKellen may have intended his characterization to be more appealing than many viewers found it, citing an interview in which McKellen discusses Richard's attractive qualities (2000: 63).

5 McKellen comments on the aptness of Loncraine's use of Jolson in the screenplay:

> When [Richard Loncraine] invited me to see the first rough-cut of *Richard III* at the studios of Interact in west London a month after shooting, I relished the double irony of the Al Jolson song which he had overlaid on the final frame of his film. Richmond and Richard simultaneously feel, in the moment their fates collide, that they are sitting on top of the world.

McKellen's remarks suggest that the song was not part of the initial conception of the scene, and that McKellen at least may have been unaware of the Cagney parallel (McKellen 1996: 286). On the other hand, Kathy Howlett cites an interview with the film's production designer, who acknowledges that the *White Heat* allusion was deliberate (2000: 222, n. 49; see Calhoun 1996: 37).

6 This film has been released on DVD by Kino Video, together with a documentary on the film's discovery, including an interview with William Buffen.

7 Robert Hamilton Ball, praising Warde's 1916 *King Lear* without having seen *Richard III*, observes that "Frederick Warde himself is surprisingly good . . . he had learned something about acting before the camera and does not especially smack of the stage" (1968: 244).

8 Bazin praised the use of long shots in deep focus, as in the films of William Wyler and Orson Welles, as opposed to the editing style pioneered by Griffith: "Depth of field is not just a stock in trade of the cameraman, it is a capital gain in the field of direction – a dialectical step forward in the history of film language" (Mast and Cohen 1985: 133).

11

SHAKESPEARE AND THE STREET

Pacino's *Looking for Richard*, Bedford's *Street King*, and the common understanding

Thomas Cartelli

> To me Shakespeare is like James Brown. . . . Shakespeare is someone to be appropriated and sampled.
>
> Oscar Kightley[1]

This essay treats several corresponding dislocations of Shakespeare: what this volume's editors have cleverly called *Shakespeare, The Movie*; Shakespeare as reconstituted by Americans and, as it were, in American (the language); and, finally, Shakespeare in relation to what is as much an idea as a specific location, that is, Shakespeare and the street. Before developing this last conceit, I want first to provide a somewhat wider context or frame of reference than the essay itself, once it begins to unwind, easily admits. In the summer of 1998 I had begun to attend an annual series of summer productions of Shakespeare in a parking lot off Ludlow Street on New York's Lower East Side that were memorable more for their conditions of performance – which involved a state of more or less constant interruption by curious pedestrians of every walk of life, children at play, and the sounds of traffic and sirens – than for the quality or originality of the productions themselves. Indeed, in many instances the productions – of *Julius Caesar* and *Othello*, among others – came to seem secondary to the unscripted dramas that invaded, punctuated, and sometimes even commented on the performances, the idioms of Spanish and Chinese casually mingling with, and occasionally overtaking, the comparatively flat line-readings spoken at full volume to little audible effect by the actors. I recall other instances when "stage" action and setting collaborated to particularly provocative effect, for example, the shock of recognition produced at the start of *Julius Caesar* (June 26, 1998) when the plebeians were beaten and berated by tribunes uniformed to resemble (and act like) police officers clearing a city park of protestors or undesirables, or the richly layered feeling that accompanied the sight of two Hasidic Jews suddenly appearing behind the space where Caesar was being assassinated to the cries of "Liberty! Freedom!"

This interpenetration of Shakespeare and a neighborhood that for well over a hundred years has been a seed-bed for a succession of immigrant cultures and communities had special resonance for me given my preoccupation with Shakespeare's early twentieth-century deployment in the project of Americanization (see the chapter entitled "Shakespeare 1916" in my 1999 book *Repositioning Shakespeare*). The clash between the avowed aims of Shakespeare in the Park(ing) Lot to bring Shakespeare into the circuit of neighborhood life and the neighborhood's obliviousness to the gesture brought back to me the extent to which the Americanization of Shakespeare remains an ongoing event of considerable complexity. And here I take my cue not from some grand theoretical intervention but from the American playwright Tony Kushner who, at a Fall 1998 symposium on "Shakespeare and American Performance" at New York's Public Theater, provocatively declared that Shakespeare is neither our contemporary nor our countryman, and that if it seems like a stretch for American actors to do Shakespeare, the fact is that it is a stretch. Kushner went on to observe that however universal he may have come (or have been made) to seem, Shakespeare's career ended about the time North America became colonized, and that America's growth came after his death. Kushner then wondered, in a distinctly Whitmanian vein, why we should look to Shakespeare to take our measure as a people or a nation, adding that if we choose to do Shakespeare, we should do him in full consciousness that for all that is the same, all that we share with him, there is just as much that renders him and us different, and hence, that if we do Shakespeare at all, we should do Shakespeare differently. For Kushner, doing Shakespeare in a presumptively "accurate" or emulative manner should seem as silly to American actors as dressing up in wigs and tights to sit in the House of Lords.

Kushner's implicitly nationalistic call for doing Shakespeare differently constituted for me a moment that could arguably be construed as "postcolonial," though I would also argue that what followed in its wake was just as decidedly postcolonial, as a succession of American actors stood up to declare how powerless they felt in the face of Shakespeare's language, and then sat in silent tribute to British director John Barton's patronizing advice to two seasoned professionals working through a scene onstage. Indeed, this alternating current of deference and difference, piety and irreverence, anxiety and aggression, has informed American attitudes towards Shakespeare from the days of Emerson and Whitman straight through Henry Clay Folger's construction of a Shakespeare Library that may at once be read as a triumphalist act of counter-colonial appropriation and as a symptom of cowed emulation marking the continued influence of Shakespeare over great stretches of the American imagination.[2] It is through this door of resounding ambivalence into a space where some of the same contrary winds of difference and deference are blowing that I would like to lead the rest of this essay.

I begin with a quotation drawn from an article published in 1996 by culture critic Margo Jefferson in the *New York Times* under the suggestive banner, "Welcoming Shakespeare into the Caliban Family" (November 12, 1996: C11). According to Jefferson:

> Shakespeare must meet America at the movies, and on equal terms. Combative, experimental and mutually seductive, whether in a mass-culture smash or a quirky art house "docudrama" like Al Pacino's current "Looking for Richard." . . . Shakespeare must adjust to city street and suburban mall English, constantly reinflected by different regions, neighborhoods, races, ethnicities and classes.

Postponing for now a considered response to the question of why Shakespeare "must meet America at the movies" (a statement that effectively conflates American culture and filmgoing), I will start by posing some collateral questions of my own that are prompted by Jefferson's connection of the popular art of "the movies" with the life and languages of popular culture, first and foremost: What does the city street, much less the suburban mall, have to do with Shakespeare or he with it? What does "the street" signify in the first place? The "street where we live," the avenue of established values and common protocols of understanding? Or the street where *we* don't, "the dirty boulevard" of hustlers and drug-dealers, of hipsters cruising for the latest fashion statement or trendiest high? Or might it represent something less specifically geo- or demo-graphic: a state of mind that ruminates, wanders, interrogates, explores; that looks (and lurks) in spaces high and low for what it takes to be the truth of experience, the street of the inquiring photographer or *flâneur*?

The "street" as I deploy it here is all these things, as much a space of interaction, negotiation, and encounter as a strictly demarcated physical place or property. It is a structure and strategy of engagement, a calculated move, intended to mark a new spot on an appropriative grid that has been rapidly expanding of late. As the "action" in Shakespeare has moved in quick succession from the study to the stage to screens large and small – televisual, cinematic, "cineplexual", and digitized – Shakespeare has emerged as privileged icon and favored site of appropriation for what Hollywood (and Kenneth Branagh Productions) no doubt deem the profitable horizons of the late adolescent suburban marketplace (see Richard Burt's *Unspeakable Shaxxxspeares* (1998) on this subject). Like other demographic phenomena in post-industrial America, the domestication of Shakespeare to appeal to the action-adventure/teen-romance/MTV end of the market has tended to leave the darker corners of urban experience and the inquiring mind to their own devices. Though Baz Luhrmann's *Romeo + Juliet* (1996) arguably brings the energy and allure of the city street to its relentlessly youth-oriented representation of "star-crossed" lovers and Michael Almereyda's *Hamlet* (2000) attempts to infuse the old play with a slacker melancholy, film *noir* moodiness, and postmodern gloss, both ventures are less engaged in staging a Shakespeare of the street, part of its comings and goings, its strains and pressures, than in translating Shakespeare into, and channeling him through, the more highly stylized pitch and rhythms of commercial marketing strategies and new communication technologies. The distantiation of Shakespeare beyond the pale of city street is particularly evident in the Almereyda *Hamlet* whose purview is that of the multinational corporation and the depersonalizing slant of the glass-walled high-rise that quite literally ascends well above the horizons of the street.

While Almereyda also impressively channels Shakespeare's language into the speech patterns of everyday discourse (making the speeches of Ethan Hawke's Hamlet seem freshly thought-out and incrementally composed, rather than being merely recited), the abrasive rhythms and textures of American urban life are more recognizably (and directly) put to work in four other cinematic appropriations of Shakespeare that attempt to bring the street to Shakespeare and Shakespeare to the street. Although I will in the following be primarily concerned with Al Pacino's *Looking for Richard* (1996), I want to start by placing it in the company of two slightly earlier films that more overtly adapt Shakespeare to the idiom of the city street – Gus Van Sant's *My Own Private Idaho* and William Reilly's *Men of Respect* (both 1991) – and end by contrasting it with the latest American avatar of *Richard III*, James Gavin Bedford's *The Street King* (aka *King Rikki*, 2002). What links these films is their effort not just to make Shakespeare viable in the popular marketplace but to find a way of translating Shakespeare into a specifically American vernacular, which involves a transformative approach to spoken language in its own right as well as a transformation or compression of language into cinematic image or gesture. In *Idaho*, the appropriative deployment of Shakespeare is most often signaled by a movement out of the speech patterns of the street into the high style of blank verse directly culled from the *Henriad*. Shakespeare is superimposed on the matter of the street in the manner of Brecht's highlighting of the movement from ordinary speech to the singing of songs. While this is not the only way Shakespeare-derived language is deployed in *Idaho* – Van Sant occasionally "translates" or transposes Shakespeare into American English paraphrase, most effectively in the sequence when his Prince Hal figure rejects "Falstaff" – it signals his film's difference both from *Men of Respect* and *The Street King* – where reductive translation into inarticulate "mafiaspeak" and Latino-accented "spanglish", respectively, are the rule rather than the exception – and *Looking for Richard*.[3] In Pacino's film, Shakespeare's language is, for the most part, "done straight" but in a manner that invites large incursions of urban American speech patterns; involves the compression of long speeches into shorter ensembles of speech-actions; and dislocates entire passages from their moorings in the Shakespearean text in order to restructure our experience of the play.

Although his approach to *Richard III* is avowedly "docudramatic", what Pacino documents in the most compelling moments of his film is how much more dramatic Shakespeare can be made by "penetrating into what at every moment the text is about," and how film itself may be better positioned than theatre to bring the truth of the speaking voice to the surface (possibly one of the reasons why it is preferable, if not entirely necessary, for Shakespeare to "meet America at the movies"). This can be achieved, according to Peter Brook (whose insights these are and who is one of the few British authorities in the film whose pronouncements are not violated by a knowing smirk or a purposeful jump-cut), when American actors stop remaining "obsessed with a British way of regarding text" – that is, as a kind of musical score – and enter into the sustained exploration of character and motivation that has been the hallmark of American acting since the high-tide period of the Method and New York's Actors Studio.[4] Brook elaborates this point at length in a clearly privileged moment in Pacino's film, claiming that:

> Every actor knows that the quieter he speaks, the closer he can be to himself. And when you play Shakespeare in close up in a film and have a mike and can really speak the verse as quietly as this [Brook demonstrates as he speaks], you are not going against the grain of verse but are going in the right direction because you are really allowing the verse to be a man speaking his inner world.

While it is unclear whether Pacino "quotes" Brook merely to articulate a position to which he has already committed himself, Brook's statements bring into focus two prevailing preoccupations of Pacino's project: (1) its Americanness, which is everywhere apparent not only in the acting choices and speech patterns of Pacino and his cast, but also in the alternating anxiety and hostility they evince regarding the authority of British acting, scholarship, and behavior (all the scholarly talking heads in the film are uncoincidentally British); and (2) its commitment to a conspicuously cinematic (and

Method-oriented) dissolving of the distance between word and feeling as a way of getting at the truth of experience.[5]

With respect to Pacino's preoccupation with the state or practice of being American, I want to make at least a small case here for a consideration of the postcoloniality of *Looking for Richard* by highlighting the internal narrative of the film's composition, the story it wants to tell not only about the embattled position of actors vis-à-vis directors, but of American actors of Shakespeare vis-à-vis British actors of Shakespeare, of the masculinized American street versus the emasculated British study, all of which may be reduced to what Margo Jefferson terms "the story of hardy, ambitious Americans who take on a powerful Old World and come out winners," or as the banner of her article implies, Caliban versus Prospero. Pacino's film combines an unusual blend of humility and deference to Shakespeare with confidence, nay arrogance, regarding the ability of actors, particularly *American* actors, to seize possession of a play to which they claim to contribute an energy and "truth" that escapes the capacity of scholars and other kinds of actors to deliver.[6] The claim Pacino makes is not unironically conveyed. He is well aware (I think) of his own lack of authority as either scholar or well-trained speaker of the verse. But he's also aware (and wants to persuade us) that the playing space Shakespeare left behind has been effectively vacated or, what amounts to the same thing, has been ineffectively filled by a theatrical and scholarly establishment that operates more as a heritage industry than as a creative force that can bring anything close to Shakespeare's originary power to the page of dramatic production. What *can* bring that power to the stage or, again, to what at this moment in time amounts to a less rarefied thing, that is, the screen, is (the argument goes) people like himself who by temperament and by training remain in close touch with a "common understanding" that it was Shakespeare's peculiar genius to appreciate and bring to bear on his own writing and productions.

While these considerations emerge (for me at least) on virtually every corner of the street that is *Looking for Richard*, they are suggestively displayed in a scene that is played more for its slapstick or farcical potential than for anything particularly significant it reveals about *Richard III*. I am speaking here of the scene when Pacino and his sidekick Frederic Kimball pay what is presented as a surprise visit to the Shakespeare birthplace and find, to their own manifest unsurprise, that no one is home and that, moreover, the beds are really too small, the rooms too threadbare and narrow to have housed so august a presence as the person of the Bard.

In his own reading of this scene, a British colleague, Chris Lawson, contends that Pacino is here endorsing the myth of the positive effects of visiting shrines, that Pacino is making a pilgrimage that involves a sincere effort both of understanding and veneration.[7] Though my own heritage as a native New Yorker may be speaking a bit too narrowly here, I think Pacino is playing this scene as what in the streets of New York would be called a "goof" – that is, a performative form of acting *out* and acting *up* premised on a studied state of unseriousness – but also to demystify the very idea that one could hope to find Shakespeare in such a setting. By contrast with both the myth and practice of bardic veneration, the film of which this forms only a small part is committed to finding new ways of looking at and for a Shakespeare that Pacino knows cannot be found in, or be limited to, a carefully reconstructed cottage in an England that seems positively geriatric in comparison to the youthfully American energy and attitude he brings to bear on it. It is for such reasons that Pacino – who constructs himself throughout as a seriously playful and playfully serious seeker-of-truth – stages his ejection from the Shakespeare birthplace at the hands of its proprietary caretakers who are invested in exercising a curatorial control over a Shakespeare that is more at home in a museum than in the open air or street. The closing comment of the middle-aged but casually dressed Kimball as he and Pacino find themselves back out on the street – "What a bummer," he opines – brings what Pacino elsewhere labels "the quest" further into the circuit of an adolescent's "excellent adventure" bumptiously but earnestly pursued by a seemingly ageless American Don and his Sancho-like sidekick.

Pacino's collateral preoccupation with the dissolving of the distance between word and feeling emerges in the primarily New York-based man-in-the-street interviews he conducts in his film and in the contrast they make with the exclusively British scholar-in-the-study sequences. They also emerge in the additional contrast Pacino is intent on staging between actors and scholar-experts. The privileging of feeling over word, directness over rhetorical display, is most powerfully evoked in a statement Pacino elicits from an anonymous gap-toothed panhandler – who claims to derive from Shakespeare the message, "If we *felt* what we said, we'd say less and mean more" – which is dramatically linked to a carefully edited comment by Vanessa Redgrave, who assesses the evolution of four hundred years of British political culture in terms of an ever-widening gap between word and feeling, the effect being to suggest that the antidote to this dissociation of sensibility is waiting in the humble confines of the American street where passion may still be said to speak. Redgrave's intervention is presented in largely voice-over form as indirect commentary on the just-concluded passionate implosions of Estelle Parsons's Queen Margaret (in a staged "rehearsal" of *Richard III*, 1.3) and as a kind of vocal bridge or caption that hovers over the succeeding imaging of yet another give-and-take discussion between Pacino and his actor-confederates. As such, her message – "The music, literally, I mean the music, and the thoughts and the concepts and the feelings have not been divorced from the words and in England you've had centuries in which word has literally been divorced from truth and that's a problem for us actors" – seems to point in two directions at once: back to the expressive immediacy of Queen Margaret's utterance and forward to the ongoing quest for truth pursued by Pacino and his band of American brothers (and sisters), which is presumably underwritten by that quest's grounding in the expressive immediacy of the street as embodied by the panhandler's commentary.[8]

Although the panhandler's statement is made with considerable support from Howard Shore's understatedly dramatic soundtrack, and seems to add a larger ethical dimension to Redgrave's magisterial pronouncement (as well as an interesting ripple to the film's prevailing anti-British bias – don't Americans also, particularly American politicians, speak with a decidedly forked tongue?), it is hard to see how Shakespeare – a playwright notably given over to the art of sustained rhetorical flourishes, of verbal *excess* and studied ambiguity – can be said to advance the idea of saying less but meaning more. What does advance this idea is Pacino's performative spin on *Richard III* which, though it mainly proceeds through a series of intense discussions and filmed rehearsals of scenes played in theatrically defined spaces, is, in the end, resolvedly cinematic and not at all consistent with the American theater's often slavishly colonial devotion to the full Shakespearean script.[9] Pacino does not, in the best moments of his film, seek to "stage" Shakespeare as much as he does to restructure our experience of the play by maximizing the dramatic potential of individual moments and sequences in the playtext, and by eliding equally significant scenes and speeches that possibly cannot sustain translation into the idiom of film. This is especially the case in the Lady Anne scene where he condenses Richard's closing speech (which he has already worked over in rehearsals) to its first three lines – capped by "I'll have her but I will not keep her long" – and a backward flourishing of his riding-crop, and in the scene in which Richard debates the arrest of Clarence and wrangles with his enemies, which Pacino intercuts with repeated imagings of King Edward writhing tormentedly on his bed. Though Pacino and his colleagues (particularly Penelope Allen in the role of Queen Elizabeth) speak – and inhabit – their lines as well as one would like, it is Pacino's preference for physicality and for fracturing the linear "screen" of text-based interpretation by means of close-ups, jump-cuts, montage, and other cinematic devices that most effectively delivers the "truth" of these scenes.

What I reluctantly term the "truth" of these scenes (and which Neil Sinyard more pointedly calls their "psychological truth") is not something Pacino arrives at spontaneously, without discussion or careful preparation. Indeed, his decision to screen Penelope Allen's spirited (and successful) defense of her powerful reading of Queen Elizabeth's resistance to Richard displays Pacino's unusual responsiveness to (and reliance on) the insights and interventions of his actors, while also demonstrating how such actors bring feeling to bear on language.[10] We move in this brief two-minute span from Pacino's statement that knowing what all the words mean doesn't really matter and Kimball's patronizing characterization of Queen Elizabeth as an "hysteric" to a much more informed understanding of what exactly is at stake in her defense of her prerogatives that is not only indebted to Allen's passionate and avowedly Method-oriented investment in the words that she speaks, but also to her convincing assessment of what exactly is at stake for Elizabeth and her family in their contention with Richard of Gloucester. Pacino edits this sequence in such a manner that Allen's objections to Kimball are intercut with roughly paraphrased readings from the text transacted by Allen and her interlocutors and full-dress filmed rehearsals of the same moments in the play. The passion of Allen's objections to Kimball's reading of the scene (the first moments of 1.3) and the cogency of her directives to the actors reading the parts of Rivers and Grey ("They know what the scoop is"; "You know damn well what's going on; if he [Edward IV] dies, that's it") carry over to the filmed rehearsals in a manner that gives considerably more strength to this woman's part than Pacino is credited with giving Lady Anne in a sequence of the film that is even more powerfully (and complicatedly) evoked.[11]

The "truth" in the case of the Lady Anne scene is the sum of its evolving parts, which we watch Pacino assemble from his casting choice (he asks for an actress young enough to make Lady Anne's vulnerability to Richard credible) to his sensitive probing of why, apart from her youth, Anne would be vulnerable to Richard (she has no sponsor or protector in the royal court: an intuitively actorly explanation of the kind that scholar-expert Emrys Jones could not provide in the micro-second of commentary editorially allotted him). In this sequence, Pacino again intercuts commentary and conversation with superimpositions and fades of full-dress rehearsals and more casual walk-throughs, while repeatedly privileging by way of repetition his sampling of facial tics, sounds, lines, and gestures. Crouching in dark corners of the film-frame, he tries on scowls, limps, and line-readings that all but announce "An actor prepares," at once striving and refusing to make a seamless transformation from Hollywood celebrity to

Shakespearean character.[12] What ensues as the scene goes forward is profoundly enhanced by the sheer intensity with which Pacino finally abandons himself to the character of Richard, and by the unusually erotic charge Pacino brings to an encounter that in other stagings tends to test an audience's capacity to abandon its disbelief. But the sequence is even more enriched by film's capacity to allow a camera to focus and circle in intimate close-up on their figures to the exclusion of all else in the frame, and (as Peter Brook notes) on the characters' ability to speak their lines with an intimacy the stage does not usually afford. Given how closely in Pacino draws the viewer, it is both shocking and exhilarating to witness how, upon Lady Anne's withdrawal, Pacino reduces an actor's dream of a 36-line speech to three lines and turns the *caesura* in the third line – "I'll have her, but I will not keep her long" – to an occasion for gleefully triumphant laughter which combines with the swinging of his riding-crop overhead to make action eloquence.

Saying less and meaning more thus translates – at least in Pacino's filming of the early scenes of the playtext – into an esthetic that shows off the power of American acting's preference for gesture over word, the body over the head, and of film's capacity to deliver, in howsoever stylized a way, the pressure and fullness of experience: the tenor and immediacy, if not the "truth", of the street. It is no coincidence that the film flattens out to something very ordinary when Pacino chooses to reproduce playtext chronology and conventional filmic realism in the closing battle scenes with Richmond. In these scenes (whose flattening is considerably abetted by Pacino's choice of the dramatically challenged Aidan Quinn to play the role of Richmond), *Looking for Richard* moves far away from the American street that was, in many respects, its inspiration and just as far from the roughness and immediacy of the play's earlier scenes which were filmed in "found" playing spaces and rehearsal studios, were the product of intense, often contentious debate, and made potent use of montage to show us things (Edward's writhing on his bed, Queen Elizabeth's passionate embrace of his corpse, etc.) that do not literally "speak" in the playtext. In the end, Pacino gets caught up in the seduction of conventional cinematic display, falls prey to the temptation to "open up" the play by allowing it the presumptive freedom of out-of-doors color, light, and panoramic spaces, and in so doing loses touch with what Neil Sinyard describes as its liberating embrace of "fragmentation, enhanced by a montage that leaps about in time and place with a mobility that only cinema can manage" (2000: 70). Although his reprising of Prospero's lines on the fading of "this insubstantial pageant" at film's end is dramatically effective, the decision itself imposes a sense of polish, refinement, and closure on a film otherwise committed to exploring the power of process, accident, and the passion and inspiration of actors themselves in *unmaking* established ways of understanding *Richard III*.

Rather than consider the ending of *Looking for Richard* a complete betrayal or contradiction of its starting premises, I would prefer to see it as a predictable concession to the conditions and conventions of commercial film-production, possibly reflective of a residual anxiety about the more experimental approach Pacino took to staging the first half of the play. A case might also be made for Pacino's effort to make a film that could, in its professedly more experimental key, nonetheless compete with the best recent British efforts in kind, the most influential of which at the time would, of course, have been Branagh's *Henry V*. We may further complicate our understanding of Pacino's hypothetical anxiety and ambition by considering the extent to which Pacino attempts to compete here with the far more potent British theatrical and cinematic "ghost" of Laurence Olivier. Although Pacino and his interlocutors never directly refer to Olivier's legendary performance in the 1955 film of *Richard III* which he, himself, directed, Olivier's ghost haunts Pacino's staging and acting from the Buckingham scene (4.2) on as Pacino pursues an increasingly more mannered and monopolistic portrayal of his character.[13]

Equally revealing here is Pacino's decision to screen his "return" to what he naively calls the same stage where *Richard III* was performed "some three hundred years ago," by which he means the Globe playhouse (where *Richard III* was *not*, of course, originally performed), then in the process of memorial reconstruction. Speaking of this spurious return to origins in his typical blend of earnestness laced with irony – "We thought we would rehearse and see maybe in a rehearsal if we could get in touch with some of those old spirits. You know, Method acting type stuff." – Pacino effectively conflates the American actor's drive to inhabit characters from the inside-out with the same embrace of the British tradition of working from the outside-in that characterizes his frequent reversion to costume drama in the last movement of his film. Pacino even departs here from his characteristic practice of discrediting his scholarly talking-heads, allowing British scholars Emrys Jones and Barbara Everett to make cinematically privileged contributions to our understanding of the scenic structure of the play's last act ("The ghost scene *is* the battle," says Jones convincingly) and of Richard's last stand: "He's like a boar who has subsumed into himself all these frightful animal images, and all that the rest have got to do is hunt the boar. And that's what they do and they get him," concludes Everett incisively.

Recalling the repeated scenes of "off-screen" antic posturing Pacino continues to insert between his screening of more polished filmic realizations of the playtext, and his delivery, in casual rehearsal dress, of Richard's powerful address to his soldiers (5.3.313–41) to no audience but the camera, I cannot, however, entirely agree with Richard Burt's contention that his other apparent concessions to an established British take on the "authentic" Shakespeare film make it seem "as if Pacino's postcolonial unconscious comes back to bite him and drag him back into Olivier's territory," or that Pacino would have done better to make "a mafia *Richard III*" instead of "an old-fashioned period film adaptation of Shakespeare, an English period film at that" (private e-mails). Burt is surely right to remark the residual postcolonial deference Pacino pays to British theatrical, filmic, and scholarly authority, but *Looking for Richard* is also more aggressively postcolonial than Burt gives it credit for, both in terms of the repeated irony it lavishes on its own emulative practices and its insistence on counter-colonizing what at times looks suspiciously like an English period film by making it "speak" in a language, pacing, and attitude that could not be more decidedly (and disruptively) American.

For such reasons among others, I would like to turn back in closing to the film's beginning and briefly consider how Pacino attempts to shape a "common" understanding of the play. The film begins portentously with the tolling of a church-bell punctuating a late fall or winter view of bare trees and a Gothic-spired church as a British-accented actor's voice speaks the lines from *The Tempest* that are reprised at the end. The church-view fades out and into that of a New York brown-brick apartment house that rises above a schoolyard where a boy shoots baskets as Pacino wanders aimlessly into the frame, dressed in black and wearing a soon-to-be-ubiquitous baseball-cap turned backwards on his head. The carefully developed montage then fades back to the church, to fingers flipping through the pages of a Shakespearean playtext, then again to the playground where Pacino turns to notice the camera as the speech concludes. At this point the film proper abruptly begins with an animated indoor scene which finds Pacino in company with his associates beginning their interrogation of *Richard III*.

Two aspects of this preface to the film are noteworthy: (1) the artful dissolving of the English pastoral scene into American urban space, which is mediated by the speaking voice of Prospero and the black-and-white pages of the playtext (as well as the contrast they make with the colorful but artless graffiti on the wall of the apartment building); and (2) the craftily conceived "look" of Pacino as he shambles aimlessly into our gaze wearing the immediately recognizable signs of adolescent laziness and studied indifference. Old world beauty, seriousness, and decorum are juxtaposed against the relaxed and sloppy standards of a new world which, as the first scene-proper develops, speaks in a lively, contentious patter as the struggle to define a common or consensus understanding of the Shakespearean playtext takes shape.

Apart from the omnipresent cap-turned-backwards on his head, Pacino's "look" and behavior change with remarkable persistence in the course of the film as he argues with his sidekick and straight man, Frederic Kimball; consults a copy of Cliffs Notes with a schoolboy's impatient incomprehension; mugs at an abashed stand-in "Shakespeare" incredulous at his shenanigans; plays the American cut up in the visit to the Shakespeare birthplace; and inhabits with astonishing intensity the persona of Richard at the same time as he speaks the role in an unabashed South Bronx accent – until he is finally rendered eerily (refreshingly?) silent and immobile by Richmond in Bosworth field, completely self-effaced and intensely present at one and the same time. An odd mix of self-mockery and self-congratulation, humility and self-assurance, modesty and preening, colors Pacino's out-of-character appearances, many of which take place in his man-in-the-street interviews where he discovers, with manifest unsurprise, that most New Yorkers know little to nothing about Shakespeare or the play he has taken it as his charge to resurrect. As he struggles to explain what the first lines of the play mean to an indifferent group of high-school students (two of whom are making out in the last row of the classroom), or good-naturedly tests an Italian immigrant's overstated knowledge of Shakespeare, Pacino's energy and commitment to the project remain undiminished, directed as they are outside the frame of the immediate encounter to the development of an understanding of the play that will, for all rights and purposes, become our own.

While *Looking for Richard* may be said to serve a self-authorizing and self-promoting function for a film star whose excess of vanity often proves distracting, it also functions as both effective teaching tool and journey of exploration: as a means, perhaps, to reach some of the disaffected and cynical young people to whom Pacino has unsuccessfully attempted to "peddle" Shakespeare on the street (and to whom he presumably attempted to market the film through the circulation of educational materials with leads like "Richard III is Alive and Well and Living on Melrose Place"). Although he dominates the proceedings in his shifting roles of film celebrity, wise fool, and Richard of Gloucester, Pacino also stages them as an ongoing matter of negotiation and debate, dialogue and disputation, in which his actors take what they need from each other, and he takes what he needs from them in order (in his words) "to communicate a Shakespeare that is about how we feel and think today": about the street more than the study, about the truth of experience more than the sanctity of the word.

The streets of East Los Angeles are the site and setting of James Gavin Bedford's *The Street King*, an otherwise very differently motivated and staged dislocation of *Richard III*. As in *Men of Respect*, which recontextualizes *Macbeth* in terms of a New York mafia subculture, Shakespeare's language is replaced by the specialized vocabulary of a site-specific (and ethnically hybridized) American vernacular in *The Street King*, which is focused on channeling *Richard III* to fit the rhythms and contours of the *chicano* gang and drug subculture of Southern California. Unlike *Men of Respect*, which attempts rather mechanically to develop its point-by-point correspondences to *Macbeth*, *The Street King* wears its Shakespearean pedigree more lightly, and tends rather to gesture, than defer, to the plot-line of *Richard III*. While the film assuredly grounds itself on *Richard III* and even employs Spanish equivalents for the names of Shakespeare's primary characters, dramatizing the drive to power of younger brother Rikki (played by Jon Seda as more hunk than hunchback) as he engineers the demise of older brothers Jorge and the current "king" of the Ortega gang, Eduardo, viewers unfamiliar with the play would be hard pressed to notice the Shakespeare connection, so seamlessly does the film otherwise conform to the established conventions of the ethnic gang/drug subculture genre of films like Martin Scorsese's *Goodfellas*, or the Brian De Palma remake of *Scarface*. In fact, *The Street King* stands in relation to *Richard III* in much the way the spray-painted reconfiguring of Shakespeare's image stands in relation to the reproduction of the Droeshout portrait that first appears on the *barrio* wail in the opening credits section of the film (see Richard Burt's Chapter 1, p. 16). As we witness this progressive act of defacement by a hand that signs itself "LCN" (the logo or signature of a brotherhood to which three members of the film's cast once belonged: Rikki, Alejandro, and good cop/bad cop, Juan Vallejo) and refashions Shakespeare's image through the addition of a goatee, shades, red bandanna, beauty-mark, and large cross ear-ring, we are disarmed of any expectation that a film that announces itself as "based on *The Tragedy of King Richard III*" will deliver anything other than an ironically debased product of that transaction.

For such reasons among others, it could be said that *The Street King* functions more as a version of what Richard Burt has called "sub-Shakespeare"[14] than as an overtly promoted or explicitly positioned appropriation of Shakespeare. The film's strategy throughout is more parodic and citational than assimilative; it "samples" selected aspects of *Richard III* without attempting to swallow the play whole, providing a series of filmic substitutions and displacements for what the playtext supplies. For filmgoers who know the play by heart, some new level of interpretive significance may be mined as we watch the "good cop" who fills the role of Richmond become the "bad cop" at the film's end, effecting an equivalence between presumed legitimacy and criminality signaled by the words "plata" and "plomo" (silver and lead, or bribes and bullets) which appear on either side of the restructured portrait of Shakespeare in the film's prologue and are reiterated by the *chicano* policeman after he shoots Rikki and appropriates his sack of drug money. Such an aim may, however, have only an incidental relation to *The Street King*'s citational strategies whose substitutions and ironic riffs on the Shakespearean original more often merely reward the knowing viewer with a double (largely parodic) perspective on the action that remains unavailable to filmgoers unprepared to read the Shakespearean signs and signals.

Some of the more successful moves in this direction involve Rikki's daring visit to the wake of his old friend Alejandro (the film's stand-in for the murdered Prince

Edward which he purportedly undertakes to retrieve a piece of Alejandro's mother's famous lemon cake to share with his buddies, but which he uses to make a date with Alejandro's surviving girlfriend, Anita (the film's stand-in for Lady Anne). Swearing oaths to his innocence in the more-sincere-than-thou manner of Richard Duke of Gloucester after having plucked a red rose from a funerary bouquet, Rikki emerges unscathed, cake in hand, anticipating his meeting with Anita where his production of the same knife he used on Alejandro proves entirely convincing. Pressing the knife into his workout-hardened stomach until it draws blood, Rikki transforms Richard's act of theatrical daring into an entirely contemporary and ethnically specific display of male vanity and macho endurance. While *The Street King* deploys the dramatically cued strategy of direct address to the camera considerably more often than Shakespeare has Richard deliver asides or soliloquies, in this instance the 36-line bravura speech that Pacino reduces to "I'll have her, but I will not keep her long" is translated into a few winks of conversational bravado followed up a few minutes later by a wryly narrated clip of Anita's visit to a tattoo parlor where she has the elaborately wrought name of Alejandro painfully erased from her own taut mid-section and replaced with the signature of her new object of devotion. Arguably of a piece with the rather vigorous misogyny that animates the film, the scene nonetheless works an acutely realized variation on the vanity that makes Lady Anne believe in Richard's love while providing a culturally specific application to the mores and practices of the East Los Angeles gang subculture.

This is not the only time that Bedford samples and elaborates on the plot of *Richard III* in a timely and inventive manner instead of merely attempting to reproduce it. For example, rather than have Rikki's brother, Eduardo, die of an unnamed illness as does Edward IV in Shakespeare's play, Bedford's script has Rikki cut Eduardo's cocaine with a foreign substance and later disguise himself as a physician in order to channel oxygen into Eduardo's IV tube, giving Rikki an added occasion to demonstrate his ruthlessness and resourcefulness and the film an opportunity to advertise its ironic take on the iconic original. Equally successful in this vein is Rikki's stage-management of his brother Jorge's arrest, solicitous visit to him in prison, and use of his own mother to deliver a secret message in Spanish to his murderers ("When flies sing, rats listen") that both echoes the prophecy about the letter "G" in *Richard III* and leads to Jorge's undoing. A later visit to the murderers made by the policeman, Juan Vallejo, gives the informed viewer an inspired sampling of Clarence's conflicted assassins that probably remains just a generic piece of throwaway humor for the uninformed filmgoer. Indeed, in this instance as elsewhere in *The Street King* – when, for example, Rikki announces that "You gotta think global for the 21st century" upon his short-lived ascension to the position of *jefe* or king of the Ortega family – it may surely be said that irony of a very cinemediated variety, as opposed to Pacino's Method-based quest for emotional truth, primarily distinguishes Bedford's effort to translate *Richard III* into the idiom of the American street.

Notes

1 Oscar Kightley is a hip-hop poet and playwright from New Zealand who claims never to have read a complete Shakespearean play. He made this comment during a plenary panel discussion entitled "Shakespeare in the Pacific" at the 6th Biennial Conference of the

Australia and New Zealand Shakespeare Association in Auckland, New Zealand, July 9, 2000. Earlier versions of the present essay were presented at that conference and also at the University of Pittsburgh, September, 2000.

2 See Michael Bristol (1990: 70–89) for an account of the founding of the Folger Library. For a fuller discussion of this entire subject, see the Introduction to Cartelli (1999: 1–23).

3 For a brilliant assessment of Van Sant's appropriations of Shakespeare in *Idaho*, see Curtis Breight 1997: 295–325. Also see Susan Wiseman's probing account of the film in the first volume of *Shakespeare, The Movie* (1997: 225–39) and my own considerably more abbreviated commentary in Cartelli (1999: 27–9). See Robert F. Willson (1992: 34–7) for a broadly informed discussion of both *Idaho* and *Men of Respect.*

4 Foster Hirsch notes that a "central problem of the [Actors] Studio" approach has been "translating emotion into words, learning how to be as turned on by a playwright's words (especially if the playwright isn't a contemporary) as by recalling a powerful image from your life." He adds that "the chasm between feeling and words . . . seems like a continuing hurdle at the Studio" (1984: 198).

5 In an unpublished paper entitled " 'What country, friends, is this?,' " Gary Jay Williams remarks an "American ambivalence about Shakespeare that is being represented in Al Pacino's *Looking for Richard.*" As he thoughtfully observes:

> in his film [Pacino] crosses his company's performance of the play dialectically with a performance of anxiety about the authenticity of Shakespeare for everyday Americans, the America from which Mr. Pacino, as a Hollywood film actor, wants and needs to derive his authenticity. Mr. Pacino is not prepared to give up either Shakespeare or America; his film gives us both unreconciled.

Williams contributed this paper to a seminar on "Shakespeare and Popular Culture" that met at the annual meeting of the Shakespeare Association of America in Cleveland in 1997 under the direction of Lynda Boose and Richard Burt.

6 Cf. Margo Jefferson:

> [*Looking for Richard*] plays with, and on, some of our favorite American myths. We love the idea that we're always searching for honesty and authenticity. And so, Mr. Pacino and company invite us to watch while they worry about plot convolutions, debate the meaning of speeches, solicit the opinions of important actors as to whether they have the training or technique to do Shakespeare at all, brood about whether we, their American audience, will care about the thing at all.
>
> (*New York Times*, November 12, 1996: C16)

7 In an article entitled "The Don Who Would Be King: *Looking for Richard*, but Finding Al," Lawson states that "by going to sites such as the Shakespeare birthplace or Globe theatre, Pacino endorses the myth that the cultural tourist can become, somehow, transfigured or altered by worshipping or paying homage at such shrines to Shakespeare" (2000: 45). Lawson delivered an earlier version of this essay at "Shakespeare on Screen: A Centenary Conference" that convened in Malaga, Spain in September, 1999.

8 The full text of the panhandler's commentary reads: "If we think words are things and we have no feelings in our words, then we say things to each other that don't mean anything. But if we *felt* what we said, we'd say less and mean more." The speech is carefully edited to conclude with his spoken (self-authenticating?) request, "Spare change," directed at a pedestrian outside the frame of the shot, which is itself immediately swallowed up to make way for the start of the film's next sequence.

9 As Foster Hirsch notes of the uncertain approach to Shakespeare of members of New York's Actors Studio, "many American actors, told for so long that they don't speak well enough to do justice to the language, have come to believe it" (1984: 200). Ironically, as my visit to the 1998 symposium on "Shakespeare and American Performance" indicated, this feeling

of insufficiency has often led American actors and directors to regard the Shakespearean text as sacrosanct and to approach it with the unquestioning fidelity of awed disciples.

10 As Sinyard observes:

> the actors struggle to get a handle on the Shakespearean verse through a modern, colloquial definition of their characters' emotional states. Penelope Allen as the Queen is particularly good at this . . . it is all an attempt to reveal what Pacino sees as the psychological truth and universality of emotion in Shakespeare's text through the actors' own explorations and discoveries.
>
> (2000: 61–2)

11 Sinyard is, however, probably right to note that "in some ways, [Allen] is stronger in the rehearsal scenes (where she fluctuates between passionate paraphrase and actual quotation) than in the extracts from the play [itself]" (2000: 61–2).

12 As Barbara Hodgdon writes, "Pacino's strategy merges with that of Richard to generate a partial, incomplete kind of re-authored man-uscript that, by showing his own body-in-process, affords an opportunity to examine how the actor's body functions as a lever to decenter, though not discard, the text-based core of Shakespeare studies" (1998: 209–10). She adds, with respect to the Lady Anne scene, that " 'I'll have her, but I will not keep her long' becomes a mantra that not only propels the actor 'into' the character but which, when the scene continues, he uses to punctuate his own (double) performance" (211).

13 According to Linda Bradley Salamon, "At the end, Pacino stands alone not in the well-deserved isolation that provides catharsis to a tragedy, but in pathos that closes in on self-pity. The character of Richard on view . . . is no less sentimental than Olivier's unhappy hunchback; he is perilously close to a victim for whom the audience is asked to make therapeutic allowance" (2000: 58).

14 In his book-in-progress, *Rechanneling Shakespeare across the Media: Post-diasporic Citations and Spin-offs from Bollywood to Hollywood.*

12

THE FAMILY TREE MOTEL

Subliming Shakespeare in *My Own Private Idaho*

Susan Wiseman

Shakespeare in Idaho

Where is "Shakespeare" in *My Own Private Idaho* (1991)? Who, what or where is the work undertaken by the bard or the shadows of the bard? This is the question this essay poses. The director, Gus Van Sant, has asserted that "the reason Scott's like he is is because of the Shakespeare, and the reason Shakespeare is in the film is to transcend time, to show that these things have always happened, everywhere" (quoted in Fuller 1993: xlii). This seems more like a retrospective claim for the transcendent qualities of Shakespeare than a consideration of the specific place of the *Henry IV* plays in the film. What place do the Shakespearean sections claim, and what implications do they have for the way the film organizes its subjects and viewers? In finding Shakespeare in the film this essay aims to tease out some of the implications of the film, concentrating on paternity and the family tree, visual versus verbal signifiers and the uncanny/sublime as these are deployed through the narrative.

It does not take much probing to find that *Idaho* is dealing with – or stylishly commodifying – some of the Big Questions of contemporary culture: questions around the family, paternity, place, home, maternity, sexuality, status, and all the elements of the masculine filmic *Bildungsroman*. Since the fatal overdose of one of the film's two stars, the twenty-three-year-old River Phoenix, it is as if Phoenix and the film have become reciprocally "about" one another. Phoenix's death, as well as his acting style, his work on the script (Van Sant describes him working "furiously" on the fireside scene), and the improvised style of the scenes where the groups of boys discuss their lives seem to refer the film back to a social world and to substantiate Van Sant's claim that those parts of the film "come directly from a number of people that I've known", "I'm not being analytical" (in Fuller 1993: xli).

But Idaho is also full of textual markers and pointers; "Shakespeare" is far from the only cultural marker in the film. It is richly intertextual – not to say overbearingly knowing – in its deployment of cultural references from popular culture to quasi-Freudian symbolism (for example the "family metaphor" that Van Sant speaks of in interview (Fuller 1993: xxxix)). "Narcolepsy," glossed for us in a pre-credit sequence, is the symptom which the film takes as the key to or metaphor for the irresolubility of violent trauma. It opens in the middle of America, in Idaho – the private, agoraphobic, landscape of the B52s' song, but also the haunted place of mining ghost towns, migrant farmworkers, salmon rivers (Miller 1976). The visuals of empty farmhouses suggest the ghostly presences of Idaho's past and, in the present, the psychic importance of the farming crisis in the mid-1980s. (Duncan Webster (1988: 28) reminds us of the 1986 Democratic Party slogan, "It wasn't just a farm. It was a family," though in this case, it is more than a family – incestuous – but less than a farm; more of a migrant's trailer.) The film prompts nostalgia for other social forms and gestures towards the life of the cowboy – always loved, always leaving, always single – in references including the song "Cattle Call," a cowboy statue at a diner, and Mike's friend's disturbed parody of a quick draw. These remind us of other models of lonely, but still possible, masculinity. In its focus on men in early adulthood, gangs, pairs or couples, even in its use of Portland, Oregon and the gang leader called Bob, the film recycles Van Sant's obsessions from *Drugstore Cowboy* (1989). *Idaho*, however, uses a script generated from many sources rather than one novel and deploys layered visual and literary references. Van Sant has commented on the origins of Scott, "I didn't fully know who he was until I saw Orson Welles's *Chimes at Midnight*" (in Fuller 1993: xxiii). But the central figures are also reminiscent of other American narratives. Mikey and Scott's journey is, as José Arroyo notes, reminiscent of road and buddy movies as well as *The Wizard of Oz* (Arroyo 1993). It even replays the drifting narrative of Twain's Huck and Jim, with Huck/Scott opting out of all those things Jim/Mikey can never have (Webster 1988: 118). And the film ends on (apparently) the same road with a replay of the story of the Good Samaritan. Indeed, *My Own Private Idaho* is a film that advertises its cultural claims. But the title also raises the question, what would it mean to live in one's own private Idaho, an internal, "private," terrain of loss and repetition, a past that can never be revisited but which, figured in spatial terms in the memory, can never be escaped either?

Amongst a plethoric and sometimes literary referentiality two elements occupy dominant and perhaps competing positions in the text: quasi-Freudian images of the past and a Shakesperean narrative of the transition to adult masculinity. As far as the *Henry IV* plays are concerned, the film seems to build on the words of Hal/Henry once he is king "I'll be your father and your brother too" (*2 Henry IV*: 5.2.57) to make an oedipal drama of fathers and brothers, past, present, and future. The ghostly presence of the *Henry IV* plays is also used to address the two adolescents' need for a path to adulthood. Even as the film carnivalizes or cannibalizes Shakespeare's texts, it uses them as a cultural anchor. In doing so, the film sets the "Shakespearean" text not only in but against the perilous journey Michael Waters (River Phoenix) makes towards resolving an impossible oedipal tangle. It would be overschematic to say that the film offers two versions of oedipal narrative, Mike's story inviting reading as a version of the Freudian uncanny in terms of the family tree, and Scott's, using the *Henry IV* plays to chart Scott's rise to power. But these twin trajectories do allow us to begin to analyze the place of "Shakespeare" in the text, and how and why the film ties "Shakespeare" to a contemporary America in a way that announces both the seriousness of the text and its hipness.

The knowingness of the film, its setting among the street-boy hustlers of Portland, Oregon, and its evident desire to slum it with Freud and Shakespeare – even as it offers viewers the pleasures of having their cultural markers in place (and I shall come back to this at the end of the essay) – also interrogates sexuality and masculinity in late-1980s America. Like Steve MacLean's first feature, *Postcards From America* (1994), *Idaho* analyzes abuse and paternity in contemporary America. As MacLean has commented, "You look at the white male backlash in America at the moment, it is all about . . . fears of disenfranchisement" (quoted in Francke 1995: 7). Both *Postcards from America* and *My Own Private Idaho* are concerned with disenfranchisement and marginality, both use visual style to associate the disenfranchised with a version of the American landscape steeped in the associations of the American sublime. *Idaho* does this through analepses using different visual orders – home movies, landscape, time-lapse photography.

Although the Scott Favor narrative is the section of the film which rereads *Henry IV*, the film opens and closes on the story of Mike Waters; the rise of Favor and the fall of Waters are clearly parallel stories but it is arguably the Waters narrative which the audience follows. The story is, more or less, as follows: Mikey and Scott seem to be friends (Mike is in love with Scott) and each hang out, working as prostitutes and sharing the life of underclass adolescents in urban America. Scott is the son of the wheelchair-bound mayor of Portland, Oregon (with no visible mother), whereas Mike is the product of no "ordinary family" – his "father" seems to have drowned himself and later he seems to actually be the son of his brother, Dick. Where Scott turns tricks for money only, Mike identifies as gay; where Scott's father searches for him and makes a contract with him for the son's reform and inheritance, Mike is attempting to untangle an impossible family tree by searching for his mother. The narrative follows first a trip back to Idaho (like a salmon returning upstream to the source of its life) to visit his brother–father, then a trip to the Family Tree Motel to search for his mother and then a trip to Italy in search of her, before ending on the return of Scott with an Italian wife to a new life in Portland. Here we have the rejection of Bob Pigeon/Falstaff in a restaurant peopled by the Portland City establishment and then the twin funerals – of Bob, conducted by street boys, and of Scott Favor's father, attended by Scott.

Such a film cannot really be considered as an adaptation of Shakespeare. It borrows from the bard, from Freudian and other narratives. Mike has a past, whereas Scott has a future and Mike's story is given a quasi-Freudian mediation, Scott's a Shakesperean. In the next sections I aim to elucidate and complicate these alliances and to end by returning to my question, what work is Shakespeare doing in Idaho?

From here to paternity: Mike's uncanny real and Scott's elective fathering

HANS: Where do you want to go?
MIKEY: I want to go home.
SCOTT: Where shall we go?
MIKEY: To visit my brother.

My Own Private Idaho opens with what turns out to be Mikey on a road in Idaho. Voice and visuals are split: in a voice-over Mike tells us that he has been there before, on this road "like a fucked up face." As he finishes his thought the camera turns to the road, then to the sky, and then switches to a fantasy/flashback from Mikey's point of view. These flashbacks are repeated throughout the film; characteristically they feature flimsy, uninhabited buildings – first the shed which, in this first sequence, is blown onto the road and smashed, then we see an abandoned gothic-style wooden bungalow, then the flimsy 1960s bungalow which seems to have been Mikey's home in his childhood and next to which his brother–father Dick lives in a caravan. The habitations seem to become increasingly transient, migratory, as they move towards Mikey's homeless present.

Van Sant's *Drugstore Cowboy* featured visions of flying, cartwheeling, buildings, trees, animals, hats. In this later film the visions are at the core of the conundrum which they both pose and partially explain. During a flashback in Rome, the "home-movie" footage of Mikey's childhood with his mother and pubertal father–brother leads our eye to the door of the house where, in wrought metalwork, we find the H that stands for home. In his visions, Mikey goes "home" to his mother's house. What might in other circumstances be read as an emphasis on the homely qualities takes on richer connotations in association with other issues in the film. The link to sexuality and desire is made clear when, early in the film, Mike has a client who pays to suck him off. We see what Mikey sees behind closed eyes: an empty house or building is taken up as in a twister, and destroyed. In part this gestures towards *The Wizard of Oz*; it is after this that his quest begins. But in terms of thematics, Mikey is presented as attempting to escape from an impossible oedipal situation through a search for his mother and desire for his brother–lover, Scott, thwarted by Scott's desire for Carmilla.

These visuals, flashbacks, reveal a problematic past – in Freud's terms, the secret "known of old and long familiar" (Freud 1955a: 217–53). The Mikey section of the narrative takes us back to what should have been hidden; during the trip to Idaho the story of Mikey's paternity is replayed in his encounter with his brother–father. In these scenes "Dick" – the (comic?) name of Mikey's brother – offers various versions of what might be interpreted as the primal scene. First, he shows Mikey a photo of "Me, you, and mom," but this turns out to be mother–father–child, as well as a mother with two sons.

Inside the caravan where Dick lives surrounded by his paintings of individuals and families, Dick and Mike propose different versions of Mike's paternity. Dick claims that Mike's father was "a lowlife cowboy fuck," shot at the cinema by their mother during a performance of the Howard Hawks western, *Rio Bravo*: "*Rio Bravo* on the big screen, John Wayne on his horse riding through the desert . . ." But Mikey interrupts: "I know who my real dad is . . . Richard, you are my dad. I know that." In refusing the elective/screen paternity of the "lowlife cowboy fuck" and by displaced association, John Wayne, Mikey is left with the literal incestuous situation, the uncanny doubling of father and brother.

Richard's elaborate story, in which an elective father is proposed by a real father, is interrupted by both Mikey's narcoleptic moments – figured for the audience as a combination of the sublime and memories of his childhood as if seen in a home movie – and by Mikey's refusals of the fantasy father in favour of the scandalous "truth." The clear narrative implication is that the narcoleptic visions, to which we also are given access, are the compensatory mechanism activated by the impossibility of any kind of successful negotiation of such a traumatic paternity.

Further signifiers suggest that the film itself may joke about the family drama, its secrecy and determining nature, in quasi-Freudian terms. When Mike and Scott leave Dick Waters (the father–brother) they are sent by their clue – a postcard – to *The Family Tree Motel*. Here Mikey is to begin his search to find his mother among the impossibly tangled and fused branches of his own family tree. But this is not all. As he and Scott arrive at the hotel, who should turn up but Hans. They met Hans earlier, after an evening with a female client, and he had offered Michael a lift in his car. This is Hans Klein, whose name coincidentally seems to translate as Little Hans – one of Freud's youngest patients, with whom he communicated through the parents, especially the father (Freud 1955b: 245). During the interview with the brother–father "Dick" and at other points – such as at the meeting with Hans at the Family Tree Motel and in Hans's interest in forms of transport and mothers – the film jokily, and apparently seriously, advertises its commitment to "the family metaphor" or Freudian narratives.

Reading the film in these terms involves a negotiation between two types of interpretation; one finds oneself at a mid-point between making a reading of the film which laboriously reads into it/makes explicit a subtextual narrative dynamic and a tracing of clues or jokes already highly thematized and framed as textual pointers. If the Shakespeare section is self-conscious in its use of *Henry IV* as a version of the family romance, then the Mike section might, too, be seen as deliberately narrating a version of the family story. The two stories are sharply distinguished and set apart in the viewer's experience, by their contrasting uses of visual codes and styles versus Shakespeareanized language.

What Mike's narrative teases out, visually, seems to be the impossibility of escape from the scandal of being fathered by his brother, a past for which he is not responsible but which leaves him without any place in a social world. His meaning is made in the past, in the conjunction of too many and contradictory meanings in the place of the "H," a home on which too many meanings home in. So what about that wrought metalwork "H" that we (and apparently also Mike) see during his visions? The sequence, as we focus on it, evidently names "home" – the house where he lived as a child, the place where he tells the German dealer in (car?) parts that he wants to go (Where do you want to go? I want to go home). In terms derived from Freudian discussion, though, we can also see Mike's visions, activated at moments of stress, as emerging from a genealogical crisis in terms of his exclusion from a place in American society, an exclusion which the café scene, a scene central to placing Mike's narrative in the context of his peers, indicates is part of a more pervasive disenfranchisement. In such terms, the "H" names the "homely" place from which Mike emerged. Freud discusses the fantasy of return to "the former . . . home of all human beings", the womb, reporting a joke in which " 'Love is home-sickness,' " and Van Sant, too, describes Mike as "trying to find the place where he was conceived" (in Fuller 1993: xliii). "H" names Mike's home, but also his history or genealogy. Accordingly, one narrative structure of the film takes us back into Mike's past, giving his impossible oedipus as a "source" for the things which prevent him from finding a full place in the social world.

In his visions, Mike and we, apparently from his point of view, see the home – bungalow or house – he lived in with his mother in his childhood. Mother's body and that signifier of mother's body, "home," are both present in the visions. These analepses also interrupt the forward movement of the narrative, providing a quite different esthetic and visual texture, without words. These silent interludes appear when Mike's present experiences touch on events from the past, events which are too traumatic to be integrated into the social/cultural narrative of life, but yet determine identity.

Mike's paternity and his relationship with his mother, as in Freud's version of the uncanny, return to haunt him. The association, for Mike, between the female body, desire for the mother, or desired and feared return to an intimate maternity, is made clear in two incidents early in the film. He sees a woman who reminds him of his mother in the street, and he collapses. He has a narcoleptic turn, too, when he is picked up by a female client. When Mike sees her he says, "This chick is living in a new car advert;" once at her home we and Mike are shown a luminous stained-glass panel of Virgin Mary and infant Jesus (the film offers us no chance to miss the point). When she tries to have sex with him, he sleeps. To be sure, later in the film Mike falls into a narcoleptic sleep when he is picked up in Italy; it is not solely the possibility of the return of the maternal that the film proposes as insurmountable. Nevertheless, these elements are present and enable – even, perhaps, invite – an audience to read Mike's predicament in terms of the specific "family metaphor" of the Freudian uncanny.

The experiences of repression and lapse are elaborated in Freud's writing on the traumatic moment when something "secretly familiar" emerges (1955a: 245). Freud plays, as the film itself appears to, on the way the German word *heimlich/unheimlich* tends to collapse into itself in such a way as the domestic, secure, familiar is also simultaneously dangerous and strange. Freud associates this feeling with the adult response to the childhood wish to return to "intra-uterine existence" and to questions of the resolution of Oedipus (1955a: 244). The homely/unhomely implications of the mother's body, for Mikey are redoubled, as it were, because of the tortuous and traumatic relations between his mother, himself, and his brother–father. This cultural confounding and excessive doubling of roles is figured in the text at the level of plot as a narcoleptic reaction to impossible stress and trauma.

This is signaled visually: the spectator sees a vision of landscape, the sublime hallucination of the barn in the wind. The "narcoleptic" gaps in the narrative are inhabited by visions which could be characterized as an estheticization of crisis as the sublime. Such interruptions of the present by the partially repressed forces of the past are discussed by Mladen Dolar in terms of a refusal to relinquish the past (Dolar 1991: 59). Dolar's reformulation of Freud offers a way to read Mike's quest for his mother in terms of just such a feared and desired return to the past. The quest is doomed but is also apparently Mike's motivating purpose. The present – adulthood, desire, and, ironically, economic exchange – is interrupted either by narcoleptic moments figured as sublime or by the heterosexual union of Scott and Carmilla at the time and place when Mike hopes to find his mother.

Idaho offers a case study in this aspect of the Freudian family romance twice: in Scott's rigid "success" and Mike's apparent failure. The constant interruption of Mike's present by the past is contrasted with the other oedipal drama; Scott's election of an "unknown, greater" father in Bob. Whereas Mike is unable to escape the paralyzing knowledge that his father is his brother, when Scott's father dies he inherits massive social and economic power, some of which is in any case destined for him on his twenty-first birthday. After the boys leave the Family Tree Motel the separation of the destinies of the two boys becomes increasingly clear; the motel, with its contradictory name, only temporarily houses both boys and the contrasting narratives which they inhabit.

From the *unheimlich* to Henry

The name, The Family Tree Motel, suggests the permanent inescapability of the family tree – however scandalous. But a "motel" is a quintessentially postmodern transient location. The name combines the film's contradictory interests in what Jean Baudrillard has called "the lyrical [American] nature of pure circulation. As against the melancholy of European analyses" (1986: 27; see also Fuller 1993: xliv). Yet as Baudrillard's comparison suggests, the two chains of association – circulation/surface and analysis/

– imply each other, and so in a similar way to the pairing of the Michael and Scott narratives. They are buddies, almost siblings, almost lovers, and Mike's narrative of the psyche contrasts with Scott's ability to turn situations to his advantage.

Where Mikey is made socially placeless by a traumatic paternity which cannot be overcome, Scott is bound in to paternity and inheritance but also free to select amongst possible fathers. Through drifting he acquires the necessary accessories of his future rule. We see Scott as initially having a complicated relationship with his biological father, the mayor ("My dad doesn't know I'm just a kid. Thinks I'm a threat"), and the narrative implies that it is the unsatisfactory nature of this paternity which has propelled him into street life and rebellion. The pairing of the narratives uses specific aspects of the *Henry IV* plays. In Mike and Scott's distinct careers *Idaho* also reworks those of Hal and Hotspur. When the film opens, Scott Favor is indeed the opposite of the Percy described in *Henry IV* as "the theme of honour's tongue" (*1 Henry IV*: 1.1.80) – but he, like Hal, is "Fortune's minion" (*1 Henry IV*: 1.1.83). Scott's narrative of succession is set out in terms of the Hal/Falstaff/Henry relationships of the *Henry IV* plays and, like Prince Hal, Scott is a cold pragmatist. He is on the street but not of it, because from the start, he is going to inherit. And, as in the *Henry IV* plays, the question of merit and money is foregrounded in Scott's unearned inheritance of his father's status. We know he is going to inherit and that he plans to transform his life; for the audience, the question is how and when this will happen.

It is through Scott's transition to adulthood that Shakespeare's history plays resonate in *Idaho* as the film reworks the play's thematization of father–son and peer relations. In Portland City we see him choosing street baron Bob Pigeon as his "real father." This is no uncomplicated paternal electivity; Scott tells Mike that Bob "was fucking in love with me." But soon after, in a monologue to camera that explicitly parallels Hal's "I know you all" first soliloquy in *1 Henry IV*, Scott vows to reform in a way which implies his eventual rejection of Bob:

PRINCE HAL: I know you all, and will awhile uphold
The unyoked humour of your idleness.
[. . .]
So when this loose behaviour I throw off,
And pay the debt I never promised,
By how much better than my word I am.
By so much shall I falsify men's hopes.

(*1 Henry IV*: 1.2.194–212)

Or, in the *Idaho*/Reeves version: "All my bad behaviour I will throw away to pay a debt." Scott's comedic election of fathers, both dead by the end of the film, contrasts with the incestuous nightmare inflicted on and implicitly determining Mike. Not only does Scott get to choose fathers, but – perhaps the ultimate triumph in oedipal struggle – when he rejects them they die. Both Scott's fathers are flawed – the Mayor has money and power but no body (he is in a wheelchair) and Bob is all body, like Falstaff, but has nothing else. In questioning paternal potential *Idaho* reworks the paternal drama of Hal/Henry/Falstaff. The arrival of Bob in Portland, Oregon (where Scott's father is mayor and, therefore, ostensibly "greater") is accompanied by Scott's election of Bob as his "real" father. However, we hear Bob describing himself as Scott's dependant: he needs Scott for a "ticket out" of street life. Bob's status as a father is predicated on a reversal of oedipal relations with "father" as suitor to son: Scott's possession of all the powerful cards in the relationship makes him partly self-fathering or self-produced. For him, fathers are a matter of temporary choice, a feature which emphasizes his potential to switch from rent boy to king, but also contrasts with Mike's paternal narrative.

Idaho presents a disintegration of economic structures into psychic and social chaos, and this differently marks the paternal and filial bodies and psyches it presents. Bob's boys, his "family" of street boys, act as an index of impossible identities being forged beyond the social margins – in economic as much as sexual terms. And the boys' clients, generationally the same as Scott's fathers and, like him, notionally part of a functioning society, are figured as parasitic upon the position of these outcasts. This is explored in the café scene in Portland where the boys tell their stories, and in the interludes in which Mikey services clients. The street offers the boys no social potential beyond prostitution; their carnival world is delimited by money and clients. Through these scenes, the film's dominant interest in the canny/uncanny sexualized buddy (and sibling) narratives of Mike and Scott is connected to a more general questioning of the economics of masculinity in contemporary America. A superficially similar range of issues is articulated in the *Henry IV* plays in terms of the relations of usurpers to feudal lords, states to servants, fathers to sons. Both parts of *Henry IV* are set against a background of rebellion and social unrest: in *2 Henry IV*, Act 4, the Earl of Westmoreland describes rebellion's proper (true) appearence as "boys and beggary", and the film suggests this, as do specific scenes (*2 Henry IV*: 3.2, the Gads Hill episode, the rejection of Falstaff). The Shakespearean section of the film is (tenuously) connected to social critique because Bob represents the leader of the boys, and it is with Bob that the Shakespeare-derived style and dialogue arrive. Bob first appears staggering and swaying out from beneath a network of flyovers when the boys have reached Portland, Oregon. The reworking of *2 Henry IV*: 3.2 also echoes the opening (and indeed the title) of Welles's *Chimes at Midnight* (1965).

His comment, "Jesus, the days we have seen," simultaneously signals Welles, Shakespeare, and the hard life of the streets. Bob's arrival inserts a Shakespearean linguistic presence into the colony of boys as the figures he speaks with are drawn into pastiche "Shakespeare." The new rhetoric "Shakespeareanizes" the hotel, making Bob's scenes there significant because of their attachment to Shakespeare, perhaps, but without "Shakespeare" ever being the language in which the boys discuss their own situation. The hotel scenes use Falstaff's relations to his boon companions to code them, in part, as a social space beyond the bounds and rule of law; but in its organization at this point the story is not of the rent boys, but scenes from Shakespeare as reworked and improvised. In a sense, one doesn't need to "know Shakespeare" to read them as intertextual. Indeed, during the editing, Van Sant cut some Shakespeare sections because, he claimed, they were "becoming like a movie within a movie" (in Fuller 1993: xxxviii).

Bob (landless knight) may be King of the Street, but the street is dangerous: it involves the boys making themselves vulnerable in cars, rooms, houses, and offers no status or income. The film interrogates the difficulty of crossing the threshold from adolescence into adulthood, gay or straight, in a moment when models of mature masculinity have vanished with cowboys and the only route to power, even safety, is through inheritance. In figuring the failure of masculinity in terms of the underworld of the *Henry IV* plays, the film is far from "imperial Shakespeare" (Wilson 1992: 34–7). To this extent the film could be said to be using Shakespeare to make a political point, or to ask, where is the place of the young male in America, now? But the boys themselves get few Shakespearean lines, and the Shakespearean dialogue tends to have a life of its own – as "Shakespeare."

Where the sublime impossibility of Mikey's situation is rendered visually, the *Henry IV* plays enter the film as stylized rather than improvised talking, dialogue, drama, and as "Shakespeare": they do seem to introduce "a movie within a movie," or to produce two cohabiting styles, one dominated by visuals, the other by voice (Chedgzoy 1995). Jack Jorgens (1977: 1) wrote of early Shakespeare silents "struggling to render great poetic drama in dumb show," but *Idaho* replaces visuals with talk: the scenes slow down and give themselves over to words (Jorgens 1977: 1). Shakespeare marks the text as a demand that the audience transfer attention to the spoken, Shakespearean, word. The film's contrasting of visual and verbal signifiers and sequences organizes, too, the differentiation of the narratives of the doomed Michael Waters and the rising Scott Favor; Michael's past is signalled in visions, Scott's control of the situation is shown in his Prince Hal-like control of dialogue and its placement in relation to Shakespeare. Unlike Mikey, who can barely speak, Scott talks to the camera on several occasions, in a gestus when the boys are covers for porn mags, and in the soliloquy when he explains that he will give up this course of life. He talks: to other characters, to us, to Carmilla in Italy. Indeed, the volte-face predicted in his address to the camera has an important linguistic aspect to it. He returns to Portland leaving Mikey in Italy, a country whose language he cannot understand but which is figured as potentially maternal (he has gone in search of his mother) (Chedgzoy 1995). To summarize: we can see the film as inviting empathy and producing Mike as the central emotional focus of the film; as José Arroyo points out, "the homosexuality that *Idaho* values the most is Mike's." Mike is the audience's empathetic focus (the fact that his narrative opens and closes the film, the style of acting, the fact that we get "inside his head" rather than Scott's monologues to camera all contribute to this); the heterosexual coupling of Carmilla and Scott replaces Mike's quest for maternity; and Scott plays a self-interested pragmatist against Michael's romantic hero. Indeed, such a reading is suggested by the popularity of the film, and as Arroyo (1993) notes, posters from the film, in gay circles. However, the place of Shakespeare in all this is complicated, even troubling, in its connection primarily to the Scott story. The question of which of the twin narratives should dominate was, it seems, hotly debated during the production of the film. Van Sant has claimed that New Line, the independent American distributors were "totally against the Shakespearean scenes" but the foreign distributors "wanted as much Shakespeare in there as we could get" (in Fuller 1993: xxxviii).

As Van Sant's comments indicate, the film has a metarelationship to Shakespeare. Even as it thematizes the struggles between fathers and sons, and to an extent offers a social critique of these issues, *Idaho* could be figured as in an oedipal relationship to the material out of which it produces itself, particularly "Shakespeare," and to be articulating its relation to "Shakespeare" in a way which invites closer analysis. How does the putting of the play through "Shakespeare," or the self-fathering of the narrative upon "Shakespeare," work in the text which narrates the failed and successful adventures in self-paternity and/or family romancing of the two boys? The film both fathers itself upon Shakespeare's text and uses the text as a moment to intervene in the questions of fatherhood, and of begetting and growing up a modern (or postmodern) man.

Marjorie Garber traces the uncanny return of Shakespeare in the way "his" ghosts haunt "our" present; she analyses Shakespeare's uncanny returns, suggesting that "he" is used in various cultural actings out of the family romance. As she puts it: "For some . . . 'Shakespeare' represents . . . a monument to be toppled . . . A related phenomenon follows the pattern of Freud's family romance, which involves the desire to subvert the father, or to replace a known parent with an unknown, greater one" (1987: 7). At first sight, it seems that this is how "Shakespeare" is working here; that, just as Derek Jarman's reworking of *Edward II* radicalizes the play's potential for a late twentieth-century audience, so putting *Idaho* through Shakespeare "radicalizes" Shakespeare, giving Shakespeare's texts new meanings in a modern world. We could see "Shakespeare" as claimed for a set of non-dominant values, wrested back from the theater audiences and returned; the conservative Shakespeare toppled, the film sets about putting a new "radical" version into place. However, as Richard Burt has argued, the only intermittent adaptation of Shakespeare's play is itself part of the film's "critique of the repressiveness of oedipalization" (1994: 338). It refuses to be fathered, exactly, but borrows and reworks.

Moreover, a reading of *Idaho* as turning Shakespeare towards a critique of sexual and economic disenfranchisement becomes more problematic when we consider the precise placing of the dialogue pastiche from the *Henry IV* plays, rather than a more general effect. Bob Pigeon speaks in "Shakespeare," and those involved in prolonged conversation with him are drawn into it. Mike, though, is not drawn into it. Nor is Bob present when the boys are telling their stories; the desperate side of the underworld is either untouched by Shakespearean language or, when it is, this results in an annexation of the Portland hotel to Shakespeare's scenes, not vice versa. The entry of "Shakespeare" into the text produces, or emphasizes, the visual/verbal split and initiates the "movie within a movie" effect derived as much from the way "Shakespeare" as a cultural anchor takes over the text as by the text's carnivalizing or radicalizing of Shakespeare.

Indeed, Mike's story is the one which might be seen as more strongly expressing social critique, and his story – although it is the center of our attention and empathy – is isolated from Shakespeareanized language. Rivers is given few Shakespearean lines and, in the scenes where he plays against Scott and Bob, not only do they have most of the dialogue, but though they are together visually and acting ensemble, it is as if there is a line down the script dividing the types of speech offered to each. Indeed, in these scenes, Mikey is virtually an audience to the exchanges of Bob and Scott.

Moreover, on a larger scale, the pairing of the two narratives of Scott and Michael tends to undermine the sense that the *Henry IV* plays are radicalized by the things they are linked to. Even though most of the parts used by *Idaho* are comic scenes suggesting the subversion of dull order, the acting out of a joyous subversiveness does not seem to be how Shakespeare is being used in *Idaho*. Although Welles – who played Falstaff – commented "Comedy can't really dominate a film made to tell this story, which is all in dark colours," there is little sense in *Idaho* that we are invited to laugh at the comic scenes, even at Bob's deception over the robbery, though these are the scenes incorporated into the film from the plays (Pearson and Uricchio 1990: 250; Cobos and Rubio 1966: 60). Rather than failing to be comedy (a criticism levelled at the Welles film) even the comic moments of *1 Henry IV* and *2 Henry IV* are incorporated in *Idaho* in order to generate seriousness and to tie the film to the "classic" narrative of Shakespeare; the comic scenes are there to be recognizably Shakespeare; Shakespearicity, not comedy, is their function.

The *Henry IV* plays do not only outline the shape of a society in crisis, they also delineate the transfer of power and control to Henry V, perhaps augmented and deepened by his knowledge of street life. It is this contrast that Idaho seizes upon to open up the question of what it means to be a man in contemporary America, fusing the mythic pasts of *Henry IV* and the cowboy community to raise the question of the possibility not only of any fulfilling resolution of Oedipus but of finding any kind of place – to live, let alone work. It retells the *Bildungsroman* of masculine achievement both ways: once in Scott's transition to power, and again in the failed paternity of Bob and the rigorous exclusion of not only Bob but Mike from Scott/Hal's transformation in the final scenes. (This worked rather differently in the script for the film, where it was explicitly stated that in the final scene, "Scott is driving the car" (Fuller 1993: 187).) And when we look at the work done by Shakespeare in the light of the pairing of the two narratives, a rather different pattern is suggested.

Scott gets to choose Bob Pigeon as his father in a paternal/sexual relationship. And then he is allowed to dispose of him – along with his own father – at the end of the film. Of course, the use of the dialogue from and referring to Shakespeare's *Henry IV* plays underlines Scott's coldness, his pragmatic princehood, and the Machiavellian utilization of experience of the underworld/underclass in making a successful entry into a "political career." Nevertheless, his trajectory is contrasted by the film with Mike's in terms which imply that, in attaining the world of money, politics, and restaurants, Scott is making some kind of superficially "successful" transition to adulthood. The mediation of his "coming of age" through the chosen key moments in the *Henry IV* narratives – the scenes in the hotel, the robbery, the rejection – underline the unearned, inherited, and, therefore, arbitrary nature of his rise from street boy to public power. However, the use of the *Henry IV* plays at these moments also serves to mark them out as tracing a rising and socially sanctioned trajectory.

The contrasting narrations of the stories of Mike and Scott is further emphasized by the way in which Mike's being locked into adolescence is figured by a verbal non- or pre-linguistic realm. His narcoleptic visions are not accompanied by dialogue; in that sense they are virtually "silent." Moreover, the trauma marks Mike's speech which, though meaningful (in both senses), is tangential, fragmentary. We find out about his story – the past – through visual materials; Scott's narrative, tied to the future, is worked out through dialogue-heavy scenes and through a formal, set-piece, rejection or murder of Bob Pigeon. This contrasting of chains of association can, at a cost, be put schematically:

> visual/silent/homosexual/adolescent (storyline: family romance with echoes of Freud)
> versus
> verbal/dialogue/heterosexual(?)/adult (storyline: family romance from Shakespeare).

Such an organization of significances troubles an understanding – which the film simultaneously seems to invite – of the film's emphasis on the centrality of the figure of Mike. It invites empathy for Mike, whose story takes up much of the film. Moreover, though vulnerable, he is still alive at least and taking his chances at the end of the film. More particularly, though, such associative links, combined with the splitting-off of the Shakespeareanized sections of the film, suggest that, although the film does address the issue of sexual identity and disenfranchisement in post-rural and post-industrial America, and does produce an ending for Mike which, in its reworking of the story of the Good Samaritan leaves the future of that narrative open to some extent, it does not use the Shakespeare sections of dialogue and performance to do so. In the light of these layered connections, the place occupied by "Shakespeare" in *Idaho* can be reassessed. On the one hand, and this is registered in the initial response of critics, the film seems to be bringing out a subtextual or latent amusing perversity in the plays. In terms of its general use of the *Henry IV* plays the film can be said to be reworking relationships in terms of a greater indeterminacy. Certainly, *Idaho* points up the potentially sexual charge of boy gangs and makes explicit the homoerotic potential to be found throughout the Henriad. And it appears to be using the most carnivalesque, anti-authoritarian, potentially politically subversive moments of the Shakespeare texts.

But this questioning use of Shakespeare at a general level in the film is not precisely underpinned or reproduced in its detail. Our understanding of Idaho's use of Shakespeare changes when we concentrate on the twin details of the actual use of Shakespearean language and the twinning of the narratives. For all that elsewhere in the text the film seems to be bringing to the surface subtextual sexual implications from the Henry plays – "boys and beggary" – the specific work of Shakespeare is to mark out the narrative of Hal's rise and to give it the cultural weight of "Shakespeare." Combined with the associations traced above, for all the questioning attitudes suggested by the rest of the film, this puts "Shakespeare" in an anchoring position; tying interpretation of the film back to cultural (intertextual) knowledge, it conserves and separates the storyline of Scott's transition from prince to king. The other Shakespearean figure, Bob/Falstaff, dies, thereby removing any "alternative" Shakespearean route. By way of micro-conclusion, the film may indeed present a critique of modern life and of the disenfranchisement of sexual identity, and one in which the future is left open. But it is not Shakespeare's language that it uses to do so; Shakespeare in *Idaho* stands by the heterosexual potential of the *Henry IV* plays and is kept separate from and contrasted with Mike's oedipal narrative.

Coda

My argument so far has been about the place of Shakespeare in a particular filmic text, not about the use of Shakespeare in film in any general sense. In 1910, Shakespeare on film was described thus: "it elevates and improves the literary taste and appreciation of the great mass of the people" (*Moving Picture World*, February, 1910, p. 257, quoted in Pearson and Uricchio (1990)). Shakespeare began his film career by making film respectable. Was Shakespeare rendered quintessentially American by film, or was America's link with Englishness reaffirmed and enriched by contact with Shakespeare? How was Shakespeare to be appropriated as cultural capital?

Obviously, the answer would depend on film and audience, but it is a question that recurs in a range of films that are not adaptations of Shakespeare but that use Shakespeare as a cultural marker. I have argued for a specific use of Shakespeare in *Idaho* but another context for this film is an emerging arthouse/mainstream narrative cinema about male homosexuality. These films – from Philadelphia to more avant-garde expositions such as *Postcards from America* – are working with a problematic cultural capital and weaving tropes, songs, and images into a set of patterns which do have generic relationships. Moments and tropes include the sublime American landscape, country music, fashion – all the elements that the first round of critics identified as "stylish" in *Idaho*; this emergent style and use of cultural capital is a wider context for the claiming and deployment of Shakespeare as cultural capital in *Idaho*.

13

WAR IS MUD

Branagh's *Dirty Harry V* and the types of political ambiguity

Donald K. Hedrick

Complexity

It requires little autocritique to unearth the social contradictions of academic left cultural criticism. A relatively unacknowledged one is the aim, on the one hand, to democratize education while, on the other hand, to participate in the process of social stratification through a credentialization separating the future cultural footsoldiers from the academostars.[1]

There are, of course, contradictions and contradictions. A particular one involving these same, future cultural workers may be more acutely felt by them now. Since graduate students presumably publish less, the contradiction is less visible even to a politically self-conscious field like cultural studies, but we see it surface in an occasional voice, such as that of Elayne Tobin in a 1995 essay about listening to depressing departmental coffee talk about new films. In the present essay I want to talk about Kenneth Branagh's *Henry V*, in part responding to the issue she raises from her perspective about current cultural critique. While there is no contractual obligation for any of us to provide our students practical political hope along with critical competency, we must try to be of assistance.

Tobin finds in such talk a continually assumed stance of being "gatekeepers to positive representation," and finds the de-illusioning papers delivered at film and Marxist conferences always to reflect an "exposing" of the same bad faith everywhere, as if we were really to expect Hollywood to represent our agendas. Her disillusionment with de-illusioning boils to a brief parody of instructions for graduate students writing about film: (1) use (preferably big European) critic A to read (preferably popular) film B; (2) expose its bad faith and Hollywood commodification; (3) along the way gesture about how meaning is unfixed; and (4) indicate that more work is to be done. Although careful not to be critically naive, Tobin seems to wish for a more optimistic practice that instead of revealing the always already commodified status of a film might rather "imagine the importance of the film's larger political functions" (Tobin 1995: 72–3). If such an optimistic wish seems merely like a narrative wish for a happy ending, one might be reminded that unhappy endings can be just as mechanically produced as happy ones. The question is rather one of the routinization and hence blunting of intellectual work.

It is also a question of what constitutes the labor of cultural criticism: is it the production of ideas, of arguments, or of theory? And it is a question of those sorts of work versus the "writing of movement" (Lyotard 1989: 187).

The critic I will ultimately turn to in thinking about these questions in the context of reading filmmaker Branagh is, sort of, Lyotard, but with William Empson reading me. What has happened to political criticism by the time of Branagh's *Henry V* might be described as a massive nuancing movement under the influences of poststructuralism, a movement which in terms of Tobin's wishes might constitute a more hopeful direction since we subsequently find in films ideological complexities (subversions, struggles) rather than monolithic exercises of absolute submission and domination. But this move seems only to have made training in critique more rather than less frustrating, if Tobin's views are any evidence.

As Norman Rabkin recounted the "distortions, deletions, and embellishments" of the Olivier *Henry V* film in order to attend both to Shakespeare's text and to a quality of interpretation (1977: 285), I want to use Branagh's film to consider political aspects of both the play as well as current "political" criticism, especially regarding the ideology of the image and the idea of complexity. In doing so, I hope to begin to suggest a way to counter an impasse rapidly reproducing that experienced by New Criticism. The latter, it might be said, after losing the historical punch of its moment, ground down into routinized readings invariably ending in tepid gestures commending the "complexity" of the text observed. But whereas New Criticism mastered the text as an ironic complexity of thematic paradox, political criticism has evolved into mastering the text as a neo-ironic and postmodern blank complexity constituting ideological paradox. Thus we read again and again of mixes of subversion and containment, domination and resistance, the utopian and the ideological, and so on.[2]

These inevitable readings begin to lack bite, at least in US academic contexts. Indeed, the old word "irony" might be used as a substitute for the new word "anxiety" used in many of these readings, with no loss of either interpretive or political force. A few tentative shifts may therefore be in order.

Mud

As an entry into the film's "politics," I begin with a striking visual feature within it, one largely unsupported by the text (but what is support?): the general prevalence of dirt. A traditional signifier of ambiguity itself, dirt also provides an ideological significance by which one can explore the sources and dynamics of cultural and political energies in this entertaining, powerful, and emotionally savvy film.[3]

Throughout the performance tradition of the play, one finds again and again a variety of means of whitewashing the war and the character of the King, but an innovation in this production is Branagh's accomplishing whitewashing chiefly by means of mud. The presence of dirt in the film – its overwhelming use on the battlefield, on the troops, and on the King himself – is certainly overdetermined. For one thing, it constitutes a traditional theatrical and filmic gesture towards historicity, or at least verisimilitude, often more than in the original playtexts (Saccio 1988: 208). We happen to know that the heavy rains and muddy fields were indeed key factors in the English victory over the armor-laden French. The battle's outcome was thus written primarily in terms of movement rather than strength – a point to which I will return later –

particularly considering the huge outnumbering of the British by the French troops. Itself a de-illusioning move, the director's manipulation of mud, like that of King Henry himself, combines the tactile and the tactical. Branagh has observed how incredibly filthy the actual battle was, as if to disillusion any film-derived fantasies about the antisepsis of war. Such a disillusionment might have productive force had it been brought into conjunction, say, with the US media and military imagery of "surgical" strikes and maneuvers in the Gulf Wars. Such wars demonstrates that even media visuals are increasingly conducted under the sign of the bureaucratic rationalization of war. I will return to the important concept of the theatricalization of war at the end of this essay.

The mud of the film, included not for historical "realism" alone, also serves intertextual and cultural uses. For one thing, the dirt of this visually dark movie is a deliberate counter to the cleaner and brighter visuals of Olivier's film of the play. Accordingly, Branagh's film begins in darkness, with stage lights gradually illuminating the behind the scenes set of modern film production, as if in an avant-garde "exposing" of the film apparatus, ho ho.[4] Branagh both bows to and competes with Olivier's exposure of the Elizabethan theatrical apparatus that opens his production, making Olivier's gesture appear somewhat naive in retrospect, and yet Branagh's gesture of competitive "realism" in no way disturbs the main story. The memory scenes of Hal with Falstaff (drawn from *Henry IV Parts 1 and 2*) are also played more darkly, although not, I believe, to cast as much doubt upon the character of the King as that same memory of the rejection serves in Shakespeare's version.

In addition, mud becomes a sliding signifier whose referent shifts from Agincourt specifically, to early modern combat generally (that's what war was like back then), to war universally and transhistorically (as hell), gathering moral and ideological associations as it goes along. Briefly put, the result of this move is a new form of whitewashing: the film implies that if war has a necessary dark or muddy side, the character of King Henry is thereby exonerated; if the King has his own dark side, on the other hand, the character of war itself is exonerated. We arrive, then, at a knotted ambiguity in which one implied critique or political interrogation is paired up with a different one, a pairing which effectively cancels out both of them. The emphasis on and the use of mud in the film, I believe, functions more strongly than do the elements of Shakespeare's text themselves to accomplish such a neutralization. It may be – and I will begin to stress the point for theoretical purposes – that the ambivalence of this film is of a different political character than the ambivalence in Shakespeare.

Both films, as it happens, produce certain ambiguous responses, but this should not surprise us, since "ambiguous" Henry V representations are all we have. A brief summary of Henry "sequels" – and all we have of historical representation here are sequels – reminds us of the variety of historically specific ways by which his charisma, along with its interrogation, has been produced, specifically through apparatuses of ambiguity.

Since what is available to us of the original King's character is only a historical representation, it may not be too austerely Foucauldian to begin the count not with the "real" King but with his achieved persona. The first Henry V, then, constituted a figure drawing cultural energies from religion as well as from the burgeoning commerce of the late Middle Ages, thereby mixing piety with ruthlessness to his opponents, and appropriating the King Arthur legends in a typical mode of medieval self-fashioning (Kinsford 1926). The complexity of the image is the direct producer of charisma, in turn producing the primary means of actual political domination. One of the main pieces of evidence for the ruthless side of the persona, of course, has become the subject of continued historical questioning, namely, the King's ordering of the killing of the prisoners of war during the Battle of Agincourt. Whether the actual King did or did not kill the French prisoners, however, was only known to Shakespeare through the second Henry V, the Henry of the Elizabethan predecessors of the play. In the chronicle sources the killing, when present, is not justified as an emotional act of retaliation, as we might expect, but as a calculated move necessary for the far outnumbered English. In one of the sources, moreover, the wholly unironic popular drama *The Famous Victories of Henry V*, there is no killing at all.

As a frequent object of scrutiny among historicist and materialist critics, Shakespeare's version of the King in *Henry V* is typically a site of contestation for the political ideas. That is, whether play, author, or audience are to be critical, approving, or ambivalent about the King, is still under debate. I wish to disturb somewhat the terms of this debate rather than to enter it directly. Of course, the play includes representation of the very issue in the figure of the Welsh captain Fluellen, who complains that the killing of prisoners is expressly against the law of war, and who even finds reason to criticize his sovereign's character through a reference to Henry's having killed the old fat knight's heart. But the complexity in Shakespeare might be assigned a different valence from that of his sources. Here I refer to Shakespeare's drawing from the popular rival to Elizabeth in the figure of the Earl of Essex, notoriously alluded to in the compliment of the Prologue. The fourth Henry of Olivier's famous film drew its monarch's specific charisma, however, from the British nationalism at the end of World War II, in a production that was explicitly dedicated to the British commandos and troops of the airborne divisions. But it drew as well from the charisma of the director-star, whose substantial reputation in both British and American films was intended to overcome the risk of producing yet another financially questionable Shakespeare film. Here, it would seem that the circumstances of performance do not particularly fuel complexity in the production of a charisma. If there is complexity at all, it is one that takes on a market character and use-value, as British patriotism must be employed for the sake of an American market. A close reading of the film along these lines might explore the film for faultlines in its marketing and appeal.

Finally, the fifth Henry V of Kenneth Branagh, while repeating some of the gestures of its predecessors, manufactures another charisma more appropriate than ever to the society of spectacle under US and international capitalism. Charisma is a phenomenon that Weber in his study of it recognized to be subject to historically determined variants.[5] Notwithstanding some theoretical resistance to "characterological criticism," in this case another look at the character of King Henry is in order. It is in his character, then, that we may encounter the play's debate about war as refracted through a residual rather than an actively dominant political issue, namely through the 1960s anti-war movement in the USA and abroad, a time significant in introducing the Clint Eastwood mystique.[6] Although some early reviewers and Shakespeareans took the film to be specifically anti-war, it might be argued that in this area is one of its particular complexities, by which Branagh maintains a stance that both reminds us of that progressive movement (like the memory of Falstaff as represented in the film – also a patronizing recollection of pathetic fun and games), but distances itself from any possible political investment in it.

Neither anti- nor pro-war, therefore, the film studiously maintains what I will preliminarily term a conservative rather than a critical ambivalence, progressive merely in the weakest sense of its openness toward some undecidability, but undecidability here really an alibi for a tactical indecision. What is ambiguous is not produced as a risk, however, as it might have been in the cases interpreted by Annabel Patterson (1989) and Steven Mullaney (1988) for some ambiguities of Renaissance theatrical representation. Although the market component of Shakespeare's version is by no means to be discounted, and heightening attention to the early modern market will no doubt increasingly bear this out for the play (see Agnew 1986; Bruster 1992), the Branagh complexity follows more directly from the consumerist principle that the customer, hawk or dove, is ultimately the rightful sovereign. The customer is always divine, and right. One reason that, despite its determination by the market, the same was not true for Shakespeare's theater is that the monarch, while perhaps somewhat analogous to a consumer by virtue of her patronage, is nevertheless not one. Her sphere is not symmetrical to the niche marketing of box office take, as just another potential ticket.

I do not want to insist overmuch on the specific interpretations here. I rather want to suggest that the different historical contexts, requiring more sustained unpacking in either case, might distinguish both the kinds of ambivalence involved as well as the progressive or reactionary political forces the different versions make available or afford. If this is so, a typology of complexities might be possible.

American clean

An unpacking of Branagh's specific ambiguity requires that his King's charisma be understood in another intertextuality, in addition to or apart from Branagh's role as Olivier's epigone. A much darker Henry than Olivier's, then, is constructed by drawing heavily from American crime and Western films,[7] in another reason for all the dirt. Of these films, Clint Eastwood's oeuvre, especially *Dirty Harry* (1971), stands out as a special impetus for the ambiguities of Branagh. The influence is brought into relief by important new studies of Eastwood: Michael Rogin's 1990 analysis of the film's importance to American foreign policy, political consensus, and collective US political amnesia; and Paul Smith's 1993 study of Eastwood as a "cultural production" perfectly embodying the values and ideology of Hollywood.

The choice of this subtext is closer to the mode of Shakespeare's rather than Olivier's version, in fact, since Essex provided for Shakespeare a quasi-outlaw figure, shortly afterward executed for his attempted overthrow of the Queen. For current US political sensibilities as the ground of this charisma, however, we might note the extent of our era's fascination with thugism, everywhere evident in political rhetoric. This has been especially evident in foreign relations: we recall Reagan telling Khadafy that he can "run but he can't hide," or other lethal language not all that anxiously lifted from the gangster and western registers.[8] We increasingly use a bullying rhetoric in handling actual or pretended bullies abroad, as US anti-diplomacy on Iraq makes clear.

Branagh seems to have developed over time his characterization of Henry, for his film King merely extends what he had earlier portrayed in an RSC version of the play, when the King became a distinctly Eastwood variant – a loner who is holy and just ("a genuinely holy man") but at the same time capable of ruthless enormity. Portrayed unsentimentally in the paradox of his personality, such a character furnishes the ambiguity generally employed as a prop in most wars, for kingship or for leadership. It is a paradox evident in editing: a tear appearing on the King's cheek during the hanging of his former friend Bardolph has mysteriously disappeared when the camera cuts back to the King after the legs finish twitching. Like mud, it is wipeable, but like ideology and screen of the society of spectacle, it is something we don't usually watch wiped. As if speeding up to jump over the slog of contradiction – sorry/not sorry – the camera's movement enforces the ideology of the visual image.

I have used dirt and mud interchangeably up to this point, drawing on the single concept analyzed by Mary Douglas in her important work on cultural taboos, *Purity and Danger* (1966). Douglas famously defines dirt as "matter out of place," that is, as a category error or violation of boundaries set up for cultural uses, one that thereby produces certain anxieties. But Douglas does not recognize the extent to which the concept itself can become dirtied in the ideological inversions of signification. Indeed, by "whitewashing" dirt, as it were, Branagh has provided the exception to her analysis, as if cleanliness were capable of being defined as itself an unnatural state, disturbing the more normative category of dirt. Nevertheless, the material difference between dirt and mud might still provide a gradation of viscosities, with mud's resulting significance as itself a second-order category error or mediation between dirt and liquid, or morally between dirt and its other – slime. To the extent that mud is privileged, slime becomes, as it were, dirty dirt, and the film fulfills this structural slot yet again in a gangster way, providing dirty rats to oppose to any who seem to be clean ones. Of course, Shakespeare provides his own traitor lords whose treasons are uncovered at the beginning of the play, but Branagh allows them not only to be tricked and then executed, but also to be roughed up as well by Henry's men, as they protect him from what momentarily looks like a physical threat just after the conspiracy of Cambridge, Scroop, and Grey is discovered. Watching this pre-emptive violence in a scene evoking the suspense of the mafia dons' meeting, the King clearly expresses his rage and contempt for their sort, but risks moral complicity as a *noir* monarch. When confronted with slime, so it would seem, one's moral rage licenses subordinates to do the dirtier work – an emblem of the US foreign policy from which this register of dirt is drawn. In battle, too, much of the film's action suggests the movie violence of the gang fight or the western brawl. By this Eastwood device Branagh captures a volatile atmosphere of a potential for instant escalation, the representation of a kind of violence often absent from war films generally, and therefore potentially more progressive in its ambiguity. The Duke of York, for instance, is ignobly dragged down by five or six French soldiers. The killing of the boys at the end of the battle, producing scenes milked for greatest human sentiment, again provides an Eastwood feel of surprise violence. Thus, Henry's rage at the end of the battle, punctuated with the textually displaced line about not being angry in France until that very moment, results in his pulling the French herald down from his horse to start to beat him up. His noble thuggery is restrained only by the interruption of the announcement of the English victory, which appears to bring Henry back to his senses. Losing control is, however, chiefly a charisma-enhancing authentication of possessing the requisite moral force and masculinity paradoxically to control violence. It is an orchestrated spontaneity, of course, not brought into conjunction by Branagh, however, with the available parallel in Henry's controversial speech threatening the town of Harfleur. There he calculatingly disclaims responsibility for the savagery that his angry soldiers, out of his control, will do to

Harfleur's greybeards, infants, and virgins should they not surrender to him. An American ambiguity is used to prevent or protect recognition of a deeper ambiguity about ruthlessness, an ambiguity more available in Shakespeare's version.

Branagh's overall take on dirt and violence seem typically directed to create and enhance the feel of a huge power continually being held in check, a representation of individual emotions barely under leash during the most unthinkable provocations – the opposite of the military situation of the play insofar as the English in it are the vastly outnumbered underdogs. By transhistorical coincidence, the same atmosphere and poetics of outrage are the result of the convergence of several artistic and political contexts: the scenarios of outrage and escalation stocking the Elizabethan revenge tradition in which Shakespeare got his career going; a decade of *Rambo* and other US revenge films, producing the classic line adopted by Reagan and others: "Go ahead. Make my day"; US self-representation justifying intervention against Third World "provocation" in the 1980s; and British nostalgic identification with and support for this feeling. Raymond Williams's notion of a "structure of feelings" (Williams 1977: Ch. 9), which might be useful for predicting and describing the ambivalent feelings of spectators, is somewhat less apt here, since this mixture is one of a dominant US imperialism but a largely residual British imperialism. In constructing the mixed feelings described earlier, Branagh inevitably relies on the assumption that moral and political mud are primarily to be characterized as emotions rather than as social relations. This helps to explain an odd disjunction in Branagh's plotting: he motivates the killing of the prisoners (the French attack on the luggage and boys) but does not follow through by having Henry kill them, as he does in the text.[9] This nevertheless marks the political unconscious of the film: actual ruthlessness is generally only in potentia (as in the Harfleur speech) or in the past (more or less the case with his treatment of Falstaff) – rather than in the present. As such, it is perceiveable more as a paradox of character than a contradiction in and marker of political action. All the unwieldy Shakespearean textual matter that does not wash off is systematically omitted: Henry's use of the former friendships with Falstaff and others to make his reform look better; the substitution of Fluellen to engage in the duel he takes on; the French King's joking comparison of Katherine to the raped French cities (5.2.308);[10] and the locker-room jokes about her sexuality.

The latter concludes the scene between Henry and Katherine that Branagh sentimentally reads as an actual falling in love, thus adding to the paradox of tough character, rather than treating the wooing itself as an exercise of power, politics by other means through the ruthlessness of charm. Also omitted is the King's business proposition to "compound a boy" with Katherine (5.2.202), a notion in which Alan Sinfield (1992) sees an example of an anxious ideological faultline regarding fear of miscegenation and nation-mixing, yet another example, as it were, of dirt. Here, however, I believe that Branagh is more in line with a neutralizing ambivalence of Shakespeare's, for I see less evidence of the "anxiety" in text or character that Sinfield, in accord with the majority of materialist, feminist, and new historicist approaches, identifies.[11] On the contrary, it seems that Shakespeare reveals how frictionlessly both the military and the emotional can be subsumed within the social intercourse of international trade. It may be that neither "anxiety" nor any other particular affect need necessarily be linked to the identification of an ambivalence or contradiction. There are complexities and there are complexities. Branagh's neutralization of the questionable dealings of the King by way of the implied apology for mud is not merely contemporary, for a similar ideological move was made by an Elizabethan lawyer who in 1599 wrote a defense of the prisoner-killing on the grounds that in "the miseries of war are all extremities justified" (quoted in Bullough 1962: 365). To counter these evil necessities and to produce a neutralizing ambivalence requires a displacement of all calculating character traits. Thus, it is not surprising that Branagh portrays all the key actions of Henry as being spontaneous: spontaneous tears, spontaneous beatings, and even spontaneous religious feelings. The realm of spontaneity is designed to contrast with the realm of politics, as we see from the church leaders of the play, who are not comical as in Olivier's version but merely cynical, apparently tainted, as are the other non-youthful figures in the film, by their years. Unlike the Shakespearean text, the film represents a true piety blind to class, by linking Henry to his men in a common religious feeling. Before battle, then, we see them all cross themselves humbly and sincerely, later spontaneously raising their voices in the "Non nobis" chorus as they trudge through the muddy, corpse-strewn battlefield, the King with a dead boy in his arms.[12] If mud de-idealizes war, it can just as soon be used in a re-idealization. Manliness, we are invited to admit, occasionally allows some tears, as Fluellen is shown to have trouble holding them in at the death of the boys. But the emotional rules for mixing feelings and separating private feelings from the political are again those of the American film tough guy, in this case recalling John Wayne's canny acting instructions that the hero, if audiences are to get choked up in empathy with him, can weep for the death of his horse but never for the death of his wife, or in this case, his boy.

In a minor character of the film, the Duke of Burgundy, Branagh furnishes the key structural negation of mud, through the suspect cleanliness noted earlier. Crucially the least muddy character of the film, Burgundy's appearance provides a visual shock when, after the scenes of the ravages of war, we encounter this pink-cheeked, chubby political minister, like the shock that Shakespeare has Hotspur feel upon encountering a perfumed, foppish lord on his battlefield. Pink, as it is in Kubrick's anti-war film *Full Metal Jacket*, becomes the primary counterhegemonic and queer signifier on the masculine battlefield, though in this case the color is implicitly stigmatized in context, whereas in Kubrick it is continually disruptive or threatening. Of course, Henry's men and Henry himself are cleaned up at this point too, but the point is that this wild bunch is made to look comically uncomfortable, no longer in their proper element as they sit at the negotiating table with the King.[13] The standpoint is again Eastwood, in a stock Western attitude toward politicians and all Easterners, buckaroos among the slick, but the adjustments that must be made with the text are new, revealing more contemporaneousness slipping in despite Branagh's efforts to evade the topical. Thus, Burgundy is seated between Henry and the French king, staging a literal position of ambivalence, as an emblem of dovish compromise in a non-player from outside the arena. A virtual British Liberal, Burgundy delivers what is transformed into a 1960s anti-war speech, deeply undercut when his remarks about French youth turning to "savages" by war are punctuated by disagreeing looks from Henry's men. Branagh introduces another distinction that further negates the possibility of national autocritique and undermines Burgundy: the French are not parodied, as in Olivier's version, but instead are identified as a military class of youthful heroes who contrast with the elderly politicians of both countries. The new nation is a nation of young, presumably the future transnational market of a New World Shakespeare. What constitutes a nation henceforth is not subject to any disturbing critique, but rather to a comforting vision of an apolitical international youth, Shakespeare having been suitably Benetonized, as in the 1990s he would be MTVized in Romeo and Juliet.

The opposition to a suspect cleanliness is furthered by radically shortening Burgundy's speech on the decay of the garden of France, whereas Olivier assents to his war-weary audience's feelings by means of panoramic vistas of nature that prolong the speech. Movement through the speech, then, if especially fast or slow, signals the ideological work of the director. The love of peace, more calculating and self-interested in Branagh's version were it not for the grim battle scenes, is valued but qualified as less than manly by Olivier, who gives Burgundy an effeminate cast. In neither film, then, is Burgundy as much disturbingly one of the guys as he is in Shakespeare's text, where the wooing scene concludes with Burgundy's difficult-to-recuperate coarse banter about Katherine's sexuality, omitted by both directors. In Branagh's film another telling moment is Henry's retort after the garden speech. While his line, saying that such a poetically envisioned peace "must be bought," lends curtness and insensitivity to his character, Branagh refigures it as merely a "pragmatic" concern, bringing the liberal down to earth, and, as it were, hence beyond dispute. With the lightest of lite ironies, the film shows Henry's men nodding in agreement with this demonstrated common sense. Politics are once again subsumed into charisma.

These examples of the dynamics of Branagh's film could be summed up as an importation of the American mud of *Dirty Harry* into the British text and film. But what specifically constitutes the importation and the ambiguity as American, since violence and revenge and war are not specifically so? It is here that the specific nature of the ambiguity might be understood in a way that could draw distinctions between ambiguities with more or less political force. Paul Smith describes the political critique of institutions found in Eastwood's *Dirty Harry* to subscribe primarily to an ideology of vigilantism, a "social phenomenon indigenous to America, having little prehistory in Britain" (1993: 92), as many commentators have observed. The ambivalence about this extends to the artistic production itself, as Smith notes that Eastwood himself approved of the politics of Harry, whereas the director of the film, Don Siegel, did not (1993: 90) – a configuration thus working against coffee talk or criticism that would seek to rate the overall politics of the film. The historical circumstances in which Branagh is operating, then, point in two directions with respect to the ambiguity he is selling to two markets: one with potential political force for an American audience (were it not for the fact that the novelty level of vigilantism would be radically diminished since the 1960s and 1970s), the other one neutralized and inapplicable for a British audience.

Of course, such neutralizations are themselves a common strategy of US political and media culture, by which true interrogations and critical perspectives are omitted, marginalized, stigmatized, pathologized, or feminized. Thus diluted, any ambiguity resides comfortably, without anxiety, in a society of spectacle where, as Guy Debord has observed, "that which appears is good and that which is good appears" (Debord 1983: sec. I, par. 12). Here we might make note of class concerns, a sphere marked again in the film by the visuals of dirt. Although it may be argued that Branagh displays some degree of sympathy, given his working-class Belfast background (Donaldson 1991: 68), it is tempered by the sensibility of one who has an interest in seeing his own success as attributable to talent and determination. The world of Bardolph, Pistol, and others in Branagh's Shakespeare appear to be dismissed as a group of losers and quitters in the realm of opportunity this Henry enters and even embodies, the realm of the superdirector and King. The type of humor Branagh permits them, moreover, signals that he wants the audience to share Henry's patrician condescension in his nostalgic rejection of his personal past as a renegade youth: the humor (humor being somewhat of a problem for Branagh in the best of circumstances) is characteristically circumscribed – no longer the humor that Shakespeare makes available as parodic and oppositional, like the bravado of Pistol in the text, but instead surprisingly bitter and defeated, as Pistol is in his final address in the film.

The lower-class counterworld is prevented by Branagh from being taken as part of the present ambiguity of the King, unlike Shakespeare's version in which Henry's rejection of Falstaff is variously tested, or even interrogated accidentally in the wordplay of Fluellen's Welsh pronunciation comparing the King to "Alexander the Pig" (4.7.13). Moreover, potentially non-genial humor in the text, such as enforced leek-eating, is suppressed. And in the striking scene of Henry disguised among his troops at night, the Branagh version merely maintains a sympathetic reading of Henry, although re-enacting the increasingly acrimonious debate with the soldiers who question the justification of the war while not knowing that they are speaking to the King himself. The lower classes serve to explain and justify, not to interrogate, domination. Of course, it might be objected that Shakespeare's version accomplishes the same, but I would suggest that the conditions of its performance would render the class politics less self-cancelling, since what would have probably been much more striking to his audience (as perhaps the first representation of this on the stage) would have been the very staging of the debate and interrogation with the King – regardless of exactly what was said in the debate or how it turned out. And, even granting their ignorance of his identity, the stage still represents an acrimonious debate between social classes, since the soldiers take him to be a lord. If this is the political force of the representation, it is worth noting that it is one about which the cultural critic can have little to say in addition, perhaps preferring, for professional reasons and publication-driven interpretation, the more textually rich cases where complexity can be unpacked in article-length fashion. At all events, in sorting out the political force of a variety of ambiguities, I hope to avoid the ready tendency to treat Shakespeare as the orginary source of a timeless politics, a tendency that would re-create what has been critiqued as a "testamentary" quality issuing from Shakespeare's era, the right of a will to extend patriarchal power indefinitely (Wilson 1993).

Branagh's attempts at neutralizing and avoiding the political are, of course, just another kind of politics, but they do not succeed on their own terms. In his 1984 RSC stage production of *Henry V*, moreover, director Adrian Noble explicitly warded off attempts to interpret the play in a specifically British military context, namely the Falklands War – in order to keep the play from being appropriated jingoistically. His ideal, an almost impermissibly political innocence, was to free the interpretation for the actors to do it "as honestly as we possibly could," thus occluding his own identification with king and politician. As Branagh writes, "It was a relief to me that we would not be burdened by the 'Post Falklands' tag that some of the press had already given the production. Our feelings about that conflict would inevitably inform our thoughts on the play but not to the point where the effect was reductive to the work" (Branagh 1988: 98). In other words, we must remain committed to complexity, an allegiance which we presumbably share with the Master playwright himself. But in contrast to the similarly glorifying Olivier film, Branagh's film achieves its own version of a glorifying charisma in a manner appropriate to capitalism's multinational corporate stage – by suppressing rather than by exploiting (as did Shakespeare and Olivier) topical application, and by appropriating whatever ideology, such as vigilantism, that possesses transnational market value under the sign of Eastwood.

One needs no especially Marxist insight to note the link between Branagh's ambivalently dirty Henry and the thuggish world of corporate capitalism, for the link has been anticipated by the filmmakers themselves. In a promotional video[14] they draw their hype from the character of the King himself, describing how Branagh thinks in a "straightforward, bold, simple, and courageous way." The director's charisma is as spontaneous as Henry's. Even more tellingly and directly, they connect the benign ambivalences of the play with those of the market itself, amusingly noting that "breaking necks is comparatively easy to breaking box office receipts in the international cinema." Thus, a Shakespeare film becomes fully equated with the English nation as an underdog competitor.

They might have gone further to note similarities between King and director, since one of the circumstances of the film's production was an actual underdog experience. In competition with American films for support, Branagh went virtually broke halfway through the production, so that it had to be completed by gaining real financial territory against enormous odds. An investment broker who stepped in for the rescue is also interviewed, and he comments on how difficult it is for a first-time director like Branagh to get money, although he adds that it certainly helps if the film is a Shakespeare film. Shakespeare, apparently, is not merely, metaphorically "cultural capital" (Bourdieu 1984: 120), but literal capital as well. And it takes no sophisticated anti-canonical theory to recognize that such a value is never absolute but relative to its market, for on the one hand, the sign of Shakespeare helped to fund production presumably among such elite investors, but on the other it was viewed as hindering consumption, the name "Shakespeare" having been entirely omitted from promotional advertisements for the film. Thus disguised, Branagh's film is a little touch of Shakespeare in the night, concealing its class and status to gain advantages over some presumably well-defined but indispensable target market from which it might build allegiance, thereby "gentling their [the audience's] condition."

War

I want to expand what I have suggested intermittently in the preceding discussion of the film, namely, that a needed project for cultural studies generally and Shakespearean political criticism particularly, barely begun here, is to explore and even to typologize the particular structure of feelings, historical and social formations that drive the production of different kinds of complexity at the political level of representation. With a view toward de-routinizing political criticism, typologizing would reveal varying sorts of political forces, whether the ambiguities are those of the author as in the conservative "esoteric" reading model of Leo Strauss (1952), those of resistant "voices" of the play in the liberal model of Annabel Patterson (1989), or those of the historical structures and residues of censorship in the poststructuralist model of Richard Burt (1993). The purpose of these suggestions is not intended, however, to create a nostalgic point of origin in Shakespeare for a progressive politics, an original political intention lost in transmission in a process like that of textual variation for editorial models more discredited now.

I think the case can be made more locally with regard to certain ambiguities. I would suggest, for instance, that in the case of Shakespeare's identification of Henry with Essex, the ambiguity is decidedly unstable. The reason is that the identification, albeit with the monarch, is in a context of threat to the contemporary monarch Elizabeth – the parallels not working out on a one-to-one basis. That ambiguity, while not exactly "progressive," nevertheless maintains more political force than those I have discussed in Branagh's version, which is more risk-free though just as much indebted to its own historical moment and its own form of the market. But there are markets and there are markets. Whether Shakespeare's play was just as much indebted to market forces as is Branagh's film remains to be investigated.

In fact, Branagh's film is more in keeping with the kind of ambivalence previously portrayed by Shakespeareans such as Rossiter and Rabkin. For Rossiter, Shakespeare shows an "essential ambivalence" in his historical vision, transcendently dissatisfied with the black-and-white political moralisms of his time because of his wider view of humanity generally (1961: 51). For Rabkin, the play's ambiguity teaches us about our deepest "hopes and fears" concerning the world of political action, and, more privately and pessimistically, that society will "never" be able to solve the problems we hope that it could (1977: 296). In each case, the human and the private are opposed to the political and the social, and the neutralizations are produced according to this juxtaposition. A political criticism focusing largely on ambivalences, however termed, is in danger of failing to distinguish among contradictions; without any means of doing so one is condemned to repeat in ever more elegant forms the model of Rabkin's analogy: the famous gestalt drawing of a duck that, with a slight shift of perspective, turns into a rabbit. In the contemporary version, domination is the duck, resistance the rabbit.

The allusion in the title of this essay to the more formalist and apolitical criticism of William Empson in his *Seven Types of Ambiguity* turns out to be less ironic than I had originally intended. A formalist critique of political criticism might recommend a project to distinguish or even taxonomize varieties of political or ideological ambivalence. It would be a project with political significance as well, however, for it might sometimes be helpful in assigning, as I have occasionally done in this essay, the degree of political force or lack of it to an individual work, although such a determination, fully contextualized, may not turn out to have any one-to-one relationship to the degree that that force is "progressive." What may be sacrificed in the process of distinguishing types is any single, totalizing model for ambivalence, such as Rabkin's spatial view of complementary themes or Greenblatt's narrative view of subversion always followed by containment. Losing their theoretical status, although not necessarily their political value, these models nevertheless retain value not as paradigms but as possible forms of ambivalence, that is, merely as different but important ways that things can and do happen.

Although I can at best only sketch such a project here, it is worth noting that Empson's formal system is itself suggestive. Terry Eagleton begins his introduction to literary theory by separating out Empson as a maverick from the New Critics he often opposed, contrasting their ironies and paradoxes, which suggest fusion and absence of threat to coherence, with Empson's ambiguities, which can never finally be pinned down. His view of ambiguity, according to Eagleton, allies him with later reader-response criticism in finding meaning not just in the work but in the context of social discourse, with every verbal nuance giving room for "alternative reactions to the same piece of language" (Eagleton 1983: 52). The emphasis, then, should be on the production of alternative meaning, not on self-cancellation of opposing meaning. That an ambiguity or complexity might provide something residual or unmanageable for ideology, moreover, might be implicit in the very form of the taxonomy he employed, since it ranged from the one extreme of fully logical, intended meanings to disordered and illogical ones – full contradiction – at the other extreme (Empson 1949: 48). From the present discussion, one could find a fully resolvable contradiction, for example, in an expectation that any prince must be both pious and ruthless, or an unresolved one in forcing the reader to question, along with the simple Fluellen, whether ruthlessness is something supplementary, the social a flaw of the personal. The possibilities of kinds of ambiguities, as reflected in the preceding discussion, might proliferate: the possibility of ambiguity accompanied or unaccompanied by "anxiety"; the possibility of ambiguity in the play to be resolved by the audience; the possibility of ambiguity resolved for one part of the audience but not for another part; the possibility of authorial confusion or division. How to keep the proliferation from becoming aporia would be the task of a responsible, affirmative cultural critique.

One might even claim that a chief assumption of any totalizing model of political complexity is that Shakespeare's representation of King Henry ratifies the basis of our institution of political critique, confirming that our basic work is to refine the critique of those ideas. It is always ideas at the heart of the critical activity. The uncovering of necessary complexities may in itself have the effect of turning the procedure into an algorithm of defeat, by which positive ideas are overwhelmed or undermined by the negative ones in the work's production or reception. The question that seems to underlie the work of the ideological critic in such cases, moreover, is whether Shakespeare (Branagh, or whoever) himself qualifies as an ideological critic, with complexity usually brought forth to demonstrate what is in fact methodologically predetermined – that he does not, that the ideas don't work. Again, it's always ideas. I think this structural situation helps account for the frustration that initiated this essay in the role of critic as gatekeeper for representations conveying positive ideas, returning us to the despair of the would-be cultural critic.

It may be, therefore, that a scenario of defeat is partly determined by an analogy or rather misanalogy between the job of the critic of ideas and the job of the writer or director. At times in the present essay I have tried to imply an alternative understanding, although it is an understanding difficult even to hint at, much less articulate. The source for this alternative is Lyotard's discussion of cinema, in which he claims that directing, rather than being a reflection of politics (as it is customarily treated in film analysis), constitutes political rule itself, or the art of politics par excellence. We might think particularly of its practices of excluding and including, of framing, and, overall, of "writing movement" (Lyotard 1989: 176). Directing doesn't, as most analysis and even the present essay at times assume, "reveal" politics. It is politics. If filmwork is more like statecraft than it is like critique, the "complexities" of positive and negative "elements" of the work are less likely to be amenable to the usual sorts of calculations designed to add up their cumulative significance, casting doubt on some of my own attempts at determining political force by taxonomizing complexity. The possibility of an entirely different, bifurcated reponse of audiences, as in the case of the British vs. American reception of Branagh's imported vigilantism, is one example in which the film's implicit rating as "progressive" or not would be rendered not simply tricky but methodologically incoherent. On the other hand, the "larger political function" of a film, in Tobin's phrase, might not be a function of what is usually regarded as the dominant placement of elements. To take a different Shakespearean example, the controversial submission of Kate at the end of *The Taming of the Shrew*, repeatedly the object of political and ideological investigation, may have much less ultimate force than the preceding representation of her refusal to be the conventional mistress or wife at the beginning. It is the habit, difficult to jettison even if the assumptions of New Criticism are no longer current, of treating the work as a discrete text containing ideas, rather than as a collection of written movements in a complicated and widespread campaign, which privileges the ending of the play, the textual parts of a work played on stage, and so on. In different terms it might be asserted that an aspect of a work might be "structural" in the sense of relational but not "structuralist" in the sense that any textual moment examined will serve as a diagnostic slice of the ideological tissue sample. Ideological critique, especially critique of the image and its power, will have to take account of this.

The quantification of complexity in a work is also rendered problematic when attention is paid only to the work itself. One might consider the example of the liberal anti-racist film *Guess Who's Coming to Dinner*, discussed at a recent seminar on the "Ideology of the Visual Image."[15] Here the discussion proceeded much on the lines of the "selling-out" model of analysis outlined by Tobin, with interpreters reading the famous interracial kiss of the film as qualified or compromised by all of the film's mechanisms of mediation. In such a predictable reading, the film's liberal audience is protected from self-critique and political change by the casting of the acceptable Sidney Poitier as the white woman's fiancé, and the writing of his character as the ideal match, a cultivated professional man, for the daughter of anxious parents Tracy and Hepburn. In the ensuing discussion of the film, however, it became clear that the usual critical approach of de-illusioning the illusion was helpless before the simple fact of this being the first Hollywood interracial kiss, and that the political force of that image of love might have at its historical moment far outweighed any of the recuperative strategies of the rest of the film, so cherished in the cultural critic's analysis, insofar as that analysis must demonstrate some novelty. Political force, in this case, is only understood intertextually, relationally and historically, as may have been the case of the scene with the disgruntled footsoldier Williams in Shakespeare's version of *Henry V*. No balance sheet of textual and discursive counterforces would necessarily neutralize such a strong visual representation at all. To allow for specific complexities in a broad historical and political context rather than to keep a balance sheet of domination and resistance requires what we hardly have at all and which I only begin to suggest here: a true political theorization of collective representation and tradition. Such theorization is all the more needed when the focus is limited, whether by convenience or by residual critical tradition, to a single text or work.

If Lyotard equates cinema direction with political rule itself as the writing of movement, one can add to this equation the writer. If ruling, directing, and playwriting are in fact one, then Henry, Shakespeare, and Branagh, rather than incommensurable categories of an analysis, are engaged in activities which, unlike the work of the cultural critic, share a formal basis in movement. Branagh's novel intuition into this complex is to recognize war itself as the writing of movement, and that its chief ally and enemy is simultaneously mud, no mere signifier. The collectivity of ambiguities, while it must be recognized in order to make the distinctions that avoid the impoverishment of a political critique of film, is at the same time what prevents a single mode of ambiguity from determining political scenarios within or without the work. Speeding up or slowing down to a standstill are in Lyotard's terms cinema at its polar extremes of absolute mobility and absolute immobility. Speeding up or slowing down to a standstill, the camera, too, registers extremes when it runs into ideology. The warworker and film-worker, unlike the cultural critic, are occupationally involved in direct dealing with movement, or movement through dirt, a resistance to theory.

Branagh, moreover, recapitulates the experience of war as work, in the exact terms of Clausewitz's well-known nineteenth-century treatise *On War*. Clausewitz saw mud metaphorically as Friktion, the quintessence of war, defined as what causes the additional energy and time required for the simplest or most obvious movement, the resistance that requires the greatest excesses of expenditure to accomplish even limited goals. It is what, moreover, makes war "real," rather than the fantasy of the rookie: "Friction is the only concept that more or less corresponds to the factors that distinguish real war from war on paper" (Clausewitz 1976: 119); and in Clausewitz's treatise it is a concept that the scientist of war employs to demythologize it and render it practical. Itself the figure of resistance, it is also what must always create a resistance to an abstraction or theorization of war: "Action in war is like movement in a resistant element" (120). Branagh's specifically filmic insight into mud, his explicit decision to "substitute rain and mud for the grass and sunshine of the earlier film" (Nightingale 1989: H18), thus furnishes more insight into war than either Olivier's or Shakespeare's versions made possible. Had Branagh been a better theoretician of his own orchestration of ambiguity and of his own identification with war-making – especially given his opening scene "exposing the apparatus" – he would have acknowledged the crucial "osmosis" that war and film have increasingly had with one another in our century, to the extent that Paul Virilio can even claim that the "theater weapon," like the demonstration message of Hiroshima, has replaced the "theater of operations" (1992: 7), and that perceptual arsenals have replaced actual ones, a "war of pictures and sounds . . . replacing the war of objects" (4). With Reagan's use of *Dirty Harry*, we come full circle to this crucial historical change, not merely as a society of spectacle but as what Nietzsche feared most, a theatocracy.

But if mud for Branagh's film constitutes a lamentably self-stabilizing ambiguity, is there any hopeful residual instability? I think Branagh for a moment recognizes one in a brief historical daydream of movement and mud that might escape his more thoroughgoing neutralization, and go beyond his pseudo-exposure of the film apparatus. In telling remarks on his reading of Shakespeare's play as "more complex . . . *darker* [italics added]" than Olivier's, Branagh's descriptions of the real horrors of the war contains a curious detail: "Irishmen ripping off their clothes and running into the battle naked in the filth. Terrible, unbelievable" (quoted in Nightingale 1989: H17–18). Failing to produce this in his visual spectacle, Branagh's intrigue with the image is, however, a little incoherent or incomplete. What, might one ask, were the motives of the muddy Irish? Are they, Branagh's own nation, a nation of mud-loving savages? Or are they performing as warriors, and simultaneously "performing" as savages, a typical resistant move by the dominated as licensed in the carnivalesque? That is, were they playing at savagery, in protective camouflage? One might speculate further about the historical case, but it hints at the loyalty problem played out in Shakespeare's play in the national rivalries of the troops, ultimately to be united in their fight with France. But Branagh's daydream stages a complicated political gesture enabling Irish support for the English, a gesture perhaps interwoven with resistances, an outdoing of English valor and boldness with a jab at "civilization." It sounds as if this is an ambiguity which, had Branagh been able to incorporate it into his production, would have performed a more politically forceful topicality than *Dirty Harry* ever could. Had it been, the contemporary identifications of the play would have been potentially skewed, with Shakespeare's French as the film's British, Shakespeare's British as the film's Irish.

But the subtext of dirt in the existing film reveals the direction of movement to neutralize opposition, omitting some of the even now potentially useful interrogations within Shakespeare's text. The techniques produce for the American-dominated market familiar structures of feeling from US film genres, not so much exclusively glorifying war as making pro-war or anti-war sentiments available to the highest bidder. And yet it is in the subliminal identification with war-making that Branagh's greatest energies are released, slogging through ideology in its manifestation as mud of the field. Individual agency is glorified in the production of an ambiguous charisma, but serving a depoliticizing point at the same time: the horror of war is acknowledged so as to redeem agency; the dark side of the King is acknowledged so as to redeem war. But if Branagh momentarily thought of himself as outside the writing of movement, outside rule, not needing the charisma of the King in order to promote himself in the international cinema, his Irishness might be allowed to stand as savage critique of the venture capitalism from which he seeks glory and to which he becomes so indebted as to be an American addictus, that is, sold into slavery after irreversible debts.

If Branagh in staging the scene is himself victimized, immobilized, and imprisoned in the visual complexity he markets, is our demystification of his complicity, like his demystification of war, any less of an illusion? "Must we then renounce the hope of finishing with the illusion, not only the cinematographic illusion but also the social and political illusions? Are they not really illusions then? Or is believing so the illusion?" (Lyotard 1989: 179–80).

Have I noted the instability of meaning? Can we get to work now?

Notes

1 I am indebted to personal correspondence with Jeffrey Williams of the *Minnesota Review* for the currency of this term. For a treatment of the contradiction that unites neo-liberals and neo-conservatives, see Michael W. Apple (1995).

2 See Greenblatt 1985, Sinfield 1992, and Jameson 1992c. For other sensible claims about the complexity that a comprehensive political criticism requires for characterizing culture, see Dollimore 1985 and Howard 1987. But the sensible model again and again works toward impasse, as in Rackin's treatment of the the histories as the impossibility of historiography, their revealed "compromised status as theatrical performances" (1990: 72), and *Henry V* as ending the two tetralogies in "a play of unresolved contradictions" (82). For further analyses of Shakespearean history and *Henry V* in terms of "entertainment value" theorized both politically and technically, see Hedrick 2002 and 2003.

3 For Tobin's desire for a "larger political significance" (1995) I might temporarily substitute a desire for a local significance, acknowledging here, in preparation for biting the hand that feeds me, the pedagogical value of Branagh's "compromised" work for introducing my

students to Shakespeare. I have seen rural students mouthing every line in advance while watching his *Much Ado*. I approve of this slavishness and think it has unrealized value for a progressive pedagogy, in specific contexts. I argue in Hedrick 2000 for a tactic of making more, not less, use of the cultural capital we have.

4 See Donaldson (1991: 62), whose article treats the muddiness of the film as well, although he sees it as representing Branagh's materialism, a claim I would not fully accept. Donaldson also notes the parallel between Henry and Branagh, with the film thus affirming "the values of professional competition and success" (71). See also Fitter 1991, who compares the film unfavorably to the more critical 1984 Adrian Noble RSC stage production that starred Branagh, and who sees the film version as "an establishment cover-up" appealing to mainstream US popular tastes (260).

5 See Weber 1968, whose opposition of charisma to rational, institutional structures is concerned with historical or epochal changes in their relationship and opposition.

6 Ambivalence needs to be distinguished by what one is ambiguous about, of course, but also at a historically salient level of abstraction. By this I mean that even though Shakespeare presses the dialogue and the action in ways that create a kind of interrogation about war, the conditions of the topic were much less strong than in the 1960s when hawks and doves, pro- and anti-movements, constituted war (not just the Vietnam War) as an issue in itself. If one generalizes an ambivalence into one about, say, institutional authority, the 1960s, as expressed in *Dirty Harry*, would offer a politically charged arena there. "Institutional authority," as an abstraction, may have less purchase as a topic for Shakespeare's audience, whereas at a different level of abstraction, namely that of the monarchy, there would be a political charge. A potential for the anti-monarchical (a potential to be historically realized) would thus be an element of representation with much more political force in an ambiguity. The problem with new historicist treatment of "power" and "authority" is not its inaccuracy (for the monarch had both), but that it sometimes provides an illegitimate interpretive power because its level of generalization is higher than warranted by the historical moment.

7 We might also note the tongue-in-cheek opening of Branagh's *Much Ado About Nothing*, in which the arrival of Don Pedro and his men on horseback lovingly spoofs the opening of *The Magnificent Seven*.

8 A subtextual association of dirt for American audiences would be Vietnam, the paradigmatic "dirty" war for hawks and doves alike. The raising of moral consciousness about war would be evident later in hypocritical inversions such as the title of the US invasion of Panama: "Operation Just Cause."

9 The editor of the Oxford *Henry V*, Gary Taylor, in arguing for placing the killing of the prisoners onstage, claims that no Elizabethan would have condemned the obvious military necessity and notes Bullough's citation of R. Crompton's 1599 defense of an action that "had been and would continue to be defended by theoreticians and soldiers" (Shakespeare 1982: 33). But the fact that it had to be defended, and that "war's miseries" are put forward as a defense, demonstrate that ideology and the historical "belief" of the time are by no means monolithic or seamless.

10 All citations from *Henry V* are from Alfred Harbage's 1969 edition of *The Complete Works*, New York: Penguin. The base text for this and most editions of the play is the folio version, which contains much of the dialogue, such as the bawdy joking about Katherine, that "muddies" the war and the character of the King.

11 Sinfield writes, "the text is implicated, necessarily, in the complexities of its culture, and manifests not only the strategies of power but also the anxieties that protrude through them" (1992: 138).

12 This emotional sequence, another element readable as a "realistic" view of the ravages of war and therefore available for an "anti-war" spectator, may also be a gibe at the corrosive cynicism of Stanley Kubrick's Vietnam War movie *Full Metal Jacket*, whose conclusion portrays the trudging GIs, having just completed an atrocity, singing the Mickey Mouse Club hymn.

13 Donaldson (1991: 65) reads this as evidence that the King's reform is marked by his being cleaned up, but I do not believe the reform motif is a crucial part of Branagh's representation of the King, nor that Branagh's demystification of war is as complete or successful as Donaldson believes.

14 *Henry V* promotional video viewed at Shakespeare Association, Philadelphia, April, 1990. Bibliographic information unavailable.

15 Seminar directed by Douglas Kellner and held at the International Association for Philosophy and Literature conference, Duquesne University, Pittsburgh, April, 1993.

14

OUT DAMNED SCOT

Dislocating *Macbeth* in transnational film and media culture

Courtney Lehmann

Exploring the effects of verisimilitude in theater and film, Walter Benjamin observes that the concept of "place" in the theater cannot, ultimately, be severed from the spectator's location beyond the footlights, despite even the most powerful illusions of *mise-en-scène*. By contrast, cinema's ability to efface its own location in time and space is the very condition of its scopic seduction. It is, according to Benjamin, a kind of representational oasis, "an orchid in the land of technology" capable of removing us from the trivium of "[o]ur taverns and our metropolitan streets, our offices and furnished rooms, our railroad stations and our factories . . . burst[ing] this prison-world asunder by the dynamite of the tenth of a second, so that now, in the midst of its far-flung ruins and debris, we calmly and adventurously go traveling" (1992: 672). Benjamin's cautiously euphoric description of the centrifugal potential of cinematic representation uncannily invokes a far more recent arrival, digital technology, which has not only changed the landscape of film production by making it widely affordable and accessible through digital distribution, but also revolutionized the act of reception as a mode of "production" in its own right. Indeed, the digital video disk (DVD) caters to the spectator's implied longing for supplemental spaces beyond the purview of the camera – provisional and performative places that invite us to construct our own film from the remnants of discarded footage, photo gallery stills, press kits, censored scenes, and multilanguage menus.[1] Accordingly, although this often highly privatized experience of home theater invokes a return to the solitary, orchid-like splendor that Benjamin ascribes to the hypnotic pull of celluloid, I would suggest that the experience of cinema today is more firmly rooted in the contested province of the thistle – a cross between a lone flower and a menacing mass of weeds – and, of course, the symbol of one place in particular: Scotland. Indeed, I shall argue that Scotland, and, more specifically, the dislocated "Scotland" that figures so prominently in twentieth-century media adaptations of Shakespeare's *Macbeth*, suggests a compelling metaphor for the transnational playground wherein the challenges and possibilities of globalization may be traversed.

In the late 1990s and the new millennium, there have been no fewer than nine, highly varied film, television, and internet adaptations of *Macbeth*, including a high-school video production available exclusively on the internet, adult straight to video and DVD spin-offs such as *In the Flesh* (Stuart Canterbury, 1998), and moderately successful independent films like *Scotland, PA* (Billy Morrissette, 2001).[2] What the adaptations I discuss have in common is not only a somewhat oblique relationship to Shakespeare's play but also a rather peculiar relationship to "Scotland": not one of them is set or shot in Scotland, and yet the idea of "Scotland" operates as a powerful metonymy for a place that is everywhere and nowhere in particular.[3] For example, the Glen Ridge High *Star Wars*-style *Macbeth* begins: "A long time ago in a galaxy far far away . . . Scotland" (Ben Concepcion, 2001). Similarly, *Scotland, PA* invokes "Scotland" only to displace it alongside the descriptive abbreviation "PA" rather than "UK." Ironically, though, the filmmakers started shooting in rural Pennsylvania only to find that they could not reproduce the look of middle America in the 1970s, and so the production moved to Nova Scotia – literally, "New Scotland." The portability of "Scotland" in the *Macbeth* films of the late 1990s and the new millennium is not, however, a mere capitulation to the hopelessness that Fredric Jameson ascribes to the postmodern condition, wherein the past can only be accessed through stereotypes that keep real history at arm's length but forever beyond our grasp (1992b: 19–20). Despite their obvious differences in production values and genre, these films more importantly suggest an attempt to map – "cognitively" and culturally – the co-ordinates of a new frontier that is not about taking the "high road" over the "low road" but, rather, about Scotland as a metaphor for the *road not taken*, a once and future landscape suspended between the imperatives of warfare and welfare, waiting upon our direction.

Taking the high(land) road

Macbeth may be known as "the Scottish play," but the Scottish film is decidedly not *Macbeth* nor, paradoxically, is it "Scottish." As Brian Pendreigh (2002) observes, Scotland has historically been invoked on film as a place that is, in point of fact, anywhere *but* Scotland. A classic example is *Brigadoon* producer Arthur Freed's conclusion that, having toured picturesque locations in the highlands, "nowhere in Scotland . . . looked quite Scottish enough" and, therefore, he "went back to Hollywood, created Scotland in the studio and filled it with Americans in tartan."[4] Despite complaints of celluloid imperialism in classic films such as *Brigadoon* (Vincente Minnelli, 1954), however, the habit of viewing Scottish scenery and history through the lens of other national fantasies dates all the way back to the *Rob Roy* films of the silent era and culminates in their 1990s' counterparts: *Rob Roy* (Michael Caton-Jones, 1995), starring Irishman Liam Neeson, and *Braveheart* (Mel Gibson, 1995), a film shot largely in Ireland starring the Australian-born "Mad Mac" himself, Mel Gibson. Although *Braveheart* in particular placed Scotland and Scottish history in an international spotlight, it did so, as Pendreigh points out, only by converting the character of William Wallace from lowlander to highlander, subscribing to the *Brigadoon* version of "Scotland" as a place of misty mountains, token tartans, and carefully cropped kilts. It seems only fitting that the film was most successful among Americans, who, quite unlike lukewarm audiences in Scotland, voted *Braveheart* the second "most important film of all time" (quoted in Pendreigh: 2002).[5] It is almost predictably ironic, then, that when the *real* Scottish film industry enjoyed a modest boom in the 1990s, marked by the release of *Shallow Grave* (Danny Boyle, 1994), this film – conspicuously shot in Edinburgh – opens with a disavowal of origins: "This could have been any city."

It is significant that this line is uttered as voice-over, for as Joan Copjec argues, voice-over issues from an uncanny off-screen space, the space of the "intemporal voice" that "cannot be situated in – nor subject to the ravages of – time or place" (1993: 185). This resolutely intemporal "place," I will ultimately argue, is the locus of the *real* Scotland, however much it may initially suggest the spectral appearances of *Brigadoon*. Voice-over narration is a staple of film noir, a genre that emerges, according to Copjec, as an attempt to cope with – and to warn of – the historical replacement of "desire" with "drive":

> the old modern order of desire, ruled over by an oedipal father, has begun to be replaced by a new order of the drive, in which we no longer have recourse to the protections against *jouissance* that the oedipal father once offered . . . Which is to say: we have ceased being a society that attempts to preserve the individual right to *jouissance*, to become a society that commands *jouissance* as a "civic" duty. "Civic" is, strictly speaking, an inappropriate adjective in this context, since these obscene importunings of contemporary society entail the destruction of the *civitas* itself . . .
>
> (1993: 182)

Shallow Grave, though by no means a noir detective film, opens with a voice-over that conveys a similar warning. For this initially comic story of middle-class twentysomethings in search of a new flatmate quickly devolves into a murder rampage when the newcomer is found dead in his room with a huge stash of money. Rather than report the incident to the authorities, the roommates attempt to eliminate everyone who poses a threat to their efforts to hoard the money for themselves; and, as in *Braveheart* and *Rob Roy*, few indeed are left standing at the film's conclusion. In hindsight, then, the line issuing from the death-inflected, disembodied voice-over – "this could be any place" – functions as a powerful warning that the fetishization of drive – of private *jouissance* – has "mortal consequences for society" as "ever smaller factions of people proclai[m] their duty-bound devotion to their own special brand of enjoyment . . ." (Copjec, 1993: 183). That the "any place" featured in *Shallow Grave* is Scotland as opposed to "Scotland" is significant, not just for the obvious admonitory suggestion that such perverse self-interest has become the rule as opposed to the exception but also for the more subtle implication that understanding the difference between the two Scotlands may, in the not-too-distant future, be the difference between life and death.

Something is rotten in the state of Scotland

The fact that *Braveheart* and *Rob Roy* have been commercially more successful than films such as *Shallow Grave* and, later, *Trainspotting* (Danny Boyle, 1996) is not due to production values alone; rather, it is their contrasting ideological values, masked as differences of genre, that constitutes the geopolitical gap between the "Scottish" film and the Scottish film. If *Shallow Grave* and *Trainspotting* suggest postmodern variations on the discomfiting themes of film noir, then *Braveheart* and *Rob Roy* are more at home among the maverick triumphs that are the topos of the American western. However, I would argue that whereas film noir confronts us with an alienating vision of a society that embraces drive over desire, the western – or, more accurately, the neo/"Scottish" western – only *pretends* to restore the reverse order. For heroes like William Wallace and Robert Roy MacGregor engage in mass military campaigns that fulfill their personal need for "revenge" and "honor," respectively, only by masking these private drives as political desires tied to land, freedom, and the sexual possession of women's bodies. The ideological upshot of *Braveheart* and *Rob Roy* is, therefore, not the isolated and, ultimately, dispensable victory of the traditional "outlaw" hero of the American western from Shane to Dirty Harry but, rather, the insidious validation of the corrupt *system* itself – a twist that is often missed in the glorification of individual courage that figures prominently in 1980s neo-westerns such as *Robocop*, *Rambo*, *Top Gun*, *Diehard*, and *Superman*.[6] In all of these films, the means – that is, drives – are never called into question so long as they achieve the *desired* ends. As Susan Jeffords explains, "the removal of a few bad individuals – whether incompetent police captains or hardened criminals such as Lex Luthor will presumably return the system to its operating purpose: serving average Americans" (1994: 20). In *Rob Roy* and *Braveheart*, we need only substitute the corrupt Scottish gentry for the "police" and the arch-evil English King Edward Longshanks for "Lex Luthor" to apply Jeffords' conclusion; in the former, an already corrupt system is shored up when Rob Roy earns the respect and protection of the gentry who wish him – and each other – dead, just as in the latter film, the one-time-traitor-turned-Scottish-king, Robert the Bruce, replaces the martyred commoner William Wallace to lead the rag-tag Scots to victory over the English. The conclusion of both "Scottish" westerns boils down to the choice of a lesser evil that ultimately does little to change the system: the unpardonable English crime of genocide gives way to the provincial Scottish acceptance of indiscriminate homicide.

Where, then, does *Macbeth* enter the picture? Ever since Orson Welles failed to keep his 1948 *Macbeth* film – originally recorded in a Scots burr – from being redubbed into "accent-free" English, subsequent film versions have blatantly called the bluff of the play's setting by featuring visibly non-Scottish locations – from Ken Hughes's Chicago-based mafia film *Joe MacBeth* (1955) to Akira Kurosawa's medieval samurai setting for *Throne of Blood* (1957) to Andrzej Wajda's Yugoslavian film *Siberian Lady Macbeth* (1961) and, finally, to Roman Polanski's hallucinatory "Playboy" *Macbeth* (1971).[7] As in the traditional western genre, these films cannot be interpreted apart from the landscapes against which they emerge. But Shakespeare's *Macbeth* is neither a traditional nor a neo-western of the Reagan/Bush Sr. era; it is, rather, a "northern" western in both its topological and sentimental climate, which is to say, *Macbeth* is a noir western that is also, unarguably, *Scottish*. What I am calling the noir western takes as its point of departure the recognition that there *never was* an old "modern order of desire, ruled over by an oedipal father" *in the first place*. Rather, like the historical predicament of pre-modern Scotland, there are only so many chieftains posing as would-be fathers among their clans, all of whom maintain varying claims to the land and the personal ascriptions of entitlement it embodies. In other words, the Scotland of Shakespeare's play, like the unevenly globalized network of late capitalism, does not revolve around the choice between two evils but the proper choice of *pleasures* in a system characterized by an excess of *jouissance*. And the range of possible articulations of drive in these films is as broad as the ideological expanse that separates the enabling heterogeneity of the Scottish clans from the oppressive singularity of the "Scottish" Ku Klux Klan. What the noir sensibility interjects into the framework of the western, then, is quite literally a change of scenery, converting the hero's mastery of the great outdoors to the menacing interior spaces – industrial and psychological – that characterize the noir anti-hero's increasingly claustrophobic sphere of action. In this spirit, the *fin-de-siècle Macbeths* I shall turn to now go one step further than their screen predecessors by dislocating Scotland from its moorings in *any place at all*, as "Scotland" becomes synonymous, for better or for worse, with a state of *mind*.

Macbeth meets Mad Max, or, the persistence of (Mel Gibson's) memory

In *Shakespeare, The Movie* (1997), Lynda E. Boose and Richard Burt cite *Clueless* (Amy Heckerling, 1995) as a symptom of Shakespeare's increasing displacement by marketing strategies that privilege, in the case of Heckerling's film, "knowing Mel Gibson's *Hamlet*" over knowing Shakespeare's *Hamlet* (1997: 8). The lure of Gibson's star persona, in other words, contains enough pop cultural capital to compensate for the fact that Cher (Alicia Silverstone) has lapsed momentarily from thunderdome to loserdom by watching a Shakespeare film in the first place. What's most curious about this episode, as Boose and Burt explain, is the fact that *Clueless* is based on the canonical Austen novel, *Emma*, which makes Cher's anti-intellectual equation of "success" with "pride in *not* knowing one's Shakespeare" a startling departure from the tradition that posits "Shakespeare and the English literary tradition . . . [as] a rallying point of national superiority" (1997: 12). Thus, *Clueless* suggests the extent to which Hollywood capitalism has infiltrated even the most intractable markets. Only two years later, Michael Bogdanov's English Shakespeare Company teamed up with Channel 4 UK to create a made-for-television version of *Macbeth* that reveals an even greater, albeit selective, dependency on Mel Gibson's star power to sell Shakespeare; for this film is nothing less than *Macbeth* shot through the lens of *Mad Max* and, perhaps, a more subtle attempt to divert attention away from the recently released *Braveheart*. Though both the gun-toting Mad Max and the broadsword-bearing William Wallace serve as intriguing screen prototypes for a 1990s Macbeth, the former implies a rationale for British colonialism, whereas the latter clearly critiques it: the lawless renegades in the *Mad Max* series are the indigenous, pleasure-seeking Others who must be "civilized" or eliminated, whereas the hedonistic marauders in *Braveheart* are the English themselves. Significantly, Bogdanov's film was released in the same year as a Scottish referendum voting for devolution and the establishment of a Scottish parliament, the first in nearly three hundred years.

Filmed on location in the Australian outback, *Mad Max* (George Miller, 1979) and its sequels, *Road Warrior* (1981), and *Beyond Thunderdome* (1985), are all set in a post-apocalyptic no-place featuring salvaged scraps of sheet-metal, motorcycles, black leather and, most memorably, Mel Gibson as the former-cop-turned-rebel-with-a-cause, seeking to avenge the murder of his wife and child. Bogdanov's setting for *Macbeth* suggests a "Scottish" variation on this theme – a dystopian *Brigadoon* that emerges from the smoke of intermittent bombs rather than whimsical highland mist, revealing, in the process, the burned-out vestiges of a once green and hilly landscape. According to the video jacket description, *Macbeth* occupies "a timeless zone," set "against a raw, urban industrial environment giving the film a surreal quality." Entering this "timeless" space as road warriors in their own right, Macbeth (Sean Pertwee) and Banquo (Michael Maloney) burst onto the scene astride motorcycles, sporting paramilitary garb replete with tartan accessories. But this is the point at which *Macbeth* and *Mad Max* appear to part company, for although Pertwee's Macbeth – with his spikey hair, tinted shades, and studied sense of road rage – bears a family resemblance to Gibson's Max, Pertwee's "Mad Mac" lacks the personal justification that is the trademark of Gibson's enraged screen personae. In reading Bogdanov's film through the lens of the noir western, however, we may discover that this Macbeth does have a battleaxe to grind after all, one that shifts our prurient gaze away from the devastated wasteland that is "Scotland" to the abject interiors that are its source, namely, "the guilty horizon of bourgeois comfort and detachment" (MacCannell 1993: 280).

The singular irony of the neo-noir revival of the early 1990s, according to Dean MacCannell, is that films such as *Public Eye* (Howard Franklin, 1992), *The Two Jakes* (Jack Nicholson, 1990), and *Barton Fink* (Joel Coen, 1991), offer a "fictional recuperation" of classic noir's interest in seamy, gritty, subproletarian city spaces "just as the actual proletarian space is historically lost" (1993: 282). The upshot for filmmakers is that they have been forced to virtualize, if not fantasize, "the imaginary boundaries of urban misery" in the form of artificial sets (1993: 282); however, the consequence for the actual occupants evicted from these spaces during the Reagan revolution is, of course, literal homelessness. It is significant, then, that in Bogdanov's film Macbeth does not come across as angry or "mad" until after his encounter with the witches – the abject threesome who are also marked as homeless. Poised over a flaming trash-heap, the witches are clad in filthy layers of tattered clothing, bandanas, and grime; they speak with thick Cockney inflections and gesture with dirty fingers poking out of hole-ridden gloves. Their open-air, makeshift dwelling is crudely assembled from discarded junk. Two of the witches are caucasian, one is black, and their capacity to horrify resides in their uncanny familiarity – they are, in other words, not otherworldly enough but, rather, altogether too *real.* Accordingly, although Bogdanov's film was received both critically and commercially as a poor imitation of Baz Luhrmann's highly successful version of *Romeo + Juliet* (1996) released the year before, I would argue that the primary shortcoming of this *Macbeth* is its failure to live up to the escapist fiction it promises. Far from inviting us into a timeless zone, Bogdanov's film is a brutally timely allegory of the *present.*

After Macbeth's encounter with the witches, the scenery that begins in the province of the wide open spaces of the western shifts almost exclusively to interiors – large, vacant, post-industrial spaces that once served as the urban playground of film noir, which, in the noir western, have become a metaphor for the dark corners of unexamined conscience. This is the psychic landscape that Dean MacCannell identifies with "senile capitalism," a capitalism that has forgotten its once enabling relationship to democratic ideals. MacCannell's provocative reflections on this unexplored tension at the very heart of film noir warrants quoting at length:

> After defeating its external enemies, fascism and communism, capitalism entered its "twilight years"; increasingly it began to turn its fading powers against its own partner, democracy, for harbouring and promoting a historically antiquated, inefficient ideological surplus. From the perspective of mature capitalism, the historical purpose of its partnership with democracy was (1) to break the privilege of aristocratic classes, making way for new entrepreneurial elites, and (2) to win the hearts and minds of socialists and others still tied to noncapitalist modes of production by offering them freedom of

> speech, choice, etcetera. Once traditional privilege is destroyed, and everyone is involved in the same system of global economic relations, there is no further need for democracy.
>
> (1993: 284)

The problem with this assertion, of course, as critics of globalization have made clear, is that not "everyone is involved" *equally* in this system, just as "drive" cannot enter into equilibrium with "desire" but instead only displace it. Significantly, in Bogdanov's *Macbeth*, it is Duncan (Philip Madoc) who is implicitly aligned with senile capitalism's uneven distribution of resources. Distinguished by his impeccably clean, non-combat wardrobe and his train of bodyguards who, later, sport slick, slim-lined suits and sunglasses – the dry-clean-only uniform of the corporate thug – Duncan suggests a portrait of senile capitalism in its worst incarnation, namely, "microfascism." As the seamy flip-side of postmodernism's exaltation of fragmentation, microfascism crystallizes as "smaller, more localized but equally exploitative power formations" made possible by an uneven global economy (Braidotti 1994: 5). This is the pseudo-medieval and distinctly postmodern fiefdom over which Duncan presides in Bogdanov's film.

Though Bogdanov's *Macbeth* fails to appeal to audiences expecting a sequel to *Romeo + Juliet,* his film is, in many ways, far more current than even Luhrmann's. For his updating of *Macbeth* is firmly rooted in a culture wherein the paternal metaphor has undergone a perverse mutation – a mutation that is encoded in the empty, abject interior spaces that pervade this film and signal its placement within the paranoid perceptual schemes of the noir universe. What is most striking about Bogdanov's approach to these interiors is the opaque quality of their emptiness; it is as if the emptiness itself is always already "filled" with a void. Lady Macbeth's chamber is a case in point: dwelling in an enormous horizontal space punctuated only with hurricane lamps and satin pillows clustered together on a dirty floor, Lady Macbeth (Greta Scaachi) reposes elegantly on the pillows in a conspicuous attempt to recover a sense of dignity long since eroded with the scraps of Duncan's royal favor. Far from being the benign, essentially absent, Oedipal father of Shakespeare's play, then, Duncan suggests the obscenely present, noir father who serves not to protect but to prevent his subjects from threatening his control of the resources. Indeed, how could such an allegedly good king allow the thanes who bleed for him to live in such grotesque urban squalor – wherein people dwell like rats in abandoned warehouses-turned-tenements, entering and exiting their vast crawl spaces through windows, scaffolding, and fire escapes? The result of a dramatic shift in the demographics of factory work in the 1990s, this post-industrial wasteland is a clear indication that the jobs have all moved away to unnamed places where the labor is cheap and the workers are infinitely replaceable. As for the loyal drones who stayed behind – Macbeth and company – their occupations, like their surroundings, appear to be Duncan's whim.[8]

At least at the beginning of the film, then, Macbeth is the figure who embodies the broken promises of senile capitalism. Prompted by the indigent witches to reflect on his own slumbering sense of self-worth and, it would seem, on Duncan's failure to provide for his kingdom, Pertwee's Macbeth can barely conceal his shock and rage when he is passed over by Duncan as the heir apparent to the throne. Even the other soldiers seem to expect Duncan to name Macbeth as his successor; but instead he singles out his son – the smug, spoiled Malcolm (Jack Davenport) – whose distinctly unsullied uniform, perfectly tilted beret, and tough-guy grimace (the product of long hours of practicing in the mirror) resembles what the young George W. Bush must have looked like when he served his cushy, dramatically abbreviated term in the Texas National Guard to avoid Vietnam. Following the forced round of applause that punctuates Duncan's unexpected announcement, Macbeth begs his leave to become "Mad Mac," violently kicking the fuselage at his feet when he is barely out of sight of the others. Like no other version of Macbeth before it, Bogdanov's film implies that Duncan gets exactly what he deserves. Indeed, the fact that the only high-tech moment in this putatively futuristic film occurs when the King's royal train enters Macbeth's "estate" via a stretch water limo – a tableau that seems to parody the lost splendor of the medieval castle moat – is a clear indication that Duncan approaches postmodernism's potentially democratic dislocations of time and space as an opportunity to revive feudal privileges. What distinguishes Bogdanov's film as a noir western, then, is the fact that such privileges are figured spatially, that is, as the masterful occupation of real and psychic space. In such a context, homelessness is not defined as the loss of "home" but as the loss of a *meaningful* relationship to space.

This is where Scotland enters the picture as a locus for imagining the possibilities of fortuitous dislocation, which I call "cinenomadicism," namely, the refusal to be bound exclusively to one "plot" of narrative, action, or land. For a short time, Macbeth seems committed to the distribution of social justice – and redistribution of resources – implied by this concept. Indeed, his murder of Duncan and, consequently, the expulsion of his privileged sons to England and Ireland, seem to leave Scotland with a clean slate, a space for renegotiating the lost contract between the free market and democratic freedoms. But under Mad Mac's leadership, "Scotland" becomes increasingly identified with nostalgia for the future, a variation on what Fredric Jameson calls "nostalgia for the present" in the form of the future that *never will be*.[9] For the bleak, post-industrial spaces that we see through the eyes of Pertwee's Macbeth suggest a perverse Dickensian fairy tale in which the ghost of capitalism future – microfascism – has already arrived. Thus, more than anything else Bogdanov's setting seems to comment cynically on the Scottish tourism boom of the 1990s, which was stimulated by the creation of *industrial* theme parks designed "to recapture the glories of Scotland's industrial past which was now vanishing fast from the real manufacturing economy" (Devine, 1999: 596). Bogdanov's film of Shakespeare's Scottish play takes up this "theme" not from the perspective of the accidental tourist but from the specter of the intentionally evicted and occupationless.

However sympathetic Macbeth may be at the beginning of the film, Mad Mac cannot be the hero of this noir western, for this genre is marked by the refusal to anthropomorphize what is, fundamentally, a corruption of space itself. Consequently, Macbeth succeeds in vanquishing Duncan's neo-feudal, micro-fascist dynasty only by falling prey to the same horizon of bourgeois comfort and detachment as his predecessor. Unlike Duncan before him and Malcolm after him, though, Macbeth never looks comfortable in his borrowed robes. Rather, he wears his gaudy suits with the self-ironizing posture of an aging rock star, attuned to every coarse crackle of his leather pants and glaring shimmer of his sateen shirts, as if he were straining under their lack of breathe-ability even as they mark him as capitalism's synthetic, that is, self-made man. Thus, when he attempts at the end of the film to restore his road warrior look with paramilitary garb and tartan trim, it is painfully obvious that the Macbeth of old, like the Scotland of the future, is a thing of the past. Indeed, in the process of wrestling with Macbeth, Macduff (Larcon Cranitch) reveals that *he* is now wearing the pants – in the form of long underwear bearing the royal Stuart tartan. But if, in the twilight years of capitalism, the clothes still make the man, in 1990s *Macbeth*s, the tartan no longer makes the Scot; for in the very instant that Macduff finishes off Macbeth, Malcolm arrives fresh from the croquet lawn of his English mansion (or is it his Texas ranch?) to take credit for the victory. Unique to Bogdanov's version, Macduff glares resentfully at the perfectly coifed Malcolm, but climbs into the hummer to join him and his henchmen anyway. Malcolm proceeds to assert his mastery over the space he inherits by abandoning it, peeling away from this scene of industrial apocalypse in search of greener, undoubtedly suburban pastures. And so the Reagan/Bush revolution returns in the form of the son who is too young to be senile but old enough to repeat Daddy's mistakes by rote. In the final scene, Macbeth is dumped by a garbage truck onto a trash heap, and the witches eagerly pillage his body in search of accessories for their nomadic dwelling, assuring us with sinister certainty that the vicious formula of this noir western will, like Macbeth's body, be recycled.

Taking the low road: Shakespeare does Scotland

The next version of *Macbeth*, Stuart Canterbury's 1998 porn-feature *In the Flesh* (written by Canterbury and Antonio Passolini), ventures a step beyond Bogdanov's *Macbeth* to explore the abject "interior" spaces that define the explicit sex film. In many respects, hard-core pornography suggests the ultimate articulation of the noir western, not only for its exploration of the forbidden territories associated with sexual transgression but also for its vision of apocalyptic capitalism – that is, consumption without (re)production – based on the fetishization of the all-important "come shot." Like Bogdanov's *Macbeth, In the Flesh* takes for its point of departure the triumph of drive over desire in a landscape that is rife with a retro-futuristic sense of déjà vu. Macbeth (Mike Horner) and Banquo (Valentino) enter the film via a military jeep, dressed in disruptive combinations of crisply decorated military jackets and tartan kilts. And, as in Bogdanov's film, they dodge flames from detonated bombs as the jarring rattle of machine gun fire pervades the air. Similarly, the witches are represented as homeless refugees – "probably shell-shocked," Banquo mutters – as the vaguely other-worldly women warm themselves over the flicker of a garbage can fire. Unlike Bogdanov's *Macbeth*, however, these indigents are not shunned as pariahs but, rather, marked as alluring threshold figures whose implied nomadicism is sexy, suggesting the ancient association of female mobility (*nomas*) with sexual promiscuity and prostitution. Clad in black latex body suits that leave nothing to the imagination, the witches beckon toward Macbeth and Banquo, inviting them to sample their wares. But contrary to our expectations for hard-core porn films, Macbeth blithely rejects their offer, paternalistically advising an all-too-eager Banquo that it is "best not to sleep with witches." Quite literally left to their own devices, the weird sisters proceed to get downright freaky among themselves, taking the viewer on a sexsploitation obstacle course that culminates in the head witch using a double-pronged dildo to pleasure the other two. In the broader context of the film, this image suggests the proverbial fork in the road – and, for Macbeth, the "road not taken" – to Scotland.

Even before Macbeth and Banquo encounter the witches, *In the Flesh* opens with a series of allusions to the "Scottish film." With the help of an establishing shot of a medieval castle façade enveloped in highland mist and a voice-over in a heavy Scots burr, the film begins with an aura of *gravitas*, as the indignant voice exclaims:

> Kings come and kings go. That's the nature of war, that's the nature of life. How many battles have been fought for next to nothing? For a piece of land, for a piece of respect, for a piece of ass – but never for peace itself. That's the big lie. And it's what men do best. As men we build out castles of power and greed and lust – and then – like beasts we knock them down.

This is the pseudo-medieval "Scotland" of *Braveheart* and *Rob Roy*: the land frozen in time, shrouded in fog, and filled with noble barbarians. But this is the last we hear of Scottish accents as the scene shifts from the pastoral haunts of haughty highlanders to the hidden pleasures of urban bohemians, as the DVD jacket promises:

> Shot on film in the exotic locale of Budapest, IN THE FLESH is a perverse twist on the classic tale of *Macbeth* – complete with greed, betrayal, madness, and of course, plenty of lust. Set in a retro-future world of castles and cars, and packed with the most beautiful new actresses Europe has to offer, this lush epic depicts the rise to power of Lord Macbeth (Mike Horner) and his insatiable wife, Lady Macbeth (Kylie Ireland). Featuring the hardest action imaginable in the most breathtaking locations, IN THE FLESH is an assault on the erotic senses, a sex spectacle of unprecedented proportions, that only Stuart Canterbury (*Dreams*, *Foolproof*) and Antonio Passolini (*Café Flesh 2*, *Devil in Miss Jones 6*) could create.

"Location," as it appears in this description, resonates as a naughty pun, since nothing in the film – from the castle interiors to the alfresco frolicking in the open air – signifies a place that is specifically "Budapest" other than the thick eastern European accents and swarthy, "Magyar" look of the cast members. Yet the artificial Budapest of *In the Flesh* has much more in common with Scotland – the land dislocated from the historical fictions I have been exploring here – than we might first realize.

Originally a borderland dividing settled cultures from nomadic ones, Hungary has historically been more deserving of the designation "Bohemia" than the Czech-populated land to the north-west, serving as a pivotal point of passage not only for Huns, Turks, and Mongols, but also for northern European tribes like the Finnish Magyars who eventually settled there. Like the "Scotland" of *Macbeth* and, as we shall see, the Hungary of *In the Flesh*, the concept of the "bohemian" is constituted precisely by its lack of a meaningful connection to place. Falsely ascribed to a nomadic people thought to live in Bohemia, the term "bohemian" emerged in association with "gypsy" which, in turn, is a word mistakenly tied to Egyptians. Nomadic in its own right, "bohemian" is a word that has accrued a variety of subversive associations over time to become a catch-all expression for "an extravagant sexual life, mobility in abode, and freedom from governing morality" (Peters 1999: 37). It seems only fitting, then, that these nomadic energies (spurred by the steady flow of capital into the former Soviet bloc) should return to Hungary and, in the process, transform Budapest into the new "Bohemia" as the center of the global porn industry. Porn, as Joseph W. Slade explains, has always been a matter of national self-interest, serving as a lucrative export for northern Europe and, in southern European countries like Spain, offering opportunities for increased tourism to cities where hard-core theaters are legal. The situation in Hungary is quite different, for unlike its European competitors, Budapest is known not only as a hothouse for Slavic beauties who "perform enthusiastically" but also as a place that welcomes the cineno-madic energies of the global market.[10] Budapest is, therefore, particularly appealing to American producers seeking to package their product as sufficiently "bohemian" – that is, dislocated from the sociopolitical imperatives of "place" – in order to circumvent GATT restrictions, which stipulate that half the programs broadcast in Europe be European in origin (in France they have to be 60 percent "French"). Under the deceptive aegis of "co-production," then, porn has become a truly multi- or, better put, *trans*national product, promiscuously following the flows of globalization so that an "American" film, for example, will "borrow the capital from a German bank, employ a Hungarian cast assembled by a European casting agency, shoot in English, distribute through a French company, and sell the product everywhere" (Slade 1997: 6).

Such a process is akin to what Dean MacCannell describes as "the perverse accommodation of capitalism by democracy" (1993: 289), a by-product of a distinctly noir environment wherein guilt – but not necessarily the pleasures associated with it – gets distributed "evenly," that is, "globally." Accordingly, the closer we look at the real conditions of production in Budapest, the more disturbing they become from the perspective of the ratio of guilt (expenditure) to pleasure (profit). Indeed, there is something vaguely sado-masochistic about the fact that Hungary, as Joseph W. Slade explains, uses porn as a means of reducing its foreign debt; in fact, the Hungarian government "actively encourages porn production because it injects revenue into the service sector" (1997: 8). Of course, this industry inflects the phrase "service sector" with distinctly bawdy overtones, which, ultimately, offer insufficient comic relief from the more sinister reality that Budapest has become such a popular site for porn films not only because of the comparatively low cost of production, but also because the women tend to be less educated and, consequently, less aware of AIDS (Slade 1997: 8). In this respect, a porn-noir western like *In the Flesh* literalizes the trope of the femme fatale which, in classic film noir, represents "desire as something that not only renders the desiring subject helpless, but also propels him or her to destruction" (Cowie 1994: 145). Yet *In the Flesh* simultaneously poses a variation on this theme. For if, as in Shakespeare's play, this film is bound to end in an apocalyptic vision of death (and indeed, in the porn noir universe, the specter of AIDS suggests the ultimate embodiment of the obscenely present, devouring father), then "survival" is not predicated on winning the war but, rather, on enjoying all the battles along the way. In this brave new "Scottish" world of bohemian sexual coalitions, Mike Horner's Macbeth is defeated *not* because he succumbs to the femme fatale but because he *doesn't:* Macbeth is the villain of this film because of his monogamous refusal to "enjoy his symptom" of globalization.

When in Scotland, do as the Bohemians do

In the Flesh is particularly fascinating for the way in which it updates Shakespeare's Scottish play to further its own ideological enterprise. The conspicuous absence of Malcolm – along with Lady Macduff's children and Banquo's son Fleance – underscores the fact that dynasties are irrelevant in the world of non-procreative and nomadic sexual relations. But the freedom from sexual orthodoxy that is the *raison d'être* of porn is precisely what Macbeth resists in this film. After Macbeth's rejection of the witches' invitation, the scene shifts to Lady Macbeth (Kylie Ireland) satisfying herself with a dildo in preparation for Macbeth's arrival. Whether she is igniting the home fires in anticipation of more pleasure with her husband or as a pre-emptive strike against his impotence, is uncertain. It is significant, then, that Lady Macbeth casts the proposition to kill Duncan (Mike Foster) in terms of a sexual bargain; not only does she threaten to leave Macbeth for a "real man" if he doesn't rise to the occasion but, worse, upon his initial refusal, she ups the ante by resolving to dress him up in her "dirty little panties" and make him her "pet," her "puppy dog." Rather than suffer this apparent humiliation, Macbeth determines to "do whatever it takes to be a man," and proceeds to engage in the standard progression from oral to vaginal to anal sex with his demanding wife. But this is the first *and* last time that Macbeth has sex in a porn film in which he is purportedly the star. Moreover, his is the most uninventive, uninspired sex scene, compared with Duncan's two-women-on-one-man before and Banquo's three-men-on-, under-, and over-one-woman after. Macbeth's sudden and seemingly irreversible decline from virility to virulence is signified most dramatically by his lack of participation in the banquet, which, in this film, takes the form of an orgy. Indeed, Macbeth can only recoil in horror at the site of Banquo's ghost participating in the tartan-trimmed flesh-fest that takes place on the long table over which he presides. In this Bacchanalian spin on Shakespeare's banquet scene, Macbeth is mortified not by Banquo's return from the dead but, rather, by the fact that he is being showed up by a ghost. The implication is that Banquo is an even more potent lover in death than he was in life, thus rendering the murder a failure and Macbeth an unlikely victim of John Ashcroft syndrome.[11]

In this "Scottish" film, then, Macbeth is what is wrong with the picture, for he is the only non-Bohemian. Consequently, Lady Macbeth's death is represented as being causally related to Macbeth's impotence.[12] Constantly assuming the sexual initiative at the beginning of the film, Lady Macbeth is, by the end, reduced to a mere spectator. Dwindling through the dungeon with candle in hand, she assumes a posture of disaffected voyeurism as the cell block denizens mock her plight with their sexual antics. The flickering and, finally, snuffing out of her "brief candle" thus signals the death of her phallic prowess. Appropriately, her masturbation and ensuing suicide in the bath tub – labeled "final fantasy" on the DVD menu – shows her dreaming of one last tryst with her once-hardy husband: the implication, according to the mercenary logic of porn, is that monogamy, not promiscuity, kills. As if to reinforce this distinctly noir suggestion, just prior to this scene Lady Macduff (Mira) is killed immediately after having sex with her well-hung Hungarian husband, which serves as foreplay to the kilt-clad Macduff's murder of Macbeth. However, the fact that Macduff (Zenza Maggie) is the implied sole survivor at the film's conclusion does not ultimately endorse the idea that monogamy kills but instead suggests that the horizon of microfascism has shifted. For in the age of AIDS, this film ultimately suggests that nomadic encounters "in the flesh" have necessarily been replaced by the prosthetic pleasures of autoeroticism. Yet these pleasures are not automatically "safer" than their bohemian counterparts, for they remind us – like the opening scene of self-detonating war instruments issuing intermittent flames – not only of the zero-sum game of suicidal terrorism, but also of the spectacle of remote control warfare with smart bombs and unmanned planes, which remains the isolationist prerogative of those nations with the most pleasure and the least guilt.

Macbeth, the comedy: from Luke Skywalker to Walker Shortbread

In 2001–2, three parodies of *Macbeth* emerged to mark the turn of the new millennium: the Glen Ridge High *Star Wars: Macbeth* (2001), *Scotland, PA* (2002), and *Macbeth, The Comedy* (dir. Allison LiCalsi, 2001); the first and last are digital films shot in a matter of days on next-to-nothing budgets, whereas *Scotland, PA* is an independent film featuring recognizable faces such as the inimitable Christopher Walken, *ER* star Maura Tierney, and *Ally McBeal* cast member James LeGros. The comedic aspect of these *Macbeths* in no way disqualifies them as noir westerns, for these are distinctly "dark comedies" that use place – often reflected in product placement – to spin sinister tales of corporate ambition even as they imagine the possibilities of a post-corporate cinenomadicism. What is most provocative about the Glen Ridge High *Star Wars: Macbeth* and *Scotland, PA* is that in contrast to the retro-futuristic worlds of Bogdanov's *Macbeth* and *In the Flesh*, these films stage their unintentional but relentless returns to the present with a detour through the past – and, more specifically, the recent past of the 1970s. In both films, however, the nostalgic focus on the more simple pleasures of bygone decades cannot ultimately insulate their *mise-en-scènes* from the ruthless pleasures of the present; for neither film can erase the specter of what Slavoj Žižek calls the "unhistorical kernel" which, by way of its inexhaustible repetition, gives the lie to every "new" epoch by dressing up the same historical crisis in different clothes (1992: 81). The central gambit of these noir westerns, then, is to mask time – and the attendant traumas of history – in spatial terms, focusing on "far far away" places in which lived temporalities are subsumed by a nostalgic fascination with space.

In peculiar respects, the Glen Ridge High School student production of *Macbeth* suggests a sequel to *In the Flesh*, for the traumatic kernel that its location can never completely repress is the notorious gang rape of a retarded girl by Glen Ridge High School jocks in 1989. Suddenly, this small, extremely affluent American town that prided itself on its above-average SAT scores, successful sports teams, and no fewer than 666 of the 3000 remaining gas lights operative in America, found itself in a seedy national spotlight. Describing the Glen Ridge community, the local Congregational Church minister explained that "[a]chievement was honored and respected almost to the point of pathology . . . whether it was the achievements of high school athletes or the achievements of corporate world conquerors" (quoted in Lefkowitz 1998: 130). Teachers, parents, and citizens in this 1.5 square-mile community were accused of turning a blind eye to the increasingly disturbing behavioral patterns they witnessed among the popular boys at Glen Ridge High, which involved parsing people – mostly women – into categories of conquest, culminating in the rape of fourteen-year-old Leslie Faber. One such objectified group, however, was comprised of mostly males: the nerds that the jocks called "giggers," a derogatory combination of "gigabyte" and "niggers." Nine years later in the spring in 1997, the giggers struck back, creating a video (digitally remastered and released in 2001) for their High School English class that represented the geeks inheriting the earth or, better put, the galaxy.

In keeping with the history of the Scottish play on screen, this version of *Macbeth* begins with the simultaneous citation and displacement of Scotland: "A long time ago in a galaxy far far away . . . Scotland." In this film, Scotland is identified as a revisionary landscape, a place of childhood nostalgia that is, in fact, no further away than the 1970s – the decade before the golden boys turned bad – when they were just kids hooked on the recently released *Star Wars* (George Lucas, 1977). Significantly, the filmmakers themselves weren't even born yet; but when they reached the age that the jocks had been when they first watched *Star Wars*, these "giggers" were bombarded with news footage of the galactic meltdown occurring in their own back yards. Their ensuing retreat in *Star Wars: Macbeth* to a space-time before they were born thus enables the filmmakers to engage in a form of nostalgia which, in Walter Benjamin's terms, is "revolutionary": by synchronizing the past with the future, *Star Wars: Macbeth* imagines thwarting the teleological march of historical inevitability that will culminate in the Glen Ridge tragedy of the late 1980s.[13] In this context, then, Scotland is identified with a once and future place in which the giggers prevail and kids with cameras are capable of digitally remastering history.

Offering a variation on the dark comedy that constitutes the American high-school experience, this film features an attractive, athletic-looking Macbeth (Ben Concepcion) being defeated by glasses-wearing, semi-preppy nerds. Following a slew of lightsaber fencing, the rather awkward "Luke Skywalker" character, Macduff (Donald Fitz-Roy), presents an African-American "Malcolm" (Robert Fuller) with Macbeth's head in a backpack. Moments later, this McForce, replete with "Hans Siward" (Raymond Perez), makes their getaway from the Glen Ridge High gymnasium (a place where geeks are never at home) by departing in a replica of the Millennium Falcon spacecraft. The implication is that this multicultural entourage is now headed "back to the future" with a clean slate, having eliminated the evildoers who will give the school and its surrounding community a bad name a decade later. What remains uncertain, however, is what these whiz kids will do when they return to the future. Indeed, given the post-Columbine release of the digital version of the Glen Ridge High School *Macbeth*, it would be difficult not to infer – even amid the fairly innocuous lightsaber battle scenes – an image of the jocks and popular kids being murdered by nerdy, trenchcoat-sporting outcasts. Yet what is markedly different about the scenario posed by *Star Wars: Macbeth* is the multiracial cast; these are not the disturbed, underachieving, neofascist white boys of Columbine High but, rather, the gifted products of transnational mergers of people, places, and profit shares in the cosmopolitan north-east. It's not surprising, then, that almost all of the cast members are currently attending Ivy League universities. But the conspicuous product placement at the end of this short film makes us wonder which "forces" will prevail when these boys leave school once and for all. Following the triumphant finale wherein the student cast is spliced into film footage of *Star Wars* itself in order to receive their rewards from a pimply-faced Princess Leia (Rebekah Heinzen), the scene suddenly cuts away to Macduff and Malcolm back at school enjoying a Coke in front of the soda machine. This moment of brotherly solidarity between young black and white men explicitly invokes another media product of the 1970s: the "I'd like to buy the world a Coke" campaign. Whether these Glen Ridge High grads teach the world "perfect harmony" or corporate conquest remains to be seen – and screened. In the meantime, they offer "Scotland" as a piece of cinenomadic real estate where, at least for now, *anyone* can be at home, as "Yoda's advice for the budding filmmaker" on their website implies: "If you have a video camera lying around, and better yet some editing equipment (pretty cheap for computers nowadays), go experiment. Be your own director, Go Hollywood . . . use a skateboard for dollying shots, or a fishing rod for special effects. . . . You don't need The Force – just some friends with a video camera."[14]

Scotland, PA is an inherently darker film that heads west from the affluent borough of Glen Ridge, New Jersey to explore the discount dreams and working class realities of dilapidated, rural Scotland county, also known as western Pennsylvania. Unlike the escapist fiction of the *Star Wars: Macbeth*, Billy Morrissette's vision of the 1970s hearkens back to the recession and disillusionment with the government that followed the Vietnam War and Watergate scandal. Here, the forces that the characters contend with are explicitly commercial, as the film tells the story of a thirtysomething couple who, trapped in the abyss of lower-management, suddenly become seized with the ambition to be the wealthiest, most successful folks in town. But the "McBeths" lack the all-important punch of pedigree and, therefore, their meteoric rise to power is short-lived. In Morrissette's film, this fundamental lack has everything to do with location, which seems to inscribe the social pathology of "going nowhere" in the non-descript topography of the land itself. Like the transitory status of Budapest, western Pennsylvania is a borderland situated between the industrial-agricultural economy of the Midwest and the slick corporate ethos of the tri-state area. By default, then, western or "Scotland" Pennsylvania is the natural habitat of "American McAnybody's" – and, perhaps, McEverybody's – "duking it out over the most popular power structure around, the small business" (Rippy 2002: B16). What makes this outrageous comedy a tragedy, as Marguerite Rippy incisively observes, is the nature of the lesson the McBeths learn from Shakespeare, namely, "that British primogeniture survives intact in American capitalism" (2002: B16). Thus, in *Scotland, PA* it is hard not to root for Joe "Mac" McBeth (James LeGros) and his wife Pat (Maura Tierney) to succeed in their quest to be *some*body's, since we cannot avoid thinking that at one time or another, "Scotland" – the place of loss, shame, and unfulfilled dreams – is somewhere we've all been before.

The fact that Morrissette stages his version of *Macbeth* as a literal tragedy of appetite situates this film firmly within the perceptual schemes of the noir universe, wherein it is not the specter of failure – and, consequently, of desire – that propels the narrative but, rather, its relentless *satisfaction*. Indeed, *Scotland, PA* draws us into the void of unfulfilled desire that lends meaning to the McBeths' loser lifestyle only to render us complicit in the formation of their super-sized drive for forbidden, deep-fried *jouissance*. Most profoundly, then, *Scotland, PA* explores the insidious symbiosis between space and ambition that is the topos of the noir western. As in Bogdanov's *Macbeth*, when we initially enter this space our sympathies lie with McBeth, since we have already seen Norm Duncan (James Rebhorn) pass him over for promotion and, worse, appoint his estranged son Malcolm (who wants nothing to do with his father or fast-food) as the new head manager. Consequently, when McBeth drowns Duncan in the deep-fat fryolater, he becomes a local hero, for once the old order of Oedipal prohibition is eliminated, the illusion of the democratic right to consume takes its place and, suddenly, enjoyment becomes the ultimate expression of " 'civic' duty" (Copjec1993: 182). With the help of the nomadic technology of the drive-through and a traveling French fry truck, McBeth's business expands exponentially. In the process, however, Pat's psychic space suffers steady constriction, an infirmity that works its way outward to the fryolater burn on her hand, which, she believes, is only worsening with time. That's because time cannot be synchronized with drive; by its very nature, it can only be identified with lack: "We're not bad people, Mac," Pat says to her husband while urging him to kill Duncan, "we're just underachievers who have to make up for lost time." But Pat will have to settle for space, for her one moment of glory occurs when, for the first time in her life, she appears content in her surroundings; drink in hand, she is buoyed up by the sheer bliss of her location which, the camera pulls back to reveal, is an above-ground pool, marking her arrival on the scene of the modest, Midwestern American dream.[15]

Unlike the other *Macbeth* films I have examined here, *Scotland, PA* is the only one that privileges place over protagonist, underscoring the notion that this is not really Mac's tragedy but PA(T)'s, the figure most identified with her surroundings. She is also quite clearly the brains in the operation but, like other women in the 1970s who were contemplating their autonomy for the first time, she still requires a man to execute – and, consequently, profit from – her plans. And though she attempts to safeguard the private moments of *jouissance* that come from her suddenly, solidly, middle-class existence, the "burn" on her hand which, unbeknownst to her, has healed *completely*, begins to drive her insane. Copjec's observations on the paranoid, increasingly claustrophobic dimensions of the noir universe are particularly apropos of Pat's predicament: "from the moment the choice of private enjoyment over community is made, one's privacy ceases to be something one savours when sheltered from prying eyes . . . and becomes instead something one visibly endures – like an unending, discomfiting rain" (Copjec1993: 183). After pharmacological creams and burner mitts fail to remove Pat's sensation of pain, a meat-cleaver does the trick, and she dies with a grin on her face. Thus, if the "burn" is the symptom of Pat's forbidden enjoyment of middle-class existence (forbidden because, based on the choices she made at nineteen, she'll never be considered classy enough to deserve this lifestyle in her thirties), her smile suggests her identification with the *sinthome*, or, "the impossible junction of enjoyment with the signifier" (Žižek 1989: 123). In other words, Pat's smile of relief signifies her liberating realization, having traversed the fantasy of her impossible class ambition, that there is nothing left for her but to identify with lack itself, for " 'beyond fantasy,' " Žižek explains, "there is no yearning . . . only drive . . . pulsating around some unbearable surplus-enjoyment" (1989: 124). Thus, Pat's violent removal of her hand is not so much the mark of a guilty conscience as it is an acceptance of the absence of desire itself – the loss of the desire to desire. As Žižek contends, "the image that most appropriately exemplifies drive is not 'blind animal thriving' but the ethical compulsion which compels us to mark repeatedly the memory of a lost Cause" (1991: 272). Scotland, Morrissette's film implies, is the place where dreams go to die.

The remainder of the film takes shape as a battle between the pseudo-Scots McDuff and McBeth or, more appropriately, *McCloud* and *McBeal*. Indeed, Christopher Walken's unlikely crime-stopping character parodies the 1970s detective series *McCloud*, whereas James LeGros's McBeth invokes his personification of Mark Albert on the recently canceled series *Ally McBeal*. Like McBeth, Mark Albert is not a leader but a follower; hence, he is drawn to phallic women (on *Ally McBeal*, he actually dates a woman whose incomplete sex-change operation leaves her with a penis). Pat McBeth is, of course, the phallic woman par excellence and, for a time, she exercises masterful control over their new-found, fast-food kingdom. But not even she could have anticipated the Loch Ness monster that McBeth becomes, roving and ravaging the open spaces that now seem too small to contain his appetites. Appropriately, then, the vegetarian McDuff steps in to restore the old order of prohibition, turning McBeth's meat joint into a health-food restaurant where no one, the film's conclusion implies, will go to eat. Fittingly, following the melodramatic showdown on the roof of the restaurant, McBeth flees, pausing in front of his car to take one last look at the neon sign that bears his name; seizing the advantage, McDuff jumps from the roof onto McBeth, impaling him on the steer horns that adorn his car. Punished in kind for grabbling the bull of social ambition by the horns, McBeth's gruesome death implies that it is not his bad deeds that destroy him, but his bad taste. This scenario might be funny if it weren't for the fact that Morrissette's film, with its Bad Company soundtrack, bell bottoms, Cameros, and *McCloud* in-jokes, actually succeeds in making us nostalgic for 1972, and even for "low-end. . . . corporate cutthroats" like the McBeths.[16] For the problem is that *Scotland, PA* can never completely escape its real location in 2002, which makes Mac and Pat's small-time, small-town McCruelty seem like child's play compared to their sequel. Indeed, what the fetishized arches of the letter "M" in this film ominously point to is what comes after "M" – "En" – as in noir and, of course, Enron, whose solution to the forgotten pact between capitalism and democracy is to steal from *everyone*, though not necessarily in equal measure. Compared with stock land, Scotland never looked so good.

If we didn't know that *Macbeth: The Comedy* was shot on location in New Brunswick, New Jersey, and New York, its setting could be just about anywhere that Walker Shortbread ships. Indeed, even more so than in *Scotland, PA*, in Allison LiCalsi's film, "Scotland" is not so much produced as it is consumed, for Walker Shortbread, Glenlivet Scotch Whisky, "mad for plaid" fashions, and "Thank God I'm SCOTTISH" placards make all the Scottish world a stage for comedy – and commodities.[17] Yet what distinguishes *Macbeth: The Comedy* from *Scotland, PA* is the fact that rather than serving as markers of distinction and separation, the product placements form a continuum between places defined as home and the marginalized spaces of exile: "have shortbread, will travel" seems to be the only social qualification for movement in this film. *Macbeth: The Comedy* thus refuses to inscribe Shakespeare's play within the structures of loss and longing that are, according to Homi Bhabha, the province of globalization. For in the process of creating access to "a range of materials and material cultures with an ease never before imagined," globalization, Bhabha contends, erodes the prospect of "being-and-belonging by virtue of the nation, a mode of experience and existence that Derrida calls a national ontopology" (1999: ix). With the exception of LiCalsi's film, the *Macbeths* of the late 1990s and new millennium ultimately suggest a conservative reaction to this loss of national ontopology in their portraits of "Scotland." For if Bogdanov's *Macbeth* and *In the Flesh* are fueled by the diasporic energies of transnational media culture and, consequently, look to Shakespeare for ontological stability, then the Glen Ridge High *Star Wars: Macbeth* and *Scotland, PA* are exilic narratives that similarly appropriate Shakespeare as a source of nostalgia for better times and places that remain, nonetheless, hopelessly out of reach. Set in neither the "retro-future" nor the recent past, *Macbeth: The Comedy* privileges not a monadic conception of "Shakespeare" but, rather, a cinenomadic idea of Scotland.[18]

As in the other noir westerns I have explored here, the through-line in LiCalsi's comedy is its preoccupation with the centrifugal energies of multinational capitalism. However, in this film, the act of conspicuous consumption is not visibly marked by class distinction, and capitalism itself is conceived of as a horizontal, rather than vertical, force. For example, although the three male witches appear homeless as they wander across the snowy countryside of New York bedroom communities, their clothes signify their bohemian lifestyle as fashionable, even willful. This utopian concept is first introduced in the opening scene, where the witches huddle together for warmth over a steaming kettle until – in a moment of unimaginable horror – a Karl Lagerfeld sweater rises to the surface of the bubbling cauldron and "Sassy sister" shrieks: "I told you it was dry clean only and now it's ruined, you bitch!" But the class markers that are absent from this seemingly non-discriminatory distribution of products are reinscribed in the frequent citations of Shakespearean verse, virtually all of which result in annoying interruptions of the dramatic action and are signaled by the sudden irruption of "serious" orchestral background music. Duncan (John Little), for example, requires Donalbain (Gerald Downey) to translate for him every time a character cites lines from the play. "You'll have to excuse my father," Donalbain explains, "Ever since verse came into fashion, he's been a bit confused." Unlike Karl Lagerfeld, however, "Shakespeare" is a brand name that is clearly out of fashion in this film. For in this bizarre vision of late capitalism as all play and no work, *Shakespeare himself* comes to be identified with the old order of prohibition – the blocking figure who interrupts the flow of consumption as characters desperately labor to produce his lines with proper accent and inflection. According to this logic, then, Malcolm (Hugh Kelly) is represented as the heir apparent only because he is the son who practices his Shakespeare recitations at every conceivable opportunity, but, like his father, he often fails to comprehend their meaning.

Suggesting a variation on the theme of *Scotland, PA*, which sets out to answer the question "What if the McBeths were alive in '75?", Allison LiCalsi's comedy asks "What if the Macbeths could say what they were really thinking in the play?" What classifies *Macbeth: The Comedy* as a noir western is, therefore, its attempt to turn Shakespeare's play inside out: to expose, in the dark recesses of each character's conscience, the thoughts that they are cloaking in the often obscure semantics of Shakespearean verse. Consequently, the film subscribes to an entertaining form of literalism that paradoxically liberates Shakespeare's metaphor-laden language from the landscape of hidden meaning, recreating it within the topos of "plain English." The effect is the equivalent of *Macbeth* on a truth serum, for every Shakespearean line is accompanied by a Stanislavskian paraphrase that tells the real story behind the words. For example, upon determining to leave Scotland, Donalbain exclaims with conviction: "I'll go to Ireland," adding, "the beer will be cheaper there." Similarly, in the process of easing Malcolm's guilt over fleeing to England, Macduff (Ted de Chatelet) calls the bluff of his own cowardice, freely confessing: "I myself only the other day deserted my wife and kids." Plot ambiguities are likewise given logical, albeit updated explanations, according to LiCalsi's parodic approach to her Shakespearean predecessor. Consequently, the "weird sisters" are not siblings but, rather, gay male fashion mongers named Sassy Sister (Michael Colby Jones), Scary Sister (Phillip Christian), and Southern Sister (Christopher Briggs); meanwhile, Macbeth (Erika Burke), whose manhood is repeatedly indicted in the play, is literally converted to a woman in a lesbian marriage with Lady Macbeth (Juliet Furness) – a scenario that also conveniently explains why the Macbeths can't produce a legitimate heir to the throne. The most unpredictable aspect of this seemingly reductive approach, however, is the way in which it deepens and complicates the psychological layers of Shakespeare's play, as this cinematic Macbeth increasingly appears to struggle against the pull of her textual destiny. In the beginning of the film, Macbeth is fully capable of either interrupting her Shakespearean outbursts *in medias res* ("'Stars hide your fires' – no, stop that!") or decoding them in her own terms ("'So foul and fair a day I have not seen.' We really kicked some ass.") But by the end, her decisive decline into insanity is signaled when she is handed the "tomorrow" soliloquy on a scroll by her servant (Lisa Rezac), and, upon reading it, compliments the verse profusely, exclaiming: "did you write that? I gotta tell ya, it's really good." Naturally, the servant takes credit for the work, claiming enthusiastically, "there's more where that came from!"

Like Shakespeare's Macbeth before her, this female Macbeth is foiled by her pathological embrace of the witches' prophecy which, ironically, she fails to interpret *literally enough*. It never occurs to her that Macduff could be the product of a C-section, or that Birnam Wood will come to Dunsinane not of its own volition but, rather, with a little help from soldiers in search of camouflage. Often seen with book in hand and citing Shakespearean verse by wrote, the witches in LiCalsi's film represent the lapse from cinematic fluidity – "an acute awareness of the nonfixity of boundaries" (Braidotti 1994: 56) – into the prescriptive assertion of textual certainty, ushering in Macbeth's tragic destiny. Ironically, in this comedy, it *is* tragic when Macbeth dies, not only because she's so likable but also because Malcolm, the new King, is devastated by her death. Indeed, he christens his reign by sobbing hysterically: "I could've changed her [from a lesbian] . . . I know I could've." And in some respects we can't help but believe him, for in this provisional space called Scotland, we are led to believe that anything is possible. Here, lesbians can be legally married, servants claim to authorize Shakespeare, homeless people sport Karl Lagerfeld fashions, and everyone "thanks God they're Scottish" – whatever that means. Indeed, whatever location this film gestures toward, we can be certain that it won't play in Peoria, but we can hope that it will emerge from the mists once and for all in another hundred years.

Conclusion: "If it isn't Scottish it's crap!" – Mike Myers

It seems only fitting that in *Macbeth: The Comedy*, it is the witches' wierdly worded prophecy that is associated with the menacing noir core of Shakespeare's play, much in the same way that film noir – despite its claims to esthetic autonomy – can never escape classification based on the detective fiction that precedes it. But if, as Marc Vernet provocatively claims, "Film noir is a collector's idea that, for the moment, can only be found in books" (1993: 26), then these recent *Macbeth*s remind us that Shakespeare, too, is a collector's item that, for the moment, can only be found in films. I would suggest, then, that it is not "Scotland" but *Shakespeare* who is the damned spot, Scot, or what you will, which these films relentlessly seek to traverse, inhabit and, ultimately, displace. But it is one thing to displace Scotland; it is something else entirely to replace Shakespeare as the "unhistorical kernel" that constitutes every new version of *Macbeth* as an unwitting act of repetition. Indeed, it should not surprise us that there is an outpouring of *Macbeth* films when, in the world at large, we are witnessing "an explosion of vested interests that claim their respective difference in the sense of regionalisms, localisms, ethnic wars, and relativism of all kinds" (Braidotti 1994: 146). Given the extent to which the horizon of reception has changed in the wake of the digital diaspora, the temptation has never been greater to retreat further into the private *jouissance* of our personal entertainment units. But the proper choice of pleasure, as Shakespeare repeatedly reminds us, lies not in reproducing the home theater of cruelty featured in *Macbeth* but, rather, in adopting a politics of movement that generates accountability from positionality. This, then, is the "damned spot" that marks the "X" – the point at which the high road and the low road meet in the recognition that *every* road can lead to the enabling dis-location that is Scotland, provided we are willing to leave the comforts of our homes.

Notes

I especially wish to thank Caroline Cox, Skip Willman, Marguerite Rippy, Allison LiCalsi, Patrick Murray, and Richard Burt.

1 My thanks to Richard Burt for letting me read his introduction and related material on digital culture and globalization from his book-in-progress, *Rechanneling Shakespeare across Media: Post-diasporic Citations and Spin-offs from Bollywood to Hollywood.*

2 In addition to the films and television adaptations I discuss, other versions include a French adult feature entitled *Macbeth* (dir. Silvio Bandinelli, 2000), *Macbeth* (dir. Jeremy Freeston, 1997), filmed in Scotland and set in the eleventh century, *Macbeth on the Estate* (dir. Penny Woolcock,1997), set in English housing projects, *Macbeth in Manhattan* (dir. Greg Lombardo, 1999), a play-within-a-film, and *Macbeth-Sangrador* (dir. Leonardo Henríquez, 1999), filmed in Venezuela. Two versions of *Lady Macbeth of Mzensk*, were also filmed, one of Dmitri Shostakovich's opera with soft-core sex scenes (dir. Petr Weigl, 1992), and the other of the short story on which the opera is based (dir. Roman Balayan, 1989). The latter is available on video but without English subtitles.

3 Richard Burt (1999: 77–125) makes the point that even Jeremy Freeston's use of Scotland in his 1997 *Macbeth* is highly mediated by *Braveheart.* On the reception of *Braveheart* in Scotland, see Maley 1998.

4 <http://www.insideout.co.uk/scots/briefhistory.shtml>.

5 *Braveheart* and *Rob Roy* also suggest conservative reactions to the multiculturalism debates of the 1990s, since these films represent places and identities that enable white men to get in on the game and "go ethnic" themselves.

6 See *Robocop* (Paul Verhoeven, 1987); *First Blood* (Ted Kotcheff, 1982); *Rambo: First Blood Part Two* (George Pan Cosmatos, 1985); *Rambo III* (Peter MacDonald, 1988); *Top Gun* (Tony Scott, 1986); *Diehard* (John McTiernan, 1988); *Superman* (Richard Donner, 1978); *Superman 2* (Richard Lester, 1980); *Superman 3* (Richard Lester, 1983); *Superman 4* (Sidney J. Furie, 1987). For a discussion of these films, see Susan Jeffords's *Hardbodies* (1994), particularly Chapter 1: "Life as a Man in the Reagan Revolution."

7 It is worth noting that Welles's *Macbeth* is now available in its "restored" form (with the Scottish accent) on both DVD and video.

8 Bogdanov's vision of Duncan as the post-industrial, obscene father may trace its imaginative origins – particularly given its production in the UK – to the Michael Gambon character in Peter Greenaway's *The Cook, the Thief, His Wife and Her Lover*, 1989.

9 See Jameson's chapter in *Postmodernism* (1992b), titled "Nostalgia for the Present."

10 For a thorough analysis of the global politics of the porn industry, see Joseph W. Slade 1997.

11 John Ashcroft was defeated in the Governor's race on November 7, 2000 by Mel Carhnahan, who died before election day but nonetheless beat Ashcroft.

12 On impotence and Shakespeare porn more generally, see Burt 1999.

13 See Benjamin 1968.

14 See <http://www.glenridge.org/Macbeth.mainpage.html>.

15 Appropriately, just before the premiere of *Scotland, PA*, Pat's (Maura Tierney's) *ER* character, recovering alcoholic Abby Lockhart, fell off the wagon after six years and drank a beer. Although her fall from grace received "jeers" in the "Picks and Pans" section of *TV Guide*, what seemed gratuitous on *ER* proved the perfect backstory to Pat McBeth's single moment of glory in *Scotland, PA*.

16 <http://www.lot47.com/scotlandpa/press_macbeth.html>.

17 I am especially grateful to Allison LiCalsi and Patrick Murray for generously providing me with a copy of *Macbeth: The Comedy*, as well as for offering detailed information about the conception and making of the film.

18 The opening credit sequence underscores this rather contestatory relationship between Shakespeare's play and LiCalsi's film. Alluding to a line at the beginning of Sam Taylor's 1929 *Taming of the Shrew* that reads "Based on the play by William Shakespeare, with additional dialogue by Sam Taylor," LiCalsi's film ups the ante with the statement: "story and additional dialogue by William Shakespeare." It seems only fitting that this allusion to a claim that mortified purists in the first-ever Shakespearean "talkie" should be revisited as an opportunity for virtually silencing Shakespeare in this millennial parody of *Macbeth.*

15

DOGME SHAKESPEARE 95

European cinema, anti-Hollywood sentiment, and the Bard

Amy Scott-Douglass

In 1995, a group of four Danish directors, Lars von Trier, Thomas Vinterberg, Søren Kragh-Jacobsen, and Kristian Levring, collectively known as the Dogme brethren, published a group statement against the Hollywood esthetic. "As never before," they claimed, "the superficial action and the superficial movie are receiving all the praise. The result is barren. An illusion of pathos and an illusion of love. Today a technological storm is raging of which the result is the elevation of cosmetics to God. By using new technology anyone at any time can wash the last grains of truth away in the deadly embrace of sensation."[1] The Dogme95 manifesto calls for a rejection of the spectacle and excess of the industry film. In the preface to their manifesto, the Dogme brethren ask, "[if] the 'supreme' task of the decadent filmmakers is to fool the audience . . . [i]s that what we are so proud of? Is that what the '100 years' have brought us? Illusions via which emotions can be communicated? . . . By the individual artist's free choice of trickery?" The manifesto advocates the purging of cinema, the eradication of screen tricks, a movement away from "the film of illusion," and a return to films that tell the truth. Endorsing what I would call a *retrolutionary* approach, a backward-looking movement in which the filmmakers attempt to improve the present state of cinema by a return to the technology of the past, the Dogme brothers swear their adherence to a "Vow of Chastity," a set of rules that restricts them from using, for example, special effects, camera filters, any unnatural lighting, or any added music.

In their rejection of tricks and illusion, the Dogme films are quite different from the plays of Shakespeare, who was never one to hesitate to use a trap door. But in their interest in drama that tells the truth, the Dogme brothers endorse a kind of Shakespearean esthetic. One thinks, for instance, of Hamlet's complaint against the groundlings "who for the most part are capable of nothing but inexplicable dumb shows and noise" (3.2.12) and his advice to the players "to hold as 'twere the mirror up to nature" (3.2.22).[2] Indeed, films by Dogme directors are often concerned with questions of perception and truth. "How do we know what we're seeing? How do we know what's true? what's right? what's normal? what's beautiful?" are questions these films ask us, films that manipulate our vision in order to present us with another way of looking at the world.[3] Bad eyesight that leads to spiritual insight and madness that leads to acuity are also themes in several English Renaissance plays. Like Kent in Shakespeare's *King Lear*, Dogme films encourage us to "see better" – to see the world, as Gloucester puts it, "feelingly" (1.1.159; 4.6.149). In this essay I discuss two of the four anchor Dogme films – Vinterberg's *The Celebration* [*Festen*] (1998) and Levring's *The King is Alive* (2000), focusing on their borrowings from Shakespeare's *Hamlet* and *King Lear* and their critical stances against Hollywood.[4] Before discussing the films themselves, however, it might be useful to consider the Dogme movement in the context of European/American debates about cinema at the turn of the millennium.

European cinemas and Hollywood

The Dogme manifesto is a postmodern collection of credos from past film movements, one that borrows heavily from the philosophies and vocabularies of statements by, in particular, neorealist and New Wave filmmakers at the same time that it faults them for their failings, claiming that "the goal was correct but the means were not!" Of particular interest is one discussion between several writers, actors and film theorists that was published in *Cahiers du Cinema* in 1965. In it, Jean-André Fieschi speaks against the kind of "spectacle" that American film had perfected, seeing "[e]xcesses of this kind" as "evidence of the irreversible victory of American cinema." Fieschi goes on to say, "it is precisely because a particular battle has been won that we must once again show ourselves to be demanding." The best way to counter Hollywood tendencies, Fieschi contends, is "certain rigid dogmatic control," of that the kind that *Cahiers* had been practicing for years (quoted in Comolli *et al.* 1986: 203). The word "dogmatic" is used several times in this discussion. Jean-Louis Comolli, *Cahiers*' editor, invokes the term in reference to *mise-en-scène*, the New Wave term for the director's method of film-making. "Once the film is made," Comolli explains, "the *mise-en-scène* has only an abstract or phantom existence. Or a dogmatic one" (quoted in Comolli *et al.* 1986: 206). Both New Wave definitions of "dogma" are relevant to the Danish film movement in that the Dogme manifesto works against Hollywood spectacle by drawing attention to what is normally left invisible: the director's creative process.

As plentiful as allusions to past cinematic movements may be, the Dogme manifesto is very much a 1990s text. The official title of the movement, "Dogme95," written as it is with no spaces in between the proper name and the last two digits of the year in which the Dogme rules went into effect, recalls the discursive convention that politicians and economists employ when referring to governmental councils and legislative texts.[5] In particular, the title "Dogme95" suggests that the movement should be regarded, at least in part, as a reaction to GATT93, the final year of the Uruguay round of General Agreement of Tariffs and Trade talks, and GATT94, the international agreement that resulted from those talks. Led by the president of the Motion Picture Association of America, Jack Valenti, who recruited Steven Spielberg and George Lucas to speak on behalf of Hollywood, the United States went into the Uruguay talks with the intention of removing all international trade restrictions on movies and other cultural commodities (Jeancolas 1998: 47–60; Mundo 1999: 134–9). Representatives of several European countries, especially France, resisted the American initiative, arguing that films are works of art and, therefore, as François Mitterand put it, "not mere merchandise [. . .] not simple commercial concerns" (quoted in Jeancolas 2000: 17). At the same time, several European film directors, among them Pedro

Almodóvar, Bernardo Bertolucci, and Wim Wenders, wrote an "open letter" to Spielberg and Martin Scorsese in which they worried that if their national and regional cinemas were denied trade restrictions like quotas and tariffs on American imports, Hollywood would quickly "annihilat[e]" them: "there will be no [. . .] European film industry left by the year 2000" (quoted in Pells 1997: 275). Ultimately, the French-led Europeans were successful: films were exempted from the GATT agreement signed in 1994, resulting in what has become known as *l'exception culturelle* or *l'exception française* (Hanley 1996). But filmmakers and filmgoers around the world would not ignore "Hollywood's inexorable drive toward a quasi monopoly, with European companies reduced to the marginal role of suppliers for special-interest audiences" (Singer 2000: 252). Anti-Hollywood sentiment continued to increase (Nowell-Smith 1998). It was out of this environment that Dogme95 was born.

In every rule of the Dogme manifesto is an implicit, tacit critique of the imperialistic dominance of the Hollywood movie industry.[6] In the late 1990s, the Dogme movement's potential for a revolution of the state of *Danish* film was not lost on Carsten Jensen, a political scientist at the University of Copenhagen:

> [T]here's another way to meet the Hollywood challenge, which is to accept that in the long run we just can't compete like that: there's just not enough money in the Danish industry to sustain that kind of defense. What we can do, though, is change the battlefield, [and] say, "We don't want to enter your competition. We'll set our own rules for filmmaking." So Dogme defines a new way of making films; or takes up an old one. But it says, "This is different. This is Danish. Not American."
>
> (Quoted in Kelly 2000: 74)

At the end of the millennium, the importance of making "not American" films was felt throughout Europe. In 1995, just three years before his death, Anatole Dauman, Polish filmmaker and one of the founders of the New Wave, wrote a public letter to "the Hollywood majors" and "French zealots," calling for a "declaration of interdependence, signed by the big names in world cinema [. . .] that would affirm the necessity of cultural pluralism as the defense of all national cinema industries, threatened with asphyxiation by American overdomination." In the same text, Dauman appealed to his fellow filmmakers "to defend cinema as art" (Dauman 1995: 28; my translation). Certainly many American filmmakers (and, for that matter, critics, theorists, and moviegoers) share the predominate European estimation that film is an art form. But, presumably, Dauman was out to convert Hollywood big shots like Spielberg and Lucas, the latter of whom has said, "I'm a craftsman. I don't make a work of art; I make a movie" (quoted in Sturhahn 1974: 28).

In the commodity versus culture, entertainment versus art, movie versus film debate, the world of Shakespeare cinema provides an especially fraught space. Shakespeare is both commodity and culture; entertainment and art; professional and poet; yet Hollywood, in aiming for mass-market audiences, has tended to focus on the former rather than the latter. Virtually all directors of Shakespeare films complain about the difficulties of dealing with Hollywood executives and the pressures that they are put under to change their films in order to make them more saleable. One thinks, for example, of Trevor Nunn's anger at being told to provide novice audiences with more plot synopsis at the beginning of his *Twelfth Night* (Buhler 2002: 152); of Ian McKellen's frustration at being contractually obliged to cast "at least two" American actors in his *Richard III* (Hopkins 2002: 50); of Kenneth Branagh's if-this-doesn't-make-them-happy-then-I-don't-know-what-they-want admission that he couldn't possibly pack more Hollywood convention into his *Much Ado about Nothing*.

Even Franco Zeffirelli, self-proclaimed popularizer of Shakespeare, has expressed mixed feelings about American cinema. In his autobiography, published in 1986, Zeffirelli wrote:

> The cinema survives because people in America still go to the movies. Cinema attendances are pretty low in Britain and Italy, though France has a viable audience for its home-made product. Yet in America that huge public, far from allowing the industry to take risks, has led to the relentless search for safe stories which fit a predictable market profile, anything that will make a killing at the box-office over the first weekend.
>
> (309)

Zeffirelli's book records his mixed feelings towards the US film industry; he alternates between declaiming against the American moviegoing public and blaming the Hollywood system while at the same time recognizing that his success as a Shakespearean film director came about largely because of the financial backing of the former and the ticket-buying practices of the latter. In many ways, Zeffirelli's Shakespeare films align with an esthetic code that is decidedly Hollywood: make sure that the cast includes as many bankable, beautiful stars as possible; cut the text to a fraction of the original; add plenty of song and visual splendor; in short, create a film that is commercially viable because of its conformity to industry film conventions.

If we were to place Zeffirelli (and certainly Branagh along with him) at one end of the spectrum of relations with Hollywood and trends in European Shakespeare on film, we might put Jean-Luc Godard at the other. When it comes to Hollywood and conventional cinema, Godard has said, "I know I'm definitely the opposition" (quoted in Sterrit 1998: 179). Quentin Tarantino has confessed that when he was a struggling actor he felt safe in putting Godard's *King Lear* (1987) on his *resumé* even though he wasn't in it because he thought, "there's no way in *hell* anyone is ever gonna see this movie!"[7] Purposefully less than marketable, Godard's film is not only a brilliant visual essay on Shakespeare's play, but also, as Peter S. Donaldson and Stephen Buhler have pointed out, the director's complaint against film as an industry and, as Godard puts it, a "Las Vegasized" America (Donaldson 1990: 189–225; Buhler 2002: 176–8). The film begins with a recording of a telephone conversation between Godard and a representative of Cannon, the Los Angeles-based film production company that, Godard thought, had betrayed him. At the end of the film, a prophecy is delivered: "Before seven years have passed, the Americans will lose everything they have in France in a great victory which God is sending to the French." This timeframe, curiously enough, corresponds with the previously mentioned Uruguay GATT negotiations, which began in 1987 (the same year in which Godard finished *King Lear*) and resulted in America's concession to France's demands in 1993.

On this axis of European directors' approaches to dealing with Hollywood, with Zeffirelli at one end and Godard at the other, the Dogme films prove difficult to place:

they tend to shift from pole to pole. While the Dogme brothers would certainly share Godard's disgust at the Las Vegasization of film, they, like Dauman, have encouraged other directors from several nations to make Dogme films, including not only Bertolucci, Bergman, and Kurosawa, but also *Hollywood* directors, in particular Spielberg and Scorsese (Roman 2001: 72, 79–80). The Dogme manifesto, it should be pointed out, is written in English, not Danish. And although neither Spielberg nor Scorsese has applied for a Dogme certificate, the Dogme website currently lists no fewer than thirty-one films that have: eight of them are Danish; eleven of them are United States productions. Critics of Dogme have faulted films like *The Celebration* for being too conventional and too market-driven (Weisberg 2000). But although the Dogme certificate has become a marketing tool and the critical and commercial success of *The Celebration* has led to more opportunities for Vinterberg and other Dogme directors, the directors still consider film as first and foremost an art form rather than a commodity. The "Vow of Chastity" ends with a sort of postscript that requires the Dogme director to "swear to refrain from personal taste" and to promise, "I am no longer an artist." Levring and Vinterberg admit that this eleventh rule, one of von Trier's contributions to the manifesto, proved impossible for them to keep. Says Levring, "the whole thing from the beginning was to get back to the *auteur* thinking. I believe that film is the director's medium. [. . .] the films I love were made by directors, not by producers" (quoted in Roman 2001: 54–5). Dogme's commitment to fighting for the rights of the independent artist over and against an overwhelmingly powerful film industry is, I would argue, especially evident not only in their minimalist approach to filmmaking but also in their uses of and borrowings from Shakespeare.

Dogmatic Shakespeare

The Celebration replicates Shakespeare's *Hamlet* in plot, structure, and character. Both Vinterberg and Mogens Rukov, Vinterberg's instructor at the Danish Film Institute and script adviser on *The Celebration*, have said that *The Celebration* is purposefully similar to *Hamlet* (quoted in Porton 1999: 18; Kelly 2000: 16). According to Rukov, *The Celebration* also contains allusions to Francis Ford Coppola's *Godfather* films (1972; 1974; 1990) as well as Ingmar Bergman's *Fanny and Alexander* [*Fanny och Alexander*] (1982) (Kelly 2000: 16), all of which, it is important to point out, borrow from Shakespeare: Coppola's tragic heroes have been compared to Macbeth and Hamlet, and in *Fanny and Alexander*, Alexander watches his ill father rehearsing the ghost in *Hamlet*; after his father dies, theatre and reality seem indistinguishable as Alexander is visited by his father's ghost and abused by his mother's new husband, Uncle Edvard.

As *The Celebration* begins, a thirtysomething named Christian, heir apparent to his father's estate and lodge, is returning home to Denmark from self-exile in Paris in order to attend his father's sixtieth birthday party. Just as Claudius and Gertrude's marriage followed a little too hotly on the heels of Hamlet Sr.'s funeral, so does patriarch Helge's self-indulgent celebration come too soon after the funeral of Christian's twin sister, Linda, who has recently drowned herself. Linda's spirit is not yet at rest, suggesting that justice has yet to be served. "There've always been ghosts in this house," says Christian's surviving sister, Helene, and just as in Shakespeare's play, this ghost comes with a message: Linda has left a note explaining that her suicide was the result of her father's incestuous abuse of her. Christian himself has come to the party with a few texts of his own: two speeches, from which he asks his father to choose. "It's a kind of 'home truth' speech," Christian says of his father's choice, and then proceeds to read what is the equivalent of Hamlet's *Mousetrap*. Called "When Dad Had His Bath," Christian's speech is a public narrative accusing Helge of raping the twins throughout their adolescence. In a subsequent speech, Christian accuses his father of murdering Linda. So this is a film that includes incest, a ghost, and a drowned sister in a story about a Christian "prince" returning home to Denmark to avenge a family member's murder at the hands of another family member.

Christian is similar to Hamlet in several details. For instance, both Hamlet and Christian make frequent use of the written word, especially as a tool for revenge. Indeed, Shakespeare's prince does a remarkable amount of writing: a memorandum of his encounter with his father's ghost; letters to Ophelia, to Gertrude, Horatio, and Claudius; a revision of Claudius's death writ; part of a play. Hamlet often discusses his life as if it were a piece of fiction in the midst of being written, as when he describes his adventures with Rosencrantz and Guildenstern as a "play" which he proved capable of rewriting (5.2.30–6). *The Celebration* highlights Hamlet's writerly tendencies more than any other adaptation of *Hamlet* that I have seen. There is no poison, no sword – Christian's only weapons against his father are words, words, words: his own texts and, eventually, his sister's. "I always thought you'd make a really good author one day," Christian's mother, Elsa, tells him, in the rebuttal that she delivers as an effort to contain any damage that might result from her son's accusations. It is not meant to be a compliment. Christian's rhetorical ability is taken as evidence that he's either lying or losing his grip on reality. *Alas, he's mad* seems to be the consensus. "He's sick in the head, Mum," says Michael, and Helge agrees, "He's sick, damn it." Helene asks her brother, point blank, "Christian, are you mad?" Christian's similarities to Hamlet don't stop there. In addition to being taken for a madman, Christian has trouble sleeping, and seems to lack interest in sex, presumably as a result of years of abuse. Helge chastises Christian for his lack of prowess: "there is so little man in you." This comment, of course, coming from a father who has repeatedly raped his children, is meant to reflect how little man there is in Helge. But even Pia, one of the "waitresses" at the lodge and Christian's eventual beloved,initially complains that he "can't even be bothered to look at a pretty girl [including herself] anymore." Certainly Christian's sexual restraint is in sharp contrast to the animalistic behavior of his brother, Michael. The virtuous Christian doesn't sleep with Pia until very late in the film, and the next morning he asks her to move in with him. Michael, on the other hand, is guilty of having an extramarital affair with Pia's friend and fellow-waitress Michelle, and when Michelle confronts Michael, he offers her hush money, threatens to fire her, and beats her up. Michael's mistreatment, most violent when directed towards women, especially Michelle and his poor wife Mette, extends to all of the staff, even to Lars, the hotel receptionist. To Christian, though, the staff members are not employees; they're friends. Helge's chef, Kim, doesn't think of Christian as his boss's son; he calls Christian "my boyhood buddy." As between Hamlet and Horatio, friendship, not patronage, provides the model for Christian's relationships.

This is not to say that Christian's relationships are all sweetness and innocence. Just as in *Hamlet* or, rather, in a Freudian interpretation of *Hamlet*, Christian demonstrates an inordinate love for a family member that borders on being incestuous. If Hamlet is in love with his mother, Christian is even more in love with his dead sister. The film suggests that Christian finally has sex with *Pia*, but it represents Christian's experience as a vision in which he converses with *Linda*'s ghost. Christian's hallucination begins when he asks for a glass of water, then passes out. The film jump cuts to Christian appearing at the foot of Pia's bed, and saying to her, "Pia my sister is here." This is far and away Christian's most poignant line of the film, and actor Ulrich Thomsen manages to deliver it with all of its nuances intact. Even after watching the scene several times, I am not sure how to punctuate the line. Is it "Pia, my sister is here" or "Pia, my sister, is here"? Is Christian telling Pia that his sister is in the house, or perhaps even in their bed? Or is Christian stating that Pia and his sister are, in effect, the same thing? "I love you," says Christian. "I love you, too" is the reply, but, again, it's not clear who's saying this: Linda or Pia. The scene cuts to Christian and Linda. "I miss you," Linda says; "I miss you too," says Christian, and the next image is of Christian waking up in bed with Pia, five hours later. By this point in the film, Vinterberg has already made the substitution of the thriving Pia for the dead Linda very clear. An early scene in which Helene finds Linda's suicide note by having Lars lie in the dead sister's bathtub and look up at the ceiling is intercut with a scene in which Pia lies in Christian's bathtub and looks up at the ceiling while immersing herself underwater. The sister/lover/bathtub montage concludes when Pia emerges from Christian's bath and, wrapped in a towel, says to him, "You fell asleep. Aren't you sleeping properly?" "Only with you," Christian replies – a curious answer, since the only thing that Christian's been holding onto in that bedroom is a glass of water. Here, and throughout the film, water is representative of Linda's spirit (as are light and air).[8] At the end of the film, while Pia is filling Christian's glass, he asks her to come live with him in Paris and then he returns the glass of water to her. What this act means is left wonderfully ambiguous: does it signify that Christian is finally free from his obsession with his sister, or does it mean that Pia is to drink in Linda's spirit and complete the process of sister/lover substitution? It is Pia who brings Linda's suicide note to Christian, it is Pia who halfway into the film whispers to the discouraged Christian "we're still here" ("we" meaning Pia and, in spirit, Linda), and it is Pia who stands behind Christian as he holds the suicide note up to Helene: not coincidentally, Pia's presentation of the ghost's reminder occurs in Vinterberg's film at the same point that Hamlet Sr.'s ghost returns in Shakespeare's play.

Levring's *The King is Alive* also includes references to *Hamlet*, but it borrows mostly from *King Lear*. Visually and aurally, it recalls Peter Brook's 1971 adaptation. Levring employs several of Brook's techniques, including jump cuts (Brook does this especially in the Tom of Bedlam scene; Levring does it throughout) and flashbacks at the end of the film (Brook cuts back to an image of Goneril in 1.1, holding an orb in her hand; Levring cuts back to individual images of each character riding in their bus). Both Brook and Levring highlight Shakespeare's motif of sight/perception and render this cinematically through out-of-focus shots, extreme close-ups, and scenes with actors falling out of the frames. The abrupt silence at certain points in both films is used to different effect by each director. In Brook's case, lack of sound establishes an eerie quality of existentialistic nothingness; in Levring's case, the silence, necessary because of the Dogme rules, underscores his reading of *King Lear* as a play about people's inability to communicate with and understand each other.

The King is Alive is about a group of tourists stranded in the desert in Namibia. One of them is Henry, a former London stage actor who somehow ended up in

California. (Henry insists that he still works in the theatre, but his luggage contains an awful lot of screenplays, which suggests his involvement in Hollywood film production, perhaps just as a reader to supplement his income.) When Henry sees the survival scenario playing out before him, he decides to busy himself by staging an adaptation of *King Lear*, and he begins to transcribe those parts of the play that he can remember, writing each character's individual lines on the backs of screenplays for feature films that go by names like *Space Killers* and *Love Story* (an act that can be read as a metaphor for Levring's Dogmatic desire to replace Hollywood junk with good films, or at the very least to finance independent films off of the backs of blockbusters). Initially, Henry offers the role of Cordelia to a young Frenchwoman named Catherine. Her refusal to play Cordelia sets off a string of rejections. The film suggests that there are two possible responses to rejection: people can either reconcile, or they can take revenge.

Indeed, one of the reasons that Henry has chosen to stage *King Lear* rather than another play is that Henry himself is trying to come to terms with his guilt and sense of loss at having rejected his own daughter, Uwina. Uwina is mentioned only once, early in the film, when Henry records a sort of spoken letter to her on his mini-tape recorder: "These past days I've been thinking of you more and more. I should've done that a long time ago. [. . .] I'm trying to imagine your life." Although Catherine and an American woman named Gina both vie for Henry's affections, neither one of them succeeds in taking the place of Uwina. The next time that Henry uses the tape recorder, he gives it to Amanda, the character who plays the Fool, with the instructions, "What I need is to hear *you*, not the Fool." Amanda *does* record her lines on tape, and Henry listens to her recorded voice in private: "Caught holy water in a dry house is better than this rain water out of doors. Good nuncle, in. Ask thy daughter's blessing. Here's a night pities neither wisemen nor fools." Just as the Fool replaces Cordelia in acts 2–4 of Shakespeare's play, so does Amanda serve as a replacement for the missing Uwina. Subsequent scenes show Amanda sitting by Henry near the fire, working on their lines, or Amanda sitting on the ground next to the enthroned Henry, watching the others rehearse. Unable to apologize to his daughter in real life, the tape recorder provides Henry with the means to facilitate a symbolic confession and reconciliation. Towards the end of the film, Henry/Lear talks into the recorder, presumably reciting Lear's lines to Cordelia in 4.7: "Pray you now, forget and forgive./I am old and foolish" (89–90).

While each stranded tourist plays a specific role in their production of *King Lear*, the correlation between the tourist and the Shakespeare character is not a matter of simple substitution. Ray plays Kent, but he becomes like Goneril's husband, Albany, when Liz attempts to cuckold him. Liz plays Goneril but she occasionally speaks Regan's lines. Catherine is Cordelia-like in her Frenchness and in her rejection of Henry, but she becomes a version of Goneril when she poisons Gina out of jealousy. Both Catherine and Liz are, at times, slightly reminiscent of Lady Macbeth; the murderous Catherine appears to be sleepwalking at one point, and Liz is unhappily childless.[9] Gina plays Cordelia, but she is also Edmund in that she is the one with the illegitimate past; moreover, although Charles/Gloucester loves her, she scorns and tricks him. Charles plays Gloucester, but he is also Goneril when he kills Gina and commits suicide. He's similar to Cordelia in that he dies from hanging, and he resembles Lear in his misogyny and preoccupation with aging.

What I find most interesting about Levring's film is its use of Shakespeare as a means to comment upon the current state of cinema. As Levring himself has pointed out,

The King is Alive is not just a film *by* a director following Dogme rules; it is a film *about* a director following Dogme rules, in that it is about a man who attempts to put on a play having been stripped of all theatrical devices: props, costumes, technological tools, even the text itself. To a certain extent, *The King is Alive* is a film about the history of film in the twentieth century. For instance, there are two Cordelias stranded in Africa. The first one is Catherine, the film's Cordelia, the bookish French woman, who is truly capable of understanding Shakespeare's verse but who ultimately refuses to accept a role in the play. The second Cordelia is the play's Cordelia, Gina, the America woman, who doesn't quite understand *King Lear* but who values Shakespeare because it's Shakespeare, and who is willing to prostitute her morals, and her body, so that the Shakespeare play can go on. The conflict between these two Cordelias can be read as a characteristic Dogmatic critique of both American and European cinema: the first Cordelia, representative of the French New Wave, has the correct approach to art and a natural affinity for Shakespeare; however, she ultimately shirks her responsibility and rejects the role she's been offered, at which point the second, techno-pop American Cordelia hungrily jumps at the chance to play the role, but, just like Hollywood, or, perhaps more accurately, just like the Dogme brothers' version of Hollywood, she lacks the intelligence or substance to deliver a quality performance. Levring establishes Gina and Catherine as representatives of Hollywood and the New Wave through references to both American films (e.g. Gina is played by Jennifer Jason Leigh, who starred as Caroline/Cordelia in *A Thousand Acres* (dir. Jocelyn Moohouse, 1997), the most recent American film adaptation of *King Lear*) and French ones (e.g. at a pivotal point, Catherine reads a novel by William Faulkner, an allusion to one of the most memorable scenes of Jean-Luc Godard's *Breathless* [*A Bout de Souffle*] (1960), in which an American woman reads Faulkner to her French boyfriend).

Levring's film attempts to reclaim Shakespeare *for* Europe, *from* Hollywood. Kunana, the African sage who watches the rehearsals of *King Lear*, says that no one understands the lines they're reciting except for Henry, an Englishman. Several scenes show Americans butchering Shakespeare's verse while Europeans roll their eyes and grunt in disgust. Not only are the Americans unable to understand Shakespeare, they're unable to understand anything European. In one pivotal scene, Gina attempts to befriend Catherine by asking her to tell a story in French. Catherine's story is a bitterly sarcastic reading of the stranded tourists' situation, in which she calls Gina a "cow" and a "Yankee bitch," and points out her "immense" and "great" "stupidity." Gina, who doesn't speak French, understands none of what Catherine is saying. When she finishes, Catherine tells Gina that her story was a "fairy tale." Gina claps her hands and squeals with delight, unaware that she has just been thoroughly insulted. She functions, in this scene, as a sort of metaphor for American moviegoing audiences who beg for stories and applaud fantastical films without questioning what they're watching, contented in their lack of understanding.

At the same time that Gina is portrayed as a dupe, it is only because of her that the Shakespeare production is able to continue. She plays Cordelia after Catherine rejects the part, and when Henry worries that he won't be able to find someone to play Gloucester, Gina promises to persuade Charles to accept the role. He eventually does so, in exchange for sex with Gina. In creating an American woman character that functions as a conduit to contemporary Shakespeare performance, Levring follows a tradition of Shakespearean film directors who invoke the American woman as a symbol of wealth or cultural capital, even as a representative of Hollywood. In films as diverse in tone and genre as *Tea with Mussolini* (1999), *Shakespeare in Love* (1998), Godard's *King Lear*, and *The King is Alive* it is *because* of the American woman that the show goes on.

In Zeffirelli's quasi-autobiographical film *Tea with Mussolini*, for instance, Zeffirelli's fictive version of himself, Luca Innocenti, has an *American* benefactress. She is, in fact, an obscenely wealthy American Jewess, named Elsa, and she has come to Italy for one reason and one reason only: to buy European art. Later in the film, though, we find that all of the paintings she has bought are fakes; for all her enthusiasm Elsa is unable to distinguish authentic art on her own.[10] This subtle commentary on Americans' inability to recognize true art establishes their place on Zeffirelli's cultural chain of being: *Tea with Mussolini* suggests that the best works of art are, not surprisingly, those that result from a happy marriage between English and Italian strengths: the English provide the beautifully poetic, morally sound plays, and the Italians, with their penchant for the visual arts, are the best suited to bring those words to life. What do the Americans provide? The money. After all, somebody has to pay for the wedding, and even if Americans aren't able to fully appreciate true art, they're plenty capable of financing it nevertheless.[11] It should be said that at the same time that the film points out Elsa's shortsightedness, she is nevertheless a character who is treated with respect and love; Elsa offers Zeffirelli/Luca the financial support that enables him to go to art school and eventually become a filmmaker. In return for her benevolence, Zeffirelli/Luca saves Elsa from the Gestapo, which is better treatment than the American woman usually receives in contemporary Shakespeare films.

Perhaps because of what she is made to represent (i.e. a container for men's displaced anxieties about Hollywood commercialism and, in some cases, fears of being dominated), the American benefactress usually ends up dying. In John Madden's *Shakespeare in Love*, the death is metaphorical; Viola (played by American Gwyneth Paltrow) resigns herself to an unhappy marriage in Virginia, her early retirement from the stage, and the end of her participation in the public sphere even as she presents Will (English actor Joseph Fiennes) with a bag full of money, making him poised to become the greatest playwright in the history of the world. Godard's *King Lear* also concludes with the death of an American woman: Cordelia (played by Molly Ringwald). According to the title cards and to William Shakespeare Jr. the Fifth's voice-over, Godard's Cordelia represents virtue (as in the virtue of the independent filmmaker) in its struggle against Lear-like power (as in the power of the film industry). Ultimately, Cordelia is killed by her father after, the suggestion is, having been raped; nevertheless, she retains her virtue, just as Godard, abused by the Cannon corporation, remained defiantly true to his art. Similarly, *The King is Alive* follows in the tradition of the sacrificial death of the American woman. But unlike Godard's Cordelia, who is associated with independent filmmaking, Levring's Gina/Cordelia is associated with Hollywood. She is not virtuous. Correspondingly, her death is brutal: she is poisoned and urinated on. Before she dies, she crawls out of her house, sliding across the sand on her belly as though she were a snake.[12]

Like Godard's *King Lear* and Levring's *The King is Alive*, *The Celebration* also contains a kind of anti-Hollywood message. Christian's challenge is to return to his father's world of corruption, incest, and false rhetoric, and to initiate a process of renewal by telling the simple truth, and by exposing the liars and purging the community of them. Christian's story is so non-rhetorical that he has to tell it several times. In a world which is used to glitz and glamour, his story is too true to be real; not fictive enough to be believed. His plight parallels that of the Dogme film director attempting to expose and offer an alternative to Hollywood corruption and decadence. Such self-referentiality is characteristic of Dogme films, and is often seen in the smallest of details. Surely it is significant, for instance, that the heroes of *The Celebration* and *The King is Alive* are in command of the written word. Christian's *Mousetrap* story and Henry's version of *King Lear*, painstakingly written out from memory, remind us that the Dogme directors are also writers, creating and producing their own screenplays, quite unlike Hollywood directors, who often film screenplays that have been written by someone else, and more similar to the French New Wave directors, who were characteristically screenplay writers and film theorists before they were directors.

The films are also similar in their treatment of Shakespeare. Vinterberg has said, "when you're a small country, you have to yell to get heard" (quoted in Kelly 2000: 120), but Dogmatic Shakespearean borrowings tend to be understated rather than explosive. There are no explicit references to Shakespeare in *The Celebration*; the name Hamlet is never mentioned. Hamlet is simply a part of Danish culture, and *The Celebration* takes as its rightful inheritance not just the plot of Shakespeare's play but also a specifically Scandinavian approach to the Hamlet story. Just as in Bergman's *Fanny and Alexander* and Gabriel Axel's *The Prince of Jutland* (1994), *The Celebration* presents a decidedly Scandinavian interpretation of *Hamlet*, with a focus on toasts and ghosts, and an ending that rewards rather than punishes Hamlet for taking revenge. Indeed, neither *The Celebration* nor *The King is Alive* advertises its Shakespearean borrowings. In *The King is Alive*, Shakespeare becomes a part of the characters' everyday lives, a means for attaining a better understanding of themselves. In this way, it is similar to Eric Rohmer's *A Tale of Winter* [*Le Conte d'Hiver*] (1992), in which intellectual discussions include references to Shakespeare as often as to Plato, and a performance of *The Winter's Tale* results in *the* crucial moment of higher understanding and intellectual clarity for the main character. In these films, Shakespeare plays are treated as philosophical texts, and the playwright is imagined as a sort of sage. How different from *Shakespeare in Love* co-writer Marc Norman's assertion that if Shakespeare were alive today, he'd be a Hollywood filmmaker: "he'd have a three-picture deal at Warner Brothers, he'd be driving a Porsche, and he'd be living in Bel-Air."[13]

While *The Celebration* and *The King is Alive* are both Dogme films that enlist Shakespeare in their critique of Hollywood, it would be misleading to ignore the differences between the two films. Vinterberg's film is in Danish, with a Danish cast and crew, written by a Danish director who lives in Denmark, and sponsored by the state-funded Danmark Radio. Levring's film is in English, with a predominately Anglo-American cast, written by a Danish director who has lived in South Africa and France, and who now resides in London. Indeed, according to the Danish government's definition, which requires at least twenty-five percent of the actors and technicians to be Danish in order for a film to receive state support (Hjørt 1996: 524), *The King is Alive* is not a Danish film. Moreover, these films belong to different phases in the Dogme movement. *The Celebration* is the first of the anchor Dogme films; *The King is Alive* is the last. In the years between the release of *The Celebration* and the production of *The King is Alive*, Dogme films became commercially viable products. Levring's budget was four times the amount of Vinterberg's, and, importantly, seventy percent of it was American money (Levring quoted in Roman 2001, 78). A comparison of Vinterberg's and

Levring's histories illustrates the difficulties that a European film movement faces and the danger of simply being bought out by Hollywood.[14] Perhaps it is because of this frustration that Levring's film seems more anti-Hollywood, more anti-American than Vinterberg's.

Acknowledgments

My thanks to Dominic Rainsford and Tim Maloney, who encouraged and responded to various drafts of this essay; to Kenneth Rothwell and José Ramon Díaz-Fernández, who coordinated the European Shakespeare films seminar at ESSE 2002, at which I presented an early draft of "Dogmatic Shakespeare"; and to the many ESSE 2002 attendees who offered useful feedback, including my fellow seminar participants and my "Danish brethren": Michael Skovmand, Niels Bugge Hansen, and Peter Mortensen.

Notes

1 The Dogme manifesto is reprinted in two published books on the history of the movement, Kelly (2000) and Roman (2001), and is also available, at least for the time being, on the official website: <http://www.dogme95.dk>.

2 All Shakespeare citations are taken from *The Complete Works of William Shakespeare*, ed. David Bevington (New York: Longman, 1997).

3 Several Dogme films feature blind or nearsighted characters, such as *The King is Alive*, von Trier's *Dancer in the Dark* (2000), and Harmony Korine's brilliant *julien donkey-boy* (1999). Additionally, the films often draw attention to the tools that we depend upon to see (e.g. mirrors, glasses) at the same time that techniques like out-of-focus shooting and the lack of artificial lighting often make it difficult actually *to see* what's happening in the films.

4 There are also also references to *King Lear* and *Macbeth* in Kragh-Jacobsen's *Mifune* [*Mifunes Sidst Sang*] (1999) and to *Othello* in both *The Celebration* and *The King is Alive*.

5 See, for example, Dunkley 1997: 28–9.

6 Indeed, the Dogme brothers' strategy is reminiscent of John Milton's tactic against the Hollywood of the seventeenth century: the Caroline court. In his own day, Milton objected to both the corrupt court system and its literature – its flowery poetry and dazzling masques. He attempted to counter the situation by advocating a kind of technical restraint: returning to a poetic style which allowed him to strip away the trappings of rhyme and rhetoric and get back to what he considered to be the truth. Milton's case illustrates how technical restraint can provide an artist with the means of making an extremely effective ideological statement.

7 Tarantino interviewed on *The Tonight Show with Jay Leno*, National Broadcasting Corporation, original air date December 9, 1997.

8 According to Vinterberg, "the sight of the water is the thing that reminds us of her" (quoted in Roman 2001: 81).

9 The suggestion that Ray is the one who is reluctant to parent a child is reminiscent of the interpretation of the Macbeths' relationship that appears in *Men of Respect* (dir. William Reilly, 1991). In that film, the implication is that Macbeth/Michael has made his wife, Ruthie, have an abortion. In *Throne of Blood*, Lady Asaji miscarries. Liz's frustration at not having a child adds a new poignancy to the line she delivers to Moses/Edmund: "this kiss [. . .] *conceive* and fare thee well" (4.2.22–4; italics mine).

10 As if to underscore the message that the US film industry and American popular audiences have been important to Zeffirelli's Shakespearean enterprises, Elsa, Luca's benefactress, is played by none other than multimedia diva Cher, who first became a star in the late 1960s, about the same time that Zeffirelli, with the help of American money, was bringing his adaptations of *The Taming of the Shrew* (1967) and *Romeo and Juliet* (1968) to movie-going masses.

The semantics of casting are telling: in spite of having won several film and TV awards, Cher is still largely considered to be a commercial success rather than an artistic one.

11 Indeed, the fictive Elsa's shopping spree for European paintings is reminiscent of the way in which real-life American moguls like Henry Huntington and Henry Clay Folger went about buying up English libraries, and especially collections of Shakespeare, in the first half of the twentieth century.

12 The treatment that Gina receives in Levring's film points to one of the weaknesses of the Dogme movement: the Dogme brothers are as *retrolutionary* in their treatment of the female subject as they are in their cinematic techniques. The language of the manifesto, for instance, entirely excludes women from *auteur* status. No wonder that Anne Wivel, originally the fifth founding member of the Dogme movement, thought of the society as "a man's club" and left because of the "male chauvinism." (This is the description of Wivel's experience according to Levring and Zentropa Managing Director Pete Aalbaek Jensen (quoted in Kelly 2000: 47, 89).) No wonder that Lone Scherfig, the only woman to direct a Dogme film, claims that she had to rely upon her "masculine side" in order to make *Italian for Beginners* [*Italiensk for Begyndere*] (2002) (quoted in Kelly 2000: 128). The king might be alive in Dogmewood, but the queen ain't.

13 Marc Norman's quote comes from one of the behind-the-scenes segments, entitled "Shakespeare in Love and on Film," on the *Shakespeare in Love* collector's edition DVD.

14 Levring's film was funded by Good Machine in New York. In 2002, Good Machine and USA Films were merged into Focus, which is owned by Universal Studios. Technically, the connection to Universal would make *The King is Alive* a Hollywood film; however, such a categorization is not irrefutable, since the film was produced almost a year before the merger. Nevertheless, even when national and independent cinemas are able to retain artistic and legal control at the level of production, there is still the possibility of studio takeover at the level of distribution. In the case of *The King is Alive*, Good Machine sold the distribution rights to IFC Films, and IFC Films handed distribution over to MGM, which had recently acquired twenty percent of Rainbow Bravo Entertainment, IFC's parent company (Hettrick). Ultimately, then, the American/Canadian DVD version of *The King is Alive*, released in October 2002, was distributed by MGM/United Artists Video, which, again, would make *The King is Alive* a Hollywood film.

16

SHAKESPEARE AND ASIA IN POSTDIASPORIC CINEMAS

Spin-offs and citations of the plays from Bollywood to Hollywood

Richard Burt

The dislocation of culture

While the concept of diaspora has gained wide academic currency among postcolonial critics since the 1990s as a way of opposing a transnational liberation to the oppressiveness of the nation-state and of turning the tables on the West, its meaning has been both expanded and redefined. Ien Ang observes that diaspora was once reserved for Jewish, Greek, and Armenian peoples, but "today the term tends to be used much more generically to refer to almost any people living outside its country of origin, be it Italians outside of Italy, Africans in the Caribbean, North America, or Western Europe, Cubans in Miami and Madrid, and Chinese all over the world" (2001: 75). A number of postcolonial critics have deconstructed diaspora as a site of identity politics, ethnic authenticity, internal coherence, sameness, and exclusion, and redefined it as border crossings, mobility, hybridity, and difference in dispersal (Chow 1994; Radhakrishnan 1996; Mishra 1997; Spivak 1996; Peters 1999; Ang 2001: 11–13, 75–92; Naficy 2001; Axel 2002). The diaspora is usually viewed by postcolonial critics as a forced migration in the twentieth century of people either from often poorer, developing Asian nations to developed, Western nations (the subaltern) or from upper, educated classes who either identify with the colonial, as in the case of V.S. Naipaul, or produce a hybrid, cosmopolitan critique of both the West and East, neither of whom, it is implied, can really understand itself except with the help of intellectuals freed from the parochialism of specific location (Rushdie 1992; Spivak 1993; Bhabha 1994; Said 1994). The celebration of diasporic cosmopolitanism has in turn generated a critique of the metropolitan-based intellectual as inauthentic and complicit with global capitalism (Dirlik 1997).

Despite the increasing centrality of disapora as a critical concept, postcolonial Shakespeare critics have not attended to it in literature, theater, or in film. Instead, the focus of postcolonial critics has been on globalization, intercultural performance, and the breakdown of oppositions between the local and the global, the foreign and the native, and so on.[1] A debate has emerged over Shakespeare's global/local reproductions. For some critics, globalization threatens to appropriate local, postcolonial productions of Shakespeare for neoliberal or neocolonial purposes. For others, globalization enables the indigenization and subversive appropriation of Shakespeare in postcolonial and developing nations. Despite their differences, critics on both sides of this debate agree that focusing on the local cases in which Shakespeare is appropriated and historicized is a corrective to a tendency to homogenize and blur differences between appropriations when attending to the global. Significant differences will blur, so the argument goes, unless we look at particular cases.[2] For critics of postcolonial Shakespeare, local analysis means attending not only to how Shakespeare is used as a means of writing back to the imperial center but to how he is used for the "natives'" own purposes. The point of focusing on the local, I take it, is not to examine how "the Other" reinvents Shakespeare to criticize the center, itself a residually Eurocentric task, but to examine how Shakespeare is used in the peripheries to reinvent foreign, postcolonial, and indigenous literary or theatrical traditions. Implicitly, critics assume that the less metropolitan the rewrite, the less the point of the rewrite is to produce a new interpretation of Shakespeare, the more the use of Shakespeare for non-Shakespearean purposes is valued (see Loomba 2001).

In this essay, I examine a range of art and mall films related to Shakespeare and Asia, including recognizable adaptations such as Michael Almereyda's *Hamlet* to acknowledged spin-offs such as *China Girl*, citations or allusions sometimes consisting of a single scene or even word (*Romeo Must Die*, *Sense and Sensibility*, *American Pie*, *The Golden Bowl*, *Moulin Rouge*, *The Emperor's Club*), and unacknowledged spin-offs that do or do not mention Shakespeare (*Dil Chahta Hai*, *The Glass House*, *Mississippi Masala*, *Monsoon Wedding*). I look at Asians in a variety of roles, including director, screenwriter, producer, and actor, in connection with a variety of Asian, British, and American cinemas. My aim is not simply to update postcolonial Shakespeare criticism by taking account of the relation between film and what Vijay Mishra (1997) has called a new "border" phase of the diaspora, to be distinguished from an older "exclusive" diaspora. I situate the films I discuss in relation to what I call the "postdisapora" in order to challenge the ways postcolonial critics have assimilated film, mass media, and new communications technologies to existing practices of postcolonial critique focused on literature and theater. Critics of Indian cinema have pointed out that Indians living in the diaspora connect back to the nation (as idealized homeland) via videos played in their homes on their VCRs (Mishra 2001: 235–69). More generally, Ang writes:

> it is only with . . . the increased possibilities for keeping in touch with the old homeland and with co-ethnics in other parts of the world through faster and cheaper jet transport, mass media, and electronic telecommunications, that migrant groups are collectively more inclined to see themselves not as minorities within nation-states, but as members of global diasporas which span national boundaries.
>
> (2000: 76)

Similarly, there has been a shift in Asian film studies from art film to popular film on the grounds that the latter has more international appeal.[3] In her study of Indian film, for example, Sumita S. Chakravarty writes: "Unlike Italian neorealism, the French New Wave, or Latin American Third Cinema esthetics, India's new cinema was neither revolutionary enough nor culturally distinct enough to influence aspiring filmmakers elsewhere. The popular cinema, on the other hand, can boast of audiences far beyond the shores of India and the pockets of diasporic Indians scattered all over the globe" (1993: 238). She then defends attention to popular, less obviously "engaged" films on grounds that "'the global' is increasingly shaped and apprehended in the realm of mass culture. And what has spawned more 'universalism' in film than Hollywood, more far-flung cultural crossings in the Third World than the Bombay film and the film song?" (1993: 308). For these critics, the diaspora, cinema, and mass media are means of advancing postcolonial critique as practiced by literary writers such as Salman Rushdie and theorists such as Gayatri Spivak, Dipesh Chakrabarty, and Homi Bhabha.

In my view, however, networks of media, communications technologies, and the disapora make these kinds of postcolonial critique obsolete.[4] Film's transnational production and reception puts it at odds with postcolonial accounts of literary and theatrical intercultural importing and exporting, appropriation, and so on precisely because they keep intact the concept of place and location even as they claim to deconstruct oppositions between foreign and native, East and West, center and margin.[5] Because film has always been international and world cultural, and now global, transnational, and hypermediated diasporic, attempts to read Asia-related cinematic citations of Shakespeare as "sly mimicry" and "ironic appropriation of master texts" (Mishra 2001: 44), to claim for them "adversarial subjectivity" (Shohat and Stam 1996: 166), and to celebrate their hybridity are all mooted. The very expansion of the concept of diaspora is, as Ang acknowledges, its "undoing" (75–92) and deconstruction as a critical concept.[6] Earlier models of diaspora assumed that there is a place of return, the adopted country was only a temporary residence. Now, that very notion of place no longer obtains (see de Sola-Morales Rubio 1992; Jameson 1992a; Auge 1995; Peters 1999; Iyer 2000; Naficy 2001). As Brian Keith Axel says, "the very common analytic posits that a homeland is originary and constitutive of a disapora, and very often supports an essentialization of origins and a fetishization of what is supposed to be found at the origin (e.g., tradition, religion, language, race). Nevertheless, for many diasporic groups, place, or place of origin, is not the primary issue" (2002: 411). Moreover, if mobility and hybridity are the overriding characteristic of the new border diaspora, characteristics that spell the end of an exclusive diaspora that managed to contain migrants in little colonies in the new countries, as Mishra and Ang insightfully argue, that very mobility and hybridity extends well beyond diasporic migrant communities, particularly when it comes to transnationalized cinemas.

While acknowledging that diasporas come from the West as well as from the East, postcolonial critics have written as if the diasporas were all Asian. The range of Shakespeare and Asia in postdiasporic cinemas is so extremely diverse that it throws into relief just how homogeneous such accounts of hybridity in postcolonial studies are, no matter how much hybridity is said to be deconstructed and inflected with difference. Current definitions of hybridity cannot coherently make sense of postdiasporic films as diverse as Ang Lee's *Sense and Sensibility*, James Ivory's *The Golden Bowl*, *Fuck Hamlet* (dir. Cheol-Mean Whoang, 1996),[7] *Romeo Must Die* (dir. Andrezj Bartkowak, 2000), and *China Girl* (dir. Abel Ferrara, 1987), which engage diasporas from Africa and Hong Kong to the United States in the twentieth century, from Italy to the United States in the nineteenth century, and from Korea to Germany in the late twentieth century. And even postcolonial Shakespeare adaptations such as BBC Four's bilingual *Twelfth Night* (dir. Tim Supple, 2003) engage multiple diasporas. In this BBC adaptation, Viola (Parminda

Nagra) and Sebastian (Ronny Jhutti) are Bollywood *filmi*-style Indian refugees shipwrecked in contemporary England. Shakespeare's language is kept, but lines occasionally appear in subtitles as the actors speak the lines in Urdu. The combination of race-blind casting (Orsino, Valentine, and the priest are played by African-British actors, Feste is played by an Indian-British actor, and Olivia and the rest of her household are white) and race as signifier complicates any attempt to read the film as a topical allegory of postcolonial immigration, legal and illegal, to Britain.[8] Moreover, the diversity of examples I discuss also suggests that the opposition between art film and popular film is still in place and it demands an account of the heterogeneity of the popular in its engagements with high-world culture. Bollywood films are marketed in the US not as popular Indian films but as foreign art films, and films like Almereyda's *Hamlet* and Ferrara's *China Girl* are hybrid engagements with both art and popular films. Film (and its video and DVD reproductions) is not an exception to the rule of postcolonialism but the medium by which Shakespeare circulates most widely, having an impact in other kinds of Shakespeare performance such as live theater. And film often simulates live Shakespeare performance (Burt 2002c) in relation to race. The debate between postcolonial critics who view the Asian Shakespeare theater productions performed in the West as tainted by imperialism and critics who defend such performances is made equally irrelevant by the fact that there is no location not subject to globalization.[9]

To be sure, "location, location, location" is still the mantra of filmmakers, but while location is often massively encoded in the films I discuss, that encoding is done with reference to various media and cinematic genres.[10] Attention to the geopolitical esthetics of the cinema (Jameson 1995) aside, film cannot usefully be mapped on to geography.[11] Diaspora is only one version of global mobility. This is not to say that everyone is diasporic, of course; it is to say that in the postdiasporic present a distinction between diasporic mobility, migration, and border crossings, on the one hand, and global mobility and migrations, on the other, is not particularly meaningful or useful when it comes to understanding cinema and mass media in general and to filmed Shakespeare in particular. Given that filmed Shakespeare is already multiracial and multinational in the West, it hardly makes sense to regard either Asian or Asia diasporic appropriations as subversive.

To refuse to acknowledge fully the way film and media have undone diaspora (either old or new) as a critical concept and shift focus on migration, media, and mobility in general is to condemn oneself to debating ad nauseum and unproductively whether a given film has an authentic or inauthentic ethnicity or, in a variation on the same, whether the film engages in the commodification of hybridity or produces a genuine hybridity, whether it domesticates the Other or preserves the Other's strangeness, as if these distinctions were clear and significant, as if the Other culture were static and existed the same way across history. Rather than "intensify the local" (Wilson and Dissanayake 1996) or find the "global in the local" (Dirlik 1997) or focus on "border crossings" to combat or demystify the complicity of Shakespeare reproductions (and academic criticism of them) with social and economic inequities produced by globalization, I want to intensify both the cinema's citation and even allegorization of Shakespeare in relation to mass media and postdiasporic placelessness. By focusing on the ways in which film and media have undone diaspora, we can break out of the log jam of current postcolonial debates and gain a deeper understanding of Shakespeare's cinematic migrations and mobility across the globe, the persistence of the national in transnational cinemas, and the end of third world cinema.

Several significant consequences follow from shifting from a model of cinematic Shakespeares based on global/local performance to one based on media and post-diaspora. In terms of Shakespeare, it means addressing his postcanonical status, the full range of citations and spin-offs from the hermeneutic to the post-hermeneutic. If Shakespeare in film (and also in theater) is now that which is not at all connected to "place" or the "local," how are we to "replace place" (Huhtamo 1999), think the alternative in a way that does not amount to a regressive account of Shakespeare's universality or to a reductive account of his global homogenization? More interesting than the infinite variety of Shakespeare's citations is the fact that registering them is so often unimportant for the plot, success, and meaningfulness of the mediatic text.[12] If most people, including academics and film critics, don't register the citations, in other words, it doesn't appear to make any difference.[13] I contend that cinematic Shakespeares function as a type of currency without any particular meaning, location, traceable source of value, but as nevertheless somehow signs of that which can be exchanged. Like economic capital itself, Shakespeare is no longer connected to a "gold standard," or to the British pound, or to any particular source of value such as Pierre Bourdieu's notion of "cultural capital." The range of cinematic Shakespeares, including the post-hermeneutic, unspeakable variety, represents precisely that which has become a mark of postdiasporic transit, media, and flex (if not flux).

Three related consequences of a postdiaspora model of film and media can be grasped by attending to Shakespeare. The first relates to space. There is a tendency to engage in somewhat superficial deconstruction in postcolonial criticism – despite moves to collapse oppositions in favor of mixing and hybridity, places and locations remain in place – a geographical orientation remains the same as orientalism and occidentalism are put into question. But the consequences of mobility and stasis seen in the Shakespeare and Asia related postdiasporic films I discuss are processes of dis-Westernization and dis-Orientalization, processes far too subtle to be explained, for example, as neo-orientalist forms of Asian "chic."

The second, related consequence of acknowledging the postdiasporic model of media and mobility is time, particularly as it involves the transnational cinemas and the marketing of cinemas as national entities. Like the superficial deconstruction of postcolonial criticism, a superficial historicism forgoes attention to the nuances and complexities of historical transformations in favor of whatever can crudely be narrated inside of binary oppositions. The result is that history amounts to twin accounts of domestication and imperialism or resistance and subversive appropriation. Diaspora is about mobility and speed, but also about slowness and, in the case of cinema distribution and impact, time lag. When it comes to Indian cinema, the reception abroad is quite different from the national reception. As Rachel Dwyer and Divia Patel note:

> while this global visual culture has succeeded in engaging the diasporic audience, there is a certain irony that, as "filmi style" is being discarded by the Hindi film industry, this is the means by which it is finally gaining the recognition it has long sought in the West. Since around 2000 "Bollywood" has become a buzz word in the West, recognized and celebrated as denoting the flamboyant attractions of the Hindi movie.
>
> (2002: 217)

A deeper irony that Dwyer and Patel note is that the attention to Bollywood has occurred at the moment it is in decline. For film critics, Bollywood's "golden age" ended in the 1970s. The 1990s has marked a serious and rapid decline and even the plagiarism of Hollywood movie scripts (Joshi 2001; Levich 2002; *Guardian* 2002). To this extent a fiction of diaspora remains within the postdiaspora, a fiction of national cinema inside of cinema's transnationalization. If the new, border diaspora is about identification with what Salman Rushdie calls "imaginary homelands," or what two postcolonial critics have called the "diasporic imaginary" (Mishra 1997; Axel 2002), a lost place, a place of no return, then the postdiaspora is the imaginary of the diasporic imaginary, not post-imaginary. In Raymond William's (1977) terms, we may glimpse a residual attachment to national film industries and products, "Indian" or authentic, at this moment of emergent globalization and transnationalization of cinema.

A postdiaspora model yields not triumphalism of national cinemas (as they become not only international but transnational) but abjection due to stasis and slowness, being stuck, in a rut, in decline. Abjection is not a function of uneven economic developments globally. To be sure, there are uneven developments when it comes to new electronic and digital communications technologies.[14] For example, the Singapore film spin-off of *Romeo and Juliet*, *Chicken Rice Wars* (dir. Cheek Kong Chea, 2000), was reproduced as a CD-ROM rather than a DVD, and the film itself only refers to MTV, while the *Romeo Must Die* and *Moulin Rouge* DVDs have actual MTV music video spin-offs on them. There is also a digital divide in the access to different visual technologies. While many diasporic Indians and increasingly upper-middle-class urban Indians have access to VCRs and DVDs, the bulk of Bollywood viewers are the subaltern masses who only have access to the cinema (and increasingly shared televisions in slums). Yet the North/South digital divide is not just a matter of across the board lags in time and access; even in remote, unmodernized parts of Asia where there is no running water or heating, one can nevertheless hook up a lap top computer or use a cell phone. Moreover, global cities like Tokyo and Singapore are more hypermediated than any in the West.

Cinematic abjection in Shakespeare related cinema runs across migration and mobility, whether Asian diasporic or Western. Consider two films involving Shakespeare that focus on American and English migration. In *The Talented Mr. Ripley*, for example, Ripley's murderous envy is signaled both by a postcard he gives Dickie that cites Macbeth's "stars hide your fires" and a later performance of Verdi's *Otello*. Ripley's use of Shakespeare is not simply a product of his abject wannabe upper-class Englishman obsession that results from his migration from the US to an ex-patriot community of Anglophilic Americans (played, in the chief roles, by an English actor, Jude Law, and by Gwyneth Paltrow, an American who usually plays Englishwomen) living in Italy. An equally abject citation of Shakespeare may be seen in the James Whale biopic, *Gods and Monsters* (dir. Bill Condon, 1998). At a party for the closeted gay director George Cukor, the elder Whale, who early in his life had migrated from England to Los Angeles, wittily embarrasses the guest of honor, but later, in a defeated moment, he cites Hamlet's "O that this too, too solid flesh would melt."[15] The cinematic abject is linked to migration *tout court*, then, not just to Asian diasporic migrations, but to migrations among Caucasians in Western cinema as well.[16]

The last consequence of the postdiaspora for Shakespeare, film and postcolonial studies I want to consider is that it calls into question Marxist and postcolonial explanations of the end of the so-called third cinema (Pines and Willemen 1989) and collapses a related opposition favored by many leftist film critics between popular memory and official history (see Gabreil 1989; Cham 2001; Landy and Villarejo 1995; Landy 1986 and 1996). Fredric Jameson has acknowledged that "the very term Third World seems to have become an embarrassment in a period in which the realities of the economic have seemed to supplant the possibilities of collective struggle, in which human agency and politics seem to have been dissolved by the global corporate institutions we call late capitalism" (1995: 186), and he excuses the failure of Third World cinema of the 1960s and 1970s by offering a series of explanations: it "could be crushed politically . . . or the filmic experiment itself could fail to take, or could be reabsorbed and co-opted by an enlarged and more ecumenical mainstream (or classic Hollywood) cinema" (1995: 187). Jameson sees the failure as resulting from external pressures: the cinema is essentially authentic, but is co-opted. Yet this account of the third cinema has no force given a postdiasporic, mediatized world and transnational cinema. For there is no automatically progressive, authentic popular memory outside of media, nor is film a repository for "popular memory" somehow outside or opposed to official history since that history is also told through the same media and just as constructed as official history.

The remainder of this chapter falls into two parts. In the first, I examine a diasporic Australian, an Indian, and two Asian diasporic film directors in order to analyze Shakespeare's place in the cinematic undoing of diaspora. In the second, I address Asian characters as racial minorities and the circulation of the abject among Caucasian characters, some ethnic minorities in their own right, in Western films directed by Caucasians.

Shakespeare goes Bollywood

With few exceptions, postcolonial Shakespeare criticism has focused almost exclusively on Shakespeare in India, and I will therefore begin by considering how exchanges between Bollywood and Hollywood in the 1990s and millennium call into question postcolonial accounts of intercultural performance. The name Bollywood, combining Bombay and Hollywood, of course marks the transnational hybridity of Bombay Indian cinema.[17] Shakespeare has become almost inescapable in Bollywood film even as Shakespeare has been decolonized and decanonized. As Indian filmmakers target an international audience in the millennium, Shakespeare – the plays, Hollywood appropriations of them, and the cultural phenomenon – is apparently unavoidable. Consider, for example, director Sanjay Leela Bansali's characterization of his remake of *Devdas* (2002), a film that had already been made three times (in 1928, 1935, and 1955). It tells the story of Devdas, a man who falls in love with a woman who is forced by her family to marry a much older man, and he then takes up with a prostitute and becomes a drunk. Bansali describes his film, which runs for almost three hours and was "made with a mainstream audience in mind" as "a cross between *Shakespeare in Love* and *Moulin Rouge*, a film that dipped into music from Bollywood films."[18] Whether Bansali's references are meant seriously or are cynical packaging to market the movie in Western, mainstream Hollywood terms, they suggest the difficulty of placing Shakespeare in Indian cinemas since the difference between Hollywood and Bollywood is being dissolved. For Bansali, a Western film that remakes Bollywood and alludes to Shakespeare, *Moulin Rouge*, becomes a model for marketing a Bollywood film in the West.[19] Bollywood directors oriented to Hollywood also make use of Shakespeare. In response to an interviewer's question posed to Subhash K. Jha, a Bollywood director well known for adapting Hollywood films, about whether his next film, *Kutumb*, would be faithful to *The Godfather*, Jha said: "Actually, it's more Shakespeare's *King Lear*, more to do with what Francis Ford Coppola said during the making of *The Godfather*" (Raaz 2003).[20] (On *King Lear* as a source for *The Godfather III*, see Burt 1999: 158.)

Similarly, in the Indian diaspora, Shakespeare is used to sell Bollywood to a global audience. A forthcoming adaptation of *Hamlet* called *Aditya*, to be directed by Tarsem Singh, director of the R.E.M. music video "Losing My Religion" and *The Cell* (2001), using an all-Bollywood cast, and shot in India and in England, is referred to in the Bollywood press as a Hollywood film. The American producer markets its lead actor, Bollywood star Hrithik Roshan, as "an Indian Hamlet", adding that Hrithik is an unfamiliar name and therefore "we will have to sell him through two known names – Hamlet and Shakespeare" (Sengupta 2001).[21] Although *Agni Varsha: The Fire and the Rain* (dir. Arjun Sajnani, 2002) was adapted from the play of the same name by Girish Karnadj based on the myth of Yavakri from the Indian epic *Mahabharata*, two major US film critics (see Holden 2002; Thomas 2002) compared the film to *Hamlet* and the official film website links both reviews.[22]

Further mixing Shakespeare and East and West cinemas and aimed both at Indian and non-Indian audiences, the Canadian film *Bollywood/Hollywood* (dir. Deepa Mehta, 2002) has a Shakespeare-quoting grandmother (Dina Pathak), and ends with the hero, Raoul (Rahul Khanna), climbing onto an old truck to propose to Sue (Lisa Ray), the heroine, "on her balcony Shakespeare-style" (Covert 2002).[23] According to the director, "*Bollywood/Hollywood* is not a Bollywood film. It is a Canadian film inspired and infused with Bollywood and Hollywood traditions" (Chhabra 2002). Mehta says she "would call it a hybrid film, a fusion film. Its composer is from Bollywood and its choreographer is from Toronto who works in Hollywood" (Pais 2002). A similar dislocation of Bollywood is registered in the UK film, *Bollywood Queen* (dir. Jeremy Wooding, 2002). According to the English director, the film, which includes a mixed English and British-Asian cast and Hindi songs, is a "*Romeo and Juliet* style drama set in London, a musical genre meets *Romeo and Juliet* . . . that reverberates around a Bollywood theme" (Anon. 2002). And the British actor Jimi Mistry, who plays the hero, an Indian dancer, in the "Hollywood Bollywood" film, *The Guru* (2002), also plays a psychotic Sikh in the UK gangland take on *King Lear, My Kingdom* (dir. Don Boyd, 2001).[24] Clearly, Bollywood as signifier of film is not identical to film produced in Bollywood film studios located in Mumbai.

Even when an Indian film director wants to market internationally what he regards as an Indian film unlike Hollywood films, the effort does not succeed in leaving Shakespeare and Western cinema behind. Consider *Taj Mahal: An Eternal Love Story* (dir. Bharat Bala, 2003), India's first film in the IMAX format, produced by US-based Scott Swofford with short filmmaker Bharat Bala as director. The film was budgeted at seven million US dollars and was shot entirely on location in northern India. "The world sees India through [Sir Richard] Attenborough's film, *Gandhi*," said Bala, adding: "But I want to show that there is more to us than that. The *Taj Mahal* is also an excellent example of human commitment. It is time we made the love story behind it as popular as Shakespeare's *Romeo and Juliet*."[25] The director wants to drop Attenborough's film as a lens Westerners use to see India, but ironically cannot escape measuring his love story against the most famous British one.[26] And Shakespeare is cited in relation to popular Bollywood movie stars. For the sixtieth birthday of her husband Amitabh Bachchan, one of Bollywood's most famous movie stars, actress Jaya Bachchan published a book entitled *To Be or Not To Be: Amitabh Bachchanon* (2002) on his life and career. In an interview, Jaya explains the meaning of the title: "Amit is indecisive in real life. Also, my father-in-law translated Shakespeare's *Hamlet* into Hindi. So in a way, this book is also a tribute to him."[27]

The circulation of Shakespeare, Bollywood, and Hollywood does not translate, as some might expect, into hegemonic impositions, neocolonialism, residual internalized colonialism, or subversive indigenizations.[28] Consider, for example, exchanges between Shakespeare and Bollywood in Luhrmann's *Moulin Rouge* and Akhtar's *Dil Chahta Hai* (*The Heart Desires*), both released in 2001. The presence of Bollywood and Shakespeare in *Moulin Rouge* demands to be understood in relation to the film's transnational production. Set in Bohemian, nineteenth-century Paris but anachronistically covering pop hits such as The Police's "Roxanne," Madonna's "Like a Virgin," Nirvana's "Smells Like Teen Spirit," and Patti Labelle's "Lady Marmalade" with tango and other dance forms, *Moulin Rouge* was financed both by Hollywood and Australian backers.[29] Moreover, the film's director and female star, Nicole Kidman, are both Australian, and its male lead, Ewan McGregor, is a Scot. Shakespeare is mentioned in relation to the film's final musical number, "Spectacular Spectacular," derived from Bollywood's Formula 44, in which an Indian courtesan chooses a penniless sitar player over the Maharajah.

Dancer Nini Legs in the Air (Caroline O'Connor) lip synchs to Hindi lyrics sung by Hindi film music queen Alka Yagnik. Nini's performance is followed by the heroine Santine's (Nicole Kidman), in which Santine covers her opening song, itself a cover of Marilyn Monroe's "Diamonds Are a Girl's Best Friend." When this number is rehearsed, the Bohemian artists' evil patron, the Duke of Monroth (Richard Roxburgh), demands it be rewritten so that the Maharajah, not the sitar player, wins the courtesan. And the heartless dancer Nini Legs in the Air sits on writer Christian's (Ewan McGregor) lap and says "Don't worry, Shakespeare. You'll get your ending . . . [apparently reassuring and consoling him] . . . once the Duke gets his . . . end . . . in!" [she laughs spitefully and he throws her off his lap angrily].[30]

Figure 16.1 Shakespeare goes Bollywood.

The force of "Shakespeare" here, hardly limited to the sarcastic and disparaging use Nini makes of it given Luhrmann's own prior film, *William Shakespeare's Romeo + Juliet*, has to do not with a particular place (the Paris of the film is a total fantasy) or time (all kinds of historical references co-exist) or particular cinematic or dance codes but a variety of media and performance styles, theater, typing, singing, and dancing chief among them. From one perspective, *Moulin Rouge* sympathizes with a writer who, like Shakespeare, is relatively powerless in the theater whose products may be rewritten by "the money." Yet from another, it is precisely the extent to which an older model of authorial universality (Shakespeare/theater) has been displaced by a new kind of transnational *auteur* (Luhrmann/digital film). The film's camp parody and reaffirmation for the Bohemian's code of truth, love, and beauty depends on and marks the displacement of Shakespeare on celluloid film adaptation by the digitalization of film.

The Shakespeare reference in conjunction with Bollywood in *Moulin Rouge* marks not only a more explicit use of Bollywood by Luhrmann but Luhrmann's move from celluloid to digital film. All of *Moulin Rouge*'s many special effects were achieved digitally. And it is worth noting that the second, special DVD edition of *William Shakespeare's Romeo + Juliet* appeared shortly *after* the release of the DVD edition of *Moulin Rouge!*. Nini Legs in the Air's reference to "Shakespeare" in conjunction with the Bollywood number that follows, registers, then, the decentering of the literary and dramatic author and the recentering of the (digital) cinematic *auteur*: Shakespeare on film itself has been transformed and abjected by a global capitalist digital culture.

In *Dil Chahta Hai*, touted as a Hollywood-Bollywood film and hence what I would call a "hyp(er)brized" cinema, Shakespeare and the Indian diaspora in Australia come together. The film draws loosely upon the Benedick and Beatrice romance in Shakespeare's *Much Ado About Nothing* (in addition to drawing on the *Three Stooges*, *Baywatch*, and MTV videos, among other Western sources).[31]

Shakespeare is first explicitly referenced in Sydney, Australia, during the first major dance number involving the Beatrice and Benedick characters, Shalini (Preity Zinta) and Aakash (Aamir Khan). As Shalini enters the frame, we see a sailboat at harbor to her right named *Much Ado*. Indians and Shakespeare, that is, meet up through a

Figure 16.2 Bollywood goes Shakespeare.

diasporic passage out of India, with Shakespeare not only in a sailboat on the water but in a theater on land as well. The film's explicit turn to Shakespeare follows a date between the characters at a cineplex in which Shalini is angry with Aakash for not appreciating a good movie, left unnamed, but identified as a romantic melodrama. Shalini then takes Aakash to the opera so that he can learn that "true love does exist." The opera is, of all things, *Troilus and Cressida*, composed by the Englishman William Walton for the BBC. Some critics who have not seen *Dil Chahta Hai* might think that it uses *Troilus* to send up the many *Romeo and Juliet* Bollywood adaptations.[32] After all, Shakespeare's most acidic and generically hybrid play could hardly be regarded by any sane person as a romance about true love. Yet such is not the case in *Dil Chahta Hai*: Shalini explains the opera's plot to Aakash as a tragic romance, and by the end of the performance, Aakash has discovered that he really is deeply in love with Shalini. If the opera is not used ironically in the film, however, its citation situates Shakespeare in a rather complex way in relation to the film's plot. The fragmented title *Much Ado* signals not only the looseness of the film's retelling of the Beatrice and Benedick plot but Shakespeare's secondariness in the present. Moreover, the *Much Ado* reference certainly brings Shakespeare's *Troilus and Cressida* to mind when we see the English opera, as does the Shakespearean spelling of Cressida in the subtitles, but Walton modeled the opera, itself imported to Sydney in the film, on Chaucer's poem *Troilus and Criseyde* rather than on Shakespeare's play directly. The opera performance indirectly suggests Shakespeare's secondariness in another way, namely, by calling into question Shalini's distinction between film (mere fluff) and live performance (high culture). Before composing *Troilus and Cressida*, Walton had written the scores for Laurence Olivier's three Shakespeare films, *Henry V* (1944), *Hamlet* (1947), and *Richard III* (1954), as well as Paul Czinner's 1936 film of *As You Like* It (when he and Olivier first met), and *Richard III* was released the same year *Troilus* premiered. It doesn't really make sense to ask how close the plot of *Dil Chahta Hai* is to *Much Ado* or to try to interpret the film as a retelling of the play, because the film's implicit point is that there is no Shakespeare original or even "Shakespeare" version to locate in a specific space or time.

Nor does it make sense to ask whether the characters who have gone to Sydney and are closer to Shakespeare are less authentic than the characters who remain exclusively in Bombay. While *Dil Chahta Hai* represents particular geographical locations, its *mise-en-scène* is relentlessly transnational (Mercedes-Benz cars, English car tires, English and Hindi languages, American slang, and so on) and it does not locate Shakespeare in a particular place (Shakespeare is both on water and land, both in Australia and India) or in a particular medium (sailboat name, live opera, and more remotely, film score). Moreover, Shakespeare in Indian cinema was tied very early on to the Parsi diaspora in India. Filmed versions of the plays were initially of Parsi theater productions, complete with songs and dances. In grasping how *Dil Chahta Hai* quietly calls attention to the way Shakespeare's plays were themselves adaptations, we may also understand why the film loosely adapts *Much Ado* rather than one of Shakespeare's other comedies. Just as the usual pastoral opposition between city (or court) and country in Shakespeare's comedies is not present in *Much Ado*, which takes place entirely in the city of Messina, so the opposition between Bombay and Sydney, between Indians and diasporic Indians does not signify in the film. The diaspora is not a site of abjection or assimilation. Shalini's and Aakash's migrations are occasioned not by crime or business failure, but by marriage and management. Aakash runs a multiracial workforce for his father's company, and is no different from his friends for having gone temporarily to Sydney. If there is no Shakespeare original but only adaptations, there is also no Indian original to be opposed to diasporic secondariness and abjection.

Shakespeare masala

Perhaps even more than Bollywood film, Indian and Asian diasporic cinemas have received the lion's share of critical attention because they are the heirs to the idea of a third cinema: diasporic films open up hybrid spaces, both for film or for criticism, from which the hybrid director or critic can explain both Hollywood and Bollywood cinemas to themselves. The Indian diasporic films of US-based and Harvard-educated director Mira Nair have been lauded in these terms, with critics arguing that Nair's hybridization allows her a critical distance on India and the West. Other critics have positioned her as inauthentic, however. She is said to engage in the commodification of hybridity (Shaha 1987; Meer 1991; Stuart 1993; Mehta 1996b; Bhavnani 2000; Sharma 2001; Bose and Varghese 2001; Feldvoss 2002). R. Rhadakrishnan condemns *Mississippi Masala*, for example, for making "light of the historical ingredients that go into making 'masala'" (1996: 208). What has gone unnoticed in these debates over Nair's films is the use of Shakespeare. Nair's *Mississippi Masala* (1991) does not directly refer to *Romeo and Juliet* but its setting of a star-crossed interracial romance in the Southern US differs little from Bollywood films such as *Bobby* (dir. Raj Kapoor, 1973) and *Henna* (dir. Randhir Kapoor, 1991) that remake the play without referring to it. To be sure, Nair's films are more Western, closer to the European-influenced art films of Satyajit Ray and Aparna Sen than to the Bollywood films of Mehboob Khan and others. Yet there is no significant difference in the way Shakespeare is used in films made by Indians based in India, either Bollywood directors such as Raj Kapoor and Romesh Sippy or art directors like Ray, and an Indian filmmaker like Nair who is based in the US. Similarly, Nair's *Monsoon Wedding* (2001), a story of an arranged wedding among wealthy Punjabis, resembles in many respects a Shakespearean comedy: the classic Bollywood "kiss in the rain" scene here functions like the transgressive sex scenes in the woods in *A Midsummer Night's Dream*; there are multiple plots with elite characters and a low, worker character, one of a group of "rude mechanicals," and maid (kind of like *A Midsummer Night's Dream* meets *As You Like It*); and the presence of a scapegoat figure (in this case a child molester) to unify the community; and the romances are totally unbelievable (not love at first sight, but at first arranged sight). Yet Shakespeare is never mentioned in the film and was probably not a conscious influence. Seeking to reconcile "ancient tradition and dot.com modernity" (DVD backcover copy), Nair's film seems clearly aimed at both Indian diasporic and Western audiences (the emphasis on sexual abuse and male bashing seem quite American). Yet *Monsoon Wedding*, shot in India, is not any closer or further from Shakespeare than Nair's earlier *Mississippi Masala*. Clearly, the effects of globalization on Indian cinema cannot confine the global to India and the Indian diaspora. And Nair's success is not to be confused with the failure of Bollywood in the US. Though many thought that Bollywood, in the wake of *Lagaan*'s good notices, was poised to be in the West what Hong Kong cinema was in the 1980s, Bollywood basically bombed.[33] *Lagaan* flopped, as did *Devdas*.

Dual audio commentary heritage Shakespeare

Taiwanese director Ang Lee's first English-language film was the adaptation of the Jane Austen novel *Sense and Sensibility* (1995). In the publicity for the film and on the DVD commentary, Lee is said to be an ideal director for the film as the Taiwan he comes from, an explosive combination of new kinds of capitalism and old kinds of paternalistic and patriarchal codes of behavior, is closer to Austen's England than the US or UK an American or a British director would have known. The film has what the co-producer calls in his DVD audio commentary a "hidden Chinese theme," and is inflected by references to China and a global perspective on eighteenth-century English society. Edward Ferrars (Hugh Grant) jokes to Elinor Dashwood (Emma Thompson), for example, that young Margaret (Emilie François) will "lead an expedition to China," and a marvelous large, China cabinet is the immediate background of the scene in which Brandon visits Elinor to give her the dirt on Willoughby. Colonel Brandon (Alan Rickman), we learn, has been to the East Indies where "the air is full of spices."

Lee is very much what used to be called a woman's director, and Emma Thompson won the Academy award for best screenplay adaptation. Thompson's screenplay adds several references to Shakespeare, not present in Jane Austen's Regency novel, including *Romeo and Juliet*, a quotation from Sonnet 116, and *Hamlet*.[34] When Marianne (Kate Winslet) and Mrs. Dashwood (Gemma Jones) discuss Elinor's growing attachment to Edward, Marianne says "to love is to burn, to be on fire . . . like Juliet, or Guinevere, or Heloise." When John Willoughby (Greg Wise) goes to court Marianne in her home, he asks the Dashwood women "Who is reading Shakespeare's sonnets?" The women respond in union: "Marianne is." When Willoughby asks her "which is your favorite?," she replies: "without a doubt, mine is 116." He then begins to recite the sonnet from memory, starting with the second sentence, "Love is not love/Which alters when it alteration finds," and she begins to recite with him: "Or bends with the remover to remove./O, no! It is an ever-fix'd mark/That looks on tempests [Willoughby says "storms"] . . . and is never shaken." Both stop as Marianne holds firm for the word "tempests" (though Willoughby has a copy of the sonnets, it is not made clear in the film who is correct). A key word for its resonance, "tempest" anticipates Marianne's later and second recitation of the sonnet's second and third line near the end of the film as she looks at Willoughby's home in the rainstorm. This time she misremembers the line as "Love is not love that alters when it alteration finds." After Colonel Brandon leaves his own picnic without explanation, *Hamlet* is referenced as Willoughby quips, "Frailty, thy name is Brandon." Literary references abound throughout Thompson's script, as does the activity of reading aloud, mostly from poems, or singing lyrics set to piano music. Marianne reads aloud to Elinor from Hartley Coleridge's "Sonnet VII." Marianne and Ferrars read aloud from "The Castaway" by William Cowper. Marianne also determines Willoughby's opinion of Sir Walter Scott at their first meeting. When Margaret has a French lesson with Elinor, Margaret repeats "le destin d'Oreste/Est de venir sans cesse adorer vos attraits" [Oreste's destiny is to come incessantly to adore your attractions] from Jean Racine's *Andromaque* (2.2.482–3). (Oreste speaks here to Hermione, whom he wishes to marry but who loves Andromaque's captor.) Brandon reads part of stanza 39 of Book V, Canto II of Edmund Spenser's epic *The Faerie Queene* to Marianne. (The Books's hero, Artegall, speaks the lines in response to the subversive, leveller giant.) Ben Jonson's poem "The Dreame" and the anonymous "Weep You No

More Sad Fountains" are set to music (composed by Patrick Doyle, who did the soundtracks for Branagh's Shakespeare films).

The literary culture of the screenplay and women's film genre might seem to harmonize particularly well diaspora and women, given Lee's interest in the female-centered melodrama. Surprisingly, however, the connections between China, Shakespeare, and literature are not mentioned in criticism of the film.[35] This omission may not be surprising as the literary references work as quite subtle "clues" to help viewers "read" the characters. For example, the story of "The Castaway" resonates with what is to happen to Elinor and Marianne, both of whom are cast off by their suitors. Often the literary references work as a kind of secondary soundtrack, which is heard behind characters speaking. For example, the first part of Brandon's quotation of *The Faerie Queene* is barely audible:

> What though the sea with waves continuall
> Doe eat the earth, it is no more at all:
> Nor is the earth the less, or loseth ought,
> For whatsoever from one place doth fall,
> Is with the tide unto another brought . . .
> (Thompson 1995: 186–7)

Brandon's nearly inaudible recitation deflects a possibly accusatory use of the lines. (Artegall's quite apt opening lines "Of things unseen how cans't thou deem aright,/ Then answered the righteous Artegall,/Sith thou misdeem'st so much of things in sight?" are not quoted.) It is only when the camera cuts to him and Marianne in close-up that we hear Artegall's more conciliatory last lines in the stanza: "Is with the tide unto an other brought:/For there is nothing lost, that may be found, if sought." Marianne smiles gratefully in response, having nearly found in Brandon what she lost in Willoughby (he reads aloud from the poem whereas Willoughby recited from memory), and this scene serves retrospectively for what is a rather abrupt shot of them coming out of the church, married, ahead of Elinor and Edward, who we have seen actually propose and accept marriage. Similarly, Margaret's repeated quotations of Oreste's phrase "sans cesse adorer vos attraits" are the background of the (incorrect) news given by the servant Thomas (Ian Brimble) about the newly wedded Mrs. Edward Ferrars, and Margaret only becomes audible as we see Elinor take in the news, becoming a kind of tragic heroine like Andromaque, who cannot let go of her dead husband, Hector. Oddly, perhaps, these lines are not in the published screenplay (Thompson 1995: 190–2), nor does the screenplay supply any of the references.

One critic (Casey 2001) sees the screenplay as a "gateway" into the novel, but this account ignores the fact that the film's literary references are all supplemental to the novel, not quotations of it: literary references are not only a gateway into the film but a means of its textualization: the film invites the audience to read the characters, and anticipates, knowingly or not, its reproduction on video and DVD and postings on Austen fan websites, since most viewers will not be able to track down the references or appreciate their meaning when viewing the film in a movie theater. In other words, the literary references, as they become increasingly muted, come to function in the film like the reverse of DVD audio commentary, in which the film soundtrack is turned way down so that the commentary may be heard. The film sides with a kind of

Elinor/Thompson supplemental process of reading and rereading rather than with an oral, performative, cinematic culture linked to Marianne/Winslet.[36] This opposition may also be read as an allegory of post-production friction between the two women stars. If literature is a major influence on character *bildung* in Austen's novel, literary references in the film mark a contestation over status among the female stars' power. Though Thompson has a double role as star and screenwriter, and though she had won an Academy Award (as Best Actress in *Howards End*) before writing and starring in *Sense and Sensibility*, the film was her first screenplay, and her mature age was a casting liability: some studios turned down the film because she was too old to play Elinor. Though the film was only Winslet's second, she won an Oscar nomination for her performance, and she almost immediately took over Thompson's literary ground, starring, this time as the lead, in another British literary adaptation, *Jude* (dir. Michael Winterbottom,1996), and while filming, becoming Thompson's younger Shakespeare replacement when playing Ophelia in Kenneth Branagh's post-Thompson divorce *Hamlet* (1996). Branagh cast Winslet without having her audition or read for the part, and their explicit nude scene Branagh's idea, may seem like Branagh lording it over Thompson.

While the DVD edition of *Sense and Sensibility* might allow for an extension of supplemental reading processes, it actually reverses the film's valuation of reading from the text over oral performance from memory: the DVD "chapters" access voiced commentaries on the film. Interestingly, the commentaries divide along gender lines. Given that Lee and Thompson were the main authors of the film, it would have made sense for them to comment on the film together.[37] Instead, there are two double commentaries, one with two women, producer Lindsay Doran and Emma Thompson, the other with two men, Ang Lee and co-producer James Schamus. Thompson and Doran do not comment on the film's literary references, nor do they comment on the Chinese theme of the film.

By contrast, the American co-producer and diasporic director periodically offer a commentary both on gender politics and on China. The commentary suggests a divergence among the men as well, however, recoding the Elinor/sense and Marianne/sensibility oppositions in the novel and film: Lee is aligned with Marianne's romantic sensibility and Schamus with Marianne's more rational sensible skepticism. In their commentary over the scene when Marianne comes into Elinor's bedroom reading from Hartley Coleridge's "Sonnet VII," Lee and Schamus discuss the lighting they used, and they turn to China.

LEE: I did enjoy those candle light scenes . . . We used a lot of Chinese lanterns.
SCHAMUS: Part of the hidden Chinese theme . . .
LEE: Laughs.
SCHAMUS: . . . that runs throughout the whole movie.
LEE: That's what I find in all those big English houses, all the best Chinese artwork is in England.
SCHAMUS: Right.
LEE: They rot. They're on the walls everywhere.

And the two then begin to offer divergent accounts of what the film is about as Schamus launches into a critique of British imperialism. I quote the exchange in full:

SCHAMUS: Totally. It's imperial booty.

LEE: One of the things I never see in China, in Taiwan . . . was . . .

SCHAMUS: Laughter

LEE: The best things were in England.

SCHAMUS: One of the interesting things about the social and political background of the book of course is that we're in the Southwest of England, and even the house that we were shooting in there was some question as to whether a large amount of the family wealth had been derived from the trading, the slave, and drug running,

LEE: Opium.

SCHAMUS: Opium. And all that good stuff on which the English empire was founded and which we Americans have taken over.

LEE: If that was what I was thinking I could never have made this movie. I'm making a movie about love.

Schamus then concedes the importance of the novel and women in opposing British imperialism, bringing up sensibility as a kind feminization of civilization. And he points out that the first economic boycott, about sugar and slavery, was led by women in a "feminized if not feminist political movement." The conversation stops as they appear to agree, but Ang actually uses a quite different word, the neologism "femalized," suggesting a more idealized view of women as leaders in love. From presenting some notion of transnational, hybridized, diasporic, and postcolonial version of the novel, Lee and Thompson's *Sense and Sensibility* and its DVD reproduction offer conflicting accounts of the film's most valued medium of critique, voice or text.

(Dis)Orient(aliz)ing Shakespeare

Costume dramas, literary adaptations, and heritage films such as Ismail Merchant's production of Ruth Prawer Jhabvala's screen adaptation of Henry James's novel, *The Golden Bowl* (dir. James Ivory, 2000), are typically viewed by academic film critics as conservative ideologically since they supposedly reinforce conservative orthodoxy: "Production values smother," as one critic puts it, "political points" (North 1999: 38; see also Harper 1994). One might easily imagine both a critique and a celebration of the film for the way it would be said either to affirm or subvert the authority of patriarchal fathers and husbands over daughters and wives, upper classes over menials, England over America, and West over East. The film would be said to legitimate or to offer a critique of the upper classes it represents, both in the activity of art collecting and in the Orientalism of costume display: in one case, the film would be faulted for reducing women to attempting to position each other as abject, either as rejected wife or rejected mistress who must migrate to New York; in the other, the struggle between women would be seen to be a product of pre-feminist patriarchal oppression.[38]

In my view, what makes the film of interest is the way its use of Shakespeare in an orientalist context "disorientalizes" the assumptions on which both of these readings rest.[39] The film references Shakespeare's *Hamlet* just after the performance of a hybridized modern ballet telling the story of an Indian Pasha (Piers Gielgud) and two Indian Queens. The ballet dancers are both Western and Indian, and the score is ascribed apocryphally to a modern European fictional composer named "Gravilka."

The older Queen (Antonia Francheschi), has an adulterous affair with a Nijinksi-like slave (Philip Willingham), and the Pasha kills him and the rest of his family when he discovers them embracing. The Queen then kills herself. After the performance, Mr. Blint (Robin Hart) says to his older female lover: "It's just like *Hamlet*." She pauses for a moment and then laughs.[40]

It would be simplistic to identify Shakespeare either with Orientialism or a critique of orientalism in the film. For the force of the comparison is far from self-evident. Is the reference to *Hamlet* meant wittily? Is it an implied critique of the play rather than the ballet, *Hamlet* disparaged for being over the top? Or is it a misreading? Is Blint just an ingratiating lap dog, a twit unable to appreciate anything more sophisticated than the popular piano pieces he plays? Whichever reading one prefers, it is clear the plot of the ballet is not really like the plot of *Hamlet* at all (the only resemblance is revenge and an adulterous affair; obvious differences are that, unlike Gertrude, the old Queen kills herself and the King survives). Yet misreading is not confined to twits in the film though it is pervasive. The ballet, the affair between the slave and older Queen, hits too close to home for Maggie Verver (Kate Beckinsale), who gets up and leaves the performance and finds her father Adam Verver (Nick Nolte), who also left because he does not like the "noise," in another room. Yet the plot of the ballet does not resemble the affair between the Prince and Charlotte, who are the same age.

Though reduced to an offhand comment, Shakespeare's tiny presence marks a space of exteriority both to recording media and to live performance. It is not surprising that a ballet about an Indian Pasha and Shakespeare should appear in this film given that Ivory and Jhabvala had earlier collaborated on *Shakespeare Wallah* (1965), the story of the Geoffrey Kendall acting troupe whose traveling Shakespeare productions can no longer compete with Indian popular cinema and movie star/fan subcultures.[41] What is striking, however, is that among a large number of highly varied performances, only the ballet and the comparison to Shakespeare's *Hamlet* are not recorded or mediatized (through painting, photography, or wax). Even at the costume ball, a different kind of live performance, the guests take turns having their photograph taken.

Ivory's *The Golden Bowl* also draws our attention to the way the historical past, whether the Renaissance past or turn-of-the-century New York, is available only through media – a medallion, photographs, slides of drawings, oil paintings, costume parties – and to the way the upper classes use these media to commemorate themselves. Throughout *The Golden Bowl*, stories of women being killed by men shadow characters in the present through a variety of media, often ironizing their ability to read the present. The film tells a story not in the novel that begins and ends with shadows cast on the wall in which the older son of an aged Italian Renaissance Duke shows him his much younger wife and his younger son (her stepson) in bed together. The Duke then has both lovers executed, and we see each beheaded in shadow as the credits roll.[42] Later, the story, based on an actual historical occurrence, comes out when Maggie is in Italy and watches a slide show. The lecturer shows a black and white slide of a painting of the original Prince Amerigo, the older man we saw at the beginning of the film who murdered his adulterous wife and younger son.

Similarly, we see a number of historical wax figures, mostly from the Renaissance, in shadow and often out of focus as Charlotte and the Prince rendezvous clandestinely at Madame Tussaud's. Beginning with a guillotine from the French Reign of Terror, the wax figures, who tend to be women and their male executioners, form a backdrop to the adulterous couple. A woman about to be beheaded is revealed as the camera moves down. Henry VIII refuses to listen to Catherine of Aragon, both of whom are cropped and out of focus behind Charlotte and the Prince. An unidentified Renaissance Queen is praying while her executioner to her left is revealed as the camera tracks right. And a large, imposing Holbein portrait of Henry VIII shadows the relationship between Charlotte and Verver near the end of the film in a tour Charlotte gives of the Verver collection, on its way to New York. As the portrait is shown from top to bottom, Charlotte comments on it in a way that suggests to the viewer she is also commenting acidly on Verver himself:

> I think you will agree with me when I say that this life size portrait of King Henry VIII, by Hans Holbein, dominates every picture in this room. Holbein's portrait is that most striking depiction of royal authority in art. But to me it is also the masculine ego in all its brutal physical strength and coldness. The subject perfectly matches Holbein's style in all its coldness, and the King's defiance of all who stood in his way, including his numerous women, who one by one went to their doom.

History casts a very long and often very dark shadow, literal and figurative, on the present lovers, who often don't see the parallel or possibly misread it if there is one. During the slideshow Maggie is trying to see metaphorically what Charlotte and the Prince are up to, but she ignores what the lecturer is saying about the original Amerigo and thus does not see how knowledge of him might give her knowledge of her husband. And the story of the ballet does not parallel the story of Maggie's marriage to the Prince except for the fact of adultery. Similarly, Charlotte and the Prince pay no attention to the wax figures, and one of the last figures we see, Charles I, appears to comes alive as his eyes turn toward them when they leave. The lovers, of course, do not know they are being watched. By the same token, it is hard for the viewer to read the relation between the past and the present. Is Fanny's husband her executioner, like the one we see in the wax museum? Or is he her servant, an executioner of those she orders to their deaths? If Fanny is indeed dressed as Mary, Queen of Scots, then the relation between costumed Queen and her executioner hardly parallels the relation between Fanny and her husband, who seem to be quite close. The meaning of the Renaissance prologue is also unclear. The parallel with Duke Amerigo is initially made by the Prince to his Italian ancestor through a medallion he gives Verver. The parallel is then later confirmed in the slideshow. Yet even later in the movie, clips of the prologue are repeated to suggest a parallel between Verver and Charlotte. The force of Charlotte's critique when commenting on a similar parallel between Verver and the Holbein Henry VIII is belied, however, by the characterization of Verver. The model Ivory and Jhabvala adopted for Verver was not the later, rapaciously acquisitive William Randolph Hearst but the cultured philanthropists Henry Clay Frick and Isabella Stewart Gardner. And given that Verver wants to take Charlotte to New York, not take her head off, her implied parallel between Henry VIII and Verver says more about her than it does about Verver.[43] While Charlotte may equate her forced migration with her execution, Merchant's transformative experience upon going to New York to study and his, Ivory's, and Jhabvala's longtime residence there, Charlotte's move at the end of the film may seem like a liberating one.

The Golden Bowl's disorientation of romance and collecting (they cannot entirely be separated or identified as forms of acquisition) returns us to the way Shakespeare, referenced only as a comment, stands outside of performance. Shakespeare can't be collected as a visual or plastic work of art. Shakespeare's exteriorization both to recording media and to live performance signals both Shakespeare's centrality and his marginality to the elite culture of the film. Yet Shakespeare is for this very reason perhaps reduced to an incidental, offhand, possibly critical remark about one of his plays, a remark whose value as a translation machine for an already Orientalist performance about another culture is also called into doubt. So if Shakespeare is saved because of his distance from Orientalism and cultural imperialism (this is not an Orientalist production of Hamlet, set in the time of the Raj), by the same token his very distance so marginalizes him that he is also beyond the space of a critique of Orientalism and cultural imperialism. The distance between the ambivalence toward canonical British Shakespeare in *Shakespeare Wallah* (the disappearance of Shakespeare from India being both a good and a bad thing; the ambivalence is the consequence of a misrecognition of the many Indian Shakespeare film adaptations and theatrical productions made and performed before 1965) and the incidental, ambiguous, and possibly meaningless reference to *Hamlet* in *The Golden Bowl* also registers the extent to which Shakespeare's position, if he has one, is now post-canonical.

Dim-sum *Romeo and Juliet*, with an order of Zeffirelli on the (west) side

Ien Ang notes that although diaspora, as a concept, tends to de-emphasize living *here* and that diasporic communities are defined as being not-here to stay, "in practice . . . this cannot be the case. All migrants have to forge an accommodation with where they find themselves relocated, and to reconcile their situation here, whether this be the United States, the Netherlands, Australia, or anywhere else. For Asians who have migrated to the West, this means coming to terms somehow with racial minority status, and acting upon it" (2001: 13–14). We can appreciate this point by turning to a number of films made by Caucasian directors. In Abel Ferrara's *China Girl* (1987), two diasporas, Italian and Chinese, come together and are interpreted in relation to a cinematic Shakespeare canon. This film takes up canonical Shakespeare at one remove from the text, in relation, that is, to canonical cinematic adaptations of *Romeo and Juliet*. Ferrara's film reclaims *Romeo and Juliet* as an Italian story not by engaging Shakespeare's canonical play but by engaging two canonical film adaptations of it, namely, the earlier American musical adaptation set in New York, *West Side Story* (dir. Jerome Robbins and Robert Wise, 1961), and Franco Zeffirelli's *Romeo and Juliet* (1968), set in Verona, Italy. Unlike the US film musical, *China Girl* is set not on a sound stage with artificial looking sets but on location in a dirty, dilapidated, and grimy Little Italy and Chinatown. The rivalry in this case is not between Puerto Ricans and Caucasians but between two immigrant groups, Italian-Americans and Hong Kong Chinese. Indeed, the film alludes directly to *West Side Story*: the Romeo character is named Tony in *China Girl* just as he is to *West Side Story*, and a fight between rival gangs parallels that of a fight in *West Side Story*. Like the balcony scene between Tony and Maria on her fire escape for the number "Tonight," Tony/Romeo calls out to Tye/Juliet from the street, the fire escape below her window serving as a balcony. *China Girl* also defines itself in some ways against the musical as more hard hitting. Whereas Maria lives at the end of *West Side Story*, both the lovers are killed in *China Girl* (by the same bullet). Along similar lines, race and ethnicity are realistically and rigidly represented and codified; whereas Natalie Wood used a fake accent and wore unconvincing make-up to sound and look like the Puerto Rican Maria, the actors in *China Girl* are cast to encode racial and ethnic "authenticity," and in addition to a kind of identity politics casting, race and ethnicity are established through images of food, as is so often the case in ethnically marked films such as *Chicken Rice Wars*, *Dim Sum: A Little Bit of Heart* (dir. Wayne Wang, 1984), *Eat a Bowl of Tea* (dir. Wayne Wang, 1989), *The Scent of Green Papaya/Mui du du xanh* (dir. Anh Hung Tran, 1993), *Chunking Express/Chongqing senlin* (dir. Kar-Wai Wong, 1994), *Eat, Drink, Man, Woman/Yin shi nan nu* (dir. Ang Lee, 1994), *Big Night* (dir. Campbell Scott and Stanley Tucci, 1996), *What's Cooking?* (dir. Gurinder Chadha, 2000), and *Tortilla Soup* (dir. Maria Ripoll, 2001; screenplay by Ang Lee), to name a few. In *China Girl*, the Chinese are identified by images of fish and the Italians by images of pizza. The Chinese Mafia own and work out of a restaurant, and Romeo and his older brother own and work in a family pizza parlor. *China Girl* is less a retelling of *Romeo and Juliet* than a meditation of the diasporic circulation of the Italian version of the story, to France and to England, then back to Italy (Zeffirelli) and to the US (*West Side Story*). The Chinatown setting and the rewriting of Romeo and Juliet as an interracial Chinese-Italian romance may be read as symptomatic of Ferrara's response to the explosion of Hong Kong cinema in the 1980s, his claim both for Italian canonical cinema and for the resurgence of Italian-American films by the likes of Francis Ford Coppola, Martin Scorcese, Brian de Palma, and Michael Cimino that had dominated the 1970s.

Like many adaptations of *Romeo and Juliet*, *China Girl* rewrites and explains Shakespeare's story of feuding families as a story of antagonism generated by the racial difference between the families, with love being the antidote to violence. Yet *China Girl*'s return of *Romeo and Juliet* to its Italian roots, here Italian-American, produces some contradictions in the film's take on racial and ethnic assimilation, setting it apart from the more idealizing multiculturalism, melting-plot model of difference celebrated in *West Side Story*. The lovers, Tony (Richard Panebianco) and Tye (Sari Chang), are both extremely pacific. Unlike the play, Tony does not even attempt to kill the Tybalt character (in this case split into two characters) in revenge for their murder of the Mercutio character (here Romeo's brother). At his brother's funeral, Tony rejects the revenge code of his brother's friends. Moreover, he consciously rejects the racism found in his brother's best friend (Michael Mancuso) and almost gets into a fight with him when he calls the Chinese people names.

Unlike *West Side Story*, however, *China Girl* does not make feuding groups morally equivalent; rather, the film makes the Chinese much less moral, at times recalling the portrait of the Chinese Mafia in the violent *Year of the Dragon* (dir. Michael Cimino, 1985), also set in New York's Chinatown. In *China Girl*, the Chinese are viewed as the aggressive predators, both in the form of the older Chinese leader, who wants to take over Little Italy progressively and quietly, and some of the younger Chinese generation, who want to do so violently by extorting Chinese who locate their restaurants in Little Italy. After chasing Tony because he dances with Tye at a disco in Chinatown (initially recalling the Capulet ball), the Chinese are confronted and beaten by the Italian gang members. Later, two of the Chinese gang up on Romeo's brother and knife him when he is unarmed. Only Mercury (Russell Wong) is as crazy as the more violent Asians. The Chinese are also presented as more foreign, less assimilated, less a part of New York. Many of the Asians speak Cantonese as well as English whereas only the two older men speak any Italian and do so quite infrequently. The Asians are also differentiated in terms of their accents as more or less foreign, more or less assimilated. The Italians also help the Chinese when the restaurant is blown up by members of the Chinese gang. The Chinese murderers cause the Virgin Mary statue to be broken during an Easter parade. Unlike New York, Hong Kong is frequently recalled but never seen.

More crucial than its relation to *West Side Story*, however, is Ferrara's relation to the Italian film version, Franco Zeffirelli's *Romeo and Juliet,* and it is in his adaptation of Zeffirelli that we can see a hollowing out of the canonical cinematic adaptation. Ferrara quotes directly from Zeffirelli's film in two scenes of *China Girl.* The first quotation from Zeffirelli's film occurs when we first see Romeo walking up toward a street home, smiling while holding and twirling a flower. This scene is replayed by Ferrara before Romeo and Juliet first make love. In this case, Tony is in a pizza parlor twirling a flower. The second scene quoted by Ferrara is the *aubade.* Zeffirelli begins the *aubade* with a close-up of the lovers. The camera then slowly pulls back and moves to the left, revealing Romeo's naked backside. Ferarra first shows the lovers in a rundown apartment with a mattress on the floor, then shows the lovers kissing in close-up, and then reverses the direction of Zeffirelli's camera, moving from the right as we see Tony's nude body on top of Tye's (also covered by a sheet).

Ferrara's claim for the canonical status of his own film depends on his film being even more Italian than Zeffirelli's. The cinematic *mise-en-scène* and style of *China Girl* allude to the less idealized and more gritty neo-realist Italian cinema that emerged after the Second Word War before Zeffirelli as well as to "masculine" Italian-American filmmakers like Martin Scorcese (*Romeo and Juliet* meets *Mean Streets*). Along the lines of Harold Bloom's theory of misreading, in which the belated poet metaleptically reverses the priority of his work and his precursor's, Ferrara implies that his version is prior not only to Shakespeare's, which is already an Anglicized adaptation of its Italian source, but to *West Side Story* (not Italian) and Zeffirelli's film (not as canonically Italian cinema as Ferrara's).

The extent to which Ferrara's legitimation of *China Girl* as canonical, in the tradition of Italian cinema, hollows out the canonically Shakespeare may already be obvious. The film's only reference to the play occurs when Tony's brother teasingly calls him "Romeo." Ferrara extends a process of evacuating Shakespeare's text already begun by Zeffirelli. Whereas Zeffirelli cut two-thirds of the play and substituted images for poetry, Ferrara cuts everything but a single word. The only other allusion to the play is a character named Mercury, but even this reference is drained of meaning since the character has no relation to Mercutio at all.

The draining of Shakespeare does not succeed in producing an Italian film, however, and Ferrara's interest in *Romeo and Juliet* and in Zeffirelli's film puts him on the side of a conciliatory relation to Chinese cinema both in the sense that it is less violent, and more romantic than Cimino's reactionary and racist *Year of the Dragon.* Indeed, it is precisely this more conciliatory relation to Hong Kong cinema which explains why *China Girl* ends twice: in the first ending, the Chinese return to Hong Kong leaving Tye alone to remain with Tony while the Italian-American gang members inexplicably let them walk; in the second, Mercury returns, equally inexplicably, and shoots both

Tony and Tye, whose corpse is then cradled by her older brother. Tony's relatives and friends are nowhere to be found.

The double ending of *China Girl* may be read as the film's inability either to repress or to acknowledge and integrate its own debt to Hong Kong cinema. *China Girl* is in many ways as much a Chinese foreign film as it is an Italian film, not only in its coding of ethnicity as food but in the way its genre is more action picture than romance. There is almost no sex in the film, and the little there is has no erotic charge. The move from canonical Shakespeare film adaptation, whether Zeffirelli or Robbins and Wise, to Ferrara's "subShakespeare" adaptation marks a double failure to make a film recognizable as Italian-American nationalist cinema (due to its use of Hong Kong cinema) and to integrate racially different and competing national cinematic styles. *China Girl* bombed, is long out of print on video, and has to date never been released on DVD. While Woo became increasingly transnational, citing Scorcese in *The Killer/Die xue shuang xiong* (1989) and stating that he has been influenced by musicals like *West Side Story* (see Cieko 1997: 230), Ferrara returned to a more exclusively Italian-American national focus, casting Harvey Keitel as the lead in *Bad Lieutenant* (1992) and including Koreans as thugs and mom and pop storeowners.

Amerasian pie/cock-asian pie

At an earlier moment in the history of criticism, one might have examined a Western film involving Asia and Shakespeare in terms of how it represented Asians and how Shakespeare helped to exclude or to include an Asian racial minority; the governing assumption would be that the closer the Asian is to Shakespeare, the more speaking lines the Asian character has, the more progressive the film.[44] Yet the films discussed thus far ask questions which call these assumptions about racial and Shakespearean authenticity into question: is Shakespeare cited in a way that is next to meaningless, transparent, effectively invisible and unnoticed? Or is he a means of organizing what we see, a kind of frame for the plot's meaning? In Shakespeare-related films where diasporic Asians are proximate to Shakespeare, are Asian characters racially marked, or are they so fully assimilated that their racial difference is invisible? And why are the Shakespeare performances live, as opposed to the highly mediatized performances and readings by the white characters?

Consider *American Pie* (dir. Paul Weitz and Chris Weitz, 1999), an apparently mindless US teen comedy centering on four computer-literate jocks who want to lose their virginity before they graduate from high school. In one short scene, an Asian-American English teacher (Clyde Kusatsu) "translates" Shakespeare's *Henry IV Parts One and Two* for the students. In a classroom, Jim Levinstein (Jason Biggs) looks to his right as we hear the English teacher (not yet seen in the film) in voice-over: "So . . . once Hal becomes King . . ." The camera then cross-cuts to a shot of Nadia (Shannon Elizabeth), a foreign student at whom Jim is staring, as the teacher continues in voice-over: "he has to take on the responsibilities of leadership." The camera then cuts to the teacher, who continues "and turn his back on his old drunken friend Falstaff. You see, Hal is going through a rite of passage much like you all are. [Camera draws back.] So make the most of the time you got [*sic*] left together. You'll miss it later. You see . . ." As the camera pulls back, the teacher's voice is drowned out by students who ignore him and begin talking together among themselves.

In this scene, two of Shakespeare's history plays are "translated" into a soundbite version by an Asian-American teacher who turns the story of Hal becoming Henry V into a version of the film's *carpe diem* plot. Shakespeare is here purely oral, though already mediated, it's fair to say, by the teensploitation film genre itself (the plots of the plays are retold in a way that makes them resemble the film's plot). Neither teacher nor students has a copy of Shakespeare's text out, the teacher is giving an adaptation, not reading the play itself.[45] And despite the pencil above the blackboard with composition processes marked on it, no one even has low-tech pencils and notepaper out either. As a purely oral, modernized story, Shakespeare is opposed in the film to knowledge gained in computers and the internet (computer cameras that allow for surveillance and show to the entire student body Nadia stripping in Jim's room and then Jim and Nadia attempting to have sex), and a book, the "Bible" (consisting of material instructing heterosexual boys how to become good lovers).[46]

Why is Shakespeare being cited in *American Pie*, then? And why is he being cited by an Asian-American teacher? The classroom scene is not about multiculturalism or affirmative action, in my view, but about Shakespeare instruction and race in a post-literary age. *American Pie* is typical in its representation of the teacher as a minority. Other examples abound, such as the black teacher in *10 Things I Hate About You* (dir. Gil Junger, 1999) or the teachers on many television programs.[47] *In American Pie*, an Asian minority is not included in a multicultural way by universalizing Shakespeare; rather, the film shows the irrelevance of race as well as the irrelevance of Shakespeare to the film's (all-white) students. For them, there is no such thing as the foreign (there's even a scene in a Sushi bar). Neither Shakespeare nor an Asian teacher are of interest. Indeed, the only foreign signifiers here are Nadia and the Union Jack to her left. Yet it is worth pointing out that Jim, a white nerd or "cock-asian," is the focus of abjection here. Nadia is comfortable having sex, while Jim inadvertently shows himself twice prematurely ejaculating to his jock friends watching Jim and Nadia have sex on their computers. The entire school laughs at Jim the next day. While the racial minority may assimilate Shakespeare and minority cuisine may be assimilated literally, there's something about Nadia and the foreign that makes white jock/cock culture gag.

Clubbing the emperor

The abjection of all pedagogy in the US, even when based on a conservative view of the foundational status of a classics curriculum, is made apparent in *The Emperor's Club* (dir. Michael Hoffman).[48] Shakespeare's *Julius Caesar* and a gifted Indian immigrant student are in many ways at the center of Hoffman's film, a kind of *Goodbye, Mr Chips* (dir. Herbert Ross, 1969) meets *Dead Poets Society* (dir. Peter Weir, 1989) meets the updated and darker *Election* (dir. Alexander Payne, 1999). Kevin Kline plays a prep school (all boys) classics teacher, Mr Hundert, who moderates an annual "Mr. Julius Caesar" contest where the three best students compete for the honor of being Mr. Julius Caesar. In a key scene, the students discuss Shakespeare's *Julius Caesar*, and a "problem" student named Sedgwick Bell, the son of a US senator, who has been assigned Brutus's part, faults the conspirators' plot. The conspirators should have killed Marc Antony, in young Bell's view. Hundert is shocked, and the two have a brief debate in class over morality and power. The students all have copies of the play, and a bust of Shakespeare figures prominently in a number of shots (also at the end of the film in the same classroom). Shakespeare's appearance in the film is hardly surprising given that Hoffman directed *A Midsummer Night's Dream* with Kline as Bottom and *Soap Dish* (1991) with Kline as an aspiring Shakespearean actor, and given Kline's own experience doing Shakespeare and referring to Shakespeare in the mall film *In and Out* (dir. Frank Oz, 1998) and art films like *Looking for Richard* (dir. Al Pacino, 1996).

An Indian student named Deepak Mehta wins the "Mr. Julius Caesar" competition twice. He is one of the four main student characters, but hardly has any lines. (He is also the student who goes into higher education, apparently as an administrator, though the student denied his place in the competition, Martin Blythe, speaks of having applied to "the academy.") Though the actor is American born, his character speaks with a rather thick accent. Another white student who Hundert fails (actually cheats of a chance to be one of the three competitors) and whose father won the Mr. JC competition when he went to the school, drops off his son (same name) at the end of the film in a classroom now conspicuously multiracial and co-ed. The loser white guys bond. In an interesting revision of Rudyard Kipling's "White Man's Burden," multicultural integration and imperialism meet (as they have in George W. Bush's cabinet), but in this case (semi-)virtuous loser white guys are content to smile at each other, apparently admiring their willing sacrifices and impotence as a truly virtuous immigrant of color and a truly evil white man surpass them.

Shakespeare, through a glass house darkly

How Shakespeare and Western postdiaspora cinemas place abjection across white and Asian races may be seen if we turn to the chiller *The Glass House* (dir. Daniel Sackheim, 2001). The film cites Shakespeare more extensively and makes the Asian diaspora more present than does *American Pie* or *The Emperor's Club*. A loose adaptation of *Hamlet* about a teenage girl named Ruby (Leelee Sobieski) who discovers that her parents were murdered by their best friends, *The Glass House* makes more extensive reference to Shakespeare and makes an Asian character closer to him than *American Pie*. Indeed, an Asian teacher named Mr. Kim (Michael Paul Chan) is the first character to mention *Hamlet* explicitly. "Hamlet senses," we hear Mr. Kim say in voice-over just after Ruby sees Mrs. Glass (Diane Lane) passed out on a heroin fix, as we cut to the classroom, "something's wrong that he alone can set right." Mr. Kim then gives the students a writing assignment: "I want two pages on *Hamlet* next Friday about what he means and whether he'll succeed."

Later in the film, after Ruby has begun to catch on to the fact that her guardian, Mr. Glass (Stellan Skarsgård), has not only killed her parents but plans to kill her and her brother as well, we return to the classroom where Mr. Kim, in classic Gothic fashion, is reading aloud Old Hamlet's speech commanding Hamlet to avenge his murder: "I could a tale unfold whose lightest word would harrow up your soul, freeze thy young blood . . ./Make thy two eyes, like stars, start from their spheres . . ./And each particular hair to stand an end . . ./If thou dids't ever thy dear father love . . ./ Revenge his foul and most unnatural murder . . . most foul" (1.5.15–27). As Mr. Kim reads the speech, Ruby becomes more and more agitated as if she, not Hamlet, were being addressed, and leaves the classroom. As we hear Mr. Kim in voice-over, Ruby calls her family attorney to follow up on an e-mail she earlier sent him.

That *Hamlet* would appear in a chiller film is hardly surprising in itself, given that *The Glass House* begins as a horror film (which it turns out Ruby and her friends are watching in a movie theater) and given the frequency with which *Hamlet* is cited in Gothic literature and in horror films such as *Dracula's Daughter* (dir. Lambert Hillyer, 1936), *A Nightmare on Elm Street 4: The Dream Master* (dir. Renny Harlin, 1988), *Bram Stoker's Dracula* (dir. Francis Ford Coppola, 1992), *Interview with a Vampire* (dir. Neil Jordan, 1994), *The Haunting of Helen Walker* (dir. Tom McLoughlin, 1995), *Gods and Monsters* (dir. Bill Condon, 1998); *Teaching Mrs. Tingle* (dir. Kevin Williamson, 1999), *The Turn of the Screw* (dir. Ben Bolt, 1999), *From Hell* (dir. Albert and Allen Hughes, 2001), and *Soul Survivors: The Killer Cut* (dir. Stephen Carpenter, 2001).[49] What is more striking is that Hamlet, an Asian teacher, and multimedia, interface, as it were.[50]

Addressing this interface requires close attention to the way Kim and Ruby are doubled, he as Old Hamlet, she as Hamlet, and to the way authority figures in the school are a racial minority and a woman. This doubling has two consequences. First, the differences between their relationship to *Hamlet*, pedagogy, and media are collapsed. Initially, the teacher is identified with Hamlet in print and with reading the book aloud; pedagogically, he allows for a certain amount of time for the students to do criticism. In the first classroom scene, for example, we see him holding a book as he moves past Ruby, who also has a book on her desk. In contrast, Ruby is allied to multimedia – printed book, other open and unidentified books, the computer – in excess of *Hamlet*. Whereas in the classroom copies of the text are on students' desks, here the printed

Figure 16.3 Computing *Hamlet*.

Figure 16.4 Filling in the blanks with *Hamlet.*

book is closed and the electronic text is open. Ruby's command of multimedia allows her to drop her *Hamlet* assignment for the one seemingly called up by the play. After Glass comes in to check up on her, we see that her *Hamlet* paper actually provides cover for another kind of research she's doing. Ruby clicks back to a window with the *L.A. Times* on it which she uses to research her parents' death in a car accident. After confirming her suspicions that her parents were murdered, Ruby returns to her *Hamlet* paper as if to confirm her internalization of Old Hamlet's call for Hamlet to revenge his murder. The cursor blinks at the sentence ending with the words "revenge drama."

Despite the different ways Kim and Ruby are connected to *Hamlet*, pedagogy, and media, however, they are also linked by parallel shots and by reading aloud in ways that collapse the differences between them. As Kim reads aloud from *Hamlet* in the second classroom scene, initially we see him holding the book, and then the camera moves in for a tight focus on his face and on his mouth as he reads it. Earlier, when researching her parent's death and discovering that they were driving a BMW when they crashed, Ruby says aloud, "My father drove a Saab." Ruby's reading practice thus parallels Mr. Kim's.

The second consequence of the doubling of Mr. Kim and Ruby as Old Hamlet and Hamlet is that the difference between Mr. Kim as Old Hamlet and Mr. Glass as Claudius also collapses. Mr. Kim's Asian origins mark him as different from the corrupt white male stepfather (a Swedish actor, incidentally, who broke out in the Danish Dogme film *Breaking the Waves*). Yet it is precisely Glass's own knowledge of *Hamlet* that allows him to discredit Ruby and Mr. Kim by setting her up to be caught as a plagiarist. Later that night, he comes back to where Ruby has been writing later that night and finds her asleep. The next morning, Ruby awakens and looks at her computer, surprised to find a finished paper on *Hamlet*. Ruby realizes that Glass has completed her paper for her and she thanks him that morning for doing it.

Just after Ruby leaves the classroom to call her attorney to follow up on her internet research, she is called to the Vice-Principal's (Rutanya Alda) office, where the Vice-Principal is reading her paper. Obviously on to the fact that the paper was not written by Ruby, the Vice-Principal asks her if "that paper [she] turned in to Mr. Kim . . . was her work . . . Nobody helped?" "No," Ruby replies, brazening it out as Mr. Kim enters the office without her seeing him. "Not even Harold Bloom?" he asks her. "'Dance of contraries' didn't sound like one of my students. I found it and other phrases in Mr. Bloom's recent book, *Shakespeare: The Invention of the Human*."

Along with the female Vice-Principal, Mr. Kim becomes another discredited authority along the lines of Glass/Claudius rather than Old Hamlet. Kim's capacity to give Ruby/Hamlet the law has been corrupted by the fact that he has been deceived by Mr. Glass. Indeed, Mr. Kim may also be deceiving Ruby as well since it is not clear that he noticed the Bloom quotations himself or with the aid of Mr. Glass. There is no racial or gender alternative authority figure, then, to the corrupt Claudius, who has also in this version corrupted his wife, making her into an accomplice to murder and then turning her into a drug-stealing, junkie doctor who eventually kills herself. Ruby's younger brother is corrupted and bought off after the foster parents give him video games. Similarly, the female social worker is deceived and Ruby's attorney Adam Begleiter (Bruce Dern) turns out to be an ineffective, Polonius-like fool. In the near final sequence, a Highway patrolman is also killed by Mr. Glass. All are obscene father figures, as Slavoj Žižek puts it. Even Ruby's character is compromised. Ruby is abject when Mr. Glass makes her feel guilty for the death of her parents. Though her guilt is overstated it is not entirely misplaced. She comes home late after staying out with her girlfriends, fails to stay in touch with them when she moves, and her "bad" reputation keeps her from making friends at her new Malibu school.

Thus there is no place to read and learn from *Hamlet* via old or new media and no racial or gender "Other" to authorize a counter-Claudius/Glass appropriation of *Hamlet*. Indeed, succeeding in the film turns on one's ability to go spectral. Visually, Mr. Kim becomes more embodied during the film, moving from the spectral Ghost in the classroom and then appearing invisibly first to Ruby in the Vice-Principal's office, before showing himself not to be the one who knows. Conversely, Mr. Glass becomes more effective the more spectral he becomes. After we see him spying on Ruby while she writes her paper, he shows up with a drink as he comments on *Hamlet*; later he writes her paper unseen. By the end of the film, it is Ruby who has learned to see Mr. Glass without him seeing her.

To be sure, the paranoid horror film necessitates the isolation of the heroine and the universal corruption of everyone else. Yet that is precisely the point, I would argue. The horror film and Shakespeare's *Hamlet* actually do separate out after Begleiter/Polonius is killed (not by Hamlet but by mobsters). *Hamlet* is a specter to be exorcised from the film to permit a more general war of spectralization between a hero and villain both morally compromised. Pedagogy and literary criticism are similarly pushed aside. It's no accident that Shakespeare is taught live, not through film, as *Hamlet* is in

Last Action Hero (dir. John McTiernan, 1993), or that a book by an anti-performance literary critic, Harold Bloom, is the one Ruby plagiarizes from and that Mr. Kim names, not an essay in *Shakespeare, The Movie* or a similar work of Shakespeare film criticism. Getting up to speed in the film means leaving *Hamlet* behind and playing out what Carol Clover (1992) calls the "final girl" scenario of the horror film. If her gender transgression makes her heroic, that is because the film follows the convention of the horror-film genre, not because it positions Ruby as the heir to female Hamlets dating back to Sarah Bernhardt and Asta Nielsen.

Why then invoke *Hamlet* and ally the play with an Asian-American character if only to exorcise the play and discredit the Asian-American's authority? The film's spectralization of Shakespeare's tragedy serves as a ruse, in my view, that enables the film to deconstruct various oppositions (Asian male versus white male; Old Hamlet versus Claudius; play versus screenplay; original criticism versus plagiarism; print versus computer, and so on) while leaving untouched a more pressing genre distinction, namely between *The Glass House* and the horror film generally. Leaving Shakespeare behind is also leaving behind the question of the copy in all its forms – from adaptation, to double, to plagiarism. Just like Ruby pushes *Hamlet* aside to do research on the web, so the film uses *Hamlet* to make room for itself, pushing aside the horror film that it opens as. Bringing in *Hamlet* to get rid of it allows *The Glass House* to appear to have avoided another kind of haunting, the serialization and hence predictability of the typical horror film. What might appear at first sight to be a critical difference between the relative invisibility of Shakespeare and Asians in *American Pie* and *The Emperor's Club*, on the one hand, and their relative visibility in *The Glass House*, on the other, is really no difference at all, since the latter's spectralization of Shakespeare has the consequence of emptying of meaning both Shakespeare and the race/gender of the person who speaks Shakespeare.

The zen art of *Hamletmachine* maintenance

In the only interpolated dialogue accompanied by a visual in Michael Almereyda's *Hamlet*, we see and hear a clip from the documentary *Peace Is Every Step: Meditation in Action: The Life and Work of Thich Nhat Hanh* (dir. Gaetano Kazuo Maida, 1998).[51] The following excerpt with Thich Nhat Hanh, a Vietnamese Buddhist monk and world peace activist who now resides in Paris, plays mostly as a voice-over. I quote it in full:

> We have the word to be. But what I propose is that a word to interbe. Interbe. Because it is not possible to be alone. To be by yourself. You need other people in order to be. You need other beings in order to be. Not only you need father, mother, but also uncle, brother, sister. Society. But you also need sunshine, river, air, trees, birds, elephants, and so, so it is impossible to be by yourself, alone. You have to be interbe with everyone and everything else. And therefore, to be means to interbe.

During the clip, Hamlet turns away from the video, holding a portable video player on which he watches black-and-white video footage he took of Ophelia in bed reading William Burroughs. Hamlet takes his cue from Thich Nhat Hanh's comments, and touched by his memories of Ophelia, is next seen composing and recomposing his poem to her late at night in a coffee shop, which we hear him read in voice-over.

Figure 16.5 Buddhist Hamlet.

The meaning of this interpolation is inseparable, I think, from a series of scenes related to Chinatown which Almereyda cut from the film. Again, I quote in full from the screenplay:

> It seemed like a fair idea to throw Hamlet, Rosencrantz, and Guildenstern into Chinatown, to admit more local reality into the movie, and so a sequence of eventually excised scenes had Hamlet running through Chinatown, pursued by his disloyal friends. He ducks into a particular nerve-jangling video parlour; R & G catch up with him in a dingy back room . . . An envelope filled with cash bought us about twenty minutes with a horde of oblivious teenage video addicts and their thrilling, deafening, death-filled games. (More disassociated images-within-images! Sleepwalkers! Enemies of consciousness! Contemporary Rosencrantzes and Guildensterns!) Earlier on the streets, we were shooting from an open van . . . when the absurdity of what we were up to fully kicked in. On the neon-lit sidewalk, standing in a crush of pedestrian traffic, amidst a sea of Asian faces, Ethan was recognized – by Gwyneth Paltrow, strolling along with Ben Affleck. For the back room scene, on a separate night, the art department threw together an impressively desolate three-walled set, replete with a live rooster rented for the occasion. (Until fairly recently, a tic-tac-toe playing rooster, electronically motivated, had been one of the arcade's featured attractions. The caged bird, [pacing across a soiled newspaper photo of Fortinbras] is one of my favorite missing images in the film.) My friend You-Fei gamely pitched in, exhorting Hamlet with Shakespearean dialogue translated into Chinese. But, despite energetic work from actors and non-actors alike, the resulting scenes weren't half as cohesive as I'd hoped. They were somehow too busy, they clotted the film's forward motion, they weren't *necessary*. Alas.
>
> (Almereyda 2000: 139)

While we may respect Almereyda's editorial judgment, cutting the scenes has a crucial effect in drawing a dividing line between media as coming into self-consciousness through a transcendental esthetic and media as going into unconsciousness via an addictive, mind-numbing, sub-esthetic. The few Asian touches remaining are aligned with transcendental, artistic characters: Hamlet, Horatio, and Ophelia. On the 'plane to England, Hamlet looks at a Polaroid of a defaced Buddhist statue (it follows a postcard of a nude painting). When Hamlet returns, we see a box with Chinese lettering on his refrigerator in Horatio's apartment.

The video clip of the documentary about Thich Nhat Hanh establishes a transcendental coding, that is for Hamlet's use of video as well as Horatio's philosophy and Ophelia's photography. Indeed, early on both Hamlet and Ophelia are linked to writing as well as visual media. He passes her notes while making a video of the press conference, and writes her letters and a poem on paper, not on e-mail or a word-processing file. She reads Burroughs and takes photographs. Almereyda has a rather sentimental take on the play: Hamlet's romantic love for Ophelia, her love for him, and their knowledge via art/media are opposed to parental and self-surveillance; that is, the film opposes Hamlet's authenticity as a lover and scholar as well as Ophelia's resistance to patriarchy by linking the two characters to print and visual media, and with a range of visual media (Polaroid photographs) as well as digital camcorders. She writes a note to him, which Laertes intercepts, and she later reads his letter. And Horatio's apartment is full of books. By contrast, it is the older generation who are allhyper-mediatized. The only time Hamlet writes on a computer is when he revises Claudius's command to have him killed by Rosencrantz and Guildenstern's laptop. Had Almereyda left the Chinatown scenes in his movie, the opposition between young and old characters in relation to techno-media would have been greatly weakened as Asia would have been on the side of the transcendent as well as the degenerate. Through the documentary clip and other images, Asia remains on the side of Hamlet, Horatio, and Ophelia.

Figure 16.6 Hamlet's polaroid photo of defaced Buddha.

Yet Almereyda's mediatization of film and video in his *Hamlet* nevertheless deconstructs this opposition, revealing both Hamlet's own narcissism and the director's as well. Consciousness is defined as Asian in the sense of being transcendental, media supplying critical distance, and in the sense of unconsciousness, media as a kind of addictive drug. Throughout the film, Almereyda draws attention to visual mass media by framing someone watching another film or image. Consider, for example, the "To be or not to be" speech, reduced to a single line in this sequence before Hamlet continues it in Blockbuster, with a teacup on the left. Yet in the Vietnamese clip, the difference between the framed clip and the movie frame dissolves as the television image occupies the entire screen. The cross-cutting and voice-over in the sequence effectively conflate the monk's consciousness with Hamlet's.

Afterwards, Hamlet shows at Claudius's office to kill and begins by looking at himself on video. After Polonius appears and talks with Hamlet, we see him turn back toward a surveillance camera. Rosalind Kraus has called video a narcissistic medium, and what seems to save Hamlet from the charge of self-absorption is that he is using media for an ethical purpose, one that involves, alternately, detection and self-examination. Yet it is the film's equation and alternation between various visual media that calls this ethical legitimation of Hamlet into question. His film footage of Ophelia is already a kind of voyeuristic surveillance hardly different from the footage he aggressively shoots at the press conference. Hamlet's wool hat, linking him to the lead singer of the band The Spin Doctors, establishes his slacking as yet another form of political spinning. What he is doing to Ophelia by videotaping her is no different in kind from what Polonius does when he wires Ophelia to spy on Hamlet. Near the end of the film, Hamlet ends his "How all occasions do inform against me" soliloquy in an airplane bathroom, staring at himself in the mirror (stage). And the film begins with Hamlet delivering the "what a work of man" speech on video he has taken of himself.

Figure 16.7 Tea or Hamlet?

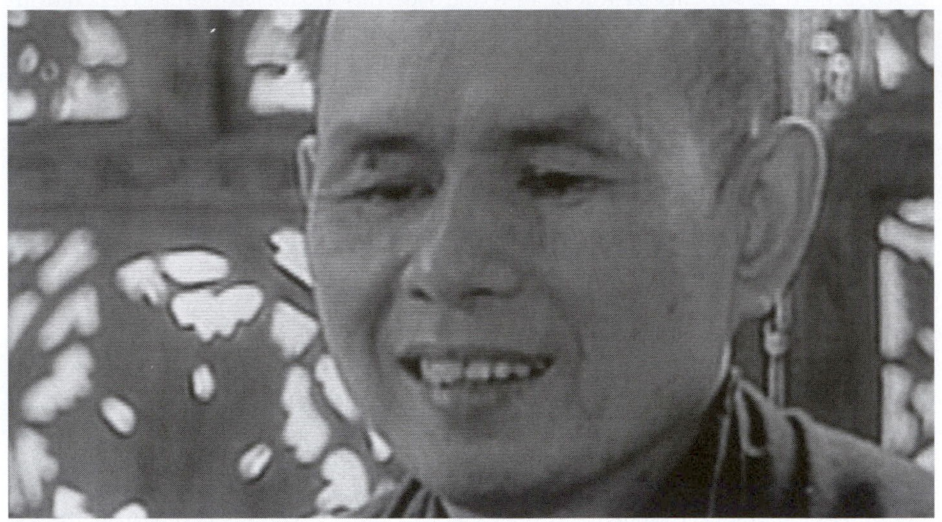

Figure 16.8 To interbe or not to interbe?

The film similarly dissolves distinctions between video and digital film when Hamlet produces *The Mousetrap*, a movie. Hamlet rents videos, not DVDs, from Blockbuster, and then produces his movie digitally, but then prints it on video. And the video-box cover in turn echoes the film-title frame near the beginning of the film, where Hamlet is also written in white "letters." The title credits of Hamlet's film reproduce this shot. Hamlet is a kind of director, with "Action," seen also as the marker of a Blockbuster section, being equated with physical action. Almereyda's editing/screenplay adapting/directing mirrors Hamlet's.

The very editing processes that make Hamlet's (inter)active command of multimedia in the film seem like self-reflective knowledge and art of being are also what open the film to a critique of its misrecognized narcissism. Hamlet sees himself everywhere, in *East of Eden* clips with James Dean; in a clip of *Return of the Crow* showing in Blockbuster; in footage of a 1950s, *Leave It to Beaver*-like nuclear family; in a film clip of Sir John Gielgud as a young man doing Hamlet in the gravedigger's scene. In the easy flow of accessible images of the film, Hamlet's time is never out of joint. Hamlet is truly posthistorical not only in his accessing of images but in the way that the mediatization of the live here implies no loss. Hamlet can stop, start, rewind, and fast forward the film of himself holding a gun in his mouth and to his head at will, all without loss. (By contrast, Ophelia burns photos of Hamlet and her, and Hamlet's letters to Ophelia end up floating in a fountain.)

The final moments of the film, as Hamlet dies, register an even more psychotic breakdown of film and video as a close-up of Hamlet's eye is intercut with video footage of Ophelia, his father, mother, and uncle, seen previously in the color film itself, now in black and white. What began as Hamlet returning the gaze with his camcorder now becomes a cross-cut mirroring of one of his eyes and film footage outside his consciousness which is positioned as if it were his memory, his consciousness. Buddhist idealism goes out the window as Hamlet meets Kurt Cobain in Nirvana.

Interestingly, it is Claudius who allegorizes a psychotic sequence of images drawn from infomercials, cartoons, and news coverage of a Bill Clinton State of the Union speech he sees on his limousine TV and draws a moral that applies to himself. As if the TV were speaking to him, he has an attack of conscience, moving into "O my offence is rank." Claudius finally blocks out the images by covering the screen with his hand, having had enough. Hamlet, however, does not see Claudius reading these images as his own story.

The problem narcissism poses in Almereyda's *Hamlet* is not simply that a Buddhist conception of "interbeing" legitimizes the voyeurism of the male gaze, equated by Laura Mulvey (1970) and others with the pornographic, male gaze; rather, Hamlet's disembodied knowledge acquired through video is the problem, *à la* Graham Dalton (James Spader) in *Sex, Lies, and Videotape*. The most sexualized moment of the film comes in the use of *Deep Throat* (dir. Gerald Damiano, 1972) footage in Hamlet's film, *The Mousetrap*. The porn actors are to be equated with what Hamlet assumes are the randy Claudius and Gertrude. Hamlet gets off (the hook) while Ophelia is left holding the letters, if not his bag, precisely because all romantic physical contact is live for Hamlet. He does embrace and kiss Ophelia at two different points, but the haptic video footage is tantalizingly intimate, tactile, and ambiguous, unlike the porn footage or the rather explicit footage of Hamlet and Ophelia having sex in Kenneth Branagh's *Hamlet*.[52] Does Hamlet's video footage of Ophelia show us a moment in which Hamlet's appearance is unwelcome and obtrusive, as if he were spying on her like another Laertes? Is that why she covers her face with her book? Or is this a moment of post-coital self-consciousness on her part? Ophelia's interiority is not the issue for Hamlet, however. His ability to use video to simulate her as live but not sexual is at one with his misrecognition of his own mediatization of "interbeing" as a live voice(-over).

Postdiasporic cinemas as the end of postcolonial Shakespeare criticism?

If cinema and media have undone the diaspora, deconstructed it so radically that post-colonial concepts of hybridity and difference may now be seen to have always already depended on an inadequate model of globalization that in turn relied on, whether overtly or not, oppositions between the Western authority and the nation-state as original and its Eastern transnational, diasporic subversion, what is postcolonial Shakespeare criticism to do when it comes to Shakespeare-related film? I am not interested in offering a prescriptive answer to this question, but I am interested in clarifying the issues related to it. To be sure, the fact that films are produced and financed transnationally does not mean that nations and national cinemas have ceased to exist, that the significance of the local entirely vanishes, or that Shakespeare cannot be used in relation to national myths represented in film.[53] Nations select the films that are nominated at the Academy Awards for "best foreign film," and there was a heated debate in India, for example, about whether *Monsoon Wedding* or *Lagaan* should have been nominated. Yet even in nationally supported cinemas, the impact of trans-nationalism marketing has undone distinctions between margin and center. The default position for Shakespeare is not universality or neo-universality, however, but cinematic abjection, and by extension the abjection of pedagogy and criticism, which fails to cross over or succeeds in doing so only by circulating obsolete concepts and critical practices.

Belatedness is the fate of postcolonial criticism in particular and criticism in general, even if it does begin to make productive use of new electronic media. If the assumptions that currently enable postcolonial Shakespeare criticism give way to a deeper understanding of the temporal and geographical complexities of Shakespeare's postdiasporic cinematic circulation and citations, that is, I should think, a salutary effect. Given that Shakespeare's own theater depended on a vast series of dislocations, from the rural to the urban, from the religious to the secular, from the free to the commercial, and so on, did it ever make sense to think of the plays as being located in the first place?

Notes

1 Similarly, Shakespeare film critics have not attended to Shakespeare in Asian cinemas nor to diasporic cinemas. Except for much older films such as James Ivory's *Shakespeare Wallah* (1965), Kurosawa's Shakespeare film adaptations and the documentary *When Hamlet Came to Mizoram* (dir. Pankaj Butalia, 1997), no Asian films or television documentaries have been discussed, nor has the Asian diaspora in Western Shakespeare-related films, apart from very brief discussions of *Hard Boiled* (dir. John Woo, 1992) and *Tombstone* (dir. George P. Cosmatos, 1993) by Breight 1997. The list of Asian and Asian diasporic films related to Shakespeare is too long to list here.

2 On this debate, see Barker *et al.* 1994; Radhakrishanan 1996: 133–54; Loomba 1997: 2001. The best contribution to this debate, to my mind, is Dirlik 1997.

3 See the end of Mishra's study of Bollywood (2001) for an example.

4 While critics like Ang 2001 rightly eschew a simplistic opposition between oppressive nation-states and liberating diasporas, they nevertheless recirculate radically compromised notions of hybridity and mimicry when discussing film, literature, and theater. The postdiaspora shows that hybridity and sly mimicry always already failed to work the way postcolonial critics have argued it has. Postcolonial critique depends on the very oppositions it wants to deconstruct, and though it often presents itself as engaging in deconstruction, it is actually affirming a series of binary oppositions that cannot be sustained, as film, even more racially than print, so clearly shows. Identifications of hybridity with subversion are always already breaking down inside of postcolonial criticism. Robert Young (1995: 27), writing that hybridity "is a key term in that wherever it emerges it suggests the impossibility of essentialism" is a typically self-defeating assertion, since it is itself completely essentialist (hybridity, that is, is essentially anti-essentialist). The problem with hybridity as a concept is not, as has sometimes been argued, that it is merely a fashionable term, that it is a false substitution for a more truly radical language, or that it depends on an ethical and hence ahistorical account of cultural difference. The problem is that there is only hybridity, particularly when it comes to Shakespeare. Hence, there is no Western, original, hegemonic, imperialist, orientalist, cinematic Shakespeare one could usefully oppose to a subversive, multicultural, anti-imperialist Asian or Asian diasporic Shakespeare cinema.

5 See, for example, the essays in Palumbo-Liu 1995.

6 Along similar lines, Axel writes "to account for the creation of the diaspora, not through a definitive relation to place, but through formations of temporality, affect, and corporeality. The diasporic imaginary, then, does not act as a new kind of place of origin but indicates a process of identification generative of diasporic subjects" (2002: 412).

7 I saw *Fuck Hamlet*, too late to be able to include a discussion of it in this chapter. The film is about an out-of-work (formerly East) German actor in Berlin who periodically rehearses lines from Hamlet's "To be or not to be" soliloquy as he has random encounters with Korean immigrants and tourists, two of whom, at the end of the film, accidentally run him down outside the Café Adler on Friedrichstrasse just after he has recited Hamlet's last speech. My thanks to Ulrike Unfug for obtaining a copy for me.

8 My thanks to Darren Pangbourne of the BBC for sending me a copy of *Twelfth Night*. The phenomenon of Shakespeare films that engage reverse diasporic immigration back to the

UK deserves more attention than I can give it in the space of this essay. In some cases, such as *Beginner's Luck* (dir. James Callis and Nick Cohen, 2001), about a young and struggling theater director (James Callis) who wants to do *The Tempest*, Shakespeare remains wholly Caucasian. Despite periodic fantasies of producing *The Tempest* like a colonial import, marked through allusions to the beach at the end of *Shakespeare in Love*, it is precisely the failure of performances of the play in a London strip club and then in an Indian restaurant that drives the director to take the performance to Paris (where it also fails). In other cases, reverse immigration has put significant pressure on the British practice of race-blind casting in Shakespeare productions. While casting in productions like the BBC *Twelfth Night* remains color-blind, race also functions (inconsistently, to be sure) as a signifier. In the TV film *Macbeth on the Estate* (dir. Penny Woolcock, 1997), for example, David Harewood, a West African actor who plays Macduff, is differentiated from Macbeth both by his race and by a prologue and epilogue that allows his perspective to frame the action of the film.

9 The point holds true for Shakespeare theater productions as well. Anthony Dawson's attempt to salvage a benign version of Shakespeare's universality by attending to the ways in which "Shakespeare shows how the historically and geographically particular . . . can be reconfigured as the universal in a thousand different locations" (2002: 190) fails precisely because the universal and location cannot be "placed."

10 On the limits of reading a film in relation to the geographical location seen in the film, see Lo 2001.

11 For attempts to reconcile film and geography, see Aitken and Zonn 1994 and Jameson 1995.

12 See also architecture theory. Ignasi de Sola-Morales Rubio writes, for example:

> This [older idea of place] produced a conservative culture of the city, imitative of the past and committed above all to any kind of recuperation, permanence, custody, and remembrance of the genius of the place. Today this situation seems to have undergone substantial modification. We are experiencing a media culture in which distances are reduced to virtual instantaneity and in which the reproduction of images by mechanisms of every kind means that they are no longer linked to any one place but float unattached over the length and breadth of the planet. At the same time, the society of ubiquity or the total village or the world of the immaterial, while giving rise to simultaneity, multiple presence, and the generation of new stimuli, also produces feelings of profound estrangement.
>
> (1992, 113)

13 Iyer 2000 mentions Shakespeare at several points in his penultimate chapter: "The Empire," 234–55.

14 See Kittler 1990 and 1999 where multimedia "discourse networks" are tied to developments in capitalism. See also Rey Chow's brilliant discussion "Media, Matter, and Migrancy," 1994: 165–80.

15 There may also be an allusion to *Lear* later in the film when Whale says "undo this button." Christopher Bram's novel *Father of Frankenstein*, on which the film is based, has several Shakespeare citations.

16 For examples, see the Shakespeare-citing Romanian giant (Gheorge Muresan) who travels to Las Vegas to make movies in *My Giant* (dir. Michael Lehmann, 1998), *Broken English* (dir. Gregor Nicolas, 1996), a diaspora film spin-off of *Romeo and Juliet* featuring Bosnians and Maoris in Australia, and the Australian child molestation victim and Shakespeare lover heroine of *Lilian's Story* (dir. Jerzy Domaradzki, 1995).

17 On Bollywood, see Mishra 2001. There are several national cinemas in India, but the only transnational one is from Bombay (the films are in Hindi and almost all have English subtitles). Nevertheless, Tamil and other regional films also cite Shakespeare.

18 "What's Wrong with Shah Rukh Khan?" 5/16/02: <http://www.1947.lt/_disk1/0000025b.htm>. See also the book by Mushtaq Sheikh, *Devdas, the Indian Hamlet* (2002). It has an epilogue by director Sanjay Leela Bhansali. And see also the opening line of a

newspaper article by Amit Roy: "London: A friend of mine, given to making provocative utterances for the sake of making provocative utterances, says that if William Shakespeare were alive today, he would be writing Bollywood scripts" (10/27/02): <http://mid-day.com/columns/amit_roy/2002/october/34832.htm>.

19 Another symptom is the website hollywoodbollywood.com. A similar back and forth movement between Indian appropriations of English Shakespeare and English Shakespeare-anizing of Indian writers begins quite early on. Though numerous Indian critics now claim, in a variation of the German claim for "unsere Shakespeare," that major Indian writers such as Kaliadaas and Tagore are "their Shakespeare"(see Srivastava 1921; Dwividi 1923; Krishnamoorthy 1972; Adarsh 1976). The first person to make the comparison between Kalidaas and Shakespeare, however, was an eighteenth-century Englishman, William Jones (17). See also Drew 1987.

20 Jha (2001) adds:

> My film will be about this man with three sons who are all partly a reflection of his personality. Coppola's Sonny Corleone had his father's anger. Fredo was the soft romantic while Michael was the patient pragmatic son. The elder son will be played by Akshay Kumar while the two other sons might be played by Abhishek Bachchan and Aftab Shivdasani. Q: How do you react to critics who say you're successful only when you adapt Hollywood films? Jha: When you seek inspiration from a Hollywood film, the whole content and approach is far more contemporary. But let me reiterate, Raaz wasn't *What Lies Beneath*, as everyone seems to think.

21 According to the American producer, this *Hamlet* is a "chilling thriller which will have a global appeal." The film uses major Bollywood actors in every role. The story is about a Rajput prince living, loving, and killing in the India of the 1850s, in the backdrop of the turbulent times when princely states were falling under the control of the British Empire. Hrithik will play Hamlet, Hollywood style. See Ratnottama Sengupta, "Hrithik will play Hamlet, Hollywood Style": <http://www.geocities.com/aboutindia2000/article/hrithik_will_play_hamlet.htm>. There has been some controversy over whether Hrithik will star. See Rakhee Gupta, "Roshan Goes Global": <http://www.tribuneindia.com/2001/20010322/main8.htm#2>; "Hollywood Will Have To Wait," *Asiaweek*, March 23, 2001, Vol. 27, No. 11: <http://www.asiaweek.com/asiaweek/magazine/nations/0,8782,102615,00.html>; Subhash K. Jha, "Hrithik not to play Hamlet, a Hollywood film," India Abroad News Service: <http://movies.indiainfo.com/scoop/hrithik.html>; "Hrithik signs Hollywood movie" (02/27/02): <http://movies.nazara.com/news/index.asp>.

22 The film flopped in India but garnered positive reviews in the US, particularly from Stephen Holden and Kevin Thomas. Holden writes: "The story's climax, echoing *Hamlet*, is a play-within-a-play performed for Paravasu and his court by a troupe of traveling players, including Aravasu, who disguises himself as a demon." For the complete reviews, go to the film website at <http://www.agnivarsha.com>.

23 A reviewer comments: "[Dina Pathak's] . . . well-placed Shakespeare lines draw a great connection between the pop-culture of Bollywood and the popular appeal of the Bard's works back in the day. Overall, Mehta proves that she can't be pigeonholed as a controversy-stirring *auteur* and that her love for Indian film transcends location" (Banerjee 2002).

24 The first time Mistry ever went to India and to Hollywood was to film *The Guru*. See <http://www.bbc.co.uk/films/2002/08/07/jimi_mistry_the_guru_interview.shtml>. For an account of Shakespeare and diasporic cinemas, see Burt forthcoming b.

25 Sitesh Debnath 2001. "Aishwarya to play Mumtaz Mahal," *Tribune of India* (05/17/01): <http://www.tribuneindia.com/2001/20010517/main8.htm>. See also <http://www.aishwarya-rai.net/movies/info/itajmahal.html>, (05/25/01). The official film website is at <http://www.tajmahalfilm.com>.

26 Allusions to Shakespeare are also frequently made by Indian film critics. For example: Gurash entitles his chapter, "Play On . . . the Music" (in Joshi 2001: 56–87); Garga entitles his fifth

chapter "The Sound and Fury" (1996); Ganguly entitles a subsection of his book on Ray "To be or not to be a *Nabina*" (2000: 61); and Chakravarty says "the second impulse . . . sought to give textual analysis a local habitation and a name" (1993: 310).

27 See Jha 2001. Bachchan also performed Shakespeare in India. "Harivansh Rai, by then a senior Hindi litterateur, improvised a theatre group from his own family members and began productions of Hindi blank verse translations of Shakespeare at the Little Theatre Gallery in New Delhi. The performances which lasted a few years attracted favourable notice in restricted circles and Amitabh came in for much praise for his roles in *Othello* and *Julius Caesar*." <http://www.3to6.com/final_retro/lamitabh4.htm>. And Bachchan stars in David Dhawan's *Bade Miyan Chote Miyan*, a remake of *The Comedy of Errors*. See Srinivasan 1998. One reviewer says that Bachchan's "father, Dr Bachchan, was the first to translate Shakespeare into Hindi verse. He dedicated his translation of *Hamlet* to his son Amitabh." See Saad El-Din 2001. See also Somaaya 1999. Bachchan's son, Abishek, has also done Shakespeare:

> I went to Boston University for two and a half years. I took up liberal arts, and then fine arts and drama . . . I was still on the Shakespeare trip! But then, I consulted my dad and he said, "Look, if you want to act, why don't you come here? Because Shakespeare doesn't work here!" . . . I took drama as a school subject. In British schools they have it as a regular term subject at the O and A levels. We did some Shakespeare, and more contemporary plays. So, yeah! I got a lot of range of plays to act in. I regret only one fact – that I never got to play Hamlet! It was a play we studied in school, and it's my favourite, but that's a dream that never came true.
>
> (Ke 2002)

28 For more on Shakespeare in Indian cinema, see Burt forthcoming b. Films I discuss include, among others, *Sholay* (*Flames*, dir. Ramesh Sippy, 1975), and *1942: A Love Story* (dir. Vidhu Vinod Chopra, 1994).

29 An Indian reviewer comments:

> *Moulin Rouge* actually seems rather Shakespearean at times. Even though the subplot of the movie is ostensibly set in India it seems more of the Shakespearean meta-theatre, i.e. point-to-the-artifice convention, and the verse-like dialogue seems more of a continuation of Luhrmann's *Romeo+ Juliet* venture.
>
> (Aparita 2001)

See also Tsering 2001 and Halter 2002.

30 Luhrmann has succeeded handsomely as a writer and director and adapter of Shakespeare, so as *auteur* and writer his position is not all like the Bohemian writer Christian's (and unlike Christian, who loses Satine to consumption, Luhrmann is happily married to his set designer, Catherine Martin).

31 MTV became a major influence; see Gokulsing and Dissanayake 1998: 21–2.

32 For spin-offs, see *Reshma Aur Shera* (*Reshma and Shera*) (dir. Sunil Dutt, 1971); *Bobby* (dir. Raj Kapoor, 1973), *Romeo in Sikkim* (dir. Kaul Karikishen, 1975); *Romeo* (dir. S.S. Nair, 1976), and *Ek Duuje Ke Liye* (*Made for Each Other*, dir. K. Balachander, 1981).

33 This confinement is attempted in the final sentence of Mishra 2001.

34 Thompson also leaves out a mention of *Hamlet* in the novel. On *Measure for Measure* in the novel, see Derry 1993. And on the literary practice of quoting Shakespeare, see Pinch 1996: 1–65, 94–7, 163–92.

35 For example, North (1999) discusses the film without considering Shakespeare and China in the film or Lee as a Taiwanese director. Conversely, Dariotis and Fung (1997) discuss the film with reference to Lee as a director but leave out of account Thompson's screenplay, Austen's novel, and Shakespeare.

36 The contrast between Elinor and Marianne is even more heightened in the screenplay by a speech of Marianne's deleted in the film. Her cut lines link her budding romance to Brandon

with reading: "Brandon has promised me the run of his library and I shall read at least six hours a day. By the end of the year I expect to have improved my learning a great deal" (Thompson 1995: 190). Marianne moves away from her oral performative mode, linked to Willoughby, as Brandon, an emotive reader of poetry, appears to be a suitable stand-in for Edward, whose reading aloud she found so disappointing.

37 The published screenplay (Thompson 1995) anticipates the DVD commentary as it includes an introduction by Doran.

38 For a discussion of the many ways the film transforms James's novel, see Mitchell 2002. And for an analysis of various kinds of cultural capital in James and in the film, see Graham 2002. Both critics find the film far less interesting than I do.

39 Even much earlier films that seem markedly Orientalist have their own kinds of complexity. For example, *The Maltese Falcon* (dir. John Huston, 1941) mixes references to Hong Kong with references to Shakespeare where sexuality complicates a gendered distinction between male Shakespeare hero and female (semi-)Asiatic heroine. Sam Spade (Humphrey Bogart) misquotes *The Tempest*: "The, uh, stuff that dreams are made of." Anticipating Elsa Bannister (Rita Hayworth) in Orson Welles's *The Lady from Shanghai* (1948), Brigid O'Shaughnessy (Mary Astor), the femme fatale, is Caucasian but linked to the Far East. Spade notices the label from O'Shaughnessy's fashionable hat, "Lucille Shop, Queen's Road C, Hong Kong," and when we see the newspaper showing ships "Arriving Today," we read that "5.35 p.m. – La Paloma from Hong Kong" has been circled. "*Hamlet* in Flames" (dir. Don Chaffey, 1957), an episode of the British television series *The New Adventures of Charlie Chan* about the sale of a "*Hamlet* Folio" stolen by a former Nazi officer while he served in France during World War II, even more explicitly links Shakespeare to a diasporic Chinese context. In this case, the complication arises from then current racially hybrid casting practices: a British actor, J. Carrol Naish, played Charlie Chan, and James Hong played his "number one son," Barry, whose accents are also reversed (Naish speaks with an unmarked accent). For another gender and racial complication, see "Lucy Meets Orson Welles" (dir. James V. Kern, 1956), where Lucille Ball appears in a magic act dressed up as a Chinese Princess named "Princess Loo See," and then upstages Welles by reciting Juliet's line "O Romeo, Romeo, wherefore art thou Romeo?"

40 Another possibly Orientalist touch may be seen at a costume ball based on parties given by the Duke and Duchess of Devonshire in the 1890s. Fanny Assingham (Anjelica Huston) attends a costume ball at the Verver London townhouse dressed as a Renaissance Queen, possibly Mary, Queen of Scots (her husband is dressed as an – her? – executioner), with a woman dressed as a Japanese Geisha in the background to Fanny's left. The costume ball in the film was based on the Devonshire House Ball on Park Lane, a grand ball given by the Duke and Duchess of Devonshire in the 1890s – the most famous of all the costume balls which were the rage at that time. They were attended by the British aristocracy and by very rich Americans – many of whom had married into the aristocracy. Lancaster House, where the ball was shot, is one of the few surviving private London townhouses: most were destroyed during World War II, or have been torn down.

41 See also *Bye Bye Brazil* (dir. Carols Diegues, 1979) for a similar story about an acting troupe in Brazil who leave Sao Paulo for the countryside only to discover that the towns there have recently installed a television set in the town square. And for a version of the same story with an Irish troupe that does parts of *Gone with the Wind* and *Othello*, see *The Playboys* (dir. Gillies MacKinnon, 1992).

42 While the Renaissance is not central to *The Golden Bowl*, Renaissance painting is central in *The Wings of the Dove*.

43 In this way, the film's making us question what we know parallels the way the novel makes us question whether Maggie ever knows that Prince and Charlotte have been having an affair.

44 In this account, a progressive film could also show critically the exclusion of Asians from Shakespeare and speech.

45 The telling of the story in terms that mirrors the students' lives is of course an index of the dumbing down of Shakespeare. See Burt 1999 and Ronell 2002.

46 See, by contrast, the earlier teen comedy, *Porky's 2* (dir. Bob Clark, 1983), in which Shakespeare and anti-racist multiculturalism come into explicit play. There is a scene in a Japanese sushi restaurant in *American Pie*, but there is no sense in the film that racism even exists.

47 For other examples, see the black teacher in the *Romeo and Juliet* episode of *Lizzie McQuire* ("Lizzie in the Middle," dir. Savage Steve Noland, Disney Channel, Season Two, Episode 46, original air date August 23, 2002) and the Asian teacher Mrs. Kwan in an episode of *DeGrassi: The Next Generation* involving *Romeo and Juliet* ("Friday Night," dir. Paul Fox, ABC, Season One, Episode 11, original air date January 27, 2002).

48 The film's website is at <http://www.theemperorsclub.com/>.

49 See Burt forthcoming a.

50 Shakespeare, race, and ethnicity come up more broadly in horror films in relation to abjection; Chinese opium, including multiple citations, and African-American directors in *From Hell*; cannibalism and vampirism in *Blade II*, with an allusion to Caliban; and vampire Lestate citing some of Othello's lines as he kills a Creole prostitute in *Interview with a Vampire*.

51 The note on the documentary says:

> This documentary directed by Gaetano Kazuo Maida and narrated by Ben Kingsley profiles the life and work of the world-renowned Buddhist monk, scholar, peace activist, and poet. Thich Nhat Hanh grew up in Vietnam during times of resistance to the French and civil war, only narrowly escaping death several times. He became known for his pioneer work promoting "engaged" Buddhism, social action on behalf of the poor and the refugees. He also served as chair of the Vietnamese Buddhist Peace Delegation to the Paris Peace Talks during the Vietnam War.

52 On "haptic visuality" and tactility, see Marks 2000: 162–90.

53 Indeed, one of the problems with the nomadic, Deleuzian model of "Shakespace" formulated by Hedrick and Reynolds 2000 is its relentless abstraction when speaking of territorialization. There's no sense of either the universal or the particular or of the global and local.

REFERENCES

Almereyda, Michael (2000) *William Shakespeare's Hamlet: A Screenplay Adaptation by Michael Almereyda*, Introduction by Ethan Hawke. London: Faber & Faber.

Anderegg, Michael (1999) *Orson Welles, Shakespeare and Popular Culture*. New York: Columbia University Press.

Anon. (n.d.a) "Kenneth Branagh: Love's Labour's Lost," *Daily Telegiraffe*. Available online at <http://members.tripod.com/~DailyTelegiraffe/branaghloveslabourslost.html>. Accessed January 3, 2003.

Anon. (n.d.b) "Kenneth Branagh: Making Love," *Daily Telegiraffe*. Available online at <http://members.tripod.com/~DailyTelegiraffe/branaghloveslabourslostmakingof.html>. Accessed January 3, 2003.

Anon. (1996) "Laurence Fishburne Stars in Movie of Shakespeare's *Othello*," *Jet* 89: 32–5.

Anon. (1999) "Shakespeare in America" in Peter Rawlings (ed.) *Americans on Shakespeare 1776–1914*. Aldershot, Hampshire: Ashgate, 159–62.

Anon. (2001) "The Story of O," *Entertainment Weekly* (August 10): 20–3.

Anon. (2002) "Born in Bollywood, Made in UK," Nrilinks.com. http://www.nrilinks.com/NRINews/EN2875.html>.

Adarsh Bala, Kum (1976) "Shakespeare and Kalidasa," *Triveni* (Madras) 44(4): 59–70.

Adelman, Janet (1992) *Suffocating Mothers: Fantasies of Maternal Origins in Shakespeare's Plays, Hamlet to The Tempest*. London and New York: Routledge.

Agnew, Jean-Christophe (1986) *Worlds Apart: Market and Theater in Anglo-American Thought 1550–1750*. Cambridge: Cambridge University Press.

Aitken, Stuart C. and Leo E. Zonn (1994) "Geographic and Cinematic Theory: Framing Spaces and Sequencing Spectacles. Re-presenting the Place Pastiche" in Stuart C. Aitken and Leo E. Zonn (eds) *Place, Power, Situation, and Spectacle: A Geography of Film*. Lanham, Md.: Rowman & Littlefield, 3–25.

Allen, Carol (2001) "In the Mouths of Babes," *The Times* (June 21): 29.

Alleva, Richard (1996) "Sliced and Diced," *Commonweal* (April 19): 18–19.

Andreae, Christopher (1993) " 'Animated Tales' of Shakespeare," *Christian Science Monitor* (January 6): 14.

Andrews, Christopher (2000) "Richard III on Film: The Subversions of the Viewer," *Literature Film Quarterly* 28(2): 82–94.

Ang, Ien (2001) *On Not Speaking Chinese: Living Between Asia and the West*. London and New York: Routledge.

Apple, Michael W. (1995) "Cultural Capital and Official Knowledge" in Michael Bérubé and Cary Nelson (eds) *Higher Education Under Fire: Politics, Economics, and the Crisis of the Humanities*. London and New York: Routledge.

Arroyo, José (1993) "Death, Desire and Identity: The Political Unconscious of 'New Queer Cinema'" in Joseph Bristow and Angelica R. Wilson (eds) *Activating Theory: Lesbian, Gay, Bisexual Politics*. London: Lawrence & Wishart.

—— (1997) "Kiss Kiss Bang Bang," *Sight and Sound* 7.3 (New Series): 6–9.

Auge, Marc (1995) *Non-Places: Introduction to an Anthropology of Supermodernity*, trans. John Howe. London: Verso.

Auslander, Philip (1999) *Liveness: Performance in a Mediatized Culture*. London and New York: Routledge.

Axel, Brian Keith (2002) "The Diasporic Imaginary," *Public Culture* 14(2): 411–28.

Bachchan, Jaya and Khalid Mohamed (2002) *To Be or Not To Be: Amitabh Bachchan*. India: Saraswathi Creations.

Bailur, Jayanti (1992) *Ruth Prawer Jhabvala: Fiction and Film*. New Delhi: Arnold.

Baker, Bob (2002) "Are these Videos Rated C for Clean or Compromised?," *Los Angeles Times*. (October 14). Available online at <http://www.calendarlive.com/cl-et-baker14oct14,0,3261253.story>.

Ball, Robert Hamilton (1968) *Shakespeare on Silent Film: A Strange Eventful History*. London: George Allen & Unwin Ltd.

Banerjee Neela (2002) "'Bollywood/Hollywood' Celebrates Double Vision," *AsianWeek*, Nov. 22–Nov. 28. Available online at <http://www.asianweek.com/2002_11_22/arts_bollywood.html>.

Barbour, Reid (1998) *English Epicures and Stoics: Ancient Legacies in Early Stuart Culture*. Amherst, Mass.: University of Massachusetts Press.

Barker, Francis, Peter Hulme, and Margaret Iversen (eds) (1994) *Colonial Discourse, Postcolonial Theory*. Manchester and New York: Manchester University Press.

Barthes, Roland (1977) "The Third Meaning: Research Notes on Some Eisenstein Stills" in *Image/Music/Text*, ed. and trans. S. Heath. New York: Hill & Wang.

Bashkoff, Tracey, Nancy Spector, Norman Bryson, and Thomas Kellein (eds) (2000) *Sugimoto Portraits*. New York: Guggenheim Museum, distributed by H.N. Abrams Inc.

Baudrillard, Jean (1986) *America*, trans. Chris Turner. London: Verso.

Bellour, Raymond (1975) "Unattainable Text" trans. Ben Brewster in Constance Penley (ed.) (2000) *The Analysis of Film*. Bloomington, Ind.: Indiana University Press.

Belton, John (1994) *American Cinema/American Culture*. New York: McGraw-Hill, Inc.

Benjamin, Walter (1968 [1940]) "Theses on the Philosophy of History" in Hannah Arendt (ed.) and Harry Zoan (trans.) *Illuminations: Essays and Reflections*. New York: Schocken Books, 253–64.

—— (1992 [1935]) "The Work of Art in the Age of Mechanical Reproduction" in Gerald Mast, Marshall Cohen, and Leo Braudy (eds) *Film Theory and Criticism*, 4th edn. New York and Oxford: Oxford University Press, 665–81.

Bhabha, Homi K. (1986) "Signs Taken for Wonders: Questions of Ambivalence and Authority under a Tree Outside Delhi, May 1817" in Henry Louis Gates, Jr. (ed.) *"Race," Writing, and Difference*. Chicago Ill.: University of Chicago Press, 163–84.

—— (1989) "The Commitment to Theory" in Jim Pines and Paul Willemen (eds.) *Questions of Third Cinema*. London: British Film Institute Publishing.

—— (1994) *The Location of Culture*. London and New York: Routledge.

—— (1999) "Arrivals and Departures" in Hamid Naficy (ed.) *Home, Exile, Homeland: Film, Media, and the Politics of Place*. New York and London: Routledge, vii–xii.

Bhandari, Aparita (2001) "Review of *Moulin Rouge*," www.mybindi.com. Available online at <http://www.mybindi.com/arts-entertainment/whatson/moulinrouge.cfm>. Accessed January 2, 2003.

Bhavnani, Kum-Kum (2000) "Organic Hybridity or Commodification of Hybridity? Comments on Mississippi Masala," *Meridians: Feminism, Race, Transnationalism* 1(1): 187–203.

Binckley, Timothy (1990) "Digital Dilemmas" in *SIGGRAPH 1990: Digital Image, Digital Cinema*, Supplemental Issue of *Leonardo: Journal of the International Society for the Arts, Sciences and Technology* 13–19.

Blackwelder, Rob (2001) "Desert Dogme: Levring Plays by the Rules in 'The King is Alive' – Part of a Minimalist Movement by Danish Filmmakers," SPLICEDwire. Available online at <http://www.splicedonline.com/01features/klevring.html>. Accessed on April 21, 2001.

Blau, Herbert (1992) *To All Appearances: Ideology and Performance*. London and New York: Routledge.

Boose, Lynda E. (1991) "Scolding Brides and Bridling Scolds: Taming the Woman's Unruly Member," *Shakespeare Quarterly* 42(2): 179–213.

Boose, Lynda E. and Richard Burt (1997) "Totally Clueless?: Shakespeare Goes Hollywood in the 1990s" in Lynda E. Boose and Richard Burt (eds) *Shakespeare, The Movie: Popularizing the Plays on Film, TV, and Video*. London and New York: Routledge, 8–22.

Bose, Purmina and Linta Varghese (2001) "Mississippi Masala, South Asian Activism, and Agency" in Wendy S. Hesford and Wendy Kozol (eds) *Haunting Violations: Feminist Criticism and the Crisis of the "Real."* Urbana, Ill.: University of Illinois Press.

Bourdieu, Pierre (1984) *Distinction: A Social Critique of the Judgement of Taste*. Cambridge, Mass.: Harvard University Press.

Bowman, James (1996) "Bard to Death," *American Spectator* (March): 58–9.

Braidotti, Rosi (1994) *Nomadic Subjects: Embodiment and Sexual Difference in Contemporary Feminist Theory*. New York: Columbia University Press.

Branagh, Kenneth (1988) "Henry V" in Russell Jackson and Robert Smallwood (eds) *Players of Shakespeare 2: Further Essays on Shakespearean Performance by Players with the Royal Shakespeare Company*. Cambridge: Cambridge University Press.

Brantley, Ben (1996) "Othello," *New York Times* (January 21): 25.

Bratlinger, Patrick (2001) *Who Killed Shakespeare? What's Happened to English since the Radical Sixties*. London and New York: Routledge.

Brecht, Bertolt (1993) *Journals 1934–1955*. London: Methuen.

Breight, Curtis (1997) "Elizabethan World Pictures" in John J. Joughin (ed.) *Shakespeare and National Culture*. Manchester: Manchester University Press, 295–325.

Bristol, Michael D. (1990) *Shakespeare's America, America's Shakespeare*. London and New York: Routledge.

—— (1996) *Big-Time Shakespeare*. London and New York: Routledge.

Brode, D. (2000) *Shakespeare in the Movies*. Oxford: Oxford University Press.

Brodie, John (1996) "Fox Doth Use its Wiles to Sell Shakespeare," *Variety* (November 11) from clipping file, Margaret Herrick Library.

Brooks, Xan (2000) "South Side Story," *Guardian* (December 8): 10.

Brown, Geoff (1992) "Bard Suffers Slings and Arrows," *Sunday Telegraph* (November 1): 12.

Browne, Ray B. (1960) "Shakespeare in American Vaudeville and Negro Minstrelsy," *American Quarterly* 12: 374–91.

Bruster, Doug (1992) *Drama and the Market in the Age of Shakespeare*. Cambridge: Cambridge University Press.

Buckley, Sandra (1991) " 'Penguin in Bondage:' A Graphic Tale of Japanese Comic Books" in Constance Penley and Andrew Ross (eds) *Technoculture*, Minneapolis, Minn.: University of Minnesota Press, 163–96.

Buhler, Stephen (2002a) "Reviving Juliet, Repackaging Romeo: Transformations of Character in Pop and Post-Pop Music," in Richard Burt (ed.) *Shakespeare After Mass Media*, New York: Palgrave, 243–64.

—— (2002b) *Shakespeare in the Cinema: Ocular Proof*. Albany, N.Y.: State University of New York Press.

Bullough, Geoffrey (ed.) (1962) *Narrative and Dramatic Sources of Shakespeare*. New York: Columbia University Press.

Bulman, J.C. and H.R. Coursen (eds) (1988) *Shakespeare on Television*. Hanover, N.H.: University Press of New England.

Burnett, Mark Thornton (2000) "Impressions of Fantasy: Adrian Noble's *A Midsummer Night's Dream*" in Mark Thornton Burnett and Ramona Wray (eds) *Shakespeare, Film, Fin de Siècle*. New York: St. Martin's Press, 89–101.

—— (2002a) " 'We Are the Makers of Manners': The Branagh Phenomenon" in Richard Burt (ed.) *Shakespeare after Mass Media*. New York: Palgrave, 83–105.

—— (2002b) " 'Fancy's Images': Reinventing Shakespeare in Christine Edzard's *The Children's Midsummer Night's Dream*," *Literature/Film Quarterly* 30(2): 166–70.

Burnett, Mark Thornton and Ramona Wray (eds) *Shakespeare, Film, Fin de Siècle*. New York: St. Martin's Press.

Burt, Richard (1993) *Licensed by Authority: Ben Jonson and the Discourses of Censorship*. Ithaca, N.Y. and London: Cornell University Press.

—— (1994) "Baroque Down: The Trauma of Censorship in Psychoanalysis and Queer Film Re-Visions of Shakespeare and Marlowe" in Michael Hattaway, Boika Sokolova, and Derek Roper (eds) *Shakespeare in the New Europe*. Sheffield: Sheffield Academic Press, 328–50.

—— (1999 [1998]) *Unspeakable ShaXXXspeares: Queer Theory and American Kiddie Culture*, 2nd edn. New York: St. Martin's Press.

—— (2000) "*Shakespeare in Love* and the End of the Shakespearean: Academic and Mass Culture Constructions of Literary Authorship" in Mark Thornton Burnett and Ramona Wray, *Shakespeare, Film, Fin de Siècle*. New York: St. Martin's Press, 203–31.

—— (2001) "T(e)en Things I Hate About Girlene Shakesploitation Flicks in the Late 1990s, or, Not So Fast Times at Shakespeare High" in Lisa Starks and Courtney Lehmann (eds) *Spectacular Shakespeare: Critical Theory and Popular Cinema*. Madison, N.J.: Fairleigh Dickinson University Press, 205–32.

—— (ed.) (2002a) *Shakespeare After Mass Media*. New York: Palgrave.

—— (2002b) "To E- or Not To E-? Disposing of Schlockspeare in the Age of Digital Media" in Richard Burt (ed.) *Shakespeare After Mass Media*. New York: Palgrave, 1–32.

—— (2002c) "Slammin' Shakespeare in Acc(id)ents yet Unknown: Liveness, Cinem(edi)a, and Racial Dis-integration," *Shakespeare Quarterly* 53: 2 (Summer), 201–26. Special issue on Shakespeare and film edited by Barbara Hodgdon.

—— (forthcoming a) " 'Scary (Movie) Quotes': Citing Shakespeare and the Cinematic Subcanny in Gothic Horror Film and Television Adaptations" in Barbara Hodgdon and W.B. Worthen (eds) *The Blackwell Companion to Shakespeare in Performance*. London: Blackwell Press.

—— (forthcoming b) "Shakespeare Goes Bollywood: Rechanneling the Bard and the Indian Cinematic Abject" in Dennis Kennedy and Yong Li Lan (eds) *Foreign Shakespeare, II*. Cambridge: Cambridge University Press.

Buss, Robin (1992) "A Palpable Hit," *Independent*: *The Sunday Review* (November 8): 33.

Butler, Judith (1993) "Endangered/Endangering: Schematic Racism and White Paranoia" in Robert Gooding-Williams (ed.) *Reading Rodney King, Reading Urban Uprising*. New York and London: Routledge, 15–22.

Butler, Shane (2002) *The Hand of Cicero*. London and New York: Routledge.

Calderwood, James L. (1971) *Shakespearean Metadrama*. Minneapolis, Minn.: University of Minnesota Press.

Calhoun, J. (1996) "Richard III," *TCI* 30 (April): 34–7.

Carruthers, Mary (1990) *The Book of Memory: A Study of Memory in Medieval Culture*. Cambridge: Cambridge University Press.

Cartelli, Thomas (1999) *Repositioning Shakespeare: National Formations, Postcolonial Appropriations*. London and New York: Routledge.

Cartmell, Deborah (2000) *Interpreting Shakespeare on Screen*. New York: St. Martin's Press.

Casey, Diana M. (2001) "Emma Thompson's *Sense and Sensibility* as Gateway to Austen's Novel" in Linda Troost and Sayre Greenfield (eds) *Jane Austen in Hollywood*. Lexington, Ky.: University Press of Kentucky, 140–7.

Cavell, Stanley (1979 [1971]) *The World Viewed: Reflections on the Ontology of Film*. Cambridge, Mass.: Harvard University Press.

—— (1982) "The Fact of Television," *Daedalus* 111(4): 75–96.

Chakrabarty, Dipesh (2000) *Provincializing Europe: Postcolonial Thought and Historical Difference*. Princeton, N.J.: Princeton University Press.

Chakravarty, Sumita S. (1993) *National Identity in Indian Popular Cinema, 1947–1987*. Austin, Tex.: University of Texas Press.

Cham, Mbye (2001) "Official History, Popular Memory: Reconfiguration of the African Past in the Films of Ousmane Sembene" in Marcia Landy (ed.) *The Historical Film: History and Memory in Media*. New Brunswick, N.J.: Rutgers University Press, 261–8.

Chamisso, Adelbert von (1964) *Reise um die Welt mit der Romanzoffischen Entdeckungsexpedition in den Jahren 1815 bis 1818* in Otto Flake (ed.) *Gesammelte Werke*. Gütersloh: Sigbert Mohn, 289–588.

Chartier, Roger, Frank Mowery, Peter Stallybrass, and Heather Wolfe (2002). "Hamlet's Tables and the Technologies of Writing in Renaissance England." Unpublished.

Chedgzoy, Kate (1995) *Shakespeare's Queer Children*. Manchester: Manchester University Press.

Chhabra, Aseem (2002) " '*Bollywood/Hollywood* is not a Bollywood film': Deepa Mehta's New Venture has the Hybrid Sensibility of India and the West," Rediffmovies.com. Nov. 21. <http://www.rediff.com/entertai/2002/nov/21deepa.htm>.

Chow, Rey (1994) *Writing Diaspora: Tactics of Intervention in Contemporary Cultural Studies*. Bloomington, Ind.: Indiana University Press.

Cieko, Anne T. (1997) "Transnational Action: John Woo, Hong Kong, Hollywood" in Hsiao-Peng and Sheldon Hsia-Peng Lu (eds) *Transnational Chinese Cinemas: Identity, Nationhood, Gender*. Honolulu, Hawaii: University of Hawaii Press, 221–37.

Clare, John (2001) "UK Schools Shelve Shakespeare?," *Daily Telegraph* (February 18).

Clausewitz, Carl von (1976 [1931]) *On War*, ed. and trans. Michael Howard and Peter Paret. Princeton, N.J.: Princeton University Press.

Clover, Carol J. (1992) *Men, Women, and Chain Saws: Gender in the Modern Horror Film*. Princeton, N.J.: Princeton University Press.

Cobos, Juan and Miguel Rubio (1966) "Welles and Falstaff," *Sight and Sound* 35 (Autumn): 159–60.

Collick, John (1989) *Shakespeare, Cinema and Society*. Manchester: Manchester University Press.

Collins, Kris (1996) "White-washing the Black-a-Moor: *Othello*, Negro Minstrelsy and Parodies of Blackness," *Journal of American Culture* 19(3): 87–101.

Comolli, Jean-Louis, Jean-André Fieschi, Gérard Guégan, Michael Mardore, Claude Ollier, and André Téchiné (1986 [1965]) "Twenty Years On: A Discussion about American Cinema and the *politique des auteurs*" in Jim Miller (ed.) and Diana Matias (trans.) *Cahiers du Cinéma: 1960–68: New Wave, New Cinema, Reevaluating Hollywood*. Cambridge, Mass.: Harvard University Press, 196–209. Originally published in *Cahiers du Cinéma* 172 (November 1965).

Cook, D. (1992) *A History of Narrative Film*, 2nd edn. New York: Norton.

Copjec, Joan (1993) "The Phenomenal Nonphenomenal: Private Space in Film Noir" in Joan Copjec (ed.) *Shades of Noir: A Reader*. London and New York: Verso, 167–97.

Corliss, Richard (1996) "Pulp Elizabethan Fiction," *Time* (January 15): 67.

Coursen, Herbert R. (1990) *Shakespearean Performance as Interpretation*. Wilmington, Del.: University of Delaware Press.

—— (2002) *Shakespeare in Space: Recent Shakespeare Productions on Screen*. New York: Peter Lang.

Covert, Andrew (2002) "Bollywood, Here I Come," *The Independent Online*, Toronto, Issue 4, 09/12. <http://www.independentweekly.net/view.php?aid=632>.

Cowie, Elizabeth (1993) "Film Noir and Women" in Joan Copjec (ed.) *Shades of Noir: A Reader*. London and New York: Verso, 121–65.

Crofts, Stephen (1998) "Concepts of National Cinema" in John Hill and Pamela Church Gibson (eds) *The Oxford Guide to Film Studies*. Oxford and New York: Oxford University Press, 385–94.

Crowl, Samuel (1992) *Shakespeare Observed: Studies in Performance on Stage and Screen*. Athens, Ohio: Ohio University Press.

—— (2000) "Flamboyant Realist: Kenneth Branagh" in Russell Jackson (ed.) *The Cambridge Companion to Shakespeare on Film*. Cambridge: Cambridge University Press, 222–38.

—— (2002) "The Marriage of Shakespeare and Hollywood: Kenneth Branagh's *Much Ado about Nothing*" in Courtney Lehmann and Lisa S. Starks (eds) *Spectacular Shakespeare: Critical Theory and Popular Cinema*. Madison, N.J.: Fairleigh Dickinson University Press, 110–24.

D'Alessandro, K.C. (1988) "Technophilia, Cyberpunk, and Cinema," paper presented to the Society for Cinema Studies, Bozeman, Montana, 1988.

Dariotis, Wei Ming and Elieen Fung (1997) "Breaking the Soy Sauce Jar: Diaspora and Displacement in the Films of Ang Lee" in Hsiao-Peng and Sheldon Hsia-Peng Lu (eds) *Transnational Chinese Cinemas: Identity, Nationhood, Gender*. Honolulu, Hawaii: University of Hawaii Press, 187–220.

Dash, Irene (1981) "Review of the BBC's *The Taming of the Shrew*," *Shakespeare on Film Newsletter* 5(2): 7ff.

Dauman, Anatole (1995) "Lettre aux 'majors' d'Hollywood . . . et à leurs zélateurs français," *Le Monde Diplomatique* (December): 28.

Dawson, Anthony (2001) "International Shakespeare" in Stanley W. Wells and Sarah Stanton (eds) *The Cambridge Companion to Shakespeare on Stage*. Cambridge: Cambridge University Press.

Dawtrey, Adam and Monica Roman (1998) " 'Love' Triangle Times 3," *Variety* (March 23) from *Shakespeare in Love* clipping file, Margaret Herrick Library.

de Sola-Morales Rubio, Ignasi (1992) "Place: Permanence or Production?" in Cynthia Davidson (ed.) and Laura Bourland (trans.) *Anywhere*. New York: Rizzoli, 108–15.

Debord, Guy (1983) *Society of the Spectacle*. Detroit, Mich.: Black & Red.

DeCordova, Richard (1990) *Picture Personalities: The Emergence of the Star System in America*. Urbana, Ill.: University of Illinois Press.

Denby, David (1996) "Bard Again," *New York*, 15 January: 48–9.

Derry, Stephen (1993) "Jane Austen's Use of Measure for Measure in Sense and Sensibility," *Persuasions* 15 (December): 37–41.

Devine, T.M. (1999) *The Scottish Nation: 1700–2000*. London and New York: Penguin.

Dhombres, Dominique (2002) "Télévision: Globalisation," *Le Monde* (October 14). Available online at <http://www.lemonde.fr/article/0,5987,3208—294184-,00.html>. Accessed January 2, 2003.

Dickson, E. Jane (1997) "American Myth Goes West: Videos," *Daily Telegraph* (June 21).

Dionne, Craig (2002) "The Shatnerification of Shakespeare: *Star Trek* and the Commonplace Tradition" in Richad Burt (ed.) *Shakespeare after Mass Media*, New York: Palgrave, 173–9.

DiPiero, Thomas (1992) "White Men Aren't," *Camera Obscura* 30: 113–37.

Dirlik, Arif (1997) *The Postcolonial Aura: Third World Criticism in the Age of Global Capitalism*. Boulder, Colo.: Westview Press.

Dobson, Michael (1992) *The Making of the National Poet: Shakespeare, Adaptation and Authorship, 1660–1769*. Oxford: Clarendon Press.

Dolar, Mladen (1991) " 'I Shall Be With You on Your Wedding Night': Lacan and the Uncanny," *October* 58: 5–23.

Dollimore, Jonathan (1985) "Introduction: Shakespeare, Cultural Materialism, and the New Historicism" in Jonathan Dollimore and Alan Sinfield (eds) *Political Shakespeare: New Essays in Cultural Materialism*, Ithaca, N.Y. and London: Cornell University Press.

Donaldson, Peter S. (1990) *Shakespearean Films/Shakespearean Directors*. Boston, Mass.: Unwin Hyman.

—— (1991) "Taking on Shakespeare: Kenneth Branagh's Henry V," *Shakespeare Quarterly* 42: 60–71.

—— (1999) " 'All Which It Inherit': Shakespeare, Globes and Global Media," *Shakespeare Survey* 52: 183–200.

—— (2002) " 'In Fair Verona': Media, Spectacle, and Performance in *William Shakespeare's Romeo + Juliet*" in Richard Burt (ed.) *Shakespeare after Mass Media*. New York: Palgrave, 59–82.

Douglas, Mary (1966) *Purity and Danger: An Analysis of Concepts of Pollution and Taboo*. New York: Praeger.

Dowling, Maurice (1834) *Othello Travestie, An Operatic Burlesque Burletta*. London: Lacy's Acting Editions.

Downing, Crystal (2000) "Misshapen Chaos of Well-Seeming Form: Baz Luhrmann's *Romeo + Juliet*," *Literature Film Quarterly* 28(2): 125–31.

Drew, John (1987) *India and the Romantic Imagination*. Delhi: Oxford University Press.

Dunkley, Graham (1997) *The Free Trade Adventure: The WTO, the Uruguay Round and Globalism: A Critique*. London and New York: Zed Books.

Dwividi, Chhynnulal (1923) *Kalidas Aur Shakespeare*. India.

Dwyer, Racel and Divia Patel (2002). *Cinema India: The Visual Culture of Hindi Film*. London: Reaktion Books.

Dyer, Richard (1979) *Stars*. London: British Film Institute Publishing.

—— (1992) *The Matter of Images: Essays on Representation.* New York and London: Routledge.
—— (2001) "Nice Young Men who Sell Antiques – Gay Men in Heritage Cinema" in Ginette Vincendeau (ed.) *Film/Literature/Heritage: A Sight and Sound Reader.* London: British Film Institute Publishing, 43–8.
Eagleton, Terry (1983) *Literary Theory: An Introduction.* Minneapolis, Minn.: University of Minnesota Press.
Eckert, Charles W. (ed.) (1972) *Focus on Shakespearean Films.* Englewood Cliffs, N.J.: Prentice-Hall.
Eisenstein, Sergei (1988) *Eisenstein on Disney*, ed. Jay Leyda and trans. Alan Upchurch. New York: Methuen, Inc.
Elsaesser, Thomas (1987) "Tales of Sound and Fury: Observations on the Family Melodrama" in Christine Gledhill (ed.) *Home Is Where the Heart Is: Studies in Melodrama and the Woman's Film.* London: British Film Institute Publishing, 43–69.
Empson, William (1949/1930) *Seven Types of Ambiguity.* New York: New Directions.
Evans, G. Blakemore (ed.) (1984) *Romeo and Juliet.* Cambridge: Cambridge University Press.
Feldvoss, Marti (2002) "Ein Portraet: Mira Nair," *Film* (April): 22–5.
Fineman, Joel (1985) "The Turning of the Shrew" in Patricia Parker and Geoffrey Hartman (eds) *Shakespeare and the Question of Theory*, New York: Methuen, 138–59.
Fitter, Chris (1991) "A Tale of Two Branaghs: Henry V, Ideology, and the Mekong Agincourt" in Ivo Kamps (ed.) *Shakespeare Left and Right.* London and New York: Routledge.
Floyd-Wilson, Mary (2003) *English Ethnicity and Race in Early Modern Drama.* Cambridge: Cambridge University Press.
Forsyth, Neil (2000) "Shakespeare the Illusionist: Filming the Supernatural," in Russell Jackson (ed.) *The Cambridge Companion to Shakespeare on Screen.* Cambridge: Cambridge University Press, 274–94.
Francke, Lizzie (1995) "Postcards from the Edgy," *Guardian* (April 6).
Freedman, Barbara (1991) *Staging the Gaze: Postmodernism, Psychoanalysis and Shakespearean Comedy*, Ithaca, N.Y.: Cornell University Press.
—— (2000) "Critical Junctures in Shakespeare Screen History: The Case of Richard III" in Russell Jackson (ed.) *The Cambridge Companion to Shakespeare on Screen.* Cambridge: Cambridge University Press.
Freud, Sigmund (1955a) "The Uncanny" in *The Standard Edition of the Complete Psychological Works*, vol. XVII, ed. James Strachey. London: Hogarth, 217–53.
—— (1955b) "Analysis of a Phobia in a Five Year Old Boy" in *The Standard Edition of the Complete Psychological Works*, vol. X, ed. James Strachey. London: Hogarth, 3–149.
Frow, John (1997) "Toute la mémoire du monde," *Time and Commodity Culture: Essays in Cultural Theory and Postmodernity.* Oxford: Clarendon Press, 218–46.
Fuller, Graham (1993) "Gus Van Sant: Swimming Against the Current: An Interview by Graham Fuller" in *Even Cowgirls Get the Blues; My Own Private Idaho.* London: Faber & Faber.
Gabriel, Teshome (1989) "Third Cinema as Guardian of Popular Memory: Towards a Third Aesthetics" in Jim Pines and Paul Willemen (eds) *Questions of Third Cinema.* London: British Film Institute Publishing.
Ganguly, Suranjan (2000) *Satyajit Ray: In Search of the Modern.* Lanham, Md.: Scarecrow Press.
Garber, Marjorie (1987) *Shakespeare's Ghost Writers.* London: Methuen.
Garga, Bhagwan Das (1996) *So Many Cinemas: The Motion Picture in India.* Mumbai, India: Eminence Designs.
Garneau, Michel (1989) *Coriolan de William Shakespeare.* Montréal: VLB Éditeur, 7–8.
Garrick, David (1981) "Catharine and Petruchio" in *The Plays of David Garrick*, vol. 3. Carbondale, Ill.: Southern Illinois University Press.
Gasché, Rodolphe (1986) *The Tain of the Mirror.* Cambridge, Mass: Harvard University Press.
Gates, Henry Louis (1995) "Thirteen Ways of Looking at a Black Man," *New Yorker* 71 (October 23): 56–65.
Gernsheim, Helmut and Alison Gernsheim (1968) *L.J.M. Daguerre: The History of the Diorama and the Daguerrotype.* New York: Dover.
Geuens, Jean-Pierre (2002) "The Digital World Picture," *Film Comment* 55(4): 16–27.

Gilmore, Michael (1998) *Differences in the Dark: American Movies and British Theater*. New York: Columbia University Press.

Gilson, Nancy (1996) "HBO Gives Shakespeare an Animated Touch," *Columbus Dispatch* (January 14): 2F.

Gokulsing, K. Moti and Wimal Dissanayake (1998) *Indian Popular Cinema: A Narrative of Cultural Change*. Stoke-on-Trent: Trentham Books.

Goldberg, Jonathan (1994) "*Romeo and Juliet*'s Open R's" in Jonathan Goldberg (ed.) *Queering the Renaissance*. Durham, N.C. and London: Duke University Press, 218–35.

Gooding-Williams, Robert (ed.) (1993). *Reading Rodney King, Reading Urban Uprising*. London and New York: Routledge.

Graham, Wendy (2002) "The Rift in the Loot: Cognitive Dissonance for the Reader of Merchant Ivory's *The Golden Bowl*" in Susan M. Griffin (ed.) *Henry James Goes to the Movies*. Lexington, Ky.: University of Kentucky Press.

Greenaway, Peter (1991) *Prospero's Books: A Film of Shakespeare's "The Tempest."* New York: Four Walls Eight Windows.

Greenblatt, Stephen (1985) "Invisible Bullets: Renaissance Authority and its Subversion, Henry IV and Henry V" in Jonathan Dollimore and Alan Sinfield (eds) *Political Shakespeare: New Essays in Cultural Materialism*, Ithaca, N.Y. and London: Cornell University Press.

Greene, Roland (1999) *Unrequited Conquests: Love and Empire in the Colonial Americas*. Chicago, Ill.: University of Chicago Press.

Grobel, Lawrence (1994) "Interview with Anthony Hopkins," *Playboy Magazine*. Available online at <http://www.concentric.net/~dysato/playboy1.htm>. Accessed January 2, 2003.

Guardian (1992) "Animation: A Visual Symphony," *Guardian: Guardian Education* (November 23): E14. <http://film.guardian.co.uk/bollywood/story/0,11871,799351,00.html>.

—— (2002) "Bollywood Accused of Stealing Plots," *Guardian* (September 26).

Hall, Kim F. (1995) *Things of Darkness: Economies of Race and Gender in Early Modern England*. Ithaca, N.Y.: Cornell University Press.

Halpern, Richard (1997) *Shakespeare Among the Moderns*. Ithaca, N.Y.: Cornell University Press.

Halter, Ed (2002) "Moulin Raj," *Village Voice*, May 6. <http://villagevoice.com>.

Hammond, A. (1981) *The Arden Shakespeare: King Richard III*. London: Methuen.

Hanley, David (1996) "France and GATT: The Real Politics of Trade Negotiations" in Tony Chafer and Brian Jenkins (eds) *France: From the Cold War to the New World Order*. London: Macmillan, 137–51.

Haraway, Donna (1985) "A Manifesto for Cyborgs: Science, Technology and Socialist Feminism in the 1980s," *Socialist Review* 80: 65–108.

Haring-Smith, Tori (1985) *From Farce to Metadrama: A Stage History of "The Taming of the Shrew," 1594–1983*. Westport, Conn.: Greenwood Press.

Harper, Sue (1994) *Picturing the Past: The Rise and Fall of the British Costume Film*. London: British Film Institute Publishing.

Harris, Dana (1999) "Much Ado About Nothing?," *Hollywood Reporter* (February 11) from *Shakespeare in Love* clipping file, Margaret Herrick Library.

Hart, Hugh (2003) Scrutinizing the Soul of a Ruthless Drug Lord: Graphic NBC Series Dissects Mexican *Kingpin*," *San Francisco Chronicle*, Sunday, January 26. <http://www.sfgate.com/cgi-bin/article.cgi?file=/chronicle/archive/2003/01/26/PK40934.DTL>.

Hedrick, Donald (2000) "Shakespeare's Enduring Immortality: The Ethical vs. the Performative Turn, or Toward a Transversal Pedagogy" in Donald Hedrick and Bryan Reynolds (eds) *Shakespeare Without Class: Misappropriations of Cultural Capital*. New York: Palgrave.

—— (2002) "Male Surplus Value," *Renaissance Drama*, n.s. 31: 85–124.

—— (2003) "Advantage, Affect, History, Henry V," *PMLA*, May.

Hedrick, Donald and Bryan Reynolds (eds) (2000) *Shakespeare Without Class: Misappropriations of Cultural Capital*. New York: Palgrave Press.

Hettrick, Scott (2002) "MGM, IFC Sign Deal," *Variety.com*, May 22. Available online at <http://www.variety.com/index.asp?layout=story&articleid=VR1117867435&categoryid=20&CS=1>. Accessed on April 28, 2003.

Higson, Andrew (1993) "Re-presenting the National Past: Nostalgia and Pastiche in the Heritage Film" in Lester Friedman (ed.) *Fires were Started: British Cinema and Thatcherism*. Minneapolis, Minn.: University of Minnesota Press, 109–29.

Hill, John (1999) "The Heritage Film: Issues and Debates" in John Hill (ed.) *British Cinema in the 1980s: Issues and Themes*. Oxford: Clarendon Press, 73–98.

Hinson, Hal (2003) "Aiming for Shakespeare (if Not *The Sopranos*)," *New York Times*, Sunday, February 2. <http://www.nytimes.com/2003/02/02/arts/television/02HINS.html>.

Hirsch, Foster (1984) *A Method to their Madness: The History of the Actor's Studio*. New York: Norton.

Hirschhorn, Clive (1981) *Hollywood Musical*. New York: Crown.

Hjørt, Mette (1996) "Danish Cinema and the Politics of Recognition" in David Bordwell and Noël Carroll (eds) *Post-theory: Reconstructing Film Studies*. Madison, Wisc.: University of Wisconsin Press, 520–32.

Hodgdon, Barbara (1990) "Kiss Me Deadly; or, The Des/Demonized Spectator" in Virginia M. Vaughan and Kent Cartwright (eds) *Othello: New Perspectives*. Madison, N.J.: Fairleigh Dickinson Press.

—— (1992) "Katherina Bound: or, Play(K)ating the Strictures of Everyday Life," *PMLA* 107(3): 38–53.

—— (1998) "Replicating Richard: Body Doubles, Body Politics," *Theatre Journal* 50(2): 207–25.

—— (1999) "*William Shakespeare's Romeo + Juliet*: Everything's Nice in America?," *Shakespeare Survey* 52: 88–98.

—— (2003) "Wooing and Winning (Or Not): Film/Shakespeare/Comedy and the Syntax of Genre" in Richard Dutton and Jean Howard (eds) *A Blackwell Companion to Shakespeare's Comedies*. Oxford: Blackwell Press.

Hoffman, Michael (1997) *A Midsummer Night's Dream* draft script, November 20, unpublished.

Holden, Stephen (2002) "Heaven and Earth at Violent Odds in an Indian Epic," *New York Times*, August 30: E1, 18.

—— (2003) "Dreaming up a Riddle for a Know-it-all," *New York Times*, February 7: <http://www.nytimes.com.2003.02/07/movies/07EVA.html>.

Holderness, Graham (1989) *Shakespeare in Performance: The Taming of the Shrew*. Manchester and New York: Manchester University Press.

hooks, bell (1997) "Whiteness in the Black Imagination" in Ruth Frankenberg (ed.) *Displacing Whiteness: Essays in Social and Cultural Crticism*. Durham, N.C.: Duke University Press, 165–79.

Hopkins, Lisa (2002) "'How Very Like the Home Life of Our Own Dear Queen': Ian McKellen's Richard III" in Courtney Lehmann and Lisa S. Starks (eds) *Spectacular Shakespeare: Critical Theory and Popular Cinema*. Madison, N.J. and Teaneck, N.J.: Fairleigh Dickinson University Press, 47–61.

Horowitz, Robert (1983) "History Comes to Life and *You Are There*" in John E. O'Connor (ed.) *American History/American Television*. New York: Frederick Ungar, 79–84.

Howard, Jean (1987) "The New Historicism in Renaissance Studies" in Arthur F. Kinney and Dan S. Collins (eds) *Renaissance Historicism*. Amherst, Mass.: University of Massachusetts Press.

Howlett, K. (2000) *Framing Shakespeare on Film*. Athens, Ohio: Ohio University Press.

Huggan, Graham (2001) *The Postcolonial Exotic: Marketing the Margins*. London and New York: Routledge.

Huhtamo, Erikki (1999) "Replacing Place" in Peter Lunenfeld (ed.) *The Digital Dialectic: New Essays on New Media*. Cambridge, Mass: MIT Press.

Iyengar, Sujata (2001) "Shakespeare in Heterolove," *Literature Film Quarterly* 29(2): 122–7.

Iyer, Pico (2000) *The Global Soul: Jet Lag, Shopping Malls, and the Search for Home*. New York: Knopf.

Jackson, Russell (1994) "Shakespeare's Comedies on Film" in Anthony Davies and Stanley Wells (eds) *Shakespeare and the Moving Image: The Plays on Film and Television*. Cambridge: Cambridge University Press, 99–120.

—— (ed.) (2000) *The Cambridge Companion to Shakespeare on Film*. Cambridge: Cambridge University Press.

Jameson, Fredric (1992a) "Allegories of Anywhere" in Cynthia Davidson (ed.) and Laura Bourland (trans.) *Anywhere*. New York: Rizzoli, 172–7.

—— (1992b [1991]) *Postmodernism, or, The Cultural Logic of Late Capitalism*. Durham, N.C.: Duke University Press.

—— (1992c) *Signatures of the Visible*. London and New York: Routledge.

—— (1995) *The Geopolitical Aesthetic: Cinema and Space in the World System*. Durham, N.C.: Duke University Press.

Jameson, Fredric and Masao Miyoshi (eds) (1998) *The Cultures of Globalization*. Durham, N.C.: Duke University Press.

Jeancolas, Jean-Pierre (1998) "From the Blum-Byrnes Agreement to the GATT Affair" in Geoffrey Nowell-Smith and Steven Ricci (eds) *Hollywood and Europe: Economics, Culture, National Identity 1945–95*. London: British Film Institute Publishing, 47–60.

—— (2000) "The Reconstruction of French Cinema" in Elizabeth Ezra and Sue Harris (eds) *France in Focus: Film and National Identity*. Oxford: Berg, 13–21.

Jefferson, Margo (1996) "Welcoming Shakespeare into the Caliban Family," *New York Times* (November 12): C11, C16.

Jeffords, Susan (1994) *Hard Bodies: Hollywood Masculinity in the Reagan Era*. New Brunswick, N.J.: Rutgers University Press.

Jenkins, Bruce (1999) "*Explosion in a Film Factory: The Cinema of Bruce Conner*" *2000 BC: The Bruce Conner Story Part II*, catalog of an exhibition held at the Walker Art Center, Minneapolis, Minnesota, October 9, 1999–January 2, 2000.

Jensen, Michael P. (2002) "No More a Fairyland: The Translation of Adrian Noble's Dream from Stage to Screen," paper presented at the Shakespeare Association of America conference, Minneapolis, Minnesota, March, unpublished.

Jha, Subhash K. (2001) "Jaya Brings Out Book on Amitabh Bachchan," *Indo-Asian News Service*, August 21. <http://www.in.news.yahoo.com/020821/43.1u1qa.html>.

Johnston, Sheila (2001) "Inner City Fairies Make Magic," *Sunday Telegraph* (June 10): 10.

—— (2002) "*My Kingdom*," *Screendaily.com*. October 10. <http://www.screendaily.com/story.asp?storyid=9797&st=My+Kingdom&s=3>.

Jones, Ann (1995) "An American Tragedy," *Women's Review of Books* 12(8): 1, 3–4.

Jones, Edward T. (1977) "ACT's *Taming of the Shrew*: A Consciousness-Raising Farce," *Shakespeare on Film Newsletter* 2(1): 4–5.

Jones, Nicholas R. (2002) "Trevor Nunn's *Twelfth Night*: Contemporary Film and Classic British Theatre," *Early Modern Literary Studies* 8(1): 38 pars. Available online at <http://www.shu.ac.uk/emls/08–1/jonetwel.htm>. Accessed on January 2, 2003.

Jorgens, Jack J. (1977) *Shakespeare on Film*. Bloomington, Ind.: University of Indiana Press.

Joshi, Lailit Mohan (ed.) (2001) *Bollywood: Popular Indian Cinema*. London: Dakini.

Kabir, Nasreen Munni (2001) *Bollywood: The Indian Cinema Story*. London: Channel 4 Books.

Kahn, Coppélia (1975) "*The Taming of the Shrew*: Shakespeare's Mirror of Marriage," *Modern Language Studies* 5: 88–102.

Kauffman, Stanley (1996) "Shrinking Shakespeare," *New Republic* (February 12): 30–1.

Ke, Dhail Akshar Prem (2002) "Unplugged," *Teens Today!* October. <http://www.india-today.com/ttoday/102000/unplugged.htm>.

Kelly, Richard (2000) *The Name of This Book is Dogme95*. London: Faber & Faber.

Kendall, Roy (1996) "Animating Shakespeare," Typescript of lecture, October, unpublished.

Kennedy, Dennis (ed.) (1993) *Foreign Shakespeare: Contemporary Performance*. Cambridge: Cambridge University Press.

—— (1998) "Shakespeare and Cultural Tourism," *Theatre Journal* 50: 175–88.

Kinnes, Sally (2001) "Children and Shakespeare Don't Mix. Who Says?," *The Times* (June 24).

Kinsford, C.L. (1926) "Henry V" in *Encyclopaedia Britannica*, 13th edn. London: Encylopaedia Britannica Co.

Kittler, Frederich, A. (1990 [1985]). *Discourse Networks: 1800/1900*, trans. Michael Metteer. Stanford, Calif: Stanford University Press.

—— (1999 [1986]) *Gramophone, Film, Typewriter*, trans. Geoffrey Winthrop-Young. Stanford, Calif.: Stanford University Press.

Kliman, Bernice (1988) "Maurice Evans' Shakespeare Productions" in J.C. Bulman, and H.R. Coursen (eds) *Shakespeare on Television*. Hanover, N.H.: University Press of New England, 91–101.

Kott, J. (1967) *Shakespeare Our Contemporary*, trans. B. Taborski. London: Methuen.

Krishnamoorthy, K. (1972) *Kālidāsa*. New York: Twayne Publishers.

Kroll, Jack (1987) "Never Gonna Dance Again: Fred Astaire Hangs up His Top Hat: 1899–1987," *Newsweek* 110 (July 6): 48.

Landy, Marcia (1986) *Fascism in Film: The Italian Commercial Cinema: 1931–1943*. Princeton, N.J.: Princeton University Press.

—— (1996) *Cinematic Uses of the Past*. Minneapolis, Minn.: University of Minnesota Press.

Landy, Marcia and Amy Villarejo (1995) *Queen Christina*. London: British Film Institute Publishing.

Lanham, Richard (1993) *The Electronic Word: Democracy, Technology, and the Arts*. Chicago, Ill.: University of Chicago Press.

Lanier, Douglas (2002a) " 'Art thou base, common and popular?': The Cultural Politics of Kenneth Branagh's *Hamlet*" in Courtney Lehmann and Lisa S. Starks (eds) *Spectacular Shakespeare: Critical Theory and Popular Cinema*. Madison, N.J.: Fairleigh Dickinson University Press, 149–71.

—— (2002b) *Shakespeare and Modern Popular Culture*. Oxford and New York: Oxford University Press.

Lawson, Chris (2000) "The Don Who Would Be King: Looking for Richard (USA, 1996), but Finding Al," *Shakespeare in the Classroom* 8(1): 44–7.

Lefkowitz, Bernard (1998) *Our Guys*. New York: Vintage.

Lehmann, Courtney (2001) "Strictly Shakespeare? Dead Letters, Ghostly Fathers, and the Cultural Pathology of Authorship in Baz Luhrmann's *William Shakespeare's Romeo + Juliet*," *Shakespeare Quarterly* 52: 189–221.

—— (2002a) "*Shakespeare in Love*: Romancing the Author, Mastering the Body" in Courtney Lehmann and Lisa S. Starks (eds) *Spectacular Shakespeare: Critical Theory and Popular Cinema*. Madison, N.J.: Fairleigh Dickinson University Press, 125–45.

—— (2002b) "Crouching Tiger, Hidden Agenda: How Shakespeare and the Renaissance are Taking the Rage out of Feminism," *Shakespeare Quarterly* 53: 260–79.

Levich, Jacob (2002) "Freedom Songs: Rediscovering Bollywood's Golden Age," *Film Comment*, special issue on "Bollywood 101" 38(3): 48–51.

Levine, Lawrence W. (1988) *Highbrow/Lowbrow: The Emergence of Cultural Hierarchy in America*. Cambridge, Mass.: Harvard University Press.

Levinson, Jill (2001) "Stoppard's Shakespeare: Textual Revisions" in Katherine E. Kelly (ed.) *The Cambridge Companion to Tom Stoppard*. Cambridge: Cambridge University Press, 154–70.

Lewis, Barbara (1992) "Bard Suffers Slings and Arrows," *Sunday Telegraph* (November 1): 12.

Liu, Alan (2002) "The Future Literary: Literature and the Culture of Information" in Karen Newman, Jay Clayton, and Marianne Hirsch (eds) *Time and the Literary*. London and New York: Routledge, 61–100.

—— (forthcoming) *The Laws of Cool*. Stanford, Calif.: Stanford University Press.

Lo, Kwai-cheung (2001) "Transnationalization of the Local in Hong Cinema" in Esther C.M. Yau (ed.) *At Full Speed: Hong Kong Cinema in a Borderless World*. Minneapolis, Minn.: University of Minnesota Press, 261–77.

Loehlin, James (2000) " 'These Violent Delights have Violent Ends': Baz Luhrmann's Millennial Shakespeare" in Mark Thornton Burnett and Ramona Wray (eds) *Shakespeare, Film, Fin de Siècle*. New York: St. Martin's Press, 203–31.

Loomba, Ania (1993) "When Hamlet Came to Mizoram" in Marianne Novy (ed.) *Cross-cultural Performances: Differences in Women's Re-Visions of Shakespeare*. Urbana, Ill.: University of Illinois Press, 257–70.

—— (1997) "Shakespearian Transformations" in John J. Joughin (ed.) *Shakespeare and National Culture*. London and New York: Routledge, 83–108.

—— (1998) *Colonialism/Post-colonialism*. London and New York: Routledge.

—— (2001) "Local-Manufacture Made-in-India Othello Fellows: Issues of Race, Hybridity, and Location in Post-colonial Shakespeares" in Ania Loomba and Orkin Martin (eds) *Post-colonial Shakespeares*. London and New York: Routledge, 143–63.

Lotman, Yu (1981) "On the Language of Animated Cartoons" in V.V. Ivanov, Yu. M. Lotman, and A.K. Zholkovsky (eds) *Film Theory and General Semiotics*. Somerton, Oxford: Russian Poetics in Translation, vol. 8, 36–9.

Lott, Eric (1993) *Love and Theft: Blackface Minstrelsy and the American Working Class*. Oxford: Oxford University Press.

Lott, Tommy L. (1999) *The Invention of Race: Black Culture and the Politics of Representation*. Oxford: Blackwell Publishers.

Low, Rachael (1985) *Film Making in 1930s Britain*. London: George Allen & Unwin.

Lyman, Rick (2002) "Revolt in the Den: DVD Sends the VCR Packing to the Attic," *New York Times* (August 26). Available online at <http://www.nytimes.com/2002/08/26/technology/26DVD.html?ex=1031706875&ei=1&en=85ea66226d01dce6>.

Lyotard, Jean-François (1989) "Acinema" in Andrew Benjamin (ed.) *The Lyotard Reader*. Oxford: Basil Blackwell.

MacCannell, Dean (1993) "Democracy's Turn: On Homeless Noir" in Joan Copjec (ed.) *Shades of* Noir*: A Reader*. London and New York: Verso, 279–97.

McCullough, Malcolm (1996) *Abstracting Craft: The Practiced Digital Hand*. Cambridge, Mass.: MIT Press.

MacDonald, Joyce Green (1994) "Acting Black: *Othello*, *Othello* Burlesques, and the Performance of Blackness," *Theatre Journal* 46: 231–49.

McGann, Jerome (2001) *Radiant Textuality: Literature after the World Wide Web*. New York: Palgrave.

McKellen, Ian (1996) *William Shakespeare's Richard III: A Screenplay*. Woodstock, N.Y.: Overlook Press.

McMillin, Scott (1988) "The Moon in the Morning and the Sun at Night: Perversity and the BBC Shakespeare" in J.C. Bulman and H.R. Coursen (eds) *Shakespeare on Television*. Hanover, N.H.: University Press of New England, 76–81.

MacPherson, Pat (1997) "The Revolution of Little Girls" in Michelle Fine, Lois Weis, Linda C. Powell, and L. Mun Wong (eds) *Off White, Readings on Race, Power, and Society*. New York and London: Routledge, 283–96.

Maguire, Laurie E. (1996) *Shakespearean Suspect Texts: the "Bad" Quartos and their Contexts*. Cambridge, Cambridge University Press.

Mahar, William J. (1999) *Behind the Burnt Cork Mask: Early Blackface Minstrelsy and Antebellum American Popular Culture*. Urbana, Ill.: University of Illinois Press.

Maley, Willy (1998) "Braveheart: Raising the Stakes of History," *Irish Review* (Summer): 22.

Malina, Roger (1990) "Digital Image – Digital Cinema: The Work of Art in the Age of Post-Mechanical Reproduction," *SIGGRAPH 1990: Digital Image, Digital Cinema*, Supplemental Issue of *Leonardo: Journal of the International Society for the Arts, Sciences and Technology*.

Manheim, R. and J. Willett (eds) (1977) *Bertolt Brecht: Plays, Poetry and Prose*, vol. 6. New York: Vintage.

Manvell, Roger (1979 [1971]) *Shakespeare and the Film*. South Brunswick, N.J.: A.S. Barnes.

—— (1987) "Shakespeare on Film" in Levi Fox (ed.) *The Shakespeare Handbook*. Boston: G.K. Hall & Co.

Marcus, Leah (1992) "The Shakespearean Editor as Shrew-Tamer," *ELR* 22(2): 177–200.

Marks, Laura U. (2000) *The Skin of the Film: Intercultural Cinema, Embodiment, and the Senses*. Durham, N.C.: Duke University Press.

Maslin, Janet (1995) "Fishburne and Branagh Confront Fate in Venice," *New York Times*, 15 December: B1, 6.

Mast, G. and M. Cohen (1985 [1974]) *Film Theory and Criticism*, 3rd edn. Oxford: Oxford University Press.

Mazdon, Lucy (2000) *Encore Hollywood: Remaking French Cinema*. London: British Film Institute Publishing.

Mehta, Binita (1996a) "Mira Nair," *BOMB* 36 (Summer): 46–9.

—— (1996b) "Emigrants Twice Displaced: Race, Color, and Identity in Mira Nair's *Mississippi Masala*" in Deepika Bahri and Mary Vasudeva (eds) *Between the Lines: South Asians and Post-Coloniality*. Philadelphia, Pa.: Temple University Press.

Meer, Ameena (1991) "*Mira Nair*," *BOMB* 36 (Summer): 46–9.
Miller, Donald C. (1976) *Ghost Towns of Idaho*. Boulder, Col.: Pruett Publishing Co.
Miller, Jonathan (1986) *Subsequent Performances*. New York: Viking.
Mishra, Vijay (1997) "The Diasporic Imaginary: Theorizing the Indian Diaspora," *Textual Practice* 10(2): 421–47.
—— (2001) *Bollywood Cinema: Temples of Desire*. London and New York: Routledge.
Mitchell, Lee Clark (2002) "Based on the Novel by Henry James: The Golden Bowl 2000" in Susan M. Griffin (ed.) *Henry James Goes to the Movies*. Lexington, Ky.: University Press of Kentucky, 281–304.
Modenessi, Alfredo Michel (2002) "(Un)doing the Book 'Without Verona Walls': A View from the Receiving End of Baz Luhrmann's *William Shakespeare's Romeo + Juliet*" in Courtney Lehmann and Lisa S. Starks (eds) *Spectacular Shakespeare: Critical Theory and Popular Cinema*. Madison, N.J.: Fairleigh Dickinson University Press, 62–85.
Monk, Claire (1995) "Sexuality and the Heritage," *Sight and Sound* 5 (October 10): 32–4.
Moody, Richard (1958) *The Astor Place Riot*. Bloomington, Ind.: Indiana University Press.
Morgann, Maurice (1963) "An Essay on the Dramatic Character of Sir John Falstaff" in D. Nichol Smith (ed.) *Eighteenth-Century Essays on Shakespeare*. Oxford: Clarendon Press, 203–83.
Morris, Peter (1972) *Shakespeare on Film*. Ottawa: Canadian Film Institute.
Morrow, Lance (1995) "A Trial for Our Times," *Time* (October 9): 8.
Morse, Margaret (1990) "An Ontology of Everyday Distraction: The Freeway, The Mall, and Television" in Patricia Mellencamp (ed.) *Logics of Television: Essays in Cultural Criticism*. Bloomington, Ind.: Indiana University Press.
Mullaney, Steven (1988) "Lying Like Truth: Riddle, Representation, and Treason" in Steven Mullaney (ed.) *The Place of the Stage: License, Play, and Power in Renaissance England*. Chicago, Ill. and London: University of Chicago Press.
Mulvey, Laura (1970) "Visual Pleasure and Narrative Cinema," rpt. in *Visual and Other Pleasures*. Bloomington, Ind.: Indiana University Press.
Mundo, Philip A. (1999) *National Politics in a Global Economy: The Domestic Sources of US Trade Policy*. Washington, D.C.: Georgetown University Press.
Naficy, Hamid (2001) *An Accented Cinema: Exilic And Diasporic Filmmaking*. Princeton, N.J.: Princeton University Press.
Nelson, Chris (2002) "The Old Days Never Looked So Good," *New York Times* (September 11). Available online at <http://www.nytimes.com/2002/09/11/arts/11RETR.html?ex=1033046156&ei=1&en=13fab5dc15d53210>.
Nelson, Tim Blake (2001) "There's a Price You Pay for Getting Too Real," *New York Times* (August 26): B8, B15.
Newman, Karen (1991) *Fashioning Femininity and English Renaissance Drama*. Chicago, Ill.: University of Chicago Press.
Nightingale, Benedict (1989) "Henry V Returns for a Monarch for this Era," *New York Times* (November 5): H17–18.
Nora, Pierre (1989) "Between Memory and History: Les Lieux de Mémoire," *Representations* 26 (Spring): 7–25.
Norman, Marc and Tom Stoppard (1998) *Shakespeare in Love: A Screenplay*. New York: Miramax Books.
North, Julian (1999) "Conservative Austen, Radical Austen: Sense and Sensibility from Text to Screen" in Deborah Cartmell and Imelda Whelehan (eds) *Adaptations: From Text to Screen, Screen to Text*. London and New York: Routledge, 38–50.
Nowell-Smith, Geoffrey (1998) "The Beautiful and the Bad: Notes on Some Actorial Stereotypes" in Geoffrey Nowell-Smith and Steven Ricci (eds) *Hollywood and Europe: Economics, Culture, National Identity 1945–95*. London: British Film Institute Publishing, 135–41.
Nugent, Helen (2002) "'Barclays Appears to have Lost the Plot," *The Times* (July 13).
Nunn, Trevor (1996) *William Shakespeare's Twelfth Night: A Screenplay*. London: Methuen Drama.

Orgel, Stephen (1986) "Prospero's Wife" in Margaret W. Ferguson, Maureen Quilligan, and Nancy J. Vickers (eds) *Rewriting the Renaissance: The Discourses of Sexual Difference in Early Modern Europe*. Chicago, Ill.: University of Chicago Press: 50–64.

Oruch, Jack (1987) "Shakespeare for the Millions: 'Kiss Me, Petruchio,'" *Shakespeare on Film Newsletter* 11(2): 7–ff.

Osborne, Laurie E. (1997) "Poetry in Motion: Animating Shakespeare" in Lynda E. Boose and Richard Burt, (eds) *Shakespeare, The Movie: Popularizing the Plays on Film, TV, and Video*. London and New York: Routledge.

—— (2002) "Clip Art: Theorizing the Shakespearean Film Clip," *Shakespeare Quarterly* 53(2): 227–40.

Pais, Arthur J. (2002) " 'It is Light, Campy, Entertaining': Deepa Mehta on What Makes *Bollywood/Hollywood* a Fusion Film," *Rediffmovies.com*. September 11. <http://www.rediff.com/entertai/2002/sep/11tor2.htm>.

Palumbo-Liu, David (ed.) (1995) *The Ethnic Canon: Histories, Institutions, and Interventions*. Minneapolis, Minn.: University of Minnesota Press.

Paster, Gail Kern (1993) *The Body Embarrassed: Drama and the Disciplines of Shame in Early Modern Europe*. Ithaca, NY: Cornell University Press.

Patterson, Annabel (1984) *Censorship and Interpretation: The Conditions of Writing and Reading in Early Modern England*. Madison, Wisc.: University of Wisconsin Press.

—— (1989) *Shakespeare and the Popular Voice*. Oxford: Basil Blackwell.

Pearson, Roberta E. and Uricchio, William (1990) "How Many Times shall Caesar Bleed in Sport: Shakespeare and the Cultural Debate about Moving Pictures," *Screen* 31(3).

Pells, Richard (1997) *Not Like Us: How Europeans Have Loved, Hated, and Transformed American Culture Since World War II*. New York: Harper Collins.

Pendleton, Thomas A. (1987) "Garrick and the Pickford-Fairbanks Shrew," *Shakespeare on Film Newsletter* 12(1): 11.

Pendreigh, Brian (2002) "From Brigadoon to Trainspotting." Available online at <http://www.insideout.co.uk/scots/briefhistory.shtml>. Last accessed September 10, 2002.

Penley, Constance and Andrew Ross (1991) *Technoculture*. Minneapolis, Minn.: University of Minnesota Press.

Peters, John Durham (1999) "Exile, Nomadicism, and Diaspora: The Stakes of Mobility in the Western Canon" in Hamid Naficy (ed.) *Home, Exile, Homeland: Film, Media, and the Politics of Place*. London and New York: Routledge, 17–41.

Pickford, Mary (1955) *Sunshine and Shadow*. Garden City, N.Y.: Doubleday & Co.

Pike-Johnson, Heidi (2002) "Reports of VHS's Death Have Been Greatly Exaggerated," *Adult Video News* 18(9): 259.

Pinch, Adela (1996) *Strange Fits of Passion: Epistemologies of Emotion, Hume to Austen*. Stanford, Calif.: Stanford University Press.

Pines, Jim and Paul Willemen (eds) (1989) *Questions of Third Cinema*. London: British Film Institute Publishing.

Porton, Richard (1999) "Something Rotten in the State of Denmark: An Interview with Thomas Vinterberg," *Cineaste* 24 (2–3): 17–19.

Prateeti Punja Ballal (1998) "Illiberal Masala: The Diasporic Distortions of Mira Nair and Dinesh D'Souza," *Weber Studies* 15(1). Available online at <http://weberstudies.weber.edu/archive/Vol.%2015.1/15.1Ballal.htm>. Accessed January 2, 2003.

Quarshie, Hugh (1999) *Second Thoughts About Othello. International Shakespeare Association Occasional Paper No. 7*. Chipping Campden: Clouds Hills Printers.

Raaz, Hit ka (2003) "Interview," *The Times of India*, Thursday, February 20. <http://times of india.indiatimes.com/cms.dll/html/uncomp/articleshow?art_id=17898037>.

Rabkin, Norman (1977) "Rabbits, Ducks and Henry V," *Shakespeare Quarterly* 28: 279–96.

Rackin, Phyllis (1990) *Stages of History: Shakespeare's English Chronicles*. Ithaca, N.J.: Cornell University Press.

Radio Times (1992) "Macbeth Moscow-Style," *Radio Times* (November 7): 29–30.

Rafferty, Terence (1995) "Fidelity and Infidelity," *New Yorker* (December 18): 127.

Readings, Bill (1997) *The University in Ruins*. Cambridge, Mass.: Harvard University Press.
Rhadakrishnan, Rajagopalan (1996) *Diasporic Meditations: Between Home and Location*. Minneapolis, Minn.: University of Minnesota Press.
Rieff, David (1991) *Los Angeles: Capital of the Third World*. New York: Simon and Schuster.
Rippy, Marguerite (2002) "A Fast-Food Shakespeare," *Chronicle of Higher Education* (April 19): B16.
Rodowick, David N. (1987) "Madness, Authority and Ideology: The Domestic Melodrama of the 1950s" in Christine Gledhill (ed.) *Home Is Where the Heart Is: Studies in Melodrama and the Woman's Film*. London: British Film Institute Publishing, 268–82.
Rogin, Michael (1990) " 'Make My Day!': Spectacle as Amnesia in Imperial Politics," *Representations* 29: 99–123.
—— (1996) *Blackface, White Noise: Jewish Immigrants in the Hollywood Melting Pot*. Berkeley, Calif.: University of California Press.
Roman, Shari (2001) *Digital Babylon: Hollywood, Indiewood and Dogme 95*. Hollywood, Calif.: Lone Eagle.
Ronell, Avital (2002) *Stupidity*. Urbana, IL: University of Illinois Press.
Rosaldo, Renato (1993 [1989]) *Culture and Truth: The Remaking of Social Analysis*, 2nd edn. Boston, Mass.: Beacon Press.
Rose, Tricia (1989) "Orality and Technology: Rap Music and Afro-American Cultural Resistance," *Popular Music and Society* 13.4: 29–40.
Rosenbaum, Ron (2002) "Shakespeare in Rewrite," *New Yorker* (May 13): 68–77.
Rossiter, A.P. (1961) *Angels with Horns*. New York: Theatre Arts Books.
Rostow, E. (1978) *Born to Lose: The Gangster Film in America*. New York and Oxford: Oxford University Press.
Rothwell, K. (2000) *A History of Shakespeare on Screen*. Cambridge: Cambridge University Press.
Rothwell, Kenneth and Annabelle Melzer (1990) *Shakespeare on Screen: An International Filmography and Videography*. New York: Neal-Schuman Publishers.
Rousuck, J. Wynn (1999) "Shakespeare Fever Burns Bright," *Baltimore Sun* (May 30): 5F.
Rubin, Susan (1984) *Animation: The Art and the Industry*. Englewood Cliffs, N.J.: Prentice-Hall, Inc.
Rushdie, Salman (1992) *Imaginary Homelands: Essays and Criticism, 1981–1991*. New York: Penguin USA.
Rutter, Carol *et al.* (1989) *Clamorous Voices: Shakespeare's Women Today*. New York: Routledge.
—— (2000) "Looking at Shakespeare's Women on Film" in Russell Jackson (ed.) *The Cambridge Companion to Shakespeare on Film*. Cambridge: Cambridge University Press, 241–60.
Saad El-Din, Mursi (2001) "Plain Talk," *Al-Ahram Weekly Online*, No. 544. July 26–August 1. <http://weekly.ahram.org.eg/2001/544/cu3.htm>.
Saccio, Peter (1988) "The Historicity of the BBC Plays" in J.L. Bulman and H.R. Coursen (eds) *Shakespeare on Television: An Anthology of Essays and Reviews*. Hanover, N.H. and London: University Press of New England.
Said, Edward (1994) *Culture and Imperialism*. New York: Vintage Books.
Salamon, Linda Bradley (2000) " 'Looking for Richard' in History: Postmodern Villainy in *Richard III* and *Scarface*," *Journal of Popular Film and Television* 28(2): 54–63.
Sanders, Julie (2002) *Novel Shakespeares: Twentieth-Century Women Novelists and Appropriation*. Manchester: Manchester University Press.
Sargeant, Amy (2000) "Making and Selling Heritage Culture: Style and Authenticity in Historical Fictions on Film and Television" in Justine Ashby and Andrew Higson (eds) *British Cinema, Past and Present*. London and New York: Routledge, 301–15.
Sawhney, Deepak Narang (ed.) (2002) *Unmasking L.A.: Third Worlds and the City*. New York: Palgrave.
Schechner, Richard (1999) "Julie Taymor: from Jacques Lecoq to The Lion King, an Interview," *Drama Review* 43(3): 36–55. Available online at <http://muse.jhu.edu/demo/tdr/43.3 schechner.html>. Accessed January 2, 2003.
Schneider, Gretchen A. (1979) "Gabriel Ravel and the Martinetti Family: The Popularity of Pantomime in 1855" in Myron Matlaw (ed.) *American Popular Entertainment: Papers and Proceedings of the Conference on the History of American Popular Entertainment*. Westport, Conn.: Greenwood Press, 241–58.

Schoenfeldt, Michael C. (1999) *Bodies and Selves in Early Modern England: Physiology and Inwardness in Spenser, Shakespeare, Herbert, and Milton*. Cambridge: Cambridge University Press.

Senelick, Laurence (1979) "George L. Fox and Bowery Pantomime" in Myron Matlaw (ed.) *American Popular Entertainment: Papers and Proceedings of the Conference on the History of American Popular Entertainment*. Westport, Conn.: Greenwood Press, 97–110.

Sengupta, Ratnottama (2001) "Hrithik Will Play Hamlet, Hollywood Style," *About India*. <http://www.geocities.com/aboutindia2000/article/hrithik_will_play_hamlet.htm>.

Serres, Michel and Bruno Latour (1995) *Conversations on Science, Culture, and Time*, trans. Roxanne Lapidus. Anne Arbor, Mich.: University of Michigan Press, 43–62.

Shadoian, J. (1977) *Dreams and Dead Ends: The American Gangster/Crime Film*. Cambridge, Mass: MIT Press.

Shaha, Amit (1987) "Dweller in Two Lands: Mira Nair, Filmmaker," *Cineaste* 15(3): 22–3.

Sharma, Alpana (2001) "Dweller in Two Lands: Mira Nair, Filmmaker," *Cineaste* 15 (3): 22–3.

Shakespeare, William (1969) *The Complete Works*, ed. Alfred Harbage. Baltimore, Md.: Penguin.

—— (1974) *The Riverside Shakespeare*, ed. G. Blakemore Evans. Boston, Mass.: Houghton Mifflin Company.

—— (1982) *Henry* V, ed. Gary Taylor. Oxford: Clarendon Press and New York: Oxford University Press.

—— (1984) *Romeo and Juliet*, ed. G. Blakemore Evans. Cambridge: Cambridge University Press.

—— (1992) *The Taming of the Shrew*, ed. Graham Holderness and Bryan Loughrey. Hertfordshire: Harvester Wheatsheaf.

—— (1994) *Macbeth* in Stanley Wells and Gary Taylor (eds) *The Oxford Shakespeare Tragedies*. Oxford: Oxford University Press, 1307–34.

—— (1997) *The Complete Works of William Shakespeare*, ed. David Bevington. New York: Longman.

—— (1997) *The Norton Shakespeare: Based on the Oxford Edition*, ed. Stephen Greenblatt *et al.* New York: W.W. Norton & Co.

—— (1998) *Love's Labour's Lost*, ed. H.R. Woudhuysen, Arden 3. Walton-on-Thames, Surrey: Thomas Nelson and Sons.

Sharma, Alpana (2001) "Body Matters: The Politics of Provocation in Mira Nair's Films," *Quarterly Review of Film and Video* 18(1): 91–103.

Sheikh, Mushtaq (2002) *Devdas, The Indian Hamlet*. India.

Shohat, Ella and Robert Stam (1996) "From the Imperial Family to the Transnational Imaginary: Media Spectatorship in the Age of Globalization" in Rob Wilson and Wimal Dissanayake (eds) *Global/Local: Cultural Production and the Transnational Imaginary*. Durham, N.C.: Duke University Press, 145–70.

Shulevitz, Judith (2003) "The Original Band of Brothers," *New York Times*, January 26: <http:www.nytimes.com/2003/01/26/books/review/26SHULEVT.html>.

Sidney, Philip (1965) *An Apology for Poetry*, ed. Geoffrey Shepherd. London: Thomas Nelson.

Silverman, Kaja (1988) *The Acoustic Mirror: The Female Voice in Psychoanalysis and Cinema*. Bloomington, Ind.: University of Indiana Press.

Sinfield, Alan (1985) "Royal Shakespeare: Theatre and the Making of Ideology" in Jonathan Dollimore and Alan Sinfield (eds) *Political Shakespeare: New Essays in Cultural Materialism*. Ithaca, N.Y.: Cornell University Press, 158–81.

—— (1992) *Faultlines: Cultural Materialism and the Politics of Dissident Reading*. Berkeley, Calif: University of California Press.

Singer, Daniel (2000 [1994]) "GATT and the Shape of Our Dreams" in Carl Bromley (ed.) *Cinema Nation: The Best Writing on Film from The Nation: 1913–2000*. New York: Thunder's Mouth Press/Nation Books, 250–5. Originally published in *Nation*, January 17, 1994.

Sinyard, Neil (2000) "Shakespeare Meets *The Godfather*: The Postmodern Populism of Al Pacino's *Looking for Richard*" in Mark Thornton Burnett and Ramona Wray (eds) *Shakespeare, Film, Fin de Siècle*. New York: St. Martin's Press, 58–72.

Slade, Joseph W. (1997) "Pornography in the Late Nineties," *Wide Angle* 19(3): 1–12.

Small, Edward S. and Eugene Levinson (1989) "Toward a Theory of Animation," *The Velvet Lighttrap: Review of Literature* 24: 67–74.

Smallwood, Robert (1996) "Directors' Shakespeare" in Jonathan Bate and Russell Jackson (eds) *Shakespeare: An Illustrated Stage History*. Oxford: Oxford University Press, 176–96.
Smith, Paul (1993) *Clint Eastwood: A Cultural Production*. Minneapolis, Minn.: University of Minnesota Press.
Somaaya, Bhawana (1999) *Amitabh Bachchan, the Legend*. India.
Spivak, Gayatri Chakravorty (1988) "Can the Subaltern Speak?" in Cary Nelson and Lawrence Grossberg (eds) *Marxism and the Interpretation of Culture*. Urbana, Ill.: University of Illinois Press, 271–313.
—— (1993) *Outside in the Teaching Machine*. London and New York: Routledge.
—— (1996) "Diasporas Old and New: Women in the Transnational World," *Textual Practice* 10(2): 245–69.
—— (2000) "The New Subaltern: A Silent Interview" in Vinayak Chaturvedi (ed.) *Mapping Subaltern Studies and the Postcolonial*. London: Verso, 324–40.
Springer, Claudia (1991) "The Pleasure of the Interface," *Screen* 32(3): 303–23.
Srinivasan, V.S. (1998) "A Comedy of Excesses," October 16, Rediffonthenet. <http://www.rediff.com/entertai/1998/oct/16miyan.htm>.
Sterrit, David (ed.) (1998) *Jean-Luc Godard: Interviews*. Jackson, Miss.: University Press of Mississippi.
Stockholder, Kay (1989) "Sexual Magic and Magical Sex," paper presented at the Institute for the Psychological Study of the Arts, Gainesville, Florida, February, unpublished.
Stockman, Oliver (2001) "A Great Film Performed by Children" (July 25). Available online at <http://us.imdb.com/CommentsShow?0289114>. Accessed January 2, 2003.
Stone, Roseanne Allucquére (1995) *The War of Desire and Technology at the Close of the Mechanical Age*. Cambridge, Mass.: MIT Press.
Strauss, Leo (1952) *Persecution and the Art of Writing*. Glencoe, Ill.: Free Press.
Stuart, Andrea (1993) "Mira Nair: A New Hybrid Cinema" in Pam Cook and Philip Dodd (eds) *Women and Film: A Sight and Sound Reader*. Philadelphia, Pa.: Temple University Press.
Sturhahn, Larry (1974) "The Filming of American Graffiti," *Filmmakers Newsletter*, March 7(5): 22.
Sullivan, Garrett (1999) " 'Be This Sweet Helen's Knell, And Now Forget Her': Forgetting, Memory and Identity in *All's Well That Ends Well*," *Shakespeare Quarterly* 50(1): 51–69.
Sutton, John (1998) *Philosophy and Memory Traces: Descartes to Connectionism*. Cambridge: Cambridge University Press.
Taub, Eric A. (2002) "Catch a Rising Star and Put It in Your Pocket," *New York Times* (January 10): G3, col. 4.
Taubin, Amy (1995) "More and Moor," *Village Voice* (December 19): 82.
—— (2001) "Character Flaws," *Village Voice* (August 29–September 4).
Taylor, Charles (2000) "The Player," review of *Love's Labour's Lost*, salon.com (June 9). Available online at <http://www.salon.com/ent/movies/feature/2000/06/09/branagh/index.html>. Accessed January 2, 2003.
Taylor, John (1994) "Murder: The Ultimate Art Form," *Esquire* 122 (September): 82.
Taylor, Neil (2000) "National and Racial Stereotypes in Shakespeare Films" in Russell Jackson (ed.) *The Cambridge Companion to Shakespeare on Film*. Cambridge: Cambridge University Press, 261–73.
Theweleit, Klaus (1987) *Male Fantasies*, vol. 2, trans. Stephen Conway. Minneapolis, Minn.: University of Minnesota Press.
Thomas, Kevin (2002) " 'The Fire and the Rain.' Is Bollywood for the Rest of Us," *Los Angeles Times*, August 30. <http://www.calendarlive.com/movies/reviews/cl-et-fire30aug30.story?coll=cl-mreview>.
Thompson, Ann (ed.) (1979) *The Taming of the Shrew*. Cambridge: Cambridge University Press.
Thompson, Emma (1995) *The Sense and Sensibility Screenplay and Diaries: Bringing Jane Austen's Novel to Film*. New York: Newmarket Press.
Tobin, Elayne (1995) "Coffee Talk," *Mediations* 19: 67–75.
Towsen, John (1976) *Clowns*. New York: Hawthorn Books.

Tsering, Lisa (2001) "Colors and Sounds of Bollywood Enlighten Moulin Rouge," *India-West* (May 31). Available online at <http://www.ncmonline.com/content/ncm/2001/may/0531colors.html>. Accessed January 2, 2003.

Turner, Bryan (1987) "A Note on Nostalgia," *Theory, Culture and Society*, 4: 1.

Uricchio, William and Roberta E. Pearson (1993) *Reframing Culture: The Case of the Vitagraph Quality Films*. Princeton, N.J.: Princeton University Press.

Van Watson, William (1992) "Shakespeare, Zeffirelli, and the Homosexual Gaze," *Literature Film Quarterly* 20(4): 308–25.

Vernet, Marc (1993) "Film Noir on the Edge of Doom" in Joan Copjec (ed.) *Shades of Noir: A Reader*. London and New York: Verso, 1–31.

Verostko, Roman (1987) "Epigenetic Painting: Software as Genotype," *Leonardo* 20(4).

Vincendeau, Ginette (ed.) (2001) *Film/Literature/Heritage: A Sight and Sound Reader*. London: British Film Institute Publishing.

Virilio, Paul (1992 [1989]) *War and Cinema: The Logistics of Perception*. London and New York: Verso.

Viswanathan, Gauri (1989) *Masks of Conquest: Literary Study and British Rule in India*. New York: Columbia University Press.

Walker, Elsie (2000) "Pop Goes the Shakespeare: Baz Luhrmann's *William Shakespeare's Romeo + Juliet*," *Literature Film Quarterly* 28(2): 132–9.

Warde, F. (1920) *Fifty Years of Make-Believe*. New York: International Press Syndicate.

Weber, Max (1968) *On Charisma and Institution Building*. Chicago and London: University of Chicago Press.

Webster, Duncan (1988) *Looka Yonder: The Imaginary America of Populist Culture*. London and New York: Routledge.

Weisberg, Niels (2000) "Great Cry and Little Wool," *POV: A Danish Journal of Film Studies* 10 (December). Available online at <http://imv.au.dk/publikationer/pov/Issue_10/POV_10cnt.html>. Accessed January 2, 2003.

Weizenbaum, Joseph (1976) *Computer Power and Human Reason*. San Francisco, Calif.: W.H. Freeman.

Wells, Matt (2002) "Channel 4 Chief Calls for Shakeup," *Guardian* (August 24). Available online at <http://media.guardian.co.uk/edinburghtvfestival/story/0,7523,780027,00.html>. Accessed January 2, 2003.

Wells, Stanley (1976) "Directors' Shakespeare," *Shakespeare Jahrbuch* 113: 64–78.

—— (1982) "Television Shakespeare," *Shakespeare Quarterly* 33: 261–77.

—— (1996) "The Challenges of Romeo and Juliet," *Shakespeare Survey* 49: 1–14.

Wells, Stanley and Gary Taylor (eds) (1988) *The Oxford Shakespeare*. Oxford: Clarendon Press.

Willems, Michele (2000) "Video and its Paradoxes," in Russell Jackson (ed.) *The Cambridge Companion to Shakespeare*. Cambridge: Cambridge University Press, 35–56.

Williams, Gary Jay (1997) *Our Moonlight Revels: A Midsummer Night's Dream in the Theatre*. Iowa City, Iowa: University of Iowa Press.

—— (1998) " 'What country, friends, is this?,' " unpublished.

Williams, Linda (1989) *Hard Core: Power, Pleasure and the Frenzy of the Visible*. Berkeley, Calif: University of California Press.

Williams, Raymond (1977) *Marxism and Literature*. New York and Oxford: Oxford University Press.

Willis, John (1621) *The Art of Memory*. London: W. Jones.

Willis, Susan (1991) *The BBC Shakespeare Plays: Making the Televised Canon*. Chapel Hill, N.C.: University of North Carolina Press.

Willson, Robert F. (1992) "Recontextualizing Shakespeare on Film: *My Own Private Idaho, Men of Respect*, and *Prospero's Books*," *Shakespeare Bulletin* 10(3): 34–7.

Wilson, Richard (1993) *Will Power: Essays on Shakespearean Authority*. Detroit, Mich.: Wayne State University Press.

Wilson, Rob and Wimal Dissanayake (eds) (1996) *Global/Local: Cultural Production and the Transnational Imaginary*. Durham, N.C.: Duke University Press.

Winokur, Mark (1996) *American Laughter: Immigrants, Ethnicity, and 1930s Hollywood Film Comedy*. New York: St. Martin's Press.

Witchel, Alex (1994) "How 'Frankenstein' Has Created a Hunk," *New York Times* (November 9): C1, C7.

Woolf, Daniel (1991) "Memory and Historical Culture in Early Modern England," *Journal of the Canadian Historical Association*, New Series 3: 283–308.

Wray, Ramona and Mark Thornton Burnett (2000). "From the Horse's Mouth: Branagh on the Bard" in Mark Thornton Burnett and Ramona Wray (eds) *Shakespeare, Film, Fin de Siècle*. New York: St. Martin's Press, 165–78.

Wyatt, Justin (1994) *High Concept: Movies and Marketing in Hollywood*. Austin, Tex.: University of Texas Press.

Yates, Frances (1964) *Giordano Bruno and the Hermetic Tradition*. New York: Random House.

—— (1966) *The Art of Memory*. Chicago, Ill.: Univeristy of Chicago Press.

Yoshimoto, Mitsuhiro (2000) *Kurosawa: Film Studies and Japanese Cinemas*. Durham, N.C.: Duke University Press.

Young, Robert J.C. (1995) *Colonial Desire: Hybridity in Theory, Culture, and Race*. London and New York: Routledge.

Zeffirelli, Franco (1986) *Zeffirelli: An Autobiography*. New York: Weidenfeld & Nicolson.

Žižek, Slavoj (1989) *The Sublime Object of Ideology*. London and New York: Verso.

—— (1991) *For They Know Not What They Do: Enjoyment as a Political Factor*. London and New York: Verso.

—— (1992) *Enjoy Your Symptom! Jacques Lacan in Hollywood and Out*. London and New York: Routledge.

—— (2001) *The Fright of Real Tears: Krzysztof Kieslowski between Theory and Post-theory*. London: BFI Publishing.

FILMOGRAPHY

Films

Aigner-Clark, Julie, dir. (2000) *Baby Shakespeare.* Buena Vista Home Video. Sound, col., 30 mins. DVD edition.

Akhtar, Farhan, dir. (2001) *Dil Chahta Hai* [*The Heart Desires*]. India. Excel Entertainment. Spark Media. Sound, col., 183 mins.

Almereyda, Michael, dir. (2000) *Hamlet.* USA. Miramax/Buena Vista Entertainment. Sound, col., 112 mins.

Anciano, Dominic and Ray Burdis, dirs. (2000) *Love, Honour and Obey.* UK. BBC. Sound, col., 93 mins.

Anon., dir. (1910) *Romeo Turns Bandit.* France. Pathé. Silent, b/w.

Anon., dir. (1911) *Bumptious as Romeo.* USA. Edison. Silent, b/w.

Anon., dir. (1923) *Juliet and Her Romeo.* UK. Butcher. Silent, b/w.

Anon., dir. (2001) *Julius Eats'er: A Vivid parody.* USA. Vivid Films. Sound, col., 340 mins.

Anon., dir. (2001) *Much Ado About Nuttin': A Vivid Parody.* USA. Vivid Films. Sound, col., 340 mins.

Axel, Gabriel, dir. (1994) *The Prince of Jutland.* Netherlands/UK/Denmark/France/Germany. Arrow Films. Sound, col., 106 mins.

Badger, Clarence, dir. (1921) *Doubling for Romeo.* USA. Goldwyn. Silent, b/w.

Balachander, K., dir. (1981) *Ek Duuje Ke Liye* [*Made for Each Other*]. India. Video Sound. Sound, col., 163 mins.

Balayan, Roman, dir. (1989) *Ledi Makbet Mtsenskogo uyezda* [*Lady Macbeth of Mzensk.*] Russia. Lizard. Sound, col., 80 mins. No English subtitles.

Baldi, Ferdinando, dir. (1976) *Get Mean.* Italy. Sound, col., 84 mins.

Bandinelli, Silvio, dir. (2000) *Macbeth.* France. Colmax. Sound, col., 83 mins.

Bansali, Sanjay Leela, dir. (2002) *Devdas.* India. Eros International. Sound, col., 165 mins.

Barjatya, Sooraj R., dir. (1989) *Maine Pyar Kiya* [*Everyone Falls in Love with Someone . . . Somehow*]. India. Rajshri Productions Ltd. Sound, col., 195 mins.

Bartkowiak, Andrzej, dir. (2000) *Romeo Must Die.* USA. Warner Bros. Sound, col., 115 mins.

Bedford, James Gavin, dir. (2002) *The Street King.* USA. Universal. Sound, col., 90 mins.

Bergman, Ingmar, dir. (1982) *Fanny och Alexander* [*Fanny and Alexander*]. Sweden/France. Swedish Film Institute/Swedish Television SVT 1/Gaumont/ Personafilm/Tobis Filmkunst. Sound, col., 309 mins.

Boyd, Don, dir. (2001) *My Kingdom.* UK/Italy. Sound, col., 117 mins.

Boyle, Danny, dir. (1994) *Shallow Grave.* UK. Rank/Figment/Channel 4/Glasgow Film Fund. Sound, col., 92 mins.

Branagh, Kenneth, dir. (1989) *Henry V.* UK. BBC/Renaissance Films. Sound, col., 138 mins.

—— (1993) *Much Ado About Nothing.* UK/USA. Renaissance Films/BBC/Samuel Goldwyn Company. Sound, col., 111 mins.

—— (1995) *In the Bleak Midwinter.* (Released in USA 1996 as *A Midwinter's Tale.*) UK/USA. Castle Rock/Midwinter Films. Sound, b/w, 99 mins.

—— (1996) *Hamlet.* UK/USA. Castle Rock/Columbia. Sound, col., 242 mins.

—— (2000) *Love's Labour's Lost*. UK/USA. Arts Council of England/Miramax/Shakespeare Film Company. Sound, col., 93 mins. DVD edition.

Brook, Peter, dir. (1971) *King Lear*. UK/Denmark. Columbia Pictures. Sound, b/w, 137 mins.

Bukhovetsky, Dmitri, dir. (1923) *Othello*. Germany. Wörner-Filmgesellschaft. Silent, b/w, 60 mins.

Burge, Stuart, dir. (1965) *Othello*. UK. BHE Films. Sound, col., 165 mins.

Callis, James and Nick Cohen, dir. (2001) *Beginner's Luck*. UK. Late Night Pictures. Sound, col., 115 mins.

Calmettes, André and James Keane (1912) *Richard III*. France/USA. Silent, b/w and col. (hand-tinted), 55 mins.

Canterbury, Stuart, dir. (1998) *In the Flesh*. USA. VCA. Sound, col., 120 mins.

Carné, Marcel, dir. (1945) *Les Enfants du Paradis* [*Children of Paradise*]. France. Pathé. Sound, b/w, 190 mins.

Castellari, Enzo G., dir. (1968) *Quella sporca storia nel west* or *Johnny Hamlet*. Italy/USA. Transvue Pictures. Sound, col., 78 mins.

Cheah, Cheek Kong, dir. (2000) *Chicken Rice War*. Singapore. Raintree Pictures. Sound, col., 100 mins. CD-ROM edition.

Chopra, Vidhu Vinod, dir. (1994) *1942: A Love Story*. India. Eros. Sound, col., 150 mins.

Clark, Bob, dir. (1983) *Porky's 2: The Next Day*. USA. Twentieth Century Fox. Sound, col., 151 mins.

Collins, Edwin J., dir. (1923) *The Taming of the Shrew*. USA. British & Colonial Kinematograph, Silent, b/w, *c.* 20 mins.

Concepcion, Ben, dir. (2001) *Star Wars: Macbeth*. USA. AriZonA Pictures. Sound, col., 17 mins. Digital film.

Condon, Bill, dir. (1998) *Gods and Monsters*. USA. Lions Gate. Sound, col., 105 mins.

Cosmatos, George P., dir. (1993) *Tombstone*. USA. Hollywood Pictures. Sound, col., 130 mins.

Diegues, Carlos, dir. (1979) *Bye Bye Brazil*. France/Brazil. Carnival/Unifilm. Sound, col., 100 mins.

Dmytryk, Edward, dir. (1954) *Broken Lance*. USA. Twentieth Century Fox. Sound, col., 96 mins.

Domaradzki, Jerzy, dir. (1995) *Lilian's Story*. Australia. Phaedra Cinema. Sound, col., 94 mins.

Dutt, Sunil, dir. (1971) *Reshma Aur Shera* [*Reshma and Shera*]. India. Ajanta Arts. Babadigital Media. Sound, col., 158 mins.

Edzard, Christine, dir. (1992) *As You Like It*. UK. Sands Films. Sound, col., 143 mins. Video.

—— (2001) *The Children's Midsummer Night's Dream*. UK. Sands Films. Sound, col., 115 mins.

Elton, Ben, dir. (2000) *Maybe Baby*. UK. BBC Films. Sound, col., 93 mins.

Farrelly, Bobby and Peter Farrelly, dirs. (1998) *There's Something About Mary*. USA. Twentieth Century Fox. Sound, col., 119 mins.

Ferrara, Abel, dir. (1987) *China Girl*. USA. Vestron Pictures. Sound, col., 89 mins.

Freeston, Jeremy, dir. (1997) *Macbeth*. UK. Cromwell Productions/Grampian Television. Sound, col., 150 mins.

Gallen, Joel, dir. (2001) *Not Another Teen Movie*. USA. Colombia. Sound, col., 89 mins.

Godard, Jean-Luc, dir. (1987) *King Lear*. USA. Cannon. Sound, col., 90 mins.

Greenaway, Peter, dir. (1991) *Prospero's Books*. France/Italy/Netherlands/UK/Japan. Allarts/Elsevier-Vendex/Film Four International/ Canal+/NHK & VPRO Television/Allarts-Cinea/Camera One-Penta. Sound, col., 124 mins.

Gregor, Nicholas, dir. (1996) *Broken English*. New Zealand. Columbia Tristar. Sound, col., 92 mins.

Griffith, D.W., dir. (1908) *The Taming of the Shrew*. USA. Biograph. Sound, b/w, 17 mins.

Hall, Peter, dir. (1968) *A Midsummer Night's Dream*. UK. Sound, col., 124 mins.

Hardwick, Gary, dir. (2003) *Deliver Us from Eva*. USA. Focus features. Sound, col., 105 mins.

Heckerling, Amy, dir. (1995) *Clueless*. USA. Paramount. Sound, col., 97 mins.

Henríquez, Leonardo, dir. (1999) *Macbeth: Sangrador*. Venezuela. Sound, col.

Hickox, Douglas, dir. (1973) *Theatre of Blood*. UK. MGM. Sound, col.

Hillyer, Lambert, dir. (1936) *Dracula's Daughter*. USA. Universal. Sound, b/w.

Hoffman, Michael, dir. (1991) *Soapdish*. USA. Paramount. Sound, col., 97 mins.

—— (1999) *William Shakespeare's A Midsummer Night's Dream*. Italy/USA. Fox Searchlight Pictures/Panoramica. Sound, col., 116 mins.

—— (2002) *The Emperor's Club*. USA. Miramax. Sound, col., 109 mins.

Henriquez, Leonardo, dir. (1999) *Macbeth: Sangrador*. Venezuela. Sound, col., 86 mins.
Hughes, Albert and Allen Hughes, dirs. (2001) *From Hell*. USA. Twentieth Century Fox. Sound, col., 121 mins.
Hughes, Ken, dir. (1955) *Joe Macbeth*. UK. Sound, b/w, 107 mins.
Huston, John, dir. (1941) *The Maltese Falcon*. USA. Warner Brothers. Sound, b/w, 101 mins.
Irvin, John, dir. (2000) *Shiner*. UK. Buena Vista. Sound, col., 99 mins.
Ivory, James, dir. (1965) *Shakespeare Wallah*. India. Merchant Ivory Productions. Sound, b/w, 115 mins.
—— (2000) *The Golden Bowl*. USA. Lions Gate Films. Sound, col., 131 mins.
James, Steve, dir. (1994) *Hoop Dreams*. USA. Fine Line. Sound, col., 170 mins.
Jordan, Neil, dir. (1994) *Interview with a Vampire*. USA. Warner Brothers. Sound, col., 123 mins.
Junger, Gil, dir. (1999) *10 Things I Hate About You*. USA. Jaret/Mad Chance/Touchstone. Sound, col., 97 mins.
Kapoor, Raj, dir. (1973) *Bobby*. India. Yashraj Films. Sound, col., 161 mins.
Karch, Roy, dir. (2002) *Hotel O*. USA. Video Team. Sound, col., 124 mins.
Karikishen, Kaul, dir. (1975) *Romeo in Sikkim*. India. Sound, col.
Keane, James, dir. (1912) *William Shakespeare's Richard III*. USA. Produced by M.B. Dudley. Silent, tinted b/w, 59 mins. Re-released 2001 with new orchestral score by Ennio Morricone. Kino Video. DVD edition.
Kern, James V. dir. (1956) "Lucy Meets Orson Welles." *I Love Lucy*. Television Series. Episode 155 (Eighth season). USA. Sound, b/w, 30 mins.
Knoesel, Klaus, dir. (2001) *Rave MacBeth*. Germany. Framewerk. Sound, col., 86 mins.
Kurosawa, Akira, dir. (1957) *Le Chateau de l'Araignee* [The Castle of the Spider's Web]. Includes Chris Marker's documentary *AK*. France. Arte Video. Sound, b/w, 105 mins. DVD.
—— (1957) *Kumonosu jo* [*Throne of Blood*]. Japan. Toho. Sound, b/w, 110 mins.
—— (1960) *The Bad Sleep Well*. Japan. Toho. Sound, b/w, 151 mins.
—— (1985) *Ran*. Japan. Toho. Sound, col., 185 mins.
Lane, Charles, Jr., dir. (1991) *True Identity*. USA. Hollywood Pictures. Sound, col., 93 mins.
Lee, Ang, dir. (1995) *Sense and Sensibility*. USA/UK. MGM/United Artists. Sound, col., 136 mins.
Lehmann, Michael, dir. (1998) *My Giant*. USA. Warner Brothers. Sound, col., 104 mins.
Levring, Kristian, dir. (2000) *The King is Alive*. USA/Denmark. Good Machine/Zentropa Entertainments. Sound, col., 108 mins.
LiCalsi, Allison L., dir. (2001) *Macbeth: The Comedy*. USA. Tristan Films. Sound, col., 91 mins.
Lombardo, Greg, dir. (1999) *Macbeth in Manhattan*. USA. Cinebard Productions/Plus Films. Sound, col., 97 mins.
Loncraine, Richard, dir. (1995) *Richard III*. USA/UK. United Artists. Sound, col., 104 mins.
Luhrmann, Baz, dir. (1996) *William Shakespeare's Romeo + Juliet*. USA. Twentieth Century Fox. Sound, col., 120 mins.
—— (2001) *Moulin Rouge!* USA/Australia. Bazmark Films/Twentieth Century Fox. Sound, col., 127 mins.
MacKinnon, Gillies, dir. (1992) *The Playboys*. UK/USA/Ireland. MGM. Sound, col., 117 mins.
Madden, John, dir. (1998) *Shakespeare in Love*. UK/USA. Bedford Falls/Miramax/Universal. Sound, col., 122 mins.
Mankiewicz, Joseph L., dir. (1949) *House of Strangers*. USA. Sound, b/w, 101 mins.
Marker, Chris, dir. (1985) *AK*. France. Arte Video. Sound, b/w, 75 mins.
Maybury, John, dir. (2003) *Marlowe*. UK/Germany. Natural Nylon. Sound, col., in production.
McTiernan, John, dir. (1993) *Last Action Hero*. USA. Columbia. Sound, col., 130 mins.
Mehta, Deepa, dir. (2002) *Bollywood/Hollywood*. Canada. Mongrel Media. Sound, col., 103 mins.
Miller, Randall, dir. (1992) *Class Act*. USA. Warner Brothers. Sound, col., 98 mins.
Moorhouse, Jocelyn, dir. (1997) *A Thousand Acres*. USA. Touchstone Pictures. Sound, col., 105 mins.
Morris, Reggie and Harry Sweet, dirs. (1924) *Romeo and Juliet*. USA. Mack Sennett/Pathé. Silent, b/w.
Morrissette, Billy, dir. (2001) *Scotland, PA*. USA. Lot 49 Films. Sound, col., 102 mins.

Nair, Mira, dir. (1991) *Mississippi Masala*. UK/USA. Columbia Tristar. Sound, col., 118 mins.
—— (2001) *Monsoon Wedding*. India/USA/France/Italy. IFC Production/Mirabai Films. Sound, col., 114 mins.
Nair, S.S., dir. (1976) *Romeo*. India. Sound.
Nelson, Tim Blake, dir. (2001) *O*. USA. Lions Gate. Sound, col., 95 mins.
Noble, Adrian, dir. (1996) *A Midsummer Night's Dream*. UK. Capitol Films. Sound, col., 105 mins.
Nunn, Trevor, dir. (1996) *Twelfth Night: Or What You Will*. UK/USA. Renaissance Films/Summit Entertainment. Sound, col., 134 mins.
—— (2001) *Merchant of Venice*. BBC.
O'Haver, Tommy, dir. (2001) *Get Over It*. USA. Miramax. Sound, col., 87 mins.
Olivier, Laurence, dir. (1944) *Henry V*. UK. Two Cities Films Ltd. Sound, col., 135 mins.
—— dir. (1948) *Hamlet*. UK. Two Cities Film Ltd. Sound, b/w, 153 mins.
—— (1955) *Richard III*. UK. London Film Productions. Sound, col., 161 mins.
Oz, Frank, dir., (1997) *In and Out*. USA. Paramount. Sound, col., 92 mins.
Pacino, Al, dir. (1996) *Looking for Richard*. USA. Twentieth Century Fox. Sound, col., 118 mins.
Parker, Oliver, dir. (1995) *Othello*. USA. Castle Rock. Sound, col., 124 mins.
Payne, Alexander dir. (1999) *Election*. USA. Paramount. Sound, col., 103 mins.
Peer, Michael (2000) *The Shakespeare Conspiracy*. Sound, col., 50 mins.
Polanski, Roman, dir. (1971) *Macbeth*. USA. Playboy. Sound, col., 140 mins.
Pool, Léa, dir. (2001) *Lost and Delirious*. USA. Lions Gate. Sound, col., 103 mins.
Reilly, William, dir. (1991) *Men of Respect*. USA. Columbia Pictures. Sound, col., 113 mins.
Richardson, Tony, dir. (1969) *Hamlet*. UK. Sound, col., 117 mins.
Ricks, Shawn (2003) *Sexspeare: The Uncensored Lusty Works of William Sexspeare*. USA. Jill Kelly Productions. Sound, col., 88 mins.
Robbins, Jerome and Robert Wise, dirs. (1961) *West Side Story*. USA. MGM. Sound, col., 151 mins.
Robinson, Bruce, dir. (1987) *Withnail and I*. UK. Hand Made Films. Criterion. Sound, col., 108 mins.
Rohmer, Eric, dir. (1992) *Le Conte d'Hiver* [*A Tale of Winter*]. France. C.E.R./Les Films du Losange/Sofiarp. Sound, col., 114 mins. Distributed on VHS in the USA by MK2 Diffusion; New Yorker Films Video (*c.* 1995).
Ross, Herbert, dir. (1969) *Goodbye, Mr. Chips*. USA. MGM. Sound, col., 151 mins.
Rozema, Patricia, dir. (1999) *Mansfield Park*. UK. Miramax. Sound, col., 112 mins.
Rubbo, Michael, dir. (2001) *Much Ado about Something*. Australia. Australian Film Commission. Sound, col., 60 mins.
Russell, Jay, dir. (2002) *Tuck Everlasting*. USA. Disney. Sound, col., 101 mins.
Sackheim, Daniel, dir. (2001) *The Glass House*. USA. Columbia Tristar. Sound, col., 107 mins.
Sajnani, Arjun, dir. (2002) *Agni Varsha* [*The Fire and the Rain*]. India. Cenebella. Sound, col., 126 mins.
Sidney, George, dir. (1953) *Kiss Me Kate*. USA. MGM. Sound, col., 109 mins.
Sippy, Ramesh (1975) *Sholay*. India. Sippy Films. Eros International. Sound, col., 205 mins.
Smith, Mel, dir. (1989) *The Tall Guy*. UK. Miramax. Sound, col., 92 mins.
Sonnenfeld, Barry, dir. (1999) *Wild Wild West*. USA. Warner Bros. Sound, col., 107 mins.
Stow, Percy, *et al.* dir. (1999) *Silent Shakespeare: King John, The Tempest, A Midsummer Night's Dream, King Lear, Twelfth Night, The Merchant of Venice, Richard III*. UK. British Film Institute, Milestone Film and Video. Original music by Laura Rossi. Silent, b/w, 88 mins.
Taylor, Sam, dir. (1929) *The Taming of the Shrew*. USA. United Artists (now Pickford Corporation). Sound, b/w, 66 mins.
Taylor, S. and Andree Madness, dir. (2001) *Naughty College Student Girls #19*. USA. New Sensations, Sound, col., 88 mins.
Taymor, Julie, dir. (1999) *Titus*. USA. Clear Blue Sky Productions/Twentieth Century Fox. Sound, col., 172 mins.
Van Sant, Gus, dir. (1991) *My Own Private Idaho*. USA. New Line. Sound, col., 86 mins. DVD edition.

Vinterberg, Thomas, dir. (1998) *Festen* [*The Celebration*]. Denmark. Danmark Radio. Sound, col., 105 mins.
Wajda, Andrzej, dir. (1961) *Siberian Lady Macbeth*. USA. Sound, b/w, 95 mins.
Waters, Mark S. (2001) *Head Over Heels*. USA. Universal. Sound, col., 86 mins.
Weigl, Petr, dir. (1992) *Lady Macbeth of Mzensk*. Image Entertainment/Carlton Entertainment. Sound, col., 100 mins.
Weir, Peter, dir. (1986) *Dead Poets Society*. USA. Touchstone. Sound, col., 128 mins.
Weitz, Paul and Weitz, Chris, dir. (1999) *American Pie*. USA. Universal. Sound, col., 96 mins.
Welles, Orson, dir. (1948) *Macbeth*. USA. Mercury Productions/Republic. Sound, b/w, 107 mins.
—— (1952) *The Tragedy of Othello: The Moor of Venice*. USA/Italy. Mercury Productions. Sound, b/w, 90 mins.
—— (1965) *Chimes at Midnight* (Swiss/USA title *Falstaff*). Spain/Switzerland. Internacional Films Española/Alpine. Sound, b/w, 115 mins.
Whang, Cheol-Mean, dir. (1996) *Fuck Hamlet*. Germany. DFFB. In German with English subtitles. Sound, b/w, 90 mins.
Williamson, Kevin, dir. (1999) *Teaching Mrs. Tingle*. USA. Miramax. Sound, col., 95 mins.
Woo, John, dir. (1992) *Hard Boiled*. Hong Kong/USA. Criterion. Sound, col., 126 mins.
Wooding, Jeremy, dir. (2002) *Bollywood Queen*. UK. Arclight Films. Sound, col., 89 mins.
Zeffirelli, Franco, dir. (1967) *The Taming of the Shrew*. USA/Italy. FAI/Royal Films/Columbia Pictures. Sound, col., 122 mins.
—— (1968) *Romeo and Juliet*. UK/Italy/USA. BHE Films/Paramount. Sound, col., 138 min.
—— (1990) *Hamlet*. USA. Warner Brothers. Sound, col., 130 mins.
—— (1999) *Tea with Mussolini*. Italy/UK. MGM. Sound, col., 117 mins.

Television programs

Bender, Jack, dir. (1998) *The Tempest*. USA. NBC Television. Vidmark/Trimark. USA. Sound, col., 88 mins.
Bogdanov, Michael, dir. (1998) *Macbeth*. UK. Channel 4. Sound, col., 87 mins.
Bolt, Ben, dir. (1999) *The Turn of the Screw*. USA. Exxon Mobil Masterpiece Theatre. Sound, col., 120 mins.
Browning, Kirk, dir. (stage dir. William Ball) (1976) *The Taming of the Shrew*. PBS Great Performances/ACT. Sound, col., 105 mins. Original air date November 10.
Butalia, Pankaj, dir. (1990) *When Hamlet Went to Mizoram*. UK. BBC. Sound, col., 52 mins.
Dixon, Christopher, dir. (1981) *Kiss Me, Petruchio*. PBS/NY Shakespeare Festival. Sound, col., 60 mins.
Edel, Uli, dir. (2002) *The King of Texas*. Turner Network Television. Sound, col., 180 mins. Original air date June 2.
Elliott, Michael, dir. (1984) *King Lear*. UK. TV. Sound, col., 158 mins.
Gambourg, Efim, dir. (1992) *Romeo and Juliet: Shakespeare: The Animated Tales*. USSR/UK/Wales. Shakespeare Animated Films Limited/Christmas Films/Soyuzmultifilm. Sound, col., 30 mins.
Greengrass, Paul, dir. (1999) *The Murder of Stephen Lawrence*. UK. ITV/BBC. Sound, col., 120 mins. Screened on PBS (Masterpiece Theatre) January 21, 2002.
Karakov, Alexei, dir. (1996) *As You Like It: Shakespeare: The Animated Tales*. Russia/UK/Wales. Christmas Films with S4C. Sound, col., 30 mins.
Leaver, Don (1976) *A Midsummer Nightmare*. TV. Sound, col., 75 mins.
Low, Adam, dir. (2001) *Kurosawa*. UK. BBC. Sound, b/w, col. 115 mins.
Lumet, Sidney, dir. (1954) "December 26, 1594: The First Command Performance of Romeo and Juliet," *You Are There*. USA. NBC-TV. Sound, b/w. 30 mins. Original air date February 21.
McLoughlin, Tom, dir. (1995) *The Haunting of Helen Walker*. USA. Sound, col. 88 mins.
Miller, Jonathan, dir. (1980) *The Taming of the Shrew*. BBC/Time-Life TV. Sound, col., 127 mins.
Muat, Marcia, dir. (1992) *Twelfth Night: Shakespeare: The Animated Tales*. USSR/UK/Wales. Shakespeare Animated Films Limited/Christmas Films/Soyuzmultifilm. Sound, col., 30 mins.

Nickell, Paul, dir. (1950) *The Taming of the Shrew*. Westinghouse Studio One Theater/NBC. Sound, col., 60 mins. Original air date June 5.

Nunn, Trevor and Philip Casson, dir. (1979) *Macbeth*. UK. Sound, col.

Orlova, Natalia, dir. (1992) *Hamlet: Shakespeare: The Animated Tales*. USSR/UK/Wales. Shakespeare Animated Films Limited/Christmas Films/Soyuzmultifilm. Sound, col., 30 mins.

—— (1996) *Richard III: Shakespeare: The Animated Tales*. Russia/UK/Wales. Christmas Films/S4C. Sound, col., 30 mins.

Saakianz, Robert, dir. (1992) *A Midsummer Night's Dream: Shakespeare: The Animated Tales*. Shakespeare Animated Films Limited/Christmas Films/Soyuzmultifilm. USSR/UK/Wales. Sound, col., 30 mins.

Sax, Geoffrey, dir. (1999) *Othello*. UK/USA/Canada. ITV/BBC. Sound, col., 100 mins. Screened on PBS (Masterpiece Theatre), January 28, 2002.

Schaefer, George, dir. (1956) *The Taming of the Shrew*. NBC Hallmark Hall of Fame. Sound, b/w.

Serebirakov, Nikolai, dir. (1992) *Macbeth: Shakespeare: The Animated Tales*. Shakespeare Animated Films Limited/Christmas Films/Soyuzmultifilm. USSR/UK/Wales. Sound, col., 30 mins.

—— (1996) *Othello: Shakespeare: The Animated Tales*. Christmas Films with S4C. Russia/UK/Wales. Sound, col., 30 mins.

Sokolov, Stanislav, dir. (1992) *The Tempest: Shakespeare: The Animated Tales*. USSR/UK/Wales. Shakespeare Animated Films Limited/Christmas Films/Soyuzmultifilm. Sound, col., 30 mins.

—— (1996) *The Winter's Tale: Shakespeare: The Animated Tales*. USSR/UK/Wales. Christmas Films with S4C. Sound, col., 30 mins.

Supple, Tim, dir. (2003) *Twelfth Night*. UK. BBC Four. Sound, col., 120 mins. Original air date January 17.

Weland, Paul, dir. (1999) *Blackadder Back and Forth V*. UK. BBC Video. Sound, col., 55 mins.

Woolcock, Penny, dir. (1997) *Macbeth on the Estate*. UK. BBC2. Sound, col., 120 mins.

Yulakov, Yuri, dir. (1996) *Julius Caesar: Shakespeare: The Animated Tales*. Christmas Films with S4C. Russia/UK/Wales. Sound, col., 30 mins.

Ziablikova, Aida, dir. (1996) *The Taming of the Shrew: Shakespeare: The Animated Tales*. Christmas Films with S4C. Russia/UK/Wales. Sound, col., 30 mins.

INDEX

ACT *see* American Conservatory Theater
Adelman, Janet 112, 115
Adelman, Ken 18
Aditya 272
Adorno, Theodor 28
Affleck, Ben 69, 293
African-Americans 26–7, 72, 73, 80–1
Agni Varsha: The Fire and the Rain 272
allegory 29, 30, 39, 43, 46
Allen, Penelope 192
Allen, Woody 78
Ally McBeal 243, 246
Almereyda, Michael 1, 8, 22, 37–55, 99; art/popular film hybridization 9, 268; Asian influence 11, 266, 292–7; the 'street' 188
Almodóvar, Pedro 253–4
ambiguity 224–5, 227
American Conservatory Theater (ACT) 122, 131
American Pie 266, 286–7, 288, 292
Americanization 186–7
anachronism 43, 44, 45
Anderegg, Michael 8, 20, 56–71
Andreae, Christopher 148
Ang, Ien 265, 266, 267, 283
animation 9, 140–53
Arroyo, José 201, 208
art 107, 254, 261
artificial intelligence 108–9, 111
As You Like It 66
As You Like It (animated version) 9, 144, 148, 150–2
As You Like It (Czinner) 275
As You Like It (Edzard) 166
Asia 7, 11, 265–303
Astaire, Fred 76, 79–80
Astor Place riot 73–4
Atkinson, Rowan 25, 26
Attenborough, Richard 272
audiences 61, 225–6
Auge, Marc 16
authenticity 17, 18, 37, 78; Branagh 43, 44; *A Midsummer Night's Dream* 155, 156
autoeroticism 112, 113, 242
Axel, Brian Keith 267
Axel, Gabriel 262

Bachchan, Amitabh 273
Bachchan, Jaya 273
The Bad Sleep Well 178
Bala, Bharat 272
Ball, Robert Hamilton 58, 123, 182
Bansali, Sanjay Leela 271
Barthes, Roland 181
Barton, John 187
Bate, Jonathan 70
Baudrillard, Jean 205
Bazin, André 184
BBC (British Broadcasting Corporation) 24, 25, 120, 122, 267–8
Beckham, David 24
Bedford, James Gavin 10, 188, 196–7
Beer, Randall 108
Bellour, Raymond 53
Bening, Annette 174, 176–7
Benjamin, Walter 231, 244
Benning, Sadie 47
Benson, Frank 183
Bergman, Ingmar 256, 262
Bertolucci, Bernardo 254, 256
Bette 22
Beymer, Richard 61
Bhabha, Homi 75, 79, 247, 267
birth metaphors 112–15
Blackadder 22, 24, 25, 26
Blair, Tony 95

Bloom, Harold 20, 285, 291, 292
Bobby 276
Bogdanov, Michael 11, 22, 28, 235–9, 245, 247
Bollywood 11, 268, 269–70, 271–6
Bollywood Queen 272
Bollywood/Hollywood 272
The Bomb-itty of Errors 21
Bond, Samantha 166
Bonham Carter, Helena 76, 83
Boose, Lynda E. 7–11, 235
Boston Public 22
Bourdieu, Pierre 269
Braidotti, Rosi 249
Branagh, Kenneth 1, 43–4, 140, 165, 188; career 77–8; *Hamlet* 24, 43, 76, 77, 80, 152, 279, 297; *Henry V* 11, 22, 23, 26, 173, 193, 213–30; Hollywood style 74, 75, 77; *In the Bleak Midwinter* 170; *Love's Labour's Lost* 8, 22–3, 24, 26, 74–82, 84, 85, 86; *Much Ado About Nothing* 26, 76–7, 81, 83, 155, 173, 175, 255; *Othello* 89, 90, 91, 96, 102
Bratlinger, Patrick 19
Braunmuller, A.R. 153
Braveheart 232, 233, 234, 235
Breathless 260
Brecht, Bertolt 56, 178, 189
Breight, Curtis 28
Brigadoon 232, 233, 235
Bristol, Michael 74
British Broadcasting Corporation (BBC) 24, 25, 120, 122, 267–8
Brodie, John 61
Broken Lance 23
Brook, Peter 163, 189, 193, 258
Budapest 240–1
Buddhism 292, 294, 296, 297
Buffy the Vampire Slayer 22
Buhler, Stephen 255
Bumptious as Romeo 58
Burbage, Richard 57
Burge, Stuart 173, 174
burlesque 58
Burnett, Mark Thornton 167
Burt, Richard 1–7, 8, 14–36, 137, 188; Asian film 11, 265–303; black popular culture 84; *Clueless* 235; cross-dressing 66–7; dumbed-down Shakespeare 74; *Looking for Richard* 194; *My Own Private Idaho* 209; poststructuralism 223; 'sub-Shakespeare' 196
Burton, Richard 120, 127
Bush, George W. 18, 19, 238, 239, 288
Butler, Judith 96
Butler, Shane 43
Bye, Bye, Birdie 102

Cagney, James 178, 179, 180
Canterbury, Stuart 239, 240
capitalism 5, 69, 265, 274; Branagh's *Henry V* 216, 223, 228; Hollywood 235; *Macbeth* 11, 247, 248; 'senile' 236–7
Cartelli, Thomas 10, 186–99
Carter, Jim 177
Casablanca 81
Cavell, Stanley 4
CD-ROMs 152–3
The Celebration 11, 253, 256–8, 261–2
Celebrity 78
Chakrabarty, Dipesh 267
Chakravarty, Sumita S. 266
Chamisso, Adelbert von 73
Chariots of Fire 177
charisma 215, 216, 217, 221, 223
Chartier, Roger 42–3
Cheney, Lynn 18
Chicken Rice Wars 270, 284
children 10, 162–4, 165–70
A Children's Midsummer Night's Dream 155, 160–2, 165–70
Children's Shakespeare 162
Chimes at Midnight 11, 78, 201, 207
China 277, 278, 279
China Girl 11, 266, 267, 268, 283–6
Chinatown 293
Chocolat 14
Christy's 72
Cimino, Michael 284, 285
Citizen Kane 78
Clare, John 21
class 155–6, 222
Clausewitz, Carl von 227
Clover, Carol 292
Clueless 15, 26, 99, 137, 235
Cochran, Johnnie 90, 94
cognitive processes 40–2
collage 46, 52
Collick, John 140
Collins, Edwin J. 123
colonialism 75, 82, 83, 85; *see also* postcolonialism

comedy 85, 120, 142; *My Own Private Idaho* 209–10; *Romeo and Juliet* 58, 62
The Comedy of Errors 21, 27, 120
Comolli, Jean-Louis 253
compassion 108, 109, 112, 113
computer technology 108, 117
Conner, Bruce 52
conservatism 17, 18, 19, 280; *Henry V* 217; *The Taming of the Shrew* 122; Zeffirelli 129
conspiracy theories 21
consumerism 217
conventions 45–6, 49
Copjec, Joan 233, 246
Coppola, Francis Ford 256, 272, 284
costume 76, 126
Cowie, Elizabeth 241
cross-dressing 66–7, 159
Crystal, Billy 76
cultural capital 211, 212, 223, 269
cultural criticism 213–14, 222, 225
cultural imperialism 28, 75, 80, 283
cultural tourism 64
Czinner, Paul 275

Daguerre, Louis 107–8
dance 76, 79, 85, 116
Dane, Clemence 66
Danes, Claire 14, 61, 62
Dauman, Anatole 254, 256
Davies, Andrew 9, 95, 101, 102
Dawson's Creek 22
De Palma, Brian 196, 284
De Quincey, Thomas 72
Dead Poet's Society 15
Dean, James 61, 296
Debord, Guy 221
deconstruction 267, 269
Deep Throat 297
Degrassi 22
democracy 236–7
Dench, Judi 23–4, 57, 68
Derrida, Jacques 113, 247
Devdas 271, 276
diaspora 11, 265, 267–8, 270, 275–6, 283, 297; *see also* postdiaspora
DiCaprio, Leonardo 14, 61, 65
digital culture 8, 30, 274
digital divide 270
digital technology 9, 107, 109, 231
digitalization 1, 2, 6, 15, 274
Dil Chahta Hai 11, 266, 273, 274–6
Dionosetti, Paola 130
Dirlik, Arif 268
dirt 214–15, 218, 219, 228
Dirty Harry 217, 221, 227, 228
Disney 142, 143
Dissanayake, Wimal 268
Dobson, Michael 120
Dogme95 1, 11, 252–64
Dolar, Mladen 205
Donaldson, Peter S. 9, 43, 58–9, 105–19, 128, 255
Donen, Stanley 75
Doran, Lindsay 279
Doubling for Romeo 58
Douglas, Mary 218
Dowling, Maurice 89
Downey, Robert Jr. 176
Drugstore Cowboy 201, 203
'dumbing-down' 74, 75, 85
Dunbar, Adrian 175
DVD 1–5, 7, 8, 39, 231, 270; *Moulin Rouge* 2–3, 270, 274; *Sense and Sensibility* 277, 278, 279, 280; *Shakespeare in Love* 67, 68; *William Shakespeare's Romeo and Juliet* 2, 3–4, 274
Dwyer, Rachel 269–70
Dyer, Richard 98, 158

Eagleton, Terry 224–5
EastEnders 22
Eastwood, Clint 216, 217, 218, 220, 221, 223
Eccleston, Christopher 95, 102
Edel, Uli 22–3
education 18–19, 20–1; *see also* pedagogy
Edward II 209
Edzard, Christine 10, 155, 160–2, 165–70, 171
Eggert, Katherine 8, 23, 72–88
Eisenstein, Sergei 142, 143, 181
Ejogo, Carmen 81
electronic media 38, 298
elitism 156, 161, 163
Elton, Ben 25
The Emperor's Club 15, 266, 287–8, 292
Empson, William 214, 224–5
eroticism: *Othello* 91; *Prospero's Books* 112, 113, 116; *The Taming of the Shrew* 133, 134; *see also* autoeroticism; homoeroticism
ethnicity 81–2, 268, 284, 286; *see also* race
Europe 11, 26, 253–6, 260

Evans, G. Blakemore 63
Evans, Maurice 127
Everett, Barbara 194
Eyre, Richard 174, 176

The Faerie Queen 277, 278
Fairbanks, Douglas Sr. 120, 121, 124, 125, 133
family romance 205, 209, 210
The Famous Victories of Henry V 216
Fanny and Alexander 256, 262
A Farewell to Arms 65
fascism 176, 177
fate 62–3
Felicity 22
femininity: *Prospero's Books* 111–12, 113; *The Taming of the Shrew* 121, 123, 127, 134
feminism 122, 135–6, 156, 158, 160, 280
Ferrara, Abel 283, 284, 285, 286
Fiennes, Joseph 68
Fieschi, Jean-André 253
film noir 188, 233, 236, 241, 249; *see also* noir western
Fine Line Features 76
Firth, Colin 24, 69
Fishburne, Lawrence 80, 89, 90, 92, 93
Folger, Henry Clay 187
'foreignization' 7
formalism 52, 224
Forrest, Edwin 74, 86
Frasier 22
Freed, Arthur 232
Freedman, Barbara 174, 182
Freeston, Jeremy 28
Freud, Sigmund 201, 203–4, 205, 209, 210
Freudian symbolism 200, 201, 202, 203–4, 205; *see also* oedipal symbolism
Frow, John 37, 38–9, 44
Fuck Hamlet 267
Full Metal Jacket 220

Gandhi 83, 86, 272
gangster movies 10, 86, 177, 178–9, 180, 181, 217
Garber, Marjorie 209
Garfield, Leon 143, 147
Garrick, David 60, 120, 125
GATT *see* General Agreement on Tariffs and Trade
gaze 114, 297
gender: *The Glass House* 292; *A Midsummer Night's Dream* 157–8; *Sense and Sensibility* 279; *The Taming of the Shrew* 120–1, 122, 126, 129, 132, 137; *see also* femininity; masculinity; women
General Agreement on Tariffs and Trade (GATT) 253, 254, 255
Gibson, Mel 15, 232, 235, 236
Gielgud, John 9, 107, 110, 112, 113, 296
The Gilmore Girls 22
Gilmore, Michael 170
Gilson, Nancy 150
Gladiator 14
The Glass House 11, 266, 288–92
Glen Ridge High School 21, 243, 244
glo-cali-zation 8, 15–17, 22, 26, 28, 30
globalization 5, 231, 237, 247, 297; digitalization 1, 2, 6; Indian cinema 270, 276; porn industry 241; postcolonial critics 265–6, 268; *see also* transnationalism
Globe Theatre 64, 65, 169
Godard, Jean-Luc 255, 256, 260, 261
The Godfather 256, 272
Gods and Monsters 270
The Golden Bowl 11, 266, 267, 280–3
Great Britain: gangster movies 86; *Looking for Richard* 189–90, 191, 193, 194; nationalism 216; 'post-postcolonial' relationship with United States 23, 24, 75, 76, 83, 86; theater affinity 170, 171; US film hegemony 74–86; *see also* United Kingdom
Greenaway, Peter 9, 105–18
Greenblatt, Stephen 70, 224
Griffith, Andy 57–8
Griffith, D.W. 123, 183
Guess Who's Coming to Dinner? 226
The Guru 272

Hall, Kim 82
Hall, Peter 24
Halpern, Richard 28–9
Hamlet 14, 42–3; Bollywood 272; Dogme films 11, 252, 253, 256–8, 262; *The Glass House* 288–92; *The Golden Bowl* 280–1, 283; *Sense and Sensibility* 277; *South Park* 21
Hamlet (Almereyda) 1, 8, 22, 37–55, 99; art/popular film hybridization 9, 268; Asian influence 11, 266, 292–7; the 'street' 188
Hamlet (animated version) 141, 148, 149
Hamlet (Branagh) 24, 43, 76, 77, 80, 152, 279, 297

Hamlet (Olivier) 15, 44, 49, 78, 126, 275
Hamlet (Richardson) 26
Hamlet (Zeffirelli) 15, 173
Hamlet: A Murder Mystery 152, 153
Hamletmachine 28
handicraft 38, 49
Haraway, Donna 105, 108–9
Hardwicke, Edward 177–8
Harry Potter books 18
Hartnett, Josh 99, 100, 102
Hawke, Ethan 9, 188
Hawkes, Terence 144
Hawks, Howard 23
Hawthorne, Nigel 76, 177
Head Over Heels 10
Hedrick, Donald K. 11, 213–30
hegemony 28, 75, 83
Henderson, Diana E. 9, 120–39
Henna 276
Henry IV 11, 200, 201, 202, 204, 206–11, 215
Henry V 11, 18
Henry V (Branagh) 11, 22, 23, 26, 173, 193, 213–30; British Shakespeare and Hollywood 77, 83, 85; flashbacks 92; resurgence of Shakespeare 1
Henry V (Noble) 222
Henry V (Olivier) 77–8, 126, 128, 161, 214, 215–16, 221, 275
heritage cinema 10, 155–6, 158, 177–8; *see also* nostalgia
Heston, Charlton 76, 126, 132
Hey Arnold! 22
high culture 16, 17, 28, 72, 73, 74; animated Shakespeare 142; heritage cinema 156; *A Midsummer Night's Dream* 163; *Othello* 89
historicism 2–3, 5, 7, 29
Hodgdon, Barbara 9, 43, 59, 89–104, 122
Hoffman, Michael 10, 155–60, 164, 170–1, 287, 288
Holderness, Graham 130, 137
Hollywood 188, 213, 217, 235; British actors 80–1; British films 74, 75, 76, 79, 80; Dogme manifesto 252, 253, 262–3; European conflict with 253–6; glo-cali-zation 15, 16–17, 28; *The King is Alive* 260, 261; Nunn complaint against 84–5, 254–5; realism 173, 174; *The Taming of the Shrew* 125
homoeroticism 96, 97, 101, 103, 211
homosexuality 10, 66, 67, 158, 208, 212
Hong Kong cinema 284, 285, 286
hooks, bell 100
Hopkins, Anthony 14
Horkheimer, Max 28
Horowitz, Robert 57
horror films 289, 291–2
House of Strangers 23
Howlett, Kathy 177
Hughes, Ken 234
humor 222
Hungary 240–1
hybridity 23, 267, 268, 271, 276, 297

imperialism 219, 288; British 279–80; cultural 28, 75, 80, 283; Hollywood 254
In the Bleak Midwinter (Branagh) 78, 170
In the Flesh 11, 231, 239–42, 243, 247
In and Out 15, 288
Indian cinema 266–7, 269–70, 271–6, 283, 297
Iraq war 18
irony: *A Children's Midsummer Night's Dream* 169; political criticism 214; *The Street King* 196; *The Taming of the Shrew* 127, 130, 131
Irving, Henry 140
Italian cinema 285
Ivan the Terrible 181
Ivory, James 267, 280, 281, 282
Iyengar, Sujata 67
Iyer, Pico 16

Jackson, Samuel L. 26, 27
Jacob, Irène 89, 90
Jacobi, Derek 80, 166, 167
Jameson, Fredric 29–30, 46–7, 232, 238, 271
Jarman, Derek 209
Jefferson, Margo 187–8, 190
Jeffords, Susan 234
Jenkins, Bruce 52
Jenkins, Harold 43
Jennings, Alex 160
Jensen, Carsten 254
Jewish entertainers 82
Jha, Subhash K. 272
Jhabvala, Ruth Prawer 280, 281, 282
Joe MacBeth 178, 234
Jolson, Al 82, 180, 181
Jones, Emrys 192, 194
Jones, James Earl 26–7
Jones, Nicholas R. 76
Jorgens, Jack 173, 208
jouissance 233, 234, 245, 246, 249

Jude 279
juggler imagery 116–17
Julia, Raul 122, 131, 132, 133
Juliet and Her Romeo 58
Julius Caesar 287, 288
Julius Caesar (animated version) 9, 142–3, 152
Julius Caesar (street version) 186
Julius Eats'er 20
Junger, Gil 99

Kaaya, Brad 99, 101
Kapoor, Raj 276
Keane, James 173, 181, 182, 183, 184
Keaton, Michael 76
Kemble, John Philip 140
Kendall, Roy 147
Kennedy, Dennis 27, 64, 174
Khan, Mehboob 276
Kidman, Nicole 273
Kightley, Oscar 186
Kimball, Frederic 190, 191, 192, 195
The King is Alive 1, 11, 28, 253, 258–63
King Lear: Dogme films 11, 253, 258–60; *The Godfather* 272; *King of Texas* 17, 22–3
King Lear (Brook) 258
King Lear (Godard) 255, 261
King, Rodney 94, 96
King of Texas 17, 22–3
Kingpin 21
Kingsley, Ben 76, 83–4, 85, 86
Kirk, Lisa 126
Kiss Me, Kate 21, 121
Kiss Me, Petruchio 122, 123, 131–3
Kittler, Friedrich 4
Kline, Kevin 15, 156, 287, 288
Kott, Jan 181
Kozintsev, Grigori 140
Kragh-Jacobsen, SØren 252
Kubrick, Stanley 220
Kurosawa 6
Kurosawa, Akira 6–7, 140, 234, 256
Kushner, Tony 187
Kutumb 272

Lagaan 276, 297
Lane, Nathan 76, 82
language 18, 27–8, 45; American vernacular 189, 196; Luhrmann's *Romeo and Juliet* 60–1; *Macbeth, The Comedy* 248; *My Own Private Idaho* 189, 209, 211; *O* 101; *Shakespeare in Love* 68–9; US devaluing of 74, 75
Lanier, Douglas 10, 154–72
Last Action Hero 15, 28, 292
Laurie, Hugh 25, 26
Law, Jude 270
Lawrence, Stephen 9, 94–5
Lawson, Chris 190
Lee, Ang 267, 277–80
Lee, Spike 104
LeGros, James 243, 245, 246
Lehmann, Courtney 11, 65, 157, 231–51
Lemmon, Jack 76
Lemmons, Kasi 104
Lester, Adrian 25, 26, 79, 80, 84
Levinson, Eugene 142
Levinson, Jill 67
Levring, Kristian 1, 11, 252, 253, 256, 258–61, 262–3
liberals 17, 18, 20
LiCalsi, Allison 247, 248, 249
The Life and Death of Richard III 173, 181–4
literalization of metaphor 142–3, 152
literary references 277–9
literature 20
Liu, Alan 20
Lizzie McGuire 22
Lodge, Thomas 152
Loehlin, James N. 10, 59, 63, 173–85
Loncraine, Richard 10, 90, 173, 174–81
Looking for Richard 10, 20, 27, 173, 187, 188–95, 288
Lotman, Yu M. 147
Lott, Tommy L. 81
love 58, 65, 121
Love Story 65
Love's Labour's Lost (Branagh) 8, 22–3, 24, 26, 74–82, 84, 85, 86
low culture 16, 17, 72, 73, 142
Lucas, George 7, 253, 254
Luhrmann, Baz 8, 11, 28, 56, 58–64, 70, 99; anachronism 44, 45; Bogdanov's *Macbeth* 236, 237; DVD menu trailers 2, 3, 7; filmic/realist mode 173; 'media allegory' 43; *Moulin Rouge* 2–3, 11, 273, 274; Shakespeare analogies 69; the 'street' 188; television 22
Lyman, Rick 2
Lyotard, J.-F. 214, 225, 226, 227, 228

McAlpine, Donald 45
Macbeth 6, 11, 21, 30, 196, 231–51
Macbeth (animated version) 141, 149
Macbeth (Bogdanov) 22, 28, 235–9, 245, 247
Macbeth (Freeston) 28
Macbeth (Nunn) 24
Macbeth (Polanski) 234
Macbeth (Welles) 78, 234
Macbeth CD-ROM 153
Macbeth, The Comedy 11, 243, 247–9
MacCannell, Dean 236–7, 241
McCullough, Malcolm 38
McElhone, Natascha 82
McGregor, Ewan 26, 273
McInnerny, Tim 175
McKellen, Ian 90, 96, 173, 174–5, 179–81, 255
MacLean, Steve 201–2
Macready, William Charles 74
Mad Max 235–6
Madden, John 8, 56, 67, 68, 69, 70
magic 105, 106–7, 109, 110, 111–13
Malcolm in the Middle 22
male body 131, 133
male gaze 297
Malina, Roger 108
Mann, Anthony 23
Manvell, Roger 22
Marker, Chris 7
Marlowe, Christopher 66
Marowitz, Charles 131
Marxism 29, 223, 270–1
Mary Poppins 79
masculinity 10, 160, 220; *My Own Private Idaho* 201, 207–8, 210; *O* 103; *Othello* 98
mass media 5, 17, 19, 20, 43, 59
Masterpiece Theater 17–18, 177
maternal symbolism 204–5
Maybe Baby 25–6
Mazurier, Charles 73
media allegory 43, 46
mediatization 171, 295, 296, 297
Mehta, Deepa 272
memory 8, 37, 38–43, 44, 49, 51, 271
Men of Respect 178, 188, 189, 196
mental memory theater 40–1, 49
Merchant, Ismail 280
The Merchant of Venice 93
The Merchant of Venice (Nunn) 17
metaphor, literalization of 142–3, 152
A Midsummer Nightmare 22
A Midsummer Night's Dream 10, 22, 25, 154–72, 276
A Midsummer Night's Dream (animated version) 141
A Midsummer Night's Dream (Hall) 24
A Midsummer Night's Dream (Hoffman) 155–60, 164, 170–1, 288
A Midsummer Night's Dream (Noble) 155, 160–5, 170
A Midwinter's Tale 78, 80
Miller, Jonathan 122, 123
minstrelsy 72–3, 80–1, 82, 85
Miramax 76
mise-en-page 41, 46
mise-en-scène 45, 231, 243, 253; Almereyda 39; Branagh 43; *China Girl* 285; *Dil Chahta Hai* 275; Keane 184; Luhrmann 59, 60; Noble 160; Willis 40, 46; Zeffirelli 60
Mishra, Vijay 266, 267
misogyny 94, 151, 152, 197, 259
Mississippi Masala 266, 276
Mistry, Jimi 272
modernity 37, 156, 157, 158, 160
Monsoon Wedding 266, 276, 297
Monty Python 22
Moody, Richard 74
Moonlighting 122, 134–5, 137
Morgann, Maurice 84
Morrissette, Billy 245, 246, 247
Morrow, Lance 89
Moulin Rouge 2–3, 11, 266, 270, 272, 273–4
MTV 58, 59, 136, 221, 270, 274
Much Ado About Nothing 274, 275
Much Ado About Nothing (Branagh) 26, 76–7, 81, 83, 155, 173, 175, 255
Much Ado About Nuttin' 20
Much Ado About Something 21
Mullaney, Steven 217
Müller, Heiner 28
multiculturalism 17, 166, 167, 284, 287, 288
multimedia 141, 152–3, 289–90, 296
Mulvey, Laura 297
The Murder of Stephen Lawrence 95
Murnau, F.W. 184
musicals 75, 76–7, 79, 84, 85
My Kingdom 272
My Own Private Idaho 10–11, 188, 189, 200–12

Naipaul, V.S. 265
Nair, Mira 276
narcissism 295, 296, 297

naturalism 160, 167, 168, 173
Nelson, Tim Blake 9, 99–100, 101, 103–4
neo-realism 285
neocolonial Shakespeare 23, 24, 266
neoconservatism 17, 18, 122
neoliberalism 266
New Criticism 214, 224, 226
new media 38, 108, 298
New Wave filmmakers 253, 254, 260, 262
Nickell, Paul 126
Nightingale, Benedict 227
No Bed for Bacon 66
Noble, Adrian 10, 155, 160–5, 170, 171, 222
noir western 234–5, 236, 238, 239, 243, 245, 247–8
Nora, Pierre 37, 38–9, 42, 43, 44, 46
Norman, Marc 24, 67–8, 262
Nosferatu 184
nostalgia 37, 39, 45, 244, 247; British films 75, 77, 78, 79; for the future 238; *A Midsummer Night's Dream* 155–6, 157, 158, 161–2, 164, 165; *see also* heritage cinema
Nugent, Helen 27
Nunn, Trevor: complaint against Hollywood 84–5, 254–5; *Macbeth* 23–4; *The Merchant of Venice* 17; *Twelfth Night* 8, 74, 75–6, 83–5, 173, 254–5

O 9, 99–104
oedipal symbolism 97, 163, 201, 205, 206–7, 208, 211; *see also* Freudian symbolism
Olivier, Lawrence 74, 77, 126, 140, 275; *Hamlet* 15, 44, 49, 78, 126, 275; *Henry V* 77–8, 126, 128, 161, 214, 215–16, 221, 275; *Othello* 78, 173, 174; *Richard III* 22, 24, 78, 180, 194
online publication 53–4
Orange County 14–15
Orgel, Stephen 113
Orientalism 280, 281, 283
Orlova, Natasha 148
Orson Welles, Shakespeare, and Popular Culture 20
Osborne, Laurie 9, 140–53
Othello 18, 26–7, 86, 89–104
Othello (animated version) 9, 143–4, 152
Othello (Davies/Sax) 9, 17, 94–9, 101, 102
Othello (Olivier) 78, 173, 174
Othello (Parker) 9, 80, 89–90, 103, 173, 174
Othello (Welles) 173
Othello: The Interactive Guide 152
Othello Travestie, An Operatic Burlesque Burletta 89
the Other 266, 268

Pacino, Al 10, 20, 27, 173, 187, 188–95, 197
Palmer, Lilli 127
Paltrow, Gwyneth 24, 68, 261, 270, 293
Papp, Joseph 122, 131, 133
Paris is Burning 70
Parker, Oliver 9, 89–91, 92, 93–4, 103, 173, 174
parody 20–1, 58, 81, 130, 196
Passolini, Antonio 239, 240
pastiche 60
Patel, Divia 269–70
Paterson, Bill 175
patriarchy 122, 125, 132, 135, 158, 222
Patterson, Annabel 217, 223
pedagogy 287, 289–90, 291; *see also* education
Pendreigh, Brian 232
Penley, Constance 111
Peter Pan 162, 165
Peters, John Durham 240
Pfifer, Mekhi 99, 100
Phoenix, River 200
photography 107
Pickford, Mary 120, 121, 124, 125
Poitier, Sidney 226
Polanski, Roman 234
political criticism 30, 214, 223–8
politics 21; *Dirty Harry* 221; *Henry V* 214, 216, 219, 221, 222; *Richard III* 176
Polonsky, Abraham 57
polychrony 8, 37, 39, 42, 54
popular culture 8, 28, 161–2, 163, 171; American 72, 73, 74, 79, 81; black 84; *A Children's Midsummer Night's Dream* 168; mass media as antithetical to 20; post–popular culture 17, 28, 29, 30; *Romeo and Juliet* 57, 58, 61; the 'street' 188; universality 15
popularization 17, 18, 20, 21, 22
pornography 20, 239–42, 297
post-mechanical reproduction 108
post-popular culture 17, 28, 29, 30
post-postcolonialism 23–4, 75, 82, 83, 84–5, 86
Postcards From America 201–2, 212
postcolonialism 11, 26, 76, 267, 268, 297–8; American Shakespeare 187, 190, 194; deconstruction 269; diaspora concept 265; globalization 265–6; third cinema 270–1
postdiaspora 266, 268–9, 270–1, 298

postmodernism 29, 237, 238; *A Midsummer Night's Dream* 156; *Romeo and Juliet* 59, 60; *The Taming of the Shrew* 130
poststructuralism 214, 223
The Prince of Jutland 262
Priscilla Queen of the Desert 45, 70
Prospero's Books 9, 105–19
The Proud Family 22
psychoanalysis *see* oedipal symbolism
puppetry 9, 141, 144–8, 166, 168
Purefoy, James 26

Quarshie, Hugh 95
Quinn, Aidan 193
quotation 53, 54

Rabkin, Norman 214, 224
race 17, 26–7, 268, 287; Asian films 286; *China Girl* 284; *The Glass House* 292; minstrelsy 81–2; *O* 99–104; *Othello* 9, 89, 90, 94, 99; *see also* ethnicity
racism 73, 91, 167, 284; *O* 104; *Othello* 94, 96, 102; police 94, 95, 98
Rackham, Arthur 162
Rafferty, Terrence 93
rap music 101
rape 102, 103
Rave Macbeth 1, 28
Ravel company 72–3
Ray, Satyajit 276
Readings, Bill 19–20
Reagan, Ronald 217, 219, 227, 239
realism 161, 173–4, 181, 215
Rebel Without a Cause 61, 64, 70
Redgrave, Vanessa 191
Reed, Vernon 108
Reeves, Keanu 76, 81
Reilly, William 188
Renaissance 281–2
representation 37, 38, 39, 40, 41
reproduction, post-mechanical 108
The Resistible Rise of Arturo Ui 178
'retrolutionary' approach 252
Rhadakrishnan, R. 276
Richard III 10, 16, 21, 173–85, 196–7
Richard III (animated version) 9, 144, 148–50, 152
Richard III (Loncraine) 10, 90, 173, 174–81
Richard III (McKellen) 255
Richard III (Olivier) 22, 24, 78, 194, 275
Richardson, Joely 25, 26
Riefenstahl, Leni 176
the Right 18
Rippy, Marguerite 245
Rob Roy 232, 233, 234
Rogin, Michael 82, 217
Rohmer, Eric 262
Romeo and Juliet 56–71; Bollywood films 272, 275, 276; *China Girl* 283, 284, 285; *Sense and Sensibility* 277; US education 18–19; *see also William Shakespeare's Romeo & Juliet*
Romeo and Juliet (animated version) 141
Romeo and Juliet (Sennett) 58
Romeo and Juliet (Zeffirelli) 58, 60, 64, 91, 283, 285
Romeo Must Die 266, 267, 270
Romeo Turns Bandit 58
A Room with a View 177
Rosaldo, Renato 75
Ross, Andrew 111
Rossiter, A.P. 224
Rotten, Johnny 24
Rousseau, Jean-Jacques 113
Rowe, Katherine 8, 37–55
Royal Shakespeare Company (RSC) 160, 161, 164, 217
Rukov, Mogens 256
Rushdie, Salman 267, 270

Sawhney, Deepak Narang 16
Scarface 178, 179, 196
Schamus, James 279–80
Schneider, Gretchen A. 73
Scorsese, Martin 75, 196, 254, 256, 284, 285, 286
Scotland 231–5, 238–42, 243, 244, 245–7, 249–50
Scotland, PA 20–1, 232, 243, 245–7, 248
Scott-Douglass, Amy 11, 252–64
Sen, Aparna 276
Sengupta, Ratnottama 272
Sense and Sensibility 26, 266, 267, 277–80
Serres, Michael 8, 37, 39, 46
sex: *Hamlet* 297; *In the Flesh* 239–42; *Othello* 90, 91, 94; *Romeo and Juliet* 69; *The Taming of the Shrew* 121–2
sexuality: *A Midsummer Night's Dream* 155, 163; *My Own Private Idaho* 201, 203, 211; *O* 102; *Othello* 92, 97; *Prospero's Books* 9, 105, 111, 112, 115–18; *Romeo and Juliet* 66–7; *The Taming of the Shrew* 122, 131, 132; *see also* eroticism

Sexy Beast 86
Shakespeare: The Animated Tales 9, 140–53
The Shakespeare Conspiracy 21
Shakespeare in Love 8, 20, 25, 56, 57, 64–70; American woman role 261; coda 63; cross-dressing 159; last scene 154; omissions 62; post–postcolonialism 23, 24
Shakespeare Wallah 281, 283
Shallow Grave 232, 233
Shaw, Fiona 124, 130
Shepherd, Cybill 134
Shohat, Ella 5, 267
shot/response shot 49, 50
Siberian Lady Macbeth 234
Siegel, Don 221
Silverman, Kaja 49
Silverstone, Alicia 76, 79, 235
Simpson, O.J. 9, 89, 90, 93, 94, 100
The Simpsons 22
simulacrum 18, 78
Sinfield, Alan 143, 219
Singer, Daniel 254
Singer, Marc 131
Singh, Tarsem 272
Sinyard, Neil 192, 193
Sippy, Romesh 276
Slade, Joseph W. 240–1
Small, Edward S. 142
Smith, Maggie 175, 179, 180
Smith, Paul 217, 221
Soap Dish 288
social relations 29
Sokolov, Stanislav 145
soliloquies 46–9, 50, 51, 125, 126
South Park 21, 22
Spall, Timothy 81
Spielberg, Steven 7, 253, 254, 256
Spivak, Gayatri 83, 267
Stallybrass, Peter 42–3
Stam, Robert 5, 267
Star Trek 22, 23
Star Wars 26, 177, 244
Star Wars: Macbeth 21, 232, 243–4, 247
Steavenson-Payne, Kate 174
stereotypes 100
Stewart, Patrick 17, 22–3
Stiles, Julia 99, 100, 135
Stockholder, Kay 111, 112, 115
Stockman, Oliver 169
Stone, Allucquére Roseanne 38
Stoppard, Tom 67–8
Strauss, Leo 223
Streep, Meryl 122, 123, 131, 132, 133
The Street King 10, 16–17, 188, 189, 196–7
'sub-Shakespeare' 196, 286
subaltern 83
subjectivity: female 122; *Othello* 91, 92; *The Taming of the Shrew* 130, 131
suspension of disbelief 158–9

Taj Mahal: An Eternal Love Story 272
A Tale of Winter 262
The Talented Mr. Ripley 14, 270
The Tall Guy 26
Taming Mrs. Shrew 121
The Taming of the Shrew 9, 120–39, 226
The Taming of the Shrew (animated version) 9, 144, 147–8, 152
The Taming of the Shrew (Collins) 123–4
The Taming of the Shrew (Griffith) 123
The Taming of the Shrew (Nickell) 126
The Taming of the Shrew (Schaefer) 127
The Taming of the Shrew (Taylor) 121, 124–5
The Taming of the Shrew (Zeffirelli) 121, 122, 124, 127–31, 132–4, 136, 137
Tarantino, Quentin 86, 255
Taubin, Amy 89, 99, 103
Taylor, Charles 76
Taylor, Elizabeth 120, 127, 128, 130, 137
Taylor, John 94
Taylor, Sam 124
Taymor, Julie 9, 44
Tea with Mussolini 261
technology 1, 29, 252; memory 8, 37–40, 42–3, 44–5, 46, 51, 52; *A Midsummer Night's Dream* 158; *Prospero's Books* 105, 106–7, 111, 118; *see also* computer technology; digital technology; multimedia
technophilia 111
teen culture 9, 58, 61, 99, 135, 188
television 8, 20, 21–2, 24; *King of Texas* 23; *Macbeth* 11; *The Taming of the Shrew* 121–2, 126–7, 131
televisualization 17
The Tempest 9, 105–19, 194
The Tempest (animated version) 141, 144, 145, 146
10 Things I Hate About You 9, 99, 122, 123, 135–7, 287
Texas Dick: Shakespeare in the Pecos 22
texts 8, 214
textuality 53, 111

theater: *The Life and Death of Richard III* 181–4; *A Midsummer Night's Dream* 154, 155, 161, 164, 170, 171
theatricality 10, 155, 156, 158–61, 169, 171
Thich Nhat Hanh 292, 294
Thomas, Kristin Scott 174, 178
Thompson, Ann 132
Thompson, Emma 25, 26, 277, 278, 279, 280
A Thousand Acres 260
Throne of Blood 6–7, 234
Tierney, Maura 243, 245
Titanic 65
Titus Andronicus 9, 44
Tobin, Elayne 213, 214, 226
Toland, Gregg 184
tragedy: animated Shakespeare 142, 152; *Othello* 90; *Romeo and Juliet* 58, 62
The Tragedy of Othello 78
The Tragical Historye of Romeus and Juliet 66
Trainspotting 26, 233
transnationalism 5, 270, 297
Traub, James 18–19
Trevis, Di 131
Triumph of the Will 176
Troilus and Cressida 275
True Identity 26
Twelfth Night 18, 154
Twelfth Night (animated version) 141, 144, 147
Twelfth Night (BBC) 267–8
Twelfth Night (Nunn) 8, 74, 75–6, 81, 83–6, 173, 254–5

United Kingdom: education 21; glo-cali-zation 17; 'post-postcolonial' relationship with United States 23, 24, 75, 76, 83, 86; race 26; *see also* Great Britain
United States: American woman role 261; audiences 72–3; film affinity 170; foreign policy 217, 218, 219; glo-cali-zation 17; political culture 221; 'post-postcolonial' relationship with Britain 23, 24, 75, 76, 83, 86; race 26; Shakespeare and the street 186–97; Shakespearean film hegemony 74–86; television 24; theatrical entertainment 72–5; *see also* Hollywood
The University in Ruins 19
urban film 10
utopian criticism 29, 30

Valenti, Jack 253
Van Dyke, Dick 79
Van Sant, Gus 10, 188, 189, 200–1, 203–4, 207–8
Vernet, Marc 249
video 52–3, 295–6, 297; "MTV style" 59; soliloquies 46–9, 50, 51
villains 80, 86
Vincendeau, Ginette 158
Vinterberg, Thomas 11, 252, 253, 256, 258, 262–3
violence: *Henry V* 218–19; *The Taming of the Shrew* 133, 147; teenage 99–100
Virilio, Paul 227
virtual handicraft 38
visual media 294, 295
voice-over 96, 110, 126, 132, 233
von Trier, Lars 252, 256

Wajda, Andrzej 234
Walken, Christopher 243, 246
Walker, Elsie 60
Walton, William 275
war 11, 215, 216, 220, 227, 228
Warde, Frederick 10, 173, 181–4
Washington, Denzel 76, 81
Waterworld 14
Wayne, John 203, 220
web-based media 53–4
Weinstein, Harvey 70
Welles, Orson 20, 21, 57, 140, 209; camera-work 184; *Chimes at Midnight* 11, 78, 201, 207; *Macbeth* 78, 234; *Othello* 173; popularization 18
Wells, Matt 24
Wells, Stanley 58, 61
Wenders, Wim 254
West Side Story 14, 58, 61, 63, 65, 283–6
The West Wing 18, 22
Westerns 22–3, 217, 233–4
Whale, James 270
White Heat 178, 179, 180
whiteness 98
Who Killed Shakespeare? 19
Will, George 18
William Shakespeare 66
William Shakespeare's Romeo & Juliet 8, 28, 56, 58–64, 69–70, 99; conventions 45–6; DVD Special Edition 2, 3–4, 274; filmic/realist mode 173; *Macbeth* comparison 236, 237; media allegory 43; omissions 61–2; *Orange*

County reference to 14, 15; the 'street' 188; television 22
Williams, Gary Jay 163
Williams, Raymond 219, 270
Williams, Robin 15, 76
Willis, Bruce 134
Willis, John 8, 40–1, 46, 49, 52
Willy Wonka and the Chocolate Factory 79
Wilson, Rob 268
Winokur, Mark 82
Winslet, Kate 277, 279
The Winter's Tale 262
The Winter's Tale (animated version) 9, 144–6, 148, 152
Wiseman, Susan 10–11, 200–12
Witchel, Alex 83
The Wizard of Oz 201, 203
women: *As You Like It* 151–2; *The Golden Bowl* 280; *A Midsummer Night's Dream* 156, 157; *Othello* 92, 93; *Prospero's Books* 111–12, 113–15, 117–18; *Sense and Sensibility* 279, 280; *The Taming of the Shrew* 120, 121–2, 124, 125; *see also* femininity; feminism; gender
Woo, John 286
writing: *Hamlet* 38, 40, 42, 43, 294; *Prospero's Books* 106; *Shakespeare in Love* 66

Year of the Dragon 284, 285
Yoshimoto, Mitsuhiro 5
You Are There 56–7, 66
youth 9, 63–4

A Zed and Two Noughts 114
Zeffirelli, Franco 58, 60, 64, 70, 91, 140; American cinema 255; *China Girl* 283, 284, 285; *Hamlet* 15, 173; popularity 75; *The Taming of the Shrew* 121, 122, 124, 127–31, 132–4, 136, 137; *Tea with Mussolini* 261
Žižek, Slavoj 5, 29–30, 243, 246, 291